Encyclopedia of
CAPITALISM

Volume III
S – Z

SYED B. HUSSAIN, Ph.D.

GENERAL EDITOR

☑®

Facts On File, Inc.

Encyclopedia of Capitalism

Facts On File, Inc.
132 West 31st Street
New York NY 1001

Library of Congress Cataloging-in-Publication Data

Encyclopedia of capitalism / Syed B. Hussain, general editor
    p. cm.
  Includes bibliographical references and index.
  ISBN 0-8160-5224-7 (alk paper)
   1. Capitalism—Encyclopedias.   I. Hussain, Syed B.

  HB501.E558 2004
  330'.03—dc22   2003064170

Facts On File books are available at special discounts when purchased in bulk quantities for businesses, associations, institutions, or sales promotions. Please call our Special Sales Department in New York at (212) 967-8800 or (800) 322-8755.

You can find Facts On File on the World Wide Web at http://www.factsonfile.com

GOLSON BOOKS, LTD.

Geoff Golson, President and Editor

Syed B. Hussain, Ph.D., General Editor, Encyclopedia of Capitalism

Kevin Hanek, Design Director

Brian Snapp, Copyeditor

Gail Liss, Indexer

PHOTO CREDITS
Bank of Sweden Prizes in Memory of Alfred Nobel: Pages 20, 193, 281, 320, 380, 488, 553, 614, 735, 780. Kenneth Gabrielsen Photography: Pages 11, 14, 27, 52, 60, 72, 75, 137, 139, 150, 152, 160, 188, 189, 212, 217, 238, 243, 248, 249, 275, 278, 281, 329, 372, 391, 413, 422, 495, 527, 556, 596, 617, 656, 659, 669, 674, 696, 708, 709, 758, 765, 768, 784, 801, 818, 831, 841, 872, 883, 889. PhotoDisc, Inc.: Pages 55, 133, 214, 269, 310, 355, 408, 433, 469, 516, 546, 675, 870, 934. U.S. Senate: 442.

Printed in the United States of America

VB PKG 10 9 8 7 6 5 4 3 2 1

This book is printed on acid-free paper.

Contents

List of Contributors   v

List of Articles   ix

Volume I
Entries A – G   1

Volume II
Entries H – R   363

Volume III
Entries S – Z   735

Glossary   937

Resource Guide   945

Appendix A: International Trade by Region   949

Appendix B: International Trade by Sector   1015

Index   1067

List of Contributors

Abugri, Benjamin
Department of Economics and Finance
Southern Connecticut University

Aka, Arsène
The Catholic University of America

Azari-Rad, H.
Department of Economics
State University of New York, New Paltz

Balak, Benjamin
Department of Economics
Rollins College

Barnhill, John
Independent Scholar

Batchelor, Bob
Independent Scholar

Becker, Klaus
Texas Tech University

Berkley, Holly
Department of History
Hardin-Simmons University

Bhattacharya, Tithi
Department of History
Purdue University

Bishop, Elizabeth
Institute for Gender and Women's Studies
American University in Cairo, Egypt

Blankenship, Cary
Department of History, Geography, Political Science
Tennessee State University

Block, Walter
Loyola University, New Orleans

Boettcher, Susan R.
Department of History
University of Texas

Borden, Timothy G.
Independent Scholar

Bradley, Robert L., Jr.
Institute for Energy Research

Braguinsky, Serguey
Department of Economics
State University of New York, Buffalo

Caplan, Bryan
Department of Economics
George Mason University

Carton, Joel
Department of Economics
Texas Tech University

Cawley, John H.
Department of Economics
Cornell University

Chen, Shehong
University of Massachusetts, Lowell

Chung, Wai-keung
Department of Sociology
University of Washington

Coelho, Alfredo
University of Montpellier, France

Cruz, Laura
Department of History
Western Carolina University

Cundiff, Kirby R.
Hillsdale College

Dadres, Susan
Department of Economics
Southern Methodist University

DeCoster, Karen
Walsh College

Dolenc, Patrick
Department of Economics
Keene State College

Dompere, Kofi Kissi
Department of Economics
Howard University

Douglas, R.M.
Department of History
Colgate University

DuBose, Mike
American Culture Studies
Bowling Green State University

Dynan, Linda
Independent Scholar

Elvins, Sarah
Department of History
University of Notre Dame

Erickson, Christian
Roosevelt University

Evrensel, Ayşe Y.
Department of Economics
Portland State University

Ewing, Bradley T.
Department of Economics
Texas Tech University

Ferguson, William
Institute for Experiential Living
Grinnell College

Foster, Kevin R.
City College of New York

Fowler, Russell
University of Tennessee, Chattanooga

Fuming, Jiang
Charles Sturt University, Australia

Gabriel, Satya J.
Department of Economics
Mount Holyoke College

Gallois, William
American University of Sharjah
United Arab Emirates

Geringer, Joseph
Essays On History

Gerlach, Jeffrey
Department of Economics
College of William & Mary

Grassl, Wolfgang
Department of Economics
Hillsdale College

Haworth, Barry
University of Louisville

Hill, Kirstin
Merrill Lynch & Company
London, England

Holst, Arthur
Widener University

Howell, Chris
Red Rocks College

Hussain, Akmal
Institute of Development Economics
Pakistan

Hussain, Syed B.,
General Editor of the Encyclopedia

Işcan, Talan
Department of Economics
Dalhousie University, Canada

Jacobson, Katherine
Department of History
Metropolitan State University

Jeitschko, Thomas D.
Department of Economics
Michigan State University

Kinni, Theodore
Independent Scholar

Kline, Audrey D.
University of Louisville

Klumpp, Tilman
Economics Department
Indiana University

Kosar, George
Brandeis University

Kozlov, Nicholas N.
Economics Department
Hofstra University

Kucsma, Kristin
Economics Department
Seton Hall University

Kypraios, Harry
Rollins College

Laberge, Yves
Institut Québécois des
Hautes Études Internationales, Canada

Larudee, Mehrene
Department of Economics
University of Kansas

Lawrence, Taresa
Howard University

Lawson, Russell M.
Independent Scholar

Lewis, David
Citrus College

Luque, Emilio
UNED University, Madrid, Spain

MacKenzie, D.W.
George Mason University

Mahmud, Tayyab
Ohio State University

Malik, Farooq
Pennsylvania State University, Berks

Matheson, Victor
Department of Economics
Williams College

Matraves, Catherine
Department of Economics and Management
Albion College

Mattson, Kevin
Department of History
Ohio University

Mazzoleni, Roberto
Department of Economics and Geography
Hofstra University

McGee, Kevin
University of Wisconsin

McGregor, Michael
Fannie Mae

Mitchell, David
George Mason University

Mocnik, Josip
Bowling Green State University

Moiz, Syed
Marian College

Moore, Karl
McGill University, Canada

Motluck, Mark E.
Anderson University

Mozayeni, Simin
State University of New York, New Paltz

Nesslein, Thomas
Urban and Regional Studies
University of Wisconsin, Green Bay

Neumann, Caryn
Department of History
Ohio State University

Odekon, Mehmet
Skidmore College

Ornelas, Emmanuel
University of Georgia

Paas, David
Hillsdale College

Palmer, Scott
RGMS Economics

Papageorgiou, Chris
Department of Economics
Louisiana State University

Petrou, Linda L.
Department of History
and Political Science
High Point University

Phelps, Chris
Ohio State University

Prieger, James E.
Department of Economics
University of California, Davis

Prono, Luca
University of Nottingham, England

Pullin, Eric
College of Business
Cardinal Stritch University

Purdy, Elizabeth
Independent Scholar

Rabbani, Mahbub
Temple University

Raman, Jaishankar
Department of Economics
Valparaiso University

Reagle, Derrick
Department of Economics
Fordham University

Robinson, Charles
Brandeis University

Rodríguez-Boetsch, Leopoldo
Portland State University

Rubel, Shawn
Independent Scholar

Saeed, Agha
University of California, Berkeley

Sagers, John
Department of History
Linfield College

Schrag, Jonathan
Harvard University

Schuster, Zeljan
School of Business
University of New Haven

Silver, Lindsay
Brandeis University

Sorrentino, John A.
Department of Economics
Temple University

Subramanian, Narayanan
Brandeis University

Sullivan, Timothy E.
Department of Economics
Towson University

Swanson, Paul
Department of Economics
and Finance
William Patterson University

Syed, Aura
Department of Political Science
Northern Michigan University

Thompson, Mark A.
Sephen F. Austin State University

Traflet, Janice
Columbia University

Troy, Michael J.
Michigan State University

Turdaliev, Nurlan
Department of Economics
McGill University

Vavrik, Ursula
Vienna University of Economics, Austria

von Ende, Terry
Texas Tech University

Walsh, John
Shinawatra University, Thailand

Weed, Charles
Department of Social Science
Keene State College

Weston, Samuel
Economics Department
University of Dallas

Whaples, Robert
Department of Economics
Wake Forest University

Wu, Xiadong
University of North Carolina, Chapel Hill

Young, Derek Rutherford
Department of History
University of Dundee, Scotland

Young, Ronald
Georgia Southern University

Zaccarini, Cristina
Adelphi University

List of Articles

A

accounting
Adams, John
Adams, John Quincy
Afghanistan
Afrocentrism
agriculture
airlines
Akerlof, George A.
Alger, Horatio, Jr.
Algeria
alienation
Allais, Maurice
Allianz
Altria (Philip Morris)
American Civil War
American Electric Power Company
American International Group
American Revolution
American Stock Exchange
Andorra
Angell, Norman
annual report
anti-globalization
antitrust
AOL Time Warner
Aquila
Arab nationalism
arbitrage
Argentina
Armenia
Arrow, Kenneth
Arthur, Chester Alan
Asian developmental state
Asian Financial Crisis
Assicurazioni Generali

Astor, John Jacob
AT&T
audit
Australia
Austria
Austrian School
autarky
automobiles
Aviva
AXA

B

Bahamas
Bahrain
Bank of America
Bank of England
Bank of France
Bank of Japan
banking, commercial
banking, consumer
banking, investment
bankruptcy
Barclays Bank
barter
Bastiat, Frederic
Beard, Charles A.
Becker, Gary S.
Belgium
Bentham, Jeremy
Berle, Adolf
Bismarck, Otto von
black market
BNP Paribas
board of directors
Boeing
Böhm-Bawerk, Eugen von

bonds
Bosnia Herzegovina
bourse
BP (British Petroleum)
Brazil
Bretton Woods
bribery
Buchanan, James
Buchanan, James M. Jr.
Burke, Edmund
Bush, George H.W.
Bush, George W.
business cycles

C
Cambodia
Canada
capital
capital accumulation
capitalism, ancient
capitalism, political
Carnegie, Andrew
carrying capacity
cartel
Carter, Jimmy
cash flow
central banks
ChevronTexaco
Chicago Board of Trade
Chicago School
chief executive officer
chief financial officer
Chile
China
China National Petroleum
Citigroup
Clark, J.B.
class structure
Clay, Henry
Cleaver, Harry M., Jr.
Cleveland, Grover
Clinton, William J.
Coase, Ronald H.
Colbert, Jean Baptiste
Colombia
colonialism
communication
company
comparative advantage
competition
competitive economics
computer
Conference of Montréal
conglomerate
conservatism

consumer
consumer behavior
contagion
contract
Coolidge, Calvin
Cooper, Peter
corruption
cost accounting
cost of information
cost, theory of
Council of Economic Advisers
credit
Credit Suisse
Cromwell, Oliver
Cuba
currency
Czech Republic

D
Dai-ichi Mutual Life Insurance
DaimlerChrysler
De Gaulle, Charles
Debreu, Gerard
debt
demand
democracy
Denison, Edward F.
Denmark
dependency theory
depreciation
depression
derivative
DeSoto, Hernando
Deutsche Bank
Deutsche Telecom
discount
discount rate
Disraeli, Benjamin
distribution
dollar
Dow Jones
drugs (pharmaceuticals)
Duke Energy
Dutch West India Company
Dynegy

E
E. ON
East India Company
econometrics
economic indicators
economic theory, classical
economic theory, Marxian
economic theory, neoclassical
economies of scale

Economist magazine
Edison, Thomas
education
Egypt
Eisenhower, Dwight D.
El Paso Company
employee benefits
employment theory
energy
Engels, E.
Engels, F.
English Civil War
ENI
Enron
enterprise
entrepreneur
equilibrium, general/partial
equity
Estonia
Ethics
Ethiopia
euro
European Central Bank
European Union
exchange rate
export and import
externalities
ExxonMobil

F
Faneuil, Peter
Fannie Mae
fascism
Federal Reserve
Federal Trade Commission
federalism
feudalism
Fiat
Fillmore, Millard
film and film industry
finance
financial institutions
financial statement
Finland
fiscal policy
Fisher, Irving
Fisk, James
Fogel, Robert W.
Ford Motor Company
Ford, Gerald
Ford, Henry
forecast
Fortis
France
France Telecom

franchising
Franklin, Benjamin
free trade
French Revolution
Frick, Henry C.
Friedman, Milton
Frisch, Ragnar
Fujitsu
functions of money

G
G8 Summit
Galbraith, John Kenneth
gambling and lotteries
game theory
gangsters
Garfield, James A.
Gates, Bill Jr.
General Agreement on Tariffs and Trade (GATT)
General Electric
General Motors
Generally Accepted Accounting Principles (GAAP)
Georgia
Germany
globalization
gold standard
goods
Gorbachev, Mikhail
Gordon, Robert J.
Gould, Jay
Grant, Ulysses
Greece
Greenspan, Alan
gross domestic product
gross national product
growth

H
Haavelmo, Trygve
Hamilton, Alexander
Hancock, John
Harding, Warren
Harrison, William Henry
Harrod, Sir Roy Forbes
Harsanyi, John C.
Hayek, Frederich von
Hayes, Rutherford
Hazlitt, Henry
health
Heckman, James J.
Heckscher, E.F.
Hegel, Georg W.F.
hegemony
Hewlett-Packard
Hicks, Sir John

Hitachi
Hobson, John A.
Hodgskin, Thomas
Home Depot
homo economicus
Honda Motor Company
Honduras
Hong Kong
Hoover, Herbert
housing
HSBC Holding PLC
Hume, David
Hundred Years' War
Hungary
HypoVereinsbank

I
imperialism
income
income distribution theories
income statement
incorporation
India
Indonesia
industrial organization
Industrial Revolution
inflation
information revolution
ING Group
insider trading
insurance
Inter-American
 Development Bank
interest rates
International Business Machines
International Monetary Fund
International Trade Centre
Iran
Iraq
Ireland
Islamic banking
Israel
Italy

J
J.P. Morgan Chase
Jackson, Andrew
Japan
Jefferson, Thomas
Jevons, W.S.
Jiang, Zemin
Jobs, Steve
Johnson, Andrew
Johnson, Lyndon B.
Jordan

K
Kahneman, Daniel
Kantorovich, Leonid V.
Kennedy, John F.
Kennedy, Joseph P.
Kenya
Keynes, John Maynard
Keynesian Economics
Klein, Lawrence R.
kleptocracy
Knight, Frank. L.
Koopmans, Tjalling
Korea, North
Korea, South
Kroger
Krugman, Paul
Kuwait
Kuznets, Simon

L
labor
Laffer Curve
laissez-faire
land
Latvia
Lenin, Vladimir I.
Leontief, Wassily
leverage
Lewis, Sir Arthur
liberalism
Liberia
libertarian
Libya
Liechtenstein
Lincoln, Abraham
liquor
Lithuania
Lloyd, Henry Demarest
Locke, John
Lucas, Robert
Luxembourg
Luxemburg, Rosa

M
MacArthur, General Douglas
Machiavelli, Niccolo
macroeconomics
Madison, James
Malaysia
Malta
Malthus, Thomas
Manifest Destiny
Marcuse, Herbert
marginal analysis
market

market efficiency
market power
marketing
Markowitz, Harry M.
Marshall Plan
Marshall, Alfred
Marx, Karl
Matsushita Electric Industrial
McFadden, Daniel L.
McKesson
McKinley, William
Medici, Cosimo de'
Mellon, Andrew
Menger, Carl
mercantilism
Merck
Merrill Lynch
Merton, Robert C.
Metro
Mexico
microeconomics
Microsoft
Mill, John Stuart
Miller, Merton M.
mining
Minsky, Hyman
Mirrlees, James A.
Mises, Ludwig von
Mitsubishi
Mitsui
Mizuho Holdings
modernization theory
Modigliani, Franco
Monaco
monetarism
monetary policy
money
monopoly
Monroe, James
Montesquieu, Charles de
moral hazard
Morgan Stanley
Morgan, John P.
Morocco
Mundell, Robert A.
Munich Re Group
Myrdal, Gunnar

N
NAFTA
NASDAQ
Nash, John F.
nationalization
NEC
Nestlé

Netherlands
New Deal
New York Stock Exchange
New Zealand
Nicaragua
Nigeria
Nikkei
Nippon Life Insurance
Nippon Telephone & Telegraph
Nissan Motor Company
Nissho Iwai
Nixon, Richard
non-alignment
nonprofit organization
North, Douglass C.
Norway

O
occupation
Ohlin, Bertil
oil
Okun's Law
Oligopoly
OPEC
Opium Wars
optimorum of market
Orientalism and Eurocentrism
ownership

P
Pakistan
Palestine
Panama Canal
Pareto optimality
partnership
patents
Pemex
Persian Gulf War
Peru
Peugeot Citroën
Philippines
Phillips Curve
physiocrats
Pierce, Franklin
planning
Poland
Polk, James
Portugal
poverty
price
price controls
price discrimination
prices, floor/ceiling
principle of diminishing returns
privatization

Procter & Gamble
producer surplus
product
production,
 individual/social
production possibilities
productivity
profit
profit maximization
Protestantism
public
public goods

Q
Quesnay, Francois
quota

R
railroads
Rand, Ayn
rationing
Reagan, Ronald
recession
regulation
Reliant Energy
Repsol YPF
research and development
resource
retail
Ricardo, David
risk
Robinson, Joan
Rockefeller, John D.
Roman Empire
Romania
Roosevelt, Franklin D.
Roosevelt, Theodore
Royal Dutch Shell Group
Russia
Russian Revolution
RWE

S
Samuelson, Paul A.
Saudi Arabia
saving
Say's Law
SBC Communications
scarcity
Scholes, Myron S.
Schultz, Theodore W.
Schumpeter, Joseph
Sears Roebuck
Securities and Exchange Commission
Selten, Reinhard

Sen, Amartya
Senior, Nassau
Serbia and Montenegro
services
Sharpe, William F.
Siemens
Simon, Herbert A.
Simon, Julian
Sinclair, Upton
Singapore
Sinopec
slavery
small business
Smith, Adam
Smith, Vernon L.
social democracy
Social Security
socialism
Solow, Robert M.
Sony
Soros, George
South Africa
Spain
Spanish American War
Spence, A. Michael
Spencer, Herbert
spice trade
sports
Sraffa, Piero
stagnation
Standard & Poor's (S&P)
Standard Oil Company
state
State Farm Insurance
static/dynamic analysis
Stigler, George J.
Stiglitz, Joseph E.
stock dividend
stock market
stockholder
Stone, Sir Richard
strikes
subsidies
subsistence theory
Suez Canal
Suez Company
Sumitomo
Summit of the Americas
Sumner, William Graham
supply
surplus
sustainable development
Sweden
Switzerland
Syria

T
Taft, William Howard
Taiwan
Target Corporation
tariff
taxes
Taylor, Zachary
technology
Thailand
Thatcher, Margaret
Third World Internationalism
Thirty Years' War
time
Tinbergen, Jan
tobacco
Tobin, James
Tokyo Electric Power
Toshiba
TotalFinaElf
tourism
Toyoda, Kiichiro
Toyota Motor Company
trade
trade barrier
Truman, Harry S
Tunisia
Turgot, A.J.R.
Turkey
Tyler, John

U
UBS
Ukraine
underground economy
unemployment
Unilever
Union of Soviet Socialist Republics
unions
United Kingdom
United Parcel Service (UPS)
United States
United States Postal Service
U.S. Steel
utilitarianism
utility
utility maximization

V
value of leisure
value theory
Van Buren, Martin
Vanderbilt, Cornelius
Vatican Bank
Veblen, Thorstein
Venezuela
venture capital
Verizon Communications
Vickrey, William
Vietnam
Vietnam War
Vivendi Universal
Volker, Paul
Volkswagen

W
wage
Wall Street
Wall Street Journal
Wal-Mart
Walras, Leon
Wang, An
War of 1812
Washington, George
welfare
Wells Fargo
Westinghouse, George
Whitney, Eli
Wilson, Woodrow
worker
World Bank
World Economic Forum
World Trade Organization
World War I
World War II
WorldCom

Y–Z
Yemen
yen
Zimbabwe
Zurich Financial Services

Encyclopedia of
CAPITALISM

VOLUME III

S

Samuelson, Paul A. (1915–)

WINNER OF THE 1970 Nobel Prize in Economics, Paul A. Samuelson was born in Gary, Indiana. He completed his undergraduate studies at the University of Chicago with a B.A. in 1935, and continued his graduate studies at Harvard University, receiving a Ph.D. in economics in 1941. Samuelson became a professor of economics at the Massachusetts Institute of Technology, where he was instrumental in building up what is now one of the leading economics departments in the world. The Nobel award was granted "for the scientific work through which he has developed static and dynamic economic theory and actively contributed to raising the level of analysis in economic science."

Most economists would agree that Samuelson has reshaped the way economic analysis is conducted. In his first major work, *Foundations of Economic Analysis* (1947), Samuelson laid out a unified approach to economic analysis using mathematics. He was able to demonstrate that, with this approach, many previous redundancies and contradictions in economic theory could efficiently be resolved. This work has led to the "mathematization" of modern economic theory—a development hailed by most academic economists, but also repeatedly criticized by some inside and especially outside of the economics profession. What these critics often overlook is that Samuelson's mathematics are not for the sake of formalism per se, but rather for the sake of making transparent what are otherwise very complex interactions.

Samuelson once remarked: "I don't care who writes a nation's laws—or crafts its advanced treaties—if I can write its economics textbooks." In this endeavor, Samuelson has had significant success. In 1948, the first edition of Samuelson's textbook *Economics: An Introductory*

Analysis was published, and in the early 2000s, it was in its 17th edition. Co-authored with William Nordhaus, this text has been widely used. In 1997, more than 4 million copies had been sold and translations of the text had appeared in more than 40 languages. Two generations of economists around the world have received some aspect of their training directly or indirectly from

Paul Samuelson, author of a standard textbook in economics, takes a keen interest in applying theory to real-world concerns.

735

this text. Due to the remarkable success of his early books, Samuelson is often considered one of the archetypes of mainstream economists of the latter half of the 20th century.

In the late 1950s and into the 1960s, Samuelson derived what he calls a "neoclassical synthesis," namely, a unified presentation of economic theory that incorporates the main economic insights from the classical period up to contemporaneous theory. In particular, Samuelson attempted to rectify what seemed to be incompatibilities between classical ECONOMIC THEORY and the recent Keynesian MACROECONOMIC theory.

His contributions in specific areas of economics and his solutions to specific problems in economic theory are associated with many modern theories in the areas of consumer choice; international trade; public goods (a single good whose benefit to one individual is largely unaffected by how many other people benefit from it at the same time—e.g., a lighthouse); production theory; finance theory; growth theory; and many modern macroeconomic theories. Samuelson has authored or co-authored more than 100 papers in the top economics journals and he still published regularly in 2003.

Samuelson has always taken a keen interest in applying economic insight to real-world concerns. He has worked in government agencies and as an advisor to many government institutions throughout his life, including the War Production Board in WORLD WAR II, the U.S. Treasury, the COUNCIL OF ECONOMIC ADVISORS, the Bureau of the Budget, and the FEDERAL RESERVE System.

BIBLIOGRAPHY. Paul A. Samuelson, *Foundations of Economic Analysis* (Harvard University Press, 1947); Paul A. Samuelson, *Economics From the Heart: A Samuelson Sampler* (Thomas Horton, 1983); Paul A. Samuelson, "Credo of a Lucky Textbook Author," *Journal of Economic Perspectives* (v.11/2, 1997); Paul A. Samuelson and William D. Nordhaus, *Economics* (McGraw-Hill, 2001); Mark Skousen, "The Perseverance of Samuelson's Economics," *Journal of Economic Perspectives* (v.11/2, 1997); "Paul Samuelson," www.nobel.se.

THOMAS D. JEITSCHKO, PH.D.
MICHIGAN STATE UNIVERSITY

Saudi Arabia

OCCUPYING MOST of the Arabian Peninsula, Saudi Arabia is at the heart of the Middle East. It is bordered on the west by the Red Sea, the north by JORDAN and IRAQ, the east by the Persian Gulf, and on the east and south by Qatar, the United Arab Emirates, Oman, and the YEMEN Republic. The peninsula is a hot and dry desert with humid coasts and rocky outcrops. Little rainfall

means desalinization plants for making fresh water are necessary.

The kingdom is an absolute monarchy of the Saudi family and has 20 million people of Arabic-speaking, Bedouin background. Formed as a country in 1926, oil was discovered in the east provinces in the 1930s, and exported after World War II. Today, Saudi Arabia is the world's largest exporter of oil with an annual trade balance of $25–50 billion, against foreign debt averages of $25 billion for 1999–2000. The currency is the Riyal. GROSS DOMESTIC PRODUCT (GDP) per capita was $8,130, and real GDP growth was 3.7 percent in 2000.

Riyadh is the modern capital of a state developing a modern infrastructure. Mecca and Medina are the two most important cities, attracting over two million Muslim pilgrims each year for the Hajj, the quintessential Islamic pilgrimage. It is important to remember that Islamic beliefs make up a key component of Muslim population economics, especially in Saudi Arabia. From a capitalist perspective, the Hajj impacts the Saudi economy like tourism and international finance, and beliefs like alms for the poor, are similar to state welfare programs. This is to say, religious beliefs often have economic impact.

The country is often embroiled in Middle East strife but usually remains neutral enough to allow oil export. Crown Prince Abdullah continues to move the economy toward privatization of the energy production sector, increased foreign investment, the creation of Saudi jobs, and an overhaul of the tax holiday system aimed at reducing corporate tax from 45–30 percent. Unemployment is high at 20 percent among 20- to 29-year-old Saudi males as many workers for the 8-billion-barrel-a-year oil production (2000) are foreign nationals. Fiscal policies are tight and Islamic, no-interest loan, banking rules apply. Most of the ministries function as family-run, state-controlled entities.

The national revenue continues to be dependent on the price of oil. Though it has significant natural gas reserves, Saudi Arabia has chosen not to export gas. Oil makes up 90 percent of its exports with the UNITED STATES and JAPAN. Imports are largely finished products for the civilian and hydrocarbon market needs with 19 percent from the United States, 9 percent from Japan, 8 percent from the UNITED KINGDOM and 7 percent from GERMANY. The 263.5 billion barrels of proven oil reserves within Saudi Arabia will last 100 years at present consumption rates.

The oil industry accounts for 45 percent of the GDP, mining for 35 percent, and manufacturing for 10 percent. The government still controls most of the economy with the domestic oil company, Saudi Aramco 100 percent state-owned. Major airlines, granaries, and metal production companies are also state-owned.

High-growth needs in domestic power and energy production sectors require billions of dollars of funding for the modernizing and privatizing Saudi state. Thus state-run oil export will continue to be the key component in the Saudi economy and will far outpace non-oil, privatization efforts. For example, in order to raise power generation capacity to 70,000 MW, a 100-billion-dollar investment is needed from 2000–20. Only the state-run oil export business can generate such funding.

Attempts to increase non-oil products have been successful in making the kingdom self-sufficient in wheat and vegetables. However, attempts to subsidize and export the surplus have been only temporarily successful. In 1992, Saudi Arabia became the world's sixth-largest exporter of wheat but internal water shortages soon cut back production. Desalinization plants proved too costly for anything but self-sufficiency needs.

Saudi membership in the ORGANIZATION OF PETRO-LEUM EXPORTING COUNTRIES (OPEC), mainly consisting of Middle Eastern, oil-producing countries, continues to be vital to the state-run economy begun in the 1960s. OPEC's ability to control oil flow and prices usually means oil prices are consistently between $20–$30 a barrel for the industrialized world. The need for oil to fuel industry and civilization in most first-world areas guarantees a market now and in the near future.

A number of factors suggest against the Saudi economy becoming fully privatized or capitalistic in nature, including the small size of the Saudi population, the nature of the global oil industry, the large desert area it controls, and the limited water supply. While Saudi Arabia can be self-sufficient and reasonably comfortable fiscally, these factors work against a traditional capitalist economy of varied industrial surplus production for internal and external consumers.

BIBLIOGRAPHY. Arabia online, www.arabia.com; R. Knauerhase, *The Saudi Arabian Economy* (Praeger, 1975); J. Presley, *A Guide to the Saudi Arabian Economy* (Sheridan House, 1989); A.D. Johany, et al., *The Saudi Arabian Economy* (Johns Hopkins University Press, 1999).

CHRIS HOWELL
RED ROCKS COLLEGE

saving

A WIDELY USED TERM with different meanings, saving for an individual may be, for example, the portion of her income that was not used for consumption. For an investor, money saved may be in the form of bonds and stocks. For a city, state, or country, saving may be the money that goes into productive uses such as building roads and parks, increasing educational standards, and building new technology.

A useful way to think about individual saving is to consider a worker in an economy who provides her labor service (say, 40 hours a week) in return for wage/income. One of the most critical decisions that the worker makes is how much of her income to spend on consumption goods and services (i.e. grocery, theater tickets, etc.) and how much to save for potential future use.

Why people save is a central question for economists, and has been the center of academic debate. Two of the most important reasons why people save are:

1. To support consumption in retirement years

2. To support consumption by their children (for bequests).

The first reason for saving (for retirement) stems from a well-known economic theory called the life-cycle hypothesis, pioneered by Franco MODIGLIANI (1963) and others. The hypothesis states that consumption and saving decisions by individuals and households, at each point in time, reflect a more or less conscious attempt to achieve the preferred distribution of consumption over the life cycle.

The second reason for saving (for bequests) stems from the notion that human beings like their children and are very motivated to work hard and save for their children's consumption. A study, by Lauren Koltikoff and Lawrence Summers (1981), concluded that the desire to make bequests was the most important motive for saving. Whether saving is for bequests or to support consumption in retirement years, it has important implications for the individual, the household and the economy as a whole.

Aggregate saving. Economists believe that a constructive way to analyze and understand saving data is by aggregating them into what is called the personal (household) saving rate. To take an example, the U.S. personal saving rate had fallen rather drastically during the 1980s. In particular, U.S. personal saving fell from 7.5 percent in 1981 to 4.1 percent in 1988. The decline in the saving rate has been a concern, as saving provides funds to finance investment projects and ultimately the production of capital (one of the key driving forces of market economies).

Several explanations have been offered for this phenomenon. One explanation consistent with the life-cycle hypothesis is that increased Social Security benefits have reduced the need to save for retirement years. A competing explanation, suggests that the increase in the access to borrowing has decreased saving for future purchase of durable goods. A final explanation is that the growing number of double-income families has significantly reduced future financial uncertainty, thus driving the saving rate down. Whatever the reason, the relatively low personal saving rate in the United States has been worrisome, especially to growth economists who believe that saving is inherently related to the economic growth and development of the country.

Since the seminal work of Robert SOLOW (1956), it has been established that the saving rate is one of the most important determinants of long-run economic growth. One way of explaining why this is the case may be to visit the process used in market economies for the production of capital (such as machinery and equipment). The neoclassical model teaches us that capital in the future is equal to the existing stock of capital (net of depreciation) plus present investment. That is, capital accumulation depends crucially on the level of investment in the economy. But investment is the result of, among other things, saving. Most of our saving (such as in the form of demand deposits etc.), is used by firms in investment projects. So there is a direct link connecting saving to investment and another one connecting investment to capital. It is then obvious that saving behavior is extremely important in the process of capital accumulation, and more generally in economic growth and development.

Given the saving rate effect on economic growth and development, economists have tried to obtain estimates across countries. The main finding is that during the period 1960–90, the variation included high saving rates associated with rich countries and low (sometimes zero) saving rates associated with poor countries.

It is possible that not only does the saving rate positively affect income, but also the reverse, that income positively affects the saving rate. One natural explanation is that saving is low in poor countries because people there simply cannot afford to save. This interpretation suggests that people in poor countries are living at the margin of subsistence, and so they cannot afford to reduce their present consumption in order to save for the future. While this argument is plausible for the poorest countries in the world, it fails once we move to richer countries. If residents of Bangladesh (average income per capita $1,050) cannot afford to save because they are on the margin of subsistence, then the same argument cannot be made about the residents of Zimbabwe (average income per capita $2,280), since they should be far above the subsistence level.

Whether for this reason or for others, the opinion that there is something about being poor that lowers the saving rate is certainly intuitively appealing.

Saving and policy. Governments can influence the private saving rates in a number of different ways. One of the most important ways is in setting up national pension plans. Programs such as Social Security in the United States, in which benefits to the elderly are prima-

rily funded by taxes on those who are currently working, do not generate saving (and thus investment). By contrast, programs in which individuals fund their own retirements by saving during their working years generate a large quantity of capital. During the early 1980s, CHILE set up this type of funded pension system, requiring workers to deposit a fraction of their earnings in an account with a private pension company. Partly as a result of this program, the private savings rate, which had been near zero at the beginning of the 1980s, had reached 17 percent by 1991. The success of the Chilean program led ARGENTINA, Bolivia, COLOMBIA, MEXICO, PERU, and Uruguay to adopt similar plans in the 1990s.

A more extreme version of this kind of pro-saving policy was implemented in SINGAPORE. Starting in the 1950s, workers were required to contribute part of their wages to a "central provident fund," which could be used to finance not only retirement but also medical expenditures and the purchase of housing. The government determined the required contribution rate, which reached a high of 40 percent of a worker's salary in the early 1980s. This forced-saving policy was an important determinant of Singapore's phenomenally high saving rate.

Not all pro-saving policies are so coercive, however. The Japanese government, for example, has relied on persuasion to get its citizens to voluntarily raise their saving rates. The government's Campaign to Encourage Diligence and Thrift (1924–26) featured posters on trains and temples, newspaper advertisements, motion pictures, radio messages, and even rallies. In addition, following WORLD WAR II, a series of pro-savings publicity campaigns were carried out by the Central Council for Savings Promotion. Included in these campaigns were programs to educate children about the importance of saving, and the creation of special banks for children within their schools. Japan has experienced one of the highest savings rates in the world in the period since World War II, although sorting out the extent to which this high saving was due to government persuasion is a not an easy task.

BIBLIOGRAPHY. Albert Ando and Modigliani Franco, "The Life Cycle Hypothesis of Saving: Aggregate Implications and Tests," *American Economic Review* (v.53, 1964); James Estelle, "New Models for Old Age Security: Experiments, Evidence and Unanswered Questions" *World Bank Research Observer* (v.13/2, 1998); Lauren Koltikoff and Lawrence Summers, "The Role of Intergenerational Transfers in Aggregate Capital Accumulation," *Journal of Political Economy* (v.89, 1981); Garon Sheldon, "Fashioning a Culture of Diligence and Thrift: Savings and Frugality Campaigns in Japan, 1900–31" *Japan's Competing Modernities* (University of Hawaii Press, 1998); Robert Solow, "A Contribution to the Theory of Economic Growth," *Quarterly Journal of Economics* (v.70, 1956); Lawrence Summer and Chris Carroll,

"Why is U.S. National Saving So Low?" *Brookings Papers on Economics Activity* (v.2, 1987).

CHRIS PAPAGEORGIOU
LOUISIANA STATE UNIVERSITY

Say's Law

IN CONTEMPORARY discussions, Say's Law of Markets, or simply Say's Law, usually refers to the concept that the production of goods or services automatically constitutes demand for a bundle of goods or services of equal market value. Thus, in aggregate, demand will always be just sufficient to absorb all production, regardless of the volume of output. Sometimes understood as a condition that holds identically at each point in time, and sometimes as the inevitable outcome of equilibrating forces, under either interpretation, it is usually summarized, following John Maynard KEYNES (1936), as the proposition that "SUPPLY creates its own DEMAND."

The rationale behind Say's Law, named for the classical French economist Jean Baptiste Say, is most easily presented in the setting of a one-period BARTER economy. In a barter economy, it is argued, Say's Law holds identically. A shoemaker, for example, may produce shoes either for himself or to exchange for other commodities. The supply of shoes produced for his own consumption obviously equals his demand for shoes, while the supply of shoes produced to exchange for other goods must exactly reflect the extent of his demand for other goods. Thus, the shoemaker's total supply equals his total demand as a simple matter of accounting. Moreover, it is the production of shoes that provides the shoemaker with the means to obtain shoes and all other goods.

While the logic of Say's Law is less transparent in a multi-period monetary economy, the essence of the argument for both the barter economy case and the more complicated case, rests on a relationship that virtually all economists agree upon: The purchasing power of the income generated by production will always exactly equal output. Provided all income is spent, this relationship will establish Say's Law.

Of course, in a barter economy, the purchasing power of income is automatically exercised. Either the shoemaker's shoes are exchanged for goods or they are consumed. In either case, the income that the shoes represent is effectively spent. In a monetary economy, however, things are not so simple. If, for instance, goods are exchanged for cash that is held for its own sake rather than being used to purchase other goods, aggregate demand will fall short of output. Similarly, if income is saved, aggregate demand will fall short of output unless that saving is channeled into investment expenditure by financial markets. Ultimately, defenders of Say's law argue that while such problems are possible in theory, they are not concerns in practice. Either as a result of behavioral relationships, or as an outcome of equilibrating forces, money is always used to purchase goods and savings always equals investment.

Although the Law of Markets bears the name of J.B. Say, it has long been recognized that the principle has distinct roots in Say's predecessors. Joseph J. Spengler (1945) has argued that Say's Law is an outgrowth of the PHYSIOCRATS' conception of circular flow, and many authors have pointed out that Adam SMITH all but enunciates the principle in his *Wealth of Nations*, which precedes Say's first published comments on the subject by more than two decades.

More controversially, several authors have suggested that it was not Say, but James Mill, father of the famous utilitarian John Stuart MILL, who first clearly enunciated the principle. Say first published his ideas in 1803 in his *Traîte d'économie politique*. However, most economic historians agree that his discussion in the first edition, though revised and expanded in later editions, did not contain a statement of what would be recognized today as Say's Law. James Mill's first published discussion of the issues surrounding Say's Law appears in 1808 in *Commerce Defended*. In contrast to Say, Mill's treatment, reiterated in later publications, is largely complete in its initial form and comes much closer to a statement of Say's Law as it is now generally understood.

An apparent consequence of Say's Law is that a nation can never produce too many goods. While nothing prevents specific goods from being temporarily oversupplied, there cannot be an excess supply (or glut) of goods in aggregate if aggregate demand is always equal to aggregate supply.

This proposition was the object of much debate among economists throughout the 1820s and 1830s, an episode that has since been labeled "the general glut controversy." Along with Mill, J.B. Say, David RICARDO, and most other economists of the day viewed general gluts as an impossibility. This followed from Say's Law in their view and meant that economic downturns and surges in unemployment must be caused by mismatches between the demand and supply of particular products.

Thomas R. MALTHUS and J.C.L. Simonde de Sismondi, both of whom were prominent economists at the time, took the opposing point of view, arguing that gluts could be both particular and general. Specifically, both argued that episodes of increased unemployment and declining wages should be viewed as situations in which aggregate demand had fallen short of aggregate supply.

While Malthus' and Sismondi's theories were decidedly more in line with modern economic theory, the defenders of Say's Law clearly won the debate over general gluts. John Stuart Mill published what was widely considered the definitive exposition of economic theory. In his *Principles of Political Economy*, he came down squarely on the side of Say's Law, effectively putting an end to the controversy.

The importance of Say's Law in recent economic history derives from its purported implications for government policy, particularly the appropriate response to a general downturn in business conditions. If Say's Law holds (the argument goes), the appropriate response to a recession is to stimulate production. Government policies that seek to end a recession by stimulating demand without addressing the incentives to produce are bound to be ineffectual, since demand ultimately derives from supply.

The successful defense of Say's Law during the general glut controversy meant that until the onset of the Great DEPRESSION, this was the predominant view among economists. In 1936, however, J.M. Keynes forever changed economic policy with the publication of his *General Theory of Employment, Interest, and Money*. According to Keynes, Say's Law theorists had things exactly backward. Rather than determining demand, production was itself determined by the level of aggregate demand. Thus, the appropriate response to a business downturn is to stimulate the demand for goods and services. In particular, Keynes' argued, the only way to end the Great Depression in a timely manner was to encourage spending on goods and services.

Although Keynes' himself rejected Say's Law, most contemporary economists view Keynesian theory as compatible with Say's Law. For most economists, the appropriate framework for economic analysis and policy prescription is a matter of the time horizon one is considering. In the long run, Say's Law holds and national income is determined by the volume of national production. In the short run, however, Keynes was right; demand is the more important determinant of national income.

BIBLIOGRAPHY. William J. Baumol, "Say's (At Least) Eight Laws, or What Say and James Mill May Really Have Meant" *Economica* (1977); Mark Blaug, ed., "Jean-Baptiste Say" *Pioneers in Economics* (Edward Elgar Publishing, 1991); John M. Keynes, *The General Theory of Employment, Interest and Money* (Macmillan, 1936); Thomas R. Malthus, *Definitions in Political Economy* (Kelley & Millman, 1954); James Mill, *Commerce Defended* (Augustus M. Kelley Publishers,1965); Jean Baptiste Say, *A Treatise on Political Economy* (J. Grigg, 1830); Joseph J. Spengler, "The Physiocrats and Say's Law of Markets," *Journal of Political Economy* (1945).

JOEL D. CARTON, PH.D.
TEXAS TECH UNIVERSITY

SBC Communications

ONE OF THE LARGEST telecommunications service providers in the United States, SBC Communications began with the formation of the Bell telephone companies in the Southwest in the late 1800s. These local telephone service companies operated as part of the AT&T system monopoly. SBC's modern history begins in 1984, when AT&T divested its local telephone service companies and the companies in Texas, Oklahoma, Kansas, Arkansas, and Missouri became Southwestern Bell. Much of SBC's growth since divestiture has been through its merger and acquisitions, which include Ameritech (in the Midwest), SNET (in Connecticut), and most recently Pacific Bell (in California and Nevada).

Beginning by offering traditional telephone service, today SBC's main lines of business also include wireless telecommunications. The company serves 58 million telephone lines and 22 million wireless customers. SBC folded its wireless operations into a joint venture with BellSouth in 2001 called Cingular. In 2001, SBC had revenue of $54 billion and assets worth $96 billion, making it the 29th largest company in the world.

The Telecommunications Act of 1996 allowed dominant local exchange carriers such as SBC to enter the long distance business after regulators deemed their markets competitive. SBC now offers long distance service in six states.

BIBLIOGRAPHY. Gerald Brock, *Telecommunication Policy for the Information Age* (Harvard University Press, 1994); Bruce Kushnick, *The Unauthorized Biography of the Baby Bells & Info-Scandal* (New Networks Institute, 1999); SBC Communications, *Annual Report* (2001).

JAMES PRIEGER, PH.D.
UNIVERSITY OF CALIFORNIA, DAVIS

scarcity

FORMING THE CENTRAL premise of economic thinking, Webster's dictionary defines scarcity as "a dearth, deficiency; state of being scarce." In economics, we use the concept of scarcity in conjunction with human needs or wants, to explain how economic theory works. Often textbooks define economics as the study of how we use our scarce resources to fulfill the unlimited needs.

The concept of scarcity is used to move the discussion into several other areas such as opportunity costs, PRODUCTION POSSIBILITIES, trade-off, efficiency, economic systems, markets and prices, and the concept of value. Thus scarcity sets the tone for much of economic thinking.

There are many things that are scarce in an economy, such as raw materials for producing goods, water, capital, machinery, goods, and human beings. Scarcity is a concept that applies to individuals as well; we have scarcity of money to purchase all of the things that we desire. We also have a scarcity of time, as there are only so many hours in a day to fulfill our tasks. The scarcity of time leads an individual to think about the opportunity cost of doing one activity as opposed to the other. Thus, we can make a rational choice about how best to use our time.

In economics, the concept of scarcity is used to further the idea of efficiency, by evaluating the actions taken in an economy to utilize the scarce resources. An economy achieves productive efficiency if it produces commodities at the least cost possible, and it achieves allocative efficiency if it produces the goods that are needed in an economy. Using these two concepts we can show how an economy is either successful in making the best use of its scarce resources or fails to achieve full potential due to inefficient use of its resources. Scarcity is thus able to explain the inefficiencies in an economy that practices discrimination of race or gender. By denying work opportunities for women and minorities, one can argue that, the UNITED STATES economy did not achieve its full potential. Since we have a limited supply of resources, it should make sense to use all available resources in satisfying the needs of the people in an economy. This is the idea behind the concept of production possibilities. Any economy can increase its output by including all potential workers and not discriminating and limiting the opportunities for a segment of the population.

The lack of availability of things is also used to explore the concept of market and prices. We are able to show how the price of a commodity often reflects the availability of a commodity. For example, the scarcity of diamonds coupled with its perceived utility results in a high price for it. The value for any commodity is arrived at by the scarcity of the commodity. Thus, areas with abundant water do not place a high value on it, while people living in a desert place a high value on water due to its scarce availability.

History gives us many examples of times when commodities become scarce. This could happen because the resources that we use to produce them are now needed in other areas, thus depriving us of the commodities that we need in our daily life. WORLD WAR II created one such situation in the United States. Since the U.S. armed forces needed metal, rubber, chemicals, and food, to fight the enemy, Americans at home faced a scarcity of many commodities. Requiring people to make sacrifices, and asking them to be frugal, among the things that were in scarce supply were rubber boots,

bicycles, birdcages, toasters, phonographs, and alarm clocks. World War II also showed how the scarcity of commodities could lead to potential inflation; policy makers initiated a period of rationing that dampened the threat of inflation. The U.S. government rationed commodities such as sugar, meat, butter, coffee, tires, gasoline, and shoes.

The country of Botswana faces a scarcity of human beings. With 35.8 percent of its population HIV positive, Botswana is losing its people at a very rapid rate. This scarcity of human resource poses a serious threat to the very survival of the country.

Capitalism and SOCIALISM base the central premise of their theories on the notion of scarcity of resources. Capitalists argue that the markets are best capable of deciding how to use scarce resources and thus governments should allow markets to perform this function unhindered. This would lead to efficiency as the highest bidder acquires the resources or goods in the market, exhibiting the clear need for such a resource or good. Karl MARX, however, argued that markets are inherently unstable and lead to the concentration of wealth and power into the hands of the wealthy. Thus, under communism the wealth of an economy can equally be shared by all, and this could lead to efficiency.

BIBLIOGRAPHY. Cynthia Crossen, "In Wartime Holidays Past, Patriots Curbed Spending," *The Wall Street Journal* (December 18, 2002); Roger Thurow, "Botswana Sees Economic Rise Leveled by Raging AIDS Crisis," *The Wall Street Journal* (August 29, 2002); Campbell McConnell and Stanley Brue, *Economics: Principles, Problems and Policies* (McGraw-Hill Irwin, 2002).

JAISHANKAR RAMAN, PH.D.
VALPARAISO UNIVERSITY

Scholes, Myron S. (1941–)

AWARDED THE 1997 Nobel Prize in Economics (with Robert C. MERTON), Myron S. Scholes was recognized for the development of the Black-Scholes option pricing model. Fischer Black, who died in 1995, was also instrumental in the development of this model. Scholes was born in Timmins, Ontario, Canada, and he had a difficult childhood, as his mother died of cancer when he was 16 and he developed scar tissue on his corneas, which gave him poor vision. This problem was corrected when he was 26 with a successful cornea transplant. Scholes attended McMaster University, graduating with a degree in economics in 1962.

For graduate school, Scholes enrolled at the University of Chicago where his graduate advisor was Merton

MILLER. His Ph.D. dissertation attempted to determine the shape of the demand curve for traded securities. After graduating from Chicago in 1968, Scholes became an assistant professor of finance at the Sloan School of Management where he worked with Paul Cootner, Franco MODIGLIANI, Stewart Myers, and Merton. He also met Black who was then a consultant with Arthur D. Little in Cambridge, Massachusetts. It was during this time period that Black, Miller, and Scholes started to develop their option pricing technology.

Scholes left Sloan and took a visiting faculty position back at Chicago in 1973, leading to a permanent position in 1974. At Chicago, he became interested in the effects of taxation on asset prices and incentives and published papers on this topic with Miller and Black. In 1983, Scholes became a permanent faculty member of the business and law schools at Stanford University.

At Stanford, Scholes continued his interest in the effects of taxation and also worked on pension planning. In 1990, he refocused his energies on derivatives when he became a special consultant to Salomon Brother's Inc. While continuing to teach and research at Stanford, he became a managing director and co-head of Salomon's fixed-income-derivative sales and trading group, and in 1994 he, Merton, John Meriwether, and several other colleagues from Salomon left to found Long-Term Capital Management.

BIBLIOGRAPHY. Nicholas Dunbar, *Inventing Money: The Story of Long-Term Capital Management and Legends Behind It* (John Wiley & Sons, 2000), F. Black and M. Scholes, "The Pricing of Options and Corporate Liabilities," *Journal of Political Economy* (v.81, 1973); John Hull, *Options, Futures, and other Derivatives* (Prentice Hall College, 2002); The Nobel e.Museum, "Autobiography of Myron S. Scholes," www.nobel.se/economics.

KIRBY R. CUNDIFF, PH.D.
HILLSDALE COLLEGE

Schultz, Theodore

THEODORE SCHULTZ is a Nobel Prize–winning economist from the University of Chicago. He won his Nobel with Arthur LEWIS for "pioneering research into economic development with particular consideration of the problems of developing countries."

Schultz grew up in the farmlands of South Dakota. WORLD WAR I disrupted his early education, but he later attended and graduated from South Dakota State College. Schultz became interested in economics as he observed the rapidly changing fortunes of farmers. He was attracted to the University of Wisconsin because of its unorthodox approach to economics. He earned his Ph.D. from Wisconsin in 1930.

Schultz began his teaching career at Iowa State College. He became chairman of his department in 1934 and edited the *Journal of Farm Economics* until 1942. He left Iowa for the University of Chicago in 1943, and stayed there until 1972. He moved to Chicago because of the suppression of a report that adversely affected dairy farmers.

During the early part of his career, Schultz focused on agricultural issues. He first studied crises in American agriculture, and then turned to developing countries. Schultz claimed that there was a counter-productive, pro-urban bias in many policies. He argued that government taxes and price ceilings on agricultural goods stifled agricultural innovation in many nations. He also noted that the U.S. government promoted such innovation.

Later in his career, Schultz turned his attention to education and human capital formation. He showed that the UNITED STATES had a considerably higher yield on investment in human capital, and that this caused rapid increases for investment in EDUCATION. Schultz also studied entrepreneurship as the ability to deal with disequilibria.

Schultz became president of the American Economics Association in 1960. He won the Francis Walker medal in 1972 and his Nobel in 1979.

BIBLIOGRAPHY. Theodore Schultz, "Nobel Lecture: The Economics of Being Poor," *The Journal of Political Economy* (v.88/4, 1980); Theodore Schultz, "The Value of the Ability to Deal with Disequilibria," *Journal of Economic Literature* (v.13/3, 1975); Theodore Schultz, "Investing in Poor People: An Economist's View," *The American Economic Review* (v.55/1-2, 1965); Theodore Schultz, *Transforming Traditional Agriculture* (University of Chicago Press, 1983).

D.W. MACKENZIE
GEORGE MASON UNIVERSITY

Schumpeter, Joseph (1883–1950)

UNANIMOUSLY CITED as one of the greatest economists and sociologists of the 20th century, Joseph Schumpeter developed the field of growth economics, argued that entrepreneurial innovation dictates business cycles, and believed that SOCIALISM is an inevitable successor of capitalism.

Joseph Alois Schumpeter was born on February 8, 1883 (the same year Karl MARX died and John Maynard KEYNES was born) in Triesch, Moravia, then part of the

Austro-Hungarian Empire and now in the Czech Republic, and died of a stroke on January 8, 1950, in Taconic, Connecticut.

Schumpeter was born to a prosperous family. His father, who died when Joseph was four, was a second-generation textile manufacturer. His mother Johanna, who moved with her son to Graz after Joseph's father died, was a daughter of a medical doctor. In 1893, Joseph's mother married a high-ranking officer in the Austro-Hungarian Army and the family moved to Vienna. His mother's short-lived remarriage enabled young Schumpeter to receive an excellent education at the Theresianum, the school for the children of the elite. He entered the University of Vienna, at the time one of the world's centers for economic research, to study law and economic history (the faculty of law taught economics). Friedrich von Wieser, Eugen von BÖHM-BAWERK, and other prominent professors sparked his interests in economy and law, but also in sociology and philosophy. Schumpeter received a doctorate in law in 1906.

After spending a year in England and marrying Gladys Ricarde Seaver, in 1907 Schumpeter went to Cairo, Egypt, where, for a couple of years, he practiced law and worked as a financial consultant. Schumpeter published his first book, *The Nature and Essence of Theoretical Economics*, in 1908 in which he provided a methodological reassessment of neoclassical static theory. With Böhm-Bawerk's help in 1909, Schumpeter became a professor at the University of Czernowitz (now called Chernivtsi in the Ukraine). From 1911–18, he worked as a political economy professor and a chair at the University of Graz. During this period Schumpeter published his early masterpiece, *The Theory of Economic Development* (1912), and several other works that made him a world-famous theoretical economist. The main focus of his early studies was the relationship between the phenomenon of economic development and entrepreneurial innovation that he believed drives the economy. Although he was not a socialist, Schumpeter started developing a theory that capitalism was doomed and socialism, or some other form of public control, was its most probable successor.

In 1919, Schumpeter briefly served as finance minister of Austria as a member of the German Socialization Commission. After being fired from the government post, largely for being perceived as fundamentally socialist, Schumpeter entered banking and investment, which proved to be disastrous, both professionally and personally. He was president of the Biedermann bank during Germany's hyperinflation. The bank collapsed in 1924 while his speculative investments with borrowed money left him with huge debts. In 1925, he re-entered academia as a professor at the University of Bonn. In 1926, the year his mother died, Schumpeter's second

wife, Annie Reisinger, died at childbirth. After recovering from grief and depression, in 1926 Schumpeter revised and published the second edition of *The Theory of Economic Development* in which he started developing a monetary theory and analyzing business cycles. He argued that it was essential to provide a dynamic theory of money and analyze cyclical development processes because they generate economic changes. In Bonn, Schumpeter focused on the study of monetary issues that he never completed. This research was only published posthumously in 1970. After firmly establishing himself as an intellectual and economic theorist, in 1932, Schumpeter became a permanent professor of economics at Harvard University.

Schumpeter left Europe and spent the last two decades of his prolific life at Harvard. The main incentive for his abandonment of the cultural world of Europe was the vibrant intellectual climate of Harvard and the opportunity to conduct empirical research on business cycles and the decline of capitalism.

In 1939, Schumpeter published the monumental two-volume work, *Business Cycles: A Theoretical, Historical, and Statistical Analysis of Capitalist Process,* that was unfortunately overshadowed by Keynes' revolutionary theory of depressions and unemployment, *General Theory of Employment, Interest, and Money* (1936), and only became prominent in the 1970s and 1980s. In *Business Cycles,* Schumpeter linked upswings and downswings of the business cycle to innovations that stimulate investment in capital-goods industries. Since new inventions are developed unevenly, business conditions are expansive and recessive. He argued that large entrepreneurial innovations cause Kondratieff Waves that last for decades. Smaller inventions cause Juglar Waves that last for approximately 10 years while Kitchin Waves are shorter still. These waves do not appear with regularity and the DEPRESSION occurred because all three cycles hit a downturn at the same time. For Schumpeter, therefore, the Depression was a part of a necessary process that leads to creative destruction and creation of new sources of economic growth.

In 1942, Schumpeter published *Capitalism, Socialism, and Democracy*, a sociological study that was considered a great success at the time. In this study, he explored the pattern of economic systems over time, focused on socio-cultural advancements, and further developed the argument that the very success of capitalism would undermine its foundations and give rise to socialism. Schumpeter disagreed with Marx that the poor would lead the revolt against capitalism. He believed that the disillusioned intellectuals, who would replace entrepreneurs as the major political force, would instigate the creation of large and powerful centralized governments that would undermine the fundamentals of capitalism.

For the rest of his life Schumpeter devoted himself to teaching and the study of history of economics. Elizabeth Boody, an economic historian specializing in Japan, who married Schumpeter in 1937, compiled and edited his research into a manuscript that was published posthumously in 1954 as *History of Economic Analysis*. This work, an authoritative account of the development of economics from ancient Greece, is still considered one of the greatest contributions to the history of economics.

BIBLIOGRAPHY. Robert Loring Allen, *Opening Doors: The Life and Work of Joseph Schumpeter* (Transaction, 1994); John Medearis, *Joseph Schumpeter's Two Theories of Democracy* (Harvard University Press, 2001); Laurence S. Moss, ed., *Joseph A. Schumpeter, Historian of Economics: Perspectives on the History of Economic Thought* (Routledge, 1996); Joseph A. Schumpeter, *Business Cycles: A Theoretical, Historical and Statistical Analysis of the Capitalist Process* (Porcupine Press, 1939); J.A. Schumpeter, *Capitalism, Socialism, and Democracy* (HarperCollins, 1942); J.A. Schumpeter, *History of Economic Analysis* (Oxford University Press, 1954); Richard Swedberg, *Schumpeter: A Biography* (Princeton University Press, 1991).

JOSIP MOCNIK
BOWLING GREEN STATE UNIVERSITY

Sears, Roebuck & Company

ALVAH CURTIS ROEBUCK and Richard W. Sears founded Sears, Roebuck & Company in 1886. Sears' foray into merchandising started inconspicuously as a side business. He began his working career as a railroad express agent in Redwood Falls, Minnesota. An ambitious fellow, Sears sold coal and lumber to his neighbors in his spare time.

Later, Sears began selling watches on a mail-order basis. He utilized his railroad contacts to expand his market. Soon thereafter, he quit his railroad job to devote his efforts to the watch business. He relocated his operations to Chicago, and opened the R.W. Sears Watch Company. In need of a repairman to fix broken watches, Sears ran a "help wanted" advertisement for a watchmaker. Alvah Curtis Roebuck responded. Sears hired him, and later a partnership developed between the two gentlemen. The company expanded on its offering of watches, and became a mail-order house.

The mail-order business was quite successful. At that time, few Americans lived in cities, and most had limited access to department stores. Sears developed the infrastructure to capture this market. The Sears catalog became a "wish book." The expansion of the railroads and the Industrial Revolution also assisted Sears in his ability to expand.

Sears had the reputation of an unscrupulous businessman. He followed the maxim of the day, *caveat emptor*, or "let the buyer beware." He utilized hard-sell tactics, inflated claims of his products in the catalogs, and introduced bogus inducements to increase sales.

In 1895, Roebuck, only 31-years-old, decided that the merchandise business was too stressful. Sears agreed to buy out his partner's one-third interest for approximately $25,000. Sears, in need of more capital, took on new partners, Julius Rosenwald, and Aaron E. Nusbaum. Rosenwald and Nusbaum operated a clothing manufacturing business, and had sold suits to Sears. Sears' marketing of clothes on a mail-order basis intrigued Rosenwald and Nusbaum. The addition of Rosenwald to the partnership changed the outlook, direction, and morality of the company. Rosenwald eventually succeeded Sears as the company leader when Sears retired in 1908.

From 1895 until 1908, the company was phenomenally successful. Over that period of time, the company realized profits of $11 million and sales grew to $41 million. Sears had an ownership interest in 10 factories.

In 1908, Sears embarked on a new product: prefabricated homes. From 1908 until 1940, Sears sold nearly 100,000 homes via both mail-order and sales offices. Its first book of homes in 1908 featured 22 different home designs, with prices ranging from $650 to $2,500. Sears' success in this venture can be attributed to its marketing strategy, its railroad networks, and building technology.

Sears continued to thrive and prosper. The company opened its first foreign retail store in Havana, Cuba, in 1942, followed by Mexico City in 1947, and then Canada in 1953. In 1973, Sears moved into its new headquarters in Chicago: The Sears Tower, a 110-story building that became the world's tallest building. The headquarters was eventually relocated to a Chicago suburb.

As of the close of fiscal year 2000, Sears operated 863 mall-based retail stores and 1,200 retail locations including hardware, outlet, tire, and battery stores. In the 2001 fiscal year, Sears reported a profit of $735 million, with sales of over $41 billion.

BIBLIOGRAPHY. D.L. Cohn, D. L. and S. Lewis, *The Good Old Days: A History of American Morals and Manners as Seen through the Sears, Roebuck Catalogs 1905 to the Present* (Simon & Schuster, 1940); A. Cooke and A. Friedman, "Ahead of Their Time: The Sears Catalogue Prefabricated Houses," *Journal of Design History* (v.14/1, 2001); E.P. Douglas, *The Coming of Age of American Business: Three Centuries of Enterprise, 1600–1900* (University of North Carolina Press, 1971); "About Sears," www.sears.com.

MARK E. MOTLUCK, J.D.
ANDERSON UNIVERSITY

Securities and Exchange Commission (SEC)

CREATED BY THE U.S. Congress in 1934, the Securities and Exchange Commission (SEC) is an independent, bipartisan, quasi-judicial agency of the federal government. It has both rule-making and enforcement authority.

The primary mission of the SEC is to protect investors and maintain the integrity of the securities markets. Investments in securities of all kinds (whether stocks, bonds, or more exotic instruments) are not guaranteed and can lose all their value. The securities laws are guided by one basic premise: full and fair disclosure of all material information. This is accomplished through two mechanisms:

1. Disclosure, issuers of securities and other parties must make available certain documents such as a prospectus or ANNUAL REPORT

2. Prohibition against misrepresentation, deceit and other fraudulent acts and practices (even where the persons involved are not required to make information available).

These two mechanisms are sometimes referred to as the registration and the anti-fraud requirements. They are distinct requirements. Everyone who is required to register must also abide by the anti-fraud rules; some persons do not have to register but are still subject to the anti-fraud rules.

Disclosure of material information is accomplished at various stages. Initial issuers of securities are required to register under the Securities Act of 1933 unless they have an exemption. Some of these issuers are public companies whose securities are held by large numbers of investors and are traded on various exchanges. These public companies are required to make continuing disclosure in quarterly and annual reports as well as other documents under the Securities Exchange Act of 1934.

The SEC also oversees key participants in the securities industry, including the various stock exchanges, the over-the-counter market, broker-dealers, investment advisors, and mutual funds. The SEC also has regulatory authority over accountants, attorneys, and other individuals to the extent they participate in the securities industry.

Persons who violate the securities laws and SEC rules are subject to civil enforcement actions by the SEC as well as possible criminal prosecution by the U.S. Department of Justice. The SEC brings more than 400 civil enforcement actions every year against both companies and individuals accused of breaking the securities laws. The alleged infractions involve providing false or misleading information, INSIDER TRADING, ACCOUNTING fraud, and other matters.

Creation of the SEC. The SEC was founded during the Great DEPRESSION of the 1930s following the stock market crash of October 1929. While some people argue that the Depression was caused by the stock market crash, the consensus of economists today is that the depression was also caused by other factors; the stock market crash was itself a result of other financial forces leading to the great depression. This led Congress to consider legal measures to reform the securities markets. An end to the Depression depended, in part, on renewed public confidence in the securities markets where business capital was raised.

Many investors had been tempted by the rags-to-riches stories of the 1920s, when some people used easy credit to purchase securities and become wealthy. Approximately 20 million large and small investors purchased stock in the 1920s, although many were not aware of the dangers inherent in the markets and were often ignorant of important information about the companies in which they purchased securities. It has been estimated that of the $50 billion in new securities offerings during the decade of the 1920s, almost one-half became worthless even before the crash of 1929.

There were primitive forms of securities regulation before Congress intervened in the 1930s. Defrauded investors could sue for damages under various common law theories, such as fraud. Many states had enacted securities regulation statutes beginning in the late 19th century. These state statutes are called Blue Sky Laws and typically require new issuers of securities to make public disclosure of information to investors. The name Blue Sky Law is allegedly based on the notion that people who purchase securities often get a financial return no better than the value of a piece of blue sky. After the 1929 stock market crash, Congress felt that these regulations were inadequate to police the large national securities markets.

As a response to the crash and to restore confidence in the capital markets of the United States, Congress passed a series of statutes. The Securities Act of 1933 was designed to regulate initial issues of securities. The Securities Exchange Act of 1934 regulates most other aspects of trading in securities. Specialized statues govern more limited aspects of the securities industry and include the Public Utility Holding Company Act of 1935, the Trust Indenture Act of 1939, the Investment Company Act of 1940, and the Investment Advisors Act of 1940. All these statutes have been amended over the decades in response to new and unique problems. For example, the Sarbanes-Oxley Act of 2002 amended the Securities Exchange Act of 1934 in the wake of financial and accounting scandals at companies such as ENRON.

Structure of the SEC. Each of the five commissioners of the SEC serves a five-year term and these terms are staggered so that one expires each year. No more than three commissioners can be from the same political party. The president appoints the chairman of the SEC from among these commissioners.

The SEC is headquartered in Washington, D.C. It has 11 regional and district offices around the United States, and a staff of over 3,000 personnel including lawyers, accountants, engineers, securities analysts, examiners, and clerical employees. These are divided among four divisions and 18 different offices.

The SEC commissioners meet as a group to interpret the securities statutes, promulgate SEC rules, and engage in enforcement actions. When the SEC promulgates rules, it acts under authority delegated by Congress and its rules generally have the force and effect of law unless they are inconsistent with the U.S. Constitution or federal statutes. When the SEC engages in enforcement actions, it acts in a quasi-judicial capacity and may conduct what amounts to trials against people charged with violations of the securities laws.

Immediately below the commission are the four divisions of the SEC. The Division of Corporation Finance is responsible for public disclosure in initial issues of securities, annual and quarterly filings by publicly traded companies, annual reports to shareholders, proxy materials sent to shareholders before their annual meetings, and documents relating to tender offers, mergers, and acquisitions. The Division of Market Regulation oversees broker-dealer firms (stock brokers), transfer and clearing agents who facilitate the transfer of securities after they are sold, and securities information processors. In addition, the Division of Market Regulation regulates the stock exchanges (such as the NEW YORK STOCK EXCHANGE and the AMERICAN STOCK EXCHANGE) as well as the National Association of Securities Dealers (NASD) and the Municipal Securities Regulation Board. The Division of Investment Management regulates investment advisors and the investment companies such as mutual funds. The Division of Enforcement investigates possible violations of the securities laws, recommends action to the Commission, and negotiates settlements of alleged violations.

Enforcement actions typically begin with a recommendation from the Division of Enforcement. The SEC conducts private investigations after receiving information from various sources including tips from the public and defrauded investors. The SEC has subpoena authority and can compel the production of evidence from a variety of persons. Based on the evidence it gathers, the SEC, through the Division of Enforcement, may recommend a formal proceeding. A trial will then be conducted before an administrative law judge who will make findings of fact and recommendations of law.

The commission reviews the determinations of the administrative law judge and may pursue three possible remedies. First, it may issue administrative remedies such as suspending or revoking the registration of a security; suspending or revoking the registration of a broker-dealer or other regulated person; and, censuring persons for misconduct and suspending them from engaging in the securities industry. Second, the commission may apply to a Federal District Court for a civil injunction prohibiting named persons from engaging in acts that violate the securities laws or SEC rules. Third, the commission may make a referral for criminal prosecution to the Department of Justice.

Securities Act of 1933. The Securities Act of 1933 is sometimes known as the "truth in securities law." Unless an issuer has an exemption, no security may be offered or sold in an initial offering without the filing of a Registration Statement with the SEC and giving each offeree a prospectus. Congress and the SEC have made it clear that registration of a security does not protect investors against loss. The SEC does not have the authority to deny registration based on the merits of a security and does not rule on the fairness of the initial price of a security or the prospects of its ultimate success.

The purpose of registration is to require the disclosure of material facts about the issuer and the security being sold so that investors can make an informed decision to buy. The process of registration does not itself guarantee the accuracy of the facts the issuer discloses, as the SEC does not have the personnel to conduct its own investigation of the underlying facts the issuer does disclose. But false and misleading statements made by an issuer or its agents are illegal. Investors who purchase or sell securities based on false or misleading information have various remedies, including rescission and restitution of the purchase price and damages for lost profits. Other participants in a securities offering such as accountants and broker-dealers may also be subject to liability along with the issuer.

Registration is accomplished on forms provided by the SEC. Information to be disclosed falls into four broad categories. First, the issuer must describe its business and properties. Second, the issuer must describe the security being offered for sale and its relationship to its capital structure. Third, the issuer must disclose information about its management. Fourth, the issuer must present certified financial statements from an independent public accountant. New companies with no operating history will have little to disclose, while existing or large companies will make long and detailed disclosures.

Every offeree and purchaser of a security subject to the Securities Act of 1933 must be given a prospectus. This document, which is often long and detailed, embodies the information contained in the registration statement but in a different format. The prospectus itself is filed with the registration statement as an addendum.

The registration statement and the prospectus are a public document once filed with the SEC. Securities analysts and other people in the industry have access to all SEC public documents and use them in their recommendations to clients on buying and selling securities. Once filed, the Division of Corporation Finance examines each registration statement and prospectus for completion and accuracy. If the SEC obtains information that indicate a registration statement or a prospectus is defective, it can require the issuer to clarify or amend its filing. In extreme cases, the SEC can issue a stop order suspending the effectiveness of a registration and prohibiting future sales of the security. If the SEC determines that a registration meets all its technical requirements, it allows the issuer to begin sales of the security to the investing public.

The filing of a registration statement with the SEC is not the only requirement for many initial issues. The individual states still maintain Blue Sky Laws, which require registration. The Securities Act of 1933 makes it clear that federal law does not pre-empt state law in this area and therefore dual regulation of initial issues exists in the United States.

There are exemptions from the Securities Act of 1933. First, some issuers and their securities are entirely exempt from all the requirements of all federal securities laws. For example, securities issued by the United States, or an individual state, are entirely exempt from both the registration and the anti-fraud requirements. Second, some securities may be exempted from the registration requirement but not the anti-fraud rules. These are usually securities issued to small groups of investors who have certain important characteristics. The philosophy behind these exemptions is based on the need for information which registration will disclose. Some investors do not need such protection since they already have access to the information, such as directors and high-level officers of the issuer. Other investors have the financial wealth to compel disclosure and they can also afford to take a loss if the investment becomes worthless. These groups of investors are sometimes called accredited investors. The SEC has promulgated various rules outlining the registration exemptions.

Securities Exchange Act of 1934. The 1934 Act extended the disclosure doctrine of investor protection. Recall that the 1933 Act only applies to initial issues of securities. Once the initial issue is sold, the 1933 Act regulations cease to apply. But many investors who purchase such initial issues will want to sell their securities in the future and others may be willing to buy. The 1934 Act governs securities traded on a public exchange or over-the-counter. The over-the-counter market has re-

cently grown to include trading by computer on the NAS-DAQ (the National Association of Securities Dealers Automatic Quotation system).

The 1934 Act requires continuing registration and disclosure by what are called registered companies. These must make quarterly and annual disclosures, as well as other disclosures of important events. Annual reports must be filed with the SEC and sent to shareholders before the annual meeting of shareholders required under state corporation law. Any person who solicits a proxy from a shareholder must register with the SEC. A proxy is the right to vote the shares of another person at a shareholder meeting. Persons who make tender offers to buy sufficient stock to take control of a company must register with the SEC once they have acquired five percent of the stock of the target company. Insider trading by directors, high-level officers, and large stockowners is regulated. Insiders must register their holdings with the SEC and report sales and purchases every month. Profits made from illegal insider trading must be paid to the company.

The SEC promulgated its famous Rule 10b-5 under the Securities Exchange Act of 1934. This rule is not the only fraud restriction contained in the various securities laws, but it has the broadest reach. Rule 10b-5 makes it unlawful to employ any device, scheme, or artifice to defraud. It also makes unlawful the making of untrue statements of material fact or the omission to state a material fact whose omission makes other statements misleading. Rule 10b-5 allows private investors to sue for securities fraud and significantly expanded the reach of the rules against fraud.

Some people, including economists, have criticized the securities laws as unnecessary and unduly burdensome. It is claimed that the securities markets operate efficiently in providing all information without the need for government intervention. Issuers of securities who fail to provide material information will be punished by the market long before the SEC can intervene to impose legal punishment. In fact, the costs of complying with SEC rules detract from the efficient functioning of the securities markets.

Congress has not adopted these criticisms of the SEC and its regulatory structure. In fact, Congress expanded the reach of SEC powers in 2002 after financial and accounting scandals brought companies such as Enron and WORLDCOM to bankruptcy. The SEC now has expanded authority to regulate accounting practices and other areas.

BIBLIOGRAPHY. *21st Century Complete Guide to the SEC* (Progressive Management, 2002); Julia K. Brazelton and Janice L. Ammons, *Enron and Beyond: Technical Analysis of Accounting, Corporate Governance, and Securities Issues* (CCH, 2002); Thomas Lee Hazen, *The Law of Securities Regulation*

(West Information Publishing Group, 2002); Richard A. Posner, *Economic Analysis of Law* (Aspen Publishers, 2002); *The Work of the SEC* (SEC, 1974).

DAVID PAAS, J.D., PH.D.
HILLSDALE COLLEGE

BIBLIOGRAPHY. J.J. O'Connor and E.F. Robertson "Reinhard Selten," MacTutor History of Mathematics Archive (University of St. Andrews, Scotland, 1996); R. Selten, "Reexamination of the Perfectness Concept of Equilibrium Points in Extensive Games," *International Journal of Game Theory* (v.4, 1975).

TILMAN KLUMPP, PH.D.
INDIANA UNIVERSITY, BLOOMINGTON

Selten, Reinhard (1930–)

GERMAN MATHEMATICIAN, economist, and Nobel laureate, Rienhard Selten was born in Breslau, Germany (now Wroclaw, Poland). He graduated from J.W. Goethe University in Frankfurt with a master's degree in mathematics in 1957, and with a Ph.D. degree in 1961. Selten was promoted to full professor at Frankfurt in 1968. He also taught at University of California, and held chaired positions at Free University in Berlin, the University of Bielefeld, and the University of Bonn.

Selten devoted much of his work to the development of game-theoretic solution concepts, used to predict the outcome of strategic problems. For his seminal work on Nash Equilibrium refinements, Selten was awarded the Bank of Sweden Prize in Economic Sciences in Memory of Alfred Nobel in 1994. He shared the prize with John NASH of the United States, and John HARSANYI of Hungary.

Searching for a Nash Equilibrium—a profile of strategies that are best responded to one another—is the most commonly used way of predicting the outcome of strategic situations (games). While Nash proved that all finite games have an equilibrium point, they frequently possess more than one. This multiplicity makes additional selection criteria desirable. Selten was the first to systematically put further restrictions on Nash's Equilibrium concept, in order to identify "reasonable" predictions.

Selten's most celebrated contributions are the solution concepts of *Trembling Hand Perfect Equilibrium* and *Subgame Perfect Equilibrium*. In the former, each player's strategic choice must be optimal even when there is a small chance that other players make mistakes (that is, they do not play their optimal strategies). The latter applies to strategic situations with a dynamic structure, requiring that each player's choice involves only threats and promises of future actions that are credible, in the sense that they are optimal once a player must make his decision.

Selten showed that all finite games have such equilibria. He published his results in several papers, his ideas were central to what became the Refinement Program in GAME THEORY: The search for ever more sophisticated rationality criteria for selecting the most reasonable prediction in a game.

Sen, Amartya (1933–)

AWARDED THE 1998 Nobel Prize in Economics, Amartya Sen is known for contributions to welfare economics, the science of how to combine individual values to decide what is best for society as a whole. Born in Bengal (India), Sen has a Ph.D. from Cambridge University and has taught at Harvard and Oxford universities.

Sen grappled with foundational questions in development economics about poverty, hunger, and inequality, their conceptualization, measurement, and cures. In *Poverty and Famines* (1981), he challenged the prevailing view that famines were caused primarily by a shortage of food. He wrote: "Starvation is the characteristic of some people not having enough food to eat. It is not the characteristic of there being not enough food to eat."

In the Great Bengal Famine of 1943, for example, food prices rapidly rose due to wartime speculation and hoarding, and farm workers' wages did not keep up; it was these sorts of factors, he said, that largely caused the famine.

Among his many contributions was to note that the POVERTY index in wide use created little incentive for governments to help the extremely poor. The index was a headcount of those below a specified income level. If a government raised the incomes of the extremely poor nearly to the poverty line, its efforts would not be reflected in a fall in the poverty headcount. Sen proposed instead the poverty gap, the total additional income needed to bring all the poor out of poverty. This index would fall if a government raised incomes of the extremely poor, giving a government recognition and motivation for doing so.

BIBLIOGRAPHY. "Amartya Sen," www.nobel.se; Amartya Sen, *Collective Choice and Social Welfare* (Holden-Day, 1970); Amartya Sen, *Poverty and Famines* (Clarendon Press, 1981); Amartya Sen, *Development as Freedom* (Knopf, 1999).

MEHRENE LARUDEE, PH.D.
UNIVERSITY OF KANSAS

Senior, Nassau (1790–1864)

BORN IN BERKSHIRE, England, Nassau Senior was originally trained as a lawyer but he gravitated to economics and, in 1821, published his first economic article on the Corn Laws (English laws restricting the trade of grain between England and other countries). In 1825, he became the first Drummond Professor of Political Economy at Oxford University. He wrote many articles on public policy, notably on the Poor Laws and the Factory Act. His major work, *An Outline of the Science of Political Economy*, was published in 1836.

Senior is best known for his abstinence theory of profit. In this theory, he attempted to explain why the rate of profit is positive and why capitalists should be the ones who receive this form of payment. This attempt must be judged successful in that abstinence theory became quite popular in 19th-century economics, particularly in England.

For Senior, abstinence meant "the conduct of a person who either abstains from the unproductive use of what he can command, or designedly prefers the production of remote to that of immediate results." Thus, capitalists will refrain from consuming part of their income so that it can be used for the production of future goods. Senior saw this as a counterpart to the labor of a worker. In both cases a cost is incurred: in the case of the worker there is the obvious cost (disutility) of the labor itself, while in the case of the capitalist there is the not-so-obvious cost (disutility) of not consuming. Senior, however, made it clear that this really is a cost to the capitalist: "To abstain from the enjoyment which is in our power, or to seek distant rather than immediate results, are among the most painful exertions of the human will." As a reward for their respective sacrifices, workers would receive wages and capitalists would receive profits.

This meant that Senior saw abstinence as one of the three factors of production. The three traditional factors of early 19th-century economics were LAND (what Senior called "natural agents"), LABOR, and CAPITAL. Senior replaced capital with abstinence, so that capital, no longer being a primary factor of production, became a result of a combination of the other three. The popularity of this theory was, no doubt, due in large part to its apologetic nature. As opposed to seeing profit as a SURPLUS, derived from the exploitation of workers, Senior saw abstinence as being productive, so that the profit paid to the capitalist who abstained, was payment for this work (abstinence as disutility), and did not indicate any sort of exploitation of workers. This not only morally justified the payment of profit, it showed that capitalism was a fair, non-exploitative economic system. This conclusion was apparently very comforting to the majority of economists of the 19th century.

In addition to his abstinence theory, Senior can be credited with being the first to have attempted to provide an axiomatic basis for economic theory. Anticipating modern developments, he tried to build up economic theory on the basis of "the four elementary propositions of the science." While theoretical advancements have long since supplanted his propositions, the idea of an axiomatic basis for the science of economics is a very modern concept, making his attempt quite noteworthy.

In his writings on public policy, Senior consistently adopted the position that all policy should be in accordance with the evolution of personal freedom. Like contemporary conservatives, he argued that an important measure of the progress of society is its level of individual freedom, and that a paramount duty of government is to preserve and enhance this freedom. Thus, he was opposed to the Poor Law relief of the able-bodied, in which the state assumed responsibility for those who should have the freedom to take responsibility for their own actions. As the driving force of the Poor Law Commission (set up in 1832) and the subsequent Poor Law Amendment Act (a milestone of English welfare regulations, passed in 1834), he was able to influence public policy in a very direct way, based on this economic philosophy. In the same vein, Senior was adamantly opposed to trade unions on the grounds that they restricted the individual liberty of workers to associate (or not associate) with whom they please.

As a final note on his philosophical adherence to what he saw as freedom—in this case his commitment to free markets—Senior gained notoriety for his argument against the Factory Act proposal of reducing the typical working day from 12 to 10 hours (i.e., he argued against the government telling firms how to conduct their business). He explained that since all the profits of cotton mills were produced in the last hour, a reduction of the working day would be devastating, with manufacturers being forced out of business. Unfortunately for Senior, this assertion that the last hour was so profitable was incorrect, and consequently he was severely criticized by his contemporaries and later famously ridiculed by Karl MARX. However, it should be said that Senior was philosophically consistent, even to the extent of defending brutally long working hours. His argument was fallacious, but his position was sound.

Senior's influence primarily comes from his theory of abstinence, which was later taken up by the much more well-known English economists John Stuart MILL and Alfred MARSHALL. However, he can be considered representative of early to mid-19th-century English political economy, as his writings on both theory and policy exemplified the prevailing dominant views on economics.

BIBLIOGRAPHY. Mark Blaug, *Economic Theory in Retrospect* (Cambridge University Press, 1978); Marian Bowley, *Nassau Senior and Classical Economics* (Octagon Books, 1967); Isaac Rubin, *A History of Economic Thought* (Ink Links, 1979); Joseph Schumpeter, *History of Economic Analysis* (Oxford University Press, 1954); Nassau Senior, *An Outline of the Science of Political Economy* (Augustus M. Kelley, 1965).

PAUL A. SWANSON
WILLIAM PATERSON UNIVERSITY

Serbia and Montenegro

A STATE KNOWN AS the Federal Republic of Yugoslavia until 2003, the country is a loose confederation of Serbia and Montenegro, two of the constituent republics of the former Socialist Federal Republic of Yugoslavia. The Socialist Yugoslavia consisted of six republics, four of which proclaimed secession in 1991–92. The remaining republics, Serbia and Montenegro, formed a joint state in 1992, claiming the legal succession of the old Yugoslav Federation. However, this idea had been abandoned, and in March 2003, the state name Yugoslavia was replaced with Serbia and Montenegro.

Serbia is the larger of two partner states with the territory of 88,316 square kilometers and with a population just above 10 million, according to the census in 2001. The majority of the population is comprised of ethnic Serbs, with sizeable Albanian and Hungarian minorities. Historically, Serbia was an agricultural economy with a dynamic livestock trade. The structural changes in Serbia's economy began in the early 20th century, when economic dependence on Austria-Hungary ended and Serbia established strong economic ties with major Western European countries. The rapid industrialization of Serbia occurred after WORLD WAR I, and especially after WORLD WAR II. In the late 1990s, the principal industries were production of electrical energy, chemical industry, textile, construction industry, machinery, and metal processing industry.

Montenegro contains an area of 13,812 square kilometers with a population around 700,000 in 2001. Montenegrins, a close ethnic kin to the Serbs, are the majority with Albanian and Muslim minorities. Traditionally, the economy of Montenegro was based on agriculture and animal husbandry. Rapid industrialization of the country occurred after World War II, with the production of electric power, iron, steel, and nonferrous metal industries. In the 1970s, tourism became the most vigorous sector of the economy.

The economy of Serbia and Montenegro suffered greatly due to international sanctions from 1992–2000.

The estimated GROSS DOMESTIC PRODUCT (GDP) was $24 billion and GDP per capita was $2,250. The inflation rate was around 40 percent and unemployment close to 30 percent. The major export items include manufactured goods and raw materials, while imports mainly consist of machinery and transport equipment, fuel and lubricants.

BIBLIOGRAPHY. Statistical Yearbook of Federal Republic of Yugoslavia (Belgrade: Statisticki zavod); Zeljan Schuster, *Historical Dictionary of the Federal Republic of Yugoslavia* (Scarecrow Press, 1999); "Serbia and Montenegro," *CIA World Factbook* (2003).

ZELJAN SCHUSTER, PH.D.
UNIVERSITY OF NEW HAVEN

services

SERVICES ARE ECONOMIC activities that yield a product that is not a physical good. As processes, services are extremely heterogeneous in nature, the intangibility of the product being the only attribute common to all services. The extent of the service sector typically grows with increasing economic development. The prevalence of services in creating wealth is therefore an indicator for the degree of structural transformation (or modernization) of capitalist economies.

A category of goods. Services are notoriously difficult to define, and a plethora of definitions have been suggested. They are conventionally portrayed as a category of GOODS that are intangible, invisible, and perishable, and that require simultaneous production and consumption, while physical goods (or commodities) are tangible, visible, and storable, and do not require direct interaction between producers and consumers. However, this characterization applies, if at all, only to personally delivered services.

Some services have elements of tangibility (e.g., the printed report of a consultant or a computer program on a diskette), visibility (e.g., haircuts or theater plays), storability (e.g., automatic telephone-answering systems or online databases) and may not require direct contact between producers and consumers (e.g., automated teller machines or online services). The production of physical goods generally involves a service component, and most products are indeed bundles that include services (e.g., automobiles are offered with warranty, service guarantees, and financing options). Conversely, complex products—such as cruise vacations or dental care—in which services predominate may also include physical goods. Neither is transience a clear criterion for separating goods and services, as may be illustrated by ice cream (a physical good) and the long-lasting effect of a medical surgery (a service).

There is no agreement on whether services are a category of final goods (or products), or rather input factors (or intermediary goods). According to the terminology of the International Organization for Standardization, services are "results" while "service delivery is an activity." Another definition, by economists Valarie Zeithaml and Mary J. Bitner, on the other hand, sees services as "deeds, processes, and performances" and thus emphasizes their process character rather than that of final products.

An alternative definition sees a service as "a change in the condition of a person, or of a good belonging to some economic unit, which is brought about as the result of the activity of some other economic unit with the prior agreement of the former person or economic unit," explains T.P. Hill in a journal article. Implicit in this conception is a focus on change and a distinction between the production of a service and its output. Changes, in contrast to goods themselves, cannot be transferred from one economic agent to another; changes can also not be owned.

For example, a composer effects changes (in paper and ink) by producing a score, which enables an orchestra to effect further changes (in bodies of air) that leave behind a residue in the form of a marketable CD. Economic value is imputed to the composer's actions (or to the actions of a designer of automobiles) on the basis of the market value of their end results, which are tradable goods. This definition ultimately implies that services as such are not any subcategory of goods and that, by implication, there are no trade-able services.

Because of the difficulty of drawing ontological boundaries between physical goods and services, and because in reality most products are bundles of both, the business literature conceives of products as placed in a spectrum that stretches from "pure" commodities to "pure" services, with nearly all products being positioned somewhere on this continuum. The more product differentiation progresses and products become augmented, the more they assume the character of wholes that can no longer be dissected into two clearly distinguishable categories of parts.

The service sector. As with other economic activities, services can be measured either on the demand side, as a share of aggregate consumption, or on the supply side, as a share of aggregate production. Since there is no generally accepted definition of services, the service sector is notoriously difficult to demarcate regardless of the method. This is why the service sector, as the "tertiary" sector, is often simply seen as the residual economic activity after the primary (agriculture and extractive industries) and secondary (manufacturing) sectors have been defined. One consequence of this categorization is that activities comprising the tertiary sector are extremely heterogeneous. The process of tertiarization, i.e., the rapid growth of the service sector at the expense of the primary and secondary sectors in practically all (and particularly in the most developed) economies, makes the absence of clear sector definitions an unwelcome fact.

As countries experience economic growth and development, the service sector typically takes up a larger share of employment and GROSS DOMESTIC PRODUCT (GDP), a process that is also referred to as structural change. In low-income countries, services contribute on average 44.9 percent to total value-added; in middle-income countries, this share is 51.9 percent, and in high-income countries, 67.3 percent. In the most advanced countries, services account for more than 70 percent of GDP. In 2001, the service share of GDP in the UNITED STATES was 73.9 percent (and in LUXEMBOURG as high as 80.1 percent). About 75 percent of employment was in the service sector including the public sector.

In the *Economic Census of the United States*, services take up chapters 41–89 in the Standard Industrial Classification (SIC) code (though only chapters 70–89 are called "Service Industries") and chapters 42–81 in the North American Industrial Classification System (NAICS). In the EUROPEAN UNION (EU), services comprise sections G to Q (chapters 50–99) of the NACE classification. The magnitudes rely on supply-side measurement.

Such service sector demarcations are by necessity arbitrary. Products that are closely related from a consumer's point of view are often categorized differently. Newspapers, for example, are usually classified in manufacturing, whereas their online versions, together with television and broadcasting, are services, though all are media products and respond to the same type of consumer demand. Tourism demand usually is for a bundle of products of which some have a more tangible (food and beverages or souvenirs) and others a more intangible character (folklore performances, transportation, or travel insurance).

Precise demand-side definitions of the sector are therefore impossible. But similar problems affect supply-side definitions. Services are not only produced by typical service businesses; manufacturers offer warranties and repair services, delivery, financing, and maintenance. Moreover, the degree of outsourcing heavily determines measurement of sector size. If, in a manufacturing firm, engineers, accountants or computer programmers are on payroll, their product is counted toward manufacturing output; if the firm outsources these tasks to specialized firms, it would be counted toward the service sector. Thus, while the size of the service sector has undoubtedly grown, and services make by far the greatest contribution to value added in most economies, its exact dimension cannot be quantified with precision.

Service classification. Several methods of classifying services have emerged. The functional method, which is generally used by international organizations and national income statistics, groups traded services—which must be distinguished from non-tradable services—according to the tasks they perform. Factor services (i.e., returns to the use of factors of production) may be contrasted with non-factor services. Functional classification also allows traded services to be separated into primary services (that is, unskilled labor services such as domestic help, guards, and the like), intermediate services (for example, transport, non-life insurance, advertising, communications, databases, and business services), and final services (such as travel, life insurance, and real estate rentals). Such classifications rely on an ad hoc taxonomy rather than on economic or behavioral criteria.

From the perspective of the demand side, a distinction between business services and consumer services is often made. Business services are those that are typically demanded by firms, e.g., insurance, financial services, and wholesaling. Consumer (or personal) services are then all residual services or those typically demanded by households (e.g., haircuts, surgery, hotel accommodation, restaurant meals, education, social work, and entertainment). More recently, the fastest-growing branches of business services, those providing knowledge and information (which includes software development, systems management, and communication), have been categorized as the knowledge-based services, or the quaternary sector of the economy. Clearly, there is a significant overlap between the two categories; service sector classifications always have a degree of artificiality.

From the perspective of the supply side, public services (i.e., those that are provided by governments of different types) may be distinguished from private services provided by participants on competitive markets. Detailed classification systems such as those underlying statistics of national accounts break service providers further down into service industries.

From an economic point of view, services can be embodied or disembodied (or splintered): "Basically one has to draw a distinction between services as embodied in the supplier of the services and requiring their physical presence where the user happens to be, and services which can be disembodied from the supplier and provided without a physical presence being necessary," explains economist Jagdish N. Bhagwati

From the perspective of international trade, services can be defined by reference to the location of producers or consumers. The GENERAL AGREEMENT ON TRADE IN SERVICES (GATS) classifies services into four modes of trade: services supplied across borders such as international telephone calls; services consumed abroad such as tourism; services provided by establishing a commercial presence in a foreign country such as a foreign branch of a commercial bank; and lastly, services provided by the movement of natural persons across borders such as consulting.

Economic issues. The traditional concept of services implies certain economic characteristics. Foremost among these has been the belief that the production of services creates lower increases in productivity than the production of commodities. Consequently, classical economists such as Adam SMITH dubbed services "unproductive labor" that could not make any lasting contribution to the accumulation of wealth. Having criticized the French PHYSIOCRATS who considered agriculture as the most productive activity, Smith considered manufacturing to be the only real "engine of growth." His argument influenced a long tradition in economics that includes Karl MARX who, in *Capital*, dismissed the economic value of services as such but admitted that they have value for the capitalist: "A writer is a productive laborer not in so far as he produces ideas, but in so far as he enriches the publisher who publishes his works, or if he is a wage-laborer for a capitalist."

Such views neglect the comparative advantage countries have historically found in the service sector. Early in the history of England, its wealth came from shipping, finance, and overseas trade because of its location. SWITZERLAND gained its pre-eminence in international finance because of its topography, geographical location, neutral policies, and strict bank secrecy. These factors, together with the natural amenities of landscape and culture, made Switzerland also one of the pioneers of tourism. Services thus hardly increase solely to absorb excess labor from production; they are frequently the objects of final consumer demand.

The notion that production of commodities (or physical goods) is of higher value than production of services betrays confusion over final products. It is not the case that services can only achieve value by becoming input factors to commodity production, as Hill's definition implies. Services such as advertising, accounting or product design are inputs to the production of other goods or services; services such as opera performances, haircuts, or television programming are, as consumer services, final products that are demanded for their own sake. The economic question is then, rather, how to explain the fact that service sector growth correlates so strongly with economic growth and development, and why structural change occurs in spite of the relatively lower capacity of services for productivity growth.

A rather skeptical answer, in the line of Smith, is in the center of the debate on services. According to William Baumol, personal (though not necessarily business) services suffer from a "cost disease" or an "unbalanced productivity growth." Due to the essentially personal and labor-intensive nature of services that admit of little or no mechanization, productivity tends to lag behind the manufacturing sector, and costs in service businesses are bound to rise over time. Baumol argued that this has three consequences:

1. Relative prices in industries with low productivity growth (such as healthcare, legal advice and law enforcement, social work, food service, or sanitation) will rise faster than prices in high-productivity industries

2. Relative employment will rise faster in industries with lower productivity growth

3. Overall productivity growth will fall as the labor force is shifted to low-productivity industries, given constant shares of output.

This model would explain why employment growth in the advanced economies has, over the recent decades, been almost exclusively in the service sector while nominal wages have fallen behind those in manufacturing and services at the same time take up growing shares of economic output. Tertiarization thus comes at a price.

However, Baumol's argument applies only to personal—or rather to embodied—services. It is disembodied (or "splintered") services such as telecommunications, software, and the production of music CDs that have been the main engine of economic growth and that explain increasing service sector shares in GDP. Disembodied services are services that can be stored; they rely on physical carrier media and are reproducible like other physical goods. Thus this type of services creates high levels of productivity increase although personal services generally may not, explains Bhagwati. Furthermore, it has been shown that productivity has been systematically underrated even in personal services. The introduction of electronic data processing, self-service operations, wage payments per output, and of more sophisticated methods of management have improved the total factor (including the labor) productivity even in personal service industries.

The two most widely misunderstood concepts in the economics of services are productivity and innovation. Measurement of productivity is hampered by the application of models developed for the primary and secondary sectors. Some service sectors such as transportation and banking have experienced significant productivity gains. It is also not true that services as such allow for little innovation, which in turn would

make them a stagnant sector of the economy. The nature of innovation in service industries is indeed distinct from the other sectors. More so than in manufacturing, it includes processes and organizational innovations, such as new forms of delivering customer value or of managing customer relationships. Service innovation and productivity gains, as exemplified in new approaches to engineering and product design, are also often not attributed to the service sector, which distorts measurement.

In international economics, it is assumed that some, though not all, services are trade-able, and that the theory of comparative advantage applies equally to the service sector. Although trade in services has historically been addressed in multilateral agreements, it has become a pivotal issue as services have emerged as a major component of world output. In 2001, services constituted about 60 percent of the world's output according to WORLD TRADE ORGANIZATION (WTO) statistics, and international trade in services continues to grow rapidly. Trade in services has increased particularly in developing countries, accounting for more than 80 percent of total export revenues for some nations. Particularly smaller nations have found it profitable to specialize on the production and trade of services for the rest of the world. In recognition of the growing importance of services in the world economy, the GATS has become the first attempt to draw international trade in services into the WTO multilateral framework of rules and market access guidelines.

Currently, two issues are at the forefront of GATS negotiations. First, WTO members disagree vehemently over the liberalization of financial sectors. Economically advanced countries are pushing for open financial markets while developing countries are resisting rapid liberalization. Second, many nations worry that liberalizing trade in services may weaken local sovereignty. Local governments clamor that open service markets will jeopardize control over land use, licensing, environmental health, and local content and production rules in media. Only further rounds of trade negotiations will resolve these issues.

Management issues. The inherent differences between services and physical goods require a different approach to services management. The intangibility of services as traditionally understood leads to a number of problems for service providers: consumers cannot test services before consumption; the results of a service often cannot be seen (e.g., insurance policies); and patenting is not possible. The inseparability of production and consumption, that characterizes many but not all services, has implications for human resource management, as consumers often cannot distinguish between a service and the person delivering it.

The heterogeneous nature of services means that mass production is impossible, that consumers' perception of service quality is highly variable, and that legal issues of warranty may arise. The time-perishable nature of services, in turn, gives the matching of supply and demand greater prominence than in the production of material goods. Many services are also subject to capacity constraints because they are, for example, produced in theaters, restaurants, cable networks, airplanes, hotels, or nature parks; all of these provide facilities that, if they remain unused, perish for that time period.

Service management has developed several strategies and tools to deal with these specificities, among which are the following:

1. Addition of material elements to service packages to increase visibility

2. Implementation of yield management systems (i.e., differential pricing and price incentives) at non-peak times so as to maximize overall capacity utilization

3. Development of reservation and flow management systems to reduce waiting

4. Increased customer participation to reduce labor input

5. Blueprinting of service delivery (i.e., development of flowcharts for service provision and training of staff to these standards)

6. Introduction of service standards and of customer guarantees and warranties (e.g., ISO 9000 standards or zero-defects programs)

7. Use of customer relationship management (CRM) and customer loyalty programs as pioneered by airlines and now widely used also in other service industries

8. Intensification of human resource management strategies such as employee empowerment and enhanced training in service delivery and customer service

9. Expansion of branding, including co-branding of services with physical goods.

Service trends. The following trends may be identified in the service sector and are likely to characterize its further development: New forms of hybrid combinations between physical goods and services will emerge, as competition forces companies to augment products by way of the inclusion of services (e.g., banking, mail, catalog shopping, and pet grooming services in retail outlets). Increased prepackaging of services will develop, which thereby become stored (e.g., self-instruction courses, do-it-yourself legal kits, medical self-testing devices, etc.). Further development of services offered and delivered on the internet will proceed (e.g., counseling, education, investment, translation, etc.).

Economists point to an enhancement of the service content in the production of physical goods, particularly due to an increasing RESEARCH AND DEVELOPMENT (R&D) intensity in product development (e.g., biotechnological and pharmaceutical products). As companies seek stronger economies from specialization, internally produced services are likely to be further replaced by externally contracted services. Expansion of franchising and other forms of distributing systems of service delivery and marketing can also be expected. Extension of services to business-to-business markets should continue; producers of intermediate goods increasingly are marketing a total product that includes associated services. And, as more countries open their service markets, under the GATS process, trade in services is expected to grow significantly. Overall, these trends would suggest that sectoral change has not yet come to an end even in highly developed economies, and that the service sector is poised for further expansion throughout the world.

BIBLIOGRAPHY. Jagdish N. Bhagwati, "Splintering and Disembodiment of Services and Developing Nations," *The World Economy* (v.7, 1984); William J. Baumol, "Macroeconomics of Unbalanced Growth: The Anatomy of Urban Crisis," *American Economic Review* (v.57, 1967); Jean-Claude Delaunay and Jean Gadrey, *Services in Economic Thought* (Kluwer Academic, 1992); Victor R. Fuchs, *The Service Economy* (Columbia University Press, 1968); F. Gallouj, *Innovation in Services* (Edward Elgar, 2003); Christian Grönroos, *Service Management and Marketing* (Swedish School of Economics, 1990); T.P. Hill, "On Goods and Services," *Review of Income and Wealth* (v.23, 1977); Christopher H. Lovelock and Lauren K. Wright, *Principles of Service Marketing and Management* (Prentice Hall, 1999); Richard Normann, *Service Management* (John Wiley & Sons, 1991); Teresa A. Swartz and Dawn Iacobucci, eds., *Handbook of Services Marketing and Management* (Sage Publications, 1999); Valarie Zeithaml and Mary J. Bitner, Services Marketing (McGraw-Hill, 2003).

WOLFGANG GRASSL
HILLSDALE COLLEGE

Sharpe, William F. (1934–)

ONE OF THREE RECIPIENTS of the 1990 Nobel Prize in Economics, William F. Sharpe (with Harry M. MARKOWITZ of the City University of New York and Merton H. MILLER of the University of Chicago) was honored for pioneering work in the theory of financial economics.

The trio, in their separate-yet-parallel research activities, added their own building blocks to the financial market theory. According to Assar Lindbeck of the Swedish Academy of Science, "The theory would have been incomplete if one of them had been missing. Together, they created a complete picture of theory for the financial market, which has had great importance in research and education."

Sharpe's contribution, called the "Capital Asset Pricing Model" and refined from earlier suggestions by Markowitz, cites a way of matching potential gain from an investment with potential risk. Since its introduction, it has become an investment standard in the securities market, continuing to be used by corporations, banking institutions, and pension fund managers.

Sharpe had barely begun to know his native Boston when his father's National Guard unit—thus, his family—relocated halfway across the United States to Texas in 1940. A year later, with the outbreak of WORLD WAR II, the Sharpes moved again, this time farther west to California. There, the family remained, long enough for Sharpe to enroll at the University of California, Berkeley, his sights set on a medical degree. Once he embarked on his course of studies, however, he realized that his interests actually lay elsewhere. Changing curriculum, he transferred to the University of California, Los Angeles, to seek a degree in business administration.

In 1955, Sharpe earned his B.A. and a year later his master's degree. He credits two particular professors at UCLA as being guiding lights to his future career: J. Fred Weston, who introduced him to the vast changes taking place in the world of finance, and Armen Alchian, a sleuth of sorts, who taught his students to question everything, to concentrate on essential elements and never surrender their own ideals. "I have attempted to emulate his approach to research ever since," Sharpe says in his autobiography.

Following a brief stint in the U.S. Army, Sharpe took a position of economist with the RAND Corporation. Besides taking part in various high-level, deep penetrating research projects, he worked on his doctorate in economics. It was at that time, while working on his dissertation, that Sharpe met Markowitz.

As Sharpe remembers, "I worked closely with him on the topic, Portfolio Analysis Based on a Simplified Model of the Relationships Among Securities. Although Harry was not on my committee, he filled a role similar to that of dissertation advisor. My debt to him is enormous."

Through most of the 1960s, Sharpe served as finance professor at the University of Washington's School of Business. During these years, the seed of what would become his Nobel achievement grew, sprouting its earliest versions in a report he wrote for the *Journal of Finance*, published in late 1964.

The year 1970 witnessed two important events in Sharpe's life. Not only was he invited to accept a teaching position at Stanford University—where he would re-main for the next quarter-century—but the publication of his book, *Portfolio Theory and Capital Market*, met with widespread praise. By 2003, Sharpe was still conducting research and working with the National Bureau of Economic Research to study bank capital adequacy, designing a new course at Stanford on international investment management, and, one of his proudest accomplishments, founding Financial Engines, a firm providing online investment advice.

BIBLIOGRAPHY. William F. Sharpe, *Portfolio Theory* (McGraw Hill, 1999); William F. Sharpe Biography, www.stanford.edu; William F. Sharpe Autobiography, www.nobel.se.

JOSEPH GERINGER
SYED B. HUSSAIN, PH.D.
UNIVERSITY OF WISCONSIN, OSHKOSH

Siemens

RANKED BY *Fortune* magazine as the 22nd largest company in the world, Siemens is a German conglomerate founded in 1847 that, in 2002, had 426,000 employees worldwide and net sales of over $90 billion.

Founded as a small manufacturer of telegraph equipment, Siemens grew in its 150-plus- year history to have over a dozen business units, including Information and Communication Networks (the largest unit), Information and Communication Mobile, Business Services, Automation and Drives, Building Technologies, Power Generation, Transportation Systems, Automotive, and Medical Solutions.

In the mid-19th century, Siemens started a program of technology research that resulted in discoveries such as a new way to generate electricity (1866). The company also inaugurated employment practices that were quite humane and somewhat radical for their time, such as an employee pension fund (1872) and an 8.5-hour workday (1891).

Some notable business and technological successes for Siemens were the first electric railway (1879); the first subway on the European continent (1896); laying the foundation for the European long-distance telephone network (1921); the first automatic traffic lights in Germany (1926); development of the first pacemaker for heart patients (1958); and the first 64-kilobit computer memory chip (1981).

Siemens's success has been both a blessing and a curse. Its diverse businesses and far-flung operations have made it hard for anyone at Siemens to know what others are doing. One contract in Malaysia was saved, for example, when a Siemens employee discovered by chance that the company had already done a similar project in Denmark and could transfer the technology.

In the late 1990s, Siemens sought to re-invent part of itself as an e-business. At the turn of the 21st century, the effort appeared to be succeeding.

BIBLIOGRAPHY. Roy Radner, "Hierarchy: The Economics of Managing" *Journal of Economic Literature* (September 1992); Leslie Hannah, "Survival and Size Mobility among the World's Largest 100 Industrial Corporations, 1912–1995," *American Economic Review* (May 1998); "All at Siemens," *The Economist* (November 5, 1998); "Electronic Glue," *The Economist* (May 31, 2001); "Waving or Drowning?" *The Economist* (July 26, 2001); "Global 500," *Fortune* (July 2002).

SCOTT PALMER, PH.D.
RGMS ECONOMICS

Simon, Herbert A. (1916–2001)

IN 1978, THE ROYAL Bank of Sweden awarded the Nobel Prize in Economics to Herbert Simon, citing his "pioneering research into the decision-making process within economic organizations."

A half-time economist by his own reckoning, Simon professed himself to be a monomaniac about decision-making, a central aspect of human activity in so many fields of scientific inquiry that a list of the fields of knowledge to which Simon contributed would include: economics, psychology, political science, sociology, public administration, organization theory, computer science, cognitive science, and philosophy.

A major stimulus to Simon's work on decision making processes was his dissatisfaction with the economists' classical theory of omniscient rationality, HOMO ECONOMICUS. When applied to the study of business activity, this theory depicted businesses as individual economic agents that make optimal choices relative to the goal of maximizing profits under constraints posed by market and technological factors. Under this approach, predictions about business decisions are made to depend exclusively on the characterization of the choice environment dictating the constraints for individual choice. The approach excludes a positive role in decision making processes for organizations and their structural features, Simon argues.

The dictum that "human behavior is intendedly rational, but boundedly so" captures Simon's preoccupation with individuals' limited ability to define goals, and to identify and rank alternative means for pursuing them. In light of individuals' bounded rationality, Simon viewed organizations as structures intended to overcome the limitations of any single individual to cope with complex decision- and-problem solving tasks.

In his 1947 book, *Administrative Behavior*, Simon describes organizations as pursuing general goals or ends by identifying generally specified means, that are themselves the ends of a set of more detailed means, and so on, in a chain of ends-means relationships. An organization pursues the resulting hierarchy of sub-goals by attributing decision-making responsibilities to individuals, as well as by providing them with information, resources, and incentives so as to favor the conformity of their decisions to the general goals of the organization.

The concept of bounded rationality was given a more precise formulation in Simon's later work by introducing the notions of "search" and "satisficing." In most choice contexts, the alternative choices are not known and given to decision makers. Rather, they have to be identified through the acquisition and processing of information, which Simon calls search.

Relatedly, Simon observes that the search for alternatives terminates with the identification of a decision or a solution to a problem well before the entire set of possible choices is explored. Instead, borrowing from research in empirical psychology, he argues that the search would stop upon identification of an alternative that achieves the decision maker's aspiration level (a notion of how good an alternative he or she should find). This process for selecting, Simon calls satisficing.

Exploiting the availability of computers during the 1950s, Simon found himself drawn to developing computational models of human reasoning and decision making. He made an early and lasting impact on the emerging fields of cognitive science and artificial intelligence.

As a half-time economist, Simon spurred and contributed to a burgeoning literature in evolutionary and institutional economics exploring the implications of bounded rationality and the organizational dimensions of decision making and problem solving. Partly under the stimulus of his work, even the dissenting majority of economists, wedded to the theory of omniscient rationality, have embraced the study of social organizations and information-processing activities.

BIBLIOGRAPHY. Herbert A. Simon, *Administrative Behavior*, MacMillan (1947); Herbert A. Simon, *Models of Man*, Wiley (1957); Herbert A. Simon, *The Sciences of the Artificial* (MIT Press, 1981); Herbert A. Simon, Massimo Egidi, and Robin Marris, *Economics, Bounded Rationality, and the Cognitive Revolution* (Edward Elgar, 1992).

ROBERTO MAZZOLENI, PH.D.
HOFSTRA UNIVERSITY

Simon, Julian (1932–98)

JULIAN SIMON IS MOST famous for "The Bet" with Paul Ehrlich. Ehrlich, a biologist with a Malthusian outlook, believed that rising world population was destined to result in higher prices and SCARCITY of resources. Simon recognized that as prices of resources rose, the profit incentive to develop new ways of harvesting those resources, or to find substitute resources, also rose. For this reason, Simon was optimistic that in the future, resources would be abundant and cheap.

In 1980, Simon offered Ehrlich the following bet to test their competing predictions. Ehrlich could choose any five metals. The two would create a hypothetical account that included $200 worth of each metal. If in 10 years the value of the hypothetical account were above its original $1000 (adjusting for inflation), Ehrlich would be declared the winner. If in ten years the value of the hypothetical account were below its original $1,000, Simon would be declared the winner. The loser would send the winner the difference between the original value of $1,000 and the final value of the account.

Ehrlich accepted the bet and chose copper, chrome, nickel, tin, and tungsten. By 1990, the price of each of the five metals was below its 1980 level. Ehrlich sent the victorious Simon a check for $576.07. Simon's victory in this bet illustrated that economics is not, as Thomas Carlyle called it, the "dismal science," but rather it offers great reason for optimism about the future: Resources will be more abundant, and standards of living higher, thanks to technological innovation; for this reason, Simon described the human intellect as "The Ultimate Resource."

Simon is also responsible for a system of allocation with which most airline travelers are familiar, offering rewards to people who voluntarily surrender their ticket on an overbooked plane. Prior to 1978, airlines dealt with the problem of overbooked flights by bumping passengers involuntarily (airlines often chose elderly and military passengers because they would be less likely to complain). For 12 years after Simon first suggested a system of compensating volunteers, airlines and the Civil Aeronautics Board were uninterested, but in 1978 Simon found a sympathetic ear in Alfred Kahn, the first economist to chair the Civil Aeronautics Board. Today, the system is in widespread use.

Simon was born in Newark, New Jersey. He was given the middle name Lincoln because he was born on that president's birthday. Simon writes in his autobiography that he was "born an economist" but he also took pride in the fact that he was not formally trained as such; as a result, he wrote, he was not instilled with conventional ideas in economics that were wrong.

He studied experimental psychology as an undergraduate at Harvard University and earned an M.B.A. and a Ph.D. from the Graduate School of Business at the University of Chicago. He served on the faculties of the University of Illinois, Hebrew University, and the University of Maryland. His research spanned the economics of advertising, population, and immigration.

BIBLIOGRAPHY. Julian L. Simon, *A Life Against the Grain* (Transaction Publishing, 2002); Julian L. Simon, *The Ultimate Resource* (Princeton University Press, 1981).

JOHN CAWLEY, PH.D.
CORNELL UNIVERSITY

Sinclair, Upton (1878–1968)

WHEN A NOVEL ABOUT the brutal exploitation of immigrant labor in Chicago meatpacking, *The Jungle*, was published in 1906, it was the year's bestseller and a worldwide sensation, translated immediately into 17 languages. Its young author, Upton Sinclair, would remain a prolific writer and opponent of capitalism throughout his life, but would never again recapture the imagination of the reading public as in that vivid early novel.

The Jungle was a metaphor for capitalism. Sinclair associated capitalism not with modernity but barbarism: the savagery of POVERTY, the primitiveness of corruption, and a dog-eat-dog world in which individual gain triumphs over common good and the powerful devour the weak. Chicago's giant meat trusts, Sinclair argued, led their workers to the slaughter as surely as cattle. To Sinclair, there was a civilized alternative to the ruthless economic jungle. The answer was SOCIALISM, a cooperative and democratic system of production.

The Jungle's nauseating images of rat feces ground up into sausages, gangrenous cattle butchered and sold, and preservatives and dyes used to disguise decomposition in canned meat resulted in a massive public outcry. Middle-class and elite readers, including Republican President Theodore ROOSEVELT, tended not to be moved by Sinclair's evocation of the plight of immigrant workers so much as disgusted by Sinclair's depictions of what they might be eating. When European nations levied trade sanctions against American meat, even the major packers sought to improve their image. The outcome was the Pure Food and Drug Act of 1906, which strengthened government rules and inspections.

Sinclair, of course, wanted capitalism overthrown, not mere amelioration of its worst effects. Jurgis Rudkus, the earnest, hardworking, daft hero of *The Jungle*, says again and again, "I will work harder," yet he falls deeper and deeper into misery until his conversion to so-

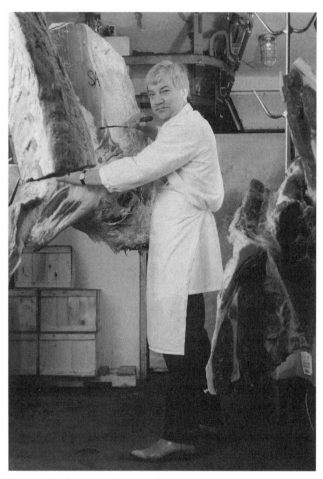

Upton Sinclair's revelations about the meatpacking industry led to increased government regulation.

age 14 and enrolled in graduate studies at Columbia University in 1897. To support his studies and his mother, Sinclair, at 15, began writing cheap mass fiction, cranking out boys' military stories under pseudonyms. The acquired habit of quick writing enabled him to produce nearly 100 books in his lifetime.

Sinclair's first novels under his own name were sentimental, romantic, and unsuccessful, but he evolved toward socialist politics and naturalism. In 1904, Sinclair published an article in *Appeal to Reason,* a socialist paper with nationwide circulation printed in Kansas, called "You Have Lost the Strike! And Now What Are You Going to Do About It?" Addressed to Chicago stockyard workers, the article held that the answer to workers' troubles was political action at the ballot box by voting for the Socialist Party. *Appeal* editor Fred Warren admired the piece and advanced Sinclair $500 so that he could travel to Chicago, the epicenter of the American industrial proletariat, to dramatize the conditions in fiction. Sinclair spent weeks interviewing workers and walking through Packingtown's giant concerns, acquiring realistic details. *The Jungle* began appearing in serial form in *Appeal to Reason* in 1905.

The hope of Sinclair and Warren was that *The Jungle* would be to wage slavery what Harriet Beecher Stowe's *Uncle Tom's Cabin* was to chattel slavery—a clarion call for abolition. *The Jungle* did not have the same precise effect, but it was phenomenally successful. Published in book form by Doubleday, it enjoyed runaway-sales success, netting Sinclair tens of thousands of dollars. He sunk his new fortunes into establishing a commune for writers and artists in Englewood, New Jersey, but the colony burnt to the ground a year later, leaving Sinclair penniless.

Sinclair wrote many novels critical of capitalism, including *King Coal* (1917), *Oil!* (1927), and *Boston* (1928), but his seriousness was somewhat undercut by his enthusiasms for telepathy and odd dietary regimes. Sinclair was arrested for protesting the massacre of miners at Ludlow, Colorado, outside John D. ROCKEFELLER's New York offices in 1914, and arrested again in California for trying to read the Constitution aloud in 1923. When he ran for governor of California in 1934, he won the Democratic primary on his program to End Poverty in California (EPIC) but lost the general contest after a heavily funded smear campaign against him.

Sinclair won a Pulitzer Prize for *Dragon's Teeth* (1942), one of the novels in his 11-volume series centered on the hero Lanny Budd. *The Jungle* continues to inspire muckraking successors, most notably Eric Schlosser's examination of the hamburger industry in *Fast Food Nation* (2001).

cialism at the end of the novel. Jurgis was a powerful counterpoint to Horatio ALGER's myths of "rags to riches," and the novel won many recruits to the cause of the left, but the novel's primary effect was conveyed by Sinclair's quip, "I aimed at the public's heart, and by accident I hit it in the stomach."

The Jungle resulted in reform for the consumer rather than equality for the worker. Modern liberal oversight aimed not at socialism but at preserving capital accumulation through regulation to prevent competitive pressures from undermining the system's stability and legitimacy. *The Jungle*, in this sense, is the quintessential novel of the Progressive Era. Not inappropriately was Sinclair grouped as a muckraker along with journalists Ida Tarbell, Ray Stannard Baker, and Lincoln Steffens.

Born in Baltimore, Maryland, to a Southern family with a long line of naval distinction, Sinclair had a childhood overshadowed by his salesman father's alcoholism. He was raised primarily by his mother in conditions of threadbare gentility. When he was 10, they moved to New York. Precocious, Sinclair attended City College at

BIBLIOGRAPHY. Upton Sinclair, *The Autobiography of Upton Sinclair* (1962); Walter Rideout, *The Radical Novel in* the United States, 1900–1954 (Columbia University Press, 1956); Leon Harris, *Upton Sinclair: American Rebel* (Ty Crowell, 1975); Greg Mitchell, *The Campaign of the Century: Upton Sinclair's Race for Governor of California and the Birth of Media Politics* (Random House, 1992).

CHRISTOPHER PHELPS, PH.D.
OHIO STATE UNIVERSITY

Singapore

A SMALL CITY-STATE located across the Johore Strait from MALAYSIA, Singapore experienced extraordinarily high levels of economic growth and technological development in the last three decades, and in the early 2000s enjoyed one of the highest GROSS NATIONAL PRODUCTS (GNP) per capita in the world.

Sir Thomas Stamford Raffles of the BRITISH EAST INDIA COMPANY established a trading post on the island of Singapore with the permission of the Malay Johore Sultanate in 1819. An 1824 treaty with the Dutch recognized British control of the island. Drawn into the world commodities market, Singapore grew quickly as a transshipment center for rubber and tin from the Malaysian hinterland bound for Europe.

When WORLD WAR I ended in 1918, the British recognized Singapore's vital strategic importance in protecting their Asian colonial interests. The British Navy developed Singapore's harbor facilities and the shipping industry flourished until war with JAPAN in 1942 ravaged the country's economic infrastructure. The British colonial regime, reinstated after WORLD WAR II in 1946 proved unable to address Singapore's labor unrest, inadequate housing, and low wages left in the war's wake. In 1959, unemployment remained at 13.5 percent

This unfavorable post-war economic climate prompted many Singaporeans to call for independence. Lee Kuan Yew, a fourth generation Singaporean of Chinese ancestry educated in England, rose to national leadership as a founder in 1954 of the People's Action Party (PAP). To aid the cause of independence, the PAP formed an anti-colonial united front with Singaporean Communists, but it soon became clear that the PAP's political ideology was dedicated to fee market capitalist rather than socialist economic development.

In June 1959, Singapore became a self-governing part of the British Commonwealth and joined with Malaya, Sarawak, and Sabah to form the Malaysian Federation in September 1963. Tensions between ethnic Malayans and Chinese over control of the new federation soon boiled over into violent confrontations and the two sides agreed on Singaporean independence from Malaysia in 1965.

Despite efforts in the 1950s to build up Singapore's industrial capacity in tin and rubber processing and maintenance support for shipping, manufacturing was only 11.9 percent of GNP in 1960 and 94 percent of Singapore's exports were re-export of goods not produced in Singapore. In the 1960s, Singapore's economy was cut off from the Malaysian market after independence, and hard hit by a1968 British announcement of military withdrawal resulting in the loss of 38,000 jobs in related industries.

Lee Kuan Yew's PAP government addressed these economic crises with a series of policies designed to attract multinational corporations and reduce Singapore's regional dependence. In a pattern similar to other high-growth Asian economies, the government of Singapore actively promoted the growth of technologically sophisticated export industries. The government gave tax incentives and access to inexpensive capital to favored industries, and kept labor costs low by shifting a large share of the responsibility for worker welfare to the state. These policies apparently worked and Singapore enjoyed an average annual real GROSS DOMESTIC PRODUCT (GDP) growth of 12.7 percent between 1965 and 1973. Although the oil shocks of the early 1970s slowed Singapore's growth, it continued to enjoy annual growth rates of 8.7 percent between 1973–79.

Realizing that much of Singapore's comparative advantage rested with its well-educated and relatively inexpensive labor force, Lee Kuan Yew's government resisted labor union demands for higher wages. In return, the government tried to appease labor by looking out for the workers' welfare with paternalistic policies in housing, healthcare, and education. Between 1960 and 1985, the Housing and Development Board built 500,000 apartments and housed 88 percent of Singapore's population.

The government also promoted the growth of Singapore's financial services industry. The Monetary Authority of Singapore established a system for offshore banking that encouraged nonresidents to deposit funds in Singapore to be invested in southeast Asia. The Stock Exchange of Singapore was established in 1973 and, in 1983, funds held by nonresidents and invested outside Singapore were granted tax exemption. Today, Singapore is the region's leading provider of financial services.

Singapore's government also used economic incentives to manipulate social practices in ways it believed would improve the country's economy. People were encouraged to buy a "stake in Singapore" and purchase homes built by the Housing and Development Board. The Central Provident Fund retirement program promoted individual and family self-reliance by holding savings in individual accounts to be returned to workers with interest upon retirement in contrast to the Social Security model of taxing the young to support the old. The government also promoted population control by charging couples higher rates for the education and health care of their third and additional children. This policy was modified in 1986 to grant tax rebates to women with college degrees who had more than two children, in an effort to supposedly raise the genetic and educational level of the population.

In the 1980s, Singapore's government responded to changes in the global economy and to pressure from Singaporeans who felt their country was over-regulated. In 1983, the government's Trade Development Board looked for new up-and-coming industries and actively promoted electronics, printing and publishing, textiles and timber processing. A severe recession caused by declining world demand for petroleum, semi-conductors, and computer components hit Singapore in 1985. This led to a decline in demand for hotels, shopping centers, and apartments built in the earlier construction boom and resulted in many facilities remaining vacant. Opposition to the PAP became more vocal and the government became concerned that it was unable to maintain the level of service that Singaporeans had come to expect.

To improve its reputation, the PAP launched two campaigns. The first campaign was primarily ideological and appealed to Singaporean identity as one of the "Asian Tigers" characterized by Confucian values, community cooperation, and successful economic development. The other campaign was more practical and attempted to privatize state-owned business and shift the burden for medical and welfare services to the private sector.

Singapore's population of 4.45 million (2001) enjoys a per capita GDP of $24,700. The $106.3 billion GDP is composed of 33 percent manufacturing and 67 percent financial and other services. Singapore's exports of $122 billion include machinery, electronics, consumer goods, chemicals, and mineral fuels. Malaysia, the UNITED STATES, HONG KONG and JAPAN are Singapore's major export markets. Singapore imports $116 billion worth of products such as machinery, equipment, petroleum, chemicals, and food.

BIBLIOGRAPHY. *CIA World Factbook: Singapore* (2002); Peter S. J. Chen, *Singapore: Development Policies and Trends* (Oxford University Press, 1983); Stephan Haggard, *Pathways from the Periphery* (Cornell University Press, 1990); Barbara Leitch LePoer, *Singapore: A Country Study* (GPO, 1991); R. S. Milne and Diane K. Mauzy, *Singapore: The Legacy of Lee Kuan Yew* (Westview Press, 1990).

JOHN SAGERS, PH.D.
LINFIELD COLLEGE

Sinopec Corporation

CHINA PETROLEUM and Chemical Corporation, better known as Sinopec Corporation, is a vertically integrated energy and chemical company. Its scope of business is wide-ranging and includes: exploration, development, production and marketing of petroleum and natural gas; refining, marketing, production and sales of petrochemicals, chemical fibers and fertilizers; storage and pipeline transportation of petroleum and natural gas; importation and exportation of petroleum, natural gas, refined oil, petrochemicals, and chemicals; research and development; and technology and information.

Sinopec is CHINA's second largest oil producer, but the country's largest producer and marketer of oil products (gasoline, diesel, and jet fuel). It also leads the way for China-supplied petrochemical products (synthetic resin, fiber, and rubber).

Sinopec was created in February 2000, pursuant to the company law of the People's Republic of China. Following international models, Sinopec sets a standardized structure of corporate governance, with centralized decision-making, delegated management, and specific business targets handled by specialized departments, or units. More than 70 subsidiaries are either wholly owned or comprised of equity participation. Among them, they operate businesses devoted to exploration and production, refining, chemicals, marketing, foreign trade, and RESEARCH AND DEVELOPMENT. The latter effort has won a national award. Some of the more important subsidiaries are Shanghai Oil Field, Ltd., Sinopec Sales Company, Ltd., and Sinopec International, Ltd.

Sinopec sees itself as a first-rate competitor in China, but aims to become a world-class competitor in its industry. Successes have been based on its early maximization of profits, its ability to deliver shareholder return, and its belief in customer satisfaction, discipline, and integrity.

Since 2001, the company has followed four main strategies: resource expansion; market expansion; investments; and cost reduction. Of the latter, Sinopec immediately demonstrated its earnestness through an overall reduction of $2 billion, and another of $1.57 billion through elimination of duplicate and unnecessary job positions.

Reported revenue (mid-year 2002) was $40 billion, making Sinopec the 86th largest company in the world.

BIBLIOGRAPHY. "Global 500: World's Largest Companies," *Fortune* (July 2002); "Sinopec to Head Wall Street," *People's Daily,* www.fpeng.peopledaily.com; Sinopec Corporation, www.sinopec.com.cn.

JOSEPH GERINGER
SYED B. HUSSAIN, PH.D.
UNIVERSITY OF WISCONSIN, OSHKOSH

slavery

STATISTICS ALONE CAN be a modest pointer to the horrors of slavery during the dawn of capitalism. America had 33,000 slaves in 1700, nearly 3 million in 1800 and over 6 million in 1850. During this period, 1.5 million slaves died during the passage to the New World, and between 10 and 20 percent died within a year of landing.

If history is the world's court, then modernity and capitalism stand accused before it for the rise of New World slavery. Scholars have suggested that it points us towards the "dark side of progress" in that the inhumanity of the system developed side by side with huge steps forward in knowledge and technique, such as the exploration of the Atlantic and the development of new navigational techniques.

At the heart of the system lay an irresolvable contradiction. The colonizers of the New World were those who rejected most strongly the old order in Europe. Yet just as unfree labor was dying out in Europe it began to develop on a massive new scale in the Americas. This contradiction was only resolved by the complete racialization of New World slavery so that skin color/ethnicity and slavery became inextricably linked.

Origins of slavery. Slavery, of course, was not invented in the 17th and 18th centuries. Apart from ancient GREECE and Rome, it had persisted in small pockets in different parts of Europe and the Middle East throughout the Middle Ages. New World slavery, however, was distinct from earlier instances of the practice in several significant ways. The buying and selling of slaves in the Ancient World (200 B.C.E. to 200 C.E.) reflected the policy of the state or particular individuals as opposed to a more generalized economic project. In other words, Roman slaves were sold because they had been captured, while in the New World African slaves were caught in order to be sold. In the Middle Ages slaves were allowed to own property, ply trade, and hold state positions.

There were also provisions and numerous instances of slaves buying back their freedom. Slavery was not confined to any particular ethnic identity. White people were frequently galley slaves in the Mediterranean navies and the actual word "slave" is derived from "Slav" pointing to the hold of the institution over Eastern Europe. Historians have shown that Africans or persons of African descent were a clear minority as slaves in 1500, but became the majority by 1700.

Slavery in the New World. The beginnings of New World slavery can be traced to the Spanish conquest of the Americas. Christopher Columbus sent some of the Arawaks people who first greeted him to be sold as slaves in the Caribbean. There were also some unsuccessful attempts to use Native Americans as slaves. Due to the severe decimation of the indigenous population of the Americas, the British Crown and colonists alike turned increasingly to a different source of labor, the buying of slaves off the coast of West Africa.

Slavery took off on a massive scale when PORTUGAL, Holland, England, and FRANCE began commercial cultivation of tobacco and sugar in their colonies. The crops demanded a huge labor force and free immigrants from Europe were not prepared to provide it.

The conquest of colonies was vital to England's economic growth and the profits of slavery paved the way for English industrialization. The capitalist development in agriculture created a landless workforce ready to emigrate or work for low wages at the newly emergent English factories. The transformation of the English economy helped to create a market for the new commodities in the colonies. Profits from the plantations assisted this economic process in certain crucial ways.

First, it raised the level of economic prosperity in their sheer scale and hence advanced industrialization. Second they provided much needed credit to the new generation of industrialists. The early industrial processes involved a lengthy turnover time, when a capitalist might have to wait a long time to realize the profits from an investment. In such circumstances credit was vital. The profits of slavery helped to lubricate this process. Financial bills, drawn on plantation products such as sugar or tobacco, began to circulate as a form of money. In the absence of sufficient institutional sources of credit, plantation funds helped to fill the gap.

Initially, it was wage labor that worked the new plantations in Barbados and elsewhere. White indentured servants from England would be contracted to work for three, five, or seven years for the plantation after which they would be free to pursue other employment. In 1638, Barbados had 2,000 indentured servants and only 200 African slaves. By 1653 there were 20,000 slaves and only 8,000 indentured servants.

White indentured servants faced enormous hardships on the estates. The work was extremely hard, conditions appalling and life expectancy was short. Escaped servants were made to serve double time for their master. A repeated escape could lead to branding. Like slaves, the servant was regarded as a piece of property and was valued according to the amount of tobacco or sugar that could be expected to be produced before the indenture expired.

The plantation owners faced two problems. As the demand for the plantation exports rose rapidly they needed more and more labor. As emigration from Britain was, by and large, voluntary it could not guarantee to meet the needs of the system. At the same time, stories drifted back of life in the colonies, which tended to discourage volunteers for the indenture system. Thus it was the growing demand for secure supplies of labor that produced the shift toward African slavery. In this context, the mid-17th century saw the rapid growth of the slave plantation in the English Caribbean.

The extremely hard conditions of the plantation colonies meant that the owners, and the colonial authorities, always faced the possibility of revolt. As long as black slaves and white servants worked alongside each other this included the possibility of joint action, however temporary. In 1676, for example, Bacon's rebellion in Virginia had involved servants, slaves, and freemen.

Rare as such risings might have been, they terrified those in authority. Increasingly, laws were passed to enforce racial segregation. Such laws helped to create a form of racial solidarity among the white colonists. Increasingly whites, even poor whites, could identify themselves as a part of the privileged race. The privilege of their color exempted them from slavery and granted them certain civil rights. The plantation owners' fear of resistance and rebellion evolved into a more general white fear of black rebellion. In these ways, slavery was crucial to forming the new racial identities in the American colonies.

These new identities and structures tended to undermine white opposition to slavery. Slavery came to be identified with black Africans. In turn, black people were identified as slaves or potential slaves. These racial divisions were sharpest in the English-speaking colonies in the Caribbean and North America. In the Spanish, Portuguese, and French territories there developed a far bigger free-black population. Here blacks could begin to demand some of the rights of the white citizen. In the English colonies such a blurring of the racial boundaries did not emerge and the number of free blacks remained small.

The scale and conditions of slavery. The deadly scale of the slave trade cannot be underscored. Between 1600–1850 about 12 million Africans were shipped across the Atlantic from West Africa to European colonies in the Caribbean and North America. The slaves were captured by raiding parties, imprisoned at coastal forts, and forced to endure a horrific voyage as human freight.

The "standard space per slave" laid down by the British-run Royal Africa Company was five feet long, 11 inches wide, and 23 inches high, for a voyage lasting 9 or 10 months. Around one in six of the slaves died on the journey. Those who survived were sold at auction into a life of brutal labor on plantations producing tobacco, sugar, and cotton. It was not only the slaves who suffered. African society as a whole was hurled back. The population of Africa stagnated and in places fell.

One estimate is that the population of about 25 million in 1850 in West and Central Africa was about a half what it would have been had there been no slave trade.

The whole process was directed by state-backed "adventurers" and bankers who became the pillars of industrial Britain. It was not only the merchants directly involved in the slave trade who gained. The "triangular trade" saw slaves carried to the Americas; sugar, tobacco, and other goods then shipped to Europe; and then European products sent to the coast of Africa to begin the triangle again. Each leg of the triangle benefited a separate group of merchants.

The early British capitalists' use of "free labor" (labor which must sell itself on the market) at home gave a vicious dynamism to their profit-making. This meant they could then exploit unfree labor on a totally new scale. There was an organic connection between free labor and slave labor structured into the capitalist system as a whole. Slave money financed the massive cotton mills where generations of "free" workers spent a vast portion of their stunted, short lives. The use of big workforces on the plantations was a model for the creation of factories in Britain. Even the use of child slaves in the Americas was the template for the use of children who were pressed into wage slavery in the mills. Infant paupers were taken from the workhouses and transferred to textile firms. As an account in 1842 says, "These children are sent off by wagon loads and are as much lost to their parents as if they were shipped for the West Indies." Calling the conditions of early industrial workers "slave-like" was no exaggeration.

In the Barbados sugar cane fields, slaves were unlikely to live for more than four or five years. Many died in their teens or early 20s. In Manchester, in 1840, the average age at death for laborers was 17. The Irish laborers, the European factory workers, and agricultural proletariat were all kin to the slave. That is why there was an almost instinctive unity between poor whites and slaves that their owners and employers made great efforts to extinguish.

Slave rebellions. Slavery first became the focus of public controversy in the 1760s and 1770s as Britain's imperial order was plunged into crisis. The loss of American plantations in 1776 was a major blow to both the Empire and the pro-slavery lobby. There was also the memory of slave rebellions.

The first turning point for the West Indian plantation regime came in 1739 in Jamaica during the First Maroon War. The British had to sue for peace after they failed to defeat an army of escaped slaves who lived "free" from then on. In 1763, rebel slaves in the Dutch colony of Berbice (Guyana) expelled their masters from the southern half of the colony. But these uprisings could be contained by the colonial powers. It was the powerful ideas carried on the wind of revolution that swept America and then France in 1789, which really set the cane fields alight.

Saint Domingue (Haiti, as it is known today) was a French slave colony and the pearl of the slave economy. In 1791, the slaves of Saint Domingue claimed their liberty when they rose up under the leadership of cattle-keeper Toussaint L'Ouverture. Toussaint turned his slave army into a magnificent fighting force, crushing the plantation owners and then the elite of the Spanish, French, and British armies.

In Paris, an insurrection gave power to the most revolutionary section of the French bourgeoisie, who condemned "the aristocracy of the skin" and decreed slavery abolished. They sent 330,000 rifles to Toussaint. The slaves inflicted huge losses on the British forces sent by Prime Minister William Pitt to retake the island for slave-owning interests everywhere. The bones of at least 20,000 British soldiers lie beneath the soil of Haiti.

The slaves forced the British to surrender and then drove them from the island. These slave rebellions coincided in Britain with the growth of the first mass working-class movement, Chartism. Anti-slavery was a massively popular movement to the great discomfort of the rulers.

Opinion regarding slavery within the ruling circles of Britain started to change after the loss of the American colonies. Arguments against slavery began to gain a foothold amongst important members of Parliament. Organizations such as the *Society of Friends* in Britain had been campaigning against the slave trade for many years. They had presented a petition to Parliament in 1783 and, in 1787, had helped form the *Society for the Abolition of the Slave Trade*. Conservative politicians like William Wilberforce (1759–1833) became loud critics of slavery within Parliament.

Most of Wilberforce's Tory colleagues, however, were opposed to any restrictions on the slave trade and when he presented his first bill to abolish the slave trade in 1791, at the House of Commons, it was easily defeated by 163 votes to 88.

Abolition of slavery. In February 1806, Lord Grenville, a leading Whig politician, argued in Parliament that the trade was "contrary to the principles of justice, humanity, and sound policy." The Abolition of the Slave Trade bill was passed in the House of Lords by 41 votes to 20. In the House of Commons it was carried by 114 to 15 and it become law on March 25, 1807.

British captains who were caught sustaining the trade were fined 100 pounds for every slave found on board. However, this did not deter the British slaver. Captains of slave ships tried to decrease the fine by throwing the slaves overboard.

One opinion of the anti-slave trade campaign was that the only way to end the suffering of the slaves was to make slavery illegal. The more conservative view held

by people such as Wilberforce was that the slaves were not "ready" to be granted their freedom.

There existed, however, more radical views on slavery. When the Society for the Abolition of the Slave Trade was set up in 1783 it had an exclusively male organization. Leaders such as Wilberforce were opposed to the participation of women. As a result women such as Elizabeth Pease, Anne Knight, Elizabeth Heyrick, and Mary Lloyd began forming women's Anti-Slavery Societies after 1823.

The anxiety that women would advocate a more radical strategy regarding slavery proved to be correct. In 1824, Elizabeth Heyrick published her pamphlet *Immediate not Gradual Abolition*, arguing passionately in favor of the immediate emancipation of the slaves in the British colonies. The Female Society for Birmingham had established a network of women's anti-slavery groups and Heyrick's pamphlet was distributed and discussed at meetings all over the country. In 1827, the Sheffield Female Society became the first anti-slavery society in Britain to call for the immediate emancipation of slaves. Other women's groups quickly followed.

Finally in 1833, the British Parliament passed the Slavery Abolition Act giving all slaves in the British Empire their freedom. The irony remained that the British government paid compensation to the slave owners in proportion to the number of slaves that they had owned.

(Editor's Note: The story of how slavery affected the development of economic and social conditions specifically in the UNITED STATES after the AMERICAN REVOLUTIONARY WAR is a long history unto itself, not the least of which was slavery's role in the AMERICAN CIVIL WAR.)

BIBLIOGRAPHY. Robin Blackburn, *The Making of New World Slavery: From the Baroque to the Modern 1492–1800* (Verso, 1997); Patrick Manning, *Slavery and African Life: Occidental, Oriental and African Slave Trades* (Cambridge University Press, 1990).

TITHI BHATTACHARYA, PH.D
PURDUE UNIVERSITY

small business

SMALL BUSINESSES ARE often considered the backbone of a capitalist economy. It is their intrinsic dependence on entrepreneurship that sets them apart and makes the performance of the small-business sector an indicator of the degree of economic freedom prevailing in market economies.

Definitions of small businesses are by necessity arbitrary. They can either be functional or based on criteria of size. Functionally, small businesses tend to be managed by owners, use legal entities of sole ownerships, partnerships, or limited-liability companies, and have weak MARKET POWER (or the ability to significantly influence market prices). They predominate in industries with many participants although they may enjoy local monopoly. Thus, the U.S. Small Business Act defines a small business concern "to be one that is independently owned and operated and which is not dominant in its field of operation."

Determination of size is effected on an industry-by-industry basis. The size of organizations can be measured in a number of ways. Relative to the industry it is competing in, the size of a business may be measured by its market share. Its relative ability to influence market prices will also depend on the concentration ratio—the distribution of large and small businesses—in the industry. In absolute terms, output and input measures of a firm alone are used to assess and compare its size, common output metrics being receipts, value added, and total assets, and the most frequent input metric being the number of employees.

The small-business sector. The demarcation of the small business sector in any economy depends on arbitrary criteria. In the United States, the Small Business Administration (SBA), an entity of the federal government, defines whether a business is small and is thus eligible for government-subsidy programs, and preferential treatment in contracting. The North American Industry Classification System (NAICS) uses these size standards, and federal agencies are bound to apply them in procurement and contracting. The standards define the largest a firm may be, together with all of its affiliates, and still be considered a small business on an industry-by-industry basis; there is no general upper limit. Numerical definitions are almost always expressed in either the number of employees or average annual receipts (with the exception of industries such as power generation, where megawatt hours is used). The most widely used size standards are 500 employees for most manufacturing and mining industries, and $6 million in average annual receipts for most non-manufacturing industries.

However, many exceptions exist. In much of farming, small businesses are limited to annual receipts of $0.75 million, in much of construction to $28.5 million, and in certain manufacturing industries to 1,000 employees or less. Wholesale merchants are limited to 100 employees, new car dealers to $24.5 million, and gasoline stations with convenience stores to $23 million. Certain service businesses, such as travel agencies, are limited to $3 million while certified public accountants may have receipts of up to $7 million, and computer-system design services may have receipts of up to $21 to qualify for this status.

Based on these definitions, small businesses in the United States comprise about 99 percent of all employers and 48 percent of private-sector employment. They produce 50 percent of GROSS DOMESTIC PRODUCT (GDP) and are the source for two-thirds of new jobs. Nearly three-quarters of all U.S. businesses have no payroll at all, being managed by self-employed persons; because non-employers account for only 3 percent of total business receipts, they are not included in most official statistics. There are strong differences by NAICS-based industries: Ninety percent of businesses in construction employing 85 percent of all construction workers are small businesses, while only 22 percent of utility companies employing 11 percent of all utility workers fall under this designation.

Since the 1970s, the number of small firms as a share of all firms has remained rather stable while large firms have generated more employment and sales. In fact, the small-business share of U.S. economic activity, as measured in terms of employment or output, is considerably less than that of comparable businesses in JAPAN, GERMANY, ITALY, the NETHERLANDS, the UNITED KINGDOM, and other European countries (1999 statistics).

In the statistics of the EUROPEAN UNION (EU), the size standards of Small and Medium-Sized Enterprises (SME) are less inclusive than in the United States (though a special subcategory of medium-sized enterprises is added). According to the official definition, each enterprise must be independent. Only up to 25 percent of the capital or the voting rights may be owned by one enterprise, or jointly by several enterprises, which are not themselves SMEs (this threshold may be exceeded if the business is held by public investment corporations, venture capital companies, or institutional investors).

Micro-enterprises have fewer than 10 dependent workers. Small businesses have between 10 and 49 dependent workers, achieve an annual revenue not exceeding €7 million, or an annual balance-sheet total not exceeding €5 million. Medium-sized businesses have between 50 and 250 dependent workers, achieve an annual revenue not exceeding €40 million, or an annual balance-sheet total not exceeding €27 million. These definitions of small business generally do not vary by industry. For domestic purposes, they may vary between member countries; but access to regional and structural funds and to other subsidies depends on the shared EU definition, which increasingly comes to dominate standards in individual member states.

More than 93 percent of the 18 million businesses registered in the EU employ fewer than 10 persons, and 49 percent of businesses have no employees. In the United States, 78 percent of all enterprises have fewer than 10 employees, which indicates the stronger role of micro-enterprises in the EU. In general, industry structure in Europe tends to be less dominated by large corporations. The German Mittelstand (literally, "middle class") is often regarded as the backbone of economic reconstruction after WORLD WAR II and as the engine behind the strong growth of exports. It is, however, not revenue or number of employees that define the Mittelstand. Rather than by firm size, businesses falling under this designation are united by a strong entrepreneurial spirit, by having their equity held predominantly by members of a family, and by being largely managed by family members with the intent of keeping the business independent.

The explanation for the fact that the overall importance of small businesses has grown while their share of the main macroeconomic aggregates has remained relatively stable, lies in the difference between static and dynamic measurement. Overall, small businesses grow and decay faster than large corporations; the smaller business sector is more dynamic and volatile than that of larger firms. When measured in terms of entry and exit, and in the change of contribution to economic performance, the small business sector is more important for the U.S. economy than simple shares of employment or output in any given year may indicate.

In the United States, small businesses are often managed as franchises, a legal form that has been accepted with greater hesitance elsewhere. In manufacturing, small businesses are also often part of a hub-and-spoke system, as suppliers to large manufacturing firms. A cluster of companies producing automotive parts has developed in the wider region around Detroit, with various forms of ties to the Big Three automobile firms.

In Europe, small firms are frequently parts of regional networks (industrial districts), specialized in particular industries, that together attempt to achieve external economies of scale in RESEARCH AND DEVELOPMENT (R&D), production, and marketing. There is, for example, a fashion network (clothing, shoes, accessories, etc.) in northern Italy and a precision-machinery network in Germany, operating as horizontal clusters of equals rather than dependent suppliers to large firms. The Italian experience with, and theoretical work on, industrial districts built on ideas of the economist Alfred MARSHALL, has become a major point of reference in the international debate on regional policy promoting endogenous development.

Entrepreneurship. Entrepreneurship and small business are not synonymous concepts, though it appears that the second implies the first. In fact, quantity and quality of entrepreneurship are independent of firm size, while the success of small firms virtually always depends on a critical level of entrepreneurship, which makes entrepreneurship a necessary, if not yet sufficient, condition for successful small business management. Small businesses can be a vehicle both for entrepreneurs in Joseph SCHUM-

PETER's sense—innovators who introduce new products and processes that change the industry—and for managerial executives or owners. The latter group includes many franchisees, shopkeepers, and persons in professional occupations, whose businesses may grow but hardly at rates that would be considered extraordinary. Thus, a physician or lawyer may, without special entrepreneurial alertness, start and manage a small professional firm that enjoys a relative regional monopoly; but without a superior degree of entrepreneurship it is unlikely to exhibit significant growth. Innovating entrepreneurs challenge incumbent firms by introducing, for example, inventions that make current technologies and products obsolete. Through this process of "creative destruction," as Schumpeter describes it, they contribute not only to growth but also to economic development.

Economic issues. Until quite recently, the prevailing wisdom was that bigger is better. The theory of the firm, which uses tools of microeconomics to analyze the structure, conduct and performance of businesses, assumes that there are advantages to size. As the average costs of production decrease when fixed costs are spread over greater output volumes, a business benefits from economies of scale.

Moreover, companies that are active in several lines of business may additionally benefit from economies of scope. In markets where consumers are price-sensitive, large firms can pass along some of their cost advantages

Restaurants are one example of small businesses in America that have annual sales of less than $6 million.

to consumers, which may drive smaller firms out of business or into market niches not served by large firms. Schumpeter described how large firms outperform their smaller counterparts in the process of innovation and competition through a strong positive feedback loop from innovation to increased R&D activities, which allows them to be the technology leaders: "What we have got to accept is that the large-scale establishment has come to be the most powerful engine of progress," Schumpeter writes.

However, neoclassical economics also assumes that there is a point of diminishing return at which increasing size no longer brings about lower costs, and further expansion may even increase costs. With increasing use of a factor of production, its marginal productivity tends to decline. As a business grows, it tends to become increasingly bureaucratic, since more resources are used to administer its own structure, rather than to produce goods and services for the satisfaction of customers. Its owner or manager is faced with the need for the specialized knowledge required to support the main operations, and to coordinate activities among the growing number of people in the organization.

Slowness to respond to changing market needs, difficulty in communication, and increasing administrative overhead costs are other problems affecting larger firms. Division of labor in the business implies coordination costs, which in turn may reduce overall efficiency. The theory of the firm thus assumes that there is an optimum firm size (or minimum efficient scale) at which average costs are minimized for a given technology.

It has been suggested that because of technological and environmental changes, smaller businesses can now often achieve the economies of scale formerly reserved for large organizations, and that optimum firm size has thus been decreased. An example can be seen in the U.S. steel industry, where giants (such as U.S. STEEL, now USX, and LTV) went through a period of serious decline because of their inability to compete with Japanese and European mills, nearly all of which were smaller and produced at lower cost. As a result of changing production technology (using electric furnaces instead of coal- or gas-fire blast furnaces), newly available raw materials (such as recycled scrap), and changes in market demand, "mini-mills," such as Nucor or Birmingham Steel developed in the United States, produce specialty steel at a more competitive cost.

More generally, the widespread adoption of flexible automation has decreased the minimum efficient scale in many industries, which has resulted in a shift from large to smaller firms. Entry by firms into an industry is apparently not even substantially deterred in capital-intensive industries in which scale economies play an important role, as smaller companies have developed strategies to make up for disadvantages in production costs.

Optimism about the economic viability of small businesses has been strengthened by economic research. Gibrat's Law of Proportionate Effect predicts that the growth rate of a given firm is independent of its size. Numerous empirical studies have tested this hypothesis. For small and new firms, there is substantial evidence suggesting that growth is actually negatively related to firm size and age. However, for larger firms, particularly those having reached the minimum efficient scale level of output, the evidence suggests that firm growth is unrelated to size and age.

Moreover, contemporary approaches to industrial economics see the growth potential of firms not exclusively determined by cost factors but also by the available resources. Smaller companies may make a comparatively better use of the competencies, knowledge, and management skills available to them and thus gain competitive advantage.

Management issues. The management challenges specific to small firms include the start-up process and growth strategies. Successful start-ups require a professional business plan deriving an analysis of expected revenue and expenditure over a period of time from a careful analysis of the company and its products, competition, market demand, and environmental factors. The entry and growth strategy of businesses must take into account factors such as the degree of competition, the start-up costs and entry barriers to be faced, and the extent of economies of scale in the industry. Where economies of scale cannot be achieved within a firm, small businesses have the opportunity of achieving them externally, particularly through cooperation on the market (e.g., in purchasing or marketing consortia).

Two constitutive decisions are the legal form in which a business shall be run and the sources of funding. Most small businesses are sole proprietorships, partnerships, or limited-liability companies. Opportunities for starting a business are often afforded by franchising and licensing. Traditional sources of funding are personal savings, loans from family or friends, small business loans from the SBA or state offices of economic development, and collateralized bank loans. Modern forms of funding include VENTURE CAPITAL, whether in the form of "business angels" (private investors of smaller amounts of equity capital) or of investment banks.

Growth need not depend on the coverage of total markets. The business strategy literature shows that focused market coverage strategies can be as profitable as broad ones. Niche strategies, through product specialization, geographic specialization, or customer specialization, give small businesses the opportunity to achieve economies of scale on a small but defensible segment of the total market. Business start-ups are likely to focus on specific segments.

As companies grow, they typically build up market share on the segments initially served (market penetration), and then either develop new products for these segments (product development) or market their existing products to new segments (market development). For most businesses, then, growth beyond a certain threshold (at which the currently served market is maximally exhausted using the current strategy) involves diversification. Small businesses typically opt for related diversification, the development of new products that are similar to or can be used in conjunction with products that the organization currently provides (e.g., line extensions such as the development of soap-filled sponges by a company manufacturing cleaning agents).

Small businesses typically prefer horizontal growth to vertical integration, since the incorporation of backward or forward linkages into the value chain incurs higher risks and costs, and is therefore the preferred strategy of larger corporations. Recently, the trend in most markets has gone in exactly this horizontal direction, as companies have increasingly outsourced input factors and services (instead of producing these themselves), thus creating new opportunities particularly for other smaller businesses. Related diversification leads to the highest levels of profitability for two reasons. Firms are generally better able to transfer a key competency to closely related products and markets due to resource specialization. Furthermore, the combination of technology and marketing to create value may produce a synergy effect. Smaller size facilitates the development of synergies between different functional parts of organizations.

Firms tend to grow in a step-function in the direction of under-utilized resources. The limits to firm growth are the limits to resources. These resources determine the industries entered and the associated profits. For small businesses, in the long run, management capacity may be the critical resource. The two demands on managerial capacity include the need to run the firm at its current size and to achieve growth. The firm's growth often slows as it adds managers due to the time required for training and integrating, which explains why small businesses are often best run by family-owners. Once these new managers are fully incorporated, growth can return.

The concept of management being both an accelerator and brake for the growth process is known as the Penrose effect. This effect is based on the idea that management has three functions, namely those of managing current operations, planning future developments, and developing future managers. An attempt by a firm to increase its rate of growth will involve:

1. A diversion of managerial efforts to planning this growth resulting from a constraint on new managers because of training needs

2. This diversion of effort results in less effective management of current operations and hence reduced current profitability

3. This reduced profitability suggests a management constraint on growth (the Penrose effect).

The smaller firms are, the less likely they are to be negatively affected by it.

Because firms typically do not employ all types of their resources at the same rate, capacity differs among resources. Excess capacity will motivate managers to expand in order to fully utilize the resource. Additional resources are subsequently required to complement the full employment of current resources. The optimal growth for a new venture, then, involves a balance between the full exploitation of existing resources and the development of new ones. Because resources tend to be specialized, the firm is most likely to grow or diversify in a direction related to its original core mission.

Public policy. In the period after WORLD WAR I, big business developed at a rapid pace. Policy in the United States was divided between allowing for the demise of small business on economic grounds, and preserving it for social and political reasons.

Following previous ANTITRUST legislation, the Robinson-Patman Act of 1936 intended to give small independent retailers a measure of protection by reining-in the market power large firms could achieve through predation. Out of precursor institutions such as the Reconstruction Finance Corporation and the Smaller War Plants Corporation, the U.S. Congress, in 1953, created the SBA, followed by affiliated support programs such as the Small Business Investment Company (SBIC). These moves to protect less-efficient small businesses, and maintain their viability, were often criticized as attempts to protect competitors rather than competition. Partially in response to such criticism, the focus of public policy has shifted away from protecting market structures toward the stimulation of entrepreneurship.

In Western Europe of the pre-World War II era, large corporations typically had smaller market shares than in the United States, and there was no comparable tradition of antitrust legislation. As a consequence, less of a need was felt for official support programs for small businesses. In the years following World War II, this situation gradually changed. Germany, for example, pioneered a very business-friendly legal framework that strengthened small business but did not institute a government bureaucracy such as the SBA. In many European countries, employers' federations, such as chambers of commerce, have assumed the role of supporting small business, and often they have access to public funds for this purpose. In Europe, too, public policy now attempts

Most small businesses, like this barber shop, are sole proprietorships, partnerships, or limited-liability companies.

to support entrepreneurship, R&D, and innovation rather than SMEs as such.

All developed countries, and many developing countries, currently support small businesses in some form. This can be through subsidies (such as grants, loans, sureties, tax breaks, training schemes, preferential contracting rules, etc.) or through regulation, which involves exemption from requirements to which other businesses are subject. In the United States, SBA, SBIC, and affiliated institutions give loans and a range of other services in support of small businesses. In addition, individual states operate similar programs, often in the form of enterprise zones. In the EU, various community programs channel loans and other subsidies to SMEs. In addition, member countries have their own assistance programs.

Throughout the Organization for Economic Cooperation and Development (OECD) countries, however, policies have changed over recent years. The focus has shifted away from instruments essentially constraining the freedom of firms to contract—through regulation, competition policy, or antitrust law. The new emphasis is on enabling the creation and commercialization of knowledge. Such policies include encouraging R&D, venture capital, new firm start-ups, and the cooperation between universities, research institutions, and small firms. In the United States, the Small Business Innovation Research (SBIR) program enacted by Congress in 1984 (as a result of the Small Business Innovation Development Act) is an example of this new approach. It requires federal agencies (such as the Department of Energy, Department of Defense, NASA, or the National Institutes of Health) to set aside a certain share of their extramural R&D budgets for SBIR, from which small businesses are to benefit.

Small-business trends. It may be argued that small firms make two indispensable contributions to the economy. First, they are an integral part of the renewal process that pervades market economies. New and small firms play a crucial role in experimentation and innovation that leads to technological change, productivity, and economic growth. Second, small firms are the essential mechanism by which millions enter the economic and social mainstream of societies based on market economies.

Small businesses, and particularly new ones, are seen more than ever as vehicles for entrepreneurship, contributing not just to employment and economic growth but also to innovation and competitive power. The focus of the debate has shifted from small businesses as a social good that should be maintained by public policy at an economic cost, to small businesses as a vehicle for entrepreneurship. In fact, economic research has established that a cost in terms of foregone economic growth will be incurred from a lack of entrepreneurship.

There is ample evidence that economic activity shifted from large to small firms in the 1970s and 1980s, a trend that has continued since. In the United States, the share of the 500 largest corporations (Fortune 500) in total employment dropped from 20 percent in 1970 to 8.5 percent in 1996 and to 7.9 percent in 1999. Increasing differentiation of consumer wants, together with the instability of markets in the 1970s, resulted in the demise of mass production and the rise of flexible specialization. From the perspective of production, this means that economies of scale have lost importance; from the perspective of industrial organization, it has led to the decentralization and vertical disintegration of large firms. Furthermore, better and more inexpensive forms of communication have lowered transaction costs, which no longer present an insurmountable disadvantage for smaller firms. As much of economic activity becomes more knowledge-intensive, the playing field is leveled further—for there is no reason to assume small firms cannot hold their own in the production and particularly the application of knowledge. All of these trends have provided for more auspicious conditions for small business than ever before.

BIBLIOGRAPHY. Zoltan J. Acs, ed., *Are Small Firms Important? Their Role and Impact* (Kluwer Academic, 1999); Zoltan J. Acs and Bernard Yeung, eds., *Small and Medium-Sized Enterprises in the Global Economy* (University of Michigan Press, 1999); David B. Audretsch, *Innovation and Industry Evolution* (MIT Press, 1995); Andrea Colli, *The History of Family Business, 1850–2000* (Cambridge University Press, 2003); Marc Dollinger, *Entrepreneurship* (Irwin, 2003); Timothy S. Hatten, *Small Business Management* (Houghton Mifflin, 2003); Leon C. Megginson, Mary Jane Byrd, and William L Megginson, *Small Business Management* (McGraw-Hill,

2003); Edith Penrose, *The Theory of the Growth of the Firm* (Oxford University Press, 1959); Norman M. Scarborough and Thomas W. Zimmerer, *Effective Small Business Management* (Prentice Hall, 2003); Joseph A. Schumpeter, *Capitalism, Socialism and Democracy* (HarperCollins, 1942); European Commission, Directorate General for Economic and Financial Affairs, www.europa.eu.int; United States Small Business Administration, www.sba.gov.

WOLFGANG GRASSL
HILLSDALE COLLEGE

Smith, Adam (1723–90)

WIDELY ACCLAIMED as the founder of modern economics, Adam Smith's importance lies not so much in the originality of his individual ideas, but in his putting these ideas together in a compendium of knowledge, *The Wealth of Nations* (1776). Unlike the work of previous economists, this book was widely read and very influential. Before his death, it had been translated into all the major European languages, and Smith was being quoted as an authority in the British Parliament.

Probably the most famous phrase associated with Smith is "the invisible hand." Smith uses this concept as part of an explanation of why businessmen will prefer to invest domestically rather than overseas when they are free to make the choice. Smith says:

> . . . and by directing that industry in such a manner as its produce is of the greatest value, he intends only his own gain, and he is in this, as in many other cases, led by an invisible hand to promote an end which was no part of his intention. Nor is it always the worse for society that it was no part of it. By pursuing his own interest he frequently promotes that of society more effectually than when he really intends to promote it. I have never known much good done by those who affected to trade for the public good.

While Smith used this expression in a specific context it has come to serve as a broad metaphor for Smith's vision of how a market economy works. It is the unintended outcome of individual actions; it is not the product of anyone's rational design. This idea has political and ethical as well as economic significance.

Smith lived during the Enlightenment, a time when many intellectuals were enthusiastic about the possibilities raised by the success of science, especially physics. Part of the impact of this scientific viewpoint was that virtually all educated people saw the natural world as driven by impersonal, non-moral forces. Gravity and inertia had replaced the gods Thor and Zeus as the world's

movers. By this time, almost no one would have thought to explain a crop failure moralistically, for example, because he had offended the rain god.

Smith's assertion that a person can promote the social good, even when he does not intend to, is a step toward explaining the social world in the manner of natural science. The goodness of one's intentions is irrelevant if the workings of the economy can be understood mechanistically.

This idea remains a source of controversy. Any number of contemporary issues, such as child labor in Third World factories owned by multinational corporations, intellectual property rights for drug companies, or the effects of globalization on the standard of living of the poor, to name a few, contain an element of moral outrage over the intentions of the responsible companies or governments. This outrage comes into conflict with economists' suggestions that well-meaning legislation or boycotts could create a worse situation.

The Wealth of Nations is a seminal document of political liberalism. It argued that a system of individual liberty is compatible with, even necessary for, national prosperity. This is still cited today by economists as a key reason for limiting the scope of government intervention into economic matters.

Most of the work in economics since Smith has been concerned with representing, refining, extending, applying, criticizing, or interpreting the invisible hand. Among the ideas to be found in modern economics that come from Smith are:

1. exchange creates wealth

2. the market is a system that regulates itself through PRICE

3. CAPITAL theory

4. international TRADE theory

Exchange creates wealth. Smith argues this in the first three chapters of *The Wealth of Nations*. Specialization and division of labor make labor more productive. This occurs for three reasons:

1. Specialization causes skills to improve

2. Less time is wasted setting up and cleaning between jobs

3. Familiarity with a particular job leads to thinking about how the job could be done better.

This leads to better techniques and to the introduction of machinery.

In order for people to specialize there must be opportunity to exchange. Why work in a pin factory, if at the end of the day all you get is lots of pins. To have a motive for being a highly productive specialized pin maker, you must believe that you can trade the excess pins you don't want for other things you do. It should be noted that logically this argument could run in either direction. Exchange depends on specialization as much as specialization depends on exchange. Smith's argument, however, is that specialization depends on exchange. In this chapter Smith also argues that the general phenomenon of increased productivity through exchange and specialization is not the result of brilliant human planning, but that it was instead a consequence of a natural human propensity to "truck, barter, and exchange." This is one expression of the idea that the market system is an unintended consequence of human action. Smith also points out that it is "not from the benevolence of the butcher, the brewer, or the baker, that we expect our dinner, but from their regard to their own interest." We are not fed by good intentions.

The market is a system regulated by prices. Here, Smith explains the theory of exchange value, and, more important, the connection between market price and social coordination. In 21st-century terms, Smith presents a vision of the economy as a self-organizing system cybernetically controlled by feedback from prices.

The central claim is that supply tends to suit itself to effectual demand. Smith defines natural price as the cost of bringing a good to market. This cost consists of wages, rents, and profits, all at their natural or normal level. Market price is what the good actually sells for. Effectual demand is the amount demanded at the natural price. Market price can deviate from natural price if supply does not equal effectual demand. For example, if too little supply is brought to market, then those who want the product and are able to pay more will bid up the market price. With market price greater than natural price, sellers of the good receive a greater than normal profit. This attracts others to this particular industry, or allows existing producers to pay higher wages and rents to attract new resources. The effect is to increase the supply of the good, driving down the price. When the market price equals the natural price, which occurs when supply equals effectual demand, there is no incentive to change the level of production.

This, then, is an EQUILIBRIUM. If this is true for all products in the economy, then a market system tends to produce exactly what people want and for which they are willing to pay the cost.

This is how a market system solves the problem of how to direct the actions of specialized workers. The self-sufficient farmer knows how much wheat to grow because he knows how much bread he wants. How does the specialized wheat farmer know how much wheat to grow, or even whether to grow wheat, rather than, say, oats, when he doesn't even know how his wheat is going to be used? Smith's answer is that he will be adequately guided by the price of wheat and the prices of his inputs. If he can earn more growing wheat than by doing something else, he can help himself and he will inadvertently serve society.

Capital theory. For Smith, division of labor and the consequent increase in labor productivity depend on two conditions: the possibility of exchange and the prior accumulation of capital. Capital is defined as that part of a person's "stock" that is reserved for the purpose of earning further revenue. Capital is divided into two major parts. Circulating capital consists of goods purchased for resale, goods meant to maintain productive labor, raw materials, and money for trade purposes. Fixed capital refers to factories and equipment, farm animals, and improvements in the land.

There are three reasons why the division of labor requires a prior accumulation of capital. First, there is a gap between the application of labor and the emergence and sale of the product. Capital is needed to sustain workers during this interval. Second is the increased productivity of specialized labor. Since a given number of specialized workers can produce more than the same number of unspecialized workers, the former need more materials per capita with which to work. These materials must be amassed beforehand if the workers are not to be idle. Finally, division of labor tends to lead to the introduction of machinery. The construction of such equipment must be performed in advance of it becoming productive.

Capital is the result of parsimonious lifestyles. Smith distinguishes between productive and unproductive labor. Productive labor adds value to a thing that it works on, while unproductive labor does not. Agricultural and manufacturing workers are productive, while menial servants are not. Wealth used to support servants merely evaporates. People with profligate lifestyles, such as rich, idle landlords, tend to use more of their wealth in the support of unproductive laborers; hence they destroy or at least do not accumulate capital.

International trade theory. Smith argues for free international trade on the same basis as he argued for noninterference with domestic exchange. It permits international specialization, hence greater prosperity. To insist on making everything domestically, such as producing wine in Scotland, would make no more sense than a farmer insisting on making his own shoes. A generation later, David RICARDO strengthened this argument with the principle of comparative advantage, which remains the core idea of international trade theory.

BIBLIOGRAPHY. Wesley C. Mitchell, *Types of Economic Theory, Volume 1* (Augustus M. Kelley, 1967); Joseph A. Schumpeter, *History of Economic Analysis* (Oxford University Press,

1964); Adam Smith, *An Inquiry into the Nature and Causes of the Wealth of Nations* (Modern Library Edition, 1937); Henry William Spiegel, *The Growth of Economic Thought* (Duke University Press, 1991).

SAMUEL WESTON, PH.D.
UNIVERSITY OF DALLAS

Smith, Vernon L. (1927–)

OF THE TWO RECIPIENTS of the 2002 Nobel Prize in Economics (along with Daniel KAHNEMAN of Princeton University), Vernon L. Smith was recognized "for having established laboratory experiments as a tool in empirical economic analysis, especially in the study of alternative market mechanisms."

Born in Witchita, Kansas in 1927 during the economic boom before the Great DEPRESSION, Smith was raised by two politically active parents. His mother was a devoted socialist, who strongly identified with, among others, Eugene Debs' beliefs. It was his parents' influence, and the Great Depression which dominated his early childhood, that led him to pursue his scientific career.

While studying for his degree in electrical engineering at the California Institute of Technology in 1949, Smith was intrigued by a general economics course, and decided to change his course of study. He received a masters degree in economics in 1952, and earned his Ph.D. at Harvard University three years later.

Smith's Prize-winning work, mainly involving laboratory experiments, both refuted and upheld some famous economic theories not tested by controlled experiments. While it was his socialist attitudes that led him to the study of economics so that he could effectively prove the inefficiencies of a capitalist system, his research undeniably showed the efficiencies of such markets. One of his earlier experiments tested one of the most fundamental aspects of modern economic study. The equilibrium price, a theoretical concept set by past economists, is the price that is equally acceptable to both sellers and buyers under perfect market competition. Using a number of subjects, Smith randomly assigned them as either a buyer or a seller for a given good and allowed them to set a price. Using the data of both the buyers and sellers, Smith concocted a "reservation price" of each good, or a lowest-acceptable selling price and a highest-acceptable buying price, respectively. Based on the distribution of the reservation prices of the given goods, Smith was able to calculate a set equilibrium price of each good. It wasn't until he published his results in 1962 that he made a surprising discovery. The prices were obtained in the laboratory were very similar to their theoretical values, even though the subjects did not have sufficient knowledge to calculate such a price. Later ex-

periments undoubtedly confirmed the agreement of the theory with the initial laboratory experiments.

Smith was also able to test the theoretical predictions of different types of auctions. In one controlled laboratory experiment, he upheld the notion, then only theoretically proven, that a seller could expect the same amount of revenue in an English auction (buyers increase their bids until no higher bid is recognized) as they could in a sealed second-bid auction (highest bidder pays second-highest bid.) Smith also refuted the theoretical equivalence of the Dutch auction (a high bid is eventually lowered into an acceptable one) and the first-price sealed auction (highest bidder pays his bid.)

Smith is the author of many essays covering a wide range of economic theories, including ones published in the *Journal of Political Economy* and the *American Economic Review*. In 2000, he compiled some of his best works for the publication *Bargaining and Market Behavior: Essays in Experimental Economics*. A year later, Smith and six of his colleagues left the University of Arizona to form the Interdisciplinary Center for Experimental Science (ICES) at George Mason University, which at the time of its inception was directed by Smith. At ICES, Smith continued to conduct controlled experiments and solidify developing economic theories.

BIBLIOGRAPHY. "Vernon L. Smith Autobiography," www.nobel.se; Vernon L. Smith, *Bargaining and Market Behavior: Essays in Experimental Economics* (Cambridge University Press, 2000); Vernon L. Smith, *Auctions and Market Institutional Design* (Cambridge University Press, 2003).

JOSEPH GERINGER
SYED B. HUSSAIN, PH.D.
UNIVERSITY OF WISCONSIN, OSHKOSH

social democracy

A POLITICAL MOVEMENT that promotes a peaceful and reformist transition from capitalism to socialism is termed a social democracy. The theoretical origin of modern social democracy as a political and economic movement dates back to Eduard Bernstein (1850–1932), a German political theorist and historian.

Bernstein argued that Marxism and the revolutionary left of his time were wrong to assume that the forces inherent to capitalism would push it first to a crisis, and then to collapse as a result of a workers' revolution. Instead, Bernstein and his fellow socialists of the time, especially those in the Social Democratic Party in GERMANY, proposed a gradual approach to power within a democratically elected political environment. They argued the effectiveness of promoting social reforms that target the well-being of the working class and economically disadvantaged, without an overthrow of the governmental system. In short, Bernstein promoted replacing capitalism with economic socialism within a politically democratic regime. The social democratic reforms and ensuing social change would strengthen the middle class and the social democratic movement. Eventually, social democracy would permanently replace capitalism.

Although social democracy became a powerful political movement upon its inception in the 19th century, it was not until after WORLD WAR II that social democrats came to power in Western European countries. Two developments related to the war helped the social democratic cause. First, the war strengthened the state, rendering the statism of social democrats familiar to many people. Second, the transition from the war economy to the peace economy called for extensive social welfare programs, increasing public interest in the social welfare state.

These two developments led to the social democrats' rise to power and to the acceptance of a new social contract between government and citizens. The new arrangement of the rights and responsibilities of citizens fostered tolerance to an increasingly progressive tax scheme, which provided the revenues necessary to finance the expanding social welfare programs. In addition, the strong economic growth in Western European countries in the 1950s and 1960s created an economic environment where the tax-and-spend policies of social democrats were tolerated by the capitalist class. Moreover, both had a common enemy in communism in the Soviet Union.

The two oil shocks in the 1970s changed the fortunes of the social democratic movement. Shrinking economies led to large budget deficits, high interest rates, unemployment, inflation, balance-of-payments problems, exchange-rate instability, and crowding-out of the private investment. Neo-liberal parties capitalized on the worsening economic situation and held social democratic governments responsible for excessive social-welfare programs, emphasizing their adverse macroeconomic effects. With the rise of the neo-liberals to power, social democracy itself, ironically, entered an era of crisis. Throughout the 1980s and early 1990s, social democrats and indeed the left in general, lost touch with the people in most industrial countries, with the exception of Scandinavia. The powerful counter-revolution staged by the neo-liberals and led by Margaret THATCHER and Ronald REAGAN, caused social democrats to lose their political and economic base. Aggressive privatization and liberalization policies implemented in the UNITED KINGDOM and the UNITED STATES, along with significant cuts in social-welfare programs, successfully brought back some semblance of economic stability and growth.

It was in the late 1990s, with the Labor Party's ascent to power in England, that social democracy was revived, although in a rather controversial manner. Growing discontent with market liberalism and increasing inequalities between economic classes led to political power changes in the industrial world. Left-of-center President Bill CLINTON, and later Tony Blair and Gerhard Schroeder, were elected to office in the United States, Britain, and Germany, respectively. Shortly after entering office, Prime Minister Tony Blair adopted the neo-social-democratic view of Anthony Giddens known as the Third Way. Anthony Giddens is a sociology professor and director of the London School of Economics and Political Science. His book, *The Third Way* (a phrase which had been used extensively during the Cold War years by European social democrats), attracted both praise and condemnation upon its publication in 1998.

The Third Way argues that market liberalism and communism have failed as economic and social systems. A political and economic system that would serve the people should emphasize economic and social justice, equality of opportunity, personal responsibility, civil society, and freedom. At the same time, the role of private business in the economy as an engine for growth should be acknowledged. Proponents of the Third Way regard it as a means of modernizing social democracy to fit the realities of the rapidly changing contemporary world of globalization and technological advancement. According to them, social democracy in the modern era cannot rely on the old tax-and-spend policies that would lead to big but not necessarily effective governments, and that would limit competition and incentives, constraining markets and technological change. *The Third Way* proposes instead a social, political and economic system that is based on a balance among the state, economic markets, and civil society. In this new social contract, it is the responsibility of the citizens to realize that they cannot indefinitely remain in a position of receivership as welfare dependents. At one point, they have to give back to society by working. On the other hand, it is the responsibility of the state to implement policies that would minimize government borrowing and inflation, maintain regulatory authority, and use supply-side measures to increase growth in the economy and thus raise employment.

The emphasis on supply-side measures in this neo-social-democratic agenda is a radical shift from the old social democratic norm of relying on Keynesian demand management policies. The shift is based on the recognition that the state needs to help private business enhance productivity and profitability in the globalized and ever-more competitive world economy. The expansion of the business sector would have net positive employment effects lessening the pressures on the domestic social welfare system.

Thus, the strategy is founded on the argument that the social benefits of a one-dollar tax cut allowed to businesses are significantly higher than a one-dollar increase in social welfare expenditures. Furthermore, the state plays an important role in enhancing the human capital of the work force and emphasizes education as a means of enriching human capabilities enabling access to gainful employment. These measures lessen the need for an extensive social welfare system and for a large state.

One of the main criticisms of the Third Way is that it takes the state from its historic role as the provider of last resort on the demand-side of the economy to a role as a partner with private business on the supply-side of the economy, leaving economically marginalized groups vulnerable. Other critics have condemned the Third Way for its narrowness since it is based primarily on Anglo-Saxon culture and experience. Nevertheless, the Third Way social democrats have been making progress in several countries. The market-oriented approach of the Third Way is being adopted to lessen the burden of large and expensive social welfare systems even in Scandinavian countries, the bastions of old social democratic welfare states. SWEDEN, NORWAY, and DENMARK are experimenting with variations of the Third Way, combining markets with reforms directed at reducing the economic burden of the welfare state.

In the last two decades of the 20th century and in the early 21st century, social democrats have been in search of a new identity. The seeming success of neo-liberalism and the failure of socialism have rendered many people skeptical of the statist policies embedded in old-fashioned social democracy. The Third Way is an attempt to regain the public's trust in social democracy by providing a non-radical, reformist alternative to market liberalism and socialism.

BIBLIOGRAPHY. A. Giddens, *The Third Way and Its Critics* (Polity Press, 2000); A. Giddens, *The Third Way: The Renewal of Social Democracy* (Polity Press, 1998); J. Petras, "The Third Way," *Monthly Review* 51 (v.10, 2000); M. Steger, *The Quest for Evolutionary Socialism: Eduard Bernstein and Social Democracy* (Cambridge University Press, 1997).

M. ODEKON
SKIDMORE COLLEGE

social security

THE TERM SOCIAL SECURITY has two meanings. In economics, it refers to the social security of a country's population; in the general UNITED STATES population, social security usually refers to the Social Security Administration.

The development of capitalist economies in northern Europe in the 18th and 19th centuries brought with it heightened levels of poverty and unemployment as livelihood came to depend on the exchange of labor for wages.

Increasing social conflict over the distribution of wealth in the context of this commoditization of labor generated a greater social demand for the state provision of relief, and a growing diasaffection of the working classes. The need to create market conditions conducive to capitalist accumulation spurred innovations in poor relief and risk management resulting in the expanded social domain associated with the institutions and social practices of social security. Accordingly, the origin of social security systems, first in Europe in the 30 years preceding WORLD WAR I, followed by North and South America, and later by colonial authorities in much of what has come to be known as the Third World, is conventionally explained in reference to the heightened insecurity of individuals attendant on the erosion of extended networks of social support, the transformation of the family, and the migration of rural labor to the cities.

In alternative accounts, social security appears variously as a "social wage," emblematic of the expansion of legal and political rights to social rights tied to citizenship; as society's demand for protection against the vicissitudes of the market. For John Maynard KEYNES and William H. Beveridge, key theoreticians of expanded social provision, the minimal guarantee of income is deemed essential to mitigating the evils of the un-regulated market and, more significantly, to regulating production and consumption for both the working and non-working population. Marxian perspectives, on the other hand, view the rapid expansion of social security in capitalist societies both as the outcome of class-struggle by workers to better the terms of their exploitation, and capital's concession to labor to ensure social and political stability and a productive work-force.

In contemporary usage, the term social security refers to social insurance and social assistance public programs designed to protect individuals and families against the contingencies of life and the vagaries of the market that result in the loss of income due. Comprising a range of measures including, old-age pensions, healthcare, public housing, unemployment, sickness benefits, child allowances, social security practices, sometimes subsumed under the larger category of the welfare state, vary widely across countries in terms of levels of benefit, coverage, administration, political legitimacy, and the particular mix of public-private means by which these goods are provisioned. Social insurance—the state distribution of benefits based on compulsory individual contributions for old-age, unemployment, and sickness—is typically seen as an earned right based on income replacement from work. In contrast, social assistance programs, providing targeted assistance to needy groups based on means/income tested basis, involved greater administrative intervention, encroachment on privacy, and generally entailed a stigmatization of recipients.

Although access to social security has been recognized as a fundamental human right (in articles 22 and 25 of the 1948 Universal Declaration of Human Rights adopted by the United Nations General Assembly), with a variety of social security systems in place in more than 170 countries today, positive evaluations of the material benefits of social security systems, particularly its role in alleviating poverty and redistributing wealth have been challenged by Marxian and neo-Marxian scholars who see social security programs predominantly in reference to the regulation of labor. Thus, expansive social security policies are seen as central to mitigating civic disorder; and minimalist ones crucial to reinforcing work norms. Contemporary scholarship, however, drawing heavily on post-structural approaches (especially the work of Michel Foucault) is increasingly concerned with social security's disciplinary and regulative functions in post-industrial societies, particularly in the context of social security cutbacks in virtually all advanced capitalist democracies at the turn of the century.

Deeply skeptical about claims about social security's effectiveness in attenuating inequality in capitalist societies, post-structural critics suggest that its primary function in society is in relation to the production of identities and their effective social management. In contrast to direct modes of the regulation of the poor (for instance, in 18th century workhouses), the modalities of power in liberal democracies rely on the production of subjects via the many micrological channels through which power operates. On these accounts, Keynesian social security programs were vital to the production of a sociopolitical order in which classifications between the deserving and the un-deserving poor, claimants and non-claimants constituted the national-citizen/worker as the normatively produced subject of liberal governance. In contrast, cutbacks in social security spending and the marketization of social provisioning currently underway in most advanced capitalist democracies in response to heightened global economic competitiveness are seen as emblematic of new practices of governance appropriate to the new spatialization of the economy as global, and the reduced capacity of the nation-state. Cutbacks in social security spending, the privatization of insurance, pensions, and health care, and the attempt to move the unemployed needy from welfare to work-fare under conditions of heightened surveillance and behavioral scrutiny constitutes, critics suggest, a new moral technology calculated to fashion a changed subjectivity in accordance with the new axis of self-governance appropriate to the economic and political rationalities of later capitalist societies.

BIBLIOGRAPHY. Martin S. Feldstein and Horst Siebert, *Social Security Pension Reform in Europe* (University of Chicago Press, 2002); Alexander Hicks, *Social Democracy and Welfare Capitalism: A Century of Income Security Politics* (Cornell University Press, 2000).

RITU VIJ
AMERICAN UNIVERSITY

socialism

THE BIRTH OF THE IDEA of the socialism grew out of important European events in the late 18th century. The participants' philosophy about the nature of society itself would lead to the full formation of the conceptual socialist ideal nearly 100 years later.

The INDUSTRIAL REVOLUTION that swept Britain, beginning in the last quarter of the 18th century, was a massive dislocation in social life: old communities were destroyed; people were forced off the land and into the tyranny of the factory; industrial diseases multiplied; hunger, poverty and illness spread; life expectancy fell. At the same time, however, several ingredients of the Industrial Revolution held out the prospect of an end to these ills. The new machinery of production that developed, especially during the early 1800s, offered the possibility of sharply reducing drudgery and toil and of massively increasing the production of wealth to eliminate poverty forever. In reality, the Industrial Revolution did no such thing. Rather than leading to an improvement in the conditions of labor, the new industry was used to increase the fortunes of a few—the new industrial capitalists. Nonetheless, some writers saw in the Industrial Revolution an enormous potential for improving the human condition. Even some well-intentioned bankers and factory owners came to believe that the forces of the Industrial Revolution should be harnessed to serve human ends.

It wasn't until the works of Karl MARX nearly 100 years later that the ideas of democracy and economics intertwined into socialism.

Marx was the first major socialist thinker who came to socialism through the struggle for democratic rights. As a young man in Germany during the early 1840s, Marx edited a newspaper, which supported the widespread extension of democratic liberties. Increasingly, Marx came to the view that the political restrictions on democracy were a result of the economic structure of society.

When the government closed down his newspaper in 1843, Marx moved to Paris. There he encountered a vibrant working class and socialist movement. Several years later, Marx moved to England where he undertook a painstaking study of the nature of the capitalist economy. Out of his experience in France and England,

Marx developed a consistently democratic and revolutionary socialist outlook.

The young Marx came increasingly to believe that no society, which was divided into exploiting employer and exploited worker could ever achieve full democracy. So long as the capitalists held the bulk of economic power in society, they would continue to dominate political life. Full democracy, Marx argued, required the overcoming of class division in society.

Marx was also the first major socialist thinker to make the principle of self-emancipation—the principle that socialism could only be brought into being by the self-mobilization and self-organization of the working class; a fundamental aspect of the socialist project. Marx's prediction of the working class leading a revolution rang true in the early 20th century, when the Bolsheviks, led by Vladimir Lenin, overthrew Czarist Russia and transformed it into a self-proclaimed socialist state. The initial system of government, as American journalist John Reed described, was inherently democratic: "At least twice a year delegates are elected from all over Russia to the All-Russian Congress of Soviets . . . This body, consisting of about 2,000 delegates, meets in the capital in the form of a great soviet, and settles upon the essentials of national policy. It elects a central executive committee, like the Central Committee of the Petrograd Soviet, which invites delegates from the central committees of all democratic organizations."

However, the brave and courageous ambitions of the state to turn Russia into a land of working class prosperity proved to be just that, ambitions. Instead of a new hope for the working class, Russia became a totalitarian state, never realizing it's full potential, and collapsing in the late 20th century.

What passed itself off as socialism was generally an elitist and authoritarian doctrine strongly resembling the anti-democratic visions of socialism. There were, of course, major national liberation struggles, such as those in China and Cuba, which freed colonial nations from the oppressive grip of a major world powers. As victories against imperialism, these movements were justly deserving of support. But the claims of the Chinese and Cuban regimes to be socialist have stained the image of genuine socialism everywhere, much like the Josef Stalin regime of the Soviet Union. History has yet to see a true, successful socialist society.

BIBLIOGRAPHY. Albert Einstein, "Why Socialism?" *Monthly Review Magazine* (May, 1949); Brian Basgen, "*Soviet History*," www.marxists.org/history/ussr; Joseph A. Schumpeter, *Capitalism, Socialism, and Democracy* (HarperCollins, 1984); Martin Malia. *The Soviet Tragedy* (Free Press, 1994).

SYED B. HUSSAIN, PH.D.
UNIVERSITY OF WISCONSIN, OSHKOSH

Solow, Robert (1924–)

BORN IN BROOKLYN, New York, to children of immigrants, Robert Merton Solow would eventually become one of the major figures of American neo-Keynesian macroeconomics. Along with Trevor Swan, he authored the seminal articles in the modern scientific literature on economic growth. In 1987, he was awarded the Nobel Prize in Economics for his work on the topic.

A good student from an early age, Solow won a scholarship to attend Harvard University in 1940 at the age of 16. After two years of schooling, he left Harvard to join the army, but at the conclusion of WORLD WAR II, he returned and began to study economics and statistics. Under the guidance of Wassily LEONTIEF, he earned a B.A. and then Ph.D. in economics from Harvard. In 1951, shortly before graduating, he accepted a position teaching statistics and ECONOMETRICS in the Massachusetts Institute of Technology economics department, where he remained until his retirement.

In 1956, Solow published his most important theoretical paper on the topic of growth, "A Contribution to the Theory of Economic Growth." In it, he showed how the then-standard model could be modified to provide a much more satisfactory account of how growth takes place.

According to the Harrod-Domar model, economic growth is inherently unstable in the sense that if the national savings rate ever deviates from its equilibrium value, the economy will be put on a path leading further away from equilibrium. Solow felt that this feature of the Harrod-Domar model was implausible, given the relatively smooth growth observed in the real world. He showed that the problem is eliminated if production is modeled with a neoclassical production function and prices in all markets are flexible. In his model, the capital-output ratio automatically adjusts to insure that the demand for output expands at the same rate as production, regardless of the savings rate.

In addition to his theoretical work on growth, Solow was the first to demonstrate that technological improvement, rather than capital accumulation and population growth, is responsible for nearly half of all economic growth.

BIBLIOGRAPHY. B. Mak Arvin and Marisa A Scigliano, "Robert Solow," *Frontiers of Economics, Nobel Laureates of the Twentieth Century* (Greenwood Press, 2002); Robert M. Solow, "A Contribution to the Theory of Economic Growth," *Quarterly Journal of Economics* (1956); Robert M. Solow, "Growth Theory and After," *American Economic Review* (v.78, 1988).

JOEL D. CARTON, PH.D.
TEXAS TECH UNIVERSITY

Sony Corporation

A PIONEER IN THE production and global distribution of consumer electronics, Sony's early growth paralleled JAPAN's dramatic recovery following defeat in WORLD WAR II. Masaru Ibuka and Akio Morita incorporated the Tokyo Telecommunications Engineering Corporation (Tokyo Tsushin Kogyo) in May 1946. In 1950, the company marketed the first magnetic tape recorder in Japan, and developed equipment for the Japan Broadcasting Company (NHK) and its first stereo radio transmission in 1952.

In 1953, Ibuka and Morita gambled on new transistor technology. Morita negotiated an agreement to license Western Electric's transistor design for a fee of $25,000. Japanese government officials, however, were reluctant to permit a small company to spend Japan's scarce reserve of dollars on such a risky venture. After several months of lobbying, the government finally issued a foreign exchange permit. The company produced the first successful transistors made in Japan in May 1954. It manufactured Japan's first all-transistor radio in 1955 and the world's first pocket-sized model in 1957.

In 1958, Tokyo Telecommunications changed its name to Sony, which was easy to pronounce in most languages. The name combined the Latin word for sound (sonus) with the English word sonny, which Ibuka and Morita associated with adventurous youth unafraid of overturning established practices. In the early 1960s, Sony was true to its rebellious image when it marketed portable 5- and 8-inch televisions in the American market while competitors built the biggest possible sets. Sony also gambled on new technology when it entered the color television market. Unwilling to simply copy RCA's shadow mask color system, Sony engineers experimented for nearly seven years to produce a brighter color picture before announcing the Trinitron in April 1968.

Sony helped to create the home-video industry with its 1975 introduction of the Betamax video tape recorder. The Sony Betamax soon came under attack when Universal Studios and Walt Disney Productions alleged that home-video recording violated television program copyrights. After a long legal battle, the U.S. Supreme Court ruled in 1984 that personal recording for later viewing was permitted under copyright law. Sony also engaged in a 12-year struggle over video format after JVC introduced the incompatible VHS system in 1976. Since availability of movie titles proved decisive in the Betamax defeat, Sony acquired CBS records in 1988 and Columbia Pictures Entertainment in 1989 to better control "software" production for its electronic devices.

Other Sony innovations include the 1979 Walkman portable stereo, the 8mm camcorder in 1985, and the 1994 PlayStation video game system. In 2002, Sony reported sales of $53.1 billion worth of electronics, video games, music, motion pictures, and financial services, making it the 37th largest company in the world.

BIBLIOGRAPHY. Nick Lyons, *The Sony Vision* (Crown, 1976); Akio Morita, *Made in Japan* (Weatherhill, 1986), Sony Corporation, "Sony History," www.sony.net; Sony Corporation, *Annual Report* (2002). "Global 500: World's Largest Companies," *Fortune* (July 2002).

JOHN SAGERS, PH.D.
LINFIELD COLLEGE

Soros, George (1930–)

A HIGHLY SUCCESSFUL investor, multibillionaire, and philanthropist, George Soros is also the author of seven books on globalization, financial markets, and what he calls the "open society." His Quantum Fund has achieved an average annual return of over 30 percent, among the highest of any investment funds.

Born in Hungary, Soros lived under Nazi occupation during WORLD WAR II and briefly under post-war communism. He then went to capitalist England and, in 1952, graduated from the London School of Economics. There, he studied under philosopher Karl Popper whose essay, "The Open Society and Its Enemies," and whose philosophy of science deeply impressed Soros.

Like Popper, Soros holds that human beings have imperfect knowledge of the world. Society is therefore likely to reach the best solutions to the world's problems only if it allows free and open debate by people of diverse views. His philanthropic efforts, beginning in 1979 and working through his Open Society Institute, have mainly been dedicated to creating institutions that support an open society. He has given enormous funding to build universities, civic organizations, and other democratic institutions in Eastern Europe and the former Soviet Union. The Open Society Institute has also funded programs in the United States, including the campaign to legalize the medical use of marijuana.

While Soros is perhaps best known for having risked $10 billion in a successful bet against the British pound in 1992, ultimately making $2 billion on the deal, he also insists that financial markets are inherently unstable and must be contained. This is because, in financial markets, unlike markets for physical goods, there is "reflexivity"—two-way causation between the thinking of players and the outcomes in the market. What players judge will happen affects what they buy and sell, and hence affects the market's behavior. But market behavior, in turn, affects players' judgments.

Players' views easily become progressively divorced from reality, leading to speculative bubbles and crashes. Apart from using the idea of reflexivity to explain why financial markets are inherently unstable, Soros also used the concept to predict turns in the market and thereby reaped large gains.

As a reformer, Soros has proposed making both the WORLD BANK and the INTERNATIONAL MONETARY FUND (IMF) less dominated by developed countries, and strengthening the International Labor Organization as a way of promoting labor rights and standards worldwide. To reduce world inequality, he also has proposed creating a global development fund administered by a board of eminent persons and funded by country contributions with special drawing rights.

BIBLIOGRAPHY. www.soros.org; "George Soros," dir. salon.com/people; George Soros, *The Crisis of Global Capitalism* (Public Affairs, 1998); George Soros, *Open Society: Reforming Global Capitalism* (Public Affairs, 2000); George Soros, *George Soros on Globalization* (Public Affairs, 2002).

MEHRENE LARUDEE, PH.D.
UNIVERSITY OF KANSAS

South Africa

THE ECONOMY OF South Africa was for many years agricultural; that is, until the late 1800s, when diamonds were discovered near Kimberley (1867) and strains of gold were found along the banks of the Witwatersrand River (1889). A whole new era opened, hopeful miners populated the country well into the 20th century. It was not until the 1940s that South Africa's two major industries, mining and agriculture, became developed enough to produce a variety of commodities. The country was still very much dependent on the rest of the world for manufactured goods. Starting with the end of WORLD WAR II, 1945, South Africa began manufacturing much of its own commodities, to the point that it became an efficient distributor of goods to major urban centers throughout the sub-Saharan region.

Since the 1940s, South Africa has experienced a series of across-the-board growth rates—high and low—from hungry years when the economy seemed doomed to failure, to years when the economy was among the highest and most enviable in the world. For example, the South Africa that existed in the early 2000s, a magnet to foreign investors, bears little resemblance to the country of only a few decades ago. Under economic sanctions, South Africa's economy struggled as foreign powers shunned the nation's policy of apartheid, or government sponsored segregation.

With apartheid behind it, the country can be described as a middle-income, developing nation with an abundant supply of resources and well-developed financial, legal, communications, energy, and transport sectors. Its stock exchange ranks among the 10 largest in the world, and is accompanied by a wide infrastructure supporting ongoing major shipment transactions with other parts of the globe.

South Africa's GROSS DOMESTIC PRODUCT (GDP) at the end of 2001 was $412 billion, with a per capita GDP of $9,400. These figures speak for themselves when comparing them with the 1991 figures—a mere decade earlier. At the end of 1991, the GDP was $131 billion and the per capita was $3,110.

But, this has been no surprise to economic forecasters monitoring the country's performance. Annual GDP growth between 1994 and 1997 fluctuated between 1.5 percent and 3.4 percent. A brief global financial crisis (1998) saw a small percentage drop, but in 1999 it quickly rebounded. The success indicated by the GDP ratios is very much due to the government's consumer inflation policies. Until 1997, inflation had been running in double digits; in 1998 it read 6.9 percent—a dramatic drop. By 2000, inflation had dipped below 6 percent.

South Africa's government explains its priorities are to upgrade its forces to better fight crime and corruption, create more jobs, provide education for those who cannot afford it, train the unskilled, house the homeless, improve and expand health care coverage, alleviate poverty and maintain growth in economy.

"South Africa continues to lack skilled labor," notes the U.S. State Department's *Country Commercial Guide to South Africa*. It lacks labor in "not only the professional fields, but also in practical technical fields. This skills' shortage results from the inherited shortcomings of the educational system (and) the departure of skilled laborers to more lucrative employment abroad."

The state of the labor force remains South Africa's greatest challenge. 2001 figures report a 30 percent unemployment rate, a leftover casualty from the apartheid period. The fight to cure poverty has also been a long, hard battle. In 1990, the government began a long-term program aimed at sustaining economic growth and redressing socioeconomic disparities. The Reconstruction and Development Program (RDP) sought to create programs to improve the daily lifestyles for the "vast majority." Under the RDP, basic human services, education, and health care policies were re-examined and solutions presented. Not long after, the RDP was dissolved as a single unit, but the work it began was divided into several governmental bodies. Improvements continued, but perhaps without a single, tightened initiative such as the RDP, the war against unemployment became less focused.

In 1996, the government issued the four-year-long Growth, Employment and Redistribution plan, better known as GEAR. GEAR committed to open markets, privatization, and an investment climate that brought a greater discipline to the economy, using MACROECONOMIC policies. Some success was evident, but by 2000 it became obvious that GEAR failed to boost formal, ongoing employment and to empower the black population with more social middle-class mobility—two of its chief objectives.

Other, strictly budgetary-type reforms paralleled GEAR's timeline. The Medium-Term Expenditure Framework and the Public Finance Management Act, both successful, gave South Africa the ability to more accurately monitor the economy. As well, trade procedures were liberalized, import tariffs lowered and, with the country's acceptance of the obligations chartered by the WORLD TRADE ORGANIZATION (WTO), a free-market system was formally adopted.

In 1999, the South African Cabinet, the European Council of Ministers and the European Commission approved the South African/European Union Trade, Development and Cooperation Agreement. According to the U.S. State Department's report on South African commerce, the pact obliges the EUROPEAN UNION (EU) to "full liberalization of 95 percent of South African imports over a 10-year period, while South Africa is to liberalize 86 percent of EU imports over a 12-year period." This includes, particularly, agricultural goods.

South Africa's agriculture accounts for about three percent of the GROSS NATIONAL PRODUCT (GNP) but comprises some 31 percent of the labor force, per 2001 estimates. Major agricultural output includes produce and meat products.

Being a country rich in minerals, South Africa is the world's largest producer and exporter of gold and platinum, the latter having overtaken the former as the biggest foreign-exchange earner for 2000. Mining has played the main role in the economic development of the country. Beyond the gold and platinum, the country is also the world's largest producer of manganese, chromium, vanadium, and alumino-sillicates. It is the globe's number-two producer of vermiculite and zirconium, and third in the diamond mine industry. During the early 2000s, the world demand has affected the prices and costs of certain mining sectors, causing transformations within the South African mining industry. Mining companies have been, for the most part, restructured and merged.

Exports reached 29.1 percent of GDP in 2001, up more than 11 percent from 1991. Major overseas trading partners are the UNITED KINGDOM, the UNITED STATES, GERMANY, ITALY, BELGIUM, and JAPAN. Because of its strategic, active investment in both the Southern African Customs Union (SACU) and the Southern African Development Community (SADC), South Africa has been able to increase its relationship—and business of trade—with fellow sub-Saharan African countries.

In 2003, a Reuters news story announced that South Africa remains an optimistic haven in the eyes of 30 of the world's economists. Polled, the experts declared that they see the country promising—and practicing—improved growth, a stable inflation, a steady rate of exchange, and lower interest rates.

On the corporate side, the U.S. State Department foresees certain businesses and non-agricultural service industries growing in the South African economy. Some of these are the cellular industry and the internet-service provider industry. The computer and software services market are expected to continue to expand. Opportunities exist for enterprising technology companies.

The tourist industry has also grown in South Africa. By the late 1990s, the World Tourism Organization ranked South Africa among the top leisure travel destinations, with six million visitors annually.

BIBLIOGRAPHY. U.S. State Department, *Country Commercial Guide to South Africa* (2000); *CIA World Factbook: South Africa* (2003); "South African Economy," www.geography.org.

JOSEPH GERINGER
SYED B. HUSSAIN, PH.D.
UNIVERSITY OF WISCONSIN, OSHKOSH

Spain

BEARING LITTLE RESEMBLANCE to the postcard land of conquistadors, vineyards, pastoral hills, and Don Quixote, the Spain of the 21st century ranks fifth economically in overall Europe and number 10 among the world's most technology-minded, industrialized nations. Its GROSS DOMESTIC PRODUCT (GDP) ended 2001 at $828 billion, effected by Spain's early membership in the EUROPEAN UNION (EU) IN 1986, and its adoption of the EURO currency in 2002.

Spain's history was shaped by Phoenicians, Romans, and Germanic tribes, which all had a strong influence on the people of the Iberian Peninsula. Perhaps the greatest artistic and intellectual ferment in Spain was under the Moors, the Islamic conquerors who crossed the Straits of Gibraltar in the early 700s and ruled the land for more than seven centuries. Universities, unique architecture and an age of religious toleration were all fostered by the Islamic rulers. After many conflicts with Christian forces, the Moors were finally ousted in 1492. That same year, Christopher Columbus crossed the Atlantic under the Spanish flag and revealed the New World to Europe.

The next century was the height of Spain's power and influence throughout the world. Some historians point to Spain as the first true worldwide empire. In addition to colonies from the Philippines to Mexico, Spanish kings controlled all or parts of what are now PORTUGAL, the NETHERLANDS, ITALY, and FRANCE. The economic realities of managing an empire did not match the country's ambitions, however, and Spain went into a decline that saw it lose nearly all of its colonial possessions by the late 1800s.

In the early part of the 20th century, Spain saw its traditional culture and economy clash with modern political and social forces. The clash culminated in 1936 with the outbreak of the Spanish Civil War. Fascist dictator Francisco Franco, with the help of fellow fascists Adolf Hitler and Benito Mussolini, emerged victorious from the civil war and ruled until his death in 1975. He left Spain in the care of King Juan Carlos I, who soon led Spain toward democracy.

With such a heritage of exploration and colonization, the Spanish administration of the early 21st century continues to support privatization of the economy—as well as liberalization and deregulation—and some tax reforms that have been helpful in sustaining growth. Although Spain's unemployment rate has reached levels of 14 percent, the worst of the EU countries, the rate has fallen steadily since the late 1990s. "Spain has been transformed in the last three decades from a rural, backward, agricultural country into a nation with a diversified economy and strong manufacturing and service sectors," explains the Spanish government. Rising from the list of periphery countries to prosperous core nations such as GERMANY, ITALY, and the UNITED KINGDOM in the early 20th century, Spain and its economy found itself exceeding those countries' growth averages later in the century.

A strong factor of Spain's economic strength is continuing legislation that promotes modernization of technology and entry into the highly competitive, aggressive circle of top European technology markets. Thus, foreign investors eye Spain's attributes with an interested eye.

Investors come from both abroad (including the UNITED STATES) and heavily from among Spain's fellow members in the EU, some 55 percent of total investment. This includes FRANCE, the NETHERLANDS, and Germany. In speaking of its economic ties to Spain, the German Embassy writes, "Spain is an attractive country for investment. . . . The Spanish economy assumes an increasingly international dimension and this has resulted in greater economic activity."

Traditionally a farming country, Spain's agricultural export (now 8 percent of the GDP) has been shrinking since the mid-1950s, subordinated by the rapid growth of manufacturing, mining, construction, and services. Agricultural output, though somewhat diminished in a modern era, has certainly not become unimportant. Products include, as they have for centuries, olives, tomatoes, grapes, sugar beets, wheat, citrus fruits, strawberries, lemons, and oranges. Olive oil is produced in quantities incomparable with the rest of the world. Wine products abound, coming especially from the rich, fertile regions of Andalucia, Rioja, and Jerez de la Frontera.

BIBLIOGRAPHY. Carlos Zaldivar and Manuel Castells, *Spain Beyond the Myths* (Alianza Editorial, 1992); " Economy of Spain," www.andalucia.com; "Port of Spain," German Embassy, www.germanemb-portofspain.de; *CIA World Factbook* (2002).

JOSEPH GERINGER
SYED B. HUSSAIN, PH.D.
UNIVERSITY OF WISCONSIN, OSHKOSH

Spanish-American War

THE SPANISH-AMERICAN War of 1898 was a turning point for the UNITED STATES. Victory over the empire of SPAIN in this brief conflict marked America's debut onto the world stage. In the aftermath of the "splendid little war," Americans emerged confident, energetic, and eager to spread their presumed blessings and values of democracy, Christianity, and unbridled capitalism to the world as the United States took its place alongside the great and powerful nations across the globe.

The background of the Spanish-American War can be traced to American interest in CUBA, a colony of the Spanish Empire in the late 19th century. Located only 90 miles south of Florida, Cuba's proximity to the Caribbean and to America proved a source of economic and security interest to the United States. In 1895, Cubans revolted against Spain for their independence. Americans, outraged with the Spanish treatment of the island residents, sympathized with the Cuban rebels.

Historians have also suggested that American business interests favored war with Spain over Cuba. War could spur business growth in the United States, end Spanish control of Cuba, and allow American merchant interests to expand their Cuban trade. A delay in intervention might cause damage to American investments in Cuba; thus, military action was required to protect economic interests. However, such economic interests were not necessarily consistent with the business community as a whole. By the late 1890s, the U.S. economy was rebounding and members of the business community feared that military involvement in Cuba would hamper the natural recovery of the market-based society.

But in general, Americans were in favor of *Cuba libre*, or free Cuba. Concerns over Cuba were intensified through the activities of the "yellow" press, journalists who sought to increase newspaper circulation by sensational treatment of news from Cuba. The reports of the yellow press enraged and mobilized Americans against Spain. Tensions between the two nations continued to grow until they erupted in war in 1898.

The immediate catalyst for military conflict was the sinking of the U.S.S. *Maine*. While visiting Havana, Cuba, the American battleship was blown up, killing 260 American sailors. Although the cause of the explosion was unknown, it moved Americans to rally against Spain and mobilize for war.

Inspired by the call to arms—"Remember the Maine!"—the American victory over Spain was easy and quick. Only 379 of the nearly 280,000 men who served in the American armed forces died from enemy action. The financial cost of the war was also small, amounting to roughly $250 million. In particular, American naval power proved crucial in destroying the Spanish fleet in the Caribbean. The war also projected the heroism of a rising Theodore ROOSEVELT who led his crew of Rough Riders up San Juan Hill on the island.

Although the war itself lasted only a few months, the effects were far-reaching. With the 1898 Treaty of Paris, a defeated Spain agreed to free Cuba and to cede Puerto Rico and Guam to the United States. Additionally, the Philippine islands, located in the Eastern Pacific, were sold to the United States for $20 million. By ac-

quiring these lands, America gained control over international resources, especially the sugar trade, and thus provided an important source of capital to the American business community.

Having established its military and economic predominance, the United States emerged from the Spanish-American War with territories in the Caribbean and in the Pacific. These new land claims ignited a debate between imperialists, supporters of a United States empire, and anti-imperialists, those against an expanded American empire. On one hand, American business interests relished the commercial advantages that control over the Philippines, Cuba, and Guam promised, but alternatively, some Americans were skeptical and anxious over the implications of an American empire.

The debate played out in the presidential election of 1898 between anti-imperialist, Democrat William Jennings Bryan, who argued that imperialism abroad would only bring despotism to domestic soil, and Republican and imperialist, William McKinley, who won a decisive victory.

The economic and political respect and recognition that the victory over Spain afforded the United States propelled the nation into the foreground of global power and inaugurated an unprecedented sense of nationalism at the dawn of the 20th century.

BIBLIOGRAPHY. David Burner, et al, *An American Portrait* (Charles Scribner's Sons, 1985); Edward J. Marolda, ed., Theodore Roosevelt, *The U.S. Navy, and the Spanish-American War* (Palgrave, 2001); Ivan Musicant, *The Spanish-American War and the Dawn of the American Century* (Henry Holt and Company, 1998); David Traxel, *1898: The Birth of the American Century* (Knopf, 1998); Irving Werstein, *1898: The Spanish-American War* (Cooper Square Publishers, 1966).

LINDSAY SILVER
BRANDEIS UNIVERSITY

Spence, Michael (1943–)

A. MICHAEL SPENCE WAS born in Montclair, New Jersey, completed his B.A. at Princeton University in 1966 and his M.A. at the University of Oxford two years later. He obtained a Ph.D. from Harvard University in 1972. Spence was awarded the Nobel Prize in Economics, jointly with George A. AKERLOF and Joseph E. STIGLITZ in 2001, for his work on signaling in markets with asymmetric information.

Spence's groundbreaking work began with his Ph.D. dissertation at Harvard, in which he developed his theory of market signaling in labor markets. To understand his theory, consider the following sce-

Michael Spence proposed that people "signaled" their value to employers by citing their achievements during job interviews.

nario: An employer has difficulty assessing the productivity of a job applicant and thus offers a wage that is based on the average ability of prospective employees. This means that workers that are highly productive end up with wages that do not reflect their high abilities. Spence pointed out that these workers may have another option. Instead of working at the average wage, they may attempt to "signal" their higher ability to the employer and demand a higher wage. In order for a signal to yield a higher wage offer, it must be the case that the signal reveals the worker's ability. The high-productivity worker has to find a credible signal that low-ability workers would find too costly, even if they were subsequently granted a very high wage.

In Spence's (deliberately highly stylized) model, education serves as such a signal. It is assumed that education is costly due to the effort spent on obtaining a degree. People who tend to be more productive, however, find it less costly to do so than people who are less productive. Thus, education levels may serve as a signal of how productive one is. It should be noted, that as a lifelong educator, Spence has been disappointed by his model being interpreted to imply that education is merely a signal and does not serve productive purposes.

It has been noted that signaling is not purely an economic phenomenon, as evidenced in biological natural selection. In order to attract mates, many animals will use resources, which by themselves serve little other purpose, to signal health and thus good genes (e.g., extravagant colorings and feather displays of male birds).

BIBLIOGRAPHY. Mark Blaug, *Great Economists since Keynes* (Barnes & Noble, 1985); Karl-Gustaf Löfgren, Torsten Persson, and Jörgen W. Weibull, "Markets with Asymmetric Information: The Contributions of George Akerlof, Michael Spence and Joseph Stiglitz," *Scandinavian Journal of Economics* (v.104/2, 2002); Michael Spence, *Market Signaling: Information Transfer in Hiring and Related Screening Processes* (Harvard University Press, 1974); Michael Spence, "Signaling in Retrospect and the Informational Structure of Markets," *American Economic Review* (v.92/3, 2002).

THOMAS D. JEITSCHKO, PH.D.
MICHIGAN STATE UNIVERSITY

Spencer, Herbert (1820–1903)

IN POPULAR THOUGHT the phrase "the survival of the fittest" has long been overwhelmingly associated with Charles Darwin's theory of evolution. In fact, it was Herbert Spencer who coined the phrase in *Principles of Biology* (1864). Indeed, Spencer set forth his theory of evolution before Darwin's theory was known and interestingly, in distinct contrast to Darwin, Spencer's evolutionary theory was derived for his contemplations on human society. For much of the 20th century, however, Spencer's writings were dismissed entirely as the product of a simple-minded and ideologically dangerous quack. In this respect, however, one must note that Spencer was a prolific scholar with a strong scientific orientation who forcefully insisted that social phenomena be studied using scientific methods.

Moreover, next to John Stuart MILL, Spencer was the most widely read nonfiction writer in English of the 19th century. At least 1 million copies of his books were sold, and his most important works were translated widely, appearing in Arabic, Chinese, French, German, Italian, Japanese, Russian, and Spanish.

Spencer's learned contemporaries often referred to his scholarship with the highest praise. For example, Darwin once stated that Spencer was "by far the greatest living philosopher in England; perhaps equal to any that have lived." And Alfred MARSHALL, the doyen of British neoclassical economics, said of Spencer, "There is probably no one who gave as strong a stimulus to the thoughts of the younger Cambridge graduates 39 or 40 years ago as he. He opened a new world of promise; he set men on high enterprise in many diverse directions; and though he may have regulated English intellectual work less than Mill did, I believe he did more toward increasing its utility."

Spencer was born in Derby, England, and had a lifespan coinciding closely to that of Queen Victoria. Of the nine children born to William George Spencer and his wife, Harriet Holmes Spencer, Herbert, the eldest, was the sole survivor. His father, a highly respected schoolteacher with strong anti-authoritarian and dissenting religious views, did much to incline Herbert toward a lifetime of nonconformity.

Initially, Herbert's formal education was carried out by his schoolteacher father and his uncle. After three years, Herbert, declined his uncle's offer to finance his studies at Cambridge University. Consequently, from age 16 on, Herbert was largely self-educated. He published his first work, *On the Proper Sphere of Government*, at age 22. Spencer tried a career as a schoolteacher, for a few months, and then was employed as a railway civil engineer for approximately four years. His true love, however, was writing on philosophy, the natural sciences, and social policy, which significant inheritances from his father and two uncles permitted him.

Spencer was a prolific writer whose interests ranged over philosophy, ethics, biology, sociology, and political economy. His grand ambition was to link these subjects together into a holistic system of thought he labeled the "synthetic philosophy." In brief, Spencer sought to apply the principle of evolutionary progress to all branches of knowledge. While most modern scholars recognize serious deficiencies and errors in Spencer's system of thought, it is worthwhile to review briefly his key contributions to political economy.

Spencer, like Karl MARX, envisioned society as evolving toward a utopia. Spencer's utopia, however, was an extreme version of LAISSEZ-FAIRE capitalism, even more extreme than that envisioned by Adam SMITH in *The Wealth of Nations* (1776). Spencer believed that such a society would best maximize the happiness or welfare of society. To his credit, Spencer made a careful distinction between the welfare of society as an entity and the total welfare of society viewed as an aggregation of the individual levels of welfare of all the members of society. Spencer, the political LIBERTARIAN, of course, argued strongly for the latter concept. In Spencer's utopia, all members of society would be free to do what they desired as long as they did not infringe on the happiness of others.

From this, it followed that the role and coercive powers of government must be sharply circumscribed. In Spencer's view, "Men developed the state for one purpose only—protection from each other and from other societies." Consequently, the proper role for government is the establishment of a legal system to enforce private contracts and to punish acts that harm others, and the establishment of a military for defensive purposes. Like Marx, as well as modern American libertarians, Spencer had a very hostile view of COLONIALISM and foreign military adventures and feared the rise of the authoritarian, highly coercive "military state." Spencer's view on the proper role of government, of course, rules out the socialist centrally planned economy as well as virtually all welfare state activities such as the supply of education, most laws regulating business, legal impediments to international trade and finance, and even laws regulating, for example, sanitary conditions. Perhaps Spencer's most controversial belief, however, was his rejection of any form of government aid to the poor, a view that came to be labeled as "Social Darwinism." A key postulate of Spencer is that all beings possess different capabilities. From this postulate, his evolutionary theory as stated in *Social Statics* (1851) led him to assert that the whole effort of nature is to rid itself of "feeble elements." And in *Man Versus the State* (1884) he stated: "It is the universal law of nature—a law that a creature not energetic enough to maintain itself must die."

Clearly, from a modern perspective his views on poverty seem extreme and cruel. Yet, Spencer did present a perceptive analysis of some key problems and dangers inherent in the vast expansion of government that took place in the first two-thirds of the 20th century. Spencer clearly saw the basic problems and deficiencies of the socialist centrally planned economy. As economic scholars such as Ludwig von MISES and Friedrich von HAYEK argued cogently and at length during the 1920s and 1930s (and a view now overwhelmingly shared by mainstream economists), a centrally planned economy results in vast inefficiencies due to massive information and incentive problems. A socialist economy, in practice, would fail to result in a workers' egalitarian utopia. Inevitably, various political and social elites of necessity would arise to run the government, to organize production, and to supervise the workers. In the early 1990s, the collapse of the socialist economies of the former Soviet Union (RUSSIA) and eastern Europe provides empirical support in this respect.

Moreover, in the latter third of the 20th century, both economic theory and much real-world experience suggest that the growth of the modern capitalist welfare state may have gone too far. A crucial element underpinning this revised view is the recognition that not only do markets sometimes fail to achieve socials goals but there exists also a wide domain of government failure. In this respect, Spencer was remarkably farsighted: He argued that the government had no way of accurately assessing and then summing the utilities of its citizens and therefore cannot legislate efficient laws, programs, and policies. The fundamental difficulties of using various democratic voting mechanisms to ascertain social preferences finally was recognized and rigorously developed by Nobel laureate Kenneth ARROW in his pathbreaking work *Social Choice and Individual Values* (1951).

In addition, Spencer clearly perceived that special-interest groups would generally dominate a democratic political process and that the outcomes emerging from the democratic political process would seldom reflect the general welfare of society, but rather the narrow interests of the strongest political pressure groups. Indeed, Spencer feared that the government bureaucracy itself would form one of the strongest pressure groups, promoting the cumulative expansion of government at the expense of society's general interest.

Finally, Spencer argued that government producers are inherently inefficient, a key reason being that such producers operate in an economic environment free from the incentives and discipline of the market. Indeed, modern economic theory has greatly weakened the case for direct government production, and much rigorous empirical research now supports the comparative efficiency of private enterprise.

While modern scholars recognize many errors and deficiencies with respect to Spencer's grand theory of science, Spencer had several important insights with respect to political economy that resonate with modern scholars. And while most will reject Social Darwinism as a scientific basis for poverty policy, many might agree with Spencer's contemporary, Mill, who strongly argued for the expansion of government-provided poor relief on the grounds that "energy and self-dependence are . . . liable to be impaired by the absence of help, as well as its excess."

In this context, it seems instructive to note that in 1992 a major campaign slogan of President Bill CLINTON's was his mantra, "We will end welfare as we know it." In 1996, the U.S. Congress passed welfare reform legislation that ended the 60-year federal welfare entitlement and replaced it with a new program, Temporary Assistance for Needy Families, with a five-year lifetime cap on benefits.

BIBLIOGRAPHY. Herbert Spencer, *The Proper Sphere of Government* (1843), *Social Statics* (1851), *The Principles of Biology* (1864), *The Man Versus the State* (Liberty Fund, 1884); J.Y.D. Peel, *Herbert Spencer: The Evolution of a Sociologist* (Gregg International, 1971); David Wiltshire, *Social and Political Thought of Herbert Spencer* (Oxford University Press, 1978); Kieran Egan, *Getting It Wrong from the Beginning: Our Progressivist Inheritance from Herbert Spencer, John Dewey, and Jean Piaget* (Yale University Press, 2002); William L. Miller, "Herbert Spencer's Theory of Welfare and Public Policy," *History of Political Economy* (v.4/1, 1972); Andrei Shleifer, "State Versus Private Ownership," *Journal of Economic Perspectives* (v.12/4, 1998); Thomas Nesslein, "Enterprise: Public Versus Private," *Encyclopedia of Public Administration and Public Policy* (Marcel Dekker, 2003).

THOMAS S. NESSLEIN
UNIVERSITY OF WISCONSIN, GREEN BAY

spice trade

THE TERM, SPICE, describes natural products from a particular region in demand beyond their point of origin because of their flavor or odor. When Vasco da Gama's crew rounded the Horn of Africa, their motivation was twofold; they risked their lives "for Christ and for spices!"

Commerce in spices was so heavily entwined in the visions and plans of European explorers and conquistadors that it is commonly seen from the Western perspective as one of the first motivators in the development of Mediterranean wealth in the late Middle Ages, and the emergence of capitalist features of the international economy after 1500. In fact, the spice trade is one of the oldest human enterprises, stretching back 3,000 years or longer. It was well underway by Old Testament times; in Genesis 37:25, the boy Joseph is sold by his brothers to spice traders.

Those spices of greatest interest to Europeans (balsam, nutmeg, ginger, cinnamon, cloves, and pepper) originated in different regions of Africa and Asia and had to be transported to their European markets. The most ancient trading centers for spices in Eurasia were located in the Molucca (Spice) Islands of Micronesia and Sabaea, a territory in Southern Arabia (the origin of the Queen of Sheba, who brought spices to King Solomon upon their marriage); the oldest common trade routes for spices, along the Indian Ocean and the Silk Road, date to the 1st century B.C.E.

Italian cities such as Venice and Genoa served as a gateway for spices to Europe. The commonplace of elementary school learning, that Europeans wanted spices to disguise the taste of spoiled preserved meats, is patently false, since eating spoiled meat sickens its consumers no matter how it tastes; rather, spices were used as preservatives, in medicines, and to improve the taste of the immature wine that everyone drank. Most importantly, they provided a sign of ostentation and luxury for those who could afford them. The culinary conventions of the wealthy in medieval and early modern Europe demanded vast quantities of spices, in proportions that modern consumers would deem unpalatable.

Spices were thought to ease digestion and enhance fertility. The assumption that the Portuguese sought independent direct access to spice markets in the East because of drastically rising prices for spices in Italy, due to the Venetian monopoly, has not been supported by recent research, which suggests that prices for pepper in particular (the spice most desired by Europeans) had been falling in the late 15th century, in line with the general decline of the Venetian economy. In fact, the Portuguese entry into the spice market seems to have raised spice prices, since their penetration into the Indian Ocean after 1498 increased the costs of regional producers in protecting their wares from seizure, and exacerbated the problem of unregulated spice traffic.

While Portuguese spice distribution initially triumphed over that of Venice, Venetian trade recovered somewhat in the short term, for at least initially, Portuguese spices were found by contemporaries to lack the potency of their Venetian competition (either because they came from different species, or because of the rigors of the ocean voyage). The Dutch and English quickly joined the Portuguese and Venetians, increasing both competition and the size of the markets they supplied. By the 1520s, however, the Venetian spice trade was practically defunct.

The creation of the Dutch East India Company ultimately gave the Dutch a near monopoly over the trade in fine spices and a heavy portion of the market for black pepper, a condition achieved not only by Dutch influence on European markets, but also due to the company's success in controlling production of spices in its colonies, influencing commodity prices by stockpiling product in years of high production, ending the Silk Road trade, and disrupting native trade arrangements

The spice trade, dominated by Portugal, Venice, England, and Holland, included pepper, cinnamon, and cloves.

for spices in the East, replacing them with Dutch ships.

Controlling the Asian markets was key, for European consumption notwithstanding, Asians are estimated to have consumed three-quarters of available spices in the early modern period. By the 1720s, the Dutch were burning pepper and nutmeg in order to maintain price levels, and the Dutch East India Company went bankrupt in the 1790s, when European spice consumption waned due to a decline in the consumption of meat and changing culinary tastes; the company had failed to move significantly into the profitable and expanding cotton trade. Additionally, by the 18th century, the French had created spice plantations in their colonies, and Americans entered the pepper trade.

By the late 19th century, different agricultural exports (especially sugar, coffee, and tea) had eclipsed spices in importance, both as a segment of world exports and as a factor in economic and political relations. The last vestige of the spice trade's former notoriety was reflected in a pepper speculation scandal in the 1930s. De-colonization finally released the spice trade from the control of European powers when it was no longer of central importance, but spice exports still account for more than 1 billion dollars of world exports.

Fernand Braudel suggested peripherally in *Civilization and Capitalism* that the spice trade was essential for the development of capitalism in its cultural and economic outcomes: Profits from long-distance trade were huge and concentrated (not dissipated among numerous middle-men, as was the case with the grain trade); the spice trade was allegedly the most efficiently organized of all the European markets and caused the expansion of distribution networks; it generated connections between two zones of the nascent world economy; and crucially, it created among Europeans the long-term interest in accumulation and consumption fundamental to the success of capitalism.

This argument is probably essentially correct, but the significance of spices as a sole cause for these events is overstated. Rather, the spice trade moved in tandem and interacted with a number of developments now considered crucial for capitalist development. The attractiveness of spices imported by Muslim traders both sustained the primacy of Muslim civilization and played an important role in eliminating Europe's "in kind" payment system and returning it to a money economy by the end of the High Middle Ages.

It has also been suggested that the desire for spices caused both the contraction of the European money supply at the end of the 15th century (the "bullion famine") and was an important factor in motivating the desire of the Spanish crown to import American silver, which expanded the European money supply (and fed a steady inflation) in the 16th century. International business contacts fed the development both of financial instruments like the bill of exchange (a means of international currency exchange and money transfer before the advent of banking), and formal and informal institutions that guaranteed the enforceability of contracts. Increased business aided the development of uniform accounting procedures.

These are all developments, however, that have their roots in the international luxury trade of the late Middle Ages; they are not specific to the spice trade. Other factors more closely define the relationship of the spice trade to the growth of capitalism, especially the founding and development of joint-stock companies like the Dutch East India and its English counterpart, which provided an initial forum for capital investment, accumulation and reinvestment, and also funded further exploration of territories unknown to Europeans via private-sector investment.

Several scholars have suggested that the early joint-stock companies were the predecessors of present-day, multi-national corporations, though others emphasize the economically conservative nature of their activities. Nowhere did the spice trade move more obviously in tandem with European trends than in the area of its relationship to MERCANTILISM, the leading economic philosophy of the early modern world, where the fortunes of the spice trade mark the highs and lows of the fortunes of this idea.

The Portuguese search for spices was fueled by the same mercantilist dictate that heated the European search for colonies, the idea that imported products should not be purchased from competitors but only be consumed if they could be drawn directly from one's own colonies. At the same time, popular demand for spices and interest in consuming foreign imports from other countries demonstrated the inability of national governments to control the developing world market; thus demand for consumption of spices played an important role in demonstrating the need for a shift from mercantilist to capitalist political economies in the early modern period.

BIBLIOGRAPHY. Ann M. Carlos and Stephen Nichols, "Giants of an Earlier Capitalism: The Early Chartered Trading Companies as Modern Multi-nationals," *Business History Review* (v.62, 1988); Andrew Dalby, *Dangerous Tastes: The Story of Spices* (University of California Press, 2000); S.R.H. Jones and Simon P. Ville, "Efficient Transactors or Rent-seeking Monopolists? The Rationale for Early Chartered Trading Companies," *Journal of Economic History* (v.56, 1996); Giles Milton, *Nathaniel's Nutmeg: How One Man's Courage Changed the Course of History* (Hodder and Stoughton, 1999); Sidney Mintz, *Sweetness and Power: The Place of Sugar in Modern History* (Viking, 1985); M.N. Pearson, ed., *Spices in the Indian Ocean World* (Aldershot: Variorum, 1996); Jeanie M. Welch, *The Spice Trade: A Bibliographic Guide to Sources of Historical and Economic Information* (Greenwood Press, 1994).

SUSAN BOETTCHER, PH.D.
UNIVERSITY OF TEXAS, AUSTIN

sports

GREATER BY FAR than any recreation in the world is the playing or viewing of the games of sport. It overshadows the lure of the cinema, the theatre or any other event designed for public consumption. Under the term "athletics," sports has become an industry in many nations, driven by not only thirst for competitive skill, but by the intrinsic engines of commercial value. Games of sport, be they indoor or outdoor, whether they constitute tossing a ball through a hoop or batting a ball over a stadium wall, draw crowds by the tens of thousands. Basic by nature, fulfilling a need for diversion, the range of sports has become much more—an exact economical science.

By modern definition, the world of sports demands that an active participant be adept in some form of physical exertion. Practicing skills, the participant also maintains a certain form of discipline to keep talent finely tuned, to play the sport to the best of her ability, and, simultaneously, follow a pre-set agenda of rules governing the contest.

Some games are based on the team concept—that is, that a number of players serve as a unit to outscore another team of like individuals. Examples of these types of sports are baseball, football, basketball, and soccer. Then there are the individually based sports, when a sole player is pitted against another demonstrating similar talents. More often than not, this genre includes golf, skiing, swimming, fencing, track, and archery.

The origin of sports is obscure. The ancient Greeks contested players against players in assorted athletic festivals, such as javelin-throwing and running. Romans, too, practiced combative fencing and swimming, but they concentrated on brawn over the Greeks' brainpower. Wrestling, which had probably begun with the cave man, was refined into an art form.

In the Middle Ages, military-minded knights jousted, lance to lance, in an effort to demonstrate might. Tournaments of swordplay, polo, and falconry became popular among the flowered society; the lower castes played soccer.

The modern sports era started in the late 19th century. Stickball, renamed baseball, and refashioned by Abner Doubleday, became the epitome of sports-like challenge in the UNITED STATES, whose good-time approach was imitated by other athletics. The Olympics, which had been played under freely ungoverned rules, were formalized in 1896.

Sports that had known only local interest have become world-known due to a widening media and an enhanced transportation system. American baseball, boxing, and bicycle-racing found new fans in Europe; bullfighting drew Americans to Spain; cricket, for years British, replayed across the Commonwealth; and hockey, initially Canadian, generated new teams in America and France.

The 20th century recreated the field of sports into something vast and eternal; sports transformed from a pastime into a fever—especially in America. The country, worn from the cares of WORLD WAR I, slid into the fun-seeking 1920s when "anything carefree," to quote a popular idiom, became the thing to do. "Sultan of Swat" Babe Ruth and "Iron Man" Lou Gehrig of the New York Yankees became bigger American heroes than George Washington. In "winning one for the Gipper," Notre Dame's Knute Rockne and his "Horsemen of the Apocalypse" lit the spotlight on collegiate sports, which have grown ever since. Outside of arena-placed sports, people found great exercise in cycling, tennis, boating, and gymnastics.

A new industry internationalized. Before long, the Federacion Internationale de Football hosted its premiere World Cup in 1930; that same year, the Commonwealth Games drew amateur players to an Olympic-like series of meets; the Pan American Games (1951) united athletes from the western hemisphere.

While women have been actively involved in sports for decades, the 20th century saw a huge effort of female competition in the professional circuits. Babe Didrikson Zaharias' golfing feats in the 1940s, for instance, helped provided a threshold for women's' progress, proving that not only men can make athletics a full-time career. Since the mid-20th century, the world has seen the once male-dominated sports clubs spin off equally professional franchises for women—the Ladies Professional Golf Association (LPGA), the Professional Women's Bowling Association (PWBA), the Women's National Basketball Association (WNBA), the Ladies Professional Bowlers Tour (LPBT), to name the largest.

Sometimes, sports have been overshadowed by politics. In the late 1930s, Adolf Hitler raged when an African-American, Jesse Owens, outran his Aryan Olympians. After some Western nations boycotted the 1980 Olympics in Moscow due to the Soviet invasion of Afghanistan, the Soviets avoided the 1984 games in Los Angeles.

The business of sports. With the new millennium, the sports industry is richer, more diversified, sharper, and more business-oriented than ever before. From college court play to the professional leagues to the international Olympic games, the industry is a balance sheet of blacks and reds.

In the United States, the sports industry generates revenues of some $100 billion annually. Like any mammoth corporation, the major professional sports leagues survive on long-range planning and, season by season, often on spontaneous decision-making. The National Football League (NFL), Major League Baseball (MLB), the National Basketball Association (NBA), the National Hockey League (NHL), the Professional Golf Association (PGA), and worldwide soccer have their cycles of ups and downs. Economic problems brought about by low gate attendance, players' salary caps, marketing costs, to name just a few, continue to keep franchise owners—and the cities in which they play—alert and vigilant. However, one factor remains constant: the better the output, the meatier the income. Not surprisingly, that factor parallels any marketable product.

More concisely, in sports it all comes down to two things, both greatly related: public interest and national exposure. Teams with the most value—that is, those that increase the fastest in value—are those with the most formidable presence. This applies to all sports. One of these presence-making devices is, of course, television.

Football. In no other sport is the media factor more obvious than in the National Football League. The NFL, the most-watched, most popular American sports commodity, outpolling baseball by nearly a 2:1 margin, collected about $77 million in television revenue in 2002, according to the Associated Press. The NFL's $2 billion ancillary television-rights contract with the DirecTV satellite service dominates other broadcast athletics. Noting those types of media figures, NFL Commissioner Paul Tagliabue expressed to *USA Today* that, "The key for us is that our programming still stands far and away above all other sports programming . . . in terms of the size of our audience, the diversity of audience strength and the demographics."

Keeping media partners happy has been a golden key. Revenue generated through television contracts, Tagliabue said, has allowed most of the networks to show a profit on their NFL coverage. Flexible scheduling has been a part of the success.

Another element of the NFL's success is its strategic policy on its players' salaries. A strict salary cap ensures that, unlike baseball and basketball, no team can outspend another over a multiple-year period. The result is that there is a constant rotation of team members; it becomes almost impossible to retain the same roster of players even after a playoff year. This keeps not only the fans hopeful that their team has a chance for the full run, but also generates interest among the media. For instance, in 2002, the strategy helped to earn major television contracts with ESPN, ABC, CBS, and Fox.

Forbes magazine noted an interesting aspect, "The NFL system ensures that every team makes money, whether they win or lose . . . The 32 NFL teams sold out 90 percent of their games this year [2002] and played a total stadium capacity of 95 percent. . . . All NFL teams prosper from this league-wide success."

Baseball. Major League Baseball (MLB) operates under less-liberal rules when it comes to the team-sharing principle; the milieu of teams share only 25 percent of the league's inter-media revenue. This may be one reason why Baseball Commissioner Bud Selig in a December 2001 meeting of the House Judiciary Committee on Capitol Hill painted a dire—if not tragic—picture of the MLB's economic problems. According to Selig, the MLB lost more than $500 million (due largely to stadium operating costs) during the 2000/2001 season despite record revenues of $3.5 billion. However, in a rebuttal that has caused somewhat of a stir between the factions, *Forbes* magazine contested Selig's figures, claiming that the MLB's misled calculations are a true case of crying wolf.

In the meantime, local media revenues remain constant for Major League Baseball games, but, again, the deals effected between teams and outlets are not as even-handed as the NFL system. Unfortunately, geography determines how successfully (or unsuccessfully) baseball clubs can market their teams to the media. Doug Pappas, who operated the internet's "Business of Baseball Pages" for the Society of American Baseball Research, wrote of the 2001/2002 season: "Media revenues are heavily affected by the size of a club's local market. The (New York) Mets and the (Arizona) Diamondbacks have identical media contracts on a per capita basis, but because the New York metropolitan area is so much larger, the Mets gross $32 million more."

Clubs based in smaller cities have fewer game opportunities open to them. While a traditional media schedule consists of 150 broadcast games, those teams located at the bottom of the roster lack staying power. The Kansas City Royals, for instance, telecast 81 games, the Cincinnati Reds 85 games—all on cable. The Montreal Expos, which lag in the rear, received no English-language coverage.

Hockey. Hockey, which originated in and is still most popular in Canada, continues to have troubles of its own. The National Hockey League (NHL) flounders. Fiscal monetary problems, growing since the turn of the millennium, have reached a point that some forecasters are predicting what has come to be known as an "Armageddon on Ice." Into the year 2003, certain franchises have reached the threshold of bankruptcy court.

The league relies on gate receipts; it does not engender the vast media revenues enjoyed by the NFL, NBA, or the popular Major League Baseball teams. Gone—at least in hiatus—are the days when the public filled seasonal seats and private boxes. The larger corporations that once gobbled up blocks of tickets a season in advance can no longer afford the luxury. The Los Angeles Kings have reportedly lost $100 million over the last eight seasons, and the Florida Panthers have recently taken out a loan for $30 million. Even the most popular teams, such as the Stanley Cup–winning New Jersey Devils, have not seen a full house for a long time. Nashville and Phoenix, at one time considered two of the NHL's biggest supporting cities, now turn out less than 13,000 spectators per game.

Television revenues are minimal for this major sport; each team is allowed a mere $6 million. Of course, this might have to do with the overall fan-barometer, which puts fan interest below the NFL, the NBA, baseball, and even the majority of popular college games.

NHL Commissioner Gary Bettman, however, has not thrown up the white flag. He sees hope in the creation of a salary cap—strangely enough players' salaries continue to be high—and a reworking of certain aspects of the game. Quoting Bettman, "We must have a system that enables our clubs to be economically stable and competitive."

Basketball. The National Basketball Association (NBA) has been, since the early 1990s, thriving—and it continues to do so. Much of the thanks go to Commissioner David Stern who took over the association's reins in 1980. Seeing a corporation sagging with financial worries (17 of the 23 teams were losing money) and other problems (high drug use among the players), he turned the situation around. Cleansing the NBA's image was important, but on its heels came Stern's explosive marketing drive—to nurture the game until it was as big and important and dynamic as anything the American sports-loving public could imagine. If some criticized his carnival master tactics, Stern proved them wrong. Since Stern's appointment, NBA's revenues have risen seven times higher, almost all the teams show a profit by season's end, and attendance has increased a whopping 60 percent.

Stern's strategy was multi-point, the main elements being to upgrade the quality of players, promote visibility in the community, peak advertising, create satisfying media coverage and spread revenue sharing. It all worked.

But, what worked best was his priority—to glorify the NBA player by selecting several role models to represent the NBA league as a whole. Stern didn't have to look deeply into the rank and file; the names popped up as colorfully as their successful—but until then sadly overlooked—talents. Larry Bird, Earvin "Magic" Johnson, Julius Irving, and Michael Jordan, each in their own season, came forth as the caryatid of good sport and winning values.

Jordan is credited, especially, for turning the game into something more palatable to the eye. Simply, his airborne style sired many imitators, and those imitators, in trying to "be like Mike," presented their own brand of backhanded shots and curving lay-ups.

Media networks—NBC, CBS, ABC, ESPN and other cable stations—clamor for NBA time. In 2003, revenue exceeded $250 million, amplifying what NBC Vice President Ken Schanzer prophesied in the early 1990s: "The NBA can be extremely profitable."

"Because of the growing interest in the NBA from fans and advertisers, the networks began to shower the league with money," says sportswriter Joshua Levin. Even though in 1980 NBA games were unheard of outside the United States, by 1989 "over 50 foreign countries could regularly view NBA games," Levin continues. "The networks more than doubled professional basketball's telecasts from 20 to 42."

Professional Golf Association. The Professional Golf Association (PGA) is the world's largest sports organization, 27,000 members strong, including the Ladies' PGA. Illustrating the popularity of the game, 2001 sales estimates show a 58-percent growth, or $58 million. If that's not a hole-in-one, it's close.

The majority of association members are club professionals. The organization conducts some 40 tournaments annually and operates four major competitions. These "notable four" are: the Ryder Cup (featuring American and European players); the PGA Championship (in which only top professionals are invited to participate); the Grand Slam (considered the toughest competition between the most aggressive players); and the Champions Tour (formerly the Seniors' Championship). Other enthusiastic championships are the British Open and the Master's Tournament.

Although golf remains one of the most-watched sports on television—combining relaxing but artful play with beautifully landscaped country clubs and courses—some media woes may crouch on the horizon, due to what *Business Week* has called "senior-itis."

The Champions Tour has a history of success, playing generally from January through October and carving up for itself pieces of the pie worth many millions. (The 2001 purse weighed in at $59 million.) Corporate sponsorship has been impressive with TD Waterhouse, 3M, MasterCard, and others. But television viewership is sinking overall despite the wide audiences that newcomers such as Tiger Woods can draw.

Soccer and the World Cup. Most famous and beloved of all international sports, soccer (also known as football) is one of the oldest in existence. According to research done by Michigan State University, "The earlier varieties of what later became soccer were played almost 3,000 years ago," and are evidenced in 1004 B.C.E. Japan and 611 A.D. China. "The early Olympic games in ancient Rome featured 27 men on a side who competed so vigorously that two-thirds of them had to be hospitalized." Today, the sport is played throughout the globe, mostly in Europe, Asia, Africa, and South America. Currently, 203 countries belong to the Switzerland-based governing body, the Federacion Internationale de Football Association, or FIFA. There are six confederations, comprised of geographically succinct countries within each—Asian, African, North Central and Caribbean, Oceanic (Australia and New Zealand), South American, and European. The African confederation is the largest with 52 members.

The price tag for soccer is non-existent. Traditionally a billion-dollar business, a net-worth-and-expense ratio cannot be determined because of the clandestine nature of each club's finances. But, one thing is certain. Over the last couple of seasons it has become apparent that, to quote *Sports Illustrated*, "Soccer's finances have gotten into a mess, as far as many major clubs and countries are concerned."

The problems are most obtrusive when reviewing the economy of the annual World Cup event, the world of soccer's annual tribute to itself. Finances have been diminishing since the collapse of ITV Digital (Britain) and KirchMedia (Germany), two long-time promoters of the games. As well, franchise clubs are disintegrating. "Fiorentina, formed 90 years ago, twice Italian champions and the first winners of the European Cup in 1961, went bankrupt," writes *Sports Illustrated*, "while several Belgian clubs suffered a similar fate."

To add to the woe, FIFA's World Youth Championship 2003 tournament has been put on hold. Originally scheduled for March/April 2003, the committee was forced to postpone the games in the United Arab Emirates due to the outbreak of war in Iraq.

The Olympics. Every four years since 1896, during the summer and winter seasons, top ranking amateurs from the world's nations meet to vie for gold-, silver- and bronze-medal rankings in the world Olympics. Across the globe, people whose countries are represented in the many events are glued to their televisions, cheering on their own. Most viewers, however, do not see what it takes—or costs—to produce the inevitable greatest athletics show on earth.

There are differences between the summer and winter games, beyond the basic agenda of sports categories. Winter Olympics involve fewer countries, fewer games, and fewer athletes. Television contracts are, therefore, less for the Winter Games.

Yet, when Utah won the opportunity to host the XIX Winter 2002 Games at Salt Lake City, for example, it was a major undertaking and had a dramatic fiscal impact.

Seventy-seven nations were involved, 78 events took place. In all, 2,399 athletes participated—886 women, 1,513 men. A media's heaven, 8,730 media personnel came to Salt Lake—2,661 press persons, 6,069 broadcasters—from around the world.

The games generated a significant amount of employment, earnings and output in the Utah economy prior to and during 2002. More specific figures come from the Governor's Olympic "Demographic and Economic Analysis" committee: Output was estimated at $2.8 billion, including all sales and Olympic-related factors. More than 22,000 jobs lasting one year were created. The jobs represented some 21.4 percent of projected employment growth, according to 2001 figures. Salaries amounted to $900 million. Fifty thousand visitors were anticipated daily; visitor spending charted at $123 million.

Although final figures are not available, prior estimates of net revenue to state and local government were anticipated at $80 million to $140 million. This range was based on models of earlier games, the 1988 Winter Games in Calgary, Canada, and the 1998 Summer Games in Atlanta, Georgia. The 2002 Olympics was expected to generate $236 million in gross state and local government tax revenue and $120 million in additional expenditures for services rendered by the state and local government.

The city of Houston, Texas, is considering hosting the 2012 Games. After preliminary analysis, Economics Professor Steven Craig of the University of Houston views the opportunity as "a significant benefit to our city (with) an economic impact of $4.3 billion to the area."

Marketing, the biggest game in town. Shoelaces, jerseys, golf balls, tennis balls, nets, cleats, caps, water bottles, socks, trading cards, and so very much more—the long list of products is inevitable and as diverse as the wide arena of sports. Every team insignia, professional, college, domestic, and foreign, seems to be popping up on just about everything one could think of, from binoculars to stocking caps to bedsheets and quilts to Christmas-tree ornaments. If one of the more popular players endorses a product or if his or her photo appears on it, then the price automatically escalates . . . a Tiger Woods cap, an Air-Jordan pair of shoes, a Shaquille O'Neal sweatsuit. The sports shops and memorabilia manufacturers aren't batting an eye to this, because in that blink they might miss a beat.

The Sports Authority, America's number one sporting goods retailer operating nearly 200 stores in the contiguous United States, finished January 2003 with a revenue base of $1.43 billion, one percent up from last quarter. And as forecasters eye 2004, they foretell of another jump up to come. Nike, designer and developer of sports footwear, totaled $7.7 billion for the last nine months of 2002. Competitor Reebok International, Ltd., earned a 5 percent increase in 2002 over the previous fiscal year, accruing $3.13 billion. Clearly, the business of sports plays a major role in the economies of capitalist societies, reaching into all aspects of entertainment, manufacturing, marketing and distribution.

BIBLIOGRAPHY. Edward F. Cone, "Playing the Global Game," *Forbes* (January, 1989); Davide Diekcevich, "All-Star Earners," *Forbes*, www.forbes.com; Hoovers Online, www.hoovers.com; *Houston Chronicle*, www.houstonchronicle.com; Mark Hyman, "Can the PGA Cure Senior-it is?" *Business Week* (December 2001); John McManus, "NBC Scoring Big With NBA Gamble," *Advertising Age* (November 1990); Michigan State University, www.msu.edu; Doug Pappas, Society of Baseball Research, www.sabr.org; Tim Pedula, "NFL Commissioner Confident Despite Depression," *USA Today* (January 12, 2002); Alan Robbins, "NHL's Troubling Times," Associated Press (July 2, 2002); *Sports Illustrated*, www.sportillustrated.com; State of Utah, *Governor's Office Olympic Planning and Budget Report*; University of Houston NewsOnline, www.uh.edu; Paul White, "Selig's Numbers Produce Doubts," *USA Today* (August 13, 2002).

JOSEPH GERINGER
INDEPENDENT SCHOLAR

Sraffa, Piero (1898–1983)

BORN IN TURIN, Italy, Piero Sraffa entered the law faculty at Turin in 1916. He completed his doctoral thesis in financial and monetary theory in 1920 and then made a trip to Britain to conduct research, where he met John Maynard KEYNES (1883–1946) for the first time. Also, in 1919, Sraffa met the Italian revolutionary, Antonio Gramsci (1891–1937), and was his close friend until Gramsci's death in prison. Both of these meetings greatly influenced Sraffa's life.

Sraffa's first essay (1926), which was first published in Italian in 1925, confronted the foundations of the orthodox analysis of Alfred MARSHALL. In 1927, he was granted a lectureship at King's College, Cambridge University. However, when Sraffa experienced anguish in presenting his unorthodox ideas, Keynes created the librarian at the Marshall Library of Economics position to keep him there.

At Cambridge, Sraffa collected and edited David RICARDO's works to produce an impressive edition. He also undertook a research project to rehabilitate classical economics. This research came to fruition with the publication of *Production of Commodities by Means of Commodities: Prelude to a Critique of Economic Theory*. In it, Sraffa solves Ricardo's problem of finding an invariable measure of value. This not only revived classical economics, but also provided the foundations for a critique of the marginal approach to capital and distribution, based on the notion of factors of production.

Production for subsistence. Sraffa starts with a simple example of a two-commodity subsistence system. Suppose that the only commodities produced and consumed in a society are corn and iron. To produce 400 units of corn, including all the necessities of workers, we need 260 units of corn and 14 units of iron. Similarly, to produce 20 units of iron, we need 140 units of corn and 6 units of iron. Then, operations for a production period (say a year) would be written as follows:

$$260 \text{ corn} + 14 \text{ iron} \oslash 400 \text{ corn}$$
$$140 \text{ corn} + 6 \text{ iron} \oslash 20 \text{ iron}$$
$$400 \text{ corn } 20 \text{ iron}$$

In this system, since 14 units of iron must exchange for 140 units of corn, the exchange (or price) ratio between them must be one unit of iron for 10 units of corn for this economy to be able to function. No other price ratios would work.

Production with surplus. Next, Sraffa examines a similar economy with a surplus. Here the same quantities of input yield output of 570 units of corn and 20 units of iron. So we will have:

260 corn + 14 iron ∅ 570 corn
140 corn + 6 iron ∅ 20 iron
400 corn 20 iron

Thus, there is a surplus of 170 units of corn. Assuming that the rate of profit (r) is equalized through competition, and that the surplus is distributed equally between the two industries, we can set the price of corn to 1 and solve for the price of iron pi in the following system:

$$(260 + 14pi)(1+r) = 570$$
$$(140 + 6pi)(1+r) = 20pi$$

The solution to this system is $pi = 14$ and r = 0.25. Note that these systems can be generalized, and that prices are determined without any reference to utility or marginalism.

Sraffa treats the whole of wages as variable and incorporates it into his system and asserts that the system can move with one degree of freedom. Thus, if wages are set, the rate of profit and all of the prices can be determined. Sraffa then proceeds to investigate the basic classical problem. Assuming that the method of production remains unchanged, what happens to prices and profits when the net national product has to be divided between laborers and capitalists? He proceeds to give the wage successive values ranging from 1 to 0. When wage (w) is equal to 1 the whole national income goes to wages and profits (r) are eliminated.

"At this level of wages the relative values of commodities are in proportion to their labor cost, that is to say to the quantity of labor which directly and indirectly has gone to produce them," explains Sraffa. Conversely, when w is equal to 0, all of the national income goes to the capitalists. However, it is important to note how profits and prices behave in the intermediate range.

Prices diverge from their labor contents in the intermediate range, and Sraffa's explanation of this phenomenon is the same as that of Ricardo and Karl MARX. He writes that "the key to the movement of relative prices consequent upon a change in wages lies in the inequality of the proportions in which labor and means of production are employed in the various industries." Prices diverge from the labor content according to the ratio of labor to means of production—composition of capital—in different industries. Prices are higher than their labor contents in industries with higher than average composition of capital, and are lower than their labor contents in those industries with lower than average compositions. Thus, only in industries with average compositions of capital prices reflect actual labor contents. The product of such an industry could potentially serve as a "standard commodity" by which the value of other commodities could be measured.

However, due to the interdependency of the production process—outputs of one industry is an input to other industries—the value of the means of production does not remain constant as the wage changes. Therefore, if a commodity is to act as an invariant measure of value, it must not only be produced with the average composition of capital but, also, the inputs into its production along with their inputs and so on in an infinite regression must be produced with the average composition of capital. Surely, such a commodity is not to be found, but a mixture of commodities—a "composite commodity"—that possesses these characteristics would be fine. Construction of such a commodity is a major theoretical contribution by Sraffa that reinvigorated classical economics.

Finally, Sraffa introduced the possibility of the reswitching of technique of production—the possibility that the same method of production may be the most profitable of a number of methods of production at more than one rate of profit (r) even though other methods are more profitable at rates in between—this fueled the "Cambridge Capital Controversy," that was very damaging to the marginal productivity theory of distribution.

BIBLIOGRAPHY. G.C. Harcourt, *Some Cambridge Controversies in the Theory of Capital* (Cambridge University Press, 1972); Ronald L. Meek, "Mr. Sraffa's Rehabilitation of Classical Economics," *Scottish Journal of Political Economy* (v.8/2, 1961); Jean-Pierre Pottier, *Piero Sraffa: Unorthodox Economist* (Routledge, 1987); Piero Sraffa, "The Laws of Returns under Competitive Conditions," *Economic Journal* (v.XXXVI, 1926); Piero Sraffa, *Production of Commodities by Means of Commodities: Prelude to a Critique of Economic Theory* (Cambridge University Press, 1960).

HAMID AZARI-RAD, PH.D.
STATE UNIVERSITY OF NEW YORK, NEW PALTZ

stagnation

THE TERM, STAGNATION, is used to describe the absence of vigorous economic activity. While orientation of various theorists differ, the idea that stagnation is a predictable fate of capitalism can be traced to the very beginnings of classical economics. The inevitability of stagnation was seen either as a natural, biological, or historical, social phenomenon. Analogously to the organic world, societies age; that is, the growth stage is followed by stagnation, and ultimately with decay. The end phase comes as a result of depletion of natural resources and/or interplay of forces intrinsic to capitalist economy and society. The common thread in the majority of theories of stagnation and breakdown is the assumption that the capitalist system is not viable without growth. Where theories differ is the belief that economic policies may overcome stagnation; the proponents of the doomsday scenario deny the possibility that economic policies are capable of defeating stagnation.

The major interest in stagnation emerged after the prolonged economic crisis of the 1930s. In particular, the works of A. Hansen (1938, 1941), P. Sweezy (1942), P. Baran (1957), Sweezy and Baran (1966), and P. Sylos-Labini are of major interest. During the economic boom of the 1960s the analysis of stagnation became less attractive to economists. However, the prolonged economic crisis of the 1970s renewed the researchers' attention to this phenomenon. The simultaneous occurrence of prolonged unemployment, overall increase in price level, i.e., INFLATION, and low productivity growth brought a new term into popularity in economics, stagflation. The focus this time was on structural changes in the world capitalistic economy.

The decline of manufacturing, the process of de-industrialization, and the inflexible corporate and bureaucratic structures were seen as the major culprits of stagnation in the modern era. Similar to the analysis of DEPRESSION, the analysts were quick to point out that the oligopolistic structures of modern capitalist economies were the principal obstacles for introduction of technological innovations. The dissatisfaction with modern societal institutions and hierarchical structure of the corporate world intensified pursuit for an alternative path of economic development. The echo of calls for alternative technologies, and particular, region-sensitive policies for economic development, appears to be a dominant argument in the current anti-globalization debate.

BIBLIOGRAPHY. David Coates, *Models of Capitalism: Growth and Stagnation in the Modern Era* (Polity Press, 2000); Burkhard Strumpel, ed., *Industrial Societies After the Stagnation of the 1970s: Taking Stock from an Interdisciplinary Perspective* (Walter de Gruyter, 1989).

ZELJAN SCHUSTER, PH.D.
UNIVERSITY OF NEW HAVEN

Standard and Poor's

A WIDELY INFLUENTIAL provider of data related to financial investments, analysis, and valuation, Standard & Poor's is known most of all for its benchmark index of U.S. economic ratings, the S&P 500.

Standard and Poor's was founded in 1941 with the merger of the Poor's Publishing Company and the Standard Statistics Bureau. In 1860, Henry Varnum Poor (1812–1905), an editor and transportation ana-

lyst, published a study on the American railroad system, *The History of the Railroads of the United States and Canada*. In part due to the book's success as a guide for investors in railroad companies, Poor went on to establish a company to provide information about American businesses to the investor in industrial concerns, who had, according to company's motto, "the right to know."

The Standard Statistics Bureau was founded in 1906 by Luthur Lee Blake to sell financial information about American companies to banks. The Bureau went on to provide previously unavailable information for the investment market, charting debt ratings first for corporate bonds, and then in 1940, for municipal bonds as well.

The central purpose of Standard and Poor's is to research and evaluate the integrity of a given company's balance sheet and performance potential, in order to judge and publish opinions on the relative merit of investing in that company. These opinions are given an alphabetic rating system, with AAA at the top of the scale and the lower value rankings (such as B or CCC) indicating less secure investment opportunities. The riskiest gradations have earned the name "junk" bonds in the market.

The S&P 500 developed over several decades in the early 20th century.

The Standard Statistics Bureau had, as early as 1923, introduced stock market indicators, intended to provide an alternative more suitable for professional investors than the popular but limited DOW JONES Industrial Average (DJIA) then in use. Initially the company rated 26 industrial groups comprised of 233 companies, calculating these figures for publication on a weekly basis. The company soon realized the need for more timely reporting, and in 1928, switched to a reporting format that could be calculated on a daily and then eventually an hourly basis, the S&P 90 Stock Composite Index, rating a group of 50 industrial, 20 railroad, and 20 utility companies. With the merger of Poor's and Burke's firms into Standard and Poor's in 1941, the company began to actively position its 90 Index as a superior alternative to the DJIA. By the early 1950s, S&P's indices had attracted considerable attention and subscribers, including several departments of the U.S. government.

The benchmark 500 figure was introduced on March 4, 1957. The stocks chosen represent not the most valuable stocks but rather a cross-section of stocks from companies representative of important patterns and leading sectors in the economy. Due to the advent of increased computational technology, the 500 index was recalculated at one-minute intervals throughout the business day. The index's presence and influence soared during the 1960s. When the U.S. Department of Commerce established its Index of Leading Economic Indicators in 1968, the S&P 500 became one of its foundational components. McGraw-Hill acquired the company in 1966.

The Standard & Poor's system of indices continued to evolve and expand from the 1960s onward, as the company cemented its central position in the financial market. In 1976, the 500 Index was restructured to reflect 400 industrial, 40 utilities, 40 financial, and 20 transportation stocks and, for the first time, to reflect stocks outside the NEW YORK STOCK EXCHANGE (NYSE). In 1986, the index began to be calculated and disseminated on 15-second intervals for the first time. In 1988, in order to reflect an increasingly dynamic and fluid U.S. economy, the number of companies within each economic sector was allowed to fluctuate (or "float"). In 2001 the company created the Global Industry Classification Standard Direct (GISD).

In 2003, the S&P 500 comprised 500 market-weighted stocks traded on the NYSE, the AMERICAN STOCK EXCHANGE (AMEX), and NASDAQ. Standard and Poor's Index Committee oversees the S&P 500. Consisting of seven members, this highly influential body meets periodically to adjust corporate membership in the 500, adding or subtracting companies in order to maintain an optimum representative mixture of stocks.

Though criticism has been voiced about its ongoing utility and competing economic indices (such as the Wilshire 5000 and the Russell 3000), the index remains virtually synonymous with the American stock market into the 21st century. Presently, the company exists in two main divisions, Ratings Services, which maintains the data indices, and Information Services, which oversees a wide array of electronic reporting media.

BIBLIOGRAPHY. Rich Blake, "Is Time Running Out for the S&P 500?" *Institutional Investor* (May 14, 2002); Susan A. Gidel, *Stock Index Futures and Options* (John Wiley & Sons, 2000); Hugh Sherwood, *How Corporate and Municipal Debt is Calculated: An Inside Look at Standard and Poor's Rating System* (John Wiley & Sons, 1976); www.standardandpoors.com.

CHARLES ROBINSON
BRANDEIS UNIVERSITY

Standard Oil Company

THE STANDARD OIL COMPANY was founded in 1882 in the early days of the petroleum industry. In 1859, Edwin L. Drake had revolutionized the industry when he discovered that he could actually drill for oil underground. Nineteenth-century Americans used oil for heating lamps, as a lubricant and in some medicines; but since there were no automobiles at that time, gaso-

line, a byproduct of the petroleum industry was simply discarded.

John D. ROCKEFELLER saw the potential for great growth in the petroleum industry and, along with his partners, Maurice B. Clark, H.M. Flagler, and S.V. Harkness, Rockefeller was soon operating Standard Oil, the largest oil refinery in Cleveland, Ohio. Rockefeller's foresight and keen business sense soon led the company to expand by purchasing other refineries, and they were soon producing over 12 million barrels a year. By 1875, Standard Oil had spread its operations across the country. A trust agreement was signed in 1879 and amended in 1882 giving the power of this huge corporation to nine men who oversaw the operations of 40 companies and who received a portion of profits. Standard had achieved a monopoly of the petroleum industry with 75 percent of the nation's refining capacity, 90 percent of the pipeline facilities and 15 percent of crude oil products. Its holdings extended to railroads, gas, copper, iron, steel shipping, and banks and trust companies. It seemed as if Standard Oil would control the entire petroleum industry, but politics soon intervened.

The state of Ohio sued Standard Oil Company, claiming that it was violating the term of its charter by operating businesses in New York, New Jersey, Kentucky, Indiana, Kansas, Nebraska, and California, in addition to Ohio. The Ohio court decided in favor of the state. However, politicians in New Jersey had recently changed their laws to allow companies chartered in the state to become holding companies owning and operating a network of companies throughout the nation. Standard Oil moved their operations to New Jersey. As the petroleum industry grew, competition became fierce, and Standard Oil developed a reputation for ruthlessly buying up other companies by any means.

In 1904, presidential candidate Theodore ROOSEVELT promised to go after huge corporations that had developed into monopolies, and the federal government sued Standard Oil New Jersey. In 1911, the Supreme Court of the United States ordered both Standard Oil Company and the American Tobacco Company to break up into a number of separate companies. The basis for the decision was the Sherman Anti-Trust Act, which had allowed Congress to regulate the operations of corporate trusts. Standard Oil became 34 separate companies, although some of the individual companies kept the name Standard Oil. John D. Rockefeller retired, but Standard Oil New Jersey continued to grow. In 1911, the company had 6,078 shareholders. By 1963, the number had grown to 702,000 and had extended its operations around the world. Mobil Oil Corporation, Amoco Corporation, Chevron Corporation, and Exxon Corporation can all trace their roots back to Standard Oil.

BIBLIOGRAPHY. Paul A. Samuelson, *Economics* (McGraw-Hill, 1973); *Standard Oil Company* (Standard Oil Company New Jersey, undated); John Steele Gordon, "The Business of America," *American Heritage* (June 2001); Ida M. Tarbell, *The History of the Standard Oil Company* (McClure, Phillips, 1904); Gary M. Walton and Hugh Rockoff, *History of the American Economy* (Dryden Press, 1998).

ELIZABETH PURDY, PH.D.
INDEPENDENT SCHOLAR

state

THE STATE IS A POLITICAL entity that comprises a set of institutions to rule, govern, and police a political unit. The state is a contract among the individuals who govern and live in the political boundaries of the state. The state in Thomas Hobbes's *Leviathan* is known as the "artificial man." It is a grouping of individuals who agree on the creation and operation of the governing body.

The Western state has its origins in Greek city-states and in the theories of Greece's most influential philosophers, Plato and Aristotle. Plato, in the *Republic*, discussed the characteristics and workings of the ideal state. In Plato's conception there would be three distinct classes within the state: the statesmen, the civilians, and the police. The rule by the statesmen would be rule by the best, that is, the aristocracy. Aristotle believed that perfection could only result when an organization is created to administer the tasks associated with government.

Adam SMITH contributed one of the more indelible views on government and the state. His LIBERTARIAN position is one that impacted later writers and indeed, 19th-century British politics. Smith (1937) writes that:

The first duty of the sovereign, that of protecting the society from the violence and invasion of other independent societies, can be performed only by means of a military force. . . . The second duty of the sovereign, that of protecting, as far as possible, every member of the society from the injustice or oppression of every other member of it, or the duty of establishing an exact administration of justice. . . . The third and last duty of the sovereign or commonwealth is that of erecting and maintaining those public institutions and those public works, which may be in the highest degree advantageous to a great society.

The state in neo-institutional economics is viewed as a device to reduce transaction costs. Ever since Ronald

COASE's (1960) famous paper on EXTERNALITIES, a world of zero transaction costs means that if property rights are well defined, parties involved in any dispute will make an agreement so that an efficient outcome results. This is a world of minimal government since only property rights need be defined. D.C. NORTH (1979) contributed one of the more important theories of the state in this vein. North sees the state very much as an organization such as the firm, and as Coase asserted (1937) in another seminal paper, the firm is a mechanism that solves the exchange problem when transaction costs are high.

North (1981) defines the state as "an organization with comparative advantage in violence, extending over a geographic area whose boundaries are determined by its power to tax constituents." The ruler in this geographic area has a monopoly as far as government is concerned but the ruler is constrained by threats of new order, opportunistic behavior of the agents of the state, and measurement costs. North clearly incorporates the transaction costs involved with the operation of a variety of organizations including the firm. One can almost picture the state as a large encompassing organization structured like a firm and created to minimize transaction costs.

Hobbes, in *Leviathan*, asserts the necessity of government and the state emerges as a struggle for power in which the strong win and get to govern. The machine created by the rulers is essential for enforcing the rules and laws of society, and the rulers erect and keep a police and judicial system. Hobbes applied geometry to his theory of the state, with an absolute ruler at the top and a hierarchy of underlings who answer to the ruler. Hobbes visualized a form of the state in which civil society is based on a set of laws and government, which rules by force and provides the clockworks by which a well-functioning society operates. Civil war in Hobbes's mind is the greatest hazard facing the sovereign because it means the suspension of civil society.

The state of nature, as the theory of the state was often called, received a thorough treatment in John LOCKE's philosophy. The right to judge and discipline people is a defining characteristic. In Locke's view, the people ought to be sovereign. The following of the rules of government constitutes the social contract. He also argued for the separation of legislative and executive powers and if these powers abuse their positions, the people have a right to overthrow the existing government. The rights of life and property are protected under natural law according to Locke.

In the natural reason argument, such as Locke's and later Jean-Jacques Rousseau's, in the original or nascent stage of mankind, anarchy reigned, but by reason people came together and formed the social contract, or the state of nature. They can come together and form what

Robert Nozick (1974) calls protective societies. And since only one protective association is feasible—one can think of this kind of state as a natural monopoly—a dominant one will be installed in power. This protective association will serve as an agent for the inhabiting individuals in protecting property and life. How would such an association arise? One answer is given in an invisible hand explanation from Nozick:

> Show how some overall pattern or design, which one would have thought had to be produced by an individual's or group's successful attempt to realize the pattern, instead was produced and maintained by a process that in no way had the overall pattern or design in mind. After Adam Smith, we shall call such explanations *invisible-hand explanations*. ("Every individual intends only his own gain, and he is in this, as in so many other case, led by an invisible hand to promote an end which he has no part his intention.") . . . Invisible-hand explanations minimize the use of notions constituting the phenomena to be explained; in contrast to the straightforward explanations, they don't explain complicated patterns by including full-blown pattern-notions as objects of people's desires or beliefs.

Thus, the invisible-hand explanation would explain the theory of the state as a group of interacting individuals, who, without intending to do so, form a society that protects themselves, from others and one another. This form of state comes without design. Competition among the societies or associations that form will give way to a prevailing governing body or sovereign. This sovereign would then consciously place a set of rules or laws that would constitute the government.

The capitalist form of state has several defining characteristics. The state acts as a MONOPOLY and as the owners of CAPITAL who exercise certain rights over the workers of the society. The state also places constraints on free markets. Since the state controls the supply of money, it also controls the means of exchange. The state sets laws by which all economic actors must follow. The state is an institution that controls the motions of capitalist society. It sets the rules that the players must follow and polices the agents of capitalist society.

BIBLIOGRAPHY. Thrainn Eggeretsson, *Economic, Behavior and Institutions* (Cambridge University Press, 1990); D.C. North, *Structure and Change in Economic History* (W.W. Norton, 1981); R. Nozick, *Anarchy, State, and Utopia* (Basic Books, 1974); A. Smith, *An Inquiry into the Nature and Cause of the Wealth of Nations* (Oxford University Press, 1976).

ZELJAN SCHUSTER, PH.D.
UNIVERSITY OF NEW HAVEN

State Farm Insurance Companies

ONE OF THE LARGEST financial institutions in the UNITED STATES, State Farm is the nation's leading auto- and home-insurance company. *Fortune* magazine ranked State Farm as the 63rd largest company in the world with revenues of nearly $47 billion in 2001. State Farm provides INSURANCE for many other products and services including, but not limited to: life, health, disability, long-term care, boats, mutual funds, and savings accounts.

State Farm was started by George J. Mecherle in 1922 because he believed that farmers, who drove less and had fewer losses than the general population, should pay less for insurance. Thus, he began State Farm as a mutual automobile insurance company owned by the policyholders in Bloomington, Illinois. Then, in 1928 another office was opened in Berkeley, California, the company's first branch office. Today, State Farm has 25 operation centers in 13 national zones.

Recently, the insurance industry has suffered multi-billion dollar losses for various reasons (State Farm included). One of the largest reasons is home mold claims. The industry, as a whole, has paid out over $1 billion in claims (and this statistic was as of May 2002, and there are still more claims). As the leading insurer of homes in the United States, State Farm has paid the largest share of the claims. To cope, State Farm began excluding mold claims and raising rates as much as 30 percent in some areas. In early 2003, State Farm was still working out what will and will not be covered in many states.

Another reason for the large insurance losses is the attacks of September 11, 2001. Shortly after the attacks all insurance companies began to raise their rates. Much of this was due to re-insurers. Re-insurers insure direct insurers such as State Farm. State Farm, however, did not suffer as dire financial effects from September 11 as some other direct insurers did, but the total monetary impact was still unknown 18 months later. Insurance analysts point out State Farm raised rates, in part, because other insurance companies were raising rates.

State Farm has also recently been a victim of several weather catastrophes. Auto claims rose dramatically in the early 2000s due to hurricanes, floods, fires, and winter storms. A sluggish economy has also caused a rise in insurance rates, and overall, for the year 2001, State Farm lost $5 billion. However, State Farm is expected to weather the difficult financial times and remain one of the leading companies in property and casualty insurance in the United States.

BIBLIOGRAPHY. Norman G. Levine, *From Life Insurance to Diversifaction* (National Underwriter Company, 1987);

www.themoldsource.com; www.statefarm.com; "Global 500," *Fortune* (July 2002).

CHRIS HOWELL
RED ROCKS COLLEGE

static and dynamic analysis

THE CONCEPTS OF STATICS and dynamics are frequently encountered in scientific analysis. In general physics, statics and dynamics have specific meanings. Statics is associated with a position of rest, and dynamics with motion. The two concepts are also encountered in economic analysis with different applied meanings and uses. In analytical economics and related fields, dynamics is sometimes associated with disequilibrium and structural adjustment, sometimes with economic growth, and sometimes with economic evolution, as well as others. The two concepts lead to static theory and dynamic theory respectively in economic analysis and hence their relative meanings are very important in understanding the whole process of economic logic.

Statics. Statics is a timeless concept in economic analysis at a given datum. A static system is one where the key endogenous variables are viewed as timeless in position. In this case the system does not evolve as time passes by, neither does it change in any significant way with time. It may, however, change due to some exogenous shock on some or all the key endogenous variables that define the state of the system. The solution to a static system always yields a single solution vector. Such a solution vector always describes a rest position of the system at a given datum.

The concept of key endogenous variables is important in defining and distinguishing statics from dynamics in economics. This importance reflects the reality that the state of the economic system composed of resource allocation, income production, and distribution is continuously evolving. For static description of the system these key endogenous variables are taken to be invariant with time.

The static state is a convenient starting point for theoretical characterization, modeling, analysis, and study in order to understand the behavior of the evolving economic system at each time point, and thus offer an opportunity to use policy variables as exogenous shocks to move the system to a desirable state when there are deviations from the desired state. The concept of staticity is a logical tool that allows the theorist to reveal the behavioral conditions of the complex economy at any point in time. Given the static characterization of

the economy we then examine conditions, regularities, and laws of behavior of the economic agents in the static state. An example of static economy is described by the condition that factors of production composed of capital, labor, and technology are given.

Dynamics. Generally, dynamics is a time-dependent variable concept of the system. In economics, a system is defined as being dynamic when the key variables describing the state of the system at every time point are themselves functions of time. Time enters either as an implicit or explicit variable of the system whose motion may involve simultaneous changes along the time path, as well as shifts of the path, due to the behavior of the time-dependent key endogenous variables.

The specific solution obtained for any posed problem in a dynamic system generally yields a set of vectors that will define a solution time path of the system. Each key endogenous variable of the system's solution is a vector that defines its path in reference to time. The key endogenous variables may be interdependent and, hence, simultaneously determine their time states and system's states with the passage of time.

Dynamic analysis is, thus, a logical extension of static analysis. They mutually define themselves. Dynamics is a generalization of statics and statics is a specificity of general dynamics. Dynamics, like statics, is a logical tool that allows the theorist to simultaneously connect and generalize the static analysis of resource allocation, income production, and distribution, not at a time point, but over time. In this way, the theorist can reveal the behavioral conditions of the complex economic system over time.

Given the dynamic characterization of the capitalist economic system by relaxing the assumption of staticity, the theorist derives theorems and laws about the behavior of economic agents in the economic system, as the key endogenous variables and the system itself move along their time paths. From such a dynamic perspective, a dynamic theory is advanced in order to derive and analyze the behavioral conditions and regularities so as to provide a framework for dynamic economic policy of the general system and the endogenous key variables.

Evolution. Evolution is a general process of change of the system whose path depends essentially on the behavior of all or some of the key endogenous variables and the information system that defines the environment of behavior. It does combine statics and dynamics. The process may or may not be time-related. When the process does not depend in an essential way on time we say the process is time invariant. If the process depends on time in an essential way, we say that the process is time-dependent.

For example, disequilibrium analysis in economics may be time-dependent or time-invariant depending on the specification of the system or a subsystem and conditions and laws of motion governing the system's behavior. Connected to statics, dynamics and evolution are comparative statics and dynamics, which fall under the general theory of sensitivity analysis.

General sensitivity analysis. Every decision or control process is optimal relative to a given environment that is described by an information set. The information set is summarized by a set of parameters that establishes the parametric space. Sensitivity analysis is devoted to the study of the effects of parameter variations or changes on both static and dynamic systems in the parametric space (in other words to study the system's behavior as the given information is altered). The resulting analyses lead to the development of sensitivity functions that depend on the system's parameters.

Comparative statics. Comparative statics is part of sensitivity analysis. It deals with comparative analysis of the behavior of key variables of equilibrium states of static system. It is thus a mathematical technique of employing static theory to analyze and compare the values and conditions of different equilibrium states when we impose changes on the parameters of the system.

The objective is to investigate the distributive behavior of the key endogenous variables of the system from one static equilibrium to another, and derive conclusions and theorems without regard to transitional process between equilibria. Alongside the comparative statics is the concept of quasistatic changes, which is a limiting process that generates the locus of equilibrium states, which defines the path of a sensitivity function. Examples in economics are the income and price consumption curves, where income and prices are the parameters that summarize the information for optimal consumption and production decisions.

Comparative dynamics. Comparative dynamics is also part of sensitivity analysis. In this analysis, the parameters are time-dependent in such a way that they define the parametric space that is changing with time. It is a mathematical method for analyzing and comparing conditions and vector values of different dynamic equilibrium paths of a dynamic system when we impose variations on the time path of any parameter. The process is to derive theorems or empirically testable propositions about the behavior of decision or control variables as they move through a dynamically parametric space.

As such, the analysis takes account of shifts of the time paths of the parameters and the rates at which the parameters move along their time paths if such rates induce shifts of the time paths. The sensitivity functions are obtained through variational methods.

The comparative analysis is much simplified if the two changes occur either independently or in isolation.

Generally then, the comparative dynamics is not different from comparative statics in the sense that both seek to derive theorems or testable propositions as the decision or control variables traverse over the parametric space. This is another way of viewing Paul SAMUELSON's correspondence principle between comparative statics and dynamics where the sensitivity functions of comparative dynamics are generalizations of those of comparative statics, all of which may be viewed in terms of simulation processes.

BIBLIOGRAPHY. R.G.D. Allen, *Macro-Economic Theory: A Mathematical Treatment* (Macmillan, 1968); Keith Culbertson, *Macroeconomic Theory and Stabilization Policy* (McGraw-Hill, 1968); John Hicks, *Methods of Dynamic Economics* (Clarendon Press, 1987); Tjalling C. Koopmans, *Three Essays on the State of Economic Science* (McGraw-Hill, 1957); Paul A. Samuelson, *Foundations of Economic Analysis* (Atheneum, 1971); R. Tomovic and M. Vukobratovic, *General Sensitivity Theory* (Elsevier, 1972); Thomas G. Windeknecht, *General Dynamical Processes: A Mathematical Introduction* (Academic Press, 1971).

KOFI KISSI DOMPERE
TARESA LAWRENCE
HOWARD UNIVERSITY

Stigler, George J. (1911–91)

IN 1982, GEORGE J. STIGLER, whom some colleagues described as the quintessential empirical economist, was awarded the Nobel Prize in Economics for his seminal studies of industrial structures, functioning of markets, and causes and effects of public regulation. Noted for his lifelong research on the workings of industry and as a champion of deregulation, his studies have raised theoretical questions about rent controls, minimum wage laws, and antitrust.

Painting a picture of Stigler's achievements, fellow Nobel laureate Milton FRIEDMAN recalls his friend's career. "He was one of the great economists of the 20th—or any other—century. . . . Intellectual history was his first field of specialization and a deep understanding of the ideas of the great economists of the past gave him a strong foundation on which to build an analysis of contemporary issues."

Raised in the Seattle-area suburb of Renton, Washington, he was the only child of European immigrants Josef and Elizabeth Hungler Stigler. Their son would remember, many years later, how his father, a brewer who had learned his trade in Bavaria, was forced to surrender his trade when Prohibition outlawed the manufacture of liquor during the 1920s. Before Joseph found his niche in real estate, he tried many other jobs; the Stigler family moved several times in the interim.

Stigler excelled in school with a clear aptitude for learning. He entered the University of Washington in 1928 and earned a B.A. four years later at the height of the Great DEPRESSION. Since job prospects were virtually nonexistent, Stigler decided to remain in academia to pursue an M.B.A.

Attending Northwestern University in Chicago, Stigler became acquainted with a new group of academics and curriculum that changed not only his career, but also his life. He discovered economics and decided to earn a doctorate.

For much of the following decades, until his death in 1991, Stigler would be associated with either Northwestern University or with what became popularly known as the CHICAGO SCHOOL of economics. Influential persons included economics professor Jacob Viner, economic historian John Nef, and economist Henry Simons, with whom Stigler would remain a lifelong friend. But, the figure who impressed him most was Frank KNIGHT, economics professor, analyst, and social philosopher who mentored him during his dissertation. Knight, Stigler said, instilled in him "a devotion to the pursuit of knowledge . . . a sense of unreserved commitment to truth."

Stigler carried that commitment with him to Iowa State University in 1936 when he accepted a position as assistant professor.

Throughout the latter half of the 1930s and the first half of the 1940s, Stigler moved between a staff membership with the University of Minnesota; a war efforts research position with the Statistical Research Group of Columbia University; and, in 1946, a professorship with Brown University. When the smoke of WORLD WAR II cleared, the Mont Pelerin Society, a global consortium aimed at preserving freedom in trade, invited Stigler along with 36 other members to Switzerland to meet on issues regarding world economics. The experience was so enlightening and upbeat that he remained a member of the society the remainder of his life.

Over the next 10 years, Stigler taught economics at Columbia University. He was persuaded to return to Chicago in 1958 by the dean of Northwestern University, Theodore Schultz. Stigler's impact on the Chicago scene proved immediate and long-lasting. Known as a tireless, succinct writer in his field—by this time he had written several books and a plethora of journal articles—he took over editorship of the *Journal of Political Economy*.

Simultaneously, he established the Industrial Organization Workshop, providing economists a key testing ground for contributions to the area of industrial organization. In 1977, he founded the Center Study of the Economy and the State. His summer periods were spent researching at Stanford's Center for Advanced Study in Behavioral Sciences.

The last two decades of his life saw Stigler as either president or director of economic associations, or taking part in government activities, such as the National Committee on Antitrust Laws and the Securities Investor Protection Corporation. This ongoing participation culminated in his receiving the National Medal of Science from President Ronald REAGAN.

BIBLIOGRAPHY. George J. Stigler, *Memoirs of an Unregulated Economist* (Basic Books, 1990); George J. Stigler, *The Organization of Industry* (University of Chicago Press, 1983); Milton Friedman, "Memories of George J. Stigler," *National Academy of Sciences Magazine*; George Stigler Autobiography, www.nobel.se.

JOSEPH GERINGER
SYED B. HUSSAIN, PH.D.
UNIVERSITY OF WISCONSIN, OSHKOSH

Stiglitz, Joseph E. (1943–)

BORN IN GARY, INDIANA, Joseph Stiglitz received his B.A. from Amherst College in 1964, and went on to get his Ph.D. from the Massachusetts Institute of Technology in 1967. By age 27, he was appointed a tenured professor of economics at Yale University, and also taught in various positions at Oxford, Stanford, Princeton, and Columbia universities.

From 1993–97, Stiglitz served on President Bill Clinton's COUNCIL OF ECONOMIC ADVISERS—first as a member (until 1995) then as chairman. From 1997–2000, Stiglitz was senior vice president and chief economist at the WORLD BANK. As one of the founders of the "Economics of Information," Stiglitz was awarded the Nobel Prize in Economics in 2001 together with George AKERLOF of the University of California, Berkeley, and A. Michael SPENCE of Stanford University. The Nobel committee cited "their analyses of markets with asymmetric information," and noted that Stiglitz "clarified the opposite type of market adjustment, where poorly informed agents extract information from the better informed. . . ." and ". . . has shown that asymmetric information can provide the key to understanding many observed market phenomena, including unemployment and credit rationing."

Stiglitz also made fundamental contributions to several subfields of economic theory—MICROECONOMICS, MACROECONOMICS, industrial organization, international economics, labor economics, financial economics, and development economics—through more than 300 papers and 26 books. Stiglitz received more than 15 honorary doctorates, held numerous international positions as a consultant to institutions or companies such as the Ford Foundation, US-AID, the Federal Reserve Board, and the Inter-American Development Bank. His notoriety with the general public, however, began toward the end of 1997, when he started a severe and open criticism of the INTERNATIONAL MONETARY FUND (IMF) and the "Washington Consensus" while still being chief economist of the World Bank. Described by economists and authors as a "rebel within the system," or "heretic among the economic policy elite," Stiglitz "challenges the policies of the international financial community" and "has undone the conventional wisdom that dominated policy-making at the World Bank, the IMF and the U.S. Treasury Department," says author Ha-Joon Chang.

The ASIAN FINANCIAL CRISIS (1997) was a defining event for Stiglitz. With respect to IMF's failure in handling, among others, the Asian or the Russian crisis (1998), Stiglitz asserts that "half a century after its foundation, it is clear that the IMF has failed in its mission." In his view, "market fanaticism," premature capital liberalization, excessive privatization ignoring social and political costs, and unbalanced trade liberalization have been the main errors within a framework of exaggerated budgetary austerity measures or "shock therapy." Stiglitz compares the IMF failures with some examples of successful experiences: CHINA, POLAND, or HUNGARY. In those three cases, the governments refused a standardized and imposed IMF-remedy and opted for national programs.

In those cases, the local governments were involved and had a more coherent and gradual approach. Stiglitz argues in favor of a broader approach and longer-term perspective in macro- and microeconomic crisis-management: Social and political costs, safety nets, the dangers of liberalization of capital markets, the value of education, macroeconomic stability, sustainable development are important aspects which have to be taken into account rather than concentrating only on budgetary or monetary parameters. Stiglitz has also taken positions on two controversial questions, world trade liberalization and globalization. In his view, trade liberalization has been at the detriment of developing countries (developed countries obliging developing countries to open their markets for industrialized goods while continuing to protect their markets for their own "sensible" goods such as textiles or agricultural products) and globalization may have had positive effects, but to a major part of the developing world, it did not bring the promised benefits but a destroyed environment, increased corruption, and social dissolution instead. "Today, globalization does not work for the poor, for the environment, for the stability of the world economy," Stiglitz says.

The way GLOBALIZATION is handled by world economic institutions is the problem, rather than globalization by itself. As for solutions, he advocates in favor of democratic (egalitarian voting rights) and transparent international institutions, development as a "democratic social learning" on the basis of durable, equitable, and democratic policies and a more positive view of government action. In July 2000, Stiglitz founded the Initiative for Policy Dialogue, a network of social science experts, to provide an alternative to the IMF and World Bank for countries in need of sound economic policy advice.

BIBLIOGRAPHY. "Joseph Stiglitz," *Columbia News,* www.columbia.edu; Ha-Joon Chang, *The Rebel Within* (Anthem Press, 2001); Interview with J. Stiglitz, *The Progressive* (June 2000); Joseph E. Stiglitz, *Globalization and Its Discontents* (W.W. Norton, 2002).

URSULA A. VAVRIK, PH.D.
UNIVERSITY OF ECONOMICS, VIENNA

stock dividend

AN AMOUNT OF CASH some companies distribute to all their common stockholders during a given year is termed a stock dividend. Traditionally, well-established companies that have constant profits (sometimes nicknamed "blue chips") usually distribute quarterly dividends. Blue chips include banks, oil companies, public services, telephone companies, insurance companies, and some income trusts and royalty trusts. Dividends can be distributed regularly (annually, quarterly, monthly) or sometimes are announced as special dividends that are given only once (for instance when a division of the company is sold). Growth companies and high-tech stocks usually choose not to pay dividends, but issue preferred shares that promise to give settled dividends if the company is profitable in the next year.

The dividend yield is a percentage that demonstrates the relative importance of a dividend compared to a stock's price. For a stockholder, it appears more lucrative to get a $1 dividend from a $10 share (10 percent yield), than a $1 dividend for a $100 share (1 percent yield), because in this first case it would cost less to benefit from the same cash distribution. Here, the dividends are the same but the yields are very different.

When the dividend is effectively paid, the amount is automatically taken off the value of every share outstanding and later given back to the stockholder. The ex-dividend date is the first day of negotiation after the dividend (the amount of the distribution) has been subtracted from the share's price. This maneuver is made before markets open. Depending on companies' policies, the cash dividend is effectively paid a few weeks after the ex-dividend date. In other words, a stockholder has to buy his shares at least one day before the ex-dividend date in order to be paid its dividend (and keep in mind the three-day delay for official delivery of shares asked by most financial institutions).

The philosophy that lies behind dividend policies could be stated (and amplified) this way: "We are a stable company that makes constant profits; these earnings could be given as premiums to some preferred employees or managers, they could as well be reinvested or used to pay our debts, but we rather choose to share these revenues with our stockholders, who are nothing less than the owners of this company." Since members of the board and employees are often stockholders of their company, they also benefit from fair dividend policies.

A good dividend, usually, is a yield superior to the current interest rates or at least 3 percent of a share's market value. If, for some reason, a share loses half its value, its dividend yield is subsequently doubled. When this situation happens, some companies are tempted to readjust their dividend policy by cutting it, as did Bank One in July 2000, MCI in June 2001, and EL PASO CORPORATION in February 2003. In these situations, history proves that some stockholders' reaction can be punitive.

Paying dividends means a company has constant profits and cash flow; it is a sign of financial health. If for some reason a share loses its value, the frustrated shareholder can still stick with the company because of its regular dividend, which is perceived as a minimal compensation for a weak market performance. Some companies constantly increase their annual dividend (MERCK, Royal Bank of Canada).

When a company cuts its dividend, this proves there are problems with earnings, insufficient cash reserves, or lack of liquidities. According to "Nightly Business Report," American Telephone and Telegraph (AT&T) caused a major commotion on December 20, 2000, when it announced it would cut its dividend for the first time, after more than 100 years. It was suddenly reduced to 3.75 cents compared to 22 cents a year earlier. For the same reasons, Trans-Canada Pipelines lost almost half of its market value in less than a week, when it said it would provisionally reduce its quarterly dividend (from 29 to 80 cents a share). These market reactions can be explained because many stockholders choose and stick with specific companies because of their generous regular dividends.

In other countries, stock dividends are treated in different ways. For example, in France, the amount of some companies' stock dividend (FRANCE TELECOM, VIVENDI UNIVERSAL) is often negotiated with their stockholders present at every annual general meeting, depending on recent profits. This situation would be impossible to imagine in the United States, where these decisions about dividend policies are made exclusively by the members of the BOARD OF DIRECTORS and imposed on stockholders without any possible negotiation. Even Warren Buffet's Berkshire Hathaway, a famously profitable enterprise, has never paid any dividend to its stockholders.

Many companies not paying dividends say they prefer to reinvest earnings into acquisitions and capital spending. These arguments are more than contestable. First, sharing profits with stockholders should never be seen as a waste or squandering, because stockholders invested their money in the first place when they bought their shares. Second, investors who get money on a regular basis from the company they own might resist the temptation to cash-in their profits when the share value improves. Third, dividend payouts are in no way to be considered as a gift to stockholders, but rather as a compensation for the risk involved in a stock investment, specially for long-term investors. Last but not least, the dividends are subtracted from a share's value; what is gained in dividends is temporarily lost in market value.

A strong dividend is sometimes presented by some financial analysts as an obstacle to growth. This is, perhaps, a fallacious and subjective argument. Better management, reasonable compensations, lower bonuses for board members, and lower expenses in general are the best ways to assure prosperity in any enterprise. In the end, a company's dividend policies are tangible proof of a company's attitude toward its stockholders.

BIBLIOGRAPHY. Geraldine and Gregory Weiss, *The Dividend Connection: How Dividends Create Value in the Stock Market* (Dearborn Trade Publishing, 1995); "Nightly Business Report," www.nbr.com; Ethan Haskel, "Bank One's Dividend Disappearing Act," www.fool.com.

YVES LABERGE, PH.D.
INSTITUT QUÉBÉCOIS DES
HAUTES ÉTUDES INTERNATIONALES

stock market

THE CONCEPT OF STOCKS, and stock markets for trade of those stocks, have great antiquity. Originally known as stock exchanges, these markets were established in specific locations for organized buying and selling of financial tools known as securities. Today securities include stocks, BONDS, futures, and options.

Predictions for future stock markets range from virtual, online markets with no members or physical stock exchanges to predictions of eclipse by new methods of raising funds for ventures. Whatever the future holds, the stocks and bonds that are offered by companies, governments, and other entities are bought, traded, and sold on stock markets around the world to help fund the growth of capitalism as the economic system of dominance today and for the last two centuries. If one key component of capitalism is surplus production, the other surely is the generation of capital to fund surplus production, and as a result of the sale of surplus production. The question of how to create initial capital surplus for investment to create the surplus production of goods for trade and profit is answered by the role of stocks and other securities traded in stock exchanges or markets around the globe.

From the time of merchant enterprises seeking riches in overseas markets the question of how to fund these risky, but extremely profitable ventures has been addressed by the concept of stock, or selling a share of the venture in return for the investor's VENTURE CAPITAL or financial backing in the amount of the share sold. But how can all of the potential investors be brought together? By forming a stock exchange or meeting area where potential investors could exchange stocks. The potential funding for enterprises was only limited by the number of investors and their capital limits. The more investors, the more venture capital for the venture. The investors also had the benefit of selling and buying stocks from other investors at these centralized exchanges or stock markets.

History of the markets. Sharing risks in overseas ventures goes back at least to the times of the Roman sea trade across the Indian Ocean. Wealthy Roman families shared in the financing of such ventures as noted in the primary source of unknown origin, "The Periplus of the Erythrian Sea." OWNERSHIP shares or stock in a company were sold for French textile mills in the 1100s. The Bank of Venice issued government bonds back in 1157. However, it was not until the Age of Exploration in Europe that the large-scale, joint-stock companies came into their own as means for complete strangers, albeit strangers with money or financing, to pool their resources by buying stock in the ideas and trade of an overseas trade company.

The Medieval and Renaissance markets in countries such as ITALY had long seen trade in securities and commodities. Most of this involved credit papers traded between banks. Even speculation of which merchants could pay up at what interest rate was common, even though usury or interest was officially discouraged in the Middle Age societies of Europe and the Middle East. Paper money in CHINA also influenced this speculation of the future about debt collection from past business deals. However, what expeditions needed was funding just for future enterprises without being tied directly to bank notes of the past, or as promise notes from gov-

ernments involved in wars. Capitalists needed capital, real funding for their future ventures. Most historians would say this was the start of capitalism.

The joint-stock company emerged as a way to spread risk for distant sea voyages that hope to make a profit from trade with foreign markets. The Columbus voyages and the Vasco de Gama voyage of 1498 are good examples of the kinds of expeditions that led to joint-stock ventures.

In Antwerp, BELGIUM, in 1531, a stock exchange involving Dutch companies and banks is noted. Antwerp was a major shipping and trading center and most early stock exchanges developed near such trade ports. Brokers gathered to trade shares and the investor could actually see the expedition representing the company and the stocks of ownership in the company that the investor held. The investor could also be present when the expedition returned laden with riches from international trade in spices and bullion, or other mediums of exchange, if the expedition returned at all. The risks of piracy, storm, and corruption were great, so only the wealthiest merchants and nobles made up the core of early joint stock investors.

The first English joint stock company, the Russia Company of 1553, was formed to fund exploration of the fabled Northwest Passage to Asia via the Arctic Ocean. The offer to buy stock in the Russia Company was much like an Initial Public Offering (IPO) of today. The expedition met with failure to reach Asia, as did the Columbus voyages, but an agreement for exclusive trade with RUSSIA was reached and the early investors reaped great riches as the stock rose. The first English, inland joint-stock companies were formed as the Mines Royal and the Mineral and Battery for mining purposes in 1568 and were associated with German metallurgists.

In 1558, the Hamburg Exchange in the German states was established and Amsterdam founded an exchange in 1619. In the 1600s, competition emerged from stock companies for the funds of the investor. In 1599 and 1600, the British and Dutch East India Companies were founded to fund trade in India, especially for pepper. The Dutch West India Company followed in 1621 to compete with British interests in the Americas.

Between 1634 and 1637 "tulip mania" gripped Holland. Speculation on the price of tulips sent prices to all time highs, but market bubbles burst every few days and lead to 95-percent price drops. In some cases, shares of a tulip bulb were being traded for the value of an entire estate! The historical episode is very similar to stock market speculation and futures of today.

In 1640, Charles I of England forced the BRITISH EAST INDIA COMPANY to sell him its stock futures on two years of pepper imports, then sold the stock at a loss for ready, short-term cash. Charles was facing revolt and was short of cash. The move is eerily similar to hostile takeovers today, and to massive stock sell-offs by CHIEF EXECUTIVE OFFICERs (CEOs) and company leaders who leave the company stock with little value.

The advent of the rumor. London and Paris established stock exchanges in the late 1600s to help combat such overt manipulation of individual stock companies. However, a different form of stock value manipulation soon took hold. The rumor! Between 1719–21, two infamous speculative episodes clearly indicated the need for official stock markets rather than speculation in joint-stock companies of trade and exploration. The Mississippi Bubble occurred when French speculators attempted to fund French trade growth associated with Louisiana, INDIA, and China. The Mississippi Company was given exclusive rights to the trade but too many notes were issued by the Banque Royal and its bubble burst even before the venture was underway. The finance minister was blamed for the subsequent withdrawal of bullion from Paris and London markets to cover the losses, and was dismissed.

The South Seas Bubble is a similar story, when the South Seas Company was set up to break the Spanish monopoly on South Seas trade. The mania that ensued produced the inevitable bubble burst. Much of the speculation was created when the company claimed it would take over the national debt of England, an unrealistic goal, if it were successful. Such claims by companies still excite speculators despite their lack of credibility. Manipulation of the market by rumor has deep historical roots.

In the 18th century, stocks were used to fund infrastructure needs of industrial civilization, and industry itself. Canals, ironworks, ports, and the like were constructed by companies that sold shares to an increasingly broad public. England was considered the leader in such stock enterprises.

The growth of world markets. By 1792, the foundations for the largest stock exchange in world economic history were being laid on the old Wall Street in New York City. The NEW YORK STOCK EXCHANGE (NYSE) as it is now known, grew from an exclusive trade agreement between a handful of merchants to the global leader of all stock markets by the 20th century.

Today, stock markets from New York to Frankfurt, from Dehli to Tokyo, help fuel the growth of global capitalism. To be traded on stock markets of today, a company's stock must be listed by attaining certain requirements. However, many stocks are no longer sold at specific exchanges and are known as unlisted and traded over the counter (OTC). This usually involves TECHNOLOGY such as telephones or computers and hint at some of the future possible changes in stock trade and stock markets.

Technology continues to transform the world of traditional stock markets into automated exchanges around the world.

In the United States, the NYSE and the American Stock Exchange (AMEX) are two of the largest, but nine regional exchanges also exist and the major OTC exchange is the emerging NASDAQ Stock Market (National Association of Securities Dealers Automated Quotation market). In Europe, the NASDAQ equivalent is the EASDAQ (European Association of Securities Dealers Automated Quotation market), which serves the EUROPEAN UNION (EU). Other major physical stock exchanges, in addition to the NYSE and AMEX, include: London, England; Paris, France; Tokyo, Japan; Frankfurt, GERMANY; Hong Kong, China; and Toronto, CANADA.

For the next few decades, the changes introduced by technology into the traditional world of physical stock exchanges will likely continue to increase the power of automated exchanges such as the NASDAQ and EASDAQ at the expense of market share for traditional exchanges such as the NYSE or London. How far the pendulum of power will swing may largely depend upon how much of a shift takes place in value and production concerning traditional surplus production of industrialization, involving real products *vs.* post-industrial production of surplus "human capital production," such as ideas or mental products.

For the moment, stock exchange transactions still involve real dealers and brokers on real stock market or exchange floors in an often chaotic environment. Dealers buy and sell from their own portfolios, or inventories of securities. Brokers execute trades representing clients and receive commissions and fees for their services. Sometimes the same person can act in both roles.

Today, corporations seek new capital from a variety of investors including banks and stock-market investors. Typically, when a corporation needs to raise capital investment they will issue new securities in a primary market with the help of investment bankers. The investment bank obtains some of the new securities at a reduced, negotiated price in return for offering the rest of the new securities for investors on the open market in an IPO. The corporation is thus guaranteed to receive its needed capital directly from investment banks in a timely fashion. The investment bank then becomes the middleman in passing on its newly purchased securities to the secondary market. The corporation is not usually involved in the trading of its stock on the secondary market or open stock exchanges where most private investors purchase stock.

Although corporations or companies may not be involved in the secondary markets they do monitor the stock value of the company on the secondary market. The better the stock performs or trades in value, the better the company's future borrowing position with investment banks will be.

Additionally, the value of corporate stock is also closely watched by the corporation's owners, its STOCK-HOLDERS. The stockholders expect a return for their investment in the form of increasing stock value on secondary markets, dividend payments associated with stock performance, or from both. Today, a company's success is measured not only by how well it performs in terms of profit and loss in capitalistic trade markets, but also by how well or poorly the company stock performs in secondary stock markets.

Stock markets today. Stocks are still the main form of securities traded in stock markets. Stocks are shares of ownership in companies owned by the stockholders. Stockholders usually receive dividends as a portion of the company's profit margin, when the company is profitable. Stockholders usually benefit by trading company stock, by buying it at a lower price and selling it at a higher price. However, stockholders face risk as well. A company usually has to suspend dividends if it is unprofitable. A stock's value may decrease below a stockholder's purchase price and may have to be sold at a lower price, considered a loss.

A company can only list its stock on one exchange and strict regulations apply to the buying and selling or trading of stocks. Some exchanges, such as the NYSE, have high requirements that can be met only by the largest of companies. For instance, to be listed and traded on the NYSE a company must have at least 1.1 million shares outstanding or available for trade, and those shares must be valued at $100 million or more. Thus, each share must stay above one dollar in value or the company may risk being delisted.

Basically, different exchanges meet not only the needs of geographical regions such as North America but also the needs of different types and sizes of companies. The NYSE lists, large, well-established companies such as GE (GENERAL ELECTRIC has been a member since 1896), or

FORD MOTOR COMPANY. The NASDAQ, lists smaller, technology-based companies with huge growth potential. AMEX usually lists small- to medium-sized companies between the extremes of NYSE and NASDAQ. Energy companies involved in oil and gas are good examples.

Much of the securities trade is conducted by brokerage firms that are called upon to execute trades by individuals and trade groups. Only members of the stock exchange can actually conduct a stock transaction and such "seats" on exchanges are limited and expensive. In 2002, an NYSE member seat for trade cost over $2 million. Membership has its privileges and brokerage firms also get to vote upon exchange policy. Such policy allows these firms to charge fees for their trade services. Still, the venture is risky as brokerage clients can default on margin loans extended by the brokerage firm.

At traditional stock exchanges, such as the NYSE, which currently has five trading floors in New York City, a typical trade revolves around a post. A stockholder or client initially places an order to trade a security such as a stock with a stockbroker of a stockbroker firm. Sometimes, institutional brokers are used if the client is a bank or institution and the purchase is in bulk. In any case, the order is moved to the stock floor by a variety of traditional and electronic methods so that a floor broker for the stockbroker firm, or institutional broker, actually carries the order to a post where all stocks associated with that company are traded. A specialist at the post will manage the auction process as different floor brokers exchange buy and sell orders or trade the company stock. The specialist informs the floor brokers of the final price agreed upon in the ongoing auction. After-hours trade also takes place when markets are closed. Such trading is highly controlled because of the time differences between different markets around the globe, and the international nature of modern transnational corporations.

Although the stock price is usually subject to supply and demand laws, the cases of historic inflation of deflation of stock value are still common today. Often companies, such as the 1719–21 French Mississippi Company, never came into existence yet reached astronomical value, and were traded on the markets of the day with great gains and losses realized by investors. Some companies may not produce a profit, but do produce cash and product flow such as Amazon.com of the early 2000s. These companies see stock price fluctuations based on the idea that stockholders and investors expect the company may, one day, produce a profit or that the stock is simply a good investment, to be bought low and sold high, based on current or future market conditions. So, in essence, the secondary stock markets are speculative as well as market-driven.

Stock values and market-trading volume are also affected and effected by non-economic events making for volatile cycles. The 1970s saw the NYSE affected by the Richard NIXON presidency scandal, the end of VIETNAM WAR, and the Jimmy CARTER presidency. The 1980s looked like an era of recovery as stock values soared, only to be burst by the October 19, 1987, DOW JONES Industrial Average drop of 508 points, the largest in history. Two days of unprecedented volume followed with a total of over 400 million shares traded. The 1990s saw the collapse of the Cold War and a further meteoric rise of market values on the NYSE. But on October 27, 1997, the Dow Jones plunged again 554 points. Another record high was achieved by the Dow on January 14, 2000 at 11,722.98 and was followed by the largest single-day gain of almost 500 points on March 16, 2000, to close at 10,630.60.

Stock markets can also influence each other. Global stocks and technology companies played a major role in the traditional NYSE, but their overvalue on the NAS-DAQ at the millennium led to stock values plummeting on April 14, 2000, by 617 points.

The terrorist attacks on the World Trade Center in New York City led to a four-day closure of the NYSE. When it reopened on September 17, 2001, a record 2.37 billion shares exchanged hands.

BIBLIOGRAPHY. E. Chancellor, *Devil Take the Hindmost: A History of Financial Speculation* (Farrar Straus & Giroux, 1999); D. Colbert, *Eyewitness to Wall Street: 400 Years of Dreamers, Schemers, Busts, and Booms* (Broadway Books, 2001); R. Davies, *A Comparative Chronology of Money from Ancient Times to Present Day* (University of Wales Press, 2002); J. Galbraith, *The Great Crash of 1929* (Mariner Books, 1997); J. Galbraith, *A Short History of Financial Euphoria* (Penguin Books, 1994); C. Giesst, *Wall Street: A History* (Oxford University Press, 1997); C. Geisst, and R. Grasso, *100 Years of Wall Street* (McGraw-Hill, 1999); J.R. Gordon, *The Great Game: The Emergence of Wall Street As a World Power, 1653–2000* (Scribner, 1999); C. Kindleberger, *Manias, Panics, and Crashes: A History of Financial Crises* (John Wiley & Sons, 2000); D. Scott, *How Wall Street Works* (McGraw-Hill, 1999); R. Sobel and B. Mitchell, *The Big Board: A History of the New York Stock Exchange* (Beard Group, 2000).

CHRIS HOWELL
RED ROCKS COLLEGE

stockholder

THE STOCKHOLDER (or shareholder) is a person (or an institution, sometimes another company) who holds at least one share of a registered company. Theoretically, the stockholder is truly a co-owner of a company, along with possibly millions of other co-owners, recognizing the fact that some companies have more than a billion shares outstanding. In other words, to buy just one single share is enough to be considered as a stockholder, and therefore to be entitled to attend the company's annual meeting, and to vote on the board of directors' propositions.

Ownership of each share allows one vote at a company's annual meeting; the shareholder may vote in person or (in advance) by mail, sometimes by telephone or through the internet. Companies always indicate how to vote according to the board of directors' recommendations, and shareholders who don't vote are understood to vote along with the company's suggestions. Stockholders automatically receive the company's ANNUAL REPORT every year; they are paid cash dividends if the company distributes STOCK DIVIDENDS to common shareholders. Some stockholders prefer to ask for a certificate of the shares they own; others just leave these proofs to their broker and therefore can sell their shares with just a phone call to their advisor.

There are many ways to get shares from a company. They can be bought through a broker or with an account from a discount broker; or obtained by employees from their specific enterprise; or sometimes bought directly from some big companies (if the buyer already owns at least one share). Some companies (such as banks) can give bonus shares instead of cash dividends if stockholders ask for this procedure. At any moment, a stockholder may give his or her shares (or a part of them) to another person, a charity, or an institution.

Occasionally, some companies write stockholders of less than 100 shares and propose that they sell their few remaining shares, or buy enough shares to get a total of 100. Shareholders are free to ignore that proposition. Usually, shares are sold by blocks of 100, but this is no obligation. Because of the transactions fees, most individual stockholders own between 100 and 10,000 shares of a company, depending on stock value.

Two opposing philosophies lie behind the relationship between stockholders and a company's BOARD OF DIRECTORS. Some companies don't hesitate to make decisions that unavoidably weaken shareholders' value, such as issuing new shares (and therefore diluting all the shares' value), reducing or cutting dividends, and giving generous premiums and performance bonuses to senior executives or directors.

Other companies are better managed and more dedicated to their shareholders, paying good dividends and listening to stockholder suggestions. A company's attitude towards its shareholders can be analyzed at the annual meeting, when a company has to present and comment on individual shareholder's propositions (usually about the directors' salary and compensation) in front of all the company's stockholders. These active shareholders see themselves as the true collective owners of a company, considering employees, directors, and members of the board as their employees.

Usually, the most important shareholders (in percentage) are institutional investors or in some cases, mutual funds; the members of the board are not always the owners of the most important amount of shares of their company.

Shareholders can behave differently from one annual meeting to another, depending on how the stock and company are performing. Individual shareholders will often complain at the meeting if the annual dividend isn't high enough (compared to the company's profits), or if executive compensations are considered too high.

Many associations of investors and shareholders exist in different countries that advocate stockholder interests. As one example, in CANADA, former provincial minister Yves Michaud was the first to denounce the high salaries of members of the board of some Canadian banks; he later founded an association of small investors, working as a pressure group to obtain more respect from the banks' executives and board members toward individual stockholders, presented as the real owners of companies. In fact, in recent years, many investors from different countries went to court to protest against accounting irregularities, or to raise other ethical issues about a company's management.

Stockholders' reactions are one of the most impossible things to control or to predict. STOCK MARKET reactions are mostly led by important institutional shareholders, whose massive moves, orders, recommendations, and advice (upgrades, downgrades of specific stocks) can influence fluctuations. In these matters, the size of some institutional stockholders can be more influential than the number of many small- and medium-shareholders. Nonetheless, there is always one buyer for every seller, depending on prices and how many shares are offered.

BIBLIOGRAPHY. Geraldine and Gregory Weiss, *The Dividend Connection: How Dividends Create Value in the Stock Market* (Dearborn Trade Publishing, 1995); Association des petits épargnants et investisseurs du Québec, www.apeiq.com; National Association of Investors (NAIC), www.investware.com; International Corporate Governance Network (ICGN), www.icgn.org.

YVES LABERGE, PH.D.
INSTITUT QUÉBÉCOIS DES
HAUTES ÉTUDES INTERNATIONALE

Stone, Sir Richard (1913–91)

A BRITISH ECONOMIST who focused on empirical measurement, Sir Richard Stone was awarded the 1984 Nobel Prize in Economics. The Nobel committee cited his "fundamental contributions to the development of national income accounts."

While Stone attended Cambridge University initially, he studied law but switched to economics because of the Great DEPRESSION. Stone believed that it was possible to make the world a better place by better understanding economics. Stone studied under Richard Kahn in King's College. There, he met John Maynard KEYNES. Stone joined Keynes' Political Economy club and attended some of the lectures that Keynes gave while writing *The General Theory of Employment, Interest, and Money.*

Stone graduated from Cambridge in 1935. He was offered an opportunity to conduct further research as a student, but moved on to a brokerage firm instead. After marrying, Stone began to publish statistical reports in *Industry Illustrated* and also co-authored one of the earliest estimates of the marginal propensity to consume.

In 1939, Stone joined the newly formed Ministry of Economic Warfare and first focused on statistics of shipping and oil. He then transferred to the Central Economic Information Service, where he met James MEADE. Meade and Stone compiled data for a rudimentary national account on expenditures, income, and saving. Stone worked on this project as Keynes' assistant in the Treasury department, during the remainder of the war.

Stone traveled to the UNITED STATES and CANADA to examine similar efforts to compile data on national accounts. He found that others had, in fact, gone into greater statistical detail than he had, and that these different approaches needed adjustment to make country comparisons possible. Stone spent three months at Princeton University, where he began to write a paper on defining and measuring national income.

After the war, Stone became the director of the department of Applied Economics at Cambridge. He also got involved in the Organization for European Economic Cooperation, working on the implementation of the MARSHALL PLAN. Stone directed the National Accounts Research Unit. Through this agency, he set up national accounts for monitoring the progress of nations under the Marshall Plan.

Stone also wrote on consumer behavior. In 1954, he published *The Measurement of Consumers' Expenditure and Behaviour in the United Kingdom, 1920–38.* The statistical techniques of this book now seem basic and standard, but were cutting edge at the time. Stone's department was clearly at the forefront of developing statistical methods in economics.

Stone directed the department of applied economics until 1955. In that year, he became the president of the Econometric Society, but lost his directorship due to the efforts of some Cambridge Keynesians. He and Alan Brown then started the Cambridge Growth Project. Stone and Brown focused on modeling the British economy. They eventually constructed one of the largest econometric models of a national economy. Stone continued his work on national income accounts for the rest of his career, which ended with his retirement in 1980.

Stone's method was explicitly empiricist: He believed that economic analysis begins with facts, out of which economists formulate hypotheses, or theories. Theoretical models should then be combined with goals for improving the existing economic system to form policies, along with a plan to implement them. Experience with policies would then cause us to reconsider the facts.

While there is nothing wrong with looking at statistical data, the complexity of economic phenomena makes empirical analysis particularly difficult. We must also consider political motivations since, as Stone notes, policy goals do enter into analysis at some point.

Stone's work on consumption and national accounts won him fame during the heyday of Keynesian economics. The decline of Keynesian economics diminished the importance of his work on consumer expenditures and behavior. His most lasting influences are in developing national income accounting and in popularizing econometric analysis in general.

BIBLIOGRAPHY. Angus Deaton, "Sir Richard Stone," *The New Palgrave of Economics* (Palgrave Macmillan, 2002); James Buchanan, "Politics without Romance: A Sketch of Positive Public Choice Theory and its Normative Implications," *IHS Journal* (v.3, 1979); F.A. Hayek, *The Theory of Complex Phenomena, Studies in Philosophy, Politics and Economics* (Simon and Schuster, 1967); Richard Stone, "The Accounts of Society," *Journal of Applied Econometrics* (v.1/1, 1986); Richard Stone, *The Role of Measurement in Economics* (Ashgate Publishing, 1994); "Richard Stone Autobiography," www.nobel.se.

D.W. MacKenzie
George Mason University

strikes

THE JOINT WITHHOLDING of labor by a group of workers in order to protest and thereby influence some activity of their employer, or some condition of employment, is termed a labor strike. The return to work typically depends upon the employer meeting a set of, usually evolving, demands, or occurs because strikers give up or are fired. A related, less common phenomenon, the lockout involves the refusal of an employer to grant entrance to the workplace until certain conditions are met, or the employer relinquishes.

To classify strikes, we may first distinguish between three broad, but not necessarily exclusive, categories:

1. Contract strikes: strikes over the provisions of a future (or possibly existing) labor contract, usually concerning wages or working conditions

2. Recognition strikes: strikes seeking employer recognition of a UNION or other organization as the bargaining agent for a group of workers

3. Political strikes: efforts by large groups of workers from several industries, sometimes joined by employers, to achieve significant political change by withholding labor or closing down sectors of the economy. Political strikes that span many industries are called general strikes.

Strikes in categories 2 and 3 above often involve wage and working condition issues as well.

Wildcat and political strikes. Within each category we may further distinguish between sanctioned strikes, called by unions or bargaining agents, and wildcat strikes, spontaneous strikes likely to arise either before unionization has been established, or during an ongoing contract period (which unions are typically required to observe by refraining from strikes). Wildcat strikes usually fail to achieve worker demands; occasionally unions have joined ongoing wildcat strikes, sometimes with success.

Political strikes most frequently arise in unstable political environments, e.g., RUSSIA before and during the 1917 revolution. The early 2000s general strikes in VENEZUELA, which demanded new elections or the resignation of President Hugo Chavez, offer a contemporary example. A less dramatic political strike occurred in South Korea in January 1997, when tens of thousands of workers struck for 23 days protesting labor reform legislation. Political strikes have complex dynamics that distinguish them from the largely economic strikes of concern in the history of capitalism.

Contract strikes emerge within established union-management relationships, whereas recognition strikes, which assume a greater historical importance, represent efforts to establish such relationships when they do not exist, or to resist employer efforts to end them. In the United States and many other industrialized countries, recognition strikes are largely a phenomenon of the past. The last great wave of recognition strikes occurred in the United States during the 1930s. Contemporary economic theory, accordingly, has tended to focus on, or be more applicable to, contract strikes.

Economic theories of strikes. On the surface, contract strikes may appear irrational: Workers lose wages and employers lose production and sales. In principle, the parties should be able to negotiate a solution that leaves them both better off than any outcome following a strike. Using similar logic, John HICKS (1933) argued that strikes primarily reflect failures of negotiation caused by inaccurate appraisals by union leadership, membership, or employers concerning the willingness or ability of the other party to hold out, or come to terms. Hicks accordingly expects the incidence of strikes to decline with bargaining experience.

More recent theory finds the notion of negotiation failure insufficient, but builds on Hick's notions of divergent information and expectations among the players. Orley Ashenfelter and George E. Johnson (1969) argue that strikes reflect internal union politics. They arise when expectations among union members prevent the leadership from signing a contract it might otherwise accept. In order to avoid internal challenges, the leadership calls a strike, which serves to reduce the membership's (initially unrealistic) expectations, until a contract can be signed. Note the decision to strike is rational for the leadership because it helps them maintain their position. Furthermore, it reflects an information problem: The membership does not understand the employer's true position.

Asymmetric information theory, advanced by David Card in 1990, takes the information dynamics of strikes further, arguing that firms know their current profit position and workers do not (in a variation, the employer does not understand the sentiment of the union membership). Firms can benefit from withholding private information, since disclosing high profits could encourage worker demands for higher wages. Strikes then force employers to reveal their true profit picture in the process of settlement: Firms with high profits yield to strike demands following a relatively short strike, whereas low-profit firms cannot yield and will endure a long strike instead. This theory predicts that high firm profits will be associated with relatively low incidence and duration of strikes.

In another variation, Melvin W. Reder and George R. Neumann proposed in 1980 that bargaining is a sequential learning process. Over time, unions and employers develop negotiating techniques, routines and procedures that reduce the incidence of strikes, but such development absorbs time and resources. The more costly the prospect of a strike to both sides, the greater incentive they have to develop negotiating protocols. Accordingly, industries with higher strike costs are expected to experience fewer strikes.

The above theories primarily address contract strikes, though internal politics and information issues may arise in recognition strikes. John Goddard offers an alternative and somewhat broader theory, stressing institutional context, which applies to both recognition and contract strikes. Goddard argues that strikes emerge as expressions of discontent by workers and their agents; strike incidence responds to conceptions of fairness and legitimacy concerning pay and the exercise of authority in the workplace. Goddard predicts that the likelihood and duration of strikes will increase with the following five factors, all else equal:

1. The levels of discontent and solidarity among workers

2. The degree to which employers emphasize cost containment and efficiency as opposed to stabilization and accommodation

3. The extent to which strikes are viewed as effective relative to workers' alternative manners of expressing discontent, such as quitting

4. The militancy of negotiators and pressure from workers

5. The degree of uncertainty and imperfect information among negotiators.

Note that argument 4 overlaps with Ashenfelter and Johnson and that 5 essentially incorporates asymmetric information theory.

In this context then, contract strikes represent efforts to voice discontent over proposed (or possibly current) contracts and conditions, while recognition strikes express more fundamental discontent concerning the state of bargaining representation for workers, or lack thereof.

Significance and history. Contract strikes obviously cause short-term disruptions in on-site production, sometimes interfering with production in linked industries and consumer activity, as in the case of significant transportation strikes or, in an earlier era, coal strikes. Aggregate effects of strikes, at least in developed economies, are less clear-cut. Two interesting questions emerge: Do strikes increase labor's overall share of income, and do strikes reduce aggregate productivity growth? Studies report mixed results. One study, for example, finds no significant impacts of strikes on labor's share of income in the United States between 1949–92, though it does find a modest positive effect of unionization on labor's share before 1980. Another study finds that the British strikes of 1970s had negligible effects on aggregate output and work efficiency, though unions had a modest negative effect on work efficiency.

In terms of the development of capitalism, recognition strikes have played a far more substantive role, at times signaling transformations of labor relations or the failure of attempts to do so. Recognition strikes have typically occurred in the early to mid-stages of industrialization, when labor relations often remained unsettled. Between 1870 and 1940, for example, the United States experienced several waves of recognition strikes, punctuated by a few key strikes. These strikes often involved considerable violence.

The strike wave of 1884–86 represented an unsuccessful movement of both skilled and unskilled workers to achieve union-bargaining status, higher wages and an 8-hour day. After a successful strike that forced railroad magnate Jay GOULD to bargain with unions in 1885, the movement began to disintegrate after an anarchist threw a bomb at a rally of strikers in Haymarket Square, Chicago, in May 1886. Significant police and judicial suppression of union activists followed; historians describe the response as a "police terror." The Pullman railway strike of 1894, which spread from Chicago into a national strike, represented a similar unsuccessful combination of skilled and unskilled workers. Over the objections of several state governors, the federal government supported the Pullman Company by sending troops to confront strikers, often violently. Strike leaders were jailed and the American Railway Union eventually dissolved. These strikes signaled the end of early attempts by mainstream unions to organize unskilled as well as skilled workers. From the 1890s through the early 1930s successful union activity centered around the American Federation of Labor (AFL), which focused on organizing skilled crafts workers (e.g., carpenters), with no significant attention to unskilled mass production workers.

During the second half of the 1930s, at the peak of Franklin ROOSEVELT's NEW DEAL, the Congress of Industrial Organizations (CIO) split from the more conservative AFL to launch a wave of confrontational recognition strikes that fundamentally transformed U.S. labor relations. By organizing large numbers of unskilled and skilled mass production workers on an industry-wide basis, CIO strikes forced many large corporations (e.g., GENERAL MOTORS, U.S. STEEL) to recognize large industrial unions for the first time, thereby belatedly achieving important goals of the 1880–90 strike waves. A considerably more peaceful wave of CIO strikes in 1945–46 reaffirmed unions' position as bargaining agents, and focused future union and strike activity on wage and working condition issues (contract issues) while it eliminated more radical notions of sharing in enterprise management from labor's agenda.

These last two strike waves initiated a postwar labor accord which generally observed the following features: Many mass-production industries bargained with national unions setting 2–3 year contracts over wages and working conditions; negotiated pay increases tended to reflect both increases in national labor productivity and inflation; at the local level, union committees met with local management to work out grievances over working conditions; management retained its discretion over investment and the overall organization of work. On the whole, management sacrificed some flexibility with respect to setting wages, detailed work assignments, and dismissal policies in order to gain relative labor peace. In 1955, the CIO merged with the AFL, forming the AFL-CIO; the merger itself reflected the relative stability of the labor accord. Subsequent strikes involved considerably less violence and usually occurred only at the end of specified 2–3 year contracts. The combative era of U.S. labor relations had ended.

Strike trends around the world. Finally, a key strike has signaled erosion of the labor accord in the post-1980 period. After the federal government broke the air-traffic controller's (PATCO) strike, a more aggressive (though nonviolent) period of strike-breaking and anti-union activity by employers has emerged, ultimately contributing to a decline in union influence.

While the institutional details concerning the realms of union bargaining, the role of government in labor relations, and the role of political parties differ significantly, many industrialized countries underwent a roughly similar process. Recognition strikes occurred during a transition period, followed by a more stable period with established bargaining procedures. The UNITED KINGDOM, like the United States, experienced a history of highly confrontational strikes. Strike waves of 1889–90, 1910–13 and 1919–20, preceded the emergence of more stable, though not necessarily calm, labor relations after the late 1920s. As in the United States, a decline in union influence followed a successful government effort to break a key strike, in this case the 1984–85 miners strike.

Finally, in SPAIN the transition from the Francisco Franco dictatorship to democracy was marked by a strike wave from 1977–84; more stable labor relations followed.

For many developing countries, political strikes and waves of economic strikes of both types have reflected unsettled labor relations, at times foreshadowing significant transformation. British and French colonies in Africa experienced strike waves, including several general strikes, from mid-1930s to the early 1950s, signaling the process of developing an urban labor force and more significantly the terminal phase of the colonial era.

In BRAZIL, the combination of industrialization in the post-1950 period with shifts in government between relatively democratic rule and military dictatorship has been associated with waves of economic and political strikes; the former typically occurring during democratic periods, and the latter arising primarily during the transition from military to democratic rule. Even in the 1980s, Brazil experienced four general strikes. In Bangladesh, a 1996 port strike followed a contested election and threatened the country's international trade and access to foreign exchange.

Overall, strikes reflect an evolving natural tendency in continuing history of capitalism. In labor relations, the interests of employers and workers coincide to the degree that they need each other to produce the output upon which their livelihoods jointly depend, yet their interests differ over the distribution of the fruits of production and at times over the organization of work. Because group dynamics in employment relations necessarily involve substantial information and collective-action problems, an almost utopian vision of settling all labor conflicts by agreeable informed bargaining, or via individual market actions of quitting one's job or dismissing a worker, will continue to elude us. Rather, the political economy of labor relations will periodically engender strikes as an important avenue for expression of discontent over wages, working conditions, authority in the workplace, and sometimes politics in society at large.

While output and wages are indeed sacrificed in the short run, the feasible alternative is worse. Accordingly, democracies permit strikes, striving to channel expressions of discontent into relatively peaceful avenues. Dictatorships, on the other hand, fearing organized dissent of any form, usually prohibit them, perhaps ultimately to their own demise.

BIBLIOGRAPHY. Orley Ashenfelter and George E. Johnson, "Bargaining Theory, Trade Unions and Industrial Strike Activity," *American Economic Review* (v.59/1, 1969); David Card, "Strikes and Wages: a Test of an Asymmetric Information Model," *Quarterly Journal of Economics* (v.105, 1990); Frederick Cooper, *On the African Waterfront* (Yale University Press, 1987); John R. Commons, et al., *History of Labor in the United States* (Macmillan, 1921); A.P. Dickerson, P.A. Geroski and K.G. Knight, "Productivity, Efficiency and Strike Activity," *International Review of Applied Economics* (v.11/1, 1997); John Goddard, "Strikes as Collective Voice: a Behavioral Analysis of Strike Activity," *Industrial and Labor Relations Review* (v.46/1, 1992); John R. Hicks, *The Theory of Wages* (Macmillan, 1932); Melvin W. Reder and George R. Neumann, "Conflict and Contract: the Case of Strikes," *Journal of Political Economy* (v.88/5, 1980); Michael Wallace, Kevin T. Leicht and Lawrence E. Raffalovich, "Unions, Strikes, and Labor's Share of Income: A Quarterly Analysis of the United States, 1949–1992," *Social Science Research* (v.28, 1999); Robert H. Zieger, *The CIO, 1935–1955* (University of North Carolina Press, 1995).

WILLIAM D. FERGUSON
GRINNELL COLLEGE

subsidies

SUBSIDIES ARE negative TAXES. They are government expenditures that aim toward increasing the supply of certain GOODS, or to increase the income of particular individuals and organizations. These expenditures get disbursed to private organizations and individuals, such as farm subsidies, food stamps, and corporate welfare. One rationale behind subsidies is that market PRICES will sometimes not reflect underlying consumer demand.

Markets move resources to their most highly valued uses when competition drives prices to marginal costs. When the additional cost of acquiring more goods equals the benefits from acquiring these goods, consumers have gained as much as they can from trading. These results from competition imply that trading benefits only the buyers and sellers who negotiate terms of trade. Buyers and sellers exclude third parties from their business completely.

Some goods end up benefiting people who do not pay for them. If someone charged admission to a field surrounding a fireworks show, people could see the same fireworks without paying from miles away. These free-riders reduce total revenue for fireworks, in this case. Since private businesses supply goods according to the profits they earn out of revenue, reduced revenue through free-riding diminishes market supply. Free-riding implies that there are social benefits to the private supply of goods. It may be economically efficient to subsidize private enterprises when social benefits exist, whether it is more efficient to pay for goods privately through individual purchases, or collectively through taxes. If the costs of excluding consumers who do not pay for goods that entrepreneurs supply are high, then we might improve economic efficiency by subsidizing their production out of general taxes, thus forcing payment by would be free-riders.

The other main rationale behind subsidies is that consumers may not have the "right" values. Some goods may have merits that many people do not appreciate. Efficient markets will undersupply such merit goods because consumers will spend too little money on goods whose positive benefits escape them, even when entrepreneurs exclude all free-riders.

One area where we might consider subsidies is education. Some contend that education makes people better citizens by instilling civic virtues in students. This may be true. However, it is important to consider the extent to which markets cover social benefits. Education increases personal lifetime income. It also provides benefits to employers by increasing worker productivity. The existence of these private benefits explains why employers and students (not to mention their parents) often pay much for tuition at private schools. If these private expenditures provide at least as much education as we need to instill civic virtues in students, then the social benefits are infra-marginal, or irrelevant to the actual amount of private supply. Social benefits require subsidies only when they extend beyond private supply. Many colleges and universities receive subsidies, but given the existence of significant private expenditures on this level of education, it is not clear how much the social benefits of education matter to economic efficiency.

Government officials can deal with extra-marginal externalities by implementing per-unit or lump-sum subsidies. Lump-sum payments have certain advantages over per-unit subsidies. It is usually simpler to disburse lump-sum payments than to implement per-unit payments. Also, lump-sum payments can result in better resources allocation. For example, a per-unit transfer to low-income families for food changes the relative prices of food with respect to other goods. The recipients of this additional income may want to use it to buy something other than food, like clothing. Given the substitution ability of different goods, subsidy recipients may be better off spending additional income from lump-sum transfers.

Since subsidies come from the political process, they might sometimes exist for purely political reasons. Businesses lobby for subsidies not to promote economic efficiency, but to increase their private profits. Narrow interests can exert considerable influence, so businesses may succeed in securing subsidies in excess of their social benefits. Some subsidies exist simply as political payoffs to those who produce private goods. Also, competition for subsidies expends real resources. This competition can dissipate much of the gains to subsidization.

For example, the U.S. government provides a subsidy to sugar farmers. By keeping the U.S. price for sugar above the world price, the sugar program costs consumers $1.4 billion per year. Individual farmers receive millions in subsidies from this program. There are surely some instances where markets supply less than ideal amounts of goods. There is no apparent reason for this to be true of sugar. The point is that neither private enterprise nor public subsidies provide ideal solutions. Subsidies promote economic efficiency only when social benefits affect the actual margin of production and when the public sector suffers from relatively small imperfections.

Another questionable justification for subsidies is to support declining industries. Following the September 11, 2001 terrorism attacks, the airline industry received large federal subsidies. Similarly, the federal government also bailed out Chrysler when it came upon hard times during the late 1970s. Subsidies helped these industries, though it is not clear that this was economically efficient. Reduced demand reflects the fact that consumers want different goods. This has the effect of pressuring producers to improve efficiency and product quality. Failing this, weak demand will result in the redirection of resources toward other, more efficient and valued industries. Subsidies counteract the effects of demand reduction, and may, in fact, be resisting the reallocation of goods to more highly valued uses. Some feel that it is worthwhile to secure certain industries and jobs in order to preserve communities and particular ways of life. While some may value these things, others realize that subsidies can seriously impair economic efficiency.

The argument can be made that art needs subsidies because there are too few who appreciate its true value. While this notion appeals to many, discerning the merits of any merit good is a difficult matter. Whose opinion should rule in determining what constitutes good art? How can we know how much of a subsidy any particular artwork merits? Markets do foster the supply of art in many ways, but given the difficulties in sorting out allegedly objective merits in art, the case for art subsidies is far from certain.

Subsidies can make income distribution more fair, or used to promote national goals. Welfare programs such as food stamps and pension programs such as Social Security subsidize private consumption. Also, there is support for subsidies for the defense and export industries, to support nationalistic political goals. Such moral and political justifications for subsidies are inherently controversial. Lobbying by interest groups can swell the size of these subsidies, justified on equity grounds with other subsidies. That is, people may want subsidies not to promote fairness or national goals, but simply as a means to gain income at the expense of those who earned it legitimately.

While subsidies may promote efficiency, equity, or political ends, there are potential problems with them. Entrepreneurs in markets have an incentive to invent methods of excluding free-riders. Entrepreneurs in politics have an incentive to increase subsidies beyond reasonable levels. The case for them is far from clear, yet subsidies exist in many forms, and are in fact a well-entrenched part of the public sector.

BIBLIOGRAPHY. James M. Buchanan and W. Craig Stubblebine, "Externality," *Economica* (v.29/116, 1962); Tyler Cowen, *In Praise of Commercial Culture* (Harvard University Press, 2000); David N. Laband and George McClintock, *The Transfer Society: Economic Expenditures on Transfer Activity* (NBN, 2001); Richard A. and Peggy B. Musgrave, *Public Finance in Theory and Practice* (McGraw-Hill, 1989); Norman Myers and Jennifer Kent, *Perverse Subsidies: How Misused Tax Dollars Harm the Environment and the Economy* (Island Press, 2001); Mancur Olson, *The Logic of Collective Action* (Harvard University Press, 1971); Gordon Tullock, "The Welfare Costs of Tariffs, Monopolies, and Theft," *The Western Journal of Economics* (1967); Ralph Turvey, "On Divergences between Social Cost and Private Cost," *Economica* (v.30/119, 1963).

D.W. MacKenzie
George Mason University

subsistence theory

THE WORD "SUBSISTENCE" refers to the basic needs of a human being: food, water, clothing, and shelter. The concept of subsistence has been used in various economic theories dating back to the writings of Thomas MALTHUS, David RICARDO, John Stuart MILL and Karl MARX. In the 20th century, Arthur Lewis has utilized this concept of subsistence to propose his two-sector growth model.

Ricardo initiated the discussion by exploring the value of commodities produced, and hence the value of labor and the wages paid to labor. He presented the argument for a subsistence theory of wages that pointed to the fact that wages paid to a worker will equal the amount needed to sustain the worker and his or her family. The necessity to sustain a family is predicated by the creation of future workers by the family.

Ricardo makes a distinction between the natural price of labor and the market price of labor. The natural price of labor is the amount of money needed to purchase commodities that will sustain the worker and his family. The market price of labor is the wage received by the worker in the market. If the market wage rate is higher than the natural wage rate, this results in the worker being able to purchase things beyond the necessities. The worker and his family is happy and prosperous and this leads to larger families and thus an eventual increase in labor. This increase in supply will cause the market wage rate to decrease. However, if the worker receives a market wage less than the natural price of labor, then the impact on the worker is severe as he is unable to sustain himself. This could lead to an increase in the suffering of the worker and his family, which in turn could reduce the number of workers available. This potential decrease in workers could increase the wage received by the worker. Thus, under the Ricardian theory, wages will automatically revert back to the level that is sufficient for a worker and his family to sustain themselves.

Malthus, using the Ricardian argument for subsistence wages, presented a dire analysis of human development. In his theory, Malthus argued that the production of food follows an arithmetic progression, while the increase in population follows a geometric progression. Thus, if the population were to increase, then the increase in population will not be sustained by the food produced. This will eventually lead to famine and pestilence and a reduction of world population.

Marx presents a different aspect of subsistence wages in his labor theory of value. Marx writes that workers are paid a wage that allows them to sustain themselves and their family. However, a worker ends up producing more output than the amount they were paid for. This, he calls surplus value and the creation of surplus value forms the central argument of this theory.

Marx presents the surplus value as a source of potential problems as the employer finds an opportunity to exploit the workers in order to extract surplus value from them. The exploitation of workers continues as long as there exists a large quantity of excess labor, that Marx calls the reserve army of labor. The conflict between the worker and owner then results in a crisis within the economy.

Marx, however, allows for an evolving definition of subsistence wages. Thus, subsistence wage can increase over the years as the social and cultural definition of what is required for subsistence changes in a society.

In the 20th century, Lewis renewed the focus on issues of subsistence wage with his two-sector growth model. This pioneering work laid the foundation for the vast literature on development economics. The theory provides a framework for a developing economy to increase economic growth using the existing resources within the nation. The Lewis model assumes that the economy is divided into two sectors, a rural agricultural sector and an urban industrial sector. The rural sector is characterized by high level of unemployment and workers earning a subsistence wage rate. The workers in this sector have very low marginal productivity. The urban sector is modern and more productive. Due to the low productivity of workers in the rural sector, labor will migrate to the urban regions in search of better wages. This will result in an increase in the output produced and an increase in the level of employment in the nation. This process of migration from the subsistence sector to the urban areas will continue until all the excess labor is exhausted.

Lewis argues that his process of urbanization of the economy will transform this economy from an agrarian rural economy to an industrial urban economy. This model aptly describes the path of economic development of the Western economies. However, it is not appropriate in describing the growth pattern for the developing economies: The process of migration is not guaranteed, the existence of large quantity of surplus labor is not true, and the capacity for the urban sector to absorb labor is neither automatic nor unlimited.

Subsistence theory has been part of the economic discourse for many centuries, it continues to intrigue economists and it provides a fertile ground for further discussion in areas such as economic development.

BIBLIOGRAPHY. Paul Halsall, *Modern History Source Book*, www.fordham.edu; Martin Schnitzer, *Comparative Economic Systems* (South-Western College Publishing, 8th Edition); Stuart Lynn, *Economic Development: Theory and Practice for a Divided World* (Prentice Hall); History of Economic Thought, cepa.newschool.edu; Michael Todaro and Stephen Smith, *Economic Development* (Addison-Wesley, 2002).

JAISHANKAR RAMAN, PH.D.
VALPARAISO UNIVERSITY

Suez Canal

ONE OF THE LONGEST and most heavily used artificial waterways in the world, the Suez Canal significantly shortens the naval route from Europe to southern Asia and eastern Africa by connecting the Red Sea and Gulf of Suez with the Mediterranean Sea. It is 101 miles (163 kilometers) long, at least 197 feet (65 meters) wide, and around 60 feet (16 meters) deep at low tide.

The Suez Canal (in Arabic, Qanât as-suways) does not take the shortest route across the Isthmus of Suez, which would make the Canal around 75 miles long, but rather makes use of four natural lakes: Lake Manzala, Lake Timsah, Great Bitter Lake, and Little Bitter Lake. The Canal has no locks since the Mediterranean Sea and Gulf of Suez have approximately the same water level. Ships transit the Suez Canal in convoys and along most of the way there is only one lane for traffic with many passing bays.

Since it is the fastest way from the northern Atlantic Ocean to the Indian Ocean, the Suez Canal has an enormous regional and global strategic importance. The canal has been extensively used and the taxes paid by the vessels represent an important source of income for the Egyptian government, which nationalized it in 1956.

The earliest initiative to create a canal connecting the Mediterranean to the Red Sea dates back to the Pharaonic age at around the 18th century B.C.E. The ancient canals, which were poorly maintained and often fell into disrepair, were mainly used for irrigation and were only passable at flood periods. Unlike the modern canal, the earliest canals linked the Red Sea to the Nile forcing the ships to sail along the river. The Persians, the Greeks, and the Romans re-excavated the canal, the latter naming it after the Emperor Trajan. The early Arabs also re-dug and extended the canal that was infrequently operational until the 8th century C.E. when it was completely abandoned and filled-up. The Venetians in the 15th century unsuccessfully tried to revive the idea of a shorter trade route to India. Napoleon Bonaparte, in the early 19th century, abandoned the re-excavation plans when the French engineers miscalculated that the Red Sea level was 10 meters above the Mediterranean Sea.

After extensive studies that disproved earlier erroneous measurements, in 1854 the former French consul in Cairo, an engineer, and canal digger Ferdinand Marie de Lesseps signed the concession with the Egyptian viceroy Said Pasha to construct a canal. The SUEZ COMPANY was formed in 1858 with authority to cut a canal and to operate it for 99 years, after which EGYPT would assume ownership. The digging started in April 1859. The extensive construction utilized modern technologies but still resembled slave-labor conditions of centuries past. More than two million workers were involved in the construction, of which around 100,000 lost their lives. The canal was opened for navigation 10 years later in 1869 with a spectacular ceremony that was attended by dignitaries from around the world. The opera *Aida* was commissioned for the occasion of inauguration.

Initially, the French and Egyptian governments jointly owned the Suez Company. Financial troubles enabled the British government to become, in 1875, a partial owner of the canal after purchasing Egypt's shares. In 1888, the Convention of Constantinople secured freedom of navigation through the Suez Canal and opened it for unrestricted international access during times of both peace and war.

Egypt's president Gamal Abdel Nasser nationalized the canal in 1956, 13 years before the original concession was due to expire, partially because the Western powers refused to finance the Aswan Dam, because of Egypt's friendly relationship with the Soviet Union. The nationalization precipitated the first modern closure of the Suez Canal, which took place 1956–57, following the Israeli attack on Egypt and the French and British occupation of the canal and surrounding area. Soon after the end of conflict and reopening of the Canal under the mandate of the United Nations, the Egyptian government paid off all the original shareholders and assumed complete control of the Suez Canal.

The second shut-down occurred from 1967–75 following the Six-Day Arab-Israeli War when Israel occupied the Sinai Peninsula and used the canal as a buffer zone. The standoff was eventually resolved in 1979 when a peace treaty was signed between Egypt and Israel allowing all ships, even the Israelis, to gain unrestricted access to the canal.

The Suez Canal continues to be modernized and enlarged. By 2010, the Egyptian government plans to reduce transit times from around 15 to 11 hours and to enable the biggest ships (like ultra-large crude carriers, ULCC, that can carry more than 300,000 tons) to pass through the Suez Canal.

BIBLIOGRAPHY. Ghislain de Diesbach, *Ferdinand de Lesseps* (Perrin, 1998); D.A. Farnie, *East and West of Suez: The Suez Canal in History, 1854–1956* (Oxford University Press, 1969); Mohamed Heikal, *Cutting the Lion's Tail: Suez Through Egyptian Eyes* (Arbor House, 1987); Lord Kinross, *Between Two Seas: The Creation of the Suez Canal* (Murray, 1969).

JOSIP MOCNIK
BOWLING GREEN STATE UNIVERSITY

Suez Company

LOCATED AT THE crossroads of Asia, Europe, and Africa, the SUEZ CANAL in EGYPT is one of the world's most important waterways and is operated by the Suez Company, ranked as the 99th largest corporation in the world by *Fortune* magazine in 2002.

The original concession to construct and operate the canal was given to Ferdinand de Lesseps in 1888 by the viceroy of Egypt. The canal was a French conception and financial gamble, though Great Britain had an interest in the canal as the shortest route to its domains in India and the East. In the 1880s, due to a revolt in Egypt, Britain was asked to station troops along the canal for protection. This temporary protection lasted 74 years.

After WORLD WAR II, Egypt was caught between the rivalry in the Middle East between the UNITED STATES and the SOVIET UNION. In an attempt to force Egypt to politically align against the Soviet Union, the United States placed conditions on the request for aid to build the Aswan Dam along the upper Nile River. Once Egypt's president, Gamal Abdel Nasser, refused the conditions, Britain became very nervous about the possibility of Soviet control over the canal. On July 26, 1956, Nasser announced that Egypt was nationalizing the Suez Canal.

While the American government attempted to resolve this problem, Great Britain, FRANCE, and ISRAEL decided on a plan to invade Egypt and take control of the canal back from Nasser's government. Historians cite that the European governments believed once the invasion occurred, the United States would go along with it. On October 29, 1956, the invasion occurred but the United States did not go along. Instead, Americans worked through the UNITED NATIONS to end the crisis with a cease-fire.

However, by the following decade, during the Arab-Israeli Six-Day War in 1967, ships were sunk by Egypt to block the waterway, and it remained closed for eight years. Today, with annual revenues of about $38 billion, the company has widened and improved the canal, handling an average of 60 vessels a day.

BIBLIOGRAPHY. "Fortune Global 500," *Fortune* (July 2002); Chister Johnsson, "The Suez War of 1956," in Alexander L. George, ed., *Avoiding War: Problems of Crisis Management* (Westview Press, 1991); Mohamed Heikal, *Cutting the Lion's Tail: Suez Through Egyptian Eyes* (Arbor House, 1987).

LINDA L. PETROU, PH.D.
HIGH POINT UNIVERSITY

Sumitomo Corporation

A HIGH-PERFORMANCE global financial company, JAPAN-based Sumitomo Corporation conducts commodity transactions in all industries utilizing worldwide networks. It also provides related customers with financing, serves as an organizer and coordinator for various high-dollar projects, and invests in various businesses from the information industry to retailing. As its website states, "Sumitomo Corporation thus shows great diversification as an Integrated Business Enterprise."

Sumitomo's basic principles and the values it professes are summed up in nine characteristics, including: integrity and sound management; integrated corporate strength; vision; change and innovation; commitment; enthusiasm; speed; human development; and professionalism.

Such values have attracted such major stockholders as the Bank of Tokyo-Mitsubishi Ltd., NEC CORPORATION, the Japan Trustee Services Bank Ltd. and the DAIICHI MUTUAL LIFE INSURANCE COMPANY.

In early 2001, Sumitomo launched its new "Step Up Plan," which is based on an earlier reform package, but takes cost-cutting and redundancy-slashing a step further. Its most important themes are, one, to expand the earning base and, two, to strategically reallocate management resources to foster higher levels of production.

Facing a slow economy both domestically and internationally, Sumitomo reported revenues of more than $77 billion in 2002, making it the 23rd largest company in the world.

BIBLIOGRAPHY. Ikujiro Nonaka, et al., *The Knowledge-Creating Company: How Japanese Companies Create the Dynamics of Innovation* (Oxford University Press, 1995); "Global 500: World's Largest Companies," *Fortune* (July 2002); Sumitomo Corporation, www.sumitomocorp.co.jp.

JOSEPH GERINGER
SYED B. HUSSAIN, PH.D
UNIVERSITY OF WISCONSIN, OSHKOSH

Summit of the Americas

PROVIDING THE UNITED STATES and its hemispheric partners a valuable mechanism, the Summit of the Americas addresses common political, economic, and social issues. By early 2003, there had been three summits of the 34 democratically elected leaders of the western hemisphere who operate with capitalistic, free-market economies, conduct multilateral international negotiations, and who reach decisions by consensus.

The basis of these summits is the shared values of democracy, human rights, and open markets, and the shared responsibility to be proactive in their defense. Before these summits were institutionalized, there had been two presidential summits. The first was in July 1956, in

Panama and brought 19 countries together under auspices of the Organization of American States. The second summit was held in Uruguay in April 1967. It was not until 27 years later that the Summit of the Americas was held in Miami in 1994. One of the major agreements that emerged from this meeting was the creation of a Free Trade Area of the Americas (FTAA). A second Summit of the Americas was held in CHILE in 1998, and the third in CANADA in 2001.

Non-governmental organizations (NGOs), including businesses and non-profit groups, are an integral part of the Summit process. There are nine ongoing negotiating groups that work and meet regularly to produce draft texts to be considered at future summits. These groups deal with such areas as market access, agricultural issues, intellectual property rights, competition policy, and investment.

Since the first summit in 1994, participants have accomplished such goals as improving anti-corruption efforts, leading to changes in civil and criminal codes in the countries that have ratified and signed the agreements. In addition, ethics rules have been implemented for public officials. There has also been an increase in counter-narcotics efforts, coordination to fight terrorism, funding of micro-enterprise initiatives, and an increase in awareness of environmental issues affecting the Americas.

In addition, progress has been made in developing common standards for telecommunication service and access. The summit process has attempted to reorganize inter-American relations by adapting debates and procedures to the new political, economic, and social conditions of the world that have come about due to the end of the Cold War. The institutionalization of a summit process in the western hemisphere has led to a modernization of the various institutions of the inter-American system, including the Organization of American States.

BIBLIOGRAPHY. Summit of the Americas, usinfo.state.gov; Summit of the Americas Information Network, www.summit-americas.org; Civil Society Participation in the Summit of the Americas, usinfo.state.gov.

LINDA L. PETROU, PH.D.
HIGH POINT UNIVERSITY

Sumner, William Graham (1840–1910)

THE SON OF AN English immigrant to the United States, Sumner was, for almost 40 years, one of the most controversial and popular professors at Yale University, thanks to his lectures on economics, political theory, and history, sociology, and anthropology. Though he later became a key thinker in the area of Social Darwinism and a supporter of LAISSER-FAIRE capitalism, arguing for minimal state intervention in economic matters, Sumner's academic beginning was linked to theological studies. After graduating from Yale, he studied theology and biblical interpretation in Britain and Germany. From 1869–72, Sumner was an active member of the American Broad Church Episcopalianism. Yet, he was soon bored with ministry, a profession with which he could not reconcile his interest in science and modernity.

His shift to secularism was accomplished when Sumner returned to Yale in 1872 as chair in political and social science. In his social and economic theory, Sunner tried to combine Social Darwinism, derived from his reading of Herbert SPENCER, with a liberalism focused on the economically acquisitive individual. Social Darwinism was an application of Darwin's ideas of natural selection and biological evolution to human society. To its theorists, the controversial social conditions of the period were natural and could not be changed. The rapid growth of an impoverished working class, the huge gap between rich and poor, the spread of urban slums were factors that highlighted how society was functioning.

Social Darwinists such as Sumner claimed that social existence was a competitive struggle among individuals possessing different natural capacities and traits. Those with better traits, the fittest, succeeded, becoming wealthy and powerful, while those who were unfit were condemned to POVERTY. Social Darwinists believed government intervention in economic and social matters must be minimal. Improving the condition of the poor would only be useful to preserve bad traits: To Sumner, the only alternative to the survival of the fittest was the survival of the unfittest. Sumner denied any sense of moral obligation to the poor, as he argued "it is not the function of the State to make men happy." Giving protection to the poorer classes meant using the state to steal from "the rich, comfortable, prosperous, virtuous, respectable, educated, and healthy" in order to give to "classes of people who have not been able to satisfy their own desires . . . [and who] do not take their achievements as a fair measure of their [property] rights."

BIBLIOGRAPHY. Robert C. Bannister, ed., *On Liberty, Society and Politics: the Essential Essays of William Graham Sumner* (Liberty Fund, 1992); Bruce Curtis, *William Graham Sumner* (Twayne Publishers, 1981); Richard Hofstadter, *Social Darwinism in American Thought* (Beacon, 1955); M.W. Taylor, *Men Versus the State: Herbert Spencer and Late Victorian Individualism* (Clarendon Press, 1992).

LUCA PRONO, PH.D.
UNIVERSITY OF NOTTINGHAM, ENGLAND

supply

ONE OF THE MOST fundamental concepts of economics, supply, in MICROECONOMIC theory, refers to the production (or output) side of markets and is understood to be a function of prices and costs of production. In macroeconomics, aggregate supply refers to the production (or output) side of economies and is, depending on the MACROECONOMIC theory, understood to depend on factors such as household savings, capital stock, labor force, and technology. Since goods and services are—with the exception of the case of household production—supplied by businesses, the "supply side" is often treated as synonymous with the business sector.

Microeconomic analysis. One of the pillars of microeconomic price theory (as developed by Alfred MARSHALL) is the law of supply: all things being equal, the quantity of a good supplied rises as the market price rises, and falls as the price falls. A supply curve of a firm is therefore positively sloped. In standard models of supply (and all other things not being equal), the dependent variable (i.e., the amount supplied) is typically a function of a number of independent variables: the good's own price; the prices of inputs used in its production; the technology of production; taxes and subsidies; and expectations of future prices and costs. If PRICE changes, the quantity supplied will change along the supply curve; if, however, one of the other determinants changes, the supply curve shifts.

The shape of the supply curve, or the price-elasticity of supply (ε_s), reflects TIME in the production process. Over the very short time, output cannot change, the supply curve is vertical, and supply is perfectly price-inelastic: $\varepsilon_s = 0$. In the short run, over which producers can increase variable inputs such as materials and LABOR, supply is price-inelastic: $\varepsilon_s < 1$, and in the long run, over which producers can increase plant and equipment, supply is price-elastic: $\varepsilon_s > 1$. In the long run, firms can enter and exit a market, all of these firms facing the same costs. As a result, the long-run market supply curve will be more elastic than in the short run, and ultimately will be horizontal at the minimum of average total cost. This means that, when DEMAND for a good increases, the long-run result will be an increase in the number of firms and in the total quantity supplied rather than an increase in price. Empirical findings confirm that many supply curves are flat—showing great elasticity—over considerable ranges of output.

In the long run, firms earn zero profit, so price equals the minimum of average total cost. This defines the condition for market EQUILIBRIUM (Case a). If demand increases, market equilibrium shifts from point A to point B, which leads both to a higher price and a larger quantity produced (Case b). In this short-run

equilibrium, price now exceeds average total cost, and firms make a profit. Over time, this profit encourages market entry, and the short-run supply curve shifts to the right, causing price to fall back to the level where it equals average total cost and profits are zero (Case c). Thus, the market reaches a new long-run equilibrium (point C), at a higher level of total output (Q_3).

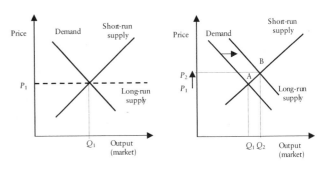

Case (a): Initial condition (very short run)   Case (b): Short-run response

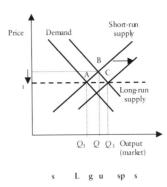

Macroeconomic analysis. Aggregate supply relates the economy's price level, measured by the GROSS DOMESTIC PRODUCT (GDP) price deflator, and aggregate domestic production, measured by real GDP. The aggregate supply relation is generally separated into long-run aggregate supply, in which all prices and wages are flexible and all markets are in equilibrium, and short-run aggregate supply, in which some prices and wages are not flexible and some markets are not in equilibrium. Different from individual or industry supply curves, the aggregate supply curve shows the amount that will be supplied by all firms in the economy at every price level.

In the past decades, there has been considerable dispute between economists in the classical tradition and Keynesians about what determines the level of aggregate supply and about the exact shape of the aggregate supply curve. Keynesians argue that the level of aggregate demand determines supply, while classical economists propose that aggregate supply is determined by supply-side factors.

Classical economists, supply-siders and monetarists hold that the shape of the curve differs between the short run and the long run. Short-run aggregate supply (SRAS) is the total real production of final goods and services available at a range of price levels, during a period of time in which some prices, especially wages, are rigid, inflexible, or otherwise in the process of adjusting. The SRAS curve therefore has a positive slope, reflecting the direct relation between the price level and aggregate real production. A higher price level is related to more real production and a lower price level is related to less real production. The general reason is similar to that of market supply curves: the opportunity cost of production.

Three specific reasons have been proposed:

1. A lower price level causes misperceptions about relative prices, and these misperceptions induce suppliers to respond to the lower price level by decreasing the quantity of goods and services supplied

2. Because wages do not adjust immediately to the price level, a lower price level makes employment and production less profitable, which induces firms to reduce the quantity of goods and services supplied

3. Because not all prices adjust instantly to changing conditions, an unexpected fall in the price level leaves some firms with higher-than-desired prices, and these depress sales and induce firms to reduce the quantity of goods and services supplied.

Overall, these explanations share the concept that output deviates from its natural rate when the price level deviates from the level that people expected.

Long-run aggregate supply (LRAS) is the total real production of final goods and services available at a range of price levels, during a period of time in which all prices, especially wages, are flexible, and have achieved their equilibrium levels. In the long run, an economy's supply of goods and services depends on its supplies of capital and labor and on the available production technology. The LRAS curve is therefore vertical, reflecting the classical view that the quantity of output (a real variable) does not depend on the level of prices (a nominal variable), or that money is neutral. In the classical view, the aggregate market automatically adjusts from short-run equilibrium, in which some prices are rigid, to long-run equilibrium. Self-correction results through shifts of the short-run aggregate supply curve caused by changes in wages and other resource prices.

Keynesians, on the other hand, do not distinguish between the short run and the long run. John Maynard KEYNES, in fact, criticized classical economics because of its alleged limitation to explaining only the long-run effects of policies. In the Keynesian model, the aggregate supply curve contains two or three segments. In the strict sense, it consists of two segments, a vertical classical range and a horizontal Keynesian range, meeting at a right angle and forming a reverse L-shape. At low levels of output, with excess capacity, firms are expected to be able to increase output without requiring price increases. An alternative version replaces the right angle intersection with a gradual transition between the two segments that is positively sloped (i.e., between points A and B in the Keynesian model below) and usually termed the intermediate range. At intermediate levels of output, firms find that to produce more output they must hire new workers, pay current workers overtime, increase wages, and use older and less efficient machinery. Consequently, they will increase output only if price increases to cover higher costs per unit. At some very high level of output, firms can no longer increase output because they have reached the physical limit of their capacity. At this point, the aggregate supply curve becomes vertical (as classical economists had predicted, though for quite different reasons).

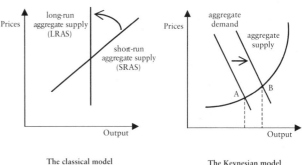

The classical model   The Keynesian model

Economic policy. The classical school believed that supply creates its own demand, a claim known as SAY'S LAW. The rationale behind it is that production of a billion dollars of output creates exactly a billion dollars of income payments that end up, in the shorter or longer run, financing a billion dollars of spending. This causes aggregate demand automatically to match aggregate supply. An increase in saving, in income not spent, causes aggregate demand to fall short of aggregate supply. But it also increases supply in the market for investment funds, which lowers the interest rate, such that ultimately extra investment offsets deficient aggregate demand. The empirical validation of Say's Law is questionable, since many economists do not regard its formulation as precise enough to allow for satisfactory testing. Its policy implication is that of free markets without government intervention.

Keynes neither believed in Say's Law nor in the automatic supply-side adjustment of markets. He objected that a fall in the interest rate causes people to increase the amount of cash they wish to hold so that not all of an increase in saving will prompt higher investment. Since it is quite possible that aggregate demand falls short of aggregate supply and any supply-side adjustment, through increased investment, will not suffice to achieve equilibrium again, monetary or fiscal policy should boost aggregate demand. In Keynes' model, the three segments of the aggregate supply curve give rise to three different reactions to fiscal policy such as government spending. When the curve is flat, the economy reacts primarily by increasing output; in the intermediary range, both output and prices increase; and when the curve is vertical, only price increases follow expansionary fiscal policy. The lesson Keynes wanted to draw is clear: Expansionary policy, such as counter-cyclical government spending, is appropriate when the economy is in a recession, but is inappropriate in a boom.

Supply-side economics reaffirmed confidence in Say's Law. This body of thought emphasizes that the principal determinant of the rate of growth of national output in both the short and long run is the allocation and efficient use of labor and capital in an economy. Consequently, it espouses economic policy measures that attempt to stimulate growth through providing incentives to work, save, and invest. In the UNITED STATES, supply-side economics emerged in the 1970s as an alternative to Keynesian demand-management policies and reached its maximum impact in the 1980s, during the presidency of Ronald REAGAN (Reaganomics). By emphasizing relative price changes rather than income changes, fiscal policy is again seen as the pivot for achieving economic growth. At the core of supply-side economics lies the conviction that by lowering the marginal tax rate, government can provide consumers with incentives to substitute work for leisure, since the substitution effect would dominate the income effect.

Contrary to Keynes' assumption that tax reductions would boost aggregate demand and fan inflation, the theory expects these incentives to shift the aggregate supply curve. Supply-side economists assume that marginal tax rates enter directly into the costs of capital and thus influence investment decisions. Excessive rates (and government regulation) not only crowd out investment, they also lead to decreasing fiscal revenue. This expectation relies on the LAFFER CURVE model, which predicts that the relationship between the marginal tax rate and fiscal revenue has the shape of an inverted U: Increasing the rate produces more revenue only up to a certain optimal threshold beyond which any further increase will actually decrease revenue, as avoidance and evasion will start to predominate. The best policy is therefore to keep taxes at rates that are low enough for households to work and save more and

for businesses to invest more. Fiscal revenue should thus be created from an expanding output at lower rates rather than from a contracting output at higher rates. This was not a new idea. Already Calvin COOLIDGE expressed it in 1924: "I am convinced that the larger incomes of the country would actually yield more revenue to the government if the basis of taxation were scientifically revised downward."

Today, supply-side economists typically argue for the elimination of provisions in the tax system that distort economic choice, such as the double taxation of investment income, the estate tax, and the "marriage penalty." They often also advocate flat tax rates set at or below the optimal rate that would maximize fiscal revenue, as a more efficient system than any based on progressive taxation. It would provide growth incentives and, through lower collection and control costs, achieve higher tax revenue. More generally, supply-side economists also espouse PRIVATIZATION and propose the elimination of regulation impeding investment, production, and trade so as to facilitate expansion of output.

What has collectively been called the new classical school of economics places the supply side in the center of their analysis, as it views BUSINESS CYCLES as largely caused by real, supply-side shocks to the economy. To a first approximation, the resulting variations in aggregate variables can be viewed as an efficient response to these shocks. According to this view, the observed relationship between money and the business cycle reflects causation going from real activity to monetary conditions, and not the other way around. These views are encapsulated in the so-called real business cycle theory, which is the most recent variant of supply-side economics. This body of thought emphasizes that real (as opposed to nominal) changes such as technology shocks, new products, new government regulations on environmental standards, changes in consumer preferences, natural resource discoveries, tax rate changes and other supply-side factors are primarily responsible for fluctuations in economic activity. Demand-side factors play a secondary and very transitory role in affecting business cycles.

BIBLIOGRAPHY. John M. Keynes, *The General Theory of Employment, Interest and Money* (1936, Prometheus Books, 1997); Lawrence R. Klein, *The Economics of Supply and Demand* (Blackwell Publishers, 1983); Lawrence B. Lindsey, *The Growth Experiment* (Basic Books, 1990); N. Gregory Mankiw, *Principles of Economics* (South-Western, 2001); Alfred Marshall, *Principles of Economics* (1890, Prometheus Books, 1997); Walter Nicholson, *Microeconomic Theory* (South-Western, 2002); Thomas Sowell, *Say's Law: An Historical Analysis* (Princeton University Press, 1972).

WOLFGANG GRASSL
HILLSDALE COLLEGE

surplus

A MARKET SITUATION where at a given price, the amount producers (i.e., firms) are willing to supply exceeds the amount consumers (i.e., individuals and households) are willing to DEMAND is termed a surplus. However, in a particular market for some good or service, there is only a surplus, or excess supply, when the current price is above the EQUILIBRIUM (or market-clearing) price.

Market forces. The law of demand states that as the price of a good or service increases (decreases), the quantity demanded of that good decreases (increases), holding all other factors constant. On the other hand, the law of supply states that as the price of a good or service increases (decreases), the quantity supplied of that good increases (decreases), holding all other factors constant. Therefore, at the market-clearing price, the quantity supplied equals the quantity demanded. That is, the market will clear.

When the price of the particular good is above the equilibrium price, producers will supply more while consumers will demand less. This phenomenon creates a surplus. However, due to market forces, the surplus will not last indefinitely. An adjustment process will take place. While the adjustment process may be slow or sticky, the market will eventually adjust to eliminate the surplus, unless there is some other force restricting the adjustment process. If there is no restriction on the adjustment process, the surplus will put pressure on the market to lower the price. As the price falls, the quantity supplied decreases and the quantity demanded increases, thus eliminating the excess supply or surplus. Price will continue to fall until it reaches the equilibrium price. If for some reason the price is below the market-clearing price, then there will be a shortage (the opposite of a surplus). When there is a shortage (or excess demand), consumers demand more than what producers are willing to supply at the given price. As a result of the shortage, there is an upward pressure on price to rise to the market-clearing price. At this market-clearing price, there is no market force pushing the price to deviate from this equilibrium and there is no shortage or surplus.

However, there is often market failure as a result of some intervention restricting the adjustment process. This intervention causes an undesirable market outcome such as a shortage or surplus. For example, the government puts PRICE restrictions in place when it believes that the market price is too high or too low. The government can impose such price restrictions as price ceilings and price floors, which cause shortages and surpluses, respectively. Effective price floors, the minimum legal price, creates a surplus and forces the market to adjust in different ways besides price. Two such examples of price floors are minimum wages and agricultural price supports.

Labor markets. The minimum wage in the UNITED STATES is a frequent topic of debate, especially among economists and policymakers. Dating back to 1938, the U.S. Congress passed the Fair Labor Standards Act to ensure workers would receive an adequate standard of living. In effect, they forced a wage restriction (i.e., minimum wage), where the government sets a minimum legal wage for what employers can pay their workers, regardless of whether employees are willing to work for less. While states are allowed to further raise the minimum wage in their respective state, and some have done so, they cannot lower the wage below the national minimum wage rate. Those who advocate policy to raise the minimum wage at the national or state level do so as a way to raise the income of the poor. Many economists oppose hikes in the minimum wage and argue that it is not a way to help the working poor or improve their standard of living. Economists and others that oppose minimum wage claim that unemployment will result from this type of policy. In addition, they argue that teenagers and low-skilled workers will be adversely affected, which is the exact group for whom advocates argue minimum wage supports.

In order to examine the effects of minimum wage, we must consider the market for labor. In the LABOR market, the price of labor is the wage rate. Firms demand labor (i.e., workers) while individuals supply the labor. As the wage rate increase (decreases), the demand for labor decreases (increases) and the supply of labor increases (decreases), holding all other factors constant. When there is no government intervention, the wage rate will adjust until the supply of labor equals the demand for labor (i.e., equilibrium in the labor market). If minimum wage is set below the equilibrium wage rate, then the particular labor market will be unaffected by the wage restriction. This is the case for many workers with substantial experience or training that are making wages well above the minimum wage. However, if the minimum wage is set above the equilibrium wage rate for a particular labor market, then the supply of labor exceeds the demand for labor. This results in a surplus of labor or unemployment.

Unemployment from minimum wage has its greatest impact on the labor market for teenagers and low-skilled workers. The wages for teenagers are usually the lowest since they lack experience and training. As a result, increases in the minimum wage will cause additional teenagers to look for jobs (at the higher wage) than might otherwise. A number of studies have shown that teenagers will drop out of school and take a job due to the hike in minimum wage. Many of these teenagers who drop out due to the increase in the minimum wage end up replacing the teenagers who had dropped out of school earlier. Consequently, some of those teenagers are unemployed, and thus, the argument goes, the minimum wage law tends to hurt the workers that it was designed to help in the first place. Of course, those workers who had jobs and managed to keep them have benefited from the increase in the minimum wage since it raised their income and standard of living.

Besides minimum wage, wage subsidies could be used to help those in need. Wage subsidies are designed to raise the standard of living by offering an earned income tax credit. This earned income tax credit is a government program that supplements the incomes of low-wage workers. While wage subsidies may be more effective than minimum wage, they have problems as well. For example, wage subsidies cost the government money. As a result, the government may raise taxes to support this program. Other programs used to eliminate this surplus of labor or unemployment provide subsidies to the particular firms that hire teenagers or low-skilled workers, or to programs that train workers to become more productive.

Agricultural markets. Agricultural price supports are another example of government intervention that results in a surplus. Farmers supply a variety of agricultural products, and since consumers have some demand for these agricultural products, a market is created. However, farmers often portray that the price of their products are too low and not enough to cover their production costs. Since farmers have substantial political power and influence, they advocate to policymak-

A surplus of shipped goods that exceeds demand should, in an unrestricted market, lower the price of such goods.

ers the need for price supports. That is, a minimum price level for their agricultural products. In many cases, the government will impose a price restriction that limits the price from falling below some specified level (i.e., price floor).

These price supports result in a surplus of agricultural products because farmers will produce more as a result of the higher price while households will demand less. Often, the government will purchase or store the surplus even though the cost to support such a program is enormous. In an effort to minimize the additional problems from the price supports, the U.S. government has developed a variety of programs to eliminate the surplus. One such program is to impose production limits or QUOTAS on farmers. However, quotas in the agricultural sector create more problems. Farmers are forced to produce their quota, which further limits their ability to rotate crops. This inability to rotate crops has an adverse affect on the soil, and thus, ultimately affects agricultural production. These problems associated with surpluses are known to policymakers, but due to the intense political pressure brought on by farmers, price restrictions on agricultural products continue to be imposed.

While government interventions in the form of price restrictions can be inefficient and result in undesirable market outcomes, this is not to say that governments should avoid any kind of policy that minimizes the changes in prices or wages. However, policymakers should be cautioned in conducting policy in response to these price changes (or changes in wages). More often than not, these changes in price (or wages) are a direct result of the market adjusting to supply and demand factors. Therefore, policy to restrict price within the market may be ineffective, if not harmful. In particular, binding price floors such as minimum wages and agricultural price supports lead to surpluses. Some of the programs used to eliminate these surpluses are costly. Alternative policies must take into account the laws of supply and demand and not hinder the market forces at work. If the government can develop such policies, they will be more effective in reaching the desired effect than price restrictions.

BIBLIOGRAPHY. Jonathon Grossman, "Fair Labor Standards Act of 1938: Maximum Struggle for a Minimum Wage," *Monthly Labor Review* (v.101, 1978); Thomas Rustici, "A Public Choice View of the Minimum Wage," *Cato Journal* (v.5, 1985); Joseph Stiglitz, *Principles of Microeconomics* (W.W. Norton, 1997); N. Gregory Mankiw, *Principles of Microeconomics* (Dryden Press, 1998); Gary Becker and Guity Becker, *The Economics of Life* (McGraw-Hill, 1997).

MARK A. THOMPSON, PH.D.
STEPHEN F. AUSTIN STATE UNIVERSITY

sustainable development

THE TERM, SUSTAINABLE development, was first mentioned in the World Conservation Strategy (1980), but the most famous definition stems from the report of the World Commission for Environment and Development, *Our Common Future* (1987) referring to development that "meets the needs of the present without compromising the ability of future generations to meet their own needs."

This definition can be considered as probably the best since it emphasizes all encompassing notions of the term or concept, the long-term perspective necessarily linked to it, as well as the aspect of inter-generational equity. It is further commonly understood that sustainable development aims to treat economic, social, and environmental concerns equally, while traditionally and still today, economic policies prevail without taking environmental and social aspects sufficiently into account.

Other important aspects of sustainable development include technological developments, respect for human rights, peace endeavors or transparent and democratic decision-making processes. Finally, a sustainable development policy approach relates to an integrated and holistic approach, considering all policy fields and all stakeholders (also called the multi-stakeholder approach) with a view to give equal weight to all policies and stakeholders involved.

History and content. The World Conservation Strategy highlights three goals of sustainable development: the conservation of important ecological processes and ecological systems, as well as the conservation of biodiversity, and the necessity to use species and ecosystems in a sustainable way. Ecological economics has been declared "the science and management of sustainability." Theories, models and principles of sustainable development including the precautionary principle, the polluter-pays principle, and factor four have been constantly developed further.

In 1992, for the first time, a world summit dealt with sustainable development issues, at the United Nations Conference for Environment and Development (UNCED) in Rio de Janeiro, Brazil. Three documents were adopted by more than 178 governments: *Agenda 21*, the *Rio Declaration on Environment and Development*, and the *Statement of Principles for Sustainable Management of Forests*.

Agenda 21 represents a comprehensive action plan for sustainable development to be adopted globally, nationally, and locally by organizations of the United Nations system, governments, and major groups. The 40 chapters of *Agenda 21* reflect an all-encompassing approach organized in four main areas, the social and economic dimensions, the conservation and management of resources for development, strengthening the role of major groups, and means of implementation. Two other important documents were agreed to in Rio, the *United Nations Framework Convention on Climate Change* and the *Biodiversity Convention* aimed at responding to increasing global environmental threats.

Ten years later, in 2002, the World Summit on Sustainable Development in Johannesburg, South Africa, took stock of the achieved goals established in *Agenda 21* and concluded that the process of implementation was slower than expected. Nevertheless, governments strongly reaffirmed their commitment to the full implementation of *Agenda 21* and "confirmed that a significant progress has been made toward a global consensus and partnership among all people of our planet." The Johannesburg Declaration on Sustainable Development further states:

> Poverty eradication, changing consumption and production patterns, and protecting and managing the natural resource base for economic and social development are overarching objectives of, and essential requirements for sustainable development. . . . The ever-increasing gap between the developed and developing worlds pose a major threat to global prosperity, security and instability. The global environment continues to suffer. . . . globalization has added a new dimension to these challenges. The rapid integration of markets, mobility of capital and significant increases in investment flows around the world have opened new challenges and opportunities for sustainable development. But the benefits and the costs of globalization are unevenly distributed, with developing countries facing special difficulties in meeting this challenge.

A Johannesburg Action Plan has been launched mainly focusing on the reduction of "biodiversity loss by 2004, to restore fisheries to their maximum sustainable yields by 2015, to establish a representative network of marine protected areas by 2012, and to improve developing countries' access to environmentally sound alternatives to ozone-depleting chemicals by 2010."

Main unsustainable trends and challenges. Probably one of the most unsustainable trends represents the current production and consumption patterns of capitalistic, industrialized countries. Just to highlight the urgency of the problem: If Western production and consumption patterns were applied to the whole world, we would need two or three planets earth. In other words, the carrying capacity of the earth has limits and therefore has to be taken into account in welfare models and in global policy making. Another key factor for unsustainable development can be seen in the lack of internalization of external cost. The fact that ecological and social externalities are not reflected accordingly, neither at macro-economic nor at microeconomic level, entails wrong market signals. The GDP as an indicator of wealth and welfare appears to show misleading results unless ecological and social issues are taken into account. Relevant studies show a distortion of GDP of up to 8 percent. Today capitalist economies are more conscious of negative environmental and social externalities, partly because demographic and economic growth and technology have made them worse. Tackling externalities is an essential function of government, ignored in communist countries and an essential means in achieving sustainable development.

A third major challenge to be mentioned consists in the proper management of urban growth in developing countries. Global unsustainable trends include climate change, biodiversity loss, soil degradation, availability of clean drinking water and diminishing fish and other natural resources, or also unstable international financial markets, growing social riots and war; sector-specific unsustainable trends can be observed in energy, transport, health, agricultural and urban or land use policies, forest management, chemical use, and food safety.

In a wider sense it can be argued that market access restrictions, in particular for disadvantaged partners could be considered as hindering factors to sustainable development. This is why the success of the negotiations in the WORLD TRADE ORGANIZATION (WTO) would represent a crucial contribution to sustainable development. It has been further observed that development, and thus sustainable development, strongly depends on certain framework conditions such as a healthy macroeconomic environment, democracy, the establishment of the rule of law, and the respect of human rights. It is also argued that a certain philosophical culture, such as proposed by Sir Karl Popper, would be advantageous for fostering development and thus sustainable development.

Policy responses. Whereas up to 10 years ago sustainable development was mainly linked to the protection of the environment, and the main global threats seemed to be environmental ones, today a more holistic approach is applied. In 1992, the United Nations established the Commission on Sustainable Development to ensure effective follow-up of UNCED and thus to deepen the process towards sustainable development. UN sub-bodies as well as the European Commission have been increasingly stressing the need for sustainable development. As a commitment to the process, sustainability strategies were elaborated at regional, national and local level (Local Agenda). Some anchored the principles of sustainable development in their treaties (EUROPEAN UNION) or national constitutions (SWITZERLAND).

In order to achieve sustainable development in the business sector, the World Business Council for Development has been launched, including more than 130 members.

BIBLIOGRAPHY. World Conservation Strategy, "Living Resource Conservation for Sustainable Development," (1980); World Commission on Environment and Development, *Our Common Future* (Oxford University Press, 1987); Robert Constanza, *The Science and Management of Sustainability* (Columbia University Press, 1992); United Nations, "The Johannesburg Declaration on Sustainable Development 2002," World Summit on Sustainable Development (Document A/CONF.199/L.6/Rev.2, 2002); Joseph E. Stiglitz, *Globalization and its Discontents* (W.W. Norton, 2002).

URSULA A. VAVRIK, PH.D.
UNIVERSITY OF ECONOMICS, VIENNA, AUSTRIA

Sweden

THROUGH ITS MIX of industrial and agricultural output, Sweden continues to demonstrate an ongoing trend of manufacturing and farming produce superiority, evident at a glance in its economic statistics. It continues to be one of the world's wealthiest countries. Transportation, modern internal and external communications, and world trade also contribute heavily to the country's economic staying power. The nation's timber and hydropower industries reach worldwide, as does its production of iron, copper, zinc, lead, and pyrite. Mines, such as those located in Kiruna and Gallivare, deliver enough abundance to make Sweden one of the globe's leading ore exporters.

Although agriculture remains a constant source of national income (roughly 3 percent throughout the 1990s), the manufacturing and engineering sectors have been the main focal points of the economic landscape, both steadily growing since the advent of WORLD WAR II. Today, they contribute some 20 percent of income.

From small but efficient mechanized farms comes a diverse export of dairy products, grain, beets, and potatoes, as well as livestock. Simultaneously, manufacturing plants generate a wide range of universal products. Iron and steel, precision equipment, processed foodstuff, and motor vehicles dominate. Natural commodities include an array of forest products, refined petroleum, and chemicals.

One-third of Sweden's GROSS NATIONAL PRODUCT (GNP)—chiefly, timber, machinery, chemicals, iron, and steel—is exported to other parts of the sphere. Foreign trade is continuous with a number of countries in Europe and the Americas. DENMARK, FINLAND, FRANCE,

GERMANY, NORWAY, the UNITED KINGDOM, and the UNITED STATES follow a principal-trade partnership with Sweden.

As Sweden has pursued a political doctrine of neutrality for the second half of the 20th century, output of its GNP has been mostly constant and enduring in the face of downswings in the world economy and other upheavals affecting the marketplace, internally and externally. Development faltered in the latter half of the 1970s, due to rising costs of petroleum and oil, and again in the early 1980s because of volatile changes in government. Over a period of several years, the krona currency suffered devaluation, as much as 16 percent. Before a return to normalcy, a recession struck the country in 1990, resulting in an industry downturn, job loss, and eroding competition that caused a 6 percent decline in the GNP. But, since that time, reform has boosted manufacturing and, as a result, exports have grown significantly.

The Swedish government has taken a vital role in re-establishing the success of its economy and reinvigorating its high standard of living. More than 90 percent of industry is privately owned, and conservative business tactics have created a unique mixture of capitalism and social welfare benefits. With a population of 8.8 million (2002), Sweden is a member of the EUROPEAN UNION (EU) with economic parity to its western European partners, but waived participation in the euro currency as of early 2003.

BIBLIOGRAPHY. *CIA World Factbook* (2003); Ministry of Finance, *Statistics: Swedish Trade Council* (2002); www.mapzones.com; John Wright, ed., *The New York Times 2003 Almanac* (St. Martin's Press, 2003).

JOSEPH GERINGER
SYED B. HUSSAIN, PH.D.
UNIVERSITY OF WISCONSIN, OSHKOSH

Switzerland

THE SWISS ECONOMY is one of the most prosperous and aggressive economies on the globe, ranking among the top 20 states in the world family of nations. Its per capita purchasing power parity ($31,700 in 2002) is among the highest and matched by its high wage scale, the envy of many in the working world. A highly successful market-based economy founded on international trade and banking, its standard of living, worker productivity, quality of education, and health care serve as models for other nations. Inflation is low and unemployment exists at moderate and low levels. Switzerland remains a safe haven for investors, because it has maintained a degree of bank secrecy and has kept up the Swiss franc's long-term external value.

Switzerland has liberal trade and investment policies and a conservative fiscal policy. Its legal system is judiciously developed, commercial law is exact, and the Swiss franc represents one of the soundest currencies in world finance. Switzerland has brought its economic practices largely into conformity with the EUROPEAN UNION (EU) to enhance international competitiveness. Although the Swiss have not pursued full EU membership in the early 2000s, they have signed agreements to further liberalize trade ties.

Switzerland had slow or even no-growth periods in the 1990s, and suffered higher levels of unemployment. However, between February 1997 and January 2002, unemployment dropped from 5.7 percent to 1.6 percent. At the time, a commercial counselor representing Switzerland in the U.S. Department of Commerce wrote, "Reaching the level of near full employment constitutes a windfall for the overall spending and consumption. A full-fledged revival in consumer or corporate spending is hence on the horizon. . . . The Swiss economy is approaching growth levels encountered in markets of competitors."

The *Confoederatio Helvetica* describes the economic structure of the country: "About two-thirds of Switzerland is covered with forests, lakes and mountains. Since Switzerland has no mineral resources, it must import, process and resell them as products. Services are the most important part of the economy." While farming is regarded as an important commodity to the overall welfare, it does not satisfy the needs of all the people, thus the country's reliance on imported GOODS.

Those employed in the agricultural industry account for only about 10 percent of the labor force, and are divided between cattle and dairy farming, about the only two agricultural offerings of any importance found within the country's limited farming region. Mineral resources are not plentiful; most raw materials and many food products are imported. Tourism, a significant addition to the economy, helps balance the national trade deficit.

The total economy of Switzerland, then, is divided into three principal sectors: agriculture, industry, and services. The United States is the second-largest importer of Swiss goods, just behind GERMANY, and is the largest foreign investor in Switzerland, and conversely, the primary destination of Swiss foreign investment. Some 200,000 American jobs depend on Swiss trade.

About 40 percent of the population is employed in industry, trade, and handicraft. This includes the machine and metal industry, watch industry, and the textile industry. Chemicals and pharmaceuticals are a strong component of this industry sector. From Basel, Switzerland's industrial city, more than 30,000 chemical and pharmaceutical products are shipped every year for export. Switzerland boasts highly qualified and well-trained workers. In general, Swiss manufacturers follow what they call a niche strategy, concentrating on perfecting a small range of top-quality products instead of a large range of mediocre ones. "As a result, even some small enterprises have been able to corner the world market in their own specialty," explains Switzerland on Sight, a Swiss information resource.

The remainder of the population (about 50 percent) is in the service sector of the economy. Comprising the majority of this sector are banking, insurance, and tourism. Swiss trading companies have demonstrated a marketing savvy throughout the major cities of the world in Europe, the Far East, Africa, and the Middle East.

Switzerland's population of 7.3 million people had a GROSS DOMESTIC PRODUCT (GDP) of $231 billion in 2002.

BIBLIOGRAPHY. *Confoederatio Helvetica*, www.about.ch/economy; Switzerland Economy, www.tn.psg.sk/economy; Switzerland On Sight, www.schweiz-in-sicht.com; U.S. Department of Commerce, "Switzerland Economy Update" (November 3, 2000); *CIA World Factbook: Switzerland* (2002).

JOSEPH GERINGER
SYED B. HUSSAIN, PH.D.
UNIVERSITY OF WISCONSIN, OSHKOSH

Syria

THE ECONOMY OF THE Syrian Arab Republic is based on agriculture (27 percent), industry (23 percent), and services (50 percent). It remains a middle-income developing country with modest rates of growth. The country has been plagued by bouts of severe drought affecting its agricultural productivity, and it has one of the highest unemployment rates in the Arab world (24 percent). Despite some national reforms to correct slow-moving enterprises and non-productive businesses, the national economy drags—hampered by poorly performing public sector firms, low investment levels, and markedly low industrial and agricultural output. To date, the planners in Damascus, its capital, have been unable to fuel the tortoise into a hare.

Adding to its troubles, Syria's population growth soars and its once vast water supply has begun, over the last decade, to become polluted. Private investment is crucial to the modernization of the country—but it is slow in coming.

Structural deficiencies in the economy addressed by the government have focused on its lack of a modern financial sector. To its credit, the government legalized private banking in late 2001 and there is now hope that commercial financial institutions may soon emerge.

Syria's import and export trade is not without merit, however. The bulk of imports consists of raw materials essential for industry, agriculture, equipment, and machinery from trade partners ITALY, GERMANY, FRANCE, Lebanon, CHINA, South KOREA, TURKEY, and the UNITED STATES. Major exports are crude oil, refined products, raw cotton, textiles, fruit and grains, shipped to GERMANY, Italy, France, Turkey, and throughout SAUDI ARABIA.

Agriculturally, Syria has 72,000 square miles of arable soil that produces wheat, barley, cotton, olives, chickpeas, and sugar beets. Most farms are privately owned and, during periods of rainfall, reap ample harvests. The marketing and shipping of all produce are both controlled by the government.

Oil—a light-grade, low-sulphur variety—has been a main fuel for the country for the last quarter century. Before the 1980s, the country manufactured a heavy-grade blend, but the discovery of light-grade has since resulted in larger exportation. According to 2002 figures, about 530,000 barrels are produced daily.

But, this production is rather modest. Damascus continues to reform and work out problems suffered by its country's economy. It realizes that its outmoded technological base, shaky infrastructure, and weak educational system make it vulnerable for future economic setbacks. Syria's GROSS DOMESTIC PRODUCT (GDP) in 2001 was $54.2 billion, with a per capita purchasing power parity of $3,200.

BIBLIOGRAPHY. Syrian economic website, www.made-in-syria.com; *CIA World Factbook: Syria* (2002); Volker Perthes, *The Political Economy of Syria Under Asad* (Tauris & Co., 1998).

JOSEPH GERINGER
SYED B. HUSSAIN, PH.D.
UNIVERSITY OF WISCONSIN, OSHKOSH

T

Taft, William Howard (1857–1930)

THE 27TH PRESIDENT of the UNITED STATES and one of three early 20th-century progressive presidents, William Howard Taft was born into a well-known Ohio family. He graduated from Yale Law School, served as a state judge, solicitor general and a federal circuit judge. In 1900, President William McKINLEY appointed Taft chairman of the Philippine Commission with the responsibility of developing a civil government for the territory acquired in the SPANISH-AMERICAN WAR. Subsequently, Taft took on the difficult task of managing the colony as the Philippines' first governor general.

In 1904, President Theodore ROOSEVELT appointed Taft secretary of war, a position he held until the Republican Party nominated him for president in 1908, his first bid for elective office. Taft was Roosevelt's chosen successor once the president decided not to seek a third term. Roosevelt felt that as a close associate, Taft would continue his own eight-year reform course. Taft's personality, however, was almost the opposite of Roosevelt's; he disliked politics, preferring to work behind the scenes. Taft's reputation in Washington, D.C., was as an effective, if not hard-working, manager. He enjoyed golf, bridge, naps, and well-prepared meals. The heaviest president, Taft weighted more than 300 pounds. Although his own ambition lay in the U.S. Supreme Court, his wife wanted him to be president. Eventually Taft realized his ambition, becoming the only former president to serve on the court, sitting as chief justice from 1921 until his death in 1930.

The Taft administration (1909–13) was torn by two factions within the Republican Party, the conservatives who relied on business for support and policy direction and former president Roosevelt's reform faction, or progressives who wanted business regulation and greater government involvement in society. Despite Roosevelt's influence, once in office Taft most often sided with the conservatives and earned the progressives' criticism for deserting Roosevelt's policies.

TARIFFS were a central issue dividing the Republicans. Conservatives wanted high tariffs to protect American manufacturers and assure necessary funds for the federal government. Reformers wanted lower tariffs to ease heavy taxation on consumption and pushed for alternative taxes. In 1909, with Taft's support, Congress passed the Payne-Aldrich Act which raised tariffs on most imports while lowering tariffs on insignificant items. With this signal of Taft's support for the conservatives, progressives attacked the act as a product of big-business special interests. Progressives started to talk about bringing back Roosevelt as president. Also in 1909, progressives persuaded Congress to pass the 16th Amendment to the Constitution, authorizing an income tax. This amendment became law in 1913, at the end of the Taft administration.

Another issue that divided conservatives and progressives was conservation. Taft's secretary of the interior proposed selling a million acres of public land. Progressives attacked the sale, pointing out that a previous sale in Alaska benefited a coal syndicate that included J.P. MORGAN. Progressives again attacked the Taft administration, calling his policies a betrayal of Roosevelt.

In 1910, Taft suffered an embarrassing defeat in off-year elections as Democrats captured control of both houses of Congress. He worked with the new Congress to enact progressive legislation including the Mann-Elkins Act that allowed the Interstate Commerce Commission (ICC) to set rates for railroads and placed telephone and telegraph companies under the ICC. Taft crafted a compromise between conservatives and progressive over the bill, but when he tried to enforce party loyalty among progressive Republicans, the progressives strengthened their anti-Taft movement.

In 1912, the Republicans re-nominated Taft for a second term with the progressive wing of the party deserting to support former President Roosevelt, the nominee of the Progressive Party. The Democratic nominee for president, Woodrow WILSON, defeated both Taft and Roosevelt.

BIBLIOGRAPHY. David H. Burton, *The Learned Presidency: Theodore Roosevelt, William Howard Taft, Woodrow Wilson* (Fairleigh Dickinson University Press, 1988); Paolo E. Coletta, *The Presidency of William Howard Taft* (University Press of Kansas,1973); Henry F. Pringle, *The Life and Times of William Howard Taft* (Easton Press, 1986); www.american-president.org.

CARY W. BLANKENSHIP, PH.D.
TENNESSEE STATE UNIVERSITY

Taiwan

THE LARGEST ISLAND off the Chinese coast, Taiwan, in prehistoric times was connected with the mainland. It became an island as a result of geological movements, and is flanked by the Pacific Ocean on its east and the Taiwan Strait on the west. The average width of the Strait between the island and CHINA's Fujian Province on the mainland is about 110 miles. Taiwan is some 250 miles long and has a width ranging from 9.5 to 90 miles, with a total area of 13,875 square miles. About two-thirds of the island is mountainous while the rest is flat. Next to Taiwan are smaller islands, including the Penghu Islands (Pescadores). The population on Taiwan is over 22 million (2000) with about 97 percent Han Chinese and the rest aboriginal.

Historical records of Taiwan can be found in Chinese history books written around 200 B.C.E. In 230 C.E., Sun Quan, a Chinese general, sent 10,000 troops to Taiwan. From then on, people from the mainland migrated to the island. In the southern Song dynasty (1127–1279), China's emperor established an administrative post in the Penghu Islands.

In 1624 and 1626, Holland and Spain invaded Taiwan, and the Dutch soon drove the Spaniards away. In 1661, Zheng Chenggong (known as Koxinga in the West), a Chinese general, defeated the Dutch troops and recovered Chinese sovereignty over Taiwan. In 1887, Taiwan was upgraded from a prefecture in Fujian Province to a province. In 1895, after having militarily defeated China and Korea in war, Japan forced China to sign away Taiwan, the Penghu Islands and occupied-Korea as Japanese colonies. When Japan was defeated at the end of WORLD WAR II, it returned Taiwan and the Penghu Islands to China and gave Korea independence according to the Cairo Declaration of 1943 and Potsdam Proclamation of 1945. The government of the Republic of China sent General Chen Yi to Taiwan as the chief officer.

In the Chinese Civil War between 1946–49, the forces led by the Chinese Communist Party (CCP) defeated the government forces led by Chiang Kai-shek. Chiang and his followers retreated from the mainland to Taiwan. In October 1949, the CCP declared the founding of the People's Republic of China (PRC). But the UNITED STATES and some of its allies continued to regard Chiang's Guomindang (GMD) government on Taiwan as the legitimate Chinese government. The outbreak of the Korean War in 1950 forced the CCP to shelf its plan to attack Taiwan. In 1954, the United States signed a Mutual Defense Treaty with Chiang's regime. The treaty allowed stationing of American troops on the island and placed Taiwan under American military protection.

On October 25, 1971, the United Nations General Assembly approved, with an absolute majority, Resolution 2758. The resolution "decides to restore all its rights to the People's Republic of China and to recognize the representatives of its government as the only legitimate representatives of China to the United Nations, and to expel forthwith the representatives of Chiang Kai-shek from . . . the United Nations."

In 1972, President Richard NIXON visited China. In the Shanghai Communiqué that resulted from the visit, the United States said that it did not challenge the position that "there is but one China and that Taiwan is a part of China." In 1979, the United States repealed the Mutual Defense Treaty, withdrew its troops, ended its official relations with Taiwan, and established diplomatic relations with the PRC on the basis that the government in Beijing was the sole legal government of China. By 2002, more than 160 countries had established official relations with Beijing on the basis that there is only one China, that the government of the PRC is the sole legal government, and that Taiwan is a part of China.

The GMD government in Taiwan carried out land reform between 1949–53. The reform reduced tenant rents, set a legal limit on the amount of land each farmer could own, required all owners to sell to the government what was beyond the limit, and sold government land to farmers with little land. With the help of American economic aid, the government had restored Taiwan's economy by mid-1950s. At the end of the decade, it began to promote export-oriented industries, while the United States and Japan helped by importing from Taiwan labor-intensive products such as clothing and plastic articles. Between 1963–72, Taiwan's GROSS DOMESTIC PRODUCT (GDP) grew at an average annual rate of 10.9 percent, making it known as one of the Four Dragons, four fast- growing economies, in Asia. In 2001, its GDP was about $273 billion. Since the late 1980s, Taiwan businesses have invested billions of U.S. dollars on the Chinese mainland.

Politically, between 1949–87, the government ruled in Taiwan with martial laws that prohibited public assembly, outlawed political criticism, and used military courts to punish actions deemed dangerous to public order. In 1987, the government started to allow its people to visit their families on the mainland. Since 1989, Taiwan has witnessed multiparty elections. The GMD is now one of the political parties competing for power.

The Chinese government has proposed a "one country, two systems" formula for unification of Taiwan with the mainland. But the government on Taiwan, which still uses the official name of the Republic of China in its current constitution, has not given it positive reaction. Family visits, tourists, and business investments connect Taiwan with the mainland.

BIBLIOGRAPHY. Hungdah Chiu, ed., *China and the Question of Taiwan: Documents and Analysis* (Praeger, 1973); Linda Chao and Ramon H. Myers, *The First Chinese Democracy: Political Life in the Republic of China on Taiwan* (Johns Hopkins University Press, 1998); Tim D. Harmon, *The Land and the People: The Republic of China* (Beyond Words Publishing, 1992).

SHEHONG CHEN, PH.D.
UNIVERSITY OF MASSACHUSETTS, LOWELL

Target Corporation

GEORGE DAYTON FOUNDED Target in 1902 in Minneapolis, Minnesota, and 100 years later Target runs 1,476 stores in 47 states. Mainly a general retail sales company, Target also manages Mervyn's, Marshall Field's, target.direct, Target Financial Services, Associated Merchandising Corporation, and Dayton's Commercial Interiors, and employs approximately 192,000 people nationwide.

Mervyn's is a "premier, promotional, middle-market, neighborhood department store," with 264 stores in 14 states, according to the company. Acquired by Target in 1978 and employing 28,000 people, Mervyn's number one geographic market is Los Angeles, California, where it has 48 stores.

Marshall Field's is a retail store chain with 32,000 employees and 64 stores in eight states. The company's major market is Chicago, where Marshall Field's has 16 stores.

The most profitable division of Target Corporation is surely Target stores, which generated 82 percent of the corporation's total revenue in 2001 from a diverse retail infrastructure ranging from normal stores to SuperTarget stores. In 2000, Target Corporation launched "target.direct," an e-commerce application that allows consumers to order directly from the Target warehouses. An e-commerce partnering agreement in 2001 with Amazon.com boosted both sales and stock prices significantly, shown partly by a 9.7 percent increase in total revenue between 2000 and 2001. For fiscal 2001, Target Corporation's total revenue was $40 billion, ranking it as the 89th largest company in the world.

BIBLIOGRAPHY. Target Corporate Profile, www.hoovers.com; www.targetcorp.com; *Target Corporation 2001 Annual Report*; "Global 500: World's Largest Companies," *Fortune* (July 2002).

ARTHUR HOLST, PH.D.
WIDENER UNIVERSITY

tariff

A TARIFF IS A TAX that a country imposes on traded goods, usually on imports but sometimes on exports. In past centuries, a tariff was most often set at a nominal fee per unit of weight or volume, such as 10 cents per pound of coffee, and this was called a specific tariff. Today, the typical tariff is an *ad valorem* tariff, calculated as a percentage of the declared value of the good. This protects government revenues if prices rise, since tariff revenues also rise.

Revenue from import tariffs was long a crucial source of government income, favored because it was easy to collect as goods entered at a port or border. Some countries also imposed export tariffs, particularly on minerals like gold, silver, or copper, because exporters could pass on most of the cost of the tariff to foreign buyers, and because mining companies, unlike manufacturing firms, could not relocate to other countries to avoid the tariff.

Import tariffs raise the price of imported goods relative to local products, and so have two effects: 1) consumers buy more local goods, and 2) the price of local goods rises. Both help local producers thrive, especially if their factories have economies of scale. For instance, in auto plants, producing a larger number of cars allows the cost of expensive machinery to be spread out over total output so each car can be sold at lower cost.

Most trade economists emphasize the parts of FREE TRADE theory that say, under certain assumptions, if a small country imposes a tariff it reduces the well-being of its population. Consumers lose by paying higher prices; producers gain by selling at higher prices; and the government gains tariff revenue. However, under certain assumptions it can be proven that the gains by producers and the government are not enough to fully offset consumers' losses. And if a country is large, so that imposing a tariff drives down world demand for the good and lowers its price, then that country can gain by imposing a tariff on imports, unless other countries retaliate with protectionist measures of their own.

Governments may impose tariffs not only to raise revenue or to nurture local industry, but to attract tariff-jumping investment. If GENERAL MOTORS (GM) wants to sell cars to Brazilians, it can either export cars to BRAZIL or set up a plant in Brazil producing for the local market. But if Brazil slaps a large tariff on imported cars, GM will more likely choose to establish an auto plant inside Brazil to avoid the tariff.

Like some other countries, the United States has tariff laws that encourage its own firms to set up assembly plants abroad using inputs made in the United States. The tariff code provision HTS 9802, also known as the production-sharing law, allows a firm that sends components out of the United States, has them assembled abroad, and then re-imports the finished good to pay a tariff only on the value added abroad. Suppose Levi's sends $15 worth of fabric, zippers and thread from the UNITED STATES to MEXICO and pays workers to make them into jeans, which it re-imports for $20. Then under HTS 9802, Levi's pays tariff only on the $5 of value added in Mexico, not on the $15 of U.S. components. Identical imported jeans made from non-U.S. components would be charged a tariff on their whole $20 value upon entering the United States. This offers U.S.-based firms an edge over other firms, of which clothing makers, electronic equipment producers, and automakers have all taken great advantage, especially in Mexico and the Caribbean Basin where the cost of transporting the components and the finished goods is low.

A few reasons for raising tariffs temporarily are recognized in existing agreements. For example, the WORLD TRADE ORGANIZATION (WTO) agreement contains provisions that prohibit one country from dumping goods in another by selling them at an unfairly low price. The country in which goods are dumped may impose a countervailing duty, a compensating tariff, on the offending country or countries. In 2002, for example, President George W. BUSH imposed a countervailing duty on steel imported into the United States from a number of countries.

BIBLIOGRAPHY. Dennis R. Appleyard and Alfred J. Field, Jr., *International Economics* (McGraw-Hill, 2001); Graham Dunkley, *The Free Trade Adventure* (Zed, 1997); U.S. International Trade Commission, *Production Sharing: Use of U.S. Components and Materials in Foreign Assembly Operations, 1994–1997*, USITC Publication 3146 (December1998).

MEHRENE LARUDEE, PH.D.
UNIVERSITY OF KANSAS

taxes

U.S. SUPREME COURT Justice Oliver Wendell Holmes, Jr. once described taxes as "what we pay for a civilized society." A more objective definition would describe taxes as the compulsory payments we make to governments, to cover those governments' expenditures on structures, services, and support payments.

There are two ways governments can raise revenues: through taxes and through fees. Fees are practical only when the beneficiaries of governmental services can be identified, and excluded from the service unless they pay the fee. For example, defense and police services cannot be financed through fees, because it would be impractical to try to limit those services only to the fee payers. In contrast, state and national parks can be fee-financed, because non-payers can easily be kept out.

Taxes are also needed to finance programs designed to assist target population groups, since charging them a fee for the service would effectively cancel out the assistance provided them. Social programs, agriculture support programs, and education programs are all examples of assistance programs for which fees make no sense. Note, however, that since the recipients of Social Security must pay into the system prior to their retirement, those earlier payroll taxes could in part be interpreted as fees for the future retirement benefits.

Nevertheless, with the possible exception of social security, the overwhelming majority of government services must necessarily be tax financed. If we want these services, and the civilized society they provide us, we must have taxes.

Types of taxes. Taxes are generally levied on any one of three behaviors: earning income, spending that income, and holding wealth. The one principal exception is a head tax, which is levied on all persons who meet the tax's qualifications (e.g., all men 18 years old or older). Taxes on earning income include the personal income tax, the corporate income tax (which, in effect, taxes the investment income of the corporation's shareholders), and payroll taxes such as the FICA (Federal Insurance Contributions Act or social security) tax. Taxes on consumption (or spending) include sales taxes, excise taxes, and tariffs on imported goods; the value added tax (VAT) could be, in effect, either an income tax or a sales tax, depending on how it treats the purchase of capital equipment. Taxes on holding wealth include wealth taxes, property taxes, and estate taxes.

Since income is either spent on consumption goods or saved, the distinction between income taxes and consumption taxes lies in their different treatments of savings. An income tax taxes the money you save when it is earned, and taxes any interest, dividend, or other returns to saving when those are earned. A consumption tax taxes savings only when they are spent. Since most people eventually spend the majority of the money they save, the difference is primarily timing: an income tax taxes that money early on, when it is earned, while a consumption tax takes that money at the end, when it is spent.

Since, however, it is always advantageous to pay taxes tomorrow rather than today—you earn interest in the meantime—a consumption tax imposes a lower effective tax rate on saved income than an income tax. Indeed, a consumption tax effectively leaves savings income untaxed. As a result, a consumption tax turns out to be exactly equivalent to a labor income tax; i.e., an income tax that exempts savings income, such as a payroll tax.

Since there are many features in the U.S. personal income tax that allow saved earnings to remain untaxed until they are spent (pensions, IRAs, 401K plans), savings income to be deferred or to remain untaxed until it is cashed in (accelerated depreciation, capital gains), and savings income to be tax-exempt (Educational and Roth IRAs), the U.S. personal income tax is in reality a hybrid between an income tax and a consumption tax. A tax that is levied on individuals like the personal income tax, but that exempts all saved income until it is spent, like a pure consumption tax, is often called a personal expenditure tax.

Consumption taxes can be either narrowly or broadly based. Excise taxes are narrowly based—they apply to a relatively limited number of consumer purchases. Excise taxes are usually not major revenue raisers, but are instead used either to discourage socially undesirable behaviors (cigarette and alcohol taxes), or to approximate user fees (gasoline taxes). Luxury taxes are similarly applied to a relatively narrow range of goods, usually to indirectly tax the wealthy. Tariffs on imports originated as essentially luxury taxes, since only the well-off could afford imported products, but are now used primarily to protect domestic producers from foreign competition.

Sales taxes and value added taxes are broadly based, although exemptions on food, housing, medical care, and other essentials are common. Many sales taxes also exempt a wide range of services. A sales tax is collected from the purchaser, added on to the purchase price at the time of sale, whereas a VAT is collected from the producer of the good and the producer's suppliers, and then incorporated into the sale price.

Since most taxes are imposed on economic transactions (the purchase/sale of consumer goods or labor/capital services), the tax could ultimately fall on either the purchaser or seller. Excise and luxury taxes, tariffs, and the VAT, which are collected from the producer/sellers of consumer goods, may be passed forward in part or full to consumers.

Similarly, sales taxes, which are collected from the consumer, may be partly or fully passed back to the producer/seller. The division of the tax depends on the elasticities of SUPPLY and DEMAND: the less-price-elastic side of the tax bears the greater portion of the tax. Since gasoline and tobacco consumers are very unresponsive to prices, most of those taxes fall on consumers as higher prices. In contrast, the demands for many luxury goods are very elastic, so the producers are, in many cases, likely to absorb most of a luxury tax.

Income taxes may likewise be divided between the suppliers of labor/capital or their employers. In fact, however, since labor supply is in the aggregate extremely price inelastic, all labor income taxes (including the employer's portion of payroll taxes) are approximately fully borne by the worker. It is less clear what the elasticity of savings supply is, but it is safe to say that the major portions of capital income taxes are borne by the saver/investor.

Fair taxation. Ideally, taxes are both efficient, in the sense of collecting the desired amount of revenue with as little impact on behavior as possible, and are fairly distributed. Broad-based taxes are more efficient than narrow taxes, since they are harder to escape: a tax on all consumption can be avoided only by saving or not earning, while a tax on jewelry can be avoided by shifting to other untaxed items. Special provisions in the tax code—the exemption of housing from sales taxes, the exemption of employer-provided insurance from income taxes, accelerated depreciation of some investments, low tax rates on dividends or capital gains—all lead to changes in behavior that are likely to be inefficient, unless the goal of the special provision was to encourage a specific behavior (e.g., educational tax credits). In general, however, the most efficient tax system will treat all forms of income, or all forms of consumption, identically.

What constitutes fair taxation depends on one's sense of fairness. At one extreme, a head tax could be considered fair—everyone enjoys equal rights and protections from government, so everyone should pay equally for government. Alternatively, if the benefits people receive from government differ, they could be taxed in proportion to their benefits—an argument that would favor the widespread use of fees. Most commonly, however, a fair tax system is defined as one where one's taxes are a function of one's ability to pay taxes.

A person's ability to pay taxes is usually measured by that person's income, although wealth or consumption could also be used. A proportionate tax collects a constant fraction of income (or consumption): a 5 percent sales tax on all purchases would be a proportionate tax relative to consumption. A 20 percent flat tax with no deductions or exemptions would be a proportionate income tax.

A tax that collects a smaller fraction of income/consumption from the rich than from the poor is a regressive tax. A head tax that collects the same amount from rich and poor alike would be extremely regressive. Most modern societies prefer progressive taxes, which collect a larger fraction of income/consumption from the rich than from the poor. The personal income tax, with its series of the tax brackets that rise with income, is clearly progressive, although a flat tax with a personal exemption would also be mildly progressive. A personal expenditure tax could be designed to be as progressive as the personal income tax.

In most societies, the majority opinion is that the ability to pay taxes rises disproportionately with income, since lower levels of income are used to satisfy more basic wants and needs than higher income levels. Therefore, in those societies where progressive taxation is preferred, the optimal tax system would be based on either corporate and personal income taxes, or personal expenditure taxes and corporate cash flows taxes (that immediately depreciate capital purchases, but allow no deduction for interest payments). Property taxes might be used to finance local government, since most local government services primarily benefit property. Estate taxes would add additional progressivity to the system, while taxing income that had previously escaped taxation (inheritances, tax shelter income, savings under a consumption tax) but which provided consumption-like benefits to the estate's owner (e.g., status, security).

Those societies which have the ability to pay taxes rising exactly proportional to income would prefer a proportional tax system. Their optimal choice would be a VAT rather than a sales tax, since the former is harder to elude, more consistently deals with the distinction between intermediate goods and final goods, and is generally applied more comprehensively. If an income-tax-like VAT is desired, capital asset purchases should receive no special treatment. A consumption-tax-like VAT would allow firms to deduct capital purchases in calculating their value added.

Only countries with poorly developed economies and limited abilities to measure and monitor production and income should rely heavily on tariffs, excise, and luxury taxes. Since these taxes only require the monitoring of specific products and national borders, they are easy to administer, and have long been favored in less developed nations (e.g., the United States, prior to the Civil War). They are, however, ultimately very inefficient taxes that create substantial behavioral shifts from taxed to untaxed goods.

Finally, a note on how high tax rates should be. It is reasonable to expect that the optimal average tax rate—i.e., the percent of GROSS DOMESTIC PRODUCT (GDP) devoted to government spending—should be higher in rich countries than in poor ones. Richer societies can afford more luxuries. Within government, that would mean not just highways, police, and national defense but social insurance programs such as Social Security and national health insurance. Nevertheless, the extreme disparity in average tax rates that we actually observe makes it difficult to determine what level may be optimal. For example, among the world's wealthiest nations, average tax rates range from around 53 percent and 45 percent in SWEDEN and FRANCE, to 38 percent in the UNITED KINGDOM, 29 percent in the UNITED STATES, and 25 percent in JAPAN. Ultimately, what is the "best" average tax rate is a political decision, and clearly the political outcomes do differ widely.

BIBLIOGRAPHY. David F. Bradford, *Untangling the Income Tax* (Harvard University Press, 1986); Harvey S. Rosen, *Public Finance* (McGraw-Hill, 2002). Joseph E. Stiglitz, *Economics of the Public Sector* (W.W. Norton, 2000); Joel Slemrod and Jon Bakija, *Taxing Ourselves* (MIT Press, 1996).

M. KEVIN MCGEE PH.D.
UNIVERSITY OF WISCONSIN, OSHKOSH

Taylor, Zachary (1784–1850)

HERO OF THE MEXICAN-AMERICAN WAR (1846–48) and 12th president of the United States, Zachory Taylor was an enigmatic figure during one of the nation's most tumultuous eras. As a military and political leader, Taylor was instrumental in the addition of the southwest to American holdings, an event that greatly enhanced the nation's wealth but spawned bitter sectional conflict over the expansion of slavery.

Born to an aristocratic Virginia family, Taylor acquired plantations in Louisiana and Mississippi, as well as more than 100 slaves. But it was in his long and illustrious military career that Taylor achieved his greatest successes. Nicknamed "Old Rough and Ready," he served with distinction in the War of 1812 (1812–15), the Black Hawk War (1832), and the Seminole War (1835–38) before commanding an army in the conflict with Mexico, which began in April 1846, when President James POLK, in deliberate provocation, ordered

Taylor's army from the Nueces River, the border between Texas and Mexico recognized by Mexico, to the Rio Grande, which the United States deemed the legitimate boundary line. From there, Taylor launched a successful invasion of northern Mexico, culminating in his celebrated victory over the much reviled Santa Anna, conqueror of the Alamo, at Buena Vista in February, 1847. The war ended the following year with the Treaty of Guadalupe-Hidalgo, which ceded Mexico's northern provinces.

These victories made Taylor a national hero and catapulted him into political office. In 1848, the contentious question of slavery's expansion into the Mexican Cession divided both Democrats and Whigs. While Democrats nominated Lewis Cass on the ambiguous platform of "popular sovereignty," Whigs tried to ignore the issue altogether and nominated the politically mysterious Taylor, who had never even voted in a national election. Taylor won handily by trading on his military status and avoiding any clear position on the slavery issue.

As president, he could not be so vague. In 1849, after gold-diggers flooded into the territory, California applied for statehood as a free state, a development that sparked a massive controversy over the political balance between North and South and the constitutionality of slavery's restriction from the West. The slave-holding Taylor shocked the nation when he actively encouraged the immediate admission of California and New Mexico as free-soil states. Viewing the situation pragmatically, he disliked the social and political chaos that reigned in the two territories while debate over their admission raged, and he saw no harm to Southern slavery in the banning of the institution in areas geographically ill-suited to its existence. He vigorously opposed the Omnibus Bill offered as a compromise by his fellow Whig, Henry Clay, because it attached to the two territories' admission extraneous measures designed to mollify Southerners.

Taylor prepared to force an intense confrontation over the bill when he died suddenly on July 9, 1850 from a brief stomach illness. His departure cleared the way for the passage of Clay's bill. The Compromise of 1850, as it came to be known, delayed, but did not prevent, the AMERICAN CIVIL WAR.

BIBLIOGRAPHY. Jack K. Bauer, *Zachary Taylor: Soldier, Planter, Statesmen of the Old Southwest* (Louisiana State University Press, 1985); David M. Potter, *The Impending Crisis, 1848–1861* (HarperCollins, 1976); Elbert B. Smith, *The Presidencies of Zachary Taylor and Millard Fillmore* (University of Kansas Press, 1988).

HOLLY A. BERKLEY, PH.D.
HARDIN-SIMMONS UNIVERSITY

technology

ALTHOUGH THE WORD technology refers to knowledge about techniques, modern parlance has stretched the definition to include embodiments of technology, either in the form of material artifacts or in the practices of collections of individuals who, together with the necessary materials and production equipment, carry out a specific process.

In both of these cases, technology refers to things or systems whose performance demonstrates knowledge about a specific technique. From either of these definitions it is easy to realize that technology is an exceedingly important part of human knowledge from the viewpoint of economic activity. For any society or civilization in history, their technology is defined at least in notional terms as their members' ability to transform resources (energy, materials, information, and so on) for the satisfaction of individual and collective goals. From the latter's perspective, it can be argued that the most important thing about technology is that it changes.

Though the process of technological change has occurred and influenced the lives of individuals throughout the history of humankind, its pace and cumulativeness during the history of what we call capitalist economies is unprecedented. Even Karl MARX, the critic of capitalism *par excellence*, was ready to concede in the *Communist Manifesto* (1848) that capitalistic society's dominant class, the bourgeoisie, "has accomplished wonders far surpassing Egyptian pyramids, Roman aqueducts, and Gothic cathedrals. . . . The bourgeoisie, during its rule of scarce 100 years, has created more massive and more colossal productive forces than have all preceding generations together."

The insights of the classical economists about the impact of technological change on the living standards of the industrializing economies have found an important quantitative validation since the middle of the 20th century. A number of pioneering studies by economists Robert SOLOW and Moses Abramovitz investigated the factors contributing to the growth of American income per capita since the late 19th century and concluded that a variety of phenomena, broadly representative of technological change, accounted for around 90 percent of that growth. These early findings have been refined over time and have prompted a number of economists to focus their research efforts on understanding the process whereby technological change occurs and affects the economy and society.

The effects of technological change are not always, or even typically, beneficial for every individual or group in society. At the very least, individuals whose work skills are rendered less valuable by specific improvements in technology are made worse off by them. The opposition to technological change arising from these considerations was a core factor behind the Luddite disturbances caused by British textile workers in 1811–13.

Along the same lines, a loud chorus of criticism has accompanied forms of technological change aimed at the mechanization and automation of work processes that have been charged with reducing the economic value of workers' skills to the advantage of their capitalist employers. While this de-skilling hypothesis underscores the economic impact of technological change, other commentators on technological change have focused on its effects on the nature of work and raised important concerns about the alienating nature of the work tasks associated with technological developments such as the introduction of the assembly line, or automated machinery.

Interestingly, early concerns about this matter were raised by that champion of the division of labor, Adam SMITH, who argued in *Wealth of Nations* that the workers' limited intellectual exertion under the division of labor would make them as "stupid and ignorant as it is possible for a human creature to become."

Smith did not draw from this fact the implication that technological change and the division of labor be arrested. Rather, he argued that the government ought to temper the adverse consequences of the division of labor by providing the common people (the workers) with the "most essential parts of education."

Together with Smith, many others perceive technological change to be a critical factor in promoting better living conditions. Yet, the persistence of poverty in many parts of the world at the beginning of the 21st century makes it clear that technological change under capitalism, no matter how impressive and unprecedented, is not a panacea. Many individuals pin their hopes for fixing pressing problems of hunger and malnutrition, diseases and epidemics on technological factors. Critics of this attitude point out that the solution, or work toward resolving many of these problems, need not await any technological fix. These arguments do not necessarily dispute the proposition that technology can help, as much as they emphasize the undisputable fact that factors other than technology crucially influence who will have access to the benefits of technology.

Attention should also be called to problems confronting modern societies that are the outcome of specific aspects of technological change. For example, the international debate over the proliferation of nuclear weapons addresses a problem created by the development of technology for nuclear-power generation. And many aspects of environmental degradation can also be traced to the consequences, perhaps unintended, of adopting new technologies on a large scale.

The burden of these few remarks is to make the point that the process of technological change is pervasive and shapes our collective destiny. Understanding its basic features provides tremendously valuable insights on the history of capitalist economies and perhaps sheds a glimmer of light on their future.

The development of technology and long waves. This necessarily brief overview of the historical record of technological change takes the viewpoint that there have been multiple technological revolutions during the last quarter of a millennium, coinciding with what scholars in the field have labeled long waves of technical change. These waves are occasioned by clusters of technological innovations that lead to temporary accelerations in the rate of economic growth. Depending on the characteristics of the technologies at the core of the revolution, these accelerations reflect increased investment activity stimulated by the availability of new methods of production, by the growth of markets for new consumer products, and the reverberations across industrial sectors. As the diffusion of the new technologies progresses, the period of faster growth draws to a close. Normal conditions set in, until a new technological revolution triggers the next wave. Most accounts identify five long waves in technological change, beginning with the one associated with the industrial revolution that swept across Great Britain at the end of the 18th century.

Among the most celebrated inventions of the INDUSTRIAL REVOLUTION is James Watt's steam engine. However, the core of the first technological revolution was represented by the variety of machines that fueled the tremendous expansion of the British cotton industry, as well as the advent of factory-based production methods. In fact, the development of innovative machinery provided an essential stimulus to the concentration of production activities in factories. The latter had to be located close to streams that could be used to generate the water power necessary for the mills to operate.

Although invented in 1769, the steam engine's economic effects were limited until the 1840s, when it became a core technology of the second technological revolution. The steam engines of the late 18th century had low fuel efficiency and required considerable amounts of coal for their operation. A bulky natural resource, coal was costly to transport, crucially reducing steam power's appeal for potential users. It is not a coincidence that the economic impact of steam engines grew at the same time that the costs of transportation fell dramatically as a result of a revolutionary transportation technology, the railroads, whose coming of age, in turn, depended on the refinement of moving steam engines! The second long wave was fueled by the broadening applications of steam power to a variety of industrial sectors, growing investment in the development of a railroad infrastructure.

Changes in the dominant sources of power generation are also the hallmark of the third wave of innovation that began in the 1880s and ended with the Great DEPRESSION of the 1930s. The core technologies of this period concerned the generation, transmission, and application of electric power. Importantly, the advent of electrical power had a dramatic impact on the design and layout of factories. As machines were progressively modified for operation by unit electric drives, factory equipment no longer needed to link with belt-and-pulley arrangements to overhead shafts whose rotary motion was regulated by a single large steam engine.

Since the late 19th century, large-scale production methods became increasingly common among the manufacturing industries producing small consumer durables and production equipment. Such developments reflected the diffusion of manufacturing by interchangeable parts (pioneered in firearms production) and of the production equipment (machine tools) needed to support such methods. Although industries such as the sewing machine, bicycle, or the typewriter preceded it in the adoption of large-scale manufacturing, the automobile industry is the manufacturing sector whose evolution is most closely associated with the rise of mass production. This fact has a great deal to do with the successful strategy adopted by Henry FORD around 1908, when he decided to bet the future of his company, the Ford Motor Co., on the decision to mass produce a single economical version of automobile. An expensive and elitist good until then, the automobile was brought to a much larger consumer market by Ford's Model T. The success of Ford's gamble propelled the automobile industry through years of tremendous growth.

The adoption and refinement of the assembly-line manufacturing method and innovations in the production equipment that automated significant portions of the manufacturing process contributed to defining the Fordist techniques of mass production that are the core of the fourth technological revolution or wave of innovation that began in the 1940s. As mass-production methods diffused widely across industries and nations, a period of sustained economic growth followed the end of World War II, coming to an end in the late 1960s. The industrialized economies entered a period of stagnation or modest growth that lasted about 20 years. Although a dominant concern for economic analysts during the 1980s was to identify the causes of the productivity slowdown, a set of technologies centered around the application of computers and telecommunications was rapidly improving and became the core of what is commonly perceived as a new, the fifth, long wave of technological innovation.

A couple of important features of the long-waves pattern of technological change should be noted. First, the pattern is typically accounted for by two kinds of phenomena, namely the bunching together of technological innovations or the extraordinarily broad impact of a

The computer and digital media are the "fifth long wave" of technological innovation.

relatively small set of technologies. In fact, the two phenomena occur together when, for example, innovation in a technology with a wide range of applications stimulates further innovations among firms in the application sectors. Examples of these so-called general-purpose technologies include the steam engine, the electrical motor, the microcomputer, and several others. Accordingly, the development of microcomputers triggered a series of innovations in industries producing products whose design could benefit from the new microcomputer designs. To mention but a few: the pocket calculator, the personal computer, computer numerical controls for manufacturing, robotics, automobile injection systems.

A second feature worthy of attention is that the approximate date marking the beginning of the long wave is typically later than the date when the core technology for the wave was invented and first demonstrated. It was noted earlier that the steam engine was a driving force for the second long wave beginning in the 1840s, while its invention dates back to 1769. Likewise, the mass-production techniques pioneered in the automobile industry as early as the 1910s led the fourth long wave in the 1940s. And the computer was invented almost half a century before the beginning of the fifth long wave in the 1990s. In fact, toward the end of the productivity slowdown period, in the late 1980s, a Nobel-Prize winning economist Robert SOLOW famously quipped that computers could be seen everywhere except in the productivity statistics. A few years later, computer technology together with telecommunications has been credited as the major factor promoting the upswing of the fifth long wave.

The pattern just highlighted is not at all unusual, for what has been said of the core technologies of the long waves is an accurate account of a pattern that applies more widely. Early studies in the economics of technical change estimated the average lag between the dates of invention and commercialization for a sample of important inventions to be around 15 years. Moreover, the economic impact of a new technology depends on its diffusion among users, a process that is far from instantaneous. Any reasonable interpretation of the lags between the appearance of a broadly defined innovative technology and the realization of its economic benefits has to bear in mind that the technology itself has almost certainly undergone important changes. As Nathan Rosenberg, an economic historian, points out, "... new technologies typically come into the world in a very primitive condition. Their eventual uses turn upon an extended improvement process that vastly expands their practical application."

Furthermore, the identity of these applications and the speed at which they become available is highly uncertain *ex ante*. More broadly, a question of fundamental interest in the study of technological change has been what factors account for the pace of technical change in different technologies and in different time periods? And, relatedly, what factors account for the qualitative pattern of improvements across the spectrum of different technologies within a certain time period?

The rate and direction of technical change. Although technical advances may be triggered by the unintended consequences of research and tinkering conducted with other purposes in mind, technical change occurs typically as a result of intentional efforts by either individuals or organizations that expend valuable resources in order to pursue specific improvements. These efforts take a variety of forms, depending on the time period and the technology area of interest. Consider Adam Smith's description of how innovative methods of production may be devised by the individuals who engage in production:

> A great part of the machines made use of in those manufactures in which labor is most subdivided, were originally the inventions of common workmen, who, being each of them employed in some very simple operation, naturally turned their thoughts toward finding out easier and readier methods of performing it.

This paragraph provides an early statement of the phenomenon of learning-by-doing, a source of technological advance that can only too easily be underrated even

in modern times. However, the intensity of innovative effort in any economy or industrial sector is typically associated with the size of its investment in RESEARCH AND DEVELOPMENT (R&D) activities in relation to the overall level of economic or industrial activity. Thus, countries' (or sectors') commitment to innovation is often gauged by their R&D intensity, the ratio between national (or sectoral) R&D spending and output, or sales. It is common to observe differences in the resulting measures of R&D intensity both across countries and across industrial sectors, and these provide the empirical basis for the widely used classification of certain sectors of the economy as high-tech sectors.

To the extent that technical advance is the result of intentional efforts, a proximate cause of the rate and direction of technological change is the allocation of R&D expenditures across fields of technology. However, this argument only pushes the questions one step back. Two factors are presumed to play an important role in shaping the allocation of R&D expenditures, referred to as: demand and appropriability conditions; and technological opportunity.

The bulk of innovative activity is pursued under the expectation of a financial reward. Such expectation is normally grounded in the belief that there is a—possibly latent—demand for the innovation, and that the innovator will be able to recover his or her investment and earn a return from selling, using, or otherwise disposing of the innovation. With respect to the first issue, suffice to say that the technology has to meet a specific present or future need of the potential users, and it has to do so better than alternative technologies. It will not be inappropriate to emphasize the role of uncertainty in this matter. Not only can the innovator's judgments of latent demand for a new technology turn out to have been mistaken, but also unexpected developments of competing technologies can divert the users' demand away from his or her products.

Meeting users' needs is not sufficient to ensure that the innovator will earn a return on the investment of his or her resources. Whether or not this will be the case depends on the appropriability conditions, namely, conditions that influence the innovator's ability to appropriate part of the innovative technology's value to the users. These conditions depend on the speed at which competitors can imitate the innovative technology or reduce its market value by introducing innovations of their own.

While obtaining a PATENT is customarily considered the primary means for innovators to protect their innovative technology from imitation, patenting is not the only, nor the most important means for appropriating the returns from R&D. Empirical studies of innovation indicate that patent protection is a crucial element of appropriability conditions only in the pharmaceutical industry. Innovators in other technology areas find that their ability to appropriate returns from R&D is enhanced either by keeping secret critical aspects of the innovation's underlying knowledge; or by learning or other first-mover advantages accruing to the firms that bring a new technology to market ahead of the competitors; or even by defending their market position with complementary investments in sales and customers' assistance. Most importantly, these studies indicate that the appropriability conditions differ considerably according to the area of technology, and whether the innovation is a product for sale to other firms or consumers, or a process intended for use by the innovators themselves in the production of other goods.

The appropriability conditions in an area of technology determine the extent to which the net benefits of an innovation accrue to the innovator or the users. Generally, innovators appropriate only part of the net overall benefits of a new technology. Therefore, the social rate of return on R&D investment exceeds the innovator's private rate of return. And when appropriability conditions are weak, private investment in R&D may not be forthcoming even if the social rate of return from such investment would warrant the commitment of R&D dollars to the pursuit of the new technology.

The divergence between private and social returns from innovation has been invoked as a justification for government interventions aimed at either subsidizing private R&D investment or funding R&D activities carried out at public research institutions or non-profit centers such as universities. Prominent among these activities is the kind of scientific and technological research referred to as basic research. This is defined by the U.S. National Science Foundation as research directed toward increases in knowledge or understanding of the fundamental aspects of phenomena and of observable facts without specific application toward processes or products in mind. Private investment in basic research is limited by the fact that its returns are highly unpredictable and rather long-term in nature.

On the other hand, the development of scientific knowledge is presumed to be valuable for society at large and therefore, worth the commitment of public resources. For example, the U.S. federal government provides funding currently for about half of all domestic basic research, down from a share as high as 70 percent in the late 1960s.

While basic research activities do not create new technologies directly, they do so indirectly by contributing to the pool of scientific knowledge. The latter is a fundamental aspect of the conditions of technological opportunity that, together with appropriability, influence the direction and rate of innovative activity. In a nutshell, the conditions of technological opportunity influence the productivity of R&D investment in a partic-

ular area of innovative activity. Thus, areas of technology characterized by high technological opportunities are those where a given amount of R&D investment is more likely to be met with technical success, and vice versa. If the conditions of technological opportunity are conceptualized as a pool of knowledge and techniques supporting innovative activity, then their influence on historical patterns in the direction and rate of technical advance hinges on how that pool changes over time and why it differs in different areas of technology. From this perspective, three sources of new technological opportunity can be identified.

The first is the advance of scientific understanding, which provides knowledge about phenomena that can be relevant to the development of new technology. For example, the development of biotechnologies in the 1970s, such as the techniques for cloning and replicating genes, rested on a body of scientific knowledge to which the discovery of DNA in 1953 made a critical contribution. Likewise, the development of telecommunication technologies based on optical fibers was enabled by, among other things, the discovery of the laser effect in 1960.

Second, technological opportunities in a specific area can benefit from technological advances originating from other sectors or originally intended for other purposes. Thus, the invention of the transistor in 1947 at Bell Laboratories while working on problems of telephone equipment, created opportunities for innovation in a variety of fields including portable radios, computers, semiconductors, and television sets.

Finally, technological opportunities are enhanced as a result of feedback from prior innovations in the same area. This feedback is particularly apparent in the trajectories of improvement typical of products characterized as technical systems, whose design consists of an assembly of inter-related components. For these products, advances in one component technology frequently hold the promise of product performance improvements that can only be achieved as other components are improved. An important example of these bottlenecks comes from the development of metal-cutting machine tools. At the turn of the 19th century, the introduction of electric motors in place of steam power made it possible to turn tools, such as a drill bit, at higher speeds. While this created the possibility of increasing the speed of metal removal in machining operations, such opportunity could not be exploited until new steel alloys were developed that could withstand higher friction.

Conditions of appropriability and of technological opportunity are considered by modern economic analysis to be key factors influencing the rate and direction of technical change. While the framework articulated by these two concepts is very useful for interpreting the past and commenting intelligently about the present, it should be realized that predictions about the future direction and pace of technical change are of a highly tentative nature. The historical record of studies of innovation suggests that the reason for this fact is only in part related to the difficulty of predicting what technical problems will be resolved in the near future. "The most intriguing part of the story . . . has been the inability to anticipate the future impact of successful innovations, even after their technical feasibility has been established," Rosenberg states.

BIBLIOGRAPHY. Christopher Freeman and Luc Soete, *The Economics of Industrial Innovation* (MIT Press, 1997); David C. Mowery and Nathan Rosenberg, *Technology and the Pursuit of Economic Growth* (Cambridge University Press, 1989); Richard R. Nelson, *The Sources of Economic Growth* (Harvard University Press, 1995); Christopher Freeman, "The Economics of Technical Change," *Cambridge Journal of Economics* (v.18/5, 1994); Nathan Rosenberg, "Uncertainty and Technological Change," Ralph Landau, et al., eds., *The Mosaic of Economic Growth* (Stanford University Press, 1996); Edwin Mansfield, *The Economics of Technological Change* (W.W. Norton, 1968); National Science Foundation, "Science and Engineering Indicators" (2001).

ROBERTO MAZZOLENI, PH.D.
HOFSTRA UNIVERSITY

Thailand

A SOUTHEAST ASIAN nation, Thailand was known for extremely high levels of economic growth in the 1980s and 1990s before weakness in its financial system contributed to the ASIAN FINANCIAL CRISIS of 1997.

Thailand, formerly known as Siam, first entered the European capitalist system through modest trade concessions to the British in the 1826 Burney Treaty. King Rama IV (r. 1851–68), seeking modern military and industrial technology to defend his country from Western colonialism in neighboring Vietnam and Burma, negotiated the 1855 Treaty of Commerce and Friendship granting Britain free trade and extraterritorial privileges. King Rama V continued his father's pro-Western policies. His government completed a railroad between Bangkok and Ayutthaya in 1897, and abolished slavery and corvée labor in 1905. In the 1930s and 1940s, the nationalist Phibun regime changed the country's name to Thailand and was forced to cooperate with the Japanese in WORLD WAR II.

After 1945, Thailand struggled to maintain political stability and adopted a more interventionist approach to economic policy. In 1955, the government levied an export tax on rice that decreased overseas demand. The government then bought surplus rice and redistributed it at artificially low prices, as a subsidy to urban workers. The coup of 1957 brought Field Marshal Sarit Thanarat to power. Sarit's regime established close relations with outside agencies such as the WORLD BANK and U.S. aid agencies. The government also underscored its dedication to free-market capitalism by reducing the role of state-owned enterprises in the economy, and founding developmental institutions in 1959 and 1960 including the Budget Bureau, National Economic Development Board, and the Board of Investment.

Through the 1960s, the government promoted the substitution of Thai manufactures for imported goods in the domestic market. The Board of Investment promoted targeted industries in the following ways:

1. government guarantees that certain firms would not be nationalized

2. permits to hire foreign professionals

3. reduced duties for imported equipment

4. tax breaks for up to 8 years

5. protective tariffs on competing goods.

Between 1960 and 1970, Thailand's average annual economic growth rate was 8.4 percent, but much of this growth may have been the result of American expenditures during the VIETNAM WAR rather than economic policy.

With the American military withdrawal from southeast Asia in the early 1970s and the Thai economy reaching the limits of import substitution, the Thai government shifted its policy focus to export promotion. Consequently, the GROSS DOMESTIC PRODUCT (GDP) growth rate declined somewhat, but was maintained at an average of 7.2 percent in the 1970s.

Between 1985 and 1995, Thailand's average growth rate climbed to 9 percent, the highest in the world. Speculative pressure undermined the country's financial and monetary system and triggered the Asian Financial Crisis of 1997. The baht, Thailand's currency, was forced to float and depreciated from 25 to 56 baht per US$1 in January 1998. The Thai economy contracted 10.2 percent in 1998, but resumed modest growth of around 4 percent per year in 1999 and 2000.

In 2001, Thailand had a population of 62.35 million people. GDP was $410 billion consisting of agriculture 11 percent, manufacturing 40 percent, and services 49 percent. Thailand's main industries today are tourism, textiles, agricultural processing, beverages, tobacco, cement, jewelry, electrical appliances, and electronics. It is the world's second-largest tungsten and third-largest tin producer.

Exports totaled $65.3 billion worth of goods including computers, transistors, seafood, and clothing. Thailand's major export markets are the UNITED STATES at 23 percent, JAPAN 14 percent, and SINGAPORE 8 percent. Imports of capital goods, intermediate manufactures, raw materials, consumer goods, fuels, and other goods totaled $62.3 billion and came from Japan at 24 percent, United States 11 percent, and Singapore 10 percent.

BIBLIOGRAPHY. *CIA World Factbook* (2002); Barbara Leitch LePoer, *Thailand: A Country Study* (U.S. Government Printing Office, 1989), Robert J. Muscat, *The Fifth Tiger: A Study of Thai Development Policy* (M.E. Sharpe, Inc., 1994), David K. Wyatt, *Thailand: A Short History* (Yale University Press, 1984).

JOHN SAGERS, PH.D.
LINFIELD COLLEGE

Thatcher, Margaret (1925–)

GREAT BRITAIN'S FIRST female prime minister, Margaret Thatcher served longer than any other British prime minister in the 20th century. In office, she initiated what became known as the Thatcher Revolution, a series of social and economic changes that dismantled many aspects of Britain's post-war welfare state.

Margaret Hilda Roberts was born the daughter of a Grantham shopkeeper. She was educated on scholarship, working her way to Oxford University, taking two degrees in chemistry and law. Her fascination with politics led her into Parliament as a Conservative in 1959 at age 34, when she argued her way into one of the best Tory seats in the country, Finchley in north London. Her quick mind led her up through the Tory ranks. She held junior ministerial posts (1961–64) before settling into a place as secretary of state for education and science in Edward Heath's cabinet.

As a woman, this could very well have been the peak of her political career. But in 1975, Thatcher boldly challenged Heath for the Tory leadership simply because the candidate of the party's right wing abandoned the contest at the last minute. The Tories were fed up with Heath and "the Ratchet Effect"—the way in which each statist advance was accepted by the Conservatives and then became a platform for a further statist advance. After two defeats in general elections, the Conservative party elected Thatcher its first woman leader in 1975.

After leading the Conservatives to an electoral victory in 1979, Thatcher became prime minister. Among her first fights: a struggle against Britain's headstrong trade unions, that had been blamed for the ruin of three governments in succession. Thatcher turned the nation's anti-union feeling into a handsome parliamentary majority and a mandate to restrict union privileges by a series of laws that effectively ended Britain's trade-union "problem" for a long time to come.

Thatcher quickly discovered that every area of the economy was open to judicious reform. Her economic policy rested on the introduction of broad changes along free-market lines. She attacked inflation by controlling the money supply and sharply reduced government spending and taxes for higher-income individuals. By the mid-1980s, PRIVATIZATION was a new term in world government, and Thatcher set about privatizing Britain's nationalized industries, which had hitherto been sacrosanct. By the end of the decade, more than 50 countries, on almost every continent, had set in motion privatization programs, floating loss-making public companies on the stock markets, and in many cases transforming them into successful private-enterprise firms. Even left-oriented countries that scorned the notion of privatization began to reduce their public sector on the sly. Governments sent administrative and legal teams to Britain to study how it was done. Some enthusiasts have suggested the Thatcher Revolution was perhaps Britain's biggest contribution to practical economics since J.M. KEYNES invented "Keynesianism," or even Adam SMITH published *The Wealth of Nations.*

Although unemployment in England during this time continued to rise to post-war highs, the declining economic output had been reversed. In 1982, when Argentina invaded the Falkland Islands, a British colony, Britain's successful prosecution of the subsequent war under Thatcher's leadership contributed to the Conservatives' win at the polls in 1983.

In foreign affairs, Thatcher was a close ally of President Ronald REAGAN, one of her earliest admirers, who achieved power 18 months after she did. He, too, began to reverse the Ratchet Effect in the United States by effective deregulation, tax-cutting, and opening-up wider market opportunities for free enterprise. Thatcher shared Reagan's antipathy to communism. She allowed the United States to station nuclear cruise missiles in Britain in 1980 and to use its air bases to bomb Libya in 1986. In 1985, she forged a historic accord with Ireland, giving it a consulting role in governing Northern Ireland.

With Reagan and Thatcher in power, the application of increased pressure on the Soviet state to force it to reform or abolish itself, or to implode, became an admissible policy. Thatcher warmly encouraged Reagan to re-arm and thereby bring RUSSIA to the negotiating table. She shared his view that Moscow ruled an "evil empire," and the sooner it was dismantled the better. Together with Reagan she pushed Soviet leader Mikhail GORBACHEV to pursue his *perestroika* liberalization policy to its limits, and so fatally to undermine the self-confidence of the Soviet elite.

In 1987, Thatcher led the Conservatives to a third consecutive electoral victory, although with a reduced majority. She proposed free-market changes to the national health and education systems and introduced a controversial per-capita poll tax to pay for local government, which fueled criticisms that she had no compassion for the poor. Disputes over the poll tax, which took effect in 1990, and over European integration led to a leadership challenge from within her party. Consequently, Thatcher resigned as prime minister, and John Major emerged as her successor.

In the years following her resignation as prime minister, Thatcher busied herself with worldwide lecture tours and writing two volumes of memoirs, *The Downing Street Years* and *The Path to Power*. In 1991, she announced she would stand down as a member of Parliament at the next general election. She was elevated to the Peerage in 1992 and took her seat in the House of Lords as Baroness Thatcher of Kesteven. She remained active in political life and lectured widely on behalf of the Thatcher Foundation until March 2002. At that time, it was announced that Lady Thatcher would never speak in public again after having suffered a number of minor strokes. However, her spokesman made clear that this did not mean Thatcher was retiring, but would continue to write articles and make her views on current issues known.

BIBLIOGRAPHY. Margaret Thatcher Biography, www.margaretthatcher.com; "Time 100: Leaders and Revolutionaries," *Time* (2002); Eric J. Evans, *Thatcher and Thatcherism* (Routledge, 1997); M. Thatcher, *The Path to Power* (HarperCollins, 1995).

SYED B. HUSSAIN, PH.D.
UNIVERSITY OF WISCONSIN, OSHKOSH

Third World Internationalism

THIRD WORLD INTERNATIONALISM is an overarching ideology of the people of Asia, Africa, and Latin America to enunciate a universal conception of life, society, government, peace, progress, and human development that is rooted in their common conception of a need for consolidating the independence and freedom of third world countries, on the one hand, and for universalization of human rights and democratization of the world order, on the other.

Primarily derived from combined humanistic experiences, needs, and values of third world peoples and expressed in terms of their mutual solidarity, Third World Internationalism is an ideological framework—a statement of moral and ethical principles—that gives meaning, shape, and coherence to the third world as the "trade union" of the poor nations in its attempt to fashion new development styles and strategies, identify new areas of collective self-reliance, and connect the three circles of identity (national, regional, and international) with each other.

This ideology has provided a common cause, solidarity, moral and diplomatic support, strategic depth, and a flexible-value orientation to the newly independent nations. This solidarity-building has occurred through a number of themes and sub-themes, including revolution (of multiple kinds), decolonization, SOCIALISM, non-capitalist paths to development, planned progress, NON-ALIGNMENT, universal disarmament, North-South relations, East-West relations, and elimination of racism from all parts of the world. Its primary motivations include attempts to reject the idea of big powers dividing the world into spheres of influence, view things from a non-military point of view, and to build societies in which freedom is both real and essential. This ideological framework also includes opposition to superimposition of governments over other governments, and it self-consciously promotes negotiations among the aligned nations to avoid war and build international peace and stability.

However, the third world (and consequently Third World Internationalism) cannot be conceptualized in sheer geographical terms. Theorizing it as a socio-economic and not a geographical category, African-American civil rights leader Malcolm X and others have argued that ethnicized poverty in the midst of Western affluence is proof of the existence of a third world in Europe and the UNITED STATES. As a mode of consciousness, Third World Internationalism deals with the issue of poverty all over the globe. It was this mode of consciousness that gave Third World Internationalism its authenticity and uniqueness.

Third Worldism and Third World Internationalism. While Third Worldism refers to a political approach premised on the (perceived) revolutionary potential of countries in Asia, Africa, and Latin America, Third World Internationalism is characterized by a loosely coordinated set of ideas and values pertaining to independence, change, and prosperity based on a non-aligned model of progress and development.

Third Worldism was premised on two main factors: conditions leading to infuriating poverty and the capacity of the revolutionary regimes to terminate the exploitation of their countries by European and other colonizers. Crystallized by the competition between the capitalist and socialist camps, on the one hand, and between RUSSIA and the Peoples' Republic of CHINA, on the other, this Third Worldism was seen manifested in a tricontinental revolutionary movement personified, in the eyes of many, by communist revolutionaries.

In comparison, Third World Internationalism was equated with the awakening of Asia, Africa, and Latin America and directed toward ending Western monopoly over power and knowledge, and using the newly gained freedom for building democratic and just societies working for mass literacy, citizen efficacy, cultural empowerment, social ennoblement, and mobilizing the intellectual, moral, and spiritual resources of the society to build life-enhancing solidarities. This mode of history making was generally associated with leaders as diverse as CUBA's Fidel Castro and SOUTH AFRICA's Nelson Mandela.

The loosening of the bipolar world system influenced by Yugoslavia defecting from the Soviet camp, FRANCE asserting its independence from the United States, and a long-term rivalry emerging between INDIA and China, introduced a conceptual complexity and pragmatic flexibility into the formulations and operations of both Third Worldism and the Third World Internationalism. By the mid-1960s, there was a quasi-consensus that all Third World countries should commit themselves to certain basic principles, but beyond that each country should have freedom and flexibility to develop its "own genius," define its own destiny, charter its own path, invent its own solutions, and create its own *modus operandi* to pursue its national interests.

Three levels of articulation. The Third World internationalist ideology was articulated at three levels, political philosophy, aesthetics, and institutional codification. Its political philosophy is loosely organized around writings of Jawaharlal Nehru, Gamal Abdel Nasser, Kwame Nkrumah, Ahmad Sukarno, Fidel Castro, Ho Chi Minh, Martin Luther King, Jr., Malcolm X, and Nelson Mandela. But one must also acknowledge the indirect yet considerable influence of M. K. Gandhi, Mao Zedong, and Zhou Enlai on the evolution of this idea system.

Its aesthetics have been articulated by an impressive array of poets, novelists, playwrights, artists, and theorists including Pablo Neruda, Rabindernath Tagore, Faiz Ahmed Faiz, Leopold Senghor, Nazim Hikmat, Nagib Mehfouz, Gabriel Garcia Marquez, C.L.R. James, Amilcar Cabral, Mehmud Darwish, Frantz Fanon, and Edward Said, to name only a few.

At the institutional level, though the international non-aligned movement has been the primary source for the enunciation, elaboration, and application of the Third World Internationalist ideology. The efficacy of this ideology has been sustained and, paradoxically, limited by regional alliances such Organization of African Unity (OAU); Economic Community of West African States (ECOWAS); Southern African American Development Coordination Council (SAADCC); South Asian Association for Regional Cooperation (SAARC); Association of Southeast Asian Nations (ASEAN); Arab League (AL); Organization of Islamic Countries (OIC); some members of the Commonwealth of Independent States (CIS); Latin American Free Trade Association (LAFTA); and even the ORGANIZATION OF PETROLEUM EXPORTING COUNTRIES (OPEC).

While the political thinkers and philosophers were focused on the establishment of a new world order, the poets, writers, and cultural theorists honed-in on the birth of a new human being; and the institutional energies were directed toward new skills, techniques, and systems of knowledge. To put it another way, the political thinkers were concerned with ideology, the aesthetes with (collective) identity, and institutional leaders with policies. The sum total of these three constitutes the corpus of Third World internationalism, an enterprise pursued through a combination of political, economic, and cultural strategies.

Political strategies: searching for nonviolent solutions. Political-strategy building by Third World Internationalists has been historically focused in four main areas: expanding opposition to colonial, neocolonial, militaristic, and hegemonic forces; choosing a mode of struggle appropriate for the context (whether armed, nonviolent or combined); calibrating partnership with socialist countries and parties; and seeking fusion of agendas and intellectual energies through greater interaction with feminist, environmentalist, and Western nuclear nonproliferation and peace movements.

The generic political strategies included: building broad-based coalitions in support of wars of independence; building collective moral, diplomatic, economic (sanctions, boycott, etc.) pressure against colonialism; exposing neocolonial schemes and structure; empowering international institutions; and strengthening the United Nations (UN) General Assembly vis-à-vis the U.N. Security Council. Such efforts to socialize support for freedom, equality, and human dignity, South Africa and PALESTINE being the prime examples, were carried out at national, regional, and international levels.

Armed struggle has been one contested component of the third world political strategy. Many of its exponents from Ho Chi Minh to Mandela have recognized and emphasized the necessity for armed struggle. "In view of the situation I have described," wrote Mandela, "the ANC was ready to depart from its 50-year-old policy to the extent that it would no longer disapprove of properly controlled violence." But at the same time, Mandela recognized that a "successful armed struggle proceeds to out-administer the adversary and not out-fight him. And that the task of out-administration was the task of out-legitimizing the enemy."

But even at the peak popularity of armed struggles, the nonviolent ideologies of Gandhi, Abul Kalam Azad, Jawaharlal Nehru, Abdul Ghaffar Khan, Martin Luther

King, Jr., and Cesar Chavez had continued to echo in the movement and served as a moral critique of the choices of "ends and means" by various national movements and their leaders.

In the last quarter of the 20th century, Third World Internationalism became increasingly more engaged with and influenced by other consciousness-raising movements such as feminism, environmentalism, and nuclear non-proliferation and disarmament campaigns. During this period, the political agenda of the Third World Internationalism has evolved into mature and critical formulations that question and seek to transform networks of power relations built around the nodal points of race, gender, and class. These more sophisticated formulations have been directed at self-criticism, creative combinations of reform and resistance, and carefully nuanced and calibrated north-south relations. Today, the movement seeks to inculcate critical sensibilities and capacities in the processes of collective identity-formation and decision-making but without suppressing internal dissent, individual choice, and unconventional thought processes.

Third World internationalism and capitalism. Poverty, redistribution of wealth, knowledge and technology transfer, health care, education, infra-structural development, debt rescheduling, and debt write-off were among the major issues that various economic strategies were supposed to address and remedy. Though the post-Cold War economic strategies of most third world countries are by and large based on capitalist models, in the past the assortment had included a patterned focus on land reform, public-sectorism, industrialization, modernization, urbanization, import-substitution, and greater control over local resources. These steps were designed to bridge the gap between the haves and have-nots within and among the nation-states.

Some of its guiding principles were power to the people, self-reliance and autonomy, and social justice. These values can be summed in terms of the following four categories:

1. Social justice based on freedom from exploitation, with human relations of egalitarianism, cooperation and respect for work

2. Economic welfare for all in a society of abundance, with special attention to raising the living standard of marginalized groups (such as women and national minorities) and regions that have been resource-poor or historically oppressed

3. Fuller participation in economic decision-making pertaining to global distribution of resources

4. Improve the bargaining power of third world countries vis-à-vis multinational corporations.

Culturally, Third World Internationalist intelligentsia has remained focused on modernization without Westernization; promoting a vaguely defined non-European approach to development and progress; and avoiding, in Franz Fanon's words, creating the "third Europe."

Fanon has argued: "A national culture under colonial domination is a contested culture whose destruction is sought in systematic fashion." The colonizers see any attachment to the disallowed cultural attributes (dress, food, songs, flag, symbols, icons, literature, values, articles of religious faith, and music, etc.) as a form of sabotage and a refusal to submit. As a related strategy, Third World Internationalism seeks to restore the public character of contested cultures by connecting them with a number of regional and interregional cultural categories and processes.

The main goals under such conditions are to protect one's culture, resist its suppression, recover its suppressed parts at the earliest opportunity, and mobilize various cultural aspects (like Gandhi's *swadeshi*, homegrown clothing movement) to reconstitute national identity and to bring about the ideological, moral, and intellectual liberation of the colonized society ahead of its political and military liberation. One of the key cultural strategies, however, has been to use larger, usually regional, culture as means to socialize the struggle and to bring depth and density to the movement.

For example, during his meeting with Castro in New York in 1960, Nasser urged him to construct a regional cultural frame like Arab nationalism to garner greater "moral and political depth of the Cuban revolution." Interestingly, Castro echoed the same ideas in an important speech from a platform he was sharing with Mandela, during Mandela's visit to Cuba in July 1991. He told his audience that Latin Americans had no choice but to unite. Otherwise, despite their greater numbers they will add up to very little because "Balkanized Latin America" cannot compete with "a very powerful and increasingly protectionist European economic community."

Perceptions and interaction with the socialist and capitalist camps. By the 1950s, it was recognized that the third world exists in both socialist and capitalist countries. China, for example, was clearly a third world country. Similarly, ghettoized racial minorities in the West were seen as third world in the bosom of the First World. And both camps recognized the advantages of creating carefully crafted common cause with the third world. China's Mao Zedong, believed that there are "three forces: one is the force of socialism; one is the force of the national independence movement; one is the force of imperialism. These forces do battle [with each other]; and the second force, the national independence movement of Nasser, and others, can cooperate with us on various problems, on the problem of peace, on the problem of imperialism; the degree [of collaboration] is not [always] the same but [they] can cooperate with us."

Likewise, American Senator Adlai Stevenson had told Nehru during a television interview on November 12, 1961, that the United States joins the third world in opposing colonialism and supporting peoples' right to self-determination and that this should be "the objective of all peoples everywhere."

While socialism was supposed to bring about a redistribution of economic resources in favor of the dispossessed, LIBERALISM was expected to bring about a wider distribution of political power in favor of the marginalized. But this ethical dualism of the two superpowers was not of much help. In reality, the Soviet Union did not favor redistribution of economic resources at the global level, and the United States did not support redistribution of political power for the marginalized.

Though this three-way relation has remained less than satisfactory and the third world intelligentsia continues to feel betrayed by both sides, in the post-Cold War situation, it is generally recognized by a number of third world leaders and intellectuals that even the implicitly coordinated competition between the superpowers did provide breathing space to various third world nations and movements.

Conclusion. One of the major contributions of Third World Internationalism has been a low-key but reasonably sustained effort to democratize the international system. While the First World has focused on democracy within nation-states, the Third World Internationalists have emphasized democracy among the nation-states.

On the other hand, most of the third world countries have been beleaguered by ethnic and religious conflicts, territorial disputes, underdevelopment, illiteracy, disease, high infant mortality rate, and brain drain. So far, it has failed in its efforts to create a synthesis of socialism and capitalism, or the liberal state and the welfare state. And, now, it faces a monumental challenge of maintaining its unity of purpose and multicultural identity during the processes of globalization. Next to the need for a moral and intellectual renaissance, this remains its biggest challenge.

BIBLIOGRAPHY. Gerard Chiland, *Revolution in the Third World* (Penguin Books, 1980); Peter Worsley, *The Third World* (University of Chicago Press, 1965); Paulo Freire, *The Pedagogy of the Oppressed* (Continuum; 2000); Franz Fanon, *The Wretched of the Earth* (Grove/Atlantic, 1976); Gunnar Myrdal, *Asian Drama: An Enquiry into the Poverty of Nations* (Vintage Books, 1972); Charles K. Wilber, ed., *The Political Economy of Development and Underdevelopment* (Random House, 1979); William A. Joseph, et al., *Third World Politics at the Crossroads* (D.C. Heath and Company, 1996); Cristobal Kay, *Latin American Theories of Development and Underdevelopment* (Routledge, 1989); Arthur Koestler, *The Yogi and the Commissar* (Macmillan, 1965); Roderick MacFarquhar, et al., *The Secret Speeches of Chairman Mao: From the Hundred Flowers to the Great Leap Forward* (Harvard University Press, 1989); Fredrick Jameson and Masoa Miyoshi, eds., *The Cultures of Globalization* (Duke University Press, 1989); Gamal Abdel Nasser, Speeches and Press Interviews (Information Department, Government of Egypt, 1962); Jawaharlal Nehru's Speeches 1957–63 (Publications Division, Government of India, 1983); Edward Said, *Culture and Imperialism* (Alfred K. Knopf, 1993).

AGHA SAEED, PH.D.
UNIVERSITY OF CALIFORNIA, BERKELEY

Thirty Years' War

A DISASTROUS SERIES of declared and undeclared wars, the Thirty Years' War began as a dispute within the German territories of the Holy Roman Empire and eventually drew all major European powers into participation, most of which were ended by the Peace of Westphalia (1648).

Conventional explanations emphasize that the war began because of constitutional problems in the Holy Roman Empire relating to the balance between Catholics and Protestants in the ranks of those who elected the Emperor (traditionally a member of the Habsburg family), and by the revolt of the Bohemians against the persecution of Lutherans by the Austrian crown. Their refusal to accept the decrees of imperial ambassadors led them to throw the ambassadors out of the window of the Hradcany palace (the "defenestration of Prague") in 1618 and elect the Protestant Elector Palatine as King of Bohemia.

These actions provoked a broad revolt in Bohemia and Austria against the Habsburgs and a strong military response; the imperial forces suppressed the rebellion at the Battle of White Mountain (1621). After the Palatine Elector retreated to salvage his German territories, the French, English, and Dutch formed a league led by Christian IV of Denmark to challenge Habsburg power (1624–27). The imperial generals, Wallenstein and Tilly, drove Christians back and the victorious empire issued an Edict of Restitution (1629) restoring all Protestant lands to Catholicism that had been Catholic in 1552. Subsidized by the French and hoping to bolster Protestantism, Swedish forces under King Gustavus Adolphus invaded Germany beginning in 1630.

Although initially successful, the Swedish forces were routed at Nördlingen in 1634 and Adolphus lost his gains. At this point, most Protestants made peace with the Habsburgs, but France pursued war with Spain, eventually weakening the Empire and allowing the Swedes to advance again. By 1648, most parties were suing for peace (though the French continued the war against Spain until 1659) and deliberated for a treaty at Münster and Osnabrück (the Catholics in one city, the Protestants in the other).

Marxist historians such as Josef Polisensky have stressed the economic causes of the war, particularly in Bohemia, arguing that the Habsburgs were traditional feudal monarchs who were challenged by the growing economic power of Protestant burgher and peasant communities there. The Habsburgs could not afford to lose control of Bohemia since it provided a crucial part of their tax base and masses of soldiers to fight the Turks. In his view, the Thirty Years' War was a military response caused by a political crisis that resulted from economic changes taking place during the transition from feudalism to capitalism.

The war was disastrous for Germany by any account. Estimates of population loss due to famine, battle, plundering, and disease range from 20–40 percent of the German population. Flourishing communities became ghost towns, the profitable Baltic and Central European grain trade was disrupted, local industry was destroyed, and tax collection was lamed. German manufactured goods disappeared from European markets. Though suppliers of military goods and shipbuilders did increase their production, such increases were sporadic and always subject to challenge in the quickly changing landscape of the war. Urban communities were forced to pay tribute in order to avoid being plundered, which heavily limited their activities. The larger picture suggests that the settlement of the Peace of Westphalia, with its failure to eliminate the Holy Roman Empire completely as a political unit (the problems of which had provoked the war in the first place) or to provide centralized authority for the Holy Roman Emperor, seriously hampered German economic and political development over the next century.

As a result of the war, the Empire was dissolved into a mass of over 200 individual territories, each with its own currency, taxes, and customs barriers. Not only did this structure destroy the beginnings of MERCANTILISM, it worked as an obstacle to trade. These barriers were not removed until the 19th century, as a consequence of the Napoleonic invasion, and the push toward German unification that created the development of numerous partial bodies and later (1867) a full *Zollverein*, which dropped the customs barriers.

Numerous contemporary accounts refer to the hordes of small merchants, peddlers, and prostitutes that followed in the wake of the different armies, seeking to draw a little profit from the situation. Bertolt Brecht's popular musical drama, *Mother Courage and Her Children* (1941) dramatized this situation by using the character of a camp follower and barkeeper during the Thirty Years' War to ruminate on the connections between war and capitalism in the WORLD WAR II era.

BIBLIOGRAPHY. E.E. Rich and C.H. Wilson, eds., *The Cambridge Economic History of Europe, Volume IV: The Economy of Expanding Europe in the Sixteenth and Seventeenth Centuries* (Cambridge University Press, 1967); R.L. Carsten, "Was there an Economic Decline in Germany before the Thirty Years' War?" *English History Review* (v.71, 1956); Henry Kamen, "The Economic and Social Consequences of the Thirty Years' War," *Past and Present* (v.39, 1968); Geoffrey Parker, *The Thirty Years' War* (Military Heritage Press, 1988); Josef V. Polisensky, *The Thirty Years' War* (University of California Press, 1971).

SUSAN R. BOETTCHER, PH.D.
UNIVERSITY OF TEXAS, AUSTIN

time

THE NOTION OF TIME is something that we take for granted. The uninterrupted marking of chronology by our watches, clocks, and increasingly our Palm Pilots, is that which merely provides a backdrop to our daily lives. The concept of time, however, much less the ways of perceiving and apprehending it, is far from constant. Different parts of the world in different historical periods have had a wide variation in their conceptualization of time.

According to Indian cosmology, time is divided into the four great cyclical ages or *yugas*, the shortest lasting for 1,000 years and the longest for 4,000. Depicted as a circle or wheel, time for the Mayans was an endlessly recurring sequence of 13-year periods or *katuns*. Even the famous Strasbourg clock of 16th-century Europe was not equivocal in its temporal rendition. Alongside its modern, mechanical devices it depicted traditional emblems and paintings, which proclaimed a different order of sequencing from those of Renaissance science.

The existence of different modes of marking time, geographically as well as historically, was at tandem with the means to do so. Nature and its accessories were the most consistent time-keepers of pre-modernity. The passing of seasons, the crowing of the rooster at dawn, the cycles of agricultural production, all faithfully served as dependable tokens of the passage of time. In most cases, however, the measurement of time according to natural markers was directly related to human experience. The familiar processes in the cycle of work and domestic chores determined temporal sequencing thus relating the rhythms of human labor to the measurement and recording of human history.

Besides experiential temporality there also existed the time of the gods. Simultaneously with the measurement of time as related to the world of material practices, there existed in most pre-modern societies, an equally important system of ritual time. It was comprehended diversely as the twinkling of the eyes of a god (India), the passage from Creation, Flood, Exile, and the birth of Christ (Judeo-Christian), or simply as the reckoning of the events of the past, either real or imaginary, relating to a larger scheme of cosmological patterns.

In this schema, time was most often an eternal and continuous chain that connected the mundane to the divine and peopled by gods, kings, and events alike. Actual historical occurrences (battles, natural disasters) merged with epics and mythologies in an unbroken design relating all pasts to all futures.

How did we arrive from this heterogeneous structure of time reckoning to our modern universe of organizing time? The heterogeneity of measuring time, each related to its own structure of social production and historical consciousness, is the most prominent difference between the world of the past and that of the modern. Modern time measurement is marked by its universal homogeneity, where differences exist only as anomalies. It is now commonly assumed that this process began in the years between 1300–1650 in Europe. The significance of this development lay in the method of calibrating hours in a metric independent of tangible occurrences with units that were uniform and interchangeable across seasons.

It is not coincidental that this development in the world of time-measurement is concurrent with the development of capitalism and urban WAGE labor in the towns of Europe. Time from this period onward is constituted irrevocably within registers of economic and monetary value. The enlargement of the monetary sphere of circulation and the organization of commercial networks over space, forced an increasingly predictable and stable measurement of time.

Municipal authorities in the early 14th century began to set up mechanical clocks in public towers. Urban employers who paid their wage workers by the day wanted not only to mark the start and end of work shifts in a public, official fashion but also to establish a standard work shift independent of the natural seasons. Workdays of uniform duration gave employers a yardstick by which they could accurately gauge changes in the productivity of labor. Historians have argued that cities that led in the textile trade, the first branch of capitalist manufacture for export, also led in the installation of clock towers.

The actual relationship between capitalism as an economic system and time as an adjunct to its mode of production can be seen in three distinct ways.

First, GOODS in a capitalist economy are produced for exchange; they must, then, have an exchange value in addition to whatever use value they may have for their owners. The measure of relative exchange value is the socially necessary (average) labor time embodied in these commodities and that same embodied labor time is also the substance of value. Labor power, or the capacity of human beings to work, becomes like all other commodities under capitalism—something the value of which is measured by the time required to produce it. Time as the measure of the exchange value of labor power renders its varied expressions homogenous and comparable from the point of view of the market.

Second, time and its prudent use are also the origin of profit. The value of the worker's labor power, under capitalism, is dependant on the amount of labor needed to reproduce it. This is usually less than the amount of labor the worker actually puts in any given workday. The difference in hours, according to Karl MARX, is the SURPLUS value that forms the source of rent, interest, and profit. It is no surprise then that from the 14th-century engravings had begun portraying time as a deadly spirit against which people fought to render an accounting of themselves.

Third, the very process of a modern mechanized workplace under capitalism, the presence at its core of labor-saving technology, creates such a homogenization of skills that the passing of moments to the clock's rhythm is the only way to measure the relative activity of different labor powers. Not only is time the measure of the exchange value of labor-power, but labor-power, too, has been made so uniform that its various forms are only distinguishable from one another by the purely quantitative yardstick of hours spent.

Time under capitalism, thus, is money. The time needed to produce goods together with the time of circulation of exchange compose the "turnover time" of capital. The faster the capital launched into circulation is recuperated the greater is the amount of profit. Thus,

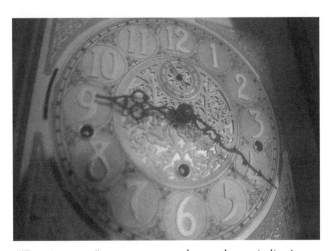

"Time is money" was never truer than under capitalism's measurement of labor productivity.

every second counts and hence the need to count every second. Since the inception of capitalism, the most contested arena of struggle between the worker and the employer has thus been over time, or the length of the workday. Just as every minute and second is counted by modern day clocks and watches, every minute and second is also accounted for. Time no longer *passes* for the global economy, it is *spent*.

BIBLIOGRAPHY. Jacques Le Goff, "Labor Time in the 'Crisis' of the 14th Century: From Medieval Time to Modern Time," *Work and Culture in the Middle Ages* (University of Chicago Press, 1980).

TITHI BHATTACHARYA, PH.D
PURDUE UNIVERSITY

Tinbergen, Jan (1903–94)

WITH RAGNAR FRISCH, Jan Tinbergen won the first Nobel Prize in Economics in 1969. The award cites their contribution to the quantification of economics via mathematical modeling and the development and application of statistical techniques for empirical testing of theory. The award credits them with providing a "rational foundation for economic policy and planning."

Tinbergen's career reflects his broad contributions. He received his doctorate from Leiden University in 1929. With Ragnar FRISCH, he founded the Econometric Society in the Netherlands in 1930. He worked in the following capacities: the Netherlands Central Bureau of Statistics (1929–45); director of the Central Planning Bureau of the Netherlands (1945–55); professor of Development Planning, Netherlands School of Economics (1955–73); chairman of the United Nations (UN) Committee for Development Planning (1966–75). During the latter periods, he also worked as an advisor for many developing countries, the Dutch development agency, and several UN agencies. In 1973, he was appointed professor of International Cooperation at the University of Leiden.

Tinbergen's earliest work concerned dynamic theory. He constructed a "cobweb" model, incorporating time-lagged responses of suppliers to prices, to explain fluctuation in agricultural prices. From 1929–45, he developed basic techniques of econometrics, being among the first to apply regression analysis to time series data, and went on to apply statistical analysis to the study of BUSINESS CYCLES. Unlike his predecessors, Tinbergen regarded the business cycle as a single dynamic phenomenon, explainable and measurable through modeling. Building on cobweb dynamics, he incorporated lagged responses to excess supply or demand into a system of equations in order to model business cycles and ultimately national economies.

In 1936, Tinbergen became the first to model an entire economy. Using regression equations to estimate parameters, he constructed a 24-equation model of the Dutch economy. He then prepared two volumes on business cycles, which empirically test investment hypotheses and statistically analyze business cycles in the United States. His Nobel award mentions these volumes as a pioneering achievement. In 1951, he developed a similar model of the UNITED KINGDOM economy. These models established the foundations for much subsequent macroeconomic forecasting. Lawrence KLEIN, well known for his forecasting models, was a student of Tinbergen's.

While at the Planning Bureau, Tinbergen applied econometric models to short-term macroeconomic policy analysis. The first to develop a unified concept of achieving multiple policy goals, he argued that nations need three policy instruments (e.g., monetary policy, fiscal policy, and one other) to achieve three fundamental policy goals: full employment, price stability, and balance-of-payments EQUILIBRIUM. His work served as a foundation for the Netherlands macroeconomic policy, for the period, and informed European policy.

After 1954, Tinbergen constructed long-term development planning models, combining macroeconomic models with disaggregated input-output models. He stressed the importance of investment in critical infrastructure and international competitiveness. Finally, beginning in the 1970s, Tinbergen turned his attention to the distribution of income, which he regarded as determined by a race between education, an equalizing force, and technological change, which usually rewards the already highly skilled. He recommended increasing education, encouraging varieties of technological change that employ the less skilled, and using tax policy to reduce income inequality.

Overall, Tinbergen contributed to development of capitalism by devising conceptual tools—dynamic modeling, econometrics, and macroeconomic modeling—and by creatively applying them to policy analysis. His work contributed to short-term macroeconomic policies used in Europe during 1950s and 1960s and to development policies of the period. While much of Tinbergen's early policy work may now be considered dated, he laid foundations for modeling, estimation, forecasting and policy analysis that endure into the current period.

BIBLIOGRAPHY. Bent Hansen, "Jan Tinbergen: An Appraisal of His Contributions to Economics," *Swedish Journal of Economics* (1969); Erik Lundberg, "Presentation Speech to the Bank of Sweden Prize in Economic Sciences in Memory of Alfred Nobel 1969," *Nobel Lectures*, www.nobel.se; Jan Tinbergen, *Statistical Testing of Business Cycle Theories* (League of

Nations, 1939); Jan Tinbergen, *Economic Policy: Principles and Design* (North Holland, 1956).

WILLIAM D. FERGUSON
GRINNELL COLLEGE

tobacco

IT HAS BEEN ESTIMATED that tobacco is the number one cause of preventable death in the United States, responsible for 400,000 deaths per year. It is the primary cause of lung cancer, bronchitis, and emphysema, and a major cause of heart disease and stroke. It has also been estimated that the total cost of smoking in the United States, which includes direct medical costs and indirect costs associated with lost earnings due to morbidity and mortality, total over $100 billion per year in 2000 dollars.

The vast majority of tobacco is consumed in the form of cigarettes, with the remainder consumed as chewing tobacco or in pipes. The smoking of tobacco imposes negative externalities on others. Chronic inhalation of second-hand smoke can cause lung cancer and heart disease in nonsmokers. Second-hand smoke has also been identified as the cause of health impairments and, most severely, Sudden Infant Death Syndrome in the children of smokers. There may also be certain positive externalities for society associated with smoking; for example, smokers tend to die younger than nonsmokers and therefore do not collect as many SOCIAL SECURITY benefits. It has been estimated that, on net, the negative EXTERNALITIES associated with smoking equaled 16 cents per pack in 1986 dollars.

Government intervention in markets has the potential to increase social welfare when consumers are not rationally making decisions. One does not judge whether an individual is rational based on whether one agrees with consumers' decisions, but by whether the individual is capable of maximizing his or her own UTILITY. Consumption of cigarettes involves three obstacles to perfect rationality: addiction, youthful irrationality, and imperfect information.

Nicotine, a chemical present in cigarettes, is addictive; the current marginal utility of consumption depends on past consumption. As a smoker develops greater tolerance for nicotine, she must smoke a greater number of cigarettes to receive the same increment of utility. If consumers are myopic—if they do not fully take into account the future consequences of their actions—then they may not realize the danger of becoming addicted when they experiment with smoking, and may benefit from policies that deter them from initiating smoking, or that reduce their consumption.

The second obstacle to perfect rationality in the market for tobacco is youthful irrationality. It is widely accepted that children are unable to take into account the future consequences of their actions. While society may trust adults to accurately assess the internal costs of smoking, it may wish to intervene for paternalistic reasons to influence the decisions of children. The inability of adolescents to accurately weigh the future health costs of smoking is relevant because the vast majority of people who ever smoke initiate the smoking when they are adolescents. For this reason, the UNITED STATES, CANADA, and many other developed countries have outlawed tobacco sales to minors and regulate advertising of tobacco to prevent it from being directed at minors.

The third obstacle to perfect rationality in the market for tobacco is imperfect information. To improve the information available to consumers, governments of developed countries have sought to disseminate information about the health harms of smoking through public health campaigns. A landmark event in tobacco markets was the publication of the U.S. Surgeon General's report on the health impact of smoking in 1964; several studies find that cigarette consumption fell significantly in response. Many developed countries now require warning labels on tobacco, stating the health risks associated with consumption.

Public health officials tend to have a different perspective on smoking than economists. Public health officials point to evidence that smoking worsens health as proof that no one should smoke. In contrast, economists believe that individuals seek to maximize their utility, not simply their health, and accept that some individuals may rationally decide to trade length of life for the pleasure derived from smoking.

A large literature in economics has been devoted to estimating the price elasticity of demand for cigarettes among different groups. Most estimates of the price elasticity of demand for cigarettes among adults fall in the range of −0.3 to −0.5, which implies that raising the price of cigarettes by 10 percent will reduce the quantity of cigarettes demanded by 3-5 percent. In contrast, recent estimates of the price elasticity of demand for cigarettes among adolescents indicate that demand is almost entirely price inelastic; the quantity of cigarettes demanded by adolescents is simply not sensitive to the price of cigarettes. It has been hypothesized that this is due either to adolescents stealing their cigarettes from their parents, "bumming" them from others, or that their demand for cigarettes is a derived demand, specifically, derived from the demand for peer acceptance.

Economists recognize two reasons for taxing tobacco. First, in order to raise tax revenue while imposing the smallest possible deadweight loss on society, one should tax the goods for which demand is most price-inelastic. Addictive goods like tobacco generally have price elasticities of demand that are relatively low. Second, to the extent that there exist externalities to society from cigarette smoking, or if there exist failures of rationality by consumers, taxes can be used to reduce smoking to socially optimal levels.

Policymakers have also sought to discourage smoking through other means of raising the "total" cost of smoking, such as clean indoor air laws that ban smoking in public places and force smokers to step outside to smoke, and laws that limit the placement of cigarette vending machines, which raise the search time associated with acquiring cigarettes.

The cigarette industry is highly concentrated; just two firms (ALTRIA/PHILIP MORRIS and R.J. Reynolds) produce roughly three-quarters of the cigarettes sold in the United States. Moreover, in the United States there are barriers to entry into farming tobacco; the federal government licenses which farmers may grow the crop and how many acres they may plant. The United States also guarantees minimum prices for tobacco to farmers. As a result of the government-enforced barriers to entry and price supports, the price of tobacco is kept above its free-market price, which, in turn, raises the price of cigarettes and lowers the quantity of cigarettes demanded.

BIBLIOGRAPHY. J. Michael McGinnis and William H. Foege, "Actual Causes of Death in the United States," *Journal of the American Medical Association* (v.270/18, 1993); Frank Chaloupka and Kenneth Warner, "The Economics of Smoking," A.J. Culyer and J.P. Newhouse, eds., *Handbook of Health Economics* (v.1B, 2000); P. DeCicca, D. Kenkel, and A. Mathios, "Putting Out the Fires: Will Higher Taxes Reduce Youth Smoking Onset?" *Journal of Political Economy* (2003); W.G. Manning, E.B. Keeler, J.P. Newhouse, E.M. Sloss, and J. Wasserman, "The Taxes of Sin: Do Smokers and Drinkers Pay Their Way?" *Journal of the American Medical Association* (v.261/11, 1989).

JOHN CAWLEY, PH.D.
CORNELL UNIVERSITY

Tobin, James (1918–2002)

ONE OF THE MAJOR figures in the neoclassical synthesis, James Tobin's life work drew together classical economic theory with Keynesian insights about macro fluctuations. Tobin was awarded the 1981 Nobel Prize in Economics for "his analysis of financial markets and their relations to expenditure decisions, employment, production, and prices," according to the Nobel Committee.

Tobin explained in his Nobel autobiography what led him to economics: "The miserable failures of capital-

ist economies in the Great DEPRESSION were root causes of worldwide social and political disasters. The Depression also spelled crisis for an economic orthodoxy unable either to explain events or prescribe remedies. The crisis triggered a fertile period of scientific ferment and revolution in economic theory." Tobin was not just a theorist. As a member of President John KENNEDY's COUNCIL OF ECONOMIC ADVISORS, he subjected his theories to the cruel testing of policymaking. The 1962 *Economic Report*, which he co-authored, marks the zenith of Keynesian macro policy.

Tobin modestly summarized his own portfolio selection theories ("Liquidity Preference as Behavior Towards Risk") as simply "don't put all your eggs in one basket," but the basic separation theorem, established for many different risky assets, underlies models of finance. The Tobin Regression ("Estimation of Relationships for Limited Dependent Variables") takes account of the fact that, in explaining household purchasing decisions of expensive items, a model must explain the (unobserved) decisions to buy a zero quantity.

The Tobin Tax on international finance, from a lecture in 1972, advocated charging a modest tax on foreign investment, which would penalize short-term investors but be inconsequential to investment with a long-term horizon.

BIBLIOGRAPHY. W.J. Baumol and J. Tobin, "The Optimal Cash Balance Proposition: Maurice Allais' Priority," *Journal of Economic Literature* (September, 1989); J. Tobin, "Liquidity Preference as Behavior Towards Risk," *Review of Economic Studies* (February, 1958); J. Tobin, "Estimation of Relationships for Limited Dependent Variables," *Econometrica* (January, 1958); J. Tobin, "A Proposal for International Monetary Reform," *Eastern Economic Journal* (July/October, 1978); "James Tobin Autobiography," www.nobel.se.

KEVIN R FOSTER, PH.D.
CITY COLLEGE OF NEW YORK

Tokyo Electric Power Company

TOKYO ELECTRIC Power Company (or TEPCO) is one of the world's largest electric utilities. It supplies power to 27 millions customers in Tokyo, Yokohama, and the rest of the huge Kanto region in JAPAN. So vast and so important is TEPCO's presence that (it is said) if TEPCO would ever suddenly extinguish its power the entire business structure of Japan would grind to a halt. Less theoretically, TEPCO possesses a generating capacity of 58,000 MW, produced by fossil fuel (56 percent), nuclear (29 percent), and hydroelectric (15 percent) power sources.

Having recently bought interest in telecommunications businesses within the region, TEPCO now offers telephone and internet services to its customer base. As well, it provides electrical construction services, owns international power generation resources, and operates an international consulting service. This consulting covers a large subject matter, from uses of renewable power to network transmission systems to systems planning and operation.

Most of TEPCO's customers regard their relationship as a "one-stop shopping" partnership, for they often look to TEPCO consultants to help them firm up areas of quality and business improvement. TEPCO's services include power quality improvement, cost reduction, environment awareness, facility management, efficiency and automation, human resource development, and safety procedures.

Though a tough competitive season, TEPCO garnered revenues of $42 billion for the period ending March 31, 2002, and ranked number 80 on *Fortune* magazine's Global 500 list of the largest companies in the world.

BIBLIOGRAPHY. "Hoover's Online," www.hoovers.com; "Global 500: World's Largest Companies," *Fortune* (July 2002); Tokyo Electric Power Company, www.tepco.co.jp.

JOSEPH GERINGER
SYED B. HUSSAIN, PH.D.
UNIVERSITY OF WISCONSIN, OSKKOSH

Toshiba Corporation

ITS NAME A WORLDWIDE presence, Toshiba's high technology and diverse electronic products are sold in Japan, North and South America, Europe, the Middle East, Africa, Asia, and Australia. Toshiba is a manufacturer and marketer of advanced products that span the sphere of information and communications through its array of products and systems, internet-based solutions and services, components, power systems, social infrastructure systems, and household appliances.

Calling itself "innovation-driven," Toshiba's umbrella objective of customer satisfaction has generated a growth quite remarkable in an industry hammered by technology companies vying for the consumer market. Its current business plan, for that matter, aims for (to quote Toshiba) "enhanced recognition as an excellent global corporation." With an eye on a technology-hungry market, Toshiba continuously monitors consumer needs for new possibilities, as shown by the company's present attention to mobile communications and networking.

Toshiba's history in communications is rich and its experience in the ever-widening market undeniable. It began in 1875 as Tanaka Seizo-sho (Tanaka Engineering Works), Japan's first manufacturer of telegraphic equipment. Evolving through various owners, name changes, and increased technology demands, it eventually became the Tokyo Electric Company, thence the Tokyo Shibaura Company in 1939. Abbreviated as "Toshiba," it officially adopted that name in 1978.

Toshiba was ranked as the 77th largest company in the world by *Fortune* magazine in July 2002, with revenues of $43 billion.

BIBLIOGRAPHY. "Toshiba," www.hoovers.com; "Global 500: The World's Largest Companies," *Fortune* (July 2002); Toshiba Corporation, www.toshiba.co.jp.

JOSEPH GERINGER
SYED B. HUSSAIN, PH.D.
UNIVERSITY OF WISCONSIN, OSHKOSH

TotalFinaElf

THE LARGEST COMPANY (as ranked by revenues) headquartered in France and one of the five largest companies in Europe, TotalFinaElf was formed in 1999 by a $46 billion hostile takeover of Elf Aquitaine, a giant French petroleum and chemical conglomerate, by Total, France's other major oil company. Combined with a merger earlier in 1999 with Petrofina, the major Belgian oil company, the new company created one of the five largest petroleum firms in the world with 2001 revenues of nearly $100 billion.

Total began in 1924 as the Compagnie Française des Pétroles (CFP), a joint venture between private investors and the French government. CFP engaged in all stages of oil production from exploration and drilling to refining and to retail distribution. CFP's major oil fields eventually included discoveries in Iraq, Algeria, Indonesia, the United Arab Emirates, and the North Sea. The brand name, Total, was used for its retail gasoline station network.

Petrofina was formed in 1920 by private investors in Belgium. Initially slated to produce and refine petroleum in Romania, discoveries in Mexico, the North Sea, Canada, and Egypt led to worldwide growth. Petrofina marketed gasoline at retail level under the name Fina and Purfina.

The ancestors of Elf-Aquitaine were three French governmental companies formed between 1939–45 to explore for oil in France and its territories. Following major oil and natural gas discoveries, refining and marketing branches were added. The different companies were merged into a single holding company in 1965 and renamed Elf in 1967. From the 1970s through the 1990s, spurred in part by the loss of its oil reserves in ALGERIA due to NATIONALIZATION, the company diversified into chemicals, health and beauty products and pharmaceuticals. PRIVATIZATION of the firm began in 1994.

Fortune magazine ranked TotalFinaElf as the 15th largest company in the world in 2002.

BIBLIOGRAPHY. M. Economides, et al., *The Color of Oil: The History, the Money and the Politics of the World's Biggest Business* (Round Oak, 2000); www.totalfinaelf.com; Alfred Chandler, *Scale and Scope: The Dynamics of Industrial Capitalism* (Belknap Press, 1990); "Global 500: The World's Largest Companies," *Fortune* (July 2002).

VICTOR MATHESON, PH.D.
WILLIAMS COLLEGE

tourism

THE ACT OF TRAVELING from one place to another, either domestically or internationally, tourism includes recreation, visiting, or any other activity that does not include paid work; it has an implication, therefore, of pleasure in traveling, often for its own sake. An anthropological approach to the subject might, in addition to this, also include a description of the tourist as representative of the "other," that is, an outsider with respect to whom local people might define themselves. The tourist dresses differently, does not speak the same language, and moves around and behaves differently than the local people.

Tourism is a very old phenomenon; there are records of citizens of the Roman Empire enjoying cultural tourism around the empire. One powerful motivation for tourism has been to complete some kind of religious pilgrimage and this continues with, for example, the Muslim tradition of the Hajj (pilgrimage to the holy city of Mecca) involving more than two million travelers per year. Pilgrimages differ from the usual idea of tourism in that they mostly involve some degree of physical hardship.

In the 18th and 19th centuries, an important means of finishing one's education for the elite of North America and Western Europe was to complete the grand tour—a lengthy process that involved visiting the cultural centers of the Mediterranean and perhaps the Near East. Other individuals might also be involved in travel for their own edification and might include visits to colonies of the home country. Such tourism was generally expensive, time-consuming, and difficult to accomplish, owing to problems in crossing borders and the great changes in climatic conditions for which people could be only ill-prepared. It was not until the middle of the 19th century that Thomas Cook arranged the first genuine tourist trips, with excursion trains in the English midlands and international journeys to the Paris Exposition of 1855. Subsequently, the necessary travel infrastructure of traveler's checks developed in conjunction with transportation technology to make travel more convenient.

Tourism of the masses. Nevertheless, tourism remained something of a preserve of the rich until the advent of cheap mass transportation, and the rise in personal disposable incomes in the decades following WORLD WAR II. The supply of short-term tourists fed the supply of related services in, for example, SPAIN for British and German tourists, and the number of people involved in what developed into a full-scale service industry has continued to increase. Tourism has moved from an individual pursuit into essentially a group activity, through what has been termed as "massification."

Massification continued into the 21st century as transportation costs continued to diminish and millions more people became able to travel as their incomes increased and travel restrictions were eased. Despite industry downturns due to terrorist attacks, disease, and war, 2002 figures indicate there were 693 million international tourist arrivals. The most popular destinations were in Europe (50 percent), the Americas (26 percent) and the Asia Pacific region (18 percent), with only 6 percent of arrivals shared by Africa, the Middle East and South Asia (World Tourism Organization, 2003). Travel is mostly between developed countries, to developed countries, or from developed countries to less-developed countries; however, more recently, people from less-developed countries have become more able to travel regionally and also to developed countries, often with a view to visiting migrant family members.

Tourism industry. The tourism industry is multidimensional, and includes such activities as providing temporary accommodation, organizing tourist activities and trips, providing transportation (by air, sea, rail, and road), and supplementary activities such as catering, retailing, and provision of cultural institutions and services. The tourism trade occurs when goods or services are sold to people from a different country or region both in their home markets, and when visiting the tourist destination. It is, therefore, an important source of export earnings. The growth of the importance of economies of scale in the tourism industry, and of the importance of vertical integration, in which firms control accommodation resorts and travel facilities, has led to the growth of mass tourism and low-cost package deals. More airports with more runways have been built, planes are larger and fly more frequently, and infrastructure within countries allows for more rapid transit of tourists.

The significance of the industry is demonstrated by the amount of money that it generates and the proportion of overall activities within an economy that are concerned with tourism. For example, more than 38 percent of all employment in the British Virgin Isles was related to tourism in 2003 and other Caribbean and island states had similarly large proportions; European states such as Malta (21 percent), Cyprus (19 percent), and Croatia (14 percent) also have very large tourism employment sectors. Large economies, too, had important tourist-related sectors: FRANCE had 5.5 percent of total employment related to tourism, ITALY 4.9 percent, the UNITED STATES 4.8 percent, and JAPAN 4.2 percent.

More than $1 billion was estimated to have been spent by the tourists of the United States and Japan in 2003, and the global total for economic activities produced by tourism was nearly $200 billion. Such an important trade has stimulated the creation of a plethora of large and small travel- and tourism-related concerns that can often be established for low cost. This has led, in some instances, to intense competition among firms. Package deals are offered for no profit or at a loss; the company seeking to recoup its costs through commissioning deals with shops and facilities specializing in tourist mementoes and goods that tourists are obliged to visit (also known as tourist traps).

Tourism can be a volatile industry since the increase in cheap air transportation, in particular, makes it more possible for people to switch destinations. The threat of terrorism, war, and disease have all had significant impacts upon the choice of destination for international visitors; with substitution of venue becoming more important than substitution of activity. The importance of the industry makes it more urgent for governments to present the "best views" of their countries and support tourism authorities to encourage inward visitors.

Tourism policy. Since tourism has become such an important industrial sector, governments have sought to establish means both to promote tourism within their own countries, and improve the ability of their people and companies to provide high-quality tourism services. This generally entails establishing a national tourism bureau or authority with a budget to promote the country and its tourism services through an international network of offices. Such agencies often work closely with established networks including national air carriers and embassies.

Upgrading skills to provide appropriate tourism services is also of considerable importance. While many tourism-related jobs are in low-wage service sectors, they can still represent attractive opportunities in many less-developed countries. However, to provide the international level of services that is often now expected, even quite junior staff needs basic training in a language such as English and some cultural sensitivity. While this level of staff development is quite feasible in developed countries, it is less likely to be possible in less-developed countries and so requires the intervention of international organizations that, while they can certainly provide the necessary inputs, are likely to retain the benefits and competencies for their own use. Developing countries need, therefore, to devote resources to developing the skills necessary for an indigenous tourism industry that will bring benefit to the host nation.

Problematic issues. Tourism has had a number of important positive impacts. These include not just the boost to employment and economic activities but, perhaps equally significantly, the exposure of people to foreign cultures and peoples has helped many people broaden their understanding of, and tolerance for, people of other cultures—although this is not universally the case. The quality of life of many people has been improved by adopting innovations and cultural practices that might not otherwise have been known apart from tourism. Similarly, recognition of the value of ethnic, and particularly minority ethnic, to the tourist industry has helped, in some cases, to preserve and to promote a sense of national and civic pride. However, not all impacts are positive. Some serious problems have arisen in the following areas:

1. *Environmental degradation.* The growth in cheap air travel has led to air and noise pollution, and the growth of airports and infrastructure to support them. The process of tourism also leads to considerable waste, especially of water resources, and also to the inappropriate discharge of waste.

2. *Enclaves.* In some cases, tourist operations can exist in isolation from local communities in tourist resorts that operate as enclaves. In these cases, tourists rarely encounter local people in a natural environment and their expenditure provides little benefit to them. The development of Dubai as a shopping and sporting destination in the United Arab Emirates, for example, provides tourists with very little interaction with nationals but a great deal of interaction with migrant workers.

3. *Tourist crime.* The presence of large numbers of comparatively rich people transplanted for a limited period of time into what might be an area of lower economic opportunities can provide a definite incentive for crimes of theft and worse. In some cases, as in EGYPT and more recently in Bali, tourists have become the victims of terrorism.

4. *Sex, drugs, and bush meat tourism.* Tourists occasionally demand goods and services they cannot have legally, or refrain from demanding at home.

Tourist locations have incentives to provide these goods and services, despite any additional cost to social cohesion or other public costs.

With a view to dealing with these issues, initiatives have been launched. One is the European Sustainable Urban Tourism Initiative, which has goals of monitoring physical heritage and environment, providing maximum access to infrastructure to both visitors and residents with a view to economic viability, while strengthening social and cultural cohesion, and minimizing adverse ecological impacts. These goals are necessary but will be more difficult to achieve away from the urban areas of developed countries. In other cases, an enforceable code of ethics, such as that proposed by the World Tourism Organization, will be helpful.

BIBLIOGRAPHY. Erik Cohen, "Thai Tourism: Trends and Transformation," *Thai Tourism: Hilltribes, Islands and Open-Ended Prostitution, Studies in Contemporary Thailand* (White Lotus Co., 1996); W. Kahlenborn, "Environmental Technology and Tourism," *Green Hotelier* (v.11, 1998); D. MacCannell, "Staged Authenticity: Arrangements of Social Space in Tourist Settings," *American Journal of Sociology* (v.79/3, 1973); K. Paskaleva-Shapiro, *Promoting Partnerships for Effective Governance of Sustainable Urban Tourism* (INTA, 2001): Pierre L. Van den Berghe, *The Quest for the Other: Ethnic Tourism in San Cristobal, Mexico* (University of Washington Press, 1994); World Tourism Organization, *Tourism Highlights 2002*, world-tourism.org; World Travel and Tourism Council, *Country League Tables*, www.wttc.org.

JOHN WALSH, PH.D.
SHINAWATRA UNIVERSITY, THAILAND

Toyoda, Kiichiro (1894–1952)

CONSIDERED THE FATHER of JAPAN's auto industry, Kiichiro Toyoda was instrumental in the establishment of TOYOTA Motor Company, Ltd. in 1935 and served as its president from 1941–50.

In 1921, after graduating from the University of Tokyo, Toyoda joined his father's firm, where he helped develop the automatic loom. In 1929, the rights to the loom were sold and provided the capital for the company's expansion into automobile manufacturing.

Inspired by the example of Henry FORD, Toyoda dreamed of mass-producing affordable passenger cars, but his plans were postponed when in 1937, the Japanese government began buying the company's vehicles for military purposes.

In difficult straits after WORLD WAR II, Toyoda sold trucks and cars to the Allied Occupational Forces. In 1947, he introduced the Model SA car, but could not return the company to profitability. By 1950, the company was virtually bankrupt and its workers in revolt. Toyoda resigned, but after the outbreak of the Korean War and large sales to the U.S. military, the company's fortunes revived. In 1952, a month after agreeing to return to lead Toyota's effort to mass-produce passenger cars, Toyoda was felled by a stroke and died.

BIBLIOGRAPHY. Tsunehiko Yui and Kazuo Wada, *The Biography of Kiichiro Toyoda* (Toyota Motor Co., 1998); Eiji Toyoda, *Toyota: Fifty Years in Motion* (Kodansha, 1987); Theodore B. Kinni and Al Ries, *Future Focus* (Capstone, 2000).

THEODORE B. KINNI
INDEPENDENT SCHOLAR

Toyota Motor Corporation

TOYOTA IS CURRENTLY the world's third largest auto manufacturer, producing a full line of models—from sedans to mini-vehicles to large trucks. Churning out products at a rate of more than 5.5 million vehicles annually (one every six seconds), Toyota sells its products in 160 countries and regions at a pace that places Toyota number 10 on *Fortune* magazine's list of Global 500, the world's largest companies in 2002.

Besides having a dozen plants located throughout its native JAPAN, Toyota claims some 55 manufacturing affiliates spread across 30 countries—several in Europe, Russia, the West Indies, Asia, Australia, Canada and the United States, including a recently announced huge production plant in San Antonio, Texas, slated for initial roll-out in 2005.

Overall, the company employs 250,000 people globally. Not only does it manufacture vehicles under its own familiar brand name, but the Lexus brand, as well.

Long a supporter of the "people community," Toyota's "Global Vision 2010" is its commitment to help create a more prosperous society. This four-point program sets the stage for a decade-long emphasis on environmental technologies, automotive safety, transportation appeal, and awareness of Toyota as a company of respect. Revenues as of 2002 totaled nearly $121 billion.

BIBLIOGRAPHY. "Toyota," www.hoovers.com; "Global 500: The World's Largest Corporations," *Fortune* (July, 2002); Toyota Motor Corporation, www.toyota.co.jp.

JOSEPH GERINGER
SYED B. HUSSAIN, PH.D.
UNIVERSITY OF WISCONSIN, OSHKOSH

trade

THE HISTORY OF TRADE can be traced to the beginning of recorded history. Archaeologists have documented trade between Egypt and Babylon as far back as 2500 B.C.E. In the beginning, trade usually involved a simple barter system with one individual or group trading one product or service for another; but as civilization progressed, so did the process by which goods were traded. In the early days of civilization, large empires generally used slave labor to produce essential goods and generated revenue by taxing conquered nations; therefore, it was unnecessary to engage in trade outside their own territories. As foreign trade developed, it was often risky because lone ships were easy prey for pirates; and some ships were attacked more than once as they transported goods. The INDUSTRIAL REVOLUTION ushered in improved methods of communication and transportation, which broadened the number of possible trading partners and expanded the kinds of goods that could be exported or imported.

British trade. As the dominant force in early industrialization, Great Britain was determined to protect its trading interests. In 1651, in response to the increase in Dutch shipping, Great Britain passed the first Navigation Act, guaranteeing that all British imports were transported on British ships. This action led to the outbreak of war with Holland in 1652. Before the English Civil War (1642-1651), the Crown received revenues from British trade and had the authority to place restrictions on trading practices. After the war, trade became more open and competition increased.

Other Navigation Acts were passed to protect British interests in trade between the colonies and the mother country. The Navigation Acts stipulated that all British colonies were subordinate to the British Parliament. In the 1770s, England continued the imperialist practice of raising revenue by taxing the American colonies. The resulting outcry of "taxation without representation" was a direct cause of the AMERICAN REVOLUTION. Ironically, the United States followed liberation from England by establishing the institution of slavery to provide labor to the Southern agricultural sector. Great Britain also placed a number of restrictions on domestic trade. For example, in 1721, Britain prohibited the importation of calico to stimulate the demand for British cotton. The same tactic was used in 1722 when cotton buttons were banned in order to boost the silk and mohair industries. By the 1860s, conflicts over free trade were often resolved through commercial treaties that provided reciprocal protection from barriers to free trade. Throughout the 20th century, Adam SMITH's work continued to influence British economic policies, particularly among the Conservative party. Margaret THATCHER's (1925-) economic advisors were known to be advocates of Smith's laissez-faire form of government. However, Great Britain pulled away from conservative politics with the election of Tony Blair (1957-) of the Labour party in 1997.

British trade theory. From the end of the Middle Ages to the late 18th century, MERCANTILISM was the dominant school of economic thought in Great Britain. The mercantilists were straightforward in their goals. They simply wanted to accumulate as much wealth as possible. To achieve these goals, mercantilists used political clout to pressure the British government to place trade restrictions wherever they were needed to promote their pursuit of wealth. The mercantilists believed that the purpose of foreign trade was to procure precious metals from other lands and bring them to Great Britain and were particularly interested in the accumulation of gold and silver.

David Hume (1711-1776) was one of the first British writers to openly criticize mercantilist policies. Hume believed that nations following mercantilist policies worked against their own self-interests. He argued that international trade benefited all nations and furthered the accumulation of wealth. The influence of Hume and his friend Smith turned the dominant school of economic thought in Britain toward classical liberalism and away from mercantilism. Classical liberalism endorsed the laissez-faire form of government promoted by the French PHYSIOCRATS who supported free trade and frowned on government interference in the economy. The role of government, as Hume and Smith saw it, was simply to maintain a stable economy by promoting free trade and punishing corruption that interfered with free competition. The publication of Smith's *The Wealth of Nations* in 1776 cemented the role of classical liberalism and its emphasis on freedom from government interference, and Smith became the strongest voice in the argument for free trade. However, Smith was a realist and understood that governments might be called upon to interfere from time to time in the interests of natural security or in response to the actions of other government's trade policies.

David RICARDO (1772-1823) expanded Smith's theories, promoting the idea of specialization among countries. Ricardo argued that "comparative advantage" dictated that countries benefited from specialization even if they could make certain goods cheaper than their trading partners. Since capital and labor were not easily transported from one nation to another, it was important to use each to the best advantage wherever it was located. Free trade, according to Ricardo, generated higher wages for both countries because each received more return for their labor costs. Contrarily, high tariffs led to a rise in prices and a loss of efficiency. Ricardo was particularly opposed to Britain's Corn Laws, which he saw as a major obstruction to free trade. John Stuart MILL (1806-1873) built on classical liberal theories, arguing that the market provided spontaneous opportunities if free from government interference. Most classical liberals accepted the need for government to help new industries with some sort of protection because older, more established industries were likely to shut them out without governmental attention. They believed that in this case the government was promoting free competition.

American trade theory. Before the American Revolution, the colonies were engaged in trade with the mother country. Abundance of natural resources provided new avenues of trade even though most of the profits were routed to England. After the Revolution, the United States became a developing nation, and conservative American writers began to promote the idea of free trade. Writer, economist, political scientist, and sociologist William Graham Sumner (1840-1910) maintained that government regulations interfered with free competition. Sumner argued that high taxation was both wasteful and inefficient. Because his focus was on the agrarian economy prevalent in the South, Thomas JEFFERSON's (1743-1826) natural instinct was to keep government interference to a minimum. As president, however, Jefferson reversed his opinion and became an active participant in government interference. As industrialization progressed in the United States, arguments over trade policies tended to break down along party lines. Republicans tended to demand protective tariffs for Northern industries, while Democrats promoted free trade to balance the interest of its Northern industrial faction against its Southern agricultural faction.

U.S. trade. Until World War I, the United States continued to develop as an industrial nation and was dependent on foreign investment to a large extent. As war began in Europe, however, the United States was placed in a unique position to provide goods to the embattled Allies. After 1918, the United States was a creditor nation and had outstripped the rest of the world in industrial output. At this point, restrictions on trade worked against American self-interest because other countries had little money to repay war debts without reciprocal trade. Trade was fairly unrestricted in the United States until 1929 with the beginning of the Great DEPRESSION. In response to Franklin ROOSEVELT's (1882-1945) NEW DEAL and the rise of the liberal economic theories of John Maynard KEYNES (1883-1946), the social welfare state signaled a move toward government regulation in most aspects of American life.

War again broke out in Europe in 1939, and the American wartime economy boomed. The United States entered the war in December 1941 after the attack on Pearl Harbor, but protected by vast oceans, American industry was in sharp contrast to the devastation suffered by Europe. In 1944, the United States hosted the BRETTON WOODS conference, which established the INTERNATIONAL MONEY FUND (IMF) and the WORLD BANK. In 1947, the United States joined other nations in creating the GENERAL AGREEMENT ON TARIFFS AND TRADE (GATT), which was aimed at abolishing restrictions on free trade on a global basis. Between 1948 and 1952, the United States provided $13 billion under the MARSHALL PLAN to aid in post-war recovery in Europe.

In the 1960s in the United States, the CHICAGO SCHOOL of economics under the leadership of Milton FRIEDMAN (1912-) attempted to overturn the Keynesian revolution and establish a return to laissez-faire economic policies. The monetarist polices of the Chicago School advocated free trade through government at the lowest level possible and placed an emphasis on controlling inflation as opposed to reducing unemployment. After the economic slump of 1987, the Chicago revolution was thwarted to some extent. Specialization continues to play a role in both domestic and foreign trade.

Global and regional trade agreements. In 1994, nations of the world came together in Morocco to establish a permanent organization to replace GATT as the promoter of free trade. The goal of what became known as the Uruguay Round was to abolish most forms of protectionism such as tariffs and entry barriers in favor of free and unrestricted trade. Specifically, the Uruguay Round extended the free trade elements of GATT, targeted the elimination of trade barriers, reduced tariffs by one-third, and opened avenues for open communication among member nations. In January 1995, the WORLD TRADE ORGANIZATION (WTO) became the instrument for implementing new global economic policies with the authority to settle trade disputes among member nations. In addition to global organizations that promote free trade, a number of regional alliances have also been formed. For example, The North Atlantic Trade Agreement (NAFTA) was formed in 1993 to promote free trade among the UNITED STATES, CANADA, and MEXICO. European countries have united under the EUROPEAN UNION (EU), and countries in Southeast Asia have created the Association of Southeast Asia Nations (ASEAN).

BIBLIOGRAPHY. Giovanni Arrighi, The Long Twentieth Century: Money, Power, and the Origins of Our Times (Verson, 1994); Roger Backhouse. Economists and the Economy: The Evolution of Economic Ideas (Transaction Publishers, 1988); Roger Backhouse, Economists and the Economy: The Evolution of Economic Ideas 1600 to the Present (Basil Blackwell, 1988); "David Hume," cepa.newschool.edu (July 2003); Graham Dunkley, The Free Trade Adventure: The Uruguay Round of Globalism: A Critique (Melbourne University Press, 1997); John Maynard Keynes, The General Theory of Employment, Interest, and Money (Harcourt, Brace, and World, 1964); Henri Miller, Free Trade (H.W. Wilson, 1996); Jerry Z. Muller, Adam Smith in His Time And Ours (The Free Press, 1993).

ELIZABETH PURDY, PH.D.
INDEPENDENT SCHOLAR

trade barrier

ANYTHING THAT INCREASES the cost of international trade, imports or exports, can be called a trade barrier. At a general level, natural and cultural obstacles to trade, such as distance or differences in language, can be considered barriers to trade, but in practice trade barriers are often regarded as only the artificially government-created costs of trade.

The most usually adopted type of trade barrier is import tariffs. They can be either *ad valorem*, when specified as a proportion of the imported value, or specific, when specified as a fixed amount per product. The practical effect of an import TARIFF is to drive a wedge between the domestic and the world price of a good, increasing the price faced by domestic consumers and producers. The implication is that a tariff reduces demand while increasing supply in the country; lower imports follow. Naturally, a tariff also generates revenues for the government.

Because tariffs are more visible and easier to monitor than other trade barriers, the WORLD TRADE ORGANIZATION (WTO) has required all countries to transform all non-tariff barriers (NTBs) into their tariff equivalents. In spite of that restriction, NTBs remain widely used.

The most prominent kind of NTB is import quotas. The effects of a quota are similar to those of a tariff, but they operate differently. Instead of introducing a wedge into prices and letting market forces adjust the import volume, as a tariff does, a quota restricts the import volume directly, then letting the market adjust the wedge between domestic and world prices. In addition to the mechanism to restrict imports, the other difference between a tariff and a quota is that the former generates tariff revenue, while the latter creates quota rents. Although the two volumes are identical, the quota rents accrue to the holders of the quota licenses. The beneficiaries are chosen by the government, which can keep the licenses and the rents for itself as it does with tariff revenues, or else distribute them to either residents or to foreigners.

Import quotas can be either global or selective. Under the former, a limit is imposed on the quantity of a good that can be imported in a given period regardless of the source of the imports. By contrast, under the latter a restriction is imposed on the quantity of the good imported from individual countries.

A type of quota that has gained popularity in recent years is the voluntary export restraints, or VERs, where the exporting country decides to "voluntarily" restrict its exports. The first and most visible case where a VER had been implemented was on the U.S. imports of automobiles from JAPAN in the 1980s. A VER is equivalent to an import quota whose rents are given to the exporting government by the importing government. One may wonder why a government may want to give away those rents, but as the U.S.-Japan case makes clear, the motivation behind a VER is the fear of triggering retaliation from the exporting country. With a VER, the importing country gives up the rents but keeps the sector protected without suffering retaliation, whereas the exporting country faces a restriction on its imports but at least obtains some rents in return.

Note that a VER, although apparently looking like a restriction imposed by a country on its exports, is in fact a restriction imposed by the importing country on its imports, albeit one that is negotiated with the exporting country. A government may nevertheless choose to restrict its own exports. In such a case, the standard instrument used is an export tax, but it is not nearly observed as often as restrictions to imports.

Many other ways to restrict imports exist, such as domestic content requirements, government procurement, and barriers often disguised as health, environment, or labor standards, such as anti-dumping measures or as administrative ("red-tape") customs difficulties. Their effects are all similar to those of import tariffs and quotas.

Trade barriers can, in principle, reflect governments' attempts to promote national welfare. This can be theoretically justifiable if the country is large enough in world markets to affect its terms of trade. It can be justifiable when there are "market failures," such as externalities or imperfect competition, as well. In practice, however, efficiency and national interest are rarely the motivation for trade barriers. Instead, the main force behind these restrictive policies is often politics—governments' desire to benefit the most influential groups in the political arena, such as organized lobbying groups, at the expense of the politically weak groups, often consumers.

BIBLIOGRAPHY. Elhanan Helpman and Paul R. Krugman, *Trade Policy and Market Structure* (MIT Press, 1989); Max Kreinin, *International Economics: A Policy Approach* (South-Western, 2003); Beth V. Yarbrough and Robert M. Yarbrough, *The World Economy: Trade and Finance* (Thomson, 2003).

EMANUEL ORNELAS, PH.D.
UNIVERSITY OF GEORGIA

Truman, Harry S (1884–1972)

THE 33RD PRESIDENT of the UNITED STATES, Harry S Truman championed capitalism in the mid-20th century Cold War struggle against communism. His administration strove to revive the WORLD WAR II-shattered economic and political structures of Europe to ensure they remained noncommunist.

Although capitalism's champion, Truman did not always champion free-market capitalists. In the U.S. Senate (1935–45), he authored legislation increasing federal regulation in transportation and aviation and identified corruption and inefficiency in war production industries. As president, Truman vetoed the Taft-Hartley Act for unfairly weakening union bargaining power. Yet, Truman had difficult relations with labor leaders, and threatened to draft striking railroad workers into the army.

Truman, son of John Anderson Truman and Martha Ellen Young, was born in Lamar, Missouri. His middle name "S" could have stood for either grandfather, Solomon Young or Anderson Shipp Truman, but in fact stood for neither (hence, no period after the S).

In 1890, the Truman family moved to Independence, Missouri. There he met Elizabeth (Bess) Wallace at the First Presbyterian Church Sunday School, whom he would wed almost 30 years later. Unlike many contemporary Missouri farm boys, Truman completed high school, graduating in 1901.

After graduation, Truman worked at several clerical jobs in Kansas City. In 1905, he joined the Missouri National Guard. In 1906, his father's Kansas City business failed. Truman returned with his family to his grandparents farm in Grandview. Truman worked the family farm for a decade.

In August 1916, Truman, then 32, volunteered for the army. He was sworn in as a member of the 129th Field Artillery regiment. In April 1917, the United States declared war on GERMANY. In 1918, Truman served in France, was promoted to captain and given command over Battery D, 129th Field Artillery Regiment, 35th Division. Truman proved an able and beloved leader, inspiring lifelong devotion from his men. In May 1919, Truman was discharged from the army and, in June, he married Bess Wallace.

The Trumans moved in with Bess's mother in Independence. Truman opened a haberdashery in Kansas City with army friend, Edward Jacobson. Truman & Jacobson experienced a short-lived success, and failed in 1922. Fifteen years later Truman's share of the store debt was fully repaid.

In 1922, Truman was elected eastern judge of the Jackson County Court, an administrative body, not a court of law, with support from Kansas City democratic political machine boss, Thomas J. Pendergast. In 1923, Truman lost re-election. Between 1923–26 he attended (without completing) Kansas City School of Law and sold memberships to Kansas City Automobile Club.

In 1926, Truman was elected presiding judge of the administrative Jackson County Court. He served two terms, from 1927–34. He brought roads, hospital, sew-

ers, and a new courthouse to Jackson County. Despite his association with Pendergast, no evidence of corruption marred his service.

In 1934, Truman ran for the U.S. Senate with Pendergast's support. He served as Senator from Missouri for a decade. Although initially scorned by the press and other senate members as "Pendergast's errand boy," Truman's diligence and well-informed participation would change that perception. While on the Interstate Commerce Committee, Truman championed two major pieces of legislation. The 1938 Civil Aeronautics Act established federal regulation of the aeronautics industry, and the 1940 Wheeler-Truman Act provided federal supervision of the railroads.

In 1941, Truman initiated and chaired a Senate Special Committee to Investigate the National Defense Program (the Truman Committee). The Truman Committee was estimated to have saved $15 billion and to have rid the country's war production effort of corruption, fraud, and inefficiency.

In 1944, Truman was elected vice president. He served for 82 days, meeting with President Franklin ROOSEVELT merely twice. In April 1945, Roosevelt died, and Truman said he felt "like the moon, the stars, and all the planets had fallen on me."

Although war continued in Europe and the Pacific, Roosevelt had not informed Truman of Allied agreements reached at Yalta, nor about the Manhattan Project. On May 7, 1945 Germany surrendered, ending the war in Europe. That summer, Truman met with Allied leaders Winston Churchill and Josef Stalin in Pottsdam, Germany. Truman's initial response to Stalin was positive. However, he quickly lost faith in Stalin's intentions as the SOVIET UNION failed to meet its promises, and opportunistically sought to take advantage of postwar chaos in Europe.

While in Pottsdam, word arrived that the atom bomb had been successfully tested. Truman decided that the use of the bomb would secure a Japanese surrender. He succeeded, although at the cost of 135,000 Japanese civilian casualties in Hiroshima and 65,00 in Nagasaki. Despite this decision, the Truman administration sought lasting peace. Among his first acts as president was creation of the United Nations.

Domestic issues were also emergent. 1946 was the most strike-torn year in American history. Truman intervened in two major strikes, coal and railroad, threatening to draft striking railway workers as they effectively shut down the U.S. economy. Congress vigorously responded with the union-limiting Taft-Hartley Act. Truman vetoed the act, but was overridden. Truman, however, chose to circumvent Taft-Harley. He ordered the government to seize the steel mills and to negotiate with steel workers during the Korean War. The U.S. Supreme Court declared the seizure illegal, given

Taft-Hartley's power to order strikers back to work for a 90-day cooling-off period.

Truman's administration was shadowed by atom and hydrogen bombs, and the experiences of two world wars. Communist leaders, Stalin in particular, were identified as aggressors likely to obtain their own nuclear arms and initiate a third world war. Thus, in 1947, communist threats to GREECE and TURKEY led to financial and military support established as the Truman Doctrine, promising U.S. support and protection to communist-threatened nations.

The Truman Doctrine was followed by the 1947 MARSHALL PLAN, a U.S.-financed, self-determined recovery in Europe. About $13 billion were provided to seven countries to resuscitate their economies and stabilize their political structures. The Soviet Union, POLAND, and Czechoslovakia walked out of initial meetings, claiming that the Marshall Plan was a thinly veiled exercise in U.S. imperialism. The concept of the Marshall Plan was extended to developing countries in Truman's second inaugural address, Point IV Plan.

In 1950, communist North KOREA, supported by CHINA and RUSSIA, crossed the 38th parallel, invading South KOREA. Truman, through the first UN military action, determined to restore the 38th parallel boundary. However, after General Douglas MACARTHUR's stunningly successful surprise attack at Inchon, the goal expanded to a communist-free Korean peninsula. Truman did not support MacArthur's vision of expanding the war, and the general was relieved of his command. The war eventually ended with a cease-fire at the 38th parallel. However, the significance of the Korean War was that it remained a Korean, not a world war.

As Truman left office, he predicted that the eventual collapse of communism would end the Cold War. He returned to Independence where he died December 26, 1972.

BIBLIOGRAPHY. American Experience, www.pbs.org; Mark O. Hatfield, *Vice Presidents of the United States, 1789–1993* (US GPO, 1997); David McCullough, *Truman* (Simon and Schuster, 1992); I.F. Stone, *The Truman Era: 1945–1952* (Little Brown, 1953); Truman Library, www.trumanlibrary.org.

LINDA DYNAN, PH.D.
INDEPENDENT SCHOLAR

Turgot, Baron Anne Robert Jacques (1727–81)

A CIVIL SERVANT, Jacques Turgot was a leading 18th-century French economic theorist. Especially notable is his early contribution to CAPITAL theory.

Turgot's success as general administrator of the city of Limoges led to appointments as minister of navy, and then as minister of finance and commerce and commissioner of public works from 1774–76. Only a few decades away from the Revolution, the French monarchy at this time was insolvent. Turgot's attempt to repair the economy involved a number of measures that would have effectively dismantled the French system of protectionism and regressive taxes (called "Colbertism" after Jean Baptiste COLBERT, 1619–83), as well as removing the medieval craft guilds and internal obstacles to trade that stifled free enterprise in France. Turgot's attempted reforms were so unpopular that he was removed from office. This could be viewed as one of the earliest attempts at economic liberalization, much later followed by Ronald REAGAN in the United States and Margaret THATCHER in Great Britain.

The term "capital" originated in Medieval Latin. It referred to the principle of a loan, as distinct from the interest. To a businessperson, it is not so important whether a yield is coming from a money loan, a piece of property, a retail outlet, or from a manufacturing operation. Hence the term further evolved to include any of these. The use of the concept of capital as an integral part of economic theory is relatively modern and roughly coeval with economics as a self-consciously separate discipline. Intellectual credit for the theoretical use of capital should probably go to the PHYSIOCRATS. But more significantly, in his *Reflections on the Formation and Distribution of Riches*, Turgot presented what economists have called the first modern discussion of capital. Turgot's discussion features a definition of the concept, a description of capital's role in the economy, and an explanation of interest.

Turgot defined capital as "moveable accumulated values" (as distinct from LAND). Capitals are accumulated by the decision to reserve a part of what is received each year. The economic function of capital is to provide advances that sustain workers in the interval between the application of labor and the sale of the resulting product. Advances are necessary in agriculture because it is "necessary to sow before reaping" in industry because workers must have tools with which to work and materials upon which to work, as well as means of subsistence while waiting for the sale of produced goods.

Turgot discussed five ways that capital can be employed. These are:

1. The purchase of land expected to yield revenue

2. Investment in agricultural undertaking, i.e., providing seed, subsistence for labor, and paying rent to landowners in hope of profit

3. Investment in an industrial undertaking

4. Investment in a commercial undertaking (buying with the intention of reselling)

5. Lending money at interest.

Turgot regarded lending at interest to be a voluntary agreement. Interest is simply the price of the use of money. Being a price, the interest rate is determined by buyers (borrowers) and sellers (lenders). It will depend on the profitability of opportunities for using the money that are available to borrowers, as well as to lenders. Economist Joseph SCHUMPETER called Turgot's theory "by far the greatest performance in the field of interest theory the 18th century produced."

BIBLIOGRAPHY. Frank A. Fetter, *Capital, Interest and Rent* (Sheed, Andrews, and NcNeel, 1997); Joseph A. Schumpeter, *History of Economic Analysis* (Oxford University Press, 1954); A.R.J Turgot, *Reflections on the Formation and Distribution of Riches* (Augustus M. Kelley, 1963).

SAMUEL C. WESTON, PH.D.
UNIVERSITY OF DALLAS

Turkey

WHILE FACING ITS SHARE of economic problems, Turkey has, over recent years, been enjoying notable economic growth in its trade and commerce, with a keen focus on modernizing its industrial output and nurturing the private sector. A free-market economy, Turkey leans toward trade with the Western markets, particularly with the UNITED STATES. Turkey's import/export ratios have shown that as its world trade expands or at least (by many indicators) remains level, its industry and services markets are strengthening. Agriculture, long a boon to the republic, remains steady—accounting for 40 percent of employment.

Into the 21st century, there have been noticeable signs that Turkey is becoming what the U.S. Commerce Department has declared one of the top 10 "big emerging markets." Being a lucrative market for U.S. exports, and also continuing to be a reliable prospective partner for joint projects and investments within Third World countries, Turkey has been included as a candidate (in 2003) for full membership in the EUROPEAN UNION (EU), the first Muslim nation to be considered. Turkey's secular government has been making long strides in reworking its legislation and industry toward moving the country in step with world demand and markets.

According to the Turkish Embassy, "Turkey remains committed to further expanding and diversifying the scope and content of its economic and commercial relations." As an example, the Turkish government is in the process of restructuring its strategy to both strengthen the ongoing stabilization of its economy and support international agreements. The country's national assembly approved a number of legislative acts that "pave the way toward broader integration of the Turkish economy with the global economy," explains the embassy.

Since the late 1980s, the private sector in business has been steadily taking a firmer hand in economic reform, but efforts are somewhat marred by haunting inflation. The government, which still oversees the basic industries of banking, transportation, and communication, continues to battle erratic spending and inflationary setbacks, beginning in the late 1990s and largely generated by deficits in the public sector. High prices have pushed consumer price inflation to 79 percent annually, since 1988. Wholesale price inflation averages 75 percent.

In response, the government continues to regulate some prices to control inflation's impact on poorer households. Certain commodities such as bread, sugar and tea are regulated, as are public utilities, including energy affiliates. Yet, the GROSS NATIONAL PRODUCT (GNP) growth rate manages to fluctuate around 6 percent.

Turkey has been promoting itself to investors and traders. Despite the weight of inflation, Turkey's economy is fast developing, evident in its growth rate. Its domestic market—a population of 67 million consumers (2002)—lures investors. Geographically, the country serves as a natural crossroad between Europe and Asia, between Eastern and Western cultures. With a strong investment record, and a highly skilled workforce, Turkey's firm cultural and historic relationships with neighboring countries puts it at an advantage in brokering East-West business and political relationships.

Turkey produces seafood, assorted vegetables, dried fruits, edible nuts, and livestock. Of services, its construction, transportation, and communications sectors are quickly rising. The manufacturing sector, too, progresses steadily ahead, its products respected for quality. The two major outputs, textiles and clothing, are almost entirely privately owned. Other products include chemicals, furniture, assorted machinery, and automotive goods. Mining generates both metallic and industrial minerals.

In 2002, Turkey had a GROSS DOMESTIC PRODUCT (GDP) of $468 billion, yielding a per capita GDP (purchasing power) of $7,000.

BIBLIOGRAPHY. Michael Lelyveld, "Turkey: Economy Spells Trouble for Russia, Iran, Azerbaijan," *Eurasia Insight* (April 4, 2002); Embassy of Turkey, "Business and Economy," www.turkey.org; *CIA World Factbook: Turkey* (2002).

JOSEPH GERINGER
SYED B. HUSSAIN, PH.D.
UNIVERSITY OF WISCONSIN, OSHKOSH

Tyler, John (1790–1862)

NICKNAMED "His Accidency," Tyler became the 10th president of the UNITED STATES in 1841, when William Henry HARRISON died just one month after assuming office. Born in Virginia, Tyler was well educated, politically experienced, and, at age 51, the youngest man to date ever to occupy the office of the presidency. His administration coincided with the opening salvos of American territorial expansion and sectional controversy over the issue of slavery.

Though he had been elected to the vice-presidency on a Whig ticket, in truth, Tyler's affiliation with the party stemmed mainly from his animosity for Andrew JACKSON in the 1830s, when Tyler served in the U.S. Senate. He shared neither the Whigs' commitment to federal direction of economic growth nor their discomfort with westward expansion. As president, he proved to be his party's worst enemy, repeatedly vetoing choice pieces of the Whig legislative agenda. Though the venerable leader of the Whig party, Henry Clay, managed to steer through Congress much of his "American System," a program of internal improvements, protective tariffs, and currency and credit reform, Tyler rejected virtually every bill Congress submitted. The only two bills Tyler signed into law were a voluntary bankruptcy law in 1841 and a new protective tariff the following year. His veto of three separate bank bills, designed to reconstruct the national bank dismantled by Andrew Jackson, led his party to expel him formally and his cabinet to resign in its entirety.

Tyler's opposition to the National Bank specifically and the American System generally emanated from his belief in state sovereignty and curtailed federal powers. He particularly disliked the proposed bank's powers to coerce a state to allow branches of the national bank to reside within its borders, and to issue loans at lower interest rates than state banks could afford. In this aversion to federal power, Tyler had more in common with the Democratic Party of his old nemesis Jackson. Finding himself politically homeless after his expulsion from the Whig folds, he began looking for inroads into the Democratic Party and positioned himself for a bid for the party's nomination in 1844.

He mounted his transition from Whig to Democrat upon an issue already dear to his heart, one that steadily gained in popularity within the Democratic Party and with the general public: westward expansion. By the 1840s the nation had been seized by "Oregon Fever," as a thousand settlers a year set out for that territory. The west as a whole soon became a symbol for economic opportunity and nationalistic pride. The Democratic Party already had a history of championing territorial expansion and stood poised to capitalize politically on the frenzy. Tyler's own claim to the expansionist mantle began in early 1844, when he initiated secret annexation negotiations with the government of the Republic of Texas, which had won independence from Mexico in 1836.

Tyler's secretary of state, the ardently pro-slavery South Carolinian, John Calhoun, introduced an annexation treaty in the Senate in April 1844. Because Calhoun explicitly linked the annexation of Texas as a slave state with the expansion of slavery, Northern opposition defeated the treaty. But Tyler maneuvered a second treaty's passage just three days before he left office in March 1845, after his failure to win the Democratic nomination for the 1844 election.

Although the annexation of Texas was the hallmark of Tyler's administration, it is also credited with settling a territorial dispute with Canada and articulating American trade interests in the Pacific with the Tyler Doctrine, a foreshadowing of the Open Door Notes of 1900. The entrance of Texas, through Tyler's efforts, into the Union inaugurated a chain of territorial acquisitions that fed the American hunger for land and fueled massive economic growth. But such progress came at the heavy price of war with MEXICO, the blood of Native American peoples, environmental destruction and political polarization between North and South over the spread of slavery.

In that conflict, Tyler eventually supported secession; he died in 1862 in Richmond, Virginia while serving in the Confederate House of Representatives.

BIBLIOGRAPHY. Daniel Walker Howe, *The Political Culture of the American Whigs* (University of Chicago Press, 1979); Norma Lois Peterson, *The Presidencies of William Henry Harrison and John Tyler* (University of Kansas Press, 1989); James L. Roark, et al., *The American Promise: A History of the United States to 1877* (St. Martin's Press, 1998); Charles Sellers, *The Market Revolution: Jacksonian America, 1815–1846* (Oxford University Press, 1991).

HOLLY A. BERKLEY, PH.D.
HARDIN-SIMMONS UNIVERSITY

U

UBS

FROM OFFICES LOCATED primarily in Europe and North America, UBS (headquartered in Zurich, SWITZERLAND) provides financial services through a number of segments. While its Swiss branch performs retail/consumer and corporate banking in Switzerland—as well as offshore private banking services—a number of other units conduct a series of related endeavors. Through these particular units, UBS provides individual and institutional asset management, brokerage duties and investment-banking, corporate finance, fixed-income services and more. Within the investment-banking and securities business, in fact, it is one of the global leaders.

Founded in June 1998, after the merger of Union Bank of Switzerland and the Swiss Bank Corporation, UBS has quickly evolved, and in 2002 employed 69,000 people across the globe. Much of the company's impressive rise has to do with its keen eye on a value-added approach to its customers who recognize its brand expertise in all corners of the world's financial industry. Having traditionally implemented its services through affiliates Warburg and Paine Webber, UBS is melding them under a "one firm" architecture, creating a single-brand UBS feel.

Among the multiple services are electronic banking (e-banking), which makes it easy for customers to carry out their banking and stock market transactions around the clock and from any geographic point. UBS's investment-funding program offers individual and comprehensive solutions throughout 20 countries. The popular Bank for Bankers service gives financial institutions unique alternatives to dealing with the complex issues surrounding the industry while maximizing their funds, focused on management and value.

UBS reported revenues of $48.5 billion in 2002 and ranked as the 59th largest company in the world.

BIBLIOGRAPHY. Thomson Financial Mutual Fund Reports (2002); "Global 500: The World's Largest Companies," *Fortune* (July 2002); Hoover's, www.hoovers.com; www.ubs.com.

JOSEPH GERINGER
SYED B. HUSSAIN, PH.D.
UNIVERSITY OF WISCONSIN. OSHKOSH

Ukraine

UKRAINE IS SITUATED in eastern Europe, consists of 603,700 square kilometers (an area slightly smaller than the state of Texas), and as of 2001, had a population of about 48 million. Ukrainians make up 73 percent of the population, with Russians as the largest minority at 22 percent. The official language is Ukrainian, but Russian is widely spoken along with Romanian, Polish, and Hungarian. Ukrainian Orthodox is the main religion.

Bordered by Belarus, HUNGARY, Moldova, POLAND, Romania, RUSSIA, and Slovakia, Ukraine's capital and largest city is Kiev. In addition to agriculture, the country's main industries include coal, electric power, ferrous and nonferrous metals, machinery and transport equipment, chemicals, and food processing. The industrial production growth rate was estimated at 12.9 percent for the year 2000.

Ukraine operates under a republic form of government, consisting of three branches: the executive, legislative, and judicial. The legislative branch consists of 450 members who serve four-year terms. One half of the members are elected by popular vote, with the remaining seats allocated on a proportional basis to those political parties that gain 4 percent or more of the national electoral vote. The head of state is the president, who is elected by popular vote to serve a five-year term. The president, with approval of the legislative branch, appoints a prime minister and deputy prime ministers.

Ukraine gained its independence from the former SOVIET UNION on August 24, 1991. The republic was the most important economic component of the former Soviet Union, and upon gaining independence, Ukraine embarked on the process of privatization and a free market economy.

Ukraine is a relatively poor country. The GROSS DOMESTIC PRODUCT (GDP) for the year 2000 is estimated at $189.4 billion. The real growth rate at that time was estimated at 6 percent. The per capita GDP was $3,850. Approximately one half of its population is below the poverty line. Inflation poses another problem. In 2000, the estimated consumer price index exceeded 25 percent. The official unemployment rate was listed at 4.3 percent as of December 1999. However this number is a bit misleading. There are a large number of unregistered and under-employed workers.

BIBLIOGRAPHY. S. Birch, *Elections and Democratization in Ukraine* (Macmillan, 2000); V.E. Kubijovy and E.J. Simmons, E. J. (1963); *Ukraine: A Concise Encyclopedia* (Ukrainian National Organization, 1963); WorldAtlas.com (2002).

MARK E. MOTLUCK, PH.D.
ANDERSON UNIVERSITY

underground economy

THE UNDERGROUND ECONOMY refers to all those aspects of economic or business activities that take place informally or illegally—in any case, beyond the knowledge and reach of the legitimate authorities. A wide range of activities fit this description, from tax evasion to moonlighting to sweatshops to dealing in illegal drugs. While the underground economy is related to the BLACK MARKET and explicitly illegal activities, it is not identical to it. However, those indulging in the underground economy will constantly be at risk both of committing and suffering from a crime which will be difficult to report.

Most people's lives are touched by the underground economy in one or more ways, and since it provides access to cheaper goods and services than would otherwise be available, there will always be a powerful incentive to use it. It is, therefore, very difficult to obtain an accurate picture of the size and importance of the underground economy; while estimates of the importance of the underground economy range from approximately 5–15 percent in Western countries, it is of considerably greater scope in many less-developed countries (LDCs). This is because many millions of people in LDCs occupy a sector that consists of "Informal units comprising small enterprises with hired workers, household enterprises using mostly family labor, and the self-employed. Production processes involve relatively high levels of working capital as against fixed capital, which in turn reflects the relatively low level of technology and skills involved," explains the International Labor Office.

In populous countries with weak governmental systems, the informal sector dominates economic activities. For example, it has been estimated to represent more than 90 percent of India's overall economy, and to involve more than 500 million people worldwide. In more developed countries as well as LDCs, the underground economy may be used to depress wages. Many restaurants, hairdressing shops, taxi-driving services, and similar industries require workers to rely on tips and gratuities to supplement their income and to keep prices low. Tips are routinely provided in cash and not always reported fully to tax authorities.

The underground economy is by no means a new phenomenon, of course. For perhaps the majority of history, the willingness of governments to try to regulate and tax international trade, for example, has stimulated smuggling which in some cases represented a majority of all trade conducted. Popular history is full of tales of local heroes who, generally with the support of local communities, conducted their business without the interference of interventionist or even unjust rulers and their agents: examples include the economic redistribution of Robin Hood and the American gangster Pretty Boy Floyd who is said to have destroyed mortgage papers as part of his bank robbery activities.

Such actions continue to be important in many parts of the world but attitudes towards them differ depending on the viewpoint of the observer: when a country is placed under sanctions, for example, those individuals who secretly supply embargoed goods might be regarded as criminals by one side and national heroes by the other. In any case, membership of the underground economy is understood to be necessitated by either the greater recompense available from avoiding the official sector, or the inability of individuals to gain access to or participate in the formal sector.

Varieties of underground economy activities. The range of activities encompassed by the underground economy includes: moonlighting, under-reporting or non-reporting of income from a second or part-time job with a view to avoiding tax and other payments; understating profit, companies deliberately mislead responsible authorities so as to reduce the amount of tax they are required to pay; understating income or assets for the purpose of obtaining social welfare; over-reporting expenditure to minimize tax payments—companies may be able to reduce their tax payments by claiming deductions for what are considered to be legitimate expenses; under-reporting or non-reporting of income earned, performed by individuals or organizations which aim to reduce liability to meet tax payments and other social costs; barter or avoiding the use of cash for the exchange of goods and services with a view to avoiding official records and hence tax payments.

Clearly, individuals and organizations can be involved in the underground economy. Estimates suggest that the activities of organizations in this respect far outweigh in monetary terms those of individuals, yet in recent years the tide of popular opinion has turned against individuals possibly involved, and greater efforts have been made to attempt to prosecute them. Some of the more insidious and important activities internationally in connection with the underground economy are illegal drug-dealing, trafficking of women and children, and counterfeiting of goods and services. While these are very vivid examples, consumers in developed countries are perhaps more likely to come into contact with the underground economy at a more mundane level: e.g., from allowing a service worker to repair an item as an informal activity without declaration, or obtaining borrowed or pirated goods without intention to profit from them. Recent cases involving peer-to-peer swapping of music files copied to computer disks demonstrates how pervasive this practice is at a comparatively low level.

Further, the popularity of the practice demonstrates openly what a cavalier attitude people are willing to take with a disputed set of laws that seem out of step with current sentiments. This is in contrast with the response articulated by very many people when confronted by corporate misdoing of a similar nature, albeit at a different scale. This is a form of double-dealing understandable by reference to the Tragedy of the Commons, in which the crucial distinction between actions is whether it destroys—or seems to destroy—resources for other people.

As a result, many forms of underground economy receive at least tacit support from members of the community in which it occurs, at least as long as they do not perceive themselves to be disadvantaged as a result. Many women in developed countries, for example, wish to balance a career with having a family and yet cannot afford the costs of official childcare and so resort to a mixture of friends and family and other sources of informal labor. In other cases, such as ITALY for example, distrust of central authorities has produced such widespread support for the underground economy that it has become endemic in society. For underground industries, such as gambling or secondary betting markets on national lotteries, a great deal of informal sector employment can be provided, often for people with a disability since selling tickets (as an example) can be managed without much physical exertion.

Social aspects of the underground economy. As described, people's attitudes to the underground economy vary depending on their proximity to it, and the ways in which they wish to use it. Frequently, those who suffer from its actions are those who are most vulnerable in any case. Many work in, or are forced to work in, factory conditions which are sweatshops; that is, according to the U.S. General Accounting Office, "an employer that violates more than one federal or state labor, industrial homework, occupational safety and health, workers' compensation, or industry registration law." Workers in such conditions may be subject to "extreme exploitation, including the absence of a living wage or benefits, poor working conditions, such as health and safety hazards, and arbitrary discipline."

If workers have crossed an international border for work, they will be subject to deportation and possible legal proceedings in the event of a dispute. This makes them subject to blackmail. Female Thai migrant workers, for example, have reported cases in which they have been subject to various types of physical and mental pressure, and little or no recourse to the law. In countries such as THAILAND and the PHILIPPINES and those of south Asia, where temporary international migration for work, and the remittances this produces, are an important source of overseas earnings, it is possible for home government agencies to collude with local employer representatives.

Most forms of child labor have now been effectively consigned to the underground economy as it is now considered an unacceptable practice in developed countries, although child labor still plays a significant role in supporting families in many countries, especially those reliant upon industries such as agriculture and small-scale retailing. The International Labor Organization has, since 1919, instituted a program of policies to which most countries adhere, ensuring that child labor is only permitted in certain, regulated situations that do not deny the child appropriate education or pose risks to health.

Economic aspects of the underground economy. Reasons why individuals might choose to participate in the underground economy, apart from sheer opportunism, include the impact of inflation or other negative economic impacts; the perception that friends and family are already involved and the legitimacy this lends to the proposition; the impact of government regulations which may appear burdensome to some; the perception of the government which might, in some cases, appear to be an inappropriate recipient of the individual's resources; and the perception of freedom or excitement in flouting regulations. Perhaps more important, particularly in the case of those living in less well-developed countries, is the inability to pay for desired goods and services at full prices and being coerced into participating in the underground economy one way or another.

The economic arguments against the underground economy are that it discriminates against those who do not participate in it and, more importantly, it reduces the amount of resources liable for use by governments through taxation and other forms of redistribution. Consequently, the underground economy generally is considered by economists to represent an inefficient allocation of resources, and to provide opportunities for rent-seeking activities that unfairly benefit some individuals to the detriment of others. Since tax evasion is held by economists to devolve to a rational choice decision featuring risk versus expected gain, it is held to be a universal phenomenon and one in which the larger the number of decisions that are made (for example if the economy is atomized, i.e., divided into a large number of small firms or individuals), the more tax evasion there will be.

Since economics holds tax evasion to be a bad thing, its conclusions are generally to increase the level of risk inherent in the decision to commit evasion by tightening tax controls or, in some cases, reducing tax levels. A similar form of analysis is brought to bear on those thought to be committing welfare fraud: since this is sub-optimal and dependent upon expectations of risk, more effort should be expended on preventing it by tightening regulations and/or decreasing the levels of benefits available, thereby making the decision less attractive.

While economics is good at providing theories, it is less able to account for the impact of cultural and historical factors on economic activities. Consequently, it cannot fully account for the persistence and importance of various kinds of underground banking, which is an important international industry linked to the troublesome practice of international money-laundering, because industry players are linked through relationships of trust, sometimes dating back centuries, but without formal institutional support to regulate transactions.

Making the informal sector formal. The informal sector is a reality of life for many millions of people worldwide. Without official recognition or regulation, they are unable to plan confidently for the future and any sudden disaster that can remove what assets they have. Further, without appropriate training and supervision in health and safety areas, they may risk injury or death to themselves and their co-workers. One of the ideas of the Nobel Prize-winner Amartya SEN is that poverty of this nature prevents people from attaining freedom and the choices that people in developed countries have come to believe are within their rights. Finding ways to bring such people within the scope of the formal sector would clearly be to the benefit of all. Achieving this goal requires policy and planning at the lower levels of society, where the micro-enterprises and individuals constituting the underground economy exist. Part of the solution can lie in the provision of credit at the micro level by suitably organized and capitalized banks, as was pioneered by the Grameen Bank in Bangladesh, and has now spread in various forms to many of the LDCs of the world.

In theses cases, the borrower—more frequently women than men—takes a small loan for the purpose of acquiring a productive asset (a cow, for example, or a sewing machine), which is then used to obtain profits to repay the loan and leave a surplus. By borrowing from a recognized bank, the assets are secured officially, and the borrower has some access to the expertise of bank staff and to guarantees of the continuing value of the asset. Other important approaches include the provision of business development services and the restructuring of social welfare systems.

Under the banner of "Decent Work for All," the International Labor Organization has sought to demonstrate the dangers inherent in people being forced to take part in the underground economy. Since many people have been forced into the informal sector as a result of economic crisis or the effects of globalization, it seems likely that the number of cases will continue to increase. Nevertheless, sustained international action, possibly supported by campaigns by concerned consumers, might be effective in bringing many people into the comparative safety of official work.

Future prospects. There seems to be little prospect of much of the underground economy emerging above ground in the future. Indeed, some forces seem to indicate that it will expand rather than decrease: globalization, urbanization, portfolio employment, and technology.

Globalization, the spread of goods and services internationally means more competitive markets, which will, in turn, force people out of traditional industries with uncompetitive practices. These people may, in many cases, lack the skills and education necessary to secure alternative official employment and may instead enter the informal sector.

Urbanization, the spread of agricultural products globally combined with increased productivity of agriculture means fewer people are required in that sector. The displaced people tend to move toward cities either permanently, or temporarily, to look for work. The work that is available is mostly in the informal sector and this will intensify as the supply of labor depresses wages, and therefore further necessitates additional income.

Portfolio employment, the reduction of labor protection laws in many countries, in combination with the increasing tendency of companies to employ temporary supply management (like the just-in-time idea) means that more people will be required to look for portfolio employment of short-term contracts, part-time work, and freelance activities to make up their income rather than one single occupation. This will complicate personal accounts and make individual transactions of less overall importance; hence, more activities are likely to go unreported.

TECHNOLOGY, the spread of information technology (IT) in particular, makes it much more convenient for people to conduct business activities internationally without intermediaries. Assignments may be contracted via email and transmitted the same way, and payment made electronically without any reference to official bodies. Similarly, IT will increasingly allow people to exchange pirated forms of intellectual property, whether for profit or not.

The underground economy is unlikely to disappear in the foreseeable future.

BIBLIOGRAPHY. Christopher Bajada, "Estimates of the Underground Economy in Australia," *Economic Record* (v.75, 1999); International Labor Organization, "Action against Child Labor: Strategies in Education," (1999), "World Employment Report," (1998); Evan T. Jones, "Illicit Business: Accounting for Smuggling in Mid-Sixteenth-Century Bristol," *The Economic History Review* (February, 2001); Amit Mitra, "Training and Skill Formation for Decent Work in the Informal Sector: Case Studies from South India," *InFocus Programme on Skills, Knowledge and Employability Working Paper* (ILO, 2002); Amartya Sen, *Development as Freedom* (Oxford University Press, 2001); Sweatshop Watch, "The Garment Industry," www.sweatshopwatch.org (2003); Jyoti Trehan, "Underground and Parallel Banking Systems," *Journal of Financial Crime* (v.10/1, 2002).

JOHN WALSH, PH.D.
SHINAWATRA UNIVERSITY, THAILAND

unemployment

DEFINED AS AN ECONOMIC CONDITION marked by the fact that some resources (LABOR, LAND, CAPITAL) are not being used, commonly understood unemployment addresses a situation where individuals actively seeking jobs remain unhired.

A WORKER who is employed is someone who holds a full-time or part-time job. A recent economics graduate who cannot find a job as an economist and is working part-time in a fast-food restaurant is still considered employed, albeit under-employed. An unemployed individual is anyone not currently employed and who is either actively looking for a job, or temporarily laid off waiting recall, or waiting to start a new job within 30 days. When unemployed and employed are added up, we have the civilian labor force. In the United States, the Bureau of Labor Statistics is responsible for the classification of individuals between unemployed and employed. This is done through surveys conducted by the Census Bureau. Anyone who did any work at all for profit or pay (whether full-time, part-time, or temporary work) during the survey week is considered employed. If a person has a job during the survey week but did not work because of sickness, weather, labor disputes, personal reasons, or vacation, he or she is still considered employed. Persons who are considered unemployed are those who did make specific efforts to find a job in the four weeks prior to the survey and who are available for work at the time of the survey.

The measure and costs of unemployment. How is unemployment measured? First the working age population is computed; it consists of all non-institutionalized (i.e., not in jails or mental hospitals) individuals above 16 years of age. The civilian labor force along with the number of employed and unemployed can then be derived, by excluding those individuals who are working but not employed (such as homemakers), discouraged workers (i.e., those who do not have jobs, would like to work but have stopped seeking employment), people in the military, etc. Statisticians and economists are then in a position to compute such important statistics as the labor force participation rate and the unemployment rate. The labor force participation rate is computed by dividing the labor force by the working age population, while the unemployment rate is the ratio of the unemployed by the labor force.

Economists, stockbrokers, and financial analysts closely watch the release of the unemployment and employment data each month. When the data show a fall in the unemployment rate, a sense of relief can be felt across the financial community. But when the data shows a rise in the unemployment rate, anxiety is felt, which often leads to adverse impacts on the major indices of the stock market. This is because unemployment is an indicator of future economic performance; it is thus an indicator of the future economic health of a country.

The measure of unemployment described above is not without problems. First, there are borderlines cases where ambiguities inevitably arise. For example, people falling on the borderline between employment and unemployment include, among others, under-employed and people working short hours involuntarily. Those falling between unemployment and economic inactivity include the discouraged workers and long-term unemployed workers no longer receiving unemployment benefits.

Second, people less than 16 years old, people in the underground economy, and homemakers are not considered employed though they may be working. Lastly, unemployment measures tend to measure only the total lack of employment in a given economy. Other aspects of unemployment such as the availability of unemployment benefits are not accounted for. This might explain why some developing countries have been found to have lower unemployment rates than developed ones: People in developing countries cannot afford to be unemployed since unemployment benefits are almost negligible. Therefore, they engage in any type of work, however insignificant or inadequate it may be. Since they are working they are not considered unemployed.

Costs of unemployment are varied. The obvious one is the lost income suffered by the unemployed. In the United States and most developed nations, this lost income is partially offset by unemployment compensation and food stamps. Another cost is the deterioration in human capital, since the unemployed is not using much of his or her human capital. A third cost is more psychic in nature: Unemployment tends to bring a loss in self-confidence and self-esteem. It is usually associated with depression.

There are different types of unemployment. The first one, frictional unemployment, arises from normal labor market turnovers. For example, when a recent college graduate comes to the job market for the first time, he or she is said to be frictionally unemployed. Another example deals with people in the process of changing jobs. Economists believe that there will always be frictional unemployment at any given point in time.

The second type of unemployment is called structural unemployment, due to deep (structural) changes occurring in some sectors of an economy. It typically translates into the elimination of one kind of job and the creation of jobs the unemployed do not have the skills for. Most of the time, structural unemployment is due to changes in technology or international competition. For example, all the workers who were employed in the steel industry in Pittsburgh, and were laid off when the industry was facing tough competition from Asia, were structurally unemployed.

The last type of unemployment is called cyclical unemployment. It occurs when there are contractions of the GROSS DOMESTIC PRODUCT (GDP). Indeed, when economic growth and income slow down, firms are making negative profit and have to lay off some workers; these workers are said to be cyclically unemployed.

As should be clear from the definitions above, structural unemployment has to do with some sectors of the economy, while cyclical unemployment is related to the economy as a whole. When there is no cyclical unemployment, the economy is said to be at full employment, a situation where the number of people looking for work exactly matches the number of jobs available. It is clear that full employment does not mean that everyone in an economy is working since there still are structurally and/or frictionally unemployed individuals in the economy. The natural rate of unemployment is the unemployment rate that prevails at full employment.

How unemployment affects the economy. In most countries unemployment data comes from either one of the two following sources: The registration data or the labor survey data. Both sources have in common a target population. Registration data is a procedure of counting a target population registered at employment exchanges; double counting of people receiving unemployment insurance benefits is avoided. Labor force surveys are surveys of the households, in which the target population is asked about his or her labor status. That is, the representative of the household is asked whether she is employed and, if not, about her recent job searches. Once the surveys are collected, appropriate statistical procedures are then used to derive an estimate of the number of people in the working age population who are employed or unemployed.

The statistics computed as a result of using the labor force survey data is called "unemployment statistics" and the one derived while using registration data is called "statistics on insurance claimants." The unemployment and employment statistics obtained from the two sources described above are almost always different. This is due to the fact that the two methods of counting the unemployed are based on different target populations and make use of different processing procedures. A large gap can be found in some countries between the number of unemployed based on registration data and the one based on survey data. Most of the time the former yields substantially lower unemployment estimates. This can be explained by many factors including:

1. The presence of individuals working in an industry not covered by the state unemployment insurance law or the presence of individuals who have just entered the labor force for the first time. These individuals are surveyed by the labor force survey but are not obviously included in the administrative records.

2. The presence of people looking for work through networks such as relatives or friends, who will not be counted when the registration data are collected but will be counted as unemployed using the labor survey data.

An important issue to be addressed is the source of unemployment. Why do we observe unemployment in an economy? Economists have proposed three main sources of unemployment: job search, job rationing, and sticky wages.

Job search is, simply put, the process of individuals looking for work. These individuals include new entrants and re-entrants to the civilian labor force. They also include people who leave their job to search for another one. When search times are prolonged, unemployment is high. For instance, when an economy is experiencing a deep contraction (recession or depression), search times tend to be prolonged and unemployment tends to increase drastically.

Job rationing is a situation where firms pay a relatively high wage (compared to the equilibrium wage rate which represents what they should pay). This "high" wage creates a surplus of labor since at that wage many people would like to work but firms would like to hire only a few of them. This surplus of workers represents the number of unemployed.

There are many reasons why firms would like to ration jobs. Two of them will be discussed here: First, firms might be "forced" to ration. For example, government laws require firms to pay any worker a wage greater than the minimum wage. To the extent that the minimum wage is set above the equilibrium real wage rate (i.e., what firms would have liked to pay), firms would hire fewer workers than normal, creating unemployment. Second, firms deliberately set wage above equilibrium wage to attract the best talent. By doing so, the firm believes that the additional cost incurred by setting wages too "high" will be outweighed by the productivity gains brought by the talented individuals. This is the foundation of the efficiency wage theory. Evidently a wage above equilibrium induces firms to hire less people, creating unemployment in an economy.

Sticky wages theory assumes that wages do not change as quickly as prices do. If there is an unexpected fall in labor demand by the firm and wages are flexible, labor will be fully absorbed but at a lower wage rate. However, if real wages are sticky in the short run, a situation where labor demanded is less than labor supplied develops and unemployment arises.

Unemployment is a fascinating topic that is no more regarded as a phenomenon largely affecting developing countries; developed countries are also affected by unemployment rates and their financial sectors pay close attention to any development in the monthly unemployment figure.

BIBLIOGRAPHY. Michael Parkin, *Macroeconomics* (Addison-Wesley Longman, 1996); Michael Edgmand, Ronald Moomaw, and Kent Olson, *Economics and Contemporary Issues* (The Dryden Press, 1998); Karl Case and Ray Fair, *Principles of Macroeconomics* (Prentice Hall, 2001).

ARSÈNE A. AKA, PH.D.
THE CATHOLIC UNIVERSITY OF AMERICA

Unilever

UNILEVER WAS FORMED in 1930 from a merger between the Lever Brothers (UNITED KINGDOM) and Margarine Unie (NETHERLANDS), the latter itself formed in 1927 from a merger between two Dutch rival margarine firms, Jurgens and Van den Bergh. In the early 2000s, Unilever had two parent companies, Unilever NV (based in Rotterdam) and Unilever PLC (based in London), but the firms operated as close to a single entity as possible, for example using the same board of directors.

Although Unilever started as a soap/detergent and margarine manufacturer, it soon began to diversify its product range, mainly via acquisition.

Today, Unilever manages worldwide brands such as Bertolli (olive oil), Hellmann's (mayonnaise), Lipton (tea), Dove (soap), and Vaseline, as well as prestige fragrances such as Calvin Klein, and some exceptionally strong local brands such as Persil detergent (UK). Unilever is the world's leader in margarine and olive oil.

In 2001, Unilever's worldwide sales were $47 billion, with operations in almost 100 countries employing 265,000 people.

In terms of regional distribution of sales, Europe accounted for 39.1 percent, North America for 26.7 percent, Africa and the Middle East for 6.2 percent, Asia and the Pacific for 15.2 percent, and Latin America for 12.8 percent. In 2001, Unilever invested about $1 billion in RESEARCH AND DEVELOPMENT (R&D) (2.5 percent of total sales), and $5 billion in marketing (14 percent of sales), and earned a net profit of $1.3 billion.

After several years of less than stellar performance, Unilever announced its five-year "Path to Growth" strategy in 2000. The aim was to restructure their product range by divesting under-performing brands, and focusing on increasing innovation and advertising of key leading brands to ensure strong growth, as well as making new acquisitions.

For example, by March 2001, Unilever had acquired Ben & Jerry's and SlimFast, and had divested 27 businesses, including Elizabeth Arden. Finally, Unilever restructured the company into two global divisions: foods, and home and personal care.

BIBLIOGRAPHY. A. Thompson, "Unilever's Acquisitions of SlimFast, Ben & Jerry's, and Bestfoods," (Harvard Business School, 2001); A. Thompson, "Unilever's Butter-Beater: Innovation for Global Diversity," (Harvard Business School, 1998); www.unilever.com.

CATHERINE MATRAVES
ALBION COLLEGE

Union of Soviet Socialist Republics (Soviet Union)

A COMMUNIST- AND Russian-controlled multinational empire, the Soviet Union existed for 69 years. The successor to the Imperial Russian Empire of the tsars, the Soviet Union (also known as the USSR) was created in 1922 and was dissolved by Mikhail GORBACHEV in December 1991. In terms of territory, it was the largest state on earth—three times the size of the UNITED STATES, located in both Europe and Asia, and covering 11 time zones from the Pacific Ocean to Eastern Europe.

After the collapse of the tsarist regime in the February 1917 Revolution, a variety of parties and movements vied for political control of the Russian Empire. Eventually the Bolsheviks, led by their leader Vladimir LENIN, seized power in the Russian city of Petrograd, carrying out the October 1917 Revolution. The Bolsheviks were the most radical group of Russian Communists who had been trying to carry out revolution. As Marxists, the Bolsheviks believed that SOCIALISM would inevitably be instituted in RUSSIA through revolution, but unlike their more moderate counterparts the Mensheviks, the Bolsheviks sought to speed up this process.

They did not want to wait perhaps decades for a capitalist, bourgeois system to dominate Russia, a country that still had a tiny middle class and had only started to industrialize on a capitalist basis. Many Marxists thought such a development was a pre-condition to introducing socialism. Instead, the Bolsheviks used a small, centrally organized, well-trained party of revolutionaries to take power in what has come to be known as the October Revolution. In 1918, they created the Russian Soviet Federated Socialist Republic (RSFSR), with a constitution that granted rights only to those who could be interpreted as serving the interests of the working class. The state they would eventually establish, the USSR, was the first communist country in history.

Lenin had seized power in the name of the soviets, or councils. These institutions had first been created during the 1905 Russian revolution, when factories and other organizations convened soviets to maintain order and security and to procure food and supplies for the people they represented. Approximately 1,000 such soviets were again established between the February and October revolutions of 1917, a chaotic period of governmental and transportation breakdown, high inflation, and food and fuel shortages. At the time, the soviets were viewed as democratic organizations designed to carry out the will of their members. Although the Bolsheviks stressed this popular institution as they built their new state, it was the Communist Party, not the soviets, that would actually run the government.

These two institutions—a government that, with some exceptions, owned or administered all institutions and enterprises, and a party that had no legal opposition—defined the organization and nature of the Soviet Union until its collapse in 1991.

The 1924 Soviet Constitution set forth the federal structure of the USSR, which, along with the RSFSR, contained 14 other socialist republics and other autonomous regions. Most authority was invested in the federal government. This new Soviet regime gave the semblance of autonomy and self-determination to the national minorities but maintained Russian control by means of Marxist ideology, which claimed to transcend issues of nationalism; after all, many Marxists simply did not consider national consciousness to be an important or lasting phenomenon in history. To its credit, the Soviet Union, through planning and coordination, built up the backward economy polity to such a degree that it claimed the mantle of superpower alongside the United States.

In 1989, no one predicted the imminent downfall of the Soviet Union, which since World War II had been, along with the United States, one of the world's two superpowers. Nevertheless, the fall of the Berlin Wall on November 9, 1989, marked a symbolic turning point in the process that eventually brought about the disintegration of the USSR. The Soviet Union's final leader, Gorbachev, sought to institute a policy of *glasnost,* or openness by allowing a freer exchange of ideas. Public criticism of the Communist Party and the government, instead of bringing about a reinvigoration of the Soviet system as Gorbachev had hoped, actually helped erode its very foundations, including the leading role that the Party was supposed to play in Soviet life. With the fall of the Berlin Wall, the USSR lost control of the Eastern European countries that had served as Communist buffer states with the capitalist, democratic West.

Meanwhile, the non-Russian soviet republics sought independence, whether slavic (Belarus, Moldova, and UKRAINE), Baltic (ESTONIA, LATVIA, and LITHUANIA), Caucasian (GEORGIA, Armenia, and Azerbaijan), or Central Asian (Kazakhstan, Kirghizstan, Tadjikistan, Turkmenistan, and Uzbekistan).

These independence movements sparked the most dramatic event of the Soviet Union's last days—the failed August 1991 coup by Communist Party hardliners to depose Gorbachev, who intended to sign a new treaty of Union members that would eliminate federal controls over the republics. A key figure in these events was Boris Yeltsin, who had been elected president of the Russian Republic and, along with his supporters, personally faced the threat of Soviet tanks that the coup plotters intended to use against their opponents. Yeltsin ended his membership in the Party and, after August, used his newfound authority and popularity to dictate his anti-Soviet agenda to Gorbachev and those who sought to maintain the Union in some form.

On December 8, 1991, Russia, Belarus, and Ukraine agreed to form the Commonwealth of Independent States, a loose confederation of almost all of the former soviet republics. The CIS made the Soviet Union obsolete, and on December 25, 1991, Gorbachev resigned his position and dissolved the USSR.

BIBLIOGRAPHY. E.H. Carr, *The Bolshevik Revolution, 1917–1923* (W.W. Norton, 1985); W.H. Chamberlin, *The Russian Revolution, 1917–1921* (Princeton University Press, 1987); M. McCauley, ed., *The Russian Revolution and the Soviet State, 1917–1921* (W.W. Norton, 1988); Robert Conquest, ed., *Soviet Nationalities Policy in Practice* (Bodley Head, 1967); R. Pipes, *The Formation of the Soviet Union* (Harvard University Press, 1964); Geoffrey Hosking, *The First Socialist Society: A History of the Soviet Union from Within* (Harvard University Press, 1993); Martin Malia, *The Soviet Tragedy: A History of Socialism in Russia, 1917–1991* (The Free Press, 1994).

GEORGE KOSAR
BRANDEIS UNIVERSITY

unions

IN THE 19TH CENTURY, labor unions formed in western Europe and the UNITED STATES in capitalistic markets to protect each individual's right to work for wages in exchange for his or her time and effort. Rather than bargain individually with those who owned the means of production—giving employees little power to negotiate—workers realized that they could gain from organizing into a collective force.

Throughout history, the relationship between laborers and owners has generally been troubled. In the midst of contention, neither side wants to give power to the opposition. When workers gained strength through organizing efforts, both employers and the state fought their attempts at reform. Confrontations between labor and management often turned violent. As a result, the history of unions is marked with brutality and bloodshed.

Economic, political, and social forces greatly influence labor unions and organization efforts. In the United States, for example, the world wars changed the nature of unionization efforts by bringing opposing sides together for a common cause. The federal government encouraged union membership in exchange for labor's support of the war efforts.

Early labor organization. As a result of war, the black plague, and famine, Europe suffered a century-long depression that began in the middle of the 14th century. Despite the harsh conditions—confronting a shortage in labor and weakened demand for merchandise—commercial institutions and labor moved closer to modern capitalism.

The shortage in labor caused manufacturing prices to rise. At the local level, artisan associations or guilds united skilled craftsmen, their apprentices, and other journeymen. Most manufacturing took place in small shops run by the artisan. Collectively, the guilds regulated output and wages, and enforced strict rules about hiring workers.

Many manufacturers reacted to the rules by moving their shops out of the cities and into the countryside where such rules were not enforced. They began hiring semi-skilled and unskilled laborers who were outside the apprentice system. These workers faced a lifetime of employment and had little chance to own their own shop or move into the artisan class. In England, the wool industry grew when industrialists built mills in rural areas and encouraged peasants to spin and weave in their homes.

After the world emerged from its long period of economic woes, industry and agriculture rebounded due to a rise in population and new technological innovations. During the reign of Elizabeth I (1558–1603), England expanded its budding textile industry, as well as shipbuilding and coal mining.

To further facilitate industrial growth, the government attempted to mobilize labor. The Statute of Artificers of 1563 ordered all able-bodied men (except scholars, gentlemen, and landowners) to learn a trade or work in agriculture. The law set apprenticeships at seven years and decreed the justices of the peace set the maximum pay rate in any given district. An employer who paid workers in excess of the rate faced punishment. The statute remained in place through the early 19th century.

Rise of modern manufacturing. As economic expansion took hold across Europe, its great mass of workers and peasants did not gain in proportion. Wage increases were not consistent with prices, which hindered purchasing power and, as a result, the standard of living dropped. In addition, technological innovation (particularly in agriculture) did not keep pace with the growing populations, which kept most European workers at the poverty line. Manufacturing in industries such as textiles and metal advanced, but workers were not the recipients of great rewards as a result.

In England, Richard Arkwright invented the first practical cotton-spinning machine, and in many respects, was the first modern manufacturer. The size of Arkwright's spinning machine required waterpower, so in 1771 he set up a large five-story factory in the tiny hamlet of Cromford. Many scholars consider this the start of the INDUSTRIAL REVOLUTION.

Arkwright had several challenges to overcome right away, primarily the lack of workers in small towns. The inventor build cottages near the factory as an enticement to workers from across Derbyshire. He advertised for weavers with large families. The houses had a weaving shed on the top floor, where the male weavers wove cotton. The women and children worked in the mill.

Like later mass production innovators, Arkwright simplified the spinning process to the point that unskilled laborers could operate the machinery. Employees at the factory worked 13-hour days from six in the morning to seven at night. Scholars have estimated that children numbered as many as two-thirds of Arkwright's 1,900 workers. Arkwright, like other factory owners, did not employ people over 40 years old.

Arkwright's primary management development was orchestrating the fixed shift system, which put laborers to work in an organized manner. However, Arkwright was also a benevolent leader. He founded a school for the children of his staff, built churches and chapels and gave workers Sundays off and helped the local community with construction projects. Arkwright supported farmers, who in turn provided fresh vegetables. He even loaned money for farmers wishing to purchase livestock.

Later, Arkwright established mills in Derbyshire, Yorkshire, Worcestershire, and Manchester. Then, he opened a mill in Scotland after a visit there revealed the abundance of waterpower. Between 1751 and 1861, Britain's total cotton export increased more than 1,000 percent, due in great part to the industry Arkwright built. By 1782, Arkwright employed more than 5,000 people in his mills.

As European economies shifted from agriculture to industry, the cities became the focal point of new social classes, with ideas and attitudes different from previous generations. At the beginning of the 19th century, workers developed a newfound class consciousness. They began asserting themselves to gain a more equitable distribution of income. By the middle of the century, workers rioted and staged strikes. When they organized into trade unions, they faced fierce resistance from their employers and governments.

Birth of unions. The working class found its first spokesman in Robert Owen (1771–1858), a former cotton mill manager and owner. Owen attempted to convince European aristocrats that providing high wages and decent living and working conditions would result in higher profits. Several unions formed after the repeal of the Combination Acts in 1824 and Owen organized them into one large union in 1834, dubbed the Grand National Consolidated Trades Union, with half-a-million members.

The new union planned a general strike to secure an eight-hour workday, but the organization suffered from internal dissension. Owen and his followers initiated a series of aggressive strikes, but rather than gain wider support, the moves instead brought the government's antipathy. In March 1834, six Dorchester laborers were sentenced to seven-years' exile in the Australian penal colony for organizing a branch of the union. Seven months later the Grand National disbanded.

Two years later, in 1836, workers turned to political means to achieve their aims. The London Working Men's Association sought parliamentary reform. In 1837, the Birmingham Political Union formed. Together the two and other groups (called Chartists) petitioned Parliament with the People's Charter, calling for various reforms, including universal male suffrage, and the secret ballot. Parliament defeated motions for the Charter in 1839 and 1842.

Riots and strikes broke out after each defeat. The government responded with repression. In 1840, after a riot in Wales where 20 activists were killed by constables, 500 Chartist leaders were jailed and several were given life imprisonment. The organization crumbled in the face of such stern measures.

Labor took less aggressive steps to exert influence after the government proved it would not accept confrontational acts. In 1845, the National Association of the United Traders for the Protection of Labor formed to mediate in disputes between workers and management. The group downplayed strikes in favor of arbitration and conciliation. In the following decades, other groups in Britain formed non-threatening cooperatives to pool resources, but without inciting those who controlled the political and social order. Groups such as the Amalgamated Society of Engineers were part of the New Model union movement, organizing skilled workers by profession. They worked to improve wages and working conditions for their own members, but did not engage in politics and rarely struck.

By the latter stages of the 19th century, many Western nations had increased industrialization efforts and challenged Britain's domination. FRANCE, GERMANY, BELGIUM, and the United States used technological innovation and natural resources to fuel their growth. Political repression, however, kept workers unorganized.

Labor efforts on the European continent were mixed. In France, unions made slow progress, primarily due to their close link to socialism. Southern European and Latin American groups were influenced by the French model and remained individualistic and fragmented. German labor unions were more cohesive and centralized than those in France. Switzerland and Austro-Hungary were like the Germans, though ethnic and political squabbles kept them from becoming true national movements. In Russia and Eastern Europe, trade unions were illegal.

In the United States, most early trade efforts took place among skilled workers. However, unskilled and semi-skilled laborers soon organized. In 1827, the Mechanics' Union of Trade Associations in Philadelphia became the first union in America to permit members from various trades. Like European employers, their American counterparts fought labor union's attempts by firing and blacklisting organizers. Unionization efforts grew until a depression in the 1830s and 1840s that undercut the movement.

In the 1850s, unions gained new life in the United States. Industrialization required great numbers of immigrant workers who streamed into the country. Skilled workers intensified their efforts. After the AMERICAN CIVIL WAR, the first truly national labor union formed, the National Labor Union (NLU), focusing on the eight-hour day and the right to organize. The NLU folded in the early 1870s, but was replaced by a new national organization, the Knights of Labor (KOL).

KOL membership peaked at 730,000 in 1886, but dropped by two-thirds over the next four years as employers and the police fought union growth and violently broke strikes. They linked organizing efforts with SOCIALISM and used the resulting "red scare" as a reason to persecute labor organizers.

Labor power ebbs and flows. In the 1890s and the early 20th century, labor rebounded and gained a solid foothold in Western nations. In Europe, union groups allied with political parties to achieve their goals. In Germany, unions were linked to the Social Democratic Party. Various labor groups in England formed the foundation of the Labor Party.

After the decline of the KOL, Samuel Gompers organized the American Federation of Labor (AFL) in 1886, supporting the aims of skilled workers. Rather than resort to aggressive tactics, AFL unions attempted to work with employers, primarily to avert the repressive tactics that had marked earlier unionization efforts. The AFL did urge union members to strike when necessary and 7,500 took place between 1890–94.

The use of new technology by big businesses focused on making the workplace more efficient, which also disrupted the lives of workers. Glass, chemicals, steel, and coal workers were forced to change processes to maximize production, regardless of how the pace affected workers. The influx of immigrant labor ensured that those who could not keep up would be replaced. Between 1897 and 1903, AFL membership jumped from 400,000 to nearly 3 million.

While the AFL mainly advocated negotiation over action, other unions affiliated with the organization were more antagonistic. The United Mine Workers of America (UMWA) used its power to win a national agreement for coal production in 1898. Other union successes, however, created anti-labor sentiment among the nation's employers. Manufacturers countered with an open-shop movement that thwarted union growth.

Many activists were frustrated by the AFL's direction and lack of action. Rather than work to change the AFL from within, they formed their own unions. In 1905 a group of 200 radical labor leaders met in Chicago, forming the Industrial Workers of the World (IWW), nicknamed the "Wobblies." Moving away from the craftsman tradition of the AFL, the IWW advocated empowering all workers, particularly the unskilled laborers excluded from the AFL. Believing that the nation's most exploited and poorest workers deserved a voice, the Wobblies called for "One Big Union" that would challenge the capitalist system, first in the United States, then later worldwide.

The Wobblies rise is best viewed as a product of the watershed events taking place in the United States in the early 20th century. The millions of immigrants moving into the nation transformed business, but also made poverty a way of life for many workers. The IWW hoped that the overthrow of capitalism would make life better for the working poor. Gompers and other AFL leaders immediately feared and despised the IWW. The Wobblies rocked the status quo and wanted immediate change, unlike the AFL's advocacy of gradual improvement. However, the Wobbly message appealed to miners, timber workers, and migratory agriculture workers, who had no place in Gompers' structure.

World War I derailed the plans of the IWW and gave the government an opportunity to link the radical union with America's overseas enemies. President Woodrow WILSON authorized a raid on IWW headquarters around the nation to capture Wobbly leaders. More than 200 were arrested on sedition and espionage charges. In 1918, 101 IWW activists went on trial and all were found guilty, with 15 sentenced to 20 years in prison.

During the WORLD WAR I era, governments rewarded unions that supported the war efforts. Wilson endorsed AFL unionization and collective bargaining in exchange for labor's aid in the conflict. With government support, the AFL organized workers in shipbuilding, steel, and meatpacking, while doubling membership between 1915 and 1919. In Britain, labor shortages during the war gave unions an unprecedented opportunity to negotiate. British unions grew to 8 million members by 1920, nearly half the non-farming workforce. In Germany and SWEDEN, union membership tripled, while it doubled in CANADA, the NETHERLANDS, and NORWAY.

After World War I, declining wages and horrible working conditions incensed European workers. They reacted to slow reform efforts by staging strikes at an alarming rate. In France, 2.5 million workers went on strike in 1919–20, while in Germany the number topped 13 million. These figures were 10–20 times the pre-war rate.

The gains were short-lived, however, as governments and industry combined to stop unionization. A postwar economic slump and high unemployment rates enabled businesses to purge labor activists and cajole unions into a less aggressive stance. In the United States, unions were driven from the major industries, including steel, automobiles, and consumer electronics. Between 1920–24, union membership decreased by 33 percent, while employers and the state combined efforts to weaken labor.

The Great DEPRESSION debilitated business worldwide, but re-energized labor. A series of strikes erupted in France in 1936, gradually moving across the nation. At the Renault factory, 35,000 workers walked out after management sped up the assembly lines in an attempt to increase efficiency. The workers occupied the factory and barricaded against police action. The Renault strike led to a series of social reform laws, giving workers a 40-hour workweek and holidays with pay. In 1937, union membership numbered 4.5 million.

In the United States, labor leaders viewed Franklin D. ROOSEVELT's victory in the 1932 presidential election as a positive sign. When the National Industrial Recovery Act (NIRA) passed, a wave of unionizing took place in the mass production industries. Although unions still faced stiff corporate opposition, the president signed the Wagner Act in 1935, which ensured union recognition. As a result, mining leader John L. Lewis formed the Committee for Industrial Organization (CIO). The CIO welcomed unskilled workers. Lewis and his allies took on both GENERAL MOTORS and U.S. STEEL by staging sit-down strikes at GM plants in Flint, Michigan, while secretly negotiating with the steel giant.

The CIO rivaled the AFL and both grew after war broke out in Europe, marking the beginning of WORLD WAR II. During the war, American unions worked with the federal government in a kind of wartime détente. Roosevelt created a National War Labor Board (NWLB), which regulated relations between workers and industry. As more men went off to fight, women and African-Americans took their places on assembly lines and in factories, which opened union ranks to these groups.

Success and failure in the postwar world. After World War II, unions in the United States staged the biggest strikes in American history. Maintaining the status quo established during the war, employers and the unions negotiated, rather than turning to violent confrontations. Collective bargaining gave workers higher wages and additional benefits, but ceded their power to management.

Technological innovations in manufacturing and competition from overseas combined to hurt organizing efforts, even though America's economy boomed after

World War II. Even the merger of the AFL and CIO in 1955 could not stop the decline of labor's influence. Unions in America had given up too much power during the global conflict and the move toward collective bargaining removed the only real tool the unions had to force action.

European union ranks swelled during and after the war, which coincided with a general political shift to the left. In the UNITED KINGDOM, the Labor Party swept to power in 1945. It nationalized the railroads, mining, and the Bank of England and established a national HEALTH care service. Similar programs sprouted up across Europe, including France.

Although union membership dropped in many European nations with the onset of the Cold War, union presence was still stronger than it had been prior to World War II. In nations where manufacturers regained equal footing, there were violent episodes as the two sides clashed. In other nations, such as Germany and AUSTRIA, where communists had influence, unions combined forces with the federal government. These relationships enabled labor leaders to gain favorable contracts for their rank and file.

The Vietnam era of the 1960s and early 1970s had different effects in Europe and the United States. The European unions showed significant gains during the time of social unrest. As a result, membership briefly jumped to over 50 percent of the labor force in both Italy and the United Kingdom. In the United States, the VIETNAM WAR deeply divided labor. The AFL-CIO supported the war, while popular leaders, such as United Autoworkers' Walter Reuther challenged that backing. The generational rift caused dissension.

The move away from industrialization in the 1970s, 1980s, and 1990s accelerated labor's decline in the United States. A series of strike losses in the 1980s and the dominance of the Republican Party in government created a negative impression of unions among many people. By the mid-1990s, union membership slipped to less than 15 percent of the non-agricultural workforce. On a positive note, however, unions have played a greater role in the service and public sectors. Teachers, police officers, and government workers have benefited from strong unions. An added gain is that women comprise about 40 percent of this membership.

Although the American labor movement has shown promise in the late 1990s and early 2000s, no nation has seen its union efforts falter like the United States. In comparison, unions in Europe and Canada still thrive, although admittedly slightly smaller than several decades ago.

The difficult relationship between labor, the state, and employers is at the heart of attempts to organize workers. Governments and businesses have traditionally been unwilling to recognize the need for unions. Furthermore, they have successfully tainted the image of unions by linking them with undemocratic and anti-capitalistic organizations and philosophies. In this centuries-old battle, unions simply cannot withstand the combined force and have had their influence chipped away.

BIBLIOGRAPHY. Christopher K Ansell, *Schism and Solidarity in Social Movements: The Politics of Labor in the French Third Republic* (Cambridge University Press, 2001); George S. Bain and Robert Price, *Profiles of Union Growth: A Comparative Statistical Portrait of Eight Countries* (Blackwell, 1980); Melvyn Dubofsky and Foster Rhea Dulles, *Labor in America: A History* (Harlan Davidson, 1999); Gerald Friedman, *State-Making and Labor Movements: France and the United States 1876–1914* (Cornell University Press, 1998); Richard Geary, *European Labour Protest, 1848–1939* (St. Martin's, 1981); David Montgomery, *The Fall of the House of Labor: The Workplace, the State, and American Labor Activism, 1865–1920* (Cambridge University Press, 1987); Daniel Nelson, *Shifting Fortunes: The Rise and Decline of American Labor, from the 1820s to the Present* (Ivan R. Dee, 1997); Robert Zieger, *The CIO, 1935–1955* (University of North Carolina Press, 1995).

BOB BATCHELOR
INDEPENDENT SCHOLAR

United Kingdom

AS THE "FIRST INDUSTRIAL NATION," the United Kingdom (UK) was until comparatively recently considered a model for emulation by developing countries. Since the 1960s, as the hapless victim of the "British disease" whose principal symptoms included low productivity, "stop-go" macroeconomic policy, and trade union militancy, it has more often been seen as an example of what to avoid.

Each of these characterizations is lacking in perspective. Happenstance rather than design played a large part in giving Britain a 50-year head start in developing a modern industrial economy; and the difficulties experienced by the United Kingdom since 1945 have been shared, to a greater or lesser degree, by many others. Rather than viewing Britain's record as unique, therefore, it should be regarded as in many ways typical of a medium-sized, Western country, albeit one that through historical accident came to occupy an especially prominent position.

After WORLD WAR II, as newly independent Third World countries confronted the challenge of developing modern economies, a great deal of effort was made to identify the conditions that had enabled Great Britain to industrialize two centuries earlier. Some commentators argued that 18th-century Britain contained a larger pool of un-invested CAPITAL than any other European country. Others pointed to social structure, noting that an unusually high proportion of the UK population, approximately a third, lived in urban centers and thus provided a large reservoir of unattached non-agricultural LABOR. Other historians again highlighted the political environment, noting that the UK government interfered less in entrepreneurial activity, and created a more favorable climate for trade than was the case elsewhere. Some academics even suggested that religion was the key factor, and that the nonconformist Protestants who made up a disproportionately large number of Britain's first generation of industrialists were inspired by their belief in individualism and hard work.

Britain's growth into industrialization. More recently, however, historians have been less preoccupied by the factors that made for Britain's launch into industrial growth, and more conscious of the incremental and often accidental character of that growth. It is now accepted that the technological advances described in numerous self-congratulatory accounts of Britain's industrial development played a relatively small part, if only because so few examples of the new machinery found their way into the manufacturing economy. On the other hand, the roots of the most important industries are acknowledged to extend much further back in time than conventional accounts once indicated. By the middle of the 17th century, coal mining was already so established that London suffered from the worst air pollution in Europe, while the use of railways (albeit horse-drawn rather than steam-driven) in manufacturing is of even earlier vintage.

The INDUSTRIAL REVOLUTION was thus an exceedingly gradual affair: between 1750 and 1850, the average annual rate of GROSS NATIONAL PRODUCT (GNP) growth in Britain was less than 2 percent. Moreover, neither the pace nor the distribution of industrial change was by any means uniform. In certain textile trades, most notably cotton, the adoption of new technology was fairly rapid. But many others, like the wool industry, lagged behind; and overall, the introduction of mechanization proceeded very unevenly. It has been estimated that as late as 1830 more than 50 percent of the industrial labor force did not work in factories, and by that date no single industry—not even cotton—had been fully mechanized.

Even during its 19th-century heyday, therefore, the picture of British industrialization was a most uneven one, with highly developed islands such as Lancashire, London, and South Wales found in areas untouched by modern technology, and in which traditional rural patterns continued well into the 20th century.

There is, however, no question that the rise of industrial society proceeded more rapidly and thoroughly

The Houses of Parliament in London have presided over centuries of economic growth in the United Kingdom.

in Britain than anywhere else in Europe. Although a heated debate continues to rage over whether industrialization improved or worsened the condition of the new urban proletariat—a controversy that in large measure is overshadowed by its protagonists' views concerning the capitalist system—the social impact of industrialization was clearly visible by the middle of the 19th century. The factory system with its unique workplace rhythms and practices had become firmly established throughout the country, a development that was accelerated by the widespread use of child labor.

Industrial social patterns. The flow of displaced agricultural workers into the burgeoning factory towns likewise brought about a revolution in traditional patterns of life. The social problems associated with early industrialization (hazardous workplaces, low wages, insecure employment, familial disruption, and above all overcrowded and unsanitary housing) are too well known to require extensive rehearsal; nevertheless, a few statistics suffice to convey much of the grim reality. In Manchester in 1842, for example, the average age of death for members of the mechanical and laboring class was a mere 17 years; while in Liverpool 20 years later the population density had reached the appalling figure of 66,000 per square mile. Nevertheless, if the growth of the British metropolitan infrastructure was outpaced—and sometimes overwhelmed—by the influx of new workers, industrialization did at least give Britain its modern character as the most urbanized large country in the world.

By 1851, the year of the Great Exhibition in London, a majority of the British population had come to live in urban environments, a stage not reached by GERMANY until 1891 and by FRANCE not until 1931. The Great Exhibition is conventionally regarded as marking the zenith of the United Kingdom's Industrial Revolution and commercial dominance over the rest of the world. Thenceforward, the country's share of global production started a steady decline that, after more than a century, had still not been arrested. This does not, in itself, mean that as early as the 1850s the British economy had begun to lose the race against its competitors. Its pre-eminence in the mid-19th century had in large measure been accidental, the result of an industrial head start of 50 years. It was inevitable, and indeed from the United Kingdom's own perspective desirable, that as other countries began to develop their own industrial sectors, Britain's hegemony should diminish in proportion. Nor did the British economy cease to grow at a healthy pace: Between 1850–70, for example, the value of exports from the United Kingdom nearly quadrupled.

Industrial under-performance. Nonetheless, there is no doubt that in the second half of the 19th century, British industrialists and manufacturers did begin to lose an excessive amount of ground to their counterparts, especially in the UNITED STATES and Germany. The reasons for this underperformance have been the subject of much debate. It is argued, most notably by Martin Wiener, that successful British businessmen were more likely than others to try to raise their social status by buying land and dissociating themselves from their plebeian trade roots. There are, however, more tangible explanations.

The disadvantage of being the first country to industrialize is that plant and machinery are also the first to become obsolete. British entrepreneurs were often slow to invest in more modern equipment, and spending on RESEARCH AND DEVELOPMENT was also low in comparison to levels in other industrial countries. Technical and managerial education were badly neglected in British schools and universities; the dominant craft tradition in manufacturing meant that most skilled workers learned their trades through lengthy apprenticeships, and thus had a vested interest in resisting new methods that might render their skills obsolete. A disproportionately high percentage of British capital was exported overseas, rather than being invested in new processes at home. British companies were also too small (only a fifth were publicly quoted in 1914) making it impossible to take full advantage of economies of scale. The cumulative result of these factors was that by the end of the 19th century, British industries that had once led the way were seriously lagging behind their foreign counterparts.

British steel output was surpassed by that of the United States in 1886 and Germany in 1893, and fell to a mere 10 percent of world production by WORLD WAR I. More ominously, the new, high-value-added technologies coming to the fore at this time—electrical goods, petrochemicals, internal combustion engines—whose advent has sometimes been described as signifying a second Industrial Revolution, failed to gain a foothold in the United Kingdom on anything like the same scale as in other major industrial nations, leaving a manufacturing sector that was already facing a growing productivity crisis over-dependent on trades that yielded low and declining rates of profit.

At the beginning of the 20th century, Britain's growing competitive disadvantage—the effects of which, to be sure, were more than compensated for by very large invisible earnings from financial services, shipping, and overseas investments—gave rise to a spirited debate on the wisdom of persisting with the country's long-established free-trade policy. Germany, France and the United States all maintained high tariff barriers against British exports; and even within the British Empire, as it industrialized, began discriminating against goods from the mother country. The advocates of protectionism, however, failed to make a compelling case on either economic or political grounds, and the United Kingdom entered WORLD WAR I as the world's last, and most faithful, devotee of 19th-century liberal orthodoxy.

The world wars. The significance of the war for Britain lay less in its unprecedented cost than in the fact that it greatly accelerated pre-existing economic trends. This is not to understate the financial stresses imposed by the world's first total war, which were on a scale neither previously seen nor imagined. Five years before the conflict began, a constitutional crisis had erupted over a proposal to raise an additional £15 million in new taxation. By 1917, the United Kingdom was spending a like sum on the war every two days. The lasting consequences of wartime mobilization, however, were only perceived after the Armistice.

Trade union membership doubled between 1914–18; thenceforward, the power of organized labor could not be overlooked in any aspect of economic and political life. The penetration of women into the paid workforce and the rise of a "pink-collar" sector, already visible by the end of the 19th century, likewise became an irreversible tide. Most important of all, perhaps, the extension of state control into every area of economic life marked a definite and permanent breach with the prewar tradition of LAISSEZ-FAIRE.

The very failure of attempts in the 1920s to restore normality by abolishing wartime controls, reverting to a currency based on gold, and resuming free trade served as confirmation that a historical watershed had been reached. In the 1930s, as a new war loomed, the United Kingdom had already adopted a system of imperial preference, abandoned fixed exchange rates, and was operating a species of primitive Keynesianism in the form of public works and rearmament projects.

If WORLD WAR I made the interventionist state indispensable, WORLD WAR II made it respectable. Despite the loss of an additional quarter of the national wealth that effectively drove the United Kingdom into nominal bankruptcy, the success of the wartime government in ensuring "fair shares" through rationing and controls over the whole of the country's economic resources was taken by its postwar successors as a sign that effective management of supply and demand had become both a political and a moral imperative. Such perceptions provided the basis for nationalization of the "commanding heights" of the economy by the Labor Party government of 1945–51. This was a somewhat ironic outcome, as hardly any businesses had been taken into public ownership during the war itself, and considering the pursuit of an undeclared quasi-corporatist strategy by successive Conservative and Labor administrations from the 1950s until the mid-1970s.

Stop-go cycles and the European community. Unhappily, increasing ambition was not always matched by increasing competence in manipulating the levers of macroeconomic policy. In the third quarter of the 20th century, a pronounced stop-go cycle, the alternation of deflationary and reflationary measures, adopted in response to rising balance of payments deficits on the one hand and rising unemployment on the other, became the most conspicuous feature of the UK economy. The impact of this oscillation, coupled with unaddressed structural deficiencies in British manufacturing, was most apparent in comparison with the record of other major European countries during the same period. Between 1951–73, the United Kingdom experienced an average annual growth rate of 2.3 percent, less than half that of its major continental competitors. Nevertheless, Britain's good fortune in escaping the devastation suffered by much of western Europe during the war meant that growth, even on so modest a scale, was sufficient to produce a degree of prosperity, a period in which Prime Minister Harold Macmillan famously observed the majority of Britons had "never had it so good." Unfortunately, it was also to produce a national complacency about the United Kingdom's economic performance that was ultimately to cost the country dearly.

After World War II, the United Kingdom consciously, and, as most outside observers now concur, shortsightedly, cold-shouldered the steps being taken by other European countries toward greater economic and political integration. This stance owed less to a sober assessment of the costs and benefits of European unity than to the powerful reinforcement given to British particularist tendencies by the experience of the war. The United Kingdom thus brusquely rejected invitations to participate in the European Coal and Steel Community, and sent only a mid-level civil servant with the status of observer to the Messina Conference that drew up plans for the European Economic Community (EEC), the forerunner to the EUROPEAN UNION (EU).

Instead, Labor and Conservative governments alike clung to the notion of the British Commonwealth as a "natural" trading community in which a symbiotic relationship existed between the industrial metropole and the primary-producing hinterland. Such a stance, however, proved unsustainable over the long term. Not only did it rest, as contemporary observers such as R.W.G. Mackay pointed out, on an outdated mercantilist philosophy, but it proceeded on the optimistic assumption that the Commonwealth countries would altruistically forgo the benefits of industrialization to provide a permanent captive market for British manufactured goods. The United Kingdom's attempt to create a rival to the EEC, in the form of a European Free Trade Area encompassing a haphazard collection of Scandinavian and Alpine countries, similarly represented the triumph of national self-regard over economic self-interest, and failed either to compete with or substitute for the Common Market. Bowing to the inevitable, Britain applied for EEC membership in 1961, only to be vetoed by a suspicious Charles DE GAULLE. Not until 1973 did the United Kingdom finally secure entry, on significantly worse terms than would have been available to the country 16 years earlier.

Even accession to the EEC, however, made little impact on the combination of underinvestment, manage-

Like the lone guard at the Tower of London, the UK economy often stands apart from the European community.

rial inefficiency, low productivity, persistent balance of payment crises and poisonous industrial relations that was known by the unflattering shorthand term "the British disease." By 1975, inflation was running at 24 percent and the British government was forced to take the humiliating step the following year of applying to the INTERNATIONAL MONETARY FUND (IMF) for a loan to stabilize the currency. Not all the United Kingdom's troubles at this time were of its own making—the OIL crisis of 1973 had a particularly unfortunate effect, arising as it did before Britain's own substantial North Sea oil deposits had begun to come on stream—but the second half of the 1970s saw all the structural problems of the British economy come home to roost. Several underperforming companies were taken into public ownership solely to prevent the rise in unemployment that would have followed their collapse; sterling fluctuated uncontrollably; and the government's unrealistic attempt to fix a nationwide wage norm resulted in a Winter of Discontent in 1978–79, in which workers in transport, the public services and, famously, the Liverpool gravediggers went on strike.

In March 1979, the Labor administration of James Callaghan became the first sitting government since 1924 to be voted out of office. In retrospect, Britain's economic record under Callaghan appears in a more favorable light than it seemed to contemporary observers. A balance of payments surplus was achieved in 1978; inflation had fallen to 7 percent in the same year; and pressure on the currency, aided by earnings from North Sea oil, had eased to such an extent that it proved unnecessary to take up the whole of the IMF loan. With memories of the Winter of Discontent fresh in people's minds, however, little notice was taken of these positive indications. The perception of an economy in permanent crisis was what mattered.

The coming of Thatcherism. In the general election of May, 1979, the Conservative administration, now led by Margaret THATCHER, was returned to office, having promised to restore British prosperity by reining back public spending, shifting from direct to indirect taxation, and, in general, applying market-based rather than Keynesian solutions to the nation's problems.

The Thatcher government's macroeconomic policy was based on the monetarist prescriptions of the Chicago economist Milton FRIEDMAN, although even the economist was subsequently to deny that he had ever advocated so doctrinaire an application of his principles. The results of this all-out monetarist attack on inflation were far from what had been expected. Despite the most determined efforts, the broad-money indicator (M3) selected by the government as its target continued to grow. So too did inflation, which nearly doubled during the first 12 months of the Thatcher administration. Intensified attempts to meet monetarist targets in 1980 and 1981 by raising interest rates had a disastrous impact upon the manufacturing sector, coupled as they were with an overvalued pound and a worldwide RECESSION. By the end of 1981, more than 20 percent of British manufacturing firms had gone out of business; economic growth moved into the negative column; and the number of unemployed rose to three million—a level not seen since the Great Depression of the 1930s. Despite a variety of efforts to massage this disturbing figure downward by changing the formula by which the number of jobless was calculated, unemployment remained at approximately the same level for another five years.

The "sado-monetarist" experiment of the early 1980s was neither disavowed nor repeated. Instead, in its second and third terms of office the Thatcher government quietly abandoned its monetary targets and set about an unannounced reflation of the economy. In the best tradition of stop-go economics, credit controls were released, interest rates lowered, and public spending increased. The budgetary and balance of payments deficits that ordinarily might evolve from such a policy were held in check by North Sea oil earnings, and by windfall receipts from the sale, at deeply discounted prices, of public utilities.

Wage inflation eased, though not eliminated, by lowered expectations on the part of workers, the result in part of stringent trade union legislation but much more importantly the existence of mass unemployment. Despite this, there was clear evidence in the latter part of the 1980s that the economy was beginning to overheat. These indications were ignored; and in the budgets of 1987 and 1988 large tax cuts injected additional purchasing power into an economy that was already in the midst of a credit-led consumer boom. The results were predictable. Inflation rose again to double digits; the jobless figures, which had abated to about half their previous level, once again approached the three million barrier; and interest rates were increased twelve consecutive times, reaching 15 percent by October 1989.

The record of Thatcher's stewardship of the economy, therefore, failed to lend credence to her oft-quoted boast to have "put the 'Great' back into Britain." Fortunately for her historical reputation, neither did that of her immediate successor. The administration of Thatcher's chosen heir, John Major, never recovered from the United Kingdom's forced withdrawal, in September, 1992, from the Exchange Rate Mechanism (ERM) of the European Monetary System, after almost exhausting the country's foreign currency reserves in a hopeless attempt to shore up the pound. If the ERM fiasco was to some extent inherited from its predecessor, most of the Major government's other wounds were self-inflicted. A badly bungled PRIVATIZATION of the railways, persistent intra-party in-fighting over relations with the EU, and a series of corruption scandals earned Major and his ministers an unshakable, though not entirely justified, reputation for incompetence, and made their electoral defeat a virtual certainty.

Britain's third way. In 1997, the United Kingdom elected a Labor administration led by Tony Blair. Preaching a Third Way between capitalism and socialism, Labor has, in practice, forsworn ideology and taken a cautious, pragmatic approach—albeit one marked by a distinct preference for free market principles—in its management of the British economy. It has been the beneficiary of a de facto devaluation of the currency following the defection from the ERM, which has improved the outlook for exports; a steady decline in unemployment, which by December 2002, had fallen to 885,000; and a low-inflation environment. It has also successfully evaded the issue of whether or not to participate in the European single currency, mindful of both the scars left by the ERM episode and the deep divisions existing within British society over European issues generally. In consequence, the United Kingdom currently finds itself in the unaccustomed position of being regarded as one of the most successful economies of the contemporary world, and the "British disease" is considered, whether by good luck or good judgment, to have been cured.

Such a verdict may be premature. While the United Kingdom's condition certainly appears healthier than in the past, persistent systemic problems remain. Many of the new jobs created since the early 1990s are part-time, short-term, and poorly paid, leading to suggestions that Britain is resigning itself to becoming the principal low-wage economy of western Europe. The education system continues to leave many—especially males, whose unemployment rate is three times that of females—inadequately prepared for work, raising concerns that a permanent urban underclass is in the process of being created. Manufacturing has barely recovered from the trauma of the 1979–81 shock, and as in the past suffers from underinvestment and low productivity.

And the question of membership of the EURO zone will sooner or later have to be faced, especially as diminishing revenues from North Sea oil removes an important crutch from the British economy. It is likely, therefore, that the growing pressures of globalization will compel the United Kingdom and its leaders to confront in the 21st century many of the hard choices that they were able to defer in the 20th.

BIBLIOGRAPHY. P. Deane, *The First Industrial Revolution* (Cambridge University Press, 1979); M. Dintenfass, *The Decline of Industrial Britain 1870–1980* (Routledge, 1992); J. Mokyr, *The British Industrial Revolution* (Westview, 1993); S. Pollard, *The Development of the British Economy 1914–1990*

(Edward Arnold, 1992); M. Wiener, *English Culture and the Decline of the Industrial Spirit* (Cambridge University Press, 1982).

R.M. Douglas
Colgate University

United Parcel Service (UPS)

UPS MARKS ITS 100-YEAR anniversary in 2007. Founded in Seattle, by 19-year-old Jim Casey, UPS has grown to become one of the global leaders in transportation. What started as a bicycle messenger service (originally named the American Messenger Company) with Casey's initial investment of $100, has grown into a company handling over 13 million shipments per day, and using an extensive fleet of aircraft and ground transportation vehicles.

UPS acquired its first car in 1913, enabling it to remain competitive as technology advanced. With the advent of automobiles and the telephone, the demand for messenger services declined. However, the United States Parcel Post system did not yet exist and as such, demand remained high for transferring packages. By 1920, UPS had adopted its present name and had expanded beyond Seattle into California, and then to the East Coast by the early 1930s. Much of UPS's success stems from Casey's early focus on competitive rates and high-quality service.

As the economy changed after WORLD WAR II, UPS moved into the common carrier business, delivering packages between both private and commercial customers. It encountered legal battles since it was in direct competition with the United States Postal Service, a violation of regulations of the Interstate Commerce Commission (ICC) regulations. UPS restarted air service in 1953, which it had briefly originated in 1923, and 25 years later the air service was available in every state in the United States. In 1975, the ICC finally granted UPS permission to serve all 48 contiguous states, utilizing cargo space on existing airlines to carry its packages.

With the onset of airline deregulation in the 1980s, UPS began to acquire its own aircraft fleet enabling expansion to next-day air service by 1985 within the United States as well as to six countries in Europe. The FAA granted UPS the authorization to fly its own planes in 1988, making UPS its own airline. UPS became the fastest growing airline and has become one of the largest 10 airlines in the United States.

The 1990s and early 2000s have seen the embrace of technology and innovation at UPS. With a rapidly changing global economy, UPS has become a leader in supply-chain management as well as logistics and distribution. As such, the UPS Logistics Group was formed in 1995, and the company introduced UPS Capital in 1998, a financial products company.

The success of UPS over the century led the company to its initial public offering on the NEW YORK STOCK EXCHANGE on November 10, 1999. UPS now holds nine companies, including Mail Boxes, Etc. From 1995 through 2001, UPS has seen total revenue increase from $21 to $30 billion, with operating profit increasing from $1.7 to $3.9 billion. In addition, basic earnings per share increased from $0.93 to $2.13.

BIBLIOGRAPHY. www.ups.com; *What Can Brown Do For You?* United Parcel Service Annual Report 2002; Hoover's, www.hoovers.com.

Audrey D. Kline, Ph.D.
University of Louisville

United States

AT THE DAWN OF THE 21st century, the United States of America had the most powerful economy and military in the world, and was the world's only real superpower. This wealth and power was grounded in extraordinary cultural and geographic diversity and a tradition of democracy and free speech. Democratic decision-making and the freedom to think and speak ideas that ran counter to the norm created a context for new innovation. The path to this state was not an easy one.

The United States was born of a violent revolution against colonial rule in 1776. It was not, however, a revolution by indigenous peoples against a conquering colonial power. Instead, the AMERICAN REVOLUTION was carried out by British subjects, the settlers of the colonies, against their nation of origin. The American colonists rebelled against the domination of their British government, which often adopted economic and political policies that ran against their interests. The new nation of the United States of America was formally recognized by the Treaty of Paris signed in 1783.

The Revolutionary War was a classic insurgency, succeeding only because of strong grassroots support from the colonial subject population. Farmers, artisans, merchants, and others joined in either direct action or indirect support of the revolutionaries. The extraordinary need for strategic planning and cooperation between colonial merchants, who supplied needed material for the war effort, and the revolutionary army helped to establish the foundation for postwar economic policies.

Many of the merchants who worked with the revolutionary army rose to prominence in the postwar economy of the new nation. Furthermore, led by the efforts of treasury secretary Alexander Hamilton, the government played an activist role in promoting a pro-growth business climate that favored these entrepreneurs. Hamilton was also a critical figure in developing the American strategy for industrialization.

An important precondition for economic growth in the new nation was to destroy the economic power of the loyalist aristocracy, wealthy landowners who had supported the continuation of British rule, and to redistribute resources to supporters of the new government. The post-revolutionary state governments, under the encouragement of the Continental Congress, confiscated the properties of loyalists and used revenues raised from the sale of such properties to supplement other sources of state funding. Some of the land confiscated from loyalists was redistributed to former soldiers returning from the war. This land redistribution, coupled with laws voiding obligations of farmers to pay feudal rents to the loyalist aristocracy, helped the expansion of family farming in the states. The expansion of family farming contributed to the growth of the domestic market in the United States, providing the basis for the growth in manufacturing.

Decentralized federalism. The postwar political leadership recognized the contradictions between building a nation founded on principles of democracy, and yet also grounded in the maintenance of slavery. In many ways, the early course of American politics was shaped by this contradiction. In particular, the country was epitomized by relatively decentralized governance. This decentralization provided a solution, albeit a temporary one, to the radically different governance requirements of the states dependent on free labor compared to those dependent upon slave labor. It provided systemic flexibility.

Decentralized federalism recognized that slavery, even if considered abhorrent by many citizens of the new nation, was a critically important source of value available for investment in the U.S. economy. There were, therefore, a number of compromises. Slavery was not abolished, but the slave trade was abolished by a number of states. The New England states, New York, and Pennsylvania committed themselves to the gradual abolition of slavery. The Southern states, dependent as they were on slave-based production, went in exactly the opposite direction, reinforcing laws that guaranteed the continuation of slavery and protected the rights of the slave masters over their human chattel. Only in an environment of political decentralization could such a sharp contradiction be maintained as long as it was in the United States.

This tension is reflected quite dramatically in agriculture. The early republic was largely agrarian. Most agricultural direct producers were either self-employed farmers or slaves. This presents a difficult environment for formulating national public policies. Policies supportive of free labor might interfere with the objectives of slave masters dependent on un-free labor. Thomas JEFFERSON tried to resolve this tension by advocating a decentralized federalism that would maximize the flexibility of each state to make its own laws. The Jeffersonian tradition is associated with an agrarian democracy of self-employed farmers, but ironically Jefferson's own agrarian experience was that of a slave master. Nevertheless, Jefferson's conception had a certain resonance in a society that had overturned a loyalist aristocracy with strong feudal traditions.

Capitalism took root in manufacturing, encouraged by the hand of government, in the form of tariff protections against foreign competition and a wide range of subsidies and special privileges. It was the textile manufacturers who saw the greatest early successes, fueled by relatively cheap slave-produced cotton. Another early success story was firearms manufacturing. The rapid expansion in firearms manufacturing was, to a significant extent, the product of governmental policy and procurement. It is not difficult to understand how the government of a new nation formed of a violent revolution would find it important to build armaments. Indeed, the government subsidized early manufacturers, partly by means of "bounties." Funds collected from foreign firms via high protective tariffs were gifted to domestic manufacturers of the same goods that had been taxed. This was part of an overall strategy of import substitution industrialization that would prove critical to the growth of capitalism in the new nation.

The basic tension between the Hamiltonian form of federalism and the decentralized federalism of Jefferson was resolved in favor of the latter with Jefferson's election. Jefferson's core constituency, the slave aristocracy of the South, deeply distrusted the federal government, which represented a potential rival to their own extraordinary power over life on their plantations, and influence over the politics of their state governments. Nonetheless, the basic tensions between the interventionist (Hamiltonian) approach and Jeffersonian LAISSEZ-FAIRE approach would come to epitomize political struggles throughout the history of the United States, extending well beyond the period of the AMERICAN CIVIL WAR when slavery ceased to be an important factor in the economy.

Self-employment and American culture. Throughout the antebellum period, agriculture remained the primary source of income for most Americans. Capitalist industrialism was a relatively less visible part of the American economic landscape, particularly outside of the largest cities. And even in the largest cities, such as New York

City, Philadelphia, Boston, and Baltimore self-employment and small scale merchants (mom-and-pop stores) remained prevalent over their larger-scale rivals for many years. In the Southern states, whose political economy was dominated by large-scale slave production, thousands of self-employed farmers and artisans and small-scale merchants played critical roles in the day-to-day economic life of most citizens. Thus, America was, in its early history, not so much a land of capitalism and slavery, but a land of the industrious, self-employed farmer and artisan. This became an important force in shaping the American character and much that has been mythologized about American culture.

The very expanse of American territory and the successful military campaign against the indigenous population served to promote self-employment, as thousands of American citizens took advantage of the frontier to migrate west, and to make their living as independent producers, either on the land, in their own workshops, or from small-scale shops. It was, therefore, difficult to develop a capitalist labor market when the potential pool of laborers could so easily pull up their roots, so to speak, and move elsewhere. The concept of the frontier, and of the freedom associated with the frontier, was another factor shaping the character of the American citizenry in complex ways.

The rapid growth of small businesses in the United States and the expansion of free enterprise to the frontier areas was supported by a highly decentralized banking system. Relatively small and autonomous state banks provided the financing for many family farms, as well as for the slave plantation system of the southern states. Bigger banks in the urban areas helped to finance industrialization but were relatively less powerful influences on economic activity in the hinterland, where most Americans lived and worked. Today the banking system in the United States remains among the most decentralized in the world.

While family farming remained relatively healthy throughout the United States in the antebellum period, expansion in slave-based production displaced many self-employed farmers from the most fertile land in the Southern states. This was more than compensated for, in the nation as a whole, by the rapid growth of family farming during the westward migration of Americans.

Export-led growth. The relatively rapid growth in population and the positive income effects of a decentralized economy were among the many factors driving development of the domestic market for agricultural and industrial goods. Another important factor in generating growth in income and domestic demand for goods and services was the export sector. Export-led growth created business opportunities and generated more revenues for existing businesses. Export-led growth was coupled with the import substitution industrialization strategy to generate rapid, even if uneven, growth in both manufacturing and agriculture during the antebellum period.

The slave plantations, in particular, focused on the production of exportable cash crops, such as cotton and tobacco. The invention and innovation of the Eli WHITNEY's cotton gin was a key technological catalyst for the growth in low-cost, slave-based cotton production that allowed U.S. planters to dramatically expand their markets, both domestic and foreign. Indeed, when one considers intra-regional export, in addition to export to foreign markets, it seems likely that most of the crops generated from the slave plantations were destined for markets outside of the region of origin. This generated sizable cash flow for the slave masters, but tended not to have quite as dramatic an impact on income growth in the region because of the sharp income inequality associated with slave-based production.

On the other hand, rapid growth in exports from family farms, whether international exports or production for the growing urban areas, generated income growth that was more egalitarian and had a more dramatic immediate impact in creating domestic demand for manufactured consumer goods.

The frontier, the railroads, and uneven regional development. The United States expanded territorially by force of arms. The indigenous populations were pushed off their lands by a combination of military force and settler violence. The expansion of the RAILROADS was an important technological component in this territorial conquest. And U.S. territory was further expanded by military aggression against MEXICO, which added California and the southwestern states to the new country.

Cattle ranchers, miners, self-employed farmers, and others moved with the railroad further and further west. As the railroads and telegraph were expanded, ports improved, and other infrastructure projects completed, it became possible to consolidate control over conquered territory and/or pursue the next stage of the expansion. The frontier mentality became an important aspect of American culture.

The expansion of the railroads was partly a consequence of the more activist (Hamiltonian) government policies of the period following the 1839–43 DEPRESSION. Among the activist measures taken was the 1850 passage of the Land Grant Act. The Act provided a grant of LAND to any corporation that agreed to lay track in the westward extension of the U.S. railroad system. The government gave away nearly four million acres of land to private corporations during this period, achieving the expected result. The railroad system was dramatically expanded which helped to create a more cohesive domestic market, to open up new territory in the west for migration, agriculture, and animal husbandry, and allowing for the sale of goods produced in the factories of the east.

The government further guaranteed the success of the new railroads by contracting with them to carry federal cargo, including mail deliveries and gold shipments. This guaranteed market for freight helped to lower the risk of investing in the railroads, making it easier to raise capital, and pushing projects into development that might otherwise have languished.

The expansion of the nation's transportation backbone provided the basis for a dramatic upward surge in agricultural production and income, as family farms were able to find markets for their output, often markets that were quite a distance from the family farm. The increased agricultural incomes were critical to expanding the domestic market in the United States, which created demand for industrial goods. The increased demand for the output from factories, and the increased quantity and lower cost of agricultural raw materials, especially slave-produced cotton, and food helped to spur the boom in manufacturing. As manufacturing expanded, this also had a positive income effect, creating further demand for both agricultural and industrial output.

Uneven regional development was reinforced during this period of economic growth. The Northern states led the way in manufacturing, while the Southern states were locked into a slave plantation-based economy. The short-term income gains to the plantations from a rise in export sales, and in sales of cotton to the textile mills of the Northeast created the illusion of prosperity. In the long term, the Southern states would significantly lag behind the Northern states in income-producing potential and in the development of infrastructure. The existence of slavery essentially retarded the industrialization of the South, hampered the building of critical infrastructure, and cost the southern states precious developmental time. The transformation of the southern economic base would have to wait until after the AMERICAN CIVIL WAR and, even then, move forward at a much slower pace than development in the North and West as the plantation system, forced to replace slavery with a form of feudalism, remained in place.

Hamiltonianism and the ascendancy of capitalism. After the Civil War, the federal government continued to play an activist role in shaping the American economy. The federal government supported the expansion of self-employed farmers and ranchers with the Homestead Act of 1862, continued to subsidize the railroads and other large business enterprises with the Timber Culture Act in 1873, the Desert Land Act in 1877, and the Timber Stone Act of 1878.

Government spending, both during and after the Civil War, stimulated growth in manufacturing industries such as coal, iron, and steel, gradually shifting the U.S. economy from an agrarian base to a more industrial one. The steel industry was particularly important during this period. Steel was a key input in both the construction of the railroads and other infrastructure, and in the development of the machine-goods industry. The innovation of new steel-making techniques helped to lower the tonnage cost of steel and had effects throughout the manufacturing economy.

The U.S. economy was not only being transformed from an agrarian one but was also shifting away from self-employment and small-scale enterprises toward corporate capitalism. Government spending and subsidies aided the rapid growth in the railroads and in manufacturing, which were organized as capitalist corporations. The corporate form of business organization, which limits the liability of owners, provided an important mechanism for raising extraordinary amounts of capital investment. The capitalist organization of work meant that it was possible to employ thousands of wage laborers within a single corporation. The legal benefits of the corporate form and the productive efficiency that came with wage labor-based production combined with the government subsidies, lower cost inputs, and expanded markets generated huge revenues for American corporations.

As corporate revenues grew it became easier to raise such funds for further business expansion. A handful of financial and industrial empires were built around this growth, led by legendary business leaders, such as Jay GOULD, James FISK, Cornelius VANDERBILT, and John D. ROCKEFELLER, who were able to marshal capital investment for their own businesses, and often used aggressive strategies for eliminating potential competitors. These early capitalist leaders have been called the robber barons because of their tactics and perceived ruthlessness.

Capitalism brought a transformation in the types of jobs available to Americans. A new middle class of white-collar workers grew up around the bureaucratic work required in large-scale corporations. The large wage-labor forces employed in manufacturing enterprises resulted in the creation of new management jobs. The growing demand for wage-labor to work in the sweatshops of New York and slaughterhouses of Chicago attracted rural people, many of whom had been self-employed, to migrate to the cities for these new jobs.

This rural-urban migration created urban metropolises where laborers and their families lived in tenement residences, often dilapidated and unhealthy places. In this case, decentralized policy making meant that the rules that determined "safe" housing were highly localized and greatly variable. Ghettos developed in the urban cities where laborers came for jobs and affordable shelter.

Industrialized wage labor was increasingly specialized to the extent that a worker might never see the final product of his labor but only a small part of it. This meant that workers who had worked for themselves, or otherwise participated in the entire production process, lost their skills over time. The resulting dissatisfaction that came with this new situation, and unsatisfactory work conditions that were often deadly in the iron and steel industries and rarely sufficient to support families, led to a push for unionization among many, though not all workers. The UNION movement, therefore, arose out of and remains an important aspect of capitalism.

U.S. capitalism, in its early history, was epitomized both by strong efforts to unionize and by severe resistance from corporate boards and managers to such efforts, including enlisting the support of the government in the suppression of unionization campaigns and strikes. In some cases, state governments sent national guard troops to assist corporate management in putting down strikes or other work actions, sometimes resulting in bloodshed.

The so-called Gilded Age from 1873–97 was an ambivalent time economically, beset by RECESSIONs and depression. It was a period of corporate takeovers and the rise of firms with monopolistic and oligopolistic market power. It was a particularly difficult time for smaller firms, self-employed farmers, and others who neither wielded much MARKET POWER nor had much influence within the halls of government. The development of these massive industrial empires had a significant impact on the character of American society. A new industrial and financial aristocracy came to prominence and celebrities, of a sort, rose in American society. These aristocrats also adopted the same political philosophy, the Jeffersonian ideal of decentralized federalism, as their political creed, although many of them continued to benefit from government policies and subsidies, including tax breaks targeted specifically at large-scale corporate enterprises and not available to smaller businesses or individuals.

The backlash against the growth of big corporate capitalist firms with extraordinary market power came in the form of government ANTITRUST legislation, including the Sherman Act, which declared monopolistic behavior illegal. The passage of the Interstate Commerce Act of 1887 formed the first regulatory agency in the federal government, the Interstate Commerce Commission, which was charged with the responsibility of regulating railroad rates.

A steady growth in the demand for cheap labor followed the advance of capitalism. Technological advances in transportation made it easier for immigrants to come to America, and the new corporate aristocracy supported relatively liberal immigration laws. Immigrant workers contributed to not only the quantity of

labor for the growing economy, but also to the creativity that went into the production of new industrial machines and new methods of organization and also into the culture of American society.

The severe decline in influence of the Southern aristocracy after the Civil War left the capitalist aristocracy without any powerful rivals in setting national economic policy. Small businesses, with the possible exception of self-employed farmers, generally had little influence on national policies. Consequently, capitalism grew quickly during the years from the close of the Civil War to WORLD WAR I. It was, in many ways, a turning point for American society, in economic, political, and cultural terms. Capitalism was dominant and would continue to be dominant, setting the course of economic life in post-Civil War U.S. society.

The New Deal. Following World War I, the United States had unprecedented economic power in the world. Government was pro-business, technological changes had lessened the domestic workload in many households, and increasing productivity meant more lax work schedules for those outside of the house. Furthermore, scientific advances led to better health and a higher average life expectancy, and children were going to school and staying for more years than they had ever been able to before, relieved from some of the pressure to join the labor force as soon as possible and help support the family.

For all of these reasons and others, there was a considerable amount of optimism about the economy. Nevertheless, in agriculture, where a significant fraction of the population still earned a living, economic conditions for the self-employed farmer continued to deteriorate. Many self-employed farmers lost their farms, unable to compete in a period of falling farm prices and mechanization of agriculture. Some of these formerly independent farmers became migrant laborers, further reflecting the continual drift away from self-employment and toward capitalism.

The optimism that had followed the end of World War I was shattered by the sharp decline in the stock market in 1929 marking the end of a speculative bubble in equity prices. The STOCK MARKET decline was followed by a decline in the output and employment in the "real economy." In this new economic landscape, the correct plan of behavior was not at all clear. Previously, the large-scale industrial and financial corporations had encouraged the government to play a limited role in the economy. President Herbert HOOVER maintained this policy in the mistaken belief that the economy would fix itself, but economic recession turned into a deep economic depression. Millions were unemployed. Without a social safety net, high levels of unemployment quickly turned into homelessness and starvation for many

Americans. The nation was in crisis and Hoover's unwavering faith in the markets did nothing to alleviate the growing despair. Franklin Delano ROOSEVELT (FDR), promising a more activist approach to solving the economic woes of America and with strong support from labor unions, was elected in a landslide in 1932.

The Roosevelt administration inaugurated a new chapter in American culture. Activist government came to be associated, perhaps for the first time, with policies designed to benefit capitalist wage-laborers. In the past, the Hamiltonian brand of activism had been designed to foster the growth of capitalist industrial and financial firms. Roosevelt's policies were called the NEW DEAL. FDR's New Deal began with legislation establishing federal institutions to regulate the banks, the stock exchange, and utilities. The hope was that such legislation would restore confidence in America's financial institutions. The New Deal continued with the passage of the National Industrial Recovery Act (NIRA), which stipulated a federal minimum wage, banned most child labor, and gave the federal government tools for combating the unemployment problem. The Wagner act of 1935 was designed to protect the rights of capitalist wage-laborers to unionize. Social Security was passed, despite strong opposition from the Republican Party. It would be a mistake to assume that New Deal legislation was simply a pro-labor set of policies.

The New Deal had its Hamiltonian overtones, as well. There was, for example, legislation to grant businesses the right to set prices for their industries. The New Deal also included the Tennessee Valley Authority (TVA) funding to develop a system that could provide cheap electricity to the nation's rural landscape. And under the Agricultural Adjustment Act, the New Deal paid farmers to control prices of their crops by limiting productions and initially destroying excess crops and livestock, driving up prices and helping both small and large farmers to generate higher revenues.

None of these policies were sufficient to pull the U.S. economy out of its most serious economic decline. As long as the directors and top managers of capitalist firms did not expect revenues and profits to grow, they were unwilling to approve new investment. The pessimism of these top leaders in business was only exacerbated by the perception of the Roosevelt administration as leaning too far in favor of labor unions, which were seen as promoting higher-cost wage-labor. In the early years of his administration, FDR made matters worse by following Hoover's example and trying to balance the federal budget in a time of declining tax revenues.

The FDR administration did eventually see the light and raised government spending in an effort to boost aggregate demand, but it was still not enough to restore business confidence. It was, in fact, WORLD WAR II that would push government spending to the point that the Depression was ended. Unemployment fell, business revenues rose, and confidence was restored during the war.

Post–World War II boom. The United States came out of World War II even more powerful than it had been after World War I. The result was another long period of optimism. Wartime rationing had suppressed consumer spending for several years, and with the growth in optimism and a booming economy, consumer spending compensated for the fall in military spending. Furthermore, the new Harry TRUMAN government would use federal funding for infrastructure improvement and spending on education, health care, and welfare including Medicare, Medicaid, and the GI bill, which provided loans to veterans to start their own businesses or continue their education. Soon, even the military was increasing its spending again. Thus, government became an increasingly important, and relatively predictable, component of aggregate demand, which reduced the degree of business uncertainty about future revenues.

The 1950s was an important period of transformation in American society. The McCarthy period served as a sort of cultural revolution against the radical politics that had grown during the Roosevelt years. Americans associated with the Communist Party of the USA were particularly targeted. In Hollywood, many writers, directors, and other screen artists were blacklisted, meaning they could not find work with the studios or financing for independent projects. The Korean War represented a hot version of the growing Cold War between the United States and its allies and the Soviet Union, CHINA, and their respective allies. These conflicts only reinforced the effects of the McCarthy era, even after McCarthy was discredited. America was also being physically transformed. Urbanization continued, but the Dwight EISENHOWER administration also funded, through the Interstate Highway Act of 1956, a dramatic increase in the highway system connecting cities and towns. The building of highways spawned the suburbanization of the nation, and helped to boost revenues for the automobile companies as car sales surged.

The John KENNEDY and Lyndon JOHNSON administrations continued the postwar transformation of America, both in terms of activist foreign policy and innovative domestic policies. The Cold War heated up again with the U.S. military intervention in the VIETNAM WAR. The Johnson administration adopted the supply-side tax cuts that Kennedy had drafted and attempted, under a barrage of criticism, to pass in order to increase consumption and stimulate the economy. Johnson's government became even more involved in the economy by passing legislation such as the Economic Opportunity Act of 1964, which included the Job Corps, and the Head Start Program for children, and increased government spending by almost $10 billion. These programs helped decrease the income gap in the United States and specifically decreased the number of Americans living in poverty. The Johnson administration was probably the most activist government since Roosevelt, and continued in the FDR tradition of using this activism to support both pro-labor and pro-business objectives.

The rise of inflation. One unfortunate result of the extended boom in the economy experienced after World War II was a rise in price INFLATION throughout the 1950s, 1960s, and 1970s, peaking in the early 1980s. Perhaps the most difficult period occurred in the 1970s when the nation experienced STAGFLATION, an economic slowdown and rise in the general level of prices caused, in part, by a sudden rise in oil prices. The VIETNAM WAR effort was also considered to be responsible for some of the economic problems of this period.

Inflation was a serious concern throughout the Eisenhower, Kennedy, and Johnson administrations but not a major political issue until Richard NIXON's presidency. Nixon attempted to stall inflation by implementing a series of PRICE CONTROLS on GOODS, WAGES, and rents. The subsequent inflation surge, when controls were lifted, discredited price controls as a tool for the federal government. During the Gerald FORD administration and every administration since, inflation has become the province of the American central bank, the FEDERAL RESERVE (Fed). The Fed used monetary policies to battle inflation, a less aggressive and often more successful tool than price controls.

Nevertheless, the Fed had only limited success. Inflation fell somewhat but the most dramatic effect was on unemployment. The problems of trying to moderate inflation, without throwing the economy into recession, became a major problem for the Fed and a key political issue. This became even more problematic with the growing power of the ORGANIZATION OF OIL EXPORTING COUNTRIES (OPEC) and the Arab oil boycott of the United States. The Jimmy CARTER administration faced stagflation, and later a crisis in IRAN after the fall of the American-supported regime of the Shah.

A superpower rises again. The Iran Hostage Crisis had a transformative effect on American politics, helping to elect Ronald REAGAN to the presidency in 1980. The Reagan presidency was marked by aggressive foreign policy actions and rhetoric. In many ways, the Reagan presidency represented a return to the "big stick" policies that have epitomized American foreign policy since the earliest days. The invasion of the tiny island of Grenada, although not significant in military terms, demonstrated that the United States had emerged from the Carter malaise that had followed the lost war in Vietnam. The Grenada invasion, interventions in Cen-

tral America, and a general perception that the Reagan administration was willing to use force in order to achieve its objectives played a key symbolic role in the resurrection of American superpower clout.

The administrations of George H.W. BUSH, William CLINTON, and George W. BUSH continued this approach, employing U.S. troops in Panama, the Persian Gulf, Kosovo, and other venues. George W. Bush took this a step beyond what his predecessors had done when he used U.S. troops to invade the strategically important Persian Gulf nation of IRAQ in 2003. The Iraq invasion was strongly opposed by many nations and, most significantly, by other permanent members of the United Nations Security Council. Thus, the Iraq invasion marked a clear move away from multilateralism in a conflict beyond the Western Hemisphere. In many ways, the George W. Bush approach represented a return to the frontier mentality of the 19th century, when the U.S. government was unlikely to stop pursuing its understanding of its national interests, regardless of world opinion.

BIBLIOGRAPHY. Charles A. Beard, *An Economic Interpretation of the Constitution of the United States* (Lawbook Exchange, 1913); William Cohen, *At Freedom's Edge: Black Mobility and the Southern White Quest for Racial Control 1864–1915* (Louisiana State University Press, 1991); Douglas Dowd, *U.S. Capitalist Development Since 1776* (M.E. Sharpe, 1993); Robert Heilbroner and Aaron Singer, *The Economic Transformation of America 1600 to the Present* (Wadsworth Publishing, 1999); Charles H. Hession and Hyman Sardy, *Ascent to Affluence* (Allyn & Bacon, 1969); Joseph A. Schumpeter, *The Theory of Economic Development* (Transaction Publishers, 1934); Charles Sellers, *The Market Revolution* (Oxford University Press, 1991); Howard Zinn, *A People's History of the United States* (HarperCollins, 1980).

SATYA J. GABRIEL
MOUNT HOLYOKE COLLEGE

United States Postal Service

THE UNITED STATES POSTAL SERVICE (USPS) has been an anomaly. In an economy dominated by COMPETITION it has enjoyed a MONOPOLY position. In an economy based on private enterprise, it is government-owned. It has played a significant role in American economic history, but has always faced detractors critical of its monopoly and practices.

The USPS traces its roots back to England's Royal Post, established for official correspondence in 1516, and was granted a monopoly when Charles I forbade private postal services in 1635. There was no regular postal service in the American colonies until, in 1692 a court favorite, Thomas Neale, was granted an exclusive license and began rudimentary service through his agent Governor Andrew Hamilton of New Jersey. In 1707, this patent was absorbed into the British Post Office.

Benjamin FRANKLIN served as deputy postmaster general for all the colonies from 1753 to 1774, expanding post roads from Maine to Florida. He was the Continental Congress's choice to head the new nation's postal system. During the Revolutionary War, the postal system deteriorated and when President George WASHINGTON appointed Samuel Osgood as the first postmaster general under the Constitution, there were only 76 post offices.

The Post Office Act of 1792 has been called one of the most important single pieces of legislation to have been enacted by Congress in the early republic. It established a system of post offices and post roads, using extremely high prices for the delivery of letters to subsidize the delivery of newspapers and the establishment of additional post offices and routes in rural areas. The Post Office soon became the largest enterprise in America and employed about three-quarters of all federal government civilian workers by 1830. One historian concludes that "it would hardly be an exaggeration to suggest that for the vast majority of Americans the postal system was the central government." Its speed impressed many Americans, as did its innovative hub-and-spoke delivery system. Subsidies that it provided to rural correspondence and especially coach lines are credited with helping to push America westward and to develop its democratic culture. The postmaster general became an influential position, joining the president's cabinet in 1829.

However, Post Office critics increasingly complained that it was inefficient and wracked by patronage problems. Many postmasters obtained their positions to benefit from the franking privilege, which allowed them to send mail for free. They were paid on a commission basis, when addressees picked up their mail, but provided no local delivery and pick-up services and often earned money by attracting traffic to their other businesses. In large cities, postmasters made substantial incomes by renting out post boxes, which freed patrons from standing in long lines to receive mail. In 1850, for example, all of Manhattan was served by one post office with 15 pick-up windows. The arrival of RAILROADS and steamboats brought considerable competition to the Post Office in the 1830s. Entrepreneurs began offering to carry private mail between cities and by 1845 carried about two-thirds of the mail. Other businesses sprang up to offer delivery of mail within cities, providing innovations including home delivery, street corner letterboxes, and postage stamps. Some argued that the system was redundant. Speaker of the House John Bell (1834–35) urged that it be privatized. The political clout of postal employees and transportation contractors, and

the desire of politicians to reward supporters with postal positions saved the Post Office, however. Congress responded in 1845 by cutting postage rates by 79 percent and by granting the Post Office a monopoly on the carriage of intercity mail, forbidding private competition. The Post Office funded the early development of the telegraph and attempted to take control of the national telegraph system, but was thwarted in this effort.

Strengthened by its intercity monopoly, the Post Office continued to expand, cutting rates again in 1855 and 1863, establishing free delivery in large cities in 1863 and inaugurating money orders in 1864. The system enhanced its efficiency by eliminating needless bookkeeping rules, which had required each piece of mail to be logged, and in 1864 switched employee payment from piece-rate to salary. In 1872, the Post Office further secured its monopoly position with legislation banning delivery of mail within cities by competitors. In 1896, it charged that railroads were transporting their own mail illegally, and in 1916, it attempted to push its monopoly position to the delivery of mail within office buildings, but these moves failed.

Expansion of services between the AMERICAN CIVIL WAR and WORLD WAR II included special delivery—speedier service at a higher price—in 1885; delivery of mail to rural mail boxes (rural free delivery) beginning in a few locations in 1896; parcel post and collect-on-delivery (COD) in 1913; and metered postage in 1920. Under the Comstock Act of 1873, material deemed obscene was banned from the mails. Postal officials were often zealous in enforcing this law, banning a wide range of items including works of literature by authors such as D.H. Lawrence and Theodore Dreiser.

The Post Office began experimenting with airmail delivery in 1918 and its subsidies played an important role in the development of the commercial aviation industry. In addition, following the Panic of 1907, the Post Office was given the responsibility of running the Postal Savings System. Established in 1910, the system was designed as a safe place for low-income savers to deposit their money. It was required by law to offer a fairly low interest rate and did not lend money, but redeposited funds in commercial banks. The Postal Savings System had an unremarkable career, attracting only about $150 million in deposits, until the Great DEPRESSION hit. During the Depression, deposits soared to over $1.2 billion as wary depositors removed their funds from banks, especially small mutual banks called building-and-loans. While these depositors were saved, the competition from risk-free postal banks crippled a key component of the banking industry, helped cause the supply, of home loans to dry up, decreased the money supply and deepened the Depression. The Postal Savings System was eliminated in 1960, largely because deposit insurance dampened its appeal.

The postal system continued to grow after World War II. The Post Office added certified mail in 1955 and implemented the use of ZIP codes in 1963. In March 1970, after the House Post Office Committee reported a compromise measure to restructure the system, the country was rocked by the first-ever nationwide strike of federal employees, as 152,000 postal workers walked out in over 600 locations, preventing mail delivery. The strike was ended when President Richard NIXON threatened to use the military to deliver the mail, negotiations resumed that granted workers substantial raises, and Congress finalized the reorganization of the system, removing the Postmaster General from the Cabinet and creating the United States Postal Service as an independent agency of the federal government.

The late 20th century brought renewed competition to the USPS. In 1979, its monopoly on express mail was lifted and private businesses, such as UPS and FedEx entered the market, easily outperforming the USPS. Simultaneously faxes and email developed as substitutes to traditional mail, which was derided as "snail mail." Between 1970 and 2002 the price of a first-class stamp soared from six cents to 37 cents, a 616 percent increase, considerably higher than the overall price increase of 467 percent.

Critics complained of slow delivery, lost mail, needless advertising and surly postal workers in an economy that increasingly stresses customer service. They argued that the USPS's inefficiencies stemmed from its slow pace of reorganizing and adopting new technology, and from a union contract that overpaid workers by 30–40 percent and gave them few incentives to work hard. In 1988, the President's Commission on Privatization recommended repealing the USPS's remaining monopoly. Other nations, led by New Zealand and including Sweden, Finland, and Great Britain, privatized with great success, but the prospect of confronting over 800,000 postal workers again dampened the fervor for privatization in Congress.

BIBLIOGRAPHY. Edward Hudgins, ed., *The Last Monopoly: Privatizing the Postal Service for the Information Age* (Cato Institute, 1996); Robert R. John, *Spreading the News: The American Postal System from Franklin to Morse* (Harvard University Press, 1995); Ross A. McReynolds, *History of the United States Post Office, 1607–1931* (University of Chicago, 1935); Maureen O'Hara and David Easley, "The Postal Savings System in the Depression," *Journal of Economic History* (v. 39, 1979); F. Robert van der Linden, *Airlines and Air Mail: The Post Office and the Birth of the Commercial Aviation Industry* (University Press of Kentucky, 2001).

ROBERT WHAPLES, PH.D.
WAKE FOREST UNIVERSITY

U.S. Steel (USX)

IN 1901, THE UNITED STATES Steel Corporation was the largest business enterprise ever launched and, after more than 100 years, it remains the largest integrated steel producer in the UNITED STATES.

Some of America's most legendary businessmen, including Andrew CARNEGIE, J.P. MORGAN, and Charles Schwab were instrumental in the formation of the U.S. Steel Corporation. Carnegie's Steel Company and the Federal Steel Company joined and formed the nucleus of U.S. Steel. Some observed that the birth of U.S. Steel was the formation of the "trust to end all trusts."

One of the most famous ANTITRUST cases decided in 1920 involved the U.S. Steel company. Like the oil and tobacco monopolies, U.S. Steel was formed by combining a large number of independent companies into a giant that held 67 percent of the nation's iron and steel market share in its first year of operation. The Supreme Court did not find the company in violation of the Sherman Antitrust Act based on mere size. The court examined the company's conduct based on evidence of monopolization by price fixing, price discrimination, or other anti-competitive behavior and didn't find any evidence of misconducts.

The company has undergone a significant diversification and restructuring since the 1980s. In 1982, the corporation became involved in the energy industry with its acquisition of Marathon Oil Company. In early 1986, it expanded its energy business when it acquired Texas Oil & Gas Corporation. In addition, the corporation entered into several steel joint-ventures with both domestic and foreign partners.

In late 1986, recognizing the fact that it had become a vastly different corporation, U.S. Steel Corporation changed its name to USX Corporation, with principal operating units involved in energy and steel. At the same time, many of the units among the corporation's diversified businesses were sold or combined into joint venture enterprises. These included chemicals and agrichemicals businesses, an oil field supply business, domestic transportation subsidiaries, and raw materials properties worldwide.

The company is preparing to expand its presence in Europe by investing in Poland at the time when the Western European steel industry is robust and Poland is preparing to join the EUROPEAN UNION in 2004.

Since early 1960s, mini-mills made a dramatic change in the market position of the steel giants. Overall, mini-mills account now for more than 25 percent of the domestic steel market. Consequently, more than 450 antiquated steel-making facilities, some dating back to the 19th century, were closed and production capacity was cut by more than 25 percent. According to the Federal Trade Commission, the industry's production costs declined by 28 percent, and labor productivity increased by 60 percent.

As a result of major structural changes in the integrated steel sector, USX has less than 11 percent of the market share, followed by Bethlehem and four companies with smaller shares that comprise the "Big Six." The stable steel OLIGOPOLY, dominated by the U.S. Steel that persisted into the early 1980s has undergone dramatic changes.

The company continued to go under structural changes in 2003. On January 30, it reaffirmed its interest in acquiring the assets of National Steel Corporation. However, implementation of its plan will depend on the approval of the Federal Trade Commission and the Untied States Department of Justice under the Hart-Scott-Rodino Antitrust Improvement Act.

Some observers believe that the recent tariff exemptions for steel would lead to inefficiencies in the steel industry. In December 2001, the U.S. International Trade Commission (USITC) recommended to President George W. BUSH to provide import relief for the U.S. steel industry. In October, they ruled that a surge of imports in 12 steel products had hurt the U.S. industry. Based on this determination, the commissioners proposed additional *ad valorem* duties ranging from 8–40 percent, quotas, and tariff-based quotas up to 20 percent. Earlier in December, USX-U.S. Steel Corporation, the largest steel company and Bethlehem Steel Corporation, the third-largest had proposed a merger and invited several of their domestic competitors to create a single steel company. The steel tariffs have already been challenged by 25 countries at the WORLD TRADE ORGANIZATION.

Recently, Professors S.W. Comanor and F.M. Scherer, from the Kennedy School of Government, have investigated the effect of government allowing U.S. Steel to maintain its large market share in the industry. They found that decentralization may have permitted more rapid technological innovation and formation of companies that could compete forcefully in world markets.

BIBLIOGRAPHY. Walter Adams and James Brooks, *The Structure of American Industry* (Prentice Hall, 1990); Richard Caves, *American Industry: Structure, Conduct, Performance* (Pearson, 1977); S. William Comanor, and F.M. Scherer, John F. Kennedy School of Government Faculty Research Working Paper: R93-5 (1993); *Industrial and Corporate Change* (v.5/1, 1996); "Trade Panel Documents Tariffs, Quotas to Help Steel Industry," *The New York Times* (December 7, 2001); United States Steel Corporation, "U.S. Steel Reaffirms Interest in Acquiring National Steel Assets," www.ussteel.com.

SIMIN MOZAYENI, PH.D.
STATE UNIVERSITY OF NEW YORK, NEW PALTZ

The American steel industry has increasingly moved from giant mills to more efficient mini-mills to forge steel.

utilitarianism

AN ETHICAL THEORY, utilitarianism states moral virtue consists of choosing to produce the greatest happiness (net of unhappiness) for society. Thus, it instructs that individual actions, as well as social policy and institutions, should all be designed to maximize society's happiness, a tenet usually called the greatest happiness principle. In his classic treatise on the subject, John Stuart MILL described the theory thus:

> The creed which accepts as the foundation of morals, Utility, or the Greatest Happiness Principle, holds that actions are right in proportion as they tend to promote happiness, wrong as they tend to produce the reverse of happiness.

While its classical advocates all denied that the theory of utilitarianism could, strictly speaking, ever be proven, their formulations of the theory all derived from a few, commonly held ideas. In particular, all of the classical Utilitarians (usually identified as Jeremy BENTHAM, Mill, and Henry Sidgwick) ascribed to the hedonistic theory of value, and all held distinctly egalitarian views of human worth. The combination of these two ideas explains their support for the greatest happiness principle.

According to the hedonistic theory of value, the only things valuable in themselves are pleasure and pain. Thus, actions have value only indirectly as means to pleasure or as means to avoid pain, and the worth of an action proceeds from the extent to which it results in a positive balance of pleasure over pain. So, the Utilitarians reasoned, if the only thing of value is the experience of pleasure or avoidance of pain, and the location of this experience (whether in person A or in person B) is unimportant, then the measure of an action's value will be the amount of pleasure that flows from it. Furthermore, the best course of action must be the one that maximizes the general happiness, understood as the simple sum of happiness of all individuals.

The hedonistic theory of value, upon which utilitarianism is based, can be traced all the way back to the Epicureans of ancient Greece. Moreover, in English philosophy, the ideas promoted by the Utilitarians first appear in Richard Cumberland's classic response to Hobbes: *De Legibus Naturae* (1672). Despite this, political philosopher and legal theorist Bentham is usually given credit for first developing the theory. Indeed, at the time, utilitarian philosophy was frequently referred to as Benthamism. Bentham presented his version of utilitarianism in the treatise, *An Introduction to the Principles of Morals and Legislation*, and used it as a basis to argue for a wide array of social and legal reforms. Later, together with his close friend James Mill, he began publishing the *Westminster Review* as a vehicle for disseminating utilitarian ideas.

In spite of Bentham's energetic efforts on behalf of the utilitarian doctrine, his formulation of the theory was a bit too crude to gain wide acceptance. John Stuart Mill's *Utilitarianism*, usually regarded as the classic statement of the doctrine, was designed in part to make Bentham's ideas more palatable. Mill had been educated by Bentham and his father. However, he rejected Bentham's view that pleasures only differed quantitatively (e.g., in intensity and duration). In addition, he insisted, pleasures can differ in quality. So, for instance, intellectual pleasures are of a higher quality than physical pleasures, and, thus, are not directly comparable to them.

Thirteen years after Mill published *Utilitarianism*, Henry Sidgwick provided the most systematic development of classical utilitarianism in his *Methods of Ethics*.

It has been pointed out by many authors that classical utilitarianism suffers from the undesirable property of obliging, under the right circumstances, behavior that most would consider morally questionable. Consider, for example, how it treats lying. While many consider lying to be unethical, classical utilitarianism asserts that it is actually the morally correct course of action provided that the happiness that results from it (or, on some interpretations, the happiness that could foreseeably result from it) outweighs its (foreseeable) adverse consequences. If, for instance, the pain I avoid by not disclosing the true reason for my absence from work exceeds the expected value of my loss of credibility and the possible general loss of confidence in the spoken word, then the classical theory says that I am morally obligated to lie.

Among others, R.F. HARROD has observed that this prescription not only runs counter to common moral intuition, but if applied in this way may actually violate the spirit of the greatest happiness principle by reducing overall happiness. The paradox arises from the fact that the damage inflicted when, for instance, one million people lie will probably be more than one million times the damage caused by one person lying, since, as lying becomes widespread the reliability of communication itself is diminished. Thus, the net effect of any single lie could be to increase overall happiness, while the net effect of lying in general is to reduce happiness. To correct this problem, Harrod suggested that the appropriate test of morality should not be whether particular acts contribute to the greatest good, but whether rules of behavior, if followed, contribute to the general good.

Accordingly, contemporary philosophers distinguish between act-utilitarianism and rule-utilitarianism. Unlike act-utilitarianism, rule-utilitarianism asserts that an action is morally good if it conforms to a rule of behavior that, if followed by all, promotes the greatest happiness. This version of the doctrine is able to sidestep the aggregation problem identified by Harrod and tends to make prescriptions more in tune with common moral intuition. While most agree that the classical utilitarians advocated a version of act-utilitarianism, modern proponents tend to be rule-utilitarians.

Among all the sciences, economics has almost surely been influenced most by the theory of utilitarianism. Even today, welfare economics, the field of economics concerned with the social desirability of alternative economic outcomes, employs the methodology of the classical utilitarians. So, for example, welfare economics confronts questions like whether a tax should be imposed or whether competitive markets are better than monopolistic ones, and in keeping with the ideas of Bentham and Mill, it attempts to answer these questions on the basis of which outcome provides the greatest happiness.

As evidence of the continuing influence of utilitarianism in economics consider the ubiquitous use economists make of Vilfredo Pareto's efficiency criterion, developed for the study of welfare economics. By definition, an outcome is said to be Pareto efficient if and only of there is no modification of the outcome that could make someone better off without making someone else worse off. Generally, economists will claim that a Pareto-efficient outcome is superior to one that is not Pareto-efficient. Of course, this follows immediately if one subscribes to the utilitarian definition of goodness, that which maximizes the sum of happiness. If, however, the social good depends upon, say, the degree to which income is evenly distributed, then it is no longer clear that Pareto efficiency is necessarily a property of socially desirable outcomes.

BIBLIOGRAPHY. Ernest Albee, *A History of English Utilitarianism* (Macmillan, 1901, 1957); Jeremy Bentham, *An Introduction to the Principles of Morals and Legislation* (Clarendon Press, 1789, 1996); Roger Crisp, *Mill on Utilitarianism* (Routledge, 1997); Roy F. Harrod, "Utilitarianism Revised," *Mind* 45 (1936); Harlan B. Miller and William H. Williams, *The Limits of Utilitarianism* (University of Minnesota Press, 1982); John Stuart Mill, *Utilitarianism* (Oxford University Press, 1861, 1998); Amartya Sen and Bernard Williams, *Utilitarianism and Beyond* (Cambridge University Press, 1982); Henry Sidgwick, *The Methods of Ethics* (University of Chicago Press, 1874, 1962); Henry Sidgwick, *Essays on Ethics and Method* (Clarendon Press, 2000); J. O. Urmson, "The Interpretation of the Moral Philosophy of J. S. Mill," *The Philosophical Quarterly* (v.3, 1953).

JOEL D. CARTON, PH.D.
TEXAS TECH UNIVERSITY

utility

THE DEGREE OF SATISFACTION of wants and needs obtained from the use or consumption of (scarce) goods and services is generally known as utility. Early social scientists regarded utility in a literal sense, as a measure of someone's happiness or well-being from the consumption of goods such as food, clothing, or shelter. It seemed that in order to understand how individuals make economic choices, one must know how much utility someone derives from a given choice.

This concept of utility is sometimes referred to as cardinal utility, meaning that it can be measured on an absolute scale like physical characteristics such as height or weight. Thus, a sentence like "I am twice as happy as you" has meaning when happiness is referred to in terms of cardinal utility. Not only did it remain unclear how cardinal utility should be measured in human beings, but the very existence of such a satisfaction measure is scientifically doubtful. These difficulties associated with the concept of cardinal utility have subsequently led to an alternative, and now prevailing, view of ordinal utility, within the preference-based approach to consumer choice theory.

The consumer's choice problem in MICROECONOMICS is to choose the "best" of several alternative bundles of consumption goods. The preference-based approach to this choice problem presumes that consumers can rank all these alternatives in order, from most preferred to least preferred. An ordinal utility function is then an assignment of numbers (utilities) to consumption bundles such that bundle *A* has higher utility than bundle *B* if and only if the consumer prefers *A* to *B*. If the consumer is indifferent between two bundles, they must have the same utility. An ordinal utility function is a mathematically convenient way to represent a person's objectives and tastes on an ordinal scale: It orders, as its name implies, different consumption choices by their desirability, without attaching significance to the magnitude of utility itself.

Thus, only statements of the form "Consuming *A* makes me happier than consuming *B*" are permissible when ordinal utility is referred to, meaning "I prefer *A* to *B*." Ordinal utility still allows for a meaningful description of consumer choice: Persons are assumed to choose their most preferred alternative, which is equivalent to finding the maximum of a utility function.

The preference-based concept of ordinal utility is most often used in the microeconomic analysis of consumer choice and demand. Sometimes, intensity of preferences (and not just their order) needs to be taken into account, however. For example, redistributive taxes typically result in a utility loss for rich persons, and in a utility gain for poor persons. A government designing and implementing such taxes must make some judgment as to how individuals' utilities should be weighed. Put differently, it must assume that individual gains and losses can be measured in utility units. This necessitates that some cardinal properties of utility must be assumed sometimes, even within the preference-based framework.

Utility functions and preference orders permit simple graphical representations as well. Consider a person who must choose among bundles that contain some amount of food and some amount of clothing, a utility function can be drawn just like contour lines on a topographical map: Similar to connecting all points on a map of the same altitude, we can connect all choices in a consumption space diagram that have the same utility. The resulting lines are called indifference curves.

The gain in utility induced by the consumption of an additional small amount of a certain good is defined as marginal utility. The concept of marginal utility is indispensable for the analysis of choice and demand in a world characterized by scarcity: It indicates what each additional unit of a good is worth to a consumer, in terms of the utility obtained from another good that could be obtained instead. Hence, marginal utility can quantify the trade-off between the consumption of one good against the consumption of another good. In particular, a person chooses optimally if the marginal utility of a dollar spent on one good equals the marginal utility of a dollar spent on another good that is also consumed.

BIBLIOGRAPHY. Amos-Web Economic Glossary, www.amosweb.com (2002); Salvador Barbera, et al., eds., *Handbook of Utility Theory* (Kluwer Academic Publishers, 1999).

TILMAN KLUMPP, PH.D.
INDIANA UNIVERSITY, BLOOMINGTON

utility maximization

THE METHOD WITH WHICH consumers choose their optimal level and distribution of consumption, given their budget constraints, is called utility maximization. In economic theory, each consumer values different choices of goods according to their UTILITY, which reflects their personal preferences. The individual's utility function gives a ranking of each choice. This relative measure of the possible combinations of goods and services is then compared to the individual's budget to determine which of the affordable choices is optimal.

Utility maximization involves two components: what the consumer prefers (utility), and what the consumer can afford (budget). Since utility functions with more than one good become complicated, three-dimensional shapes, the utility function is represented in two-dimensional space as an indifference curve. Indifference curves draw a line through those combinations of goods and services between which the consumer is exactly indifferent (i.e., neither preferring one nor the other). Each indifference curve represents a different level of utility, so utility maximization can be seen as the consumer choosing the highest indifference curve that fits their budget.

The slope of the indifference is called the Marginal Rate of Substitution (MRS), and reflects the amount of one good that would be sacrificed to obtain another unit of the other good. [Δgood 2/(-Δgood 1), or in words the gain in good 2 per loss of good 1].

The MRS is also identical to the ratio of the marginal utility (MU, the additional utility for a 1 unit increase) of each good. A one unit loss of good 1 yields a utility loss of MU_1. To stay on the indifference curve, the consumer must add enough units of good 2 to make up that utility. Since each unit of good 2 adds MU_2, MRS = Δgood 2/(-Δgood 1)=MU_1/MU_2.

The budget constraint confines one's choices to those combinations of goods and services that are affordable. Consumers are usually assumed to prefer more of a good to less, so that without a budget constraint consumers would just keep moving to higher and higher levels of consumption. The budget constraint puts a limit on consumption, and this limit is determined by the individual's income (M) and the prices of the available goods and services (P_1 and P_2 in this example). If the consumer spent all her money on good 1, she could afford M/P_1 units. If the consumer spent all her money on good 2, she could afford M/P_2 units. It is normally assumed that unless the goods are identical (perfect substitutes) then a consumer would be on a higher indifference curve by consuming a combination of goods and services.

All the combinations of the two goods in our example that are affordable fit the budget constraint:

$$P_1(\text{good 1}) + P_2(\text{good 2}) \leq M$$

Since we assumed before that consumers prefer more than less, we can quickly rule out all those combinations of goods and services which do not spend the consumers entire income (you can't take it with you) and only consider those combination that satisfy the equality:

$$P_1(\text{good 1}) + P_2(\text{good 2}) = M$$

This gives the equation of a line with a slope of P_1/P_2. Of those points on the edge of the affordable set, the consumer has the highest utility at the point where the MRS of the indifference curve equals the slope of the budget constraint. This means that the budget constraint is just tangent to the highest indifference curve that it reaches, making it the optimal level of consumption. Therefore at this point:

$$MU_1/MU_2 = P_1/P_2$$

or

$$MU_1/P_1 = MU_2/P_2$$

The second formulation may be more intuitive since it states that per dollar, a consumer should get the same marginal utility from each good.

To verify this solution, consider the case where marginal utility per dollar is not equal. For example, our consumer (let's call him Mike) is a student choosing books at a bookstore and is spending a $500 allotment from his parents between textbooks and novels. Textbooks are expensive (P_T = $100) and novels are cheaper (P_N = $20), so Mike chooses three textbooks and 10 novels. Mike has five classes, so his marginal utility of a fourth textbook is high (MU_T = 15), and while marginal utility of novels is somewhat lower (MU_N = 2). Is Mike spending optimally?

To answer this, we have our two criteria:

1. The entire budget must be spent

2. MRS = P_1/P_2.

First, we see that Mike did spend all his parents money as is optimal for his utility maximization [$100(3) + $20(10) = $500].

On the second criterion, however, Mike did not do so well. MRS = 15/2 = 7.5 while P_T/P_N= 100/20 = 5. Since marginal utility for texts is so high, even given the higher price, Mike would have a higher total utility by giving up novels and switching to texts. To get one more text, Mike would have to give up 5 novels, losing 10 units of utility. The marginal utility of the text, though, is 15, giving Mike a net increase of 5 units of utility.

At the optimum, where the per-dollar value of marginal utility is equated, this improvement would no longer be possible. This result from utility maximization is analogous to capital budgeting decisions where investments are made where they yield the highest marginal product per dollar.

BIBLIOGRAPHY. William Baumol and Alan Blinder, *Microeconomics: Principles and Policy,* 9th ed. (South-Western, 2002); Dominick Salvatore, *Microeconomics* (Oxford University Press, 2003); Hal R. Varian, *Microeconomic Analysis* (Norton, 2002).

DERRICK REAGLE, PH.D.
FORDHAM UNIVERSITY

V

value of leisure

HOUSEHOLDS HAVE A limited amount of time available to them in which to work, not work, consume, play, sleep, enjoy time off, and so on. For instance, in any one particular day there are only 24 hours available to a person or household in which to participate in these activities. Thus, households face a time constraint in which they must make decisions regarding how they will allocate their time among various and competing activities.

Leisure is that time in which a household (or person) is not involved in labor market activity. Thus, leisure is time spent in non-labor market activity. The amount of utility or satisfaction that is derived from non-labor market activity is the value of leisure. In particular, economists often try to quantify the value of leisure in dollar terms. One way in which to place a dollar value on a person's leisure is to consider the opportunity cost of their time. Opportunity cost is simply the value of the person's next best alternative or the value of what must be given up in order to do or have something. Thus, opportunity cost involves sacrifice and clearly one must sacrifice something in order to spend some time in leisure. Often, we describe the time that someone spends in non-labor market activity as if he or she were consuming leisure.

In this sense, the value of one hour's worth of leisure is the opportunity cost of that hour. If, for example, one has the opportunity to work for some hourly wage but chooses to spend that hour in leisure, then that person has given up the opportunity to earn income. The opportunity cost of consuming the hour of leisure is simply the dollar value of income that could have been earned. Presumably, the income that was given up, or foregone, could have been used to purchase goods and services.

Consequently, the opportunity cost of leisure in this case is also equal to what this person could have otherwise consumed.

As another example, consider someone who may choose to spend time acquiring education, an activity in which a person is not typically paid but which is likely

The value of leisure, for example hiking, is equal to the opportunity cost of work not done while hiking.

to increase a person's future income earning potential. In this case, a person who chooses to acquire education instead of consuming leisure may be thought of as placing a lower value on leisure than an otherwise similar person who chooses not to go to school and instead spends time in non-labor market activities.

BIBLIOGRAPHY. G. Becker, "Theory of the Allocation of Time," *Economic Journal* (v.75, 1965); J.M. Barron, M. Lowenstein, and G.J. Lynch, *Macroeconomics* (Addison-Wesley, 1989); R.E. Hall, and J.B. Taylor, *Macroeconomics* (W.W. Norton & Company, 1997).

BRADLEY T. EWING, PH.D.
TEXAS TECH UNIVERSITY

value theory

FOR OVER TWO CENTURIES economists have argued about value theory, debating the source of "value" and the difference between relative prices of goods and services. Two major views have emerged: the labor theory of value and the utility theory of value. Though the controversy is mostly forgotten in contemporary economics textbooks, each approach continues to develop models and analyses consistent with its view.

We think of value as synonymous with price, but this was not always the case. Early political economists (e.g., Adam SMITH, David RICARDO, and Karl MARX) recognized several categories of value. They analyzed exchange value, use value, and value in contexts that suggested each term was distinct. In contemporary terms, exchange value is equivalent to price, use value describes utility (or usefulness), and value is the common property goods and services share that enables them to be exchanged in market transactions. The nature of this common property is the source of the controversy. One perspective contends that because all commodities are products of human labor, labor is the source of value. The other approach observes that all commodities are useful; therefore, usefulness must be the source of value. We consider each perspective in more detail.

The labor approach. Smith provided an early foundation for the labor approach, although he used at least three different theories of value in his *Wealth of Nations*—a labor-quantity theory, a labor-disutility theory, and a cost theory. Smith rejected the utility approach because of what has been called the "paradox of value." In his words: "Nothing is more useful than water: but it will purchase scarce any thing; scarce any thing can be had in exchange for it. A diamond, on the contrary, has scarce any value in use; but a very great quantity of other goods may frequently be had in exchange for it."

Ricardo built his analysis on Smith's labor-quantity approach, contending that the quantity of labor embodied in a product determined its value. Although Ricardo recognized that machinery contributed to production, he viewed this as "past labor" (labor performed in an earlier time period.)

The labor theory of value received its most extensive treatment in the work of Marx, who expanded on Ricardo's analysis, giving it a specific historical context (i.e., the labor theory of value applies to capitalism) and distinguishing between labor (work performed) and labor power (the capacity to work). Marx linked the labor theory of value to his theory of exploitation and class conflict. If labor is the source of value, then all non-labor income (e.g., profits) is parasitic and comes at labor's expense.

The utility approach. The utility theory also has roots that reach far back in history. Aristotle viewed use value and exchange value as closely linked, and numerous theorists including Jeremy BENTHAM and Jean Baptiste Say adopted the utility approach around the time of Smith and Ricardo. Nevertheless, the utility approach didn't receive widespread recognition until William Stanley JEVONS, Carl MENGER, and Leon WALRAS each independently developed the concept of marginal utility in the 1870s. Marginal utility resolves Smith's paradox of value. Since marginal utility refers to the utility received from the last unit, it's clear that the first diamond has greater marginal utility than the umpteenth glass of water.

Initially, economists subscribed to a cardinal notion of utility, believing that utility could be quantified and measured in a precise fashion. Early in the 20th century cardinal utility was replaced with ordinal utility, or the idea that commodities can be ranked in order of preference. Today's version of the utility theory rests on this ordinal approach.

Implications. Why does value theory matter? Perhaps the most important reason is because value theory provides the foundation for other levels of economic analysis. While the labor approach emphasizes the sphere of production and the human relationships in the production process, the utility approach emphasizes market exchange, a realm where everyone enters voluntarily and no one leaves worse off than they started. As one author has noted, the labor theory of value ". . . is in essence an expression of the idea that the fundamental relationships into which men enter with one another in the field of production ultimately determine the relationships into which they enter in the field of exchange."

One need only contrast the images of a sweatshop with a farmers' market to recognize that the different emphases matter. For example, the labor theory of value inevitably leads to an exploitive theory of profits, while the neoclassical utility theory of value complements the claim that factors of production (e.g., land, labor, capital) receive income shares equal to the value of their contributions to the finished product.

The two theories of value contribute to distinct paradigms that build different models, ask different questions, and reach different conclusions about capitalism. Understanding the value theory debate provides an important tool for critically evaluating these differences and assessing the merits of each paradigm's conclusions and policy recommendations.

BIBLIOGRAPHY. Mark Blaug, *Economic Theory in Retrospect* (Cambridge University Press, 1985); E.K. Hunt, *History of Economic Thought* (HarperCollins, 1992); Ronald Meek, *Studies in the Labor Theory of Value* (Monthly Review Press, 1956); Joseph A. Schumpeter, *History of Economic Analysis* (Oxford University Press, 1954); Adam Smith, *An Inquiry into the Nature and Causes of The Wealth of Nations*, University of Chicago Press, 1976).

PATRICK DOLENC, PH.D.
KEENE STATE COLLEGE

Van Buren, Martin (1782–1862)

THE EIGHTH PRESIDENT of the UNITED STATES, Martin Van Buren was born in Kinderhook, New York, the son of an old-stock Dutch farmer. A lawyer by trade, he was elected to the U.S. Senate in 1821, to the New York governorship in 1828, before becoming Andrew JACKSON's secretary of state and eventually vice president. Van Buren's mastery of the new democratic politics of the Jacksonian period was second only to the era's namesake; his ability to reach consensus with opponents through behind-the-scene maneuvers led observers to label him a "sly fox" and a "little magician." Like Jackson, he also championed limited government and LAISSEZ-FAIRE political economy, and his policies facilitated the rampant, often chaotic economic growth of the antebellum period.

Van Buren was indispensable to the Democratic Party from its birth. He largely engineered Jackson's victory in New York during the presidential campaign of 1828. As Jackson's secretary of state, Van Buren secured a major foreign policy achievement by negotiating the re-opening of U.S. trade with the British West Indies in 1830. Leading up to the 1832 election, Van Buren shrewdly outmaneuvered his chief rival in the administration, John Calhoun, to win the vice presidency. Van Buren's political skill and insight, and his personal

and political loyalty to the president early on, made him Jackson's choice for his successor in 1836.

Van Buren's loyalty would persist even into his own administration, and even when the negative results of his predecessor's policies fell on Van Buren's shoulders. Van Buren assumed office under the gathering storm of economic DEPRESSION; the Panic of 1837 would cloud his entire administration and be the major cause of his defeat in 1840. Thousands of businesses, banks and farms were lost, as the economy collapsed under a deluge of over-extended credit, runaway inflation, and bad currency.

Van Buren's Whig opponents quickly blamed the crisis on Jackson's destruction of the Bank of the United States, which had been the economy's controlling center. Van Buren faced enormous pressure to repeal part of Jackson's program, especially the Specie Circular of 1836, which mandated that the purchase of public lands be made in hard currency. Though Jackson intended the measure to curb rampant land speculation, it had actually increased the power of the land speculator, since the average land buyer, void of hard currency, no longer had the option of buying from the government. By 1837, even many Democrats demanded the repeal of the law, yet Van Buren stood by Jackson's policy.

Instead, he called Congress into special session for the fall of 1837 and introduced a series of bills designed to alleviate the nation's economic calamities. The capstone of his program was the Independent Treasury System (also called the Sub-Treasury), which sought the complete divorce of the federal government from private business and banking. The bill proposed the removal of federal specie from "pet" state banks, where they had been placed upon the Bank of the United States' destruction, and their placement in government-owned depositories. Though Whigs opposed the bill because they claimed it shirked the federal government's responsibility to provide a sound currency, Van Buren's strict interpretation of the Constitution recognized no such responsibility. In his mind, the Sub-Treasury system would keep the federal government entirely out of the private sector while securing federal funds. After suffering initial defeat in Congress, the bill finally passed both houses in June 1840. Even more than the policies of Jackson, Van Buren's Independent Treasury plan embodied the Jacksonian commitment to laissez-faire government.

In 1840, Van Buren, still plagued by the economic crisis, suffered defeat to his Whig opponent, William Henry HARRISON. After leaving office, he would find new prominence as an anti-slavery supporter in the mounting sectional conflict leading up to the AMERICAN CIVIL WAR. In 1848, Van Buren left the Democratic Party and ran for president on the Free Soil Party's ticket. He won 10 percent of the popular vote and carried his home state of New York.

BIBIOGRAPHY. Marvin Meyers, *The Jacksonian Persuasion: Politics and Belief* (Stanford University Press, 1957); John Niven, *Martin Van Buren: The Romantic Age of American Politics* (Oxford University Press, 1984); Charles Sellers, *The Market Revolution: Jacksonian America, 1815–1846* (Oxford University Press, 1991); Glyndon G. Van Deusen, *The Jacksonian Era, 1828–1848* (Waveland Press, 1959); Major L. Wilson, *The Presidency of Martin Van Buren* (University Press of Kansas, 1984).

HOLLY A. BERKLEY, PH.D.
HARDIN-SIMMONS UNIVERSITY

Vanderbilt, Cornelius (1794–1877)

CORNELIUS VANDERBILT lived an American tale of rags to riches. Born into poverty, Vanderbilt became a shipping magnate, railroad tycoon, and founder of an American dynasty. By age 11, Vanderbilt had quit school to help his father farm and ferry produce from Staten Island to New York City. Shortly before Vanderbilt's 16th birthday, he borrowed $100 from his mother and bought a sailboat to operate a ferry service between New York City and Staten Island.

Vanderbilt soon offered lower prices and greater reliability than his competitors. During the WAR OF 1812, Vanderbilt's ferries ran British blockades to deliver supplies to the U.S. Army and American civilians. His profits from these wartime activities allowed Vanderbilt to expand into the shipping business. Feeling economically secure, he married his first cousin Sophia Johnson in 1813, and subsequently fathered a dozen children.

In 1817, faced with increasing competition from steamboats, Vanderbilt sold his sailboats and took a job as captain of the *Bellona*, a New Jersey-based steamboat owned by Thomas Gibbons, a wealthy lawyer. Vanderbilt used the federally licensed *Bellona* to ferry passengers from New York City to New Brunswick, New Jersey, where his wife Sophia ran a tavern at the ferry station. In 1819, however, a New York court ordered Vanderbilt to stop serving New York City. The court found that the state legislature, in 1807, had granted a MONOPOLY over steamboat traffic serving New York ports to Robert Fulton and Robert Livingston, and that Vanderbilt's activities infringed on that monopoly. In *Gibbons v. Ogden* (1824), the United States Supreme Court sided with Vanderbilt, broke the Fulton-Livingston interstate shipping monopoly, and established the supremacy of the U.S. Congress over state legislatures in regulating interstate commerce.

In 1829, Vanderbilt left Gibbons to start his own steamboat business. He began a line from New York to Philadelphia, undercutting prices to the point that his competitors paid him to stop running it. He repeated these tactics on the Hudson River, and again, his competitors paid him to leave the market. Finally, Vanderbilt settled his business on the Long Island Sound, where by the 1840s he was operating over 100 steamboats.

During the California Gold Rush (1849–50), Commodore Vanderbilt, as he was now called, saw another money-making opportunity. At this time, there were two time-consuming transit routes to California from the east: a sea route around the tip of South America, or an overland stagecoach route across the country. Vanderbilt saw a short cut through Nicaragua.

In 1851, Vanderbilt paid the Nicaraguan government $10,000 for a charter to cross their country and formed the Accessory Transit Company. He established a route to California that was shorter and less expensive than the alternatives. While vacationing in Europe, Vanderbilt lost contact with his subordinates in charge of the Nicaraguan route. They betrayed him to William Walker, a "filibuster" (a soldier of fortune who sought to incorporate Nicaragua into the MANIFEST DESTINY expansion of U.S. territory) who gained control of the Accessory Transit Company. Vanderbilt eventually regained control of his company, at which time his rivals paid him not to run his route.

In 1855, Vanderbilt successfully began running large steamships across the Atlantic. He later profited from the Union government's use and purchase of his ships during the AMERICAN CIVIL WAR.

In 1857, Vanderbilt began investing in the New York and Harlem railroad (NY&H), and soon became one of its directors. He championed a plan to extend the NY&H railroad line to run the full length of Manhattan island. In 1862, however, Vanderbilt's longtime rival Daniel Drew conspired to drive down the price of NY&H stock by convincing state legislators to block Vanderbilt's planned extension of the line. Vanderbilt foiled Drew's plan by purchasing all the NY&H stock on the market, thereby cornering the market and reinforcing the price of the stock. The legislature later reversed its decision and permitted extension of the line. Drew tried to repeat this scheme in 1864, but Vanderbilt again succeeded in cornering the market for NY&H stock, thwarting Drew and financially ruining numerous New York legislators.

In 1863, Vanderbilt intervened when a similar scheme was launched against the Hudson River Railroad (HRRR), which ran along the east side of the river to Albany, New York. Vanderbilt cornered the market in HRRR stock, and took control of the railroad. By 1865, he was the railroad's president. He constructed a railroad bridge across the Hudson so that both the NY&H and the HRRR entered Albany. In 1867, Vanderbilt extended his New York railroad empire by acquiring the New York Central Railroad (NYCRR), and merging it into the HRRR.

Vanderbilt next sought to extend his railroad empire beyond the state of New York by taking over the Erie Railroad, one of the two existing railroad lines that then connected the East Coast with Chicago. To do so, Vanderbilt initiated the "Erie wars" of 1868–69, in which Vanderbilt sought to buy a controlling share of Erie's outstanding stock, while Vanderbilt's old antagonist Drew, an Erie director, printed more Erie stock and dumped it on the market. In the end, Vanderbilt paid Drew about $1.5 million and failed to acquire control of the Erie railroad. Together, Vanderbilt and Drew left Drew's partners Jay GOULD and Jim FISK with the practically worthless Erie stock, and substantial legal liability for stock fraud.

Despite failing to gain control of the Erie, Vanderbilt did gain control of the Lake Shore and the Michigan Southern and Northern Indiana railroads. These acquisitions completed a consolidated railway from New York City to Chicago.

In his late years, Vanderbilt married a young southern cousin, Frankie Crawford. Despite Vanderbilt's lack of interest in philanthropy, Frankie convinced him to make a $1 million gift to found and endow Vanderbilt University in Tennessee. When Vanderbilt died on January 4, 1877, he was the richest man in America. He left the bulk of his $105 million estate to his son William Henry, who had been instrumental in achieving Vanderbilt's railroad successes.

BIBLIOGRAPHY. Louis Auchincloss, *The Vanderbilt Era: Profiles of a Gilded Age* (Charles Scribner's Sons, 1989); George Dangerfield, George, "The Steamboat Case," *Quarrels that Have Shaped the Constitution* (Harpers Torchbook, 1964); Edwin P. Hoyt, *The Vanderbilts and Their Fortunes* (Doubleday, 1962); Keith Poole, voteview.uh.edu; Arthur D. Howden Smith, *Commodore Vanderbilt* (Philip Allan & Co., 1928).

LINDA DYNAN, PH.D.
INDEPENDENT SCHOLAR

Vatican Bank

LITTLE PUBLIC INFORMATION is available about the organization and finances of the Vatican Bank. This is due, in a broad, way to the dual nature of the Vatican, which, as the home of the Papacy, is the spiritual center of the Roman Catholic Church, yet is also a temporal institution. The Vatican City, located in Rome, ITALY, is a

sovereign state with its own government, legal system (based on canon law), bureaucracy (known as the Roman Curia), citizenry, currency, flag, diplomatic corps, media, and Papal bodyguard (the Swiss Guard).

The Vatican is governed by the Pope of Rome, with the advice of the College of Cardinals. The Vatican Bank functions in both of these spheres, as a temporal bank for Vatican financial assets, as well as an institution created to serve the spiritual works of the Catholic Church worldwide.

The Vatican Bank's official title is the Institute for Works of Religion. It was originally established in 1887 by Pope Leo XIII as part of the Vatican's efforts to re-organize and manage the church's affairs after the Papal States and Rome were annexed by the unified Kingdom of Italy. The bank serves the officials and citizens of Vatican City and Roman Catholic institutions worldwide. In response to scandals and suspicions about the bank's activities, the bank was given a more transparent and organized governing apparatus—a lay director appointed by a supervisory council of five banking experts who were selected by five cardinals, all of whom are commissioned by the Pope to oversee the bank's activities.

These reforms resulted from a variety of allegations about the bank. As an institution with both secular and spiritual aspects, and that is tied to Vatican City yet also international in nature, it has been in a position for abuse and corruption. The most well-publicized scandal involved its relations in the 1970s and 1980s with the Banco Ambrosiano, that collapsed financially in 1982. Other allegations include money laundering, bribery, and the concealment of assets seized from concentration camp victims in WORLD WAR II. The Vatican's unique institutional reach across national boundaries enhances the bank's notoriety, at the same time that it remains a valuable institution for maintaining Catholic religious orders, charities, and other organizations around the world.

BIBLIOGRAPHY. Thomas J. Reese, *Inside the Vatican: The Politics and Organization of the Catholic Church* (Harvard University Press, 1996); Peter Hebblethwaite, *In the Vatican* (Adler & Adler, 1986); Eric O. Hanson, *The Catholic Church in World Politics* (Princeton University Press, 1987); Elizabeth M. Lynskey, *The Government of the Catholic Church* (P.J. Kennedy & Sons, New York, 1952).

GEORGE KOSAR
BRANDEIS UNIVERSITY

Veblen, Thorstein (1857–1929)

AN ECCENTRIC, A NONCONFORMIST, a master of satire, frequently described as a very strange man,

Thorstein Veblen brought a new approach to economic analysis, founded a school of thought known as Institutionalism, and is now accepted as one of the great economists (though he was not much appreciated during his own lifetime.) He earned a doctorate in philosophy at Yale University, received a postdoctoral fellowship at Cornell University, and was appointed as an instructor of economics at the University of Chicago, but never attained tenure at a major university. The two reasons often cited for his lack of professional success are his unconventional ideas and his personality.

According to Joseph Dorfman, Veblen viewed the economy as one from another planet might, largely because he was raised by Norwegian immigrant parents on an isolated farm. Robert Heilbroner calls Veblen's alienation from society the keynote to his life. Stephen Edgell offers a different interpretation, suggesting that Veblen's multicultural life made him quite cosmopolitan and a global thinker with no disciplinary boundaries.

Whether due to his own alienation or a sincere belief that existing economic theory had it all wrong, Veblen strove in his writings to offer a new way of thinking. He believed that a key assumption underlying economic thinking from Adam SMITH through Alfred MARSHALL is that there is harmony in the system. Smith's emphasis on the invisible hand and Marshall's emphasis on market equilibrium imply the existence of natural laws that can be identified using economic analysis. Veblen argued that economic and social behavior evolve in response to existing institutions, defined as our ways of thinking. Rather than assuming institutions as given, he intended to examine and explain the particular institutions of a culture in order to see clearly the economic forces they created.

Veblen published his most widely read book, *The Theory of the Leisure Class*, in 1899 after rewriting much of it to satisfy editorial demands. He set out to discover why and how the leisure class had evolved and why members of this class garner such respect and admiration from other members of society. Classical economists had not bothered with such trivial questions, accepting it as obvious that in the competitive struggle of economic life, some succeeded and, when they did, they naturally took advantage of the opportunity to spend their time as pleasantly as possible, far from the onerous burden of having to work for a living. Veblen questioned the basic assumption that leisure is inherently more enjoyable than work.

Based on extensive reading about other cultures, Veblen considered the possibility that productive activities are as pleasant a way to pass the time as leisure activities. He saw that in some cultures, pride of workmanship drove men to try and outdo each other and that leisure, if tolerated, was certainly not admired. The next stage of evolution came as a predatory class developed, with members who used force and cunning to take rather than produce. Warriors, who were admired for their skills though they produced nothing useful for society, were the members of the first leisure class. Whereas society had not been able to afford a nonproductive class in its early stages, economic progress eventually allowed it and the aggressive nature of people fostered it. Heilbroner observes that "the irksomeness of work, which the classical economists thought to be inherent in the nature of man himself, Veblen saw as the degradation of a once honored way of life under the impact of a predatory spirit." Moving on to modern life, and keeping in mind that the society under his gaze was marked by robber barons and captains of industry, Veblen gave us a way of interpreting our own behavior that is both enlightening and repellant. Cindy Lin makes the compelling argument that F. Scott Fitzgerald was inspired by Veblen's description of the leisure class when he wrote *The Great Gatsby*. The message that both Veblen and Fitzgerald convey is that there is nothing particularly rewarding about a life of leisure, that, in fact, such a life can be sad, bitter, and destructive.

Veblen introduced and used the terms conspicuous consumption, conspicuous leisure, conspicuous waste, and pecuniary emulation to describe why people did what they did in the modern society he sought to understand. Just as warriors and tribal leaders had been honored in earlier cultures, those with the predatory powers to accumulate wealth were held in high esteem in the culture of Veblen's time. Unfortunately, financial success cannot bring respect and admiration until it is seen and recognized by the other members of society. Thus, it was imperative that those who had achieved success find a way to let others see it.

Enjoying a good meal provides a certain amount of utility and a consumer will naturally pay a price consistent with this utility. To a classical economist, then, the price someone will pay for a meal can be explained by the amount of utility derived from its consumption. Veblen argued that, while this might be true in many cases, there were also examples of conspicuous consumption to be found in something as basic as the human need for sustenance. Dining in public view in a very expensive restaurant can provide an opportunity to advertise one's success, that, in turn, gives the consumer what he is really after: admiration and respect, not just dinner.

Veblen provides numerous examples of conspicuous consumption, many of them humorous and entertaining. The homes we live in, the cars we drive, and the clothes we wear all provide a clear indication of our success. Since in Veblen's time it was almost exclusively the male of the household involved in building financial success, it fell to the female of the household to properly display and advertise this success. The ideal according to Veblen was to have a wife who dressed well and never engaged in any sort of work. In fact, he saw the number of servants employed in a household as an important indicator of that household's success.

The Theory of the Business Enterprise was published in 1904, but was not embraced by the intellectual community as *The Theory of the Leisure Class* had been. In his new book, Veblen put forth the argument that there exists a fundamental conflict between making money and making goods, and that the businessman, far from being the driving force behind production, is actually intent on sabotaging the entire system. He provides numerous examples to support his contention, examples in which the quality of products or services is an unimportant part of the business leader's plan to dominate an industry, and his use of elaborate financial schemes to create money from nothing. Veblen would have been wonderfully fascinated with the fate of Enron and other corporations that followed almost exactly the pattern of behavior he laid out nearly a century ago.

Veblen developed an extensive framework to explain the behavior of professors, deans, and university presidents in *Higher Learning in America* (1918). His views that university presidents and boards are more interested in buildings, grounds, and real estate than in educational programs and policies, and that resources are wasted on athletic programs and ceremonies that are not of use to society, did not endear him to the academic community. However, he was offered the presidency of the American Economic Association a few years later, in belated recognition of his contributions. He turned down this opportunity on the grounds that it had not come when he needed it.

Veblen's institutional approach emphasizes the need for economic analysis to be dynamic and for economists to understand that human behavior evolves over time as social mores and habits of thought change. He would not advocate that modern economists simply devote themselves to finding new examples of conspicuous consumption or corporate misdeeds, but rather that they identify the next stage of evolution and explain what is happening and why.

Probably the most important legacy of Veblen is our current emphasis on empirical research. Whether we realize it or not, we are responding to Veblen's demand that we take a more open-minded approach, even if it is largely due to the enormous increase in computing power and data availability.

BIBLIOGRAPHY. Thorstein Veblen, *The Theory of the Leisure Class* (1899, Dover Publications, 1994); Thorstein Veblen, *Theory of Business Enterprise* (Augustus Kelley, 1904); Joseph Dorfman, *Thorstein Veblen and His America* (Augustus Kelley, 1934); Mark Blaug, *Great Economists Before Keynes: An Introduction to the Lives and Works of One Hundred Great Economists of the Past* (Cambridge University Press, 1986); Robert L. Heilbroner, *The Worldly Philosophers: The Lives, Times, and Ideas of the Great Economic Thinkers* (Touchstone, 1992); Harry Landreth and David C. Colander, *History of Economic Thought* (Edward Elgar, 1994); Cindy Lin, "Thorstein Veblen and The Great Gatsby," *Journal of Economic Issues* (June, 1999); Stephen Edgell, *Veblen in Perspective: His Life and Thought* (M.E. Sharpe, 2002).

SUSAN DADRES, PH.D.
SOUTHERN METHODIST UNIVERSITY

Venezuela

LOCATED BY THE Caribbean Sea in the northern part of South America, Venezuela's economy in the 20th century was dominated by the development of its oil industry. Its heavy dependence on the oil industry stifled economic diversification and added to its political corruption and resistance to democratization.

Venezuela has progressed from colonization to independence. During his third voyage to the New World, Christopher Columbus landed on the location of present-day Venezuela on the northern coast of the South American continent in 1498. Although Columbus issued reports of great natural wealth in the region, its lack of gold or silver meant that the Spanish Crown lacked serious rivals for dominance in the region throughout the 16th century. Some development by the Spanish took place after 1556, but the region remained sparsely settled by Europeans over the next three centuries.

At the time that Venezuela declared independence, along with its neighboring colonies, from SPAIN in 1810, its economy remained primarily agricultural with some cattle ranches and a few trading posts. After a period as a member of the Gran Colombia coalition, Venezuela formally declared independence in 1830. Political unrest plagued the country, most notably during the Federal War (1859–63). After a series of repressive dictatorships, the democratically elected administration of Romulo Gallegos was overthrown by military coup in 1948 after less than a year in office, and it was not until 1958 that democracy firmly took hold in Venezuela. In the half century since then, Venezuela has remained one of the most stable nations in South America, although the military remained a potent threat to civilian rule.

The discovery of oil in Venezuela in the early 20th century transformed the economy of the country. Through major investments by international oil companies, Venezuela was exporting oil by 1918, and by 1928, was the largest oil exporter in Latin America. Through the 1930s, Venezuela was the third-largest oil producer in the world, after the UNITED STATES and the SOVIET UNION. A founding member of the ORGANIZATION OF PE-

TROLEUM EXPORTING COUNTRIES (OPEC) cartel in 1960, Venezuela's economy became firmly yoked to the volatile oil market in the 1970s and 1980s. Compounding the problems brought on by its oil dependency and lack of economic diversification, the country's political leaders kept the country mired in corruption, inefficiency, and a bloated civil service. The country also suffered instability as a trans-shipment point for the illegal drug trade originating in COLOMBIA.

Austerity measures induced by decades of overspending and a sudden drop in oil prices in the late 1980s brought civil unrest and an attempted military coup in 1992. The leader of that coup, Hugo Chávez Frias, was democratically elected as a civilian leader in 1998, and again in 2000, on a pledge to stem corruption and spread economic development to rural areas. Oil revenues remained the source of about 80 percent of the country's export earnings and a third of its GROSS DOMESTIC PRODUCT (GDP).

BIBLIOGRAPHY. Fernando Coronil, *The Magical State: Nature, Money, and Modernity in Venezuela* (University of Chicago Press, 1997); Javier Corrales, *Presidents without Parties: The Politics of Economic Reform in Argentina and Venezuela in the 1990s* (Pennsylvania State University Press, 2002); Richard Gott, *In the Shadow of the Liberator: Hugo Chavez and the Transformation of Venezuela* (Verso, 2001); Terry L. Karl, *The Paradox of Plenty: Oil Booms and Petro-States* (University of California Press, 1997).

TIMOTHY G. BORDEN, PH.D.
INDEPENDENT SCHOLAR

venture capital

MODERN VENTURE CAPITAL came into existence in the United States in the 1950s. In the late 1990s, the business practice of venture capitalism predominated in the Silicon Valley area of California, but into the 21st century, it is no longer an exclusive investment concept experienced by the American business community. Several European and east Asian countries have developed individual derivations of venture capital industries. Therefore, they have taken on a markedly different conception from those in the United States, and the meaning of venture capitalism has become broadly defined on a global scale.

The venture capital business. Jean Witter first used "venture capital" as a term in a public forum during a presidential address to the 1939 Investment Bankers Association of America convention. Witter highlighted the need for new forms of venture capital to spur economic growth and revitalization. The effect of the onset of venture capitalism has produced a specialized form of finance. The risky investment of capital goes to support small, privately owned firms judged to have the potential for fast growth.

Venture capital invests in funding, or is available for investments. These investments are, by nature, funneled into enterprises that offer the probability of profit with accompanying high risks of no return. Indeed, venture capital was once known also as risk capital. Venture capitalists downplay the immense risks associated with this type of investing. Instead, they may operate very similarly to a gambler with a grandiose belief of always having all success and no failure in the market. No one can know with absolute certainty the effects of what Adam SMITH described as "the invisible hand on the market," nevertheless many venture investors focus on the assurance of a substantial profit. Venture capitalists can be falsely self-assured in the investor's knowledge and business sense.

A venture capital firm is an investment company with a calculated means to invest its shareholders' money in startups and other risky, but potentially very profitable ventures. Many venture-capital success stories have become household names. For example, Cisco, Amazon, Lotus, eBay, Intel, Netscape, Sun Microsystems, and Yahoo!, all received venture capital funding. All venture capital has not been exclusively in the technology industry (information technology, internet, telecoms, wireless communications, and computer software); firms such as Starbucks (coffee retailer) and Staples (office products) were also fueled by venture capital investment.

The investments made by venture capital firms may be categorized by the stage at which financing is provided. The first three may be referred to as early-stage financing and the remaining three as later-stage financing: seed financing usually involves a small amount of capital provided to an inventor, or entrepreneur to prove a concept; start-up financing provides funds to companies for use in product development and initial marketing; expansion financing includes working capital for the initial expansion of a company, or for major growth expansion, and financing for a company expecting to go public within six months to a year; leverage-buyout financing includes funds to acquire a product line, or business from either a public, or private company, utilizing a significant amount of debt and little, or no equity; acquisition financing provides financing to obtain control, possession, or ownership of a private portfolio company.

Venture capitalists were instrumental in the enormous expansion of the number of "dot-com" start-ups in the late 1990s. Because the internet was a new and untried business venue with enormous potential, many analysts with hindsight state that standard businesses rules were too frequently suspended in what was a very optimistic market. Internet-based enterprises were expected to enjoy an unprecedented measure of success; many venture capitalists were said to have encouraged dot-coms to focus on scaling upward, rather than on realizing early profits.

As the dot-com bubble of optimism burst, the venture-capital investment decision-making process has reverted to its initial discipline that requires an extensive and arduous analysis to examine management capabilities, financial health, market trends, and its own investment strategy; sometimes a venture capital firm must be adaptable to choice and structuring of investment.

Although venture capital investment is relatively small in relation to GROSS DOMESTIC PRODUCT (GDP), it is a major source of funding for new technology-based firms. Firms using venture capital are given financial support at a crucial moment to create radical innovations for the market place.

The U.S. venture capital industry. One of the most important challenges to new entrepreneurs in the innovation process is acquiring start-up capital, yet most start-up companies, characteristically, may not have access to public, or credit-oriented institutional funding.

Venture capitalists purchase equity securities and assist in the development of new products and/or services. They add value to the company through active participation. Venture capital investments are high risk with expected high rewards. Frequently, these high-risk investments are made from the long-term perspective. Venture capital, thus, can aid the growth of promising small firms. In supporting vulnerable companies, venture capital can facilitate the introduction of new products and technologies.

When considering an investment, venture capitalists cautiously screen the technical and business merits of the proposed firm. Most often, venture capitalists only invest a small stake in the business they appraise, employing and utilizing long-term financial analysis. Going forward, they actively work as a management partner with the firm. Typically, an experienced investment corporation provides more than just cash, but also offers the start-up company a wealth of experience and expertise from past endeavors.

Venture capitalists mitigate the risk of venture investing by developing a portfolio of young companies in a single-venture fund. The practice has expanded to include co-investing with other professional venture capital firms to defray potential risk and losses. In addition, many venture partnerships will manage multiple funds simultaneously. For decades, venture capitalists have nurtured the growth of America's high technology and entrepreneurial communities. The remarkable results of this business venture, when successful, are significant job creation, economic growth, and international competitiveness.

Venture capitalists strongly favored particular regions in the United States. Venture capitalist activity in California, Massachusetts, and New York together account for nearly 65 percent of the nation's venture investment, while together the top 10 states account for over 95 percent. Thus, regions with large venture capital investments develop agglomerate economies.

The pool of funds managed by venture capital firms rose considerably during the 1980s. It was during this era that venture capitalism emerged as a truly important source of financing for small innovative firms. These entrepreneurial backers differ from one another by reputation, years of operation, previous experience, acquired knowledge of the general partners, preference for lead, or follow-on investment, and the invested company's track record.

When compared to the 1980s, the early 1990s experienced a RECESSION, as investor interest waned and the amount of venture capital disbursed to companies declined. Soon after, during 1992, investors regained the confidence they needed to fund upstart entities and disbursements began to rise again. Both investor and venture capital disbursements reached record levels by the late 1990s, but by 2001 the data shows total managed venture-capital entities declined again.

In the United States (and in Europe), almost all venture funds are institutionally backed limited partnerships—wealthy individuals, pension funds, and corporate investors. Though in America the largest contributions for venture capital spending come from large institutional investors, outside the United States, banks tend to be the industry's largest funding sources. It should not be assumed that all investor funds originate in the native country of the venture capital firm itself. In fact, there are substantial and increasingly important cross-border flows of raising funds. In an increasingly global economy, both inflows and outflows are not exclusive to one nation.

The leading recipients of venture capital in the United States continue to be computer-technology businesses, those engaged in hardware or software production, including computer-related services such as computer training and support. Further, along with telecommunications venues, medical/health-care-related firms have also attracted large amounts of venture capital.

The vitality of venture capital. There are at least five institutional forces that affect the vitality and dynamics of the venture capital industry: financial market structure, human resources availability, source of opportunities, supporting institutions, and the government policy of the venture organization.

The financial market structure includes the presence of a liquid initial public offering (IPO), which provides venture capitalists with exit mechanisms to gather their successful investments. Typically, an IPO is the most profitable exiting opportunity for venture capitalists.

The human resources availability is important because venture capital can only flourish with an adequate supply of entrepreneurs and skilled capitalists. Therefore, the country's entrepreneurial tradition, and the social recognition of the entrepreneur, the flexibility of the human resources system, and the security of the jobs in large firms are central issues in the development of the industry. Source of opportunities means the availability of opportunities related to the RESEARCH AND DEVELOPMENT (R&D) environment, access to expert consultation, and the R&D outcome.

Supporting institutions involves establishing a network among a rich array of firms and professionals. This team of consultants specialize in tasks that benefit entrepreneurs, subcontractors, executive recruiters, lawyers, financial executives, and so on—the creation and self-reinforcement of these specialized institutions are a vital issue in the dynamics of venture capital development. Additionally, the role of geographical proximity in the diffusion of information and the construction of social networks is particularly important to understand types of regional development.

Government policies can influence the size and structure of the venture capital industry. Governments can take promotional measures; make use of taxes to regulate venture investments directly, or adopt laws that stimulate more supporting institutions. Governing bodies also can provide legislation to support markets (i.e., financial, labor, etc.). In addition, governments can promote venture-capital investments by adopting specific policies leading to the development of some key industries (biotechnology, pharmaceuticals, high-tech, etc.).

Venture capital funds. In the early days of venture capital, the perception was of high net-worth individuals interested in providing the capital required for developing an idea, discovery, or invention. Individuals with insufficient credit to market their idea, or discovery, often are red-flagged by banks. Banks act conservatively and categorize venture capital as an unacceptable risk to support. Formalized partnerships, or venture capital funds, were created between and among venture capitalist operations. Over the years, the more generic term "private equity investing" was coined to include a wide range of transactions involved in investing in corporations that generate high return opportunities.

Venture capital investments are generally staged, so venture capital firms typically raise their capital not on a continual basis, but rather through multiple rounds. Limited partners pay venture capitalists annual management fees between 1 percent and 3 percent of their investment. Once a fund is terminated, usually within 10 years, the general partner receives an interest of around 20 percent.

Venture capital entities can have many structures. Venture capital firms can be independent, run by teams of private individuals (commonly termed "angels" and "angel clubs"), or can be captive, a subsidiary of a financial institution, such as a bank or insurance company, or other corporate entities making investments on behalf of the parent group, its clients, as well as outside investors. Sources of revenue can vary with venture capitalism. Independent venture capital firms raise capital from various external sources, normally institutional sources, on a competitive basis. As a consequence, the financial inflows might be more dependent upon their success, making it essential for independent venture capital firms to obtain superior investment returns to signal their competence. Therefore, revenue from external sources could affect a venture capitalist's investment strategy. The investing strategy for venture capitalists desiring a large profit margin, while still retaining a sense of security, is to invest in later-stage firms in order to avoid making too many high-risk technology investments, and to have an acceptable risk diversification. High-tech investments are particularly unattractive to risk-averse investors (even if they can offer high-return with a long-term horizon), instead more safe non-technology intensive investments are considered to yield better profits in a short-term horizon.

Agency theory is the most common framework adopted to analyze the relationship between venture capitalists and entrepreneurs. Insiders in the firms in which venture capitalists invest have tacit, confidential knowledge of their opportunities that is rarely shared with outsiders of the organization. Information asymmetries make venture capital investing very labor intensive. The process of raising money and then channeling funds into the venture requires lengthy periods of time, noted to be significantly prevalent in recent fiscal years. Venture companies were able to raise funds during bullish markets, and in bearish markets when few sound investment opportunities are worth pursuing.

The globalization of venture capital industry. Venture capital is not equally available to entrepreneurs in all countries. In the 1980s and late 1990s, European entrepreneurs and financiers watched across the Atlantic with skepticism as America's high-tech growth market powered the U.S. economy. The European business community attributed the American exponential growth to the flourishing venture capital foundations. This conclusion did not bolster their confidence in their own venture capital firms to fuel their own economies. The European stock markets clung firmly to the belief that only a company with a track record of profit should be admitted to a stock market. It was decidedly a bad-business practice to fund such significantly risky ventures, despite the increasing economic integration in the EUROPEAN UNION and a sustained period of low interest rates across Europe.

The U.S. venture capital pool remains the largest in the world by either absolute size, or relative comparison to other economic data. In 2001, 62 percent of global private equity was invested in North America, 21 percent was invested in western Europe, 12 percent in Asia Pacific, 2 percent in Middle East and Africa. Private equity includes venture capital, buyout funds, mezzanine debt funds, and special situation funds. Venture capital is a substantial component of private equity. (In 2001, in the United States, the $59.7-billion pool of private equity included $41.9 billion of venture capital.) Over the years, private equity and venture capital markets have been subject to strong cyclical fluctuations.

William Bygrave and Jeffrey Timmons (1992) describe several cycles that have marked the U.S. venture capital experience. A very slow beginning in the 1940s eventually led to a boom in the 1960s. A short but quick downturn at the start of the 1990s was followed by another boom. The experience outside the United States has been marked by analogous ups and downs, over a shorter period of time beginning in the 1970s. Over time, IPOs are the most important force behind the cyclical swings in the venture capital industry. Also, early- and later-stage venture capital investments are affected quite differently by the determinants of venture capital activity. In addition, over time, IPOs explain less of the year-to-year fluctuations in early stage rather than in later-stage investments.

There still appears to be a very strong nationalistic or home bias in the venture capital industry in general. This is expressed in two ways. First, venture capitalists tend to invest in their home country. The costs of monitoring distant companies can at least partly explain why the home bias might affect investments. Second, venture capitalists also seek to exit their investments from their home country. This can again be partly explained by the time and effort it takes to sell a business. An IPO in a foreign country involves more cost and effort than an IPO in the home country.

Across countries, some segments of the venture capital market behave quite differently from others. The need for a more differentiated approach to venture capital is especially important, in that they concern two areas. These are early-stage investing, and government involvement. Several studies have tried to analyze the globalization of the venture capital industry. These studies also address the question of what are the peculiar elements of a global market for emerging venture capital. William L. Megginson (2003) found that at least super-

ficial convergence is occurring among North America and Western countries in funding levels, investment patterns, and realized returns. Surprisingly, the author concludes that no integrated global venture capital market is emerging, nor is one likely to emerge in the near future. Even vastly larger public-capital markets can remain effectively segmented from each other, despite massive cross-border capital flows. National public equity markets are much more segmented from each other than are national-debt markets; it only stands to reason that national private-equity markets like venture capital will be even less globally integrated. Finally, huge differences remain in the relative national importance of stock and bond markets.

These differences in markets are the end result of differences in legal systems and regulatory environment. In the same order of ideas, Colin Mayer (2002) concluded that, contrary to the United States, European countries opted for high levels of investor protection and low levels of diversity of investments. To stimulate high technology sectors within the European market it would be judicious to change the substance of the European approach to investing.

In the incidence of this new era, promoting employment and innovation has been a primary objective of national economic policy. Because of rapid advancements in technology, nations are becoming globalized, and venture capital has been a vital source of risk finance for companies in the United States and in Europe. These experiences over the past quarter-century show that the successful stimulation of entrepreneurs requires an integrated system of positive legislation, liberalization, and tax incentives. A process of economic vitality that cannot be underestimated is the importance of trading in the stock markets. Public trading of shares is a vital force behind growth in companies. National rivalries have slowed the integration of Europe's stock markets, but the pressure of competition has put the process underway (e.g., the creation of a pan-European stock market named "Euronext" was a major step in this process).

Most studies indicate that the successful diffusion of venture capital depends on the business opportunities that permit large capital gains. Venture-capital backed companies can provide high returns. However, despite success stories a lot of the deals fail. It is said that only one out of 10 emerging companies succeeds. There have been frequent criticisms of venture capitalists. These assertions state that capital venture companies harbor disloyalties to an organization and destabilize growth within an entity. Unity within members of a young company is tenuous as high turnover/departure of upper-level managers and even entire research teams from existing firms derail product development teams.

While research in the venture capital field progressed over the last few years, many unsolved, or unanswered questions remain, such as: what is the true correlation between risk and returns, the means of the internationalization of venture capital (e.g., is it because of global fund raising, or nationalistic public policies?) namely in banking-oriented economies such as GERMANY or JAPAN. Another inquiry refers to the relationship between venture capital, and its real impact (innovation, and subsequent job growth).

For many venture capitalists the start of the new century was not easy. In 2002, many of the largest and most successful U.S. capital funds decided to release their limited partners from a number of agreed-upon capital calls. Thereby, smaller and newer firms were forced to leave the business entirely. The cyclical nature of downs and ups of the venture capital industry became evident once again with more losses than gains from actions formally described. In the global context, the significance of business practices raises the question of whether venture capital in smaller markets will survive.

BIBLIOGRAPHY. William Bygrave and Jeffrey Timmons, *Venture Capital at the Crossroads* (Harvard Business School Press, 1992); Richard Florida and Martin Kenney, *The Breakthrough Illusion* (Basic Books, 1990); Paul Gompers, "Optimal Investment Monitoring and the Staging of Venture Capital," *Journal of Finance* (v.50, 1995); Paul Gompers and Josh Lerner, *The Venture Capital Cycle* (MIT Press, 1999); Paul Gompers and Josh Lerner, "The Venture Capital Revolution," *Journal of Economic Perspectives* (v.15/2, 2001); Thomas F. Hellman, "A Theory of Strategic Venture Investing," *Journal of Financial Economics* (v.64/2, 2002); Colin Mayer, "Financing the New Economy," *Information Economics and Policy* (v.14, 2002); William L. Megginson, "Venture Capital and Private Equity," *Corporate Finance* (South-Western, 2003); PriceWaterhouseCooopers, www.pwcmoneytree.com; Martha L. Reiner, "The Transformation of Venture Capital: A History of Venture Capital Organization in the United States," Ph.D. Dissertation, University of California, Berkeley (1989).

ALFREDO MANUEL COELHO
UNIVERSITY OF MONTPELLIER, FRANCE

Verizon Communications

ONE OF THE LARGEST telecommunications service providers in the world, Verizon traces its lineage to the formation of the Bell telephone companies in New York and other Eastern states in the late 1800s. These local telephone exchange carriers operated as part of the AT&T monopoly. Verizon's modern history begins in 1984, under the name of Bell Atlantic, when AT&T divested its regional telephone operating companies and formed the "Baby Bells."

Much of Verizon's growth since divestiture has been through merger. NYNEX, another Baby Bell, merged with Bell Atlantic in 1997. In 2000, Bell Atlantic merged with GTE, the largest independent (non-Bell) local telephone service provider, and took the name Verizon. At the same time, Verizon and Vodafone Airtouch combined their United States wireless communications assets.

Today, Verizon's main lines of business are domestic telecommunications and wireless services, international telecommunications, and information services. The company is the largest player in the local phone service and wireless markets in the United States, with 132 million telephone lines served and 29 million wireless customers across the nation. In 2001, Verizon had revenues of $67 billion and assets worth $171 billion, which earned it a top-ten ranking in the Fortune 500.

The Telecommunications Act of 1996 allowed dominant local exchange carriers such as Verizon to enter the long distance business after regulators deemed their markets competitive. Bell Atlantic was the first of the Bell operating companies to receive approval, and began offering long distance service in New York in late 1999.

Verizon has invested in international wireless and wireline ventures in 19 countries in the Americas, Europe, Asia and the Pacific. Verizon is also the world's largest print and online telephone directory publisher. Other information services offered include directory services for online providers such as internet search engines and portals.

BIBLIOGRAPHY. Gerald Brock, *Telecommunication Policy for the Information Age* (1994); Bruce Kushnick, *The Unauthorized Biography of the Baby Bells & Info-Scandal* (1999); Verizon Communications, Annual Report (2001).

JAMES PRIEGER, PH.D.
UNIVERSITY OF CALIFORNIA, DAVIS

Vickrey, William (1914–96)

CANADIAN ECONOMIST and Nobel laureate, born in Victoria, British Columbia, William S. Vickrey graduated from Yale University in 1935 with a B.S., and from Columbia University in 1937 with an M.A. degree. He began teaching at Columbia in 1946 and was awarded a Ph.D. in economics in 1948. Vickrey became a full professor in 1958, and a chaired professor in 1971.

A distinguished economics scholar, Vickrey also served as a consultant on many public policy projects. As a conscientious objector during WORLD WAR II, Vickrey spent part of his alternative service working as an advisor on tax policy in Puerto Rico. He later worked on assignments for the Twentieth Century Fund, the City of New York, and the United Nations, and served as a member of the National Academy of Sciences, president of the American Economic Association, and as Fellow of the Econometric Society. For his seminal work on auction theory, Vickrey was awarded the Nobel Prize in Economics on October 8, 1996 (jointly with James A. MIRRLEES of England). Two days after the prize announcement, Vickrey died in Hastings-on-Hudson, New York.

Vickrey pioneered the analysis of incentives under asymmetric information in the context of auctions. Vickrey's most celebrated contribution to economics is the second-price auction, or Vickrey Auction: Suppose a single object must be sold to one of several potential buyers. It is socially optimal to allocate the object to the person who has the highest willingness to pay for it, if this person bears the social cost implied by the fact that the object cannot be sold to somebody else, or be retained by the seller, at the same time (an opportunity cost). Often, a buyer knows his willingness to pay far better than the seller does—it is the buyer's private information that he typically does not want to reveal to the seller. It is hence a great challenge for economists to design market mechanisms that achieve the socially optimal outcome, even in the presence of asymmetric information.

Vickrey's mechanism implements the social optimum in the above problem in a strikingly simple and elegant way. In the Vickrey auction, each potential buyer is asked to submit a bid for the object. The good is then allocated to the highest bidder, who is required to pay the second-highest bid as the price. It is easy to see that under these rules, every bidder maximizes his own benefit by submitting a bid that equals his true private valuation for the object. Since nobody can win the good and control its price at the same time, bidding one's true valuation maximizes the chance of winning at a price that is below one's valuation. Consequently, the object is won by the person who values it the most. Moreover, since the payment by the winning bidder equals the second-highest valuation in the market, the winner pays the social opportunity cost.

Vickrey's original design is not used often in today's auction markets. Under certain conditions, however, it is equivalent (in terms of bidding behavior and outcomes) to other, more widely used auction forms.

Vickrey's work paved the way for the lively research area of auction theory, or auction design, that by now has resulted in many important applications, including U.S. and European spectrum auctions, treasury auctions, and auctions for offshore oil drilling rights.

BIBLIOGRAPHY. William Vickrey Biography (The Nobel Foundation, 1996); W. Vickrey, "Counterspeculation, Auctions, and Competitive Sealed Tenders," *Journal of Finance* (v.16/8, 1961).

TILMAN KLUMPP, PH.D.
INDIANA UNIVERSITY, BLOOMINGTON

Vietnam

WHEN THE VIETNAM WAR ended in 1975, the communist government extended the North's centrally planned economy to the South. A series of bad harvests and Vietnam's military intervention in Cambodia, however, led to an economic crisis. This forced individuals and agricultural collectives to circumvent quotas and produce goods for market, a movement popularly known as "fence breaking." Communist leaders admitted in 1979 the necessity of modest reforms and began to liberalize retail trade. Communist Party General Secretary Le Duan's death in 1986 opened the way for further liberalization under the slogan "renovation."

Vietnam negotiated an end to the UNITED STATES' economic embargo in 1994 and restored diplomatic relations the following year. From 1993 to 1997, GROSS DOMESTIC PRODUCT (GDP) growth rates averaged around 9 percent per year. The 1997 ASIAN FINANCIAL CRISIS prompted the government to reassess the dangers of an unbridled market economy and to slow the pace of reform. The 2001 United States-Vietnam Bilateral Trade Agreement is expected to improve Vietnam's exports to the United States and to bring further legal and structural reform to Vietnam.

In 2001, the real GDP growth rate was 4.7 percent and industrial production including food processing, garments, shoes, machines, mining, and cement grew an estimated 10.4 percent. Agricultural products included rice, corn, potatoes, rubber, soybeans, coffee, tea, bananas, and sugar. Vietnam exports crude oil, fish, rice, coffee, rubber, tea, clothing, and shoes. Its main export markets are JAPAN at 18.1 percent, CHINA 10.6 percent, AUSTRALIA 8.8 percent and SINGAPORE 6.1 percent. In 2002, Vietnam's population was estimated at 81,098,416 and GDP was approximately $168.1 billion.

BIBLIOGRAPHY. Central Intelligence Agency, "Vietnam" *CIA World Factbook* (2002); William J. Duiker, *The Communist Road to Power in Vietnam* (Westview, 1996), Adam Fforde and Stefan de Vylder, *From Plan to Market: The Economic Transition in Vietnam* (Westview, 1996).

JOHN SAGERS, PH.D.
LINFIELD COLLEGE

Vietnam War

CONSIDERED THE LONGEST war the UNITED STATES has fought so far, the Vietnam War is also one of the few wars from which America did not come out as a winner. It cost 57,605 American lives and wounded 303,700 soldiers. It split the American nation and led to violent demonstrations that also cost lives. The war revealed the ineffectiveness of U.S. Cold War foreign policy and triggered a major rethinking of its global strategy.

America's involvement in VIETNAM was preceded by the French effort to reassert colonial control in southeast Asia after WORLD WAR II. As a part of European imperialist expansion, FRANCE established itself in southeast Asia (present-day Vietnam, Laos, and Cambodia) and claimed the region as its protectorate in the 1880s. France called its colonial possession Indochina. During World War II, the Nazi-controlled French Vichy government collaborated with the Japanese and allowed Japan to occupy Indochina. In 1941, the Vietminh (Vietnamese Independence League) was founded under the leadership of Ho Chi Minh, a member of the Indochina Communist Party. The Vietminh spearheaded a nationalist movement against both the French and Japanese for an independent Vietnam. On September 2, 1945, after Japan surrendered, Ho Chi Minh and the Vietminh declared the independence of Vietnam and founded the Democratic Republic of Vietnam (DRV). France, however, decided to reclaim Vietnam as its colonial possession and attempted to wipe out the Vietminh.

Despite its theoretical support for national self-determination, the United States did not support Vietnam's independence, nor did it oppose the French effort at reasserting colonial control. When the KOREAN WAR broke out in June 1950, the United States decided to aid the French in Vietnam as a comprehensive effort to contain the spread of communism. Between 1952 and 1954, American aid to the French in Vietnam amounted to $2.6 billion.

The war between the French and the Vietminh came to an end in 1954. At Dienbienphu, a village in northwest Vietnam, the French garrison was finally captured by Vietminh forces after a two-month siege. The Geneva Conference held in the same year formally ended French control in Vietnam. The Geneva Accord, the result of the Geneva Conference, temporarily divided Vietnam at the 17th parallel and scheduled to unify the country after a nationwide election in two years. The Geneva Accord was signed by all the other parties present at the conference except the United States and the Bao Dai government of South Vietnam.

Determined to support a pro-American government in South Vietnam against the spread of communism, the United States turned to Ngo Dinh Diem, a Vietnamese Catholic who had collaborated with the Japanese and, since 1950, had lived in Europe and America. Diem went back to South Vietnam and became premier in the South Vietnamese government. The Dwight EISENHOWER administration not only gave financial aid to Diem, it also started to send military advisors to train South Vietnamese troops. In 1955, Diem created the Republic of Vietnam, pushed Bao Dai aside, and made himself president in a rigged election in South Vietnam. Diem then refused to participate in the nationwide election stipulated in the Geneva Accords.

By 1961, President John KENNEDY was told that despite American aid, Diem only controlled 40 percent of South Vietnam. Diem's rule in South Vietnam was authoritarian and ineffective. His Catholic beliefs set him apart from the majority of the population, who were Buddhists. His support of the landlord class disappointed peasants who had been longing for land reform. His program of forcing peasants into government-controlled villages (called agrovilles or strategic hamlets) in an effort to prevent communist infiltration further estranged the peasant class.

Meanwhile, North Vietnamese communists infiltrated into the South to organize revolts against the American-backed Diem regime. In December 1960, the National Liberation Front (NLF) was formed in the south and provided leadership in the struggle against Americans and Diem. The Diem regime called the NLF "Vietcong" (a derogatory appellation meaning Vietnamese communists). The NLF quickly attracted many supporters, both communists and non-communists, in the South. With material support transported along the Ho Chi Minh Trails from the North to the South, the NLF fought against the South Vietnamese and American troops in a guerrilla war.

The Kennedy administration's response to the NLF revolts was to dispatch Green Berets, special forces trained to fight rebels in places such as Vietnam. By 1963, Kennedy had sent more than 16,000 American troops to South Vietnam. The Green Berets, in addition to American military advisors and aid, did not help the situation in South Vietnam. Diem's suppressive policies against his own people, that caused demonstrations (including those by Buddhist priests), and his inability to effectively deal with Northern infiltration led to a coup staged by his own generals (and with U.S. encouragement) on November 1, 1963. Diem died in the coup and Kennedy was assassinated three weeks later.

Lyndon JOHNSON, who became president after Kennedy's assassination, officially announced that the United States would help South Vietnam to win its war against communism. However, the new regime in South Vietnam proved to be as ineffective as the Diem government in dealing with communist infiltration. The Johnson administration, in early 1964, deliberated over using America's superior air power to bomb North Vietnam to stop its war in the South.

The pretext for Johnson's decision to bomb North Vietnam came in the Gulf of Tonkin Incident. On August 2 and 4, 1964, American destroyers *Maddox* and *Turner Joy* were allegedly torpedoed by North Vietnamese patrol boats in the international waters of the Gulf of Tonkin. Johnson ordered American planes to bomb North Vietnamese ships and bases as a response to the alleged attacks. On August 7, the U.S. Congress passed the Gulf of Tonkin Resolution, authorizing Johnson to "take all necessary measures to repel any armed attack against forces of the United States."

In response, CHINA stepped up its already substantial aid to North Vietnam, committing itself to the effort of driving away American military forces from Vietnam. Meanwhile, the SOVIET UNION sent advanced weapons to defend North Vietnam from America's air warfare.

America's war in Vietnam further escalated in early 1965 when ground troops were sent to Vietnam and in 1966 when American B-52s started to bomb North Vietnam. By the end of the year, 160,000 American troops were in Vietnam. At the height of the war, 543,000 American troops were fighting in Vietnam and the American cost of the war jumped from $8 billion in 1966 to $21 billion in 1967. Between 1965 and 1967, American planes dropped more bomb tonnage on Vietnam than the total bomb tonnage the Allies dropped on Europe in World War II.

As the United States deepened its commitment in 1965, university and college students throughout the country started to organize protests against the government's policy. In the next several years, anti-war protests joined the civil-rights movement to pressure the government to end the war in Vietnam and discrimination against African-Americans and other minorities. Martin Luther King, Jr., publicly spoke out against U.S. involvement in Vietnam. In October 1967, about 100,000 people protested outside the Pentagon. Yet, the Johnson administration pleaded for public support and told the nation that the United States was winning the war. He said he could already see the "light at the end of the tunnel."

Contrary to what the government had been saying, the NLF's surprise attack in South Vietnam in January 1968, revealed to the American people that the United States was far from winning the military conflict. During the Vietnamese New Year, Tet, the NLF with support from the North fought their way into Saigon, the South Vietnamese capital, and engaged in combat inside the U.S. Embassy compound. Although the American-supported South came out of the Tet Offensive victorious, televised images of the war's brutality further deepened opposition. More and more Americans questioned the involvement in Vietnam.

On March 31, 1968, Johnson declared on national television that he would limit the bombing of North Vietnam as a gesture to get Ho Chi Minh to the negoti-ating table. Yet, he had no intention of withdrawing American troops from South Vietnam, for preserving South Vietnam as a nation against communism was still an important part of America's foreign policy. In May 1968, peace talks began between the United States and North Vietnam but by October, the talks had stalled over the postwar political nature of South Vietnam.

The U.S. presidential elections in 1968 were much affected by the war in Vietnam. After the Tet Offensive in March, Johnson announced to the nation that he would not seek re-election. The deeply divided nation would witness the assassinations of King and Robert Kennedy within the year. The Democratic convention in Chicago was held amidst violent protests outside the conventional hall and deep divisions among delegates. The Democratic nominee Hubert Humphrey, burdened by his party's failures to win the war in Vietnam and to end domestic violence, was defeated by Republican Richard NIXON. The Republican candidate promised the nation to somehow withdraw American troops from Vietnam while still maintaining an independent non-communist South Vietnam.

The Nixon administration tried new tactics in Vietnam. It ordered the secret bombing of Cambodia in an attempt to destroy the Ho Chi Minh Trail. Meanwhile, Nixon announced a Vietnamization policy, which was to shift the burden of defeating the communists onto the South Vietnam military, with large American aid, and to reduce American military presence there. By the end of 1971, Nixon had reduced American troops in Vietnam from 543,000 in 1969 to 139,000. But, when the secret bombing finally led to an invasion of Cambodia in April 1970, the American public, particularly college students, organized large-scale protests against the widening of the war. At Kent State University, Ohio National Guard troops fired on student protesters, killing four. Nixon, however, persisted with his tactics and further widened the war when, in 1971, he launched an attack on Laos for the same purpose of stopping North Vietnamese supplies to the South.

Nixon's new tactics were not successful. South Vietnam depended on huge American aid to maintain its large army. The North Vietnamese government refused to withdraw its support to the NLF or talk about a divided Vietnam. The North remained determined to defeat the South Vietnamese regime supported by the United States and to unify the country under a national dispensation.

The frustration in Vietnam prompted the Nixon administration to take an overall inventory of America's Cold War foreign policy. As a result, the administration signaled to the People's Republic of China, which the United States had refused to recognize since its founding in 1949, that it was willing to talk with its leaders. In July 1971, Nixon shocked the world when he announced that he was going to visit China the following

February. The development of Chinese-American relations destroyed the bipolar international system, which had been dominated by U.S.-Soviet Union tensions.

U.S. envoy Henry Kissinger's negotiations with North Vietnamese representatives continued intermittently in 1972 as the United States continued to bomb North Vietnam and as communist forces and supplies continued to enter the South. In January 1973, Kissinger and Le Duc Tho, the head of the North Vietnamese delegation, signed an agreement. According to the agreement, the United States would withdraw all its troops from South Vietnam; the two sides would exchange prisoners of war; an international commission would supervise the truce; and a coalition of various factions in Vietnam would conduct elections in the South.

On April 30, 1975, communist forces took Saigon and renamed it Ho Chi Minh City to honor the nationalist leader who had died in 1969. Vietnam was finally a unified country.

America's long war in Vietnam had enormous economic costs, diverting domestic funding into the war. As the war progressed and developed in the late 1960s, inflation and interest rates began to soar. Johnson, who also had wanted to conduct a War on Poverty and build a social support system for all Americans called the Great Society, was continually distracted by the war and passage of his economic legislation was stalled. Nixon, also trying to balance the cost of war with domestic concerns attempted to control inflation with wage and price controls, but fared not much better.

Not only had the United States lost a war, more importantly it proved incapable of fully supplanting, whether it should or not, a system of its own choice on another nation.

BIBLIOGRAPHY. George McT. Kahin, *Intervention: How America Became Involved in Vietnam* (Knopf, 1986); George C. Herring, *America's Longest War: The United States and Vietnam, 1950–1975* (McGraw-Hill, 2002); David Halberstam, *The Best and Brightest* (Random House, 1972); Michael H. Hunt, *Lyndon Johnson's War: America's Cold War Crusade in Vietnam, 1945–1968* (Hill and Wang, 1996); Patrick J. Hearden, *The Tragedy of Vietnam* (HarperCollins, 1991); Jayne S. Werner and Luu Doan Huynh, eds., *The Vietnam War: Vietnamese and American Perspectives* (M.E. Sharpe, 1993).

SHEHONG CHEN, PH.D.
UNIVERSITY OF MASSACHUSETTS, LOWELL

separate entities: Vivendi Environnement, Universal Music Group, Vivendi Universal Publishing, Vivendi Universal Entertainment, Canal Plus Group, Cegetel Group, Vivendi Telecom International and Vivendi Universal Net. Employing 381,000 workers around the world, Vivendi had an estimated income of €3.8 billion in 2001.

Environmental Services and Television & Film are the biggest revenue generators. Vivendi Environnement brought in €1.5 billion in the first half of 2002 and Vivendi Universal Entertainment & Canal Group (both are television and film) took in €600 million. The third largest generator is Telecommunications. Cegetel Group and Vivendi Telecom International brought in a combined total of €400 million in the first half of 2002.

Vivendi Environnement is a world leader in environmental services, providing water, waste management, energy, and transportation services. As just one example of Vivendi's reach, the water division has over 110 million customers in more than 100 countries. Its waste management division, Onyx, is the number 1 company in Europe and number 3 in the world, providing 70 million people with waste services. Connex, its transportation services group, counts more than 1 billion passenger miles.

After an acquisition spree in 2001, Vivendi Universal ran into several financial difficulties. It acquired Uproar Inc, Maroc Telecom, EMusic.com, Houghton Mifflin, and MP3.com. After some corporate restructuring, including firing half of its Paris office, and selling much of its privately held stock, Vivendi Universal solidified its position as a mega-media conglomerate with the approval of a €1.9 billion loan.

As of late 2002, the company was still negotiating legal issues with French telecommunications giant Vodafone. Selling many of the acquisitions of the year before, Vivendi Universal was under investigation by the United States Attorney's Office in New York City for accounting discrepancies.

BIBLIOGRAPHY. David Lieberman, "Vivendi Likely To Be a Hot Topic in Sun Valley," *USA Today* (July 2002); www.vivendiuniversal.com.

ARTHUR HOLST, PH.D.
WIDENER UNIVERSITY

Vivendi Universal

ONE OF THE LARGEST French companies, Vivendi Universal delegates its corporate responsibilities to eight

Volcker, Paul A. (1927–)

ASTUTE, CONTROVERSIAL, and some say brilliant, proponents of Paul A. Volcker describe him as one of

America's true heroes—a great, gutsy economist whose knowledge of the market and no-fear values affected the American economy for the better at a time when indecision and economic fears had Wall Street locked in apprehension.

Volcker took the chair of the FEDERAL RESERVE Board in 1979, when inflation had skyrocketed (at more than 13 percent). He prescribed harsh measures, including implementation of a monetary policy that produced soaring interest rates (much to the public's combustive reaction) and a recession (again received by a growling public), Volcker nonetheless proved that his strategy tamed inflation, after all. In fact, he had laid a cornerstone of economic rejuvenation.

Since Volcker's time, the U.S. economy has grown throughout the majority of subsequent quarters and inflation has never repeated the frightening levels of the 1970s.

Born in New Jersey, Volcker spent much of his childhood in the town of Teaneck, the son of a well-liked city manager who had rescued the town from bankruptcy. "My father made a big impact on my life because he was the central governmental figure in town," Volcker told interviewer Ben Wattenberg. "I didn't go out with the other boys and aim rocks at the street lamps for fear of ending up in my father's office being chastised."

After high school, Volcker attended Princeton University, then Harvard, and completed his studies at the London School of Economics. In his earliest college months he had been unsure of a direction and pondered a public administration career, but at Princeton, he took courses that fired his imagination. By the time he entered Harvard's Kennedy School, he preferred fewer administrative courses to concentrate solely on economics.

To complete his doctorate, he went to London in 1950. "My dissertation was going to be on comparing the transmission of monetary policy in Britain and in the United States," Volcker explained, "because Britain had a very different structure of the banking system."

The city of London intrigued him, but he never wrote the dissertation. Volcker's career over the next decade hop-scotched between civil servant and central banker; he moved among an elite line of political movers-and-shakers who respected his broad economic background with an emphasis on international market expertise. A towering figure in metaphor, he was also one physically. At 6-foot-7-inches, Volcker's presence at any political, social gathering drew people toward him.

During President Richard NIXON's term, Volcker served as under-secretary of the U.S. Treasury. Then, in 1979, President Jimmy CARTER offered him the position of the office of chairman of the Federal Reserve Bank.

The position was the capstone of any economist's career, but it was not an enviable niche. The country's economy teetered on a bleak plateau; inflation spiraled upward; Wall Street trading had been dropping off significantly since 1976; the Carter administration was at a loss economically. Nevertheless, Volcker accepted the challenge with gusto.

Change was subtle and economic forecasters, at first, doubted Volcker's strategy of firmly controlling the money belt. But, the success of his measures soon became evident. Interest rates tightened, inflation figures eventually dipped until, by mid-1981, it was 9.7 percent. As Ronald REAGAN was elected over Carter in 1980, the new administration allowed Volcker to work uninterrupted. On August 17, 1982, economist Henry Kaufman announced that the worst was over. Thanks to Volcker, a base for sustained growth lay in place. Wall Street breathed a sigh of relief as the Dow Jones Industrial Average celebrated the largest single-day rise in the market's history.

Retiring in 1989, Volcker was succeeded by current (2003) Federal Reserve chairman, Alan GREENSPAN.

BIBLIOGRAPHY. "Paul Volcker" *Encyclopedia of World Biography* (McGraw-Hill, 1986); Interview with Paul Volcker, *The Think Tank* (September 9, 2000); Barbara Garrison, "Paul Volcker" *UpDate* (v.20/15, University of Delaware, 2001).

JOSEPH GERINGER
SYED B. HUSSAIN, PH.D.
UNIVERSITY OF WISCONSIN, OSHKOSH

Volkswagen

RANKED AS THE 21st-largest company in the world in 2002 by *Fortune* magazine, the German automobile manufacturing company was founded in 1937 to construct affordable "People's Cars," or Volkswagen. The earliest designs for what became the signature Volkswagen were created by engineer Ferdinand Porsche in the early 1930s. Porsche's innovative suspension system, considerably lighter than anything designed up to that time, promised to allow for the production of smaller and less expensive cars. This goal matched the aspirations of Adolf Hitler's new government, which wanted to build small and economical cars priced within the reach of most German families. In 1934, Porsche accepted a commission from the government to develop the people's car, later known as the KdF-Wagen (Kraft durch Freude Wagen, or "Strength Through Joy" car). The company was founded May 27, 1937, and its first factory was producing cars by 1938 near the city of Wolfsburg; the first commercial KdF-Wagen appeared one year later.

Volkswagen produced a variety of vehicles for the Nazi government during WORLD WAR II and following GERMANY's surrender, the company was overseen by the British military-occupation government before being handed back to the new West German government in 1949. As West Germany rebuilt after the war, Volkswagen emerged as the centerpiece of the country's auto industry. The company expanded international operations in the 1950s, entering CANADA in 1952, BRAZIL in 1953, and the UNITED STATES in 1955. North American sales were initially very slow, until a strikingly successful advertising campaign was launched in 1959 that dubbed the car "the Beetle," creating a cultural icon and a tremendously successful product line.

Though Volkswagen enjoyed great success and the Beetle was, for a time, the bestselling car in the world, by the 1970s the company's designs had not changed for many years and sales had seriously slumped. Averting bankruptcy, the company reorganized and rebounded by introducing new models such as the Golf and Passat. Volkswagen continued to expand its international ventures in South America and Asia into the 1990s, while flagging North American sales helped encourage the introduction of the "New Beetle" in 1997. Volkswagen further expanded its reach into the luxury-car market with the purchase of Bentley, Rolls Royce, and Bugatti manufacturers in the 1990s. Volkswagen reported over $79 billion in revenue for 2001.

BIBLIOGRAPHY. Phil Patton, *Bug: The Strange Mutations of the World's Most Famous Automobile* (Simon and Schuster, 2002); Ivan Hirst and Karl Ludvigson, *Battle for the Beetle* (Bentley, 2000); Walter Henry Nelson, *Small Wonder: The Amazing Story of the Volkswagen* (Little-Brown, 1970).

CHARLES ROBINSON
BRANDEIS UNIVERSITY

W

wage

AS WORKERS LEFT the agricultural sector to seek employment during the early days of the INDUSTRIAL REVOLUTION, the wage rate became a major economic issue. In line with their practice of influencing government to improve their own profits, the mercantilists promoted government regulations to keep wages down. They believed that when wages were down, WORKERS would work longer hours and produce more goods. Since goods were less expensive, more would be sold, and profits would increase accordingly. Workers had little control over how much they were paid until trade unions were established; and even then, wages fluctuated according to the health of the overall economic scene, the availability of workers, the supply of surplus goods, and the ups and downs of prices of particular goods.

Adam Smith (1723–90). After the publication of Adam SMITH's *An Inquiry into the Nature and Causes of The Wealth of Nations* in 1776, classical economics replaced MERCANTILISM as the predominant economic theory. Unlike mercantilists who saw wages simply in relation to their own profits, classical economists attempted to explain wages as a single element of the economic system. Smith defined wages as the revenue derived from LABOR and rent as the revenue produced from land. His theory of value stated that the amount of rent for land, plus the wages paid to workers, equaled the profit that the capitalist could make. He believed that wages tend to settle near the subsistence level; and according to Smith, the subsistence wage was "the lowest wage consistent with common humanity."

He believed that workers often lost their share in the profits as population increased. Population increases, of course, resulted in a larger pool of workers and in increased drains on the wages of particular families. Wages were likely to be higher in countries that were experiencing economic growth because employers were forced to compete for their services. For example, wages were much higher in the UNITED STATES than in England, and higher in England than in Scotland. He thought that wages should be adjusted to the type of work. For example, higher wages should be paid for work that was dangerous, for jobs that required intensive training, and for tasks that no one was likely to choose to do. Higher wages were also necessary when work might be irregular, such as with a construction worker who worked according to weather conditions. Positions that required a lot of trust such as doctors and lawyers also deserved higher wages. In occupations where only a limited number were successful, Smith believed only high wages would attract potential workers. In contemporary terms, this rationale would explain why entertainment and sports figures are so highly paid.

Smith contended that wages as well as profit and rent depended on the supply of available GOODS in relation to the demand for those goods. Whenever goods were stockpiled, wages rose but profits fell. He argued that conflict over the wage rate arose when employers kept wages low while workers attempted to raise rates as high as possible. Workers were likely to work harder when wages were higher because they were more motivated. In response to his question of what made nations wealthy, Smith determined that wealth derived from the economic progress of the people. He maintained that if workers were prosperous, production would improve and living standards and wages would remain high. Smith was committed to FREE TRADE and was opposed to government attempts to regulate wages. He contended that whenever government tried to legislate a wage rate, it usually failed to do it properly.

David Ricardo (1772–1823). Like Smith, David RI-CARDO was concerned with how nations became prosperous, he believed that the law of distribution was determined by the wages that workers received, the profits commanded by the capitalists, and rents collected by landowners. Ricardo's Labor Theory of Value, which greatly influenced Karl MARX, stated that the wage rate was determined by the cost of food, which in turn was based on the costs of production. It followed, then, that the cost of labor to produce a product influenced overall production costs. In 1817, in the *Principles of Political Economy and Taxation*, Ricardo developed what became known as his "iron law of wages."

He maintained that increases in population produced a greater supply of labor, which in turn caused wages to fall below a subsistence level, where they tended to stabilize. Since the goal of the worker was to take care of dependents and, hopefully, have enough of the extras to which they had all become accustomed, subsistence wages were never enough. The result was misery and sometimes starvation. Reduced population would then cause wages to rise again. As workers became accustomed to a new standard of living, the cycle would be repeated. Ricardo maintained that higher wages were not bound to raise prices. Sometimes, he believed, higher wages simply lowered profits for capitalists. However, Ricardo agreed with Smith that wages should be controlled by free competition and not through government regulation.

Other classical liberals. Thomas MALTHUS (1776–1834) argued that high wages and high prices tended to limit population growth, while low wages and low prices were likely to increase population. However, if population increased, as it was bound to, wages would settle at the subsistence level. Workers were happiest, Malthus thought, when high wages and high prices were accompanied by an increased demand for labor. Under these circumstances, workers were able to buy food and perhaps some of the luxuries of life.

John Stuart MILL (1806–73) defined profit as the difference between wages paid to laborers and the value of the product produced by the laborer. Because Mill, like other classical economists, believed in the idea of scarce resources, he initially argued that there was a limit on the amount of total wages that it was possible to pay. Mill later backed away from this idea and decided that capitalists set their own limits on wages.

Karl Marx (1818–83). Marx rejected the Malthusian ideas on population, calling them a "libel on the human race." His ideas on wages were heavily influence by his friend Friedrich ENGELS who had coined the term "wage slavery." Engels had worked in a factory in England and witnessed first-hand the conditions of workers. Marx saw the average price of wage labor as the minimum wage, or that wage which allowed the worker just enough money to survive. He argued that when wages rose too high, capitalists responded with new labor-saving machines that decreased the number of workers needed and forced wages back to the subsistence level. Marx was convinced that capitalism would destroy itself as the proletariat (workers) revolted against the bourgeoisie (capitalists). However, as industrialization progressed, higher wages, shorter work hours, and improved working conditions decreased the amount of ALIENATION felt by most workers.

John Maynard Keynes (1883–1946). Keynes rejected classical economic views that the market was self-regulating, and advocated government activism. When the economy became sluggish, classical economic theory called for negotiating with workers to accept lower wages in order to increase employment. While Keynes agreed that reducing wages would increase employment, he thought that the real wage was dependent on either the state or on effective demand and not on bargaining for a money wage.

Workers, in his view, were more likely to accept having less to spend because of rising prices than they were to accept a cut in the amount they placed in their pockets on payday. As Keynes saw it, full employment was possible only through wage reduction; but inflation could follow full employment with its accompanying increase in wages. According to Keynes, the solution to dealing with severe economic crisis like the Great DE-PRESSION was for the government to intervene. Keynes was an advocate of using public works to stimulate employment. This theory was the guiding principle of Franklin D. ROOSEVELT's (1882–1945) NEW DEAL. Because of the Great Depression, the private sector was not hiring, so the government hired Americans to write, paint, build roads, etc. Roosevelt, like Keynes, believed that once people were employed their wages would stimulate the economy through the purchase of food, clothing, and entertainment. Keynes' impact on economic theory was so great that it launched what became known as the Keynesian Revolution.

BIBLIOGRAPHY. Mark Blaug, *John Maynard Keynes: Life, Ideas, Legacy* (St. Martin's Press, 1990); Giovanni A. Caravale, *The Legacy of Ricardo* (Basic Books, 1985); John Kenneth Galbraith, *Economics in Perspective* (Houghton-Mifflin, 1987); Robert L. Heilbroner, *The Worldly Philosophers: The Lives, Times, and Ideas of the Great Economic Thinkers* (Simon & Schuster, 1972); Karl Marx, *The Communist Manifesto,* (Regnery, 1950); James Medoff and Andrew Harless, *The Indebted Society* (Little Brown, 1996); Louis Putterman, *Dollars and Change: Economics in Context* (Yale University Press, 2001); D.D. Raphael, "Smith," *Three Great Economists* (Oxford University Press, 1997); David Ricardo, *The Princi-*

ples of Political Economy and Taxation (J.M. Dent, 1911); Eric B. Ross, *The Malthus Factor: Population, Poverty and Politics in Capitalist Development* (Zed Books, 1998); Paul A. Samuelson, *Economics* (McGraw-Hill, 1973); Robert Skidelsky, "Keynes," and Donald Winch, "Malthus," *Three Great Economists* (Oxford University Press, 1997).

ELIZABETH PURDY, PH.D.
INDEPENDENT SCHOLAR

Wal-Mart

FROM THE FIRST WAL-MART discount department store in Rogers, Arkansas in 1962, Sam Walton built a chain of stores that ranked as the largest retailer in the United States at the time of his death in 1992. In 2002, Wal-Mart ranked as the largest company in the world with sales of $219 billion according to *Fortune* magazine. In the decade after Walton's death, Wal-Mart continued to rank as the nation's biggest retailer and largest private employer in the world, with well over one million employees. Although the chain faced criticism over its employment policies and competitive practices, it remained one of the few consistently profitable entities in the volatile retail sector.

The story of Wal-Mart is really the story of Samuel Moore Walton, born in Kingfisher, Oklahoma on March 29, 1918 to Thomas and Nannia Lee (Thompson) Walton. Along with his brother, James (Bud), Walton learned frugality from his parents; the lessons were reinforced as he accompanied his father, a mortgage and insurance agent, as he foreclosed on farms in Missouri, where the family lived during the Great DEPRESSION. After completing his bachelor's degree in economics at the University of Missouri in 1940, Walton worked as a manager trainee at a J.C. Penney's store in Iowa. In 1943, he married Helen Robson, the daughter of a wealthy Oklahoma rancher, lawyer, and businessman. With his wife's family putting up a major stake, Walton bought a retail franchise from the Ben Franklin variety store chain in 1945 and opened up his first store in Newport, Arkansas. He eventually held more than a dozen Ben Franklin franchises in the south-central United States, almost all of which were located in towns of fewer than 10,000 people.

Over the next decade, Walton developed the competitive strategies that he would later implement in the Wal-Mart chain. Regularly checking up on his competitors, Walton made a point of visiting other discount stores to take note of their stock, prices, and displays. Looking for the lowest possible prices on his merchandise, Walton also began buying directly from manufacturers and wholesalers instead of distributors, even though the habit drew the ire of Ben Franklin executives. At the heart of Walton's retail philosophy was the strategy of selling goods at a high volume with a small profit on each sale.

In June 1962, Walton opened the first store to bear the Wal-Mart name in Rogers, Arkansas. By 1969 he had 18 Wal-Mart stores in Oklahoma, Missouri, and Arkansas. As he had with most of his Ben Franklin franchises, Walton located the stores in small towns with little retail competition or in still-rural areas outside of major cities. Although his first stores sold mostly off-brand, irregular, and discontinued merchandise, Walton's growing clout allowed him to sell more brand-name consumer items by the end of the 1960s. The chain's sales volume and mostly rural- and small-town locations forced Walton to open his own warehouse and distribution system in 1969; although he resisted making the investment, the company's control of its distribution eventually gave it an edge over its competitors, such as K-Mart, which were slower and had less flexibility in getting goods on the store shelves.

In 1970, Wal-Mart became a publicly traded corporation, which allowed it to expand rapidly during the decade. By 1973, it had 55 stores in five south-central states and in 1979 it passed the $1 billion mark in sales. Expanding even through economic downturns, Wal-Mart emerged as the nation's largest retailer in 1991 and expanded its operations into Mexico and Europe. Although its low prices were popular with consumers, Wal-Mart's strategy of cost-cutting also raised controversy.

As a low-wage employer that offered few benefits to its employees, Wal-Mart was routinely accused of keeping its workers near or below the poverty level. The company's contracts with known sweatshop operators in the United States, Central America, and Asia made headlines throughout the 1990s. Its actions to prevent the unionization of its work force—including the firing of union supporters and closing of departments that had voted to unionize—resulted in hundreds of complaints to the National Labor Relations Board over its union-busting tactics. In 2002, an Oregon federal jury found Wal-Mart guilty of consistently forcing its employees to work overtime without paying them; 39 similar cases had yet to be tried. The company was also accused of destroying the commercial life of many small towns, where retailers could not compete with Wal-Mart's volume and prices. By the late 1990s, local movements to prevent Wal-Marts from opening had sprung up throughout the United States and watchdog groups continually publicized the company's ties to horrific conditions in sweatshops around the world.

After Walton's death from cancer in 1992, his four children continued to be active in Wal-Mart's management of 3,244 discount, supercenter, Sam's Club warehouse, and small neighborhood market stores in the United States and 4,414 stores in Europe, Central and South America, Canada, and China in 2002.

BIBLIOGRAPHY. Bob Ortega, *In Sam We Trust: The Untold Story of Sam Walton and How Wal-Mart Is Devouring America* (Times Business, 1998); Vance H. Trimble, *Sam Walton: The Inside Story of America's Richest Man* (Dutton, 1990); Sandra S. Vance and Roy V. Scott, *Wal-Mart: A History of Sam Walton's Retailing Phenomenon* (Twayne, 1994); Sam Walton with John Huey, *Sam Walton: Made in America: My Story* (Doubleday, 1992).

TIMOTHY G. BORDEN, PH.D.
TOLEDO, OH

Wall Street Journal

A DAILY NEWSPAPER published in the UNITED STATES in print and electronic format by Dow Jones and Company, the *Wall Street Journal* has remained one of the most influential and respected business periodicals since its foundation in 1889.

The *Wall Street Journal* was created by three young reporters from the Kiernan news agency in New York City with shared interests in reporting the American industrial and financial landscape: Charles H. Dow (1851–1902), Edward D. Jones (1856–1920), and Charles M. Bergstrasser. Dow and Jones were the first two collaborators, but they proved cash-poor, bringing on Bergstrasser for financial assistance to found DOW JONES and Company in 1882. The company's mission was to research fluctuations in American business and provide concise, objective reports for investors. For its clientele, it churned out a two-page financial review, the *Customers' Afternoon Letter*. Over the next few years, Dow and Jones realized the need for more detailed and extensive business news reporting of the changes in the volatile stock market, evolving the *Letter* into a more robust form as the *Wall Street Journal*.

The first edition of the *Wall Street Journal* appeared on July 8, 1889, running four pages and costing two cents. The new paper's mission was "to give fully and fairly the daily news attending the fluctuations in prices of stocks, bonds, and some classes of commodities." One of its chief features was the regular publication, beginning on October 7, 1896, of its famous Average, at first merely a daily averaging of the status of 11 industrial stocks. Before its appearance, while investors could track individual company's performances on a day-to-day basis in the stock market, there was no central index for charting the performance of the entire market itself. Even though the *Journal* greatly facilitated the transmis-

sion of financial news to its customers, Dow Jones saw the need for even greater speed, establishing the Dow Jones News Service, which transmitted financial data across telegraph wires in the famous broad-tape and ticker system. In addition to journalism focused upon the day's financial news and trends, the *Wall Street Journal* featured extensive tables of stock prices.

The *Journal* retained its journalistic structure and editorial outlook after the founding partners sold their interests to the journalist Clarence W. Barron in 1902; under Barron and a series of influential individuals including Kenneth "Casey" Hogate, the newspaper maintained its reputation for integrity and accuracy in business reporting while gradually expanding its focus beyond business and finance. By the time of WORLD WAR I, the newspaper's circulation had risen to nearly 20,000. After the war, the paper's reach continued to expand, as *Barron's Financial Weekly* was spun-off in 1921 targeting money managers, and a West Coast edition of the *Journal* appeared in 1929. Though the turmoil of the Great DEPRESSION was a sharp blow to the *Wall Street Journal*'s circulation in 1929, the newspaper survived and, indeed, expanded its coverage and circulation over the next few years.

Bernard "Barney" Kilgore became the managing editor at the *Journal* in 1941, and, under his direction, the paper assumed the shape it held through the end of the century. Under Kilgore, circulation surpassed 100,000 and the *Wall Street Journal* expanded in two directions following WORLD WAR II.

First, it began to truly extend its topical coverage beyond explicitly business-oriented subject matter, as its parent company Dow Jones spun off sister publications targeted at a general readership, such as the *National Observer*, founded in 1962, and through the acquisition of regional newspaper companies, especially the Ottoway group in the 1970s.

Second, the *Journal* benefited from technological leaps and bounds to expand its distribution to become a truly national daily newspaper. Technological advancements in printing and communications greatly facilitated the late-20th-century transformation of the newspaper. The *Journal* first became a true national paper in 1955, when identical editions began to be simultaneously printed in multiple facilities around the United States. Circulation surpassed 500,000 by the mid-1950s and the 1 million mark in 1966. On August 30, 1974, for the first time, an orbiting communications satellite was used for a plant-to-plan transmission of newspaper copy and layout.

The *Journal*'s focus and format continued to evolve through the end of the 20th century. As its parent company Dow Jones continued to expand internationally, so too did the *Wall Street Journal*. In 1980, a second section was added to the paper with a rotating section of topics and a third section followed in 1988. The *Asian Wall Street Journal* was founded in 1976, and a European edition was begun in Brussels, Belgium in 1983. The *Journal* expanded into syndicated radio as well during the 1980s, with the "Wall Street Journal Report" premiering in 1980, and the "Dow Jones Money Report" in 1987. The *Wall Street Journal* began electronic publication with the establishment of WSJ.com in 1996. *Wall Street Journal Sunday* began publication in 1999 as a syndicated column in many American newspapers.

BIBLIOGRAPHY. Frances Neilson, *What's News: Dow Jones* (Chilton, 1973); Jerry M. Rosenberg, *Inside the Wall Street Journal* (Macmillan, 1987); Edward E. Scharff, *Worldly Power: The Making of the Wall Street Journal* (Beaufort Books, 1986); Lloyd Wendt, *The Wall Street Journal: The Story of Dow Jones & the Nation's Business Newspaper* (Rand McNally, 1982); Frances X. Daly, *The Power & the Money* (Birch Lane Press, 1993); www.wsj.com.

CHARLES ROBINSON
BRANDEIS UNIVERSITY

Walras, Léon (1834–1910)

FOUNDER OF THE MODERN theory of general economic EQUILIBRIUM, Marie-Esprit Léon Walras' rigorous mathematical formulation of the mechanics of the price system is a landmark in economics. In the early 20th century, economic scholars such as Joseph SCHUMPETER had already labeled him, "the greatest economist of all time," an arguable title that still stands sturdy today, a century later. Recommended by peers for one of the century's earliest Nobel Prizes, Walras died before he could be considered.

Walras (pronounced *Val*-rass) was born in Evreaux, FRANCE, the son of Louise de Sainte Beauve and Antoine-August Walras, a well-known philosopher and proto-marginalist. For years, the elder Walras had long professed, through his many writings on the subject of scarcity, that mathematicians alone held the key to the advancement of economics. His thoughts, revolutionary at the time, had sparked both a following and condemnation from the economic inner circle. Most assuredly, with the birth of Leon, he hoped that his son would defend and advance his teachings.

But, as a little boy growing up in the pastoral countryside of southern France, Walras exhibited little if any interest in his father's domain. His early school years at Caen School were quite ordinary, not showing any of the brilliance that would later emerge and place him in the forefront of his field. He eventually earned a Bachelor of Letters in Science, but after entering into a field of engineering study at the School of Mines in Paris, he soured at his would-be career, finding it uninteresting and too rigid for his tastes. For, once in Paris, his outlook had changed drastically. He had become acquainted with a host of friends outside the scholastic world who frequented the Bohemian cafes and coffeehouses, and who reveled in the colorful world of *la dramatique*. Walras dropped out of engineering school and, much against his father's wishes, explored the Parisian nightlife where, in 1855, he set himself up as a critic of the arts. He even wrote a novel, *Francis Saveur*, which garnered some literary accolades.

Despite his father's entreaties, Walras continued his creative life apart from anything his erudite father would have approved of. He moved in with a young lady named Célestine Fehrbach, with whom he produced two daughters out of wedlock. (They would eventually wed.) As a young columnist writing under a pseudonym of "Paul" for *La Gazette de Lausanne*, many of his articles attacked the then-popular artistic culture. Occasionally, his articles departed the ethereal to focus on philosophy and business. In 1860, he wrote a brilliant article attacking the radical economic/anarchist teachings of Pierre-Josef Proudhon.

Two years earlier, to appease his father, Walras had promised to consider a future in economics—that is, to familiarize himself with his father's and other economists' teachings. Many a night, long into the dark hours, Walras' lamp burned as he poured over thick tomes and complex theories.

It was also during this period that Walras left *La Gazette* to write for another newspaper, the popular Paris-wide *La Presse*, but his political views clashed with the conservative views of the editorial board. He was promptly terminated. Feeling that his journalistic points of view were restricted, he sought other employment. In 1861, he accepted a clerkship with a railway company. Pay was meager and supplied neither his family's food bill nor his ailing wife's constant medical bills.

Several times between 1861–69, Walras applied for an academic position, but lacked the educational credentials. For extra income, he contributed to newspapers such as the well-read *L'Independent de la Moselle*. His articles, now centered chiefly on taxation and financing cooperatives, caught the eye of lead reformers who offered him the opportunity to speak at a conference at Lausanne, Switzerland, and elsewhere in neighboring France. In 1870, an impressed Swiss government offered Walras the position of economics instructor at the University of Lausanne. He would remain there until he retired in 1892.

At Lausanne, he started his notes on what would become *Elements of Pure Economics* (1874). The book argued in defense of a mathematical, multi-market economy and the marginalist subjective theories his father had expressed. *Elements* provides the author's definition of the scope of economics, the subjective VALUE THEORY and the mathematical method. With some customization to suit the changing demands of the 20th century, Walras' teachings present the basic, mainstream essence of today's economic equilibrium theory.

Sadly, the credit Walras so richly deserved did not come to him in his lifetime. Economists, tending to encompass newer doctrines, disregarded his *Elements*, as well as his other significant works—such as *Equations of Capitalism* (1877) and *Mathematical Theories of Social Classes* (1883). His health failing, Walras retired from teaching to live a life of obscurity until his death in 1910.

Interest once again rose in his work in the 1930s when a series of economic historians from Lausanne rediscovered his work and its value. Thanks to scholars who demanded the first English translation of *Elements* (1954), Walras' brilliance spread to a whole new generation.

BIBLIOGRAPHY. Leon Walras, William Jaffe, trans., *Elements of Pure Economics* (Augustus M. Kelley Publishers, 1969); "Biography of Leon Walras," The History of Economic Thought, Johns Hopkins University, www.econ.jhu.edu; Mark Blaug, "Leon Walras (1834–1910)," Queens University of Kingston, qed.econ.queensu.ca/walrus.

JOSEPH GERINGER
SYED B. HUSSAIN, PH.D.
UNIVERSITY OF WISCONSIN, OSHKOSH

Wang, An (1920–90)

AN INVENTOR, A BUSINESSMAN, and a philanthropist, An Wang grew up in a well-to-do family and received an education at some of the best Chinese schools, including Jiao Tong University (known as CHINA's MIT). He came to the United States in 1945 and earned a Ph.D. in applied physics at Harvard University in 1948.

Wang worked as a researcher in the Harvard Computation Laboratory where he invented magnetic memory cores. By precisely controlling the flow of magnetic energy, the memory cores provided a solution to the problem of data storage, a cutting-edge contribution to the computer revolution. In 1951, he left Harvard and started Wang Laboratories in Boston, Massachusetts. With $600 as capital, Wang, the sole proprietor, began to make magnetic memory cores in a 200-square-foot office furnished with a table, a chair, and a phone.

In 1955, he received a patent for his magnetic memory cores and Wang Labs became a corporation. In 1965, Wang introduced logarithmic calculating instrument (LOCI), a modern calculator, to the world. LOCI was an instantly successful commodity. In 1967, the company sold $4,259,000 worth of calculators. In the same year, Wang Labs became a public corporation,

whose stock value rose from $12.50 per share at opening to $40.50 at closing on its first day of trading. In 1971, Wang Labs developed an automatic typewriter with editing functions, which was the forerunner of modern word-processing system. This automatic typewriter was further developed and in 1976, the company introduced to the market the Word Processing System (WPS), a word processor with a screen.

The WPS was "the first computer with which an ordinary person could interact," said Wang. This user-friendly machine brought Wang quick fortunes. In the early 1980s, Wang Labs ranked the 11th largest American computer manufacturer, with a work force of 24,800; in 1984, Wang was the fifth-richest person in the United States, with a personal wealth of $1.6 billion.

The expansion of business brought Wang to Lowell, Massachusetts, near Boston. In 1976, he bought a piece of land in Lowell for a production site; two years later, he moved his company's headquarters there. Wang Labs created job opportunities: in the early 1980s, it employed 14,000 local residents, and drew many other business companies to settle in Lowell, thus resurrecting the town from an enduring economic depression.

Besides being an inventor and a successful capitalist, Wang was also a philanthropist. He believed that "a sense of satisfaction comes from service to one's community." He founded the Wang Institute, a graduate school offering a graduate degree in software engineering. At MIT, he financially supported a program that offered fellowships to engineers from China; at Harvard, he donated $1 million to the Fairbank Center to promote understanding of Chinese culture. For the city of Boston, his money helped to build the Wang Center for the Performing Arts and the outpatient care unit of Massachusetts General Hospital. Together with his scientific inventions, Wang left behind a substantial cultural and technological legacy.

Wang was presented the Medal of Liberty by President Ronald Reagan in 1986. In 1988, Wang was inducted into the National Inventors Hall of Fame.

BIBLIOGRAPHY. An Wang, *Lessons: An Autobiography* (Addison-Wesley, 1986); Charles C. Kenney, *Riding the Runaway Horse: The Rise and Decline of Wang Laboratories* (Little, Brown & Company, 1992).

SHEHONG CHEN, PH.D.
UNIVERSITY OF MASSACHUSETTS, LOWELL

War of 1812

THE WAR OF 1812 arose from tensions between the UNITED STATES and the UNITED KINGDOM reaching back to the AMERICAN REVOLUTION (1775–83), and was complicated by the Napoleonic Wars between Britain and FRANCE.

England, motivated by the desire to hamper Franco-American commerce, greatly curtailed American trade in the Caribbean through restrictive policies and by seizing American ships and sailors. The Jay Treaty of 1794, negotiated by George WASHINGTON's pro-British, Federalist administration, temporarily eased tensions by restoring Anglo-American trade and defining the United States' neutral status in the European conflicts. But the capture and impressment of American sailors continued; when the commercial agreements of the Jay Treaty expired and the British resumed their discriminatory trade policies, Republican Thomas JEFFERSON was far less tolerant.

At his urging, the U.S. Congress passed the Embargo Act of 1807, which closed all American ports to foreign trade. This measure, built on the assumption that England needed American trade, instead crippled the American economy while having very little impact on the British. When James MADISON became president in 1809, he eased the embargo slightly, but continued Jefferson's overall policy of economic retaliation. As this proved continually ineffective, Congress declared war on June 18, 1812. The vote was the closest for any war in American history; Federalists were overwhelmingly against a military conflict, fearing it would irreparably damage commercial relations with England, which they deemed vital to the United States' economic development.

The war was a major military challenge for the young nation; its army and navy were still woefully small, inexperienced and under-funded, and the American public was unenthusiastic. The initial strategy of a Canadian invasion went disastrously wrong. Not only did CANADA remain in British hands, by the end of 1812, the British had conquered sizable territory in the northwestern United States, including the outposts of Detroit and Ft. Dearborn on the Great Lakes.

By the summer of 1814, the United States had scored two notable retaliatory victories at the Battles of York in Canada (April, 1813) and Plattsburgh in New York (August, 1814). But by that time, the British had opened a new front on the Chesapeake Bay with a dramatic invasion of Washington, D.C. The British army set fire to much of the city, including the capitol and the executive mansion, before marching toward Baltimore. Forts McHenry and Covington managed to keep the British Navy at bay. It was while viewing the heavy bombardment of Fort McHenry that Francis Scott Key penned the words to the "Star-Spangled Banner."

The naval war went much better for the United States, an irony since the British Navy was the world's best and thought to be invincible. Early on, the super-frigate *U.S.S. Constitution* scored two impressive victories off the coasts of Halifax, Canada, and Brazil. All told, the U.S. navy won 13 of 25 naval engagements, a better navy record than any other nation against the British.

The last major campaign of the war took place at New Orleans, where the British launched an attack in December 1814. The climactic battle occurred on January 8, when American forces under General Andrew Jackson overwhelmingly repelled the British offensive. Unbeknownst to its participants, the battle actually took place after the conclusion of the Treaty of Ghent, which ended the war. Nevertheless, the win at New Orleans helped legitimize an overall American victory, which was largely due to British fatigue rather than American military superiority. It also made a national hero out of future President Andrew JACKSON.

Although the war was of little military consequence, it is seen as a pivotal event in the political and economic life of the United States. Politically, the war saw the demise of the Federalist Party, already out of step with the democratic trend of American politics, then completely undone by its opposition to the war. The war also ushered in a new economic nationalism within the Republican Party, which had previously been the party of state sovereignty and strict LAISSEZ-FAIRE. In the aftermath of the war, these "new Republicans" approved a re-charter of the national bank, internal improvements and a new protective TARIFF. In addition to these political trends, the war's disruption of foreign trade stimulated American industry and manufacturing, accelerating capitalist development.

BIBLIOGRAPHY. Harry L. Coles, *The War of 1812* (University of Chicago Press, 1965); George Dangerfield, *The Awakening of American Nationalism, 1815–1826* (Waveland Press, 1965); Donald R. Hickey, *The War of 1812: A Forgotten Conflict* (University of Illinois Press, 1989); Marshall Smelser, *The Democratic Republic, 1801–1815* (HarperCollins, 1968).

HOLLY A. BERKLEY, PH.D.
HARDIN-SIMMONS UNIVERSITY

Washington, George (1732–99)

COMMANDER OF THE Continental Army during the AMERICAN REVOLUTION and first president of the UNITED STATES, George Washington played an essential role in the founding and grounding of the United States as an independent nation. His graceful wielding of military and political power gave his countrymen, highly suspicious of centralized power, the confidence needed for the creation of an effective, strong, federal government.

Washington's administration provided the crucial political and economic stability that ensured the success of the American experiment.

Washington was born to a Virginia farming family of modest means. He first gained notoriety and prestige during the French and Indian War (1754–63), in which he commanded a force against the French in the Ohio River Valley. By the time of the American Revolution, Washington was an affluent and well-respected member of the Virginia House of Burgesses. When fighting broke out in 1775, the Second Continental Congress unanimously selected him to command the yet-to-be created Continental Army. Accepting reluctantly, he faced the daunting task of constructing a national army from the volunteers of the Massachusetts militia skilled enough to match the British.

It would be the first of many challenges. Washington's army suffered numerous defeats, and faced a chronic shortage of manpower, funding, and supplies. The nadir came in the winter of 1777–78 at Valley Forge, where Washington's army had fled after the British invaded Philadelphia. By that time, Washington's men had barely enough food to prevent starvation and were barefoot in the snow. He is credited for holding the army together through deprivation, desertion, and demoralization and eventually leading it on to victory. In 1781, British commander George Cornwallis surrendered to Washington and his French allies at Yorktown, on the Virginia coast.

Upon the war's conclusion, Washington planned to retire quietly, but his near mythic status as the liberator of the United States made him indispensable to the new nation. When the Constitutional Convention of 1787 discussed the creation of an executive branch, it was with Washington in mind. The idea that he would fill and define the authoritative position eased many fears that the presidency might become a dictatorship. Washington was the quintessential republican, the symbol of an enlightened, naturally elite leader who assumed power sacrificially. He was inaugurated as the nation's first president in New York on April 30, 1789.

One of Washington's best decisions as president was his selection of Alexander HAMILTON as his secretary of treasury. With the president's support, Hamilton devised a plan for putting the United States on firm financial footing through the sound management of the nation's debt. His Reports on Public Credit recommended the full funding of debts to foreign nations and to public creditors, and the establishment of a national bank. Their passage radically improved American credit, stimulated economic growth and tied wealthy Americans to the federal government, thereby better ensuring its stability and legitimacy.

Politically, Washington mediated a series of conflicts and crises, both domestic and foreign. On the diplomatic front, Washington's administration managed threats from the British, French and Spanish, successfully kept the United States out of European wars, and restored and improved Anglo-American trade with the Jay Treaty of 1794. In that year, he also confronted a domestic challenge by skillfully subduing the revolt against a federal excise tax on whiskey by Pennsylvania farmers. Balancing deference to the popular will and governmental authority, Washington first sent in commissioners to negotiate with the rebels. By the time he ordered 13,000 militia men into action, the Whiskey Rebellion was all but over, and no violence was necessary. Washington showed similar diplomacy in straddling the growing rift within his administration between supporters of Hamilton and a faction, led by James MADISON and Thomas JEFFERSON, over Hamilton's policies and the United States' stance on the FRENCH REVOLUTION. As the first party system, comprising Federalists and Republicans, coalesced, Washington identified with the Federalists. But he retained his distaste for partisan politics, which he believed indicated the demise of civic virtue, and remained a largely neutral arbiter in the political wrangling of the era.

Disillusioned with the bitter party battles that had developed by 1796, Washington chose to retire rather than run for re-election. His farewell address is widely regarded as a distilled expression of republican ideals. He appealed for an allegiance to country above that to party, section or state and urged pursuit of national self-interest and neutrality in matters of foreign policy. When he died on December 13, 1799, he was deeply mourned as the revered, almost worshiped, father of his nation.

BIBLIOGRAPHY. Richard Brookhiser, *Founding Father: Rediscovering George Washington* (Free Press, 1996); Stanley Elkins and Eric McKitrick, *The Age of Federalism: The Early American Republic, 1788–1800* (Oxford University Press, 1993); Joseph Ellis, *Founding Brothers: The Revolutionary Generation* (Vintage Books, 2000); James Thomas Flexner, *Washington: The Indispensable Man* (Little, Brown, 1969); John C. Miller, *The Federalist Era, 1789–1801* (Waveland Press, 1960).

HOLLY A. BERKLEY, PH.D.
HARDIN-SIMMONS UNIVERSITY

welfare

THOUGH *WELFARE* MAY conjure images such as the government-supported aid to the poor, the term has a more pronounced focus in the study of capitalism. Welfare economics is the combination of economic concepts with utilitarian political philosophy to determine which economic policies and institutions are "best" for promoting human happiness.

Classical economists (such as Adam SMITH and Karl MARX) and their predecessors (such as Josiah Child, Richard Cantillon, and the PHYSIOCRATS) openly supported specific economic policies and saw certain social conditions as better or worse than others. Modern economists, however, see economics as a value-free science, like physics.

Physics, for example, tells us how to make atomic bombs, but has nothing to say about whether making bombs is good or bad. Physicists do have opinions about the morality of bomb making, but those opinions reflect their personal moral beliefs rather than their expertise as physicists.

Likewise, economics tells us that quotas on imported goods will protect the jobs of people in industries that face import competition, but at the expense of consumers who pay higher prices for goods produced by the protected industries. Mainstream economics has nothing to say about which is better: to let some workers lose their jobs so that consumers can enjoy lower prices, or to make consumers pay more so that the workers can keep their jobs.

Welfare economics attempts to answer such questions. Relying on the utilitarian view that policies should aim at producing the largest total quantity of happiness in society, welfare economics tries to determine which economic policies produce the largest total of human happiness.

A typical application of welfare economics is to evaluate the distribution of income in society. The economic idea of marginal utility states that people who have many units of X tend to value an extra unit of X less than people who have only a few units of X. For example, a person who has just eaten a full meal will tend to get less satisfaction from eating a piece of bread than would a person who hadn't eaten in two days. Likewise, welfare economics supposes that someone with a large amount of money will get less happiness from each dollar than would someone with only a small amount of money. Transferring the dollar from the rich person to the poor person would, on this view, increase the total amount of happiness in society. On this basis, some— but not all—welfare economists support welfare government programs.

Welfare economists realize that some of their assumptions are difficult to justify. A long and tortuous debate has raged over whether "amounts of happiness" can be measured in the manner required to determine that one policy produces more total happiness than another. Other contentious issues are whether the amount of happiness enjoyed by one person can be meaningfully compared with the amount of happiness enjoyed by another, or whether such measurements and comparisons are even necessary.

However, because of the impact of economic policy in promoting human happiness, welfare economics continues to be an important branch of economics. As welfare economics concepts and techniques are improved, economics may be able to make even greater contributions to human society.

BIBLIOGRAPHY. Paul Samuelson, *Foundations of Economic Analysis* (Harvard University Press, 1983) Jeremy Bentham, *The Principles of Morals and Legislation* (Prometheus Books, 1988). John Stuart Mill, *On Liberty and Utilitarianism* (Bantam Classics, 1993); A.C. Pigou, "Some Aspects of Welfare Economics," *American Economic Review* (June, 1951); Murray N. Rothbard, "Toward a Reconstruction of Utility and Welfare Economics," *On Freedom and Free Enterprise: The Economics of Free Enterprise* (Van Nostrand, 1956).

SCOTT PALMER, PH.D.
RGMS ECONOMICS

Wells Fargo

AN EXPRESS, POSTAL, and banking service, Wells Fargo was formed in 1852 to profit from the California Gold Rush. Wells Fargo played a major role in the development of the American west by serving as the chief communications conduit between the eastern and western UNITED STATES. Eventually pushed out of the postal and express services by the government, Wells Fargo shifted its business plan to focus solely on banking in 1918. It operated quietly for decades before becoming one of the nation's largest banks through a series of mergers.

Wells Fargo began when two men spotted an opportunity. In 1852, while California boomed in a gold-seeking frenzy, the directors of American Express debated whether to extend their mail and package service to the west. The company had grown by providing fast and reliable delivery that the U.S. government did not offer, and two American Express directors, Henry Wells (1805–78) and William Fargo, (1818–81) saw similar business opportunities in this rapidly developing region. When American Express refused to expand, Wells and Fargo formed a joint stock association in New York on March 18, 1852, and modeled the company after American Express. The new company specialized in shipping gold dust, bullion, specie, letters, packages, parcels, and freight of all kinds from New York to San Francisco. It gradually expanded to service most of the west.

Wells Fargo became so popular because the delivery service provided by the U.S. POSTAL SERVICE was so poor.

Wells Fargo had a broader reach and provided greater efficiency, a fact that the United States recognized by not challenging the company's interference with the government MONOPOLY on mail service. With more green Wells Fargo mailboxes on western streets than red government ones, the company delivered the bulk of the mail west of Salt Lake City and Albuquerque.

The company cultivated its reputation for speedy service. Many letters were carried by Pony Express, a business that Wells Fargo bought in 1861 and operated for only a short time before the advent of the transcontinental railroad. Pony Express riders dodged Native Americans and robbers while racing to the next station to switch ponies or rest. The work of the riders was dangerous, but glamorous, and publicity given to the riders added to the prestige of Wells Fargo. Stagecoaches operated by the company faced the same hazards as the riders. The stagecoaches numbered 2,500 in 1866 and traveled the 1,913-mile journey from Kansas to California. Most of the coaches had been acquired through mergers. They carried passengers as well as the famed green ironbound boxes, which were guarded by armed company messengers, and were much sought-after by robbers. By 1895, the Post Office had become a strong competitor and Wells Fargo ended its letter service but continued its express service.

Wells Fargo's use of express refrigerator railroad cars in 1897 brought fresh vegetables and fruits to the northeast. Besides helping to improve the health of Americans, the company stabilized the citrus fruit industry enabling it to develop into one of the most important perishable crop concerns in the country. In 1918, the government consolidated 10,000 Wells Fargo express offices as a wartime measure, forcing the company to develop its commercial banking side.

Wells Fargo Bank joined Union Trust, grew slowly until merging with American Trust Company in 1960 to become the nation's 11th largest bank. The firm helped introduce MasterCard in 1967, offered online banking in 1989, but achieved most of its growth through mergers. It joined Crocker National Bank in 1986, and merged with midwest banking giant Norwest in 1998 to create a $186 billion diversified financial services company.

Wells Fargo became a success through excellent service and shrewd marketing. More of a consolidator than an innovator, Wells Fargo achieved dominance largely by adding value to other businesses.

BIBLIOGRAPHY. Philip L. Fradkin, *Stagecoach: Wells Fargo and the American West* (Simon & Schuster, 2002); Wells Fargo Historical Services, *Wells Fargo: Since 1852* (2000).

CARYN E. NEUMANN, PH.D.
OHIO STATE UNIVERSITY

Westinghouse, George (1846–1914)

BORN NEAR SCHENECTADY, New York, George Westinghouse, Jr. became one of the United States' preeminent inventors during the Age of Invention of the late-19th century. His father was a skilled mechanic with numerous patents of his own; the young Westinghouse followed in his footsteps early on, preferring to tinker with machines than attend to his scholastic duties. He dropped out of school at 14, served in the navy during the AMERICAN CIVIL WAR, and briefly attended college after its conclusion. He patented his first invention, a rotary steam engine, in 1865.

In 1869, Westinghouse witnessed a collision between two trains unable to stop quickly, and the idea for his most famous invention was born. Later that year, he took out the first patent on a air-brake system for trains that allowed a single train engineer to apply the brakes on all the train's cars simultaneously. The system worked by transporting compressed air from a steam-powered pump to a network of pipes leading to the brake shoes of each car. At first he had trouble selling his idea to skeptical railroad companies; he had to fund his system's first demonstration and insure the trains involved in the case of damage. But by the mid-1890s his brake system had been installed on over 400,000 cars and 27,000 engines, making Westinghouse extraordinarily wealthy and greatly facilitating safe train travel.

He next immersed himself in electrical invention. Westinghouse had been in the audience of inventors when Thomas EDISON debuted his incandescent electrical lamp in 1878. But his electrical system employed direct current, which limited the distance electricity could be transmitted from a central power source. Westinghouse thought he could do better, and in 1886 he devised an alternating current that transmitted electricity over a long distance. He and Edison became fierce competitors over whose system would electrify the United States. Westinghouse established the Westinghouse Electric Company and hired other inventors to assist him in perfecting his alternating current. Among them was Nikola Tesla, a Hungarian immigrant who invented an electrical motor that used alternating electricity to power mechanical devices. By the 1890s Westinghouse's firm had proven that the benefits of alternating current outweighed those of Edison's direct current. In 1893, a hydroelectric plant that employed Westinghouse and Tesla's inventions was constructed at Niagara Falls and transmitted electricity over a 22-mile distance. By the turn of the century, power plants across the country running on alternating currents could send 30,000 volts of electricity up to 75 miles away.

By the time of his death in 1914, Westinghouse had patented more than 400 inventions. Westinghouse's inventions helped fuel the larger process of industrial growth and economic development in the Gilded Age. His air brakes facilitated the era's transportation boom, which linked markets and aided the flow of goods and people across the country. His electrical innovations made cheap electricity widely available and applicable as a source of power, revolutionizing leisure, work and production.

BIBLIOGRAPHY. Sean Dennis Cashman, *America in the Gilded Age* (New York University Press, 1984); C.J. Hylander, *American Inventors* (1934); Mark Wahlgren Summers, *The Gilded Age, or, The Hazard of New Functions* (Prentice Hall, 1997).

HOLLY A. BERKLEY, PH.D.
HARDIN-SIMMONS UNIVERSITY

Whitney, Eli (1765–1825)

ELI WHITNEY'S NAME became synonymous with American ingenuity after his invention of the cotton gin, a device that separated cotton seeds from fiber. His invention made cotton "king" in the South: production of the short-staple cotton (a variety which grew well in North America but was difficult to clean) rose exponentially because of his innovation.

Born in Massachusetts, Whitney studied at Yale University and worked as a schoolteacher to support himself. He headed south in 1793, and while a guest at a Georgia plantation learned of the challenges posed by cotton production. He devised a model for a machine that used a roller with wire teeth and a slotted sieve to tear the cotton fibers away from the seeds. A revolving brush caught the cleaned cotton, and the seeds dropped into a separate compartment. The contraption allowed one person to separate more cotton in a single day than a hundred workers doing it by hand. In 1794, Whitney applied for a patent on his invention.

Whitney's mechanical ingenuity did not, however, ensure his business success. Many planters were excited by the potential of the gin and quickly pirated his invention. Whitney and his partner, plantation manager Phineas Miller, tried in vain to recoup their losses in court. Yet, even if the cotton gin did not make Whitney's personal fortune, it transformed the nation's economy. By the 1850s, three-quarters of the world's supply of cotton came from the American South.

Whitney's invention also affected the entrenchment of SLAVERY. Cotton production was well suited to the Southern plantation system. Slavery had been in decline by 1790, but the cotton boom prompted planters to import more slaves into the Southern states before the legal closure of the slave trade in 1808. The cotton gin further encouraged farmers to focus on a single cash crop and work the land until it was exhausted, then move to new land, a devastating agricultural practice.

After the cotton gin debacle, Whitney turned to the manufacture of firearms. He was awarded a federal contract for 10,000 muskets in 1798, largely because he proposed a more standardized practice of manufacturing that would cut down on the hand-finishing typically required of guns. Whitney is sometimes credited with developing the idea of interchangeable parts for manufactured goods. This is not quite correct: although Whitney staged an 1801 demonstration for government officials, including John ADAMS and Thomas JEFFERSON, suggesting his musket was made up of standardized parts, his own arms factory was never able to put this principle fully into practice. He is better recognized as an early publicist of mechanization and interchangeability, ideas that in turn influenced others, including Samuel Colt and Henry FORD.

BIBLIOGRAPHY. David A. Hounshell, *From the American System to Mass Production, 1800–1932: The Development of Manufacturing Technology in the United States* (Johns Hopkins University Press, 1984); Constance Green, *Eli Whitney and the Birth of American Technology* (Little, Brown, 1956); Jeannette Mirsky and Allan Nevins, *The World of Eli Whitney* (Macmillan, 1952).

SARAH ELVINS
UNIVERSITY OF NOTRE DAME

Wilson, Woodrow (1856–1924)

THE FIRST DEMOCRATIC president of the 20th century and the only true academic elected to the office, Woodrow Wilson has a complicated historical legacy. Although he was admired for his moral piety, his critics found fault with his elitism. Both his strengths and weaknesses would reveal themselves during his difficult terms in office, years characterized by his progressive economic agenda, American excursions in Latin America, WORLD WAR I and its aftermath, and ultimately his own poor health.

(Thomas) Woodrow Wilson was born in Staunton, Virginia to Presbyterian Minister Joseph Ruggles Wilson and Janet (Jessie) Woodrow. At a young age, Wilson determined that he wanted to enter politics. He attended the College of New Jersey, now Princeton University, and enjoyed a successful academic career through his graduation in 1879. Wilson went on to the University of

Virginia Law School and practiced law briefly before enrolling in post-graduate studies at Johns Hopkins University in Baltimore. Wilson earned his Ph.D. in history in 1886.

In 1890, after holding professorial positions at other eastern universities, Wilson was appointed professor of jurisprudence and political economy at Princeton University. He published a series of books and developed a unique set of political values. Consistent with the moral imperatives of the progressive era, Wilson was concerned with reforming the abuses of industrial capitalism. To this end, he advocated the pursuit of "social order" through "representative government." Neither a liberal nor a conservative, Wilson was entirely committed to the preservation of a just society; however, his conception of social justice stopped at the color line: a white Southerner of the late 19th century, Wilson was a white supremacist who sanctioned racial segregation.

In 1902, Wilson was elected president of Princeton University, a position that propelled him into the national spotlight. By 1910 he resigned at the urging of New Jersey political operatives who helped him win the governorship. By 1911, the Democratic Party had nominated him for president. In part due to the split in the Republican Party between candidates President William Howard TAFT and former President Teddy ROOSEVELT, Wilson was elected to office on his platform of progressive-era policies and his own brand of liberal democracy, which he labeled "The New Freedom."

The New Freedom has been described by historians as a middle-class imperative, complemented by rural and labor support, to preserve and strengthen the democratic, capitalist society by progressive initiatives that included lower tariffs, an improved banking system, stronger business regulation and protection for unions and workers. To this end, during his first term in office, Wilson oversaw the creation of the various economic reforms, including the Underwood Tariff Act that reduced tariff rates and instituted an income tax; the Federal Reserve Act that established a central bank to monitor the nation's finances; the Clayton Anti-Trust Act that strengthened antitrust regulations; and the creation of the Federal Trade Commission that shored up government regulation of business.

When shaky governments in Latin America and the Caribbean hampered their ability to repay debts owed to American investors, Wilson sought to enforce effective financial supervision over various countries through military intervention. Though his forays into Haiti, the Dominican Republic and Nicaragua had merits, American intervention in Mexico was unsuccessful and eventually resulted in a Mexican-American skirmish incited by rebel General Pancho Villa.

The year 1914 was eventful for Wilson both personally and professionally. In August of that year, his wife, Alice, passed away. Though devastated by her death, Wilson rebounded seven months later when he met Edith Bolling Galt, a widow from Washington, D.C. After only two months of courtship, Wilson announced their engagement.

Also in 1914, Western Europe became embroiled in the military conflict that would become World War I. Although Wilson maintained American neutrality in an attempt to preserve his role as a world mediator, the United States increasingly offered economic assistance to the Allied forces. Growing hostility between the United States and Germany was intensified in the spring of 1915 when a German submarine sank the *Lusitania*, a British passenger liner. Amid the ongoing struggle, Wilson was renominated for president in 1916. Bolstered by the slogan, "He kept us out of the war," Wilson defeated Republican Charles Evans Hughes by a narrow margin.

However, German aggression persisted and in April 1917, Wilson signed the declaration of war. In January of the following year, Wilson proposed his "Fourteen Points" for a postwar settlement. This doctrine for peace included open diplomacy, self-determination for nation-states, and the creation of an international League of Nations. An instrumental player in drafting the Treaty of Versailles in Europe, which officially ended the war in 1919, Wilson pushed his peacetime agenda.

Upon returning to the United States following the negotiations, Wilson tried to arouse national support for the treaty and especially the League of Nations; however, he met great opposition in Congress, particularly from Senator Henry Cabot Lodge. Wilson's exhaustive efforts to ignite public opinion ultimately took their toll on his health. On September 26, 1919, he suffered a paralytic stroke. As he recovered, Wilson's wife Edith directed many of his political affairs leading many to speculate about the extent of her influence.

Although Wilson remained in office until 1921, the stroke had left him virtually unable to govern and the duration of his administration was plagued by postwar inflation and labor strikes. However, his progressive tenure did see the passage of both the 18th Amendment, Prohibition, and the 19th Amendment, which secured women's suffrage.

BIBLIOGRAPHY. Richard Hofstader, *The American Political Tradition and the Men Who Made It* (Vintage, 1989); Silas Bent McKinley, *Woodrow Wilson: A Biography* (Praeger, 1957); James M. McPherson, ed., "To the Best of My Ability," *The American Presidents* (Dorling Kindersley, 2000).

LINDSAY SILVER
BRANDEIS UNIVERSITY

worker

BEFORE THE INDUSTRIAL REVOLUTION, most people worked in agriculture. In this context, the term "worker," as it is understood today, had little meaning. It was only as people left the land and moved to cities to work in factories for long hours in repetitive jobs for little pay that the term "worker" signified a distinction between the "servants of industry" and the profit-making capitalists. Economists, philosophers, and writers have attempted in a variety of ways to explain the role of the worker in the capitalistic society.

Classical economics. Classical LIBERALISM or classical economics became the predominant school of thought during the last quarter of the 18th century. John LOCKE (1632–1704), the founder of classical liberalism, argued that each individual has a property in his or her own person. Therefore, the worker owns the results of LABOR produced through effort. Locke believed that God commanded individuals to labor; and since no one could labor hard enough to gain ownership of all land, each should be satisfied with a moderate portion.

Adam SMITH (1723–90) and David RICARDO (1772–1823), the founders of classical economics, were concerned with understanding how the capitalist economic system worked and how it affected the wealth of a nation as a whole. Smith believed that all the different elements of the economic system were connected. The capitalist paid WAGES to the worker, who in turn paid rent to the landlord. The circle was completed when both the worker and the landlord purchased various GOODS from the capitalist. The worker naturally wanted to make the highest wage possible but was prevented from doing so by both the capitalist and the landlord who were after the highest profits possible. Unlike Locke, Smith argued that the worker did not own all that he or she produced because the capitalist who owned the place of production, the machinery, and raw materials with which goods were produced also owned a share in the finished product. Smith recognized that the lives of workers were not always happy. He wrote of the "stultifying effect of mass production" and believed that doing the same task over and over made workers both stupid and ignorant. Smith accepted the responsibility of government to issue regulations for worker protection. He was concerned that young boys were put to work in factories without receiving an education and feared that they would grow up with no moral restraints. He saw education as a way to improve the lives of workers to keep them from being viewed as extensions of the machinery they operated.

Ricardo maintained that the goal of the worker was simply to have enough money to take care of his dependents at the standard of living to which they were accustomed. On the whole, Ricardo saw the worker as cog in the machinery of industrialization. He argued that increased wages always resulted in increased population, with its subsequent drain on limited resources. Ricardo opposed government regulations that helped the poor survive and was against trade UNIONS because he believed that workers often lost jobs when unions negotiated for higher wages. Even though Ricardo could see the effect of capitalism on workers, he believed that workers contributed to their own demeaning lives through inherent weakness.

Between 1750–1850, land that had been in common use was enclosed to allow more progressive methods of farming. While the results were beneficial to landowners, they were often disastrous to agricultural families. Losing their livelihood forced people into the cities in hopes of high wages and a larger share of available resources. As the 19th century began, Great Britain was the center of manufacturing. In London, the population more than quadrupled from 1800–80. When workers were left with no means of support, the government used Poor Laws or public workhouses as a way to deal with the poor and unemployed.

The results were often degrading and inhumane for the workers and their families. Writer Charles Dickens described his experience as a young boy in a workhouse in his novel *Oliver Twist*. Essayist and historian Thomas Carlyle estimated that, at one point, over 2 million of England's 15 million workers were housed in workhouses and poorhouse prisons. Generally, the poor were willing to do almost anything to stay out of workhouses. Some of the poor already had jobs, but the pay was insufficient to support the workers and their families. A number of reformers, such as Robert Owen (1771–1858) argued that higher wages would not only break the cycle of poverty but it would also help the economy as well because workers would buy more goods, which would then help the British economy.

Thomas Robert MALTHUS (1776–1834) who strongly endorsed the classical liberal belief in scarce resources contended that capitalists were always likely to possess the lion's share of those resources, so what was left for poor workers would never be enough to lift them out of their miserable state. John Stuart MILL (1806–1873), on the other hand, believed that if workers were educated so that they developed a sense of social class and understood the value of freedom of association, they would reject the capitalist system and establish their own cooperatives, allowing the workers to share the profits rather than making capitalists richer.

Socialism. Like Locke, Karl MARX (1818–83) believed that each worker owned the fruits of his or her labor. Not having control of one's own labor, Marx thought, resulted in exploited workers who became more wretched as the number of goods produced increased.

However, increased production made workers poorer and did not improve their lives. According to Marx, the worst kind of labor was that which the worker performed over and over. He believed that such actions robbed the worker of a sense of pride in the work performed. Marx wrote in the *Communist Manifest* that after a time the worker simply became an appendage of the machine, enslaved by the capitalist and by the means of production. The wheels of capitalism, Marx argued, were greased by greed and self-interest, with workers treated as commodities. This inhuman treatment resulted in a feeling of estrangement and ALIENATION. This alienation extended not only to the objects produced but also to the individual's role in society and government. However, the worker continued to be bound to the work as a means of survival.

Marx opens the *Communist Manifesto,* which he co-wrote with Friedrich ENGELS, with the warning that the specter of communism is haunting Europe. In this work, Marx describes all history as the history of class struggle: the battle between the bourgeoisie (capitalists) and the proletariat (workers). Because of the greed of the capitalists, the worker is always exploited and victimized. The goal of socialism, Marx insisted, was not to abolish private property but to abolish the mistreatment of workers that resulted from unchecked capitalism. He argued that at least nine-tenths of the population owned no property. Marx's labor theory of value states that the value of a product is derived from the labor involved in producing it. He maintained that the worker earns the subsistence wage in the first six hours of the working day. The rest of the workday was spent in SURPLUS value, which provided excess profit for the capitalist rather than higher wages for the worker.

The *Communist Manifesto* called for "working men of all countries to unite."

This unity would occur, according to Marx, through the stages in the war between the proletariat (workers) and the bourgeoisie (capitalists). In the beginning, individual workers began to be dissatisfied, possibly directing anger toward the factory owner rather than toward the capitalist system. As soon as economic crisis occurred—perhaps through reduced wages and personal deprivations—riots might occur, drawing a group of workers together. As the situation worsened, workers would band together and form a political party to influence legislation aimed at helping workers. When the changes were not drastic enough to suit the workers, a revolutionary class developed, and the goal of this class was to overthrow the existing system.

Marxist theories led to the introduction of communism in the SOVIET UNION, CHINA, CUBA, and much of Eastern Europe. Most Western countries contain elements of socialist thought, and socialist parties continue to thrive. In the UNITED STATES, however, socialist thought never gained prominence. While socialists were active in the 1920s and the Communist Party of the USA was a definite presence in the United States during the 1930s, SOCIALISM was virtually nonexistent after August 1939, when the Soviet Union signed a non-aggression pact with GERMANY as WORLD WAR II began, leaving American socialists stunned and disillusioned. Many reasons have been given for the absence of socialism in the United States. In the early days of the INDUSTRIAL REVOLUTION, land was still plentiful, so people could always go west instead of working for subsistence wages in a factory. The United States also has a relatively open class system and universal suffrage, and Democrats and Republicans have a tendency to incorporate third-party platforms, so American workers have never felt alienated from the political and economic systems in the way that Marx predicted.

BIBLIOGRAPHY. Bernard Caravan, *Economics for Beginners* (Pantheon, 1983); Gregory Claeys, *Machinery, Money and the Millennium: From Moral Economy to Socialism, 1850–1860* (Polity Press, 1987); "Charles Dickens' London," www.fidnet.com; John Kenneth Galbraith, *Economics in Perspective* (Houghton-Mifflin, 1997); Robert L. Heilbroner, *The Worldly Philosophers: The Lives, Times, and Ideas of The Great Economic Thinkers* (Simon and Schuster, 1972); John Locke, *The Second Treatise of Government* (Bobbs-Merrill, 1952); Karl Marx and Friedrich Engels, *The Communist Manifesto* (Washington Square Press, 1965); Karl Marx, "Selection from Economic and Philosophic Manuscripts of 1844," *Classical Political Theories from Plato to Marx* (Macmillan, 1990); Louis Putterman, *Dollars and Change: Economics in Context* (Yale University Press, 2001); Eric B. Ross, *The Malthus Factor: Population, Poverty, and Politics in Capitalist Development* (Zed Books, 1998); D.D. Raphael, "Smith," Robert Skidelsky, "Keynes," and Donald Winch, "Malthus," in *Three Great Economists* (Oxford University Press, 1997); "The Workhouse," www.workhouses.org.uk.

ELIZABETH PURDY, PH.D.
INDEPENDENT SCHOLAR

World Bank

THE WORLD BANK was founded in 1944 during the United Nations Monetary and Financial Conference (or BRETTON WOODS conference). According to the articles of agreement its chief goals were "to assist in the reconstruction and development of territories of members by facilitating the investment of capital for productive purposes [and] to promote private foreign investment by means of guarantees or participation in loans [and] to supplement private investment by providing, on suitable conditions, finance for productive purposes out of its own capital."

As such, it is one of the world's largest sources of economic assistance to developing countries, while also providing technical assistance, policy advice, and supervision for the implementation of free-market reforms. In conjunction with the INTERNATIONAL MONETARY FUND (IMF) and the WORLD TRADE ORGANIZATION (WTO), the bank plays a major role in overseeing economic policy, the reformation of public institutions within developing nations, and in shaping global macroeconomic agendas.

Though related to the United Nations, the bank functions independently of the General Assembly and Security Council. The bank is owned by 184 member nations, who are represented by a board of governors and a Washington, D.C.-based board of directors. The governors are usually their countries' foreign ministers or central bank governors. The power to make actual decisions rests mainly with the 24-member board of directors. The UNITED STATES, FRANCE, the UNITED KINGDOM, GERMANY, and JAPAN appoint their own executive directors. The remaining countries are divided into regions, each of which elects an executive director. Throughout its history, the president of the World Bank has been an American.

Five institutions comprise the World Bank Group: the International Bank for Reconstruction and Development (IBRD), the International Development Association (IDA), the International Finance Corporation (IFC), the Multilateral Investment Guarantee Agency (MIGA), and the International Centre for Settlement of Investment Disputes (ICSID). The IBRD provides market rate loans to middle-income developing countries and creditworthy lower-income ones. The IBRD finances most of its funds via global capital markets. The IDA provides interest-free long-term loans, technical assistance, and policy advice to low-income developing countries in the areas of education, rural development, and health. The IDA's loans are financed via contributions from developed countries. The IFC, in conjunction with private investors, provides loans, loan guarantees, and equity financing to businesses in developing countries. The MIGA provides loan guarantees and insurance to foreign investors against loss caused by non-commercial risk in developing countries. The ICSID oversees settlements of investment disputes between foreign investors and the host developing countries. These settlements are achieved through conciliation or arbitration.

World Bank decisions. In the decision-making process of the bank, member countries act as shareholders. However, each country does not have an equal share. Rather, a country's capital subscription determines their voting power. And since a country's capital subscription is determined by its economic resources, the wealthier the country the greater the voting power, which in turn leads to developing countries holding only a small per-centage of voting power. Thus, the countries most in need of the bank's financial support and advice may not have the necessary voting voice to receive such.

The bank's funds come from member nations' capital subscriptions, bond flotations on global capital markets, and net earnings accrued from interest payments on IBRD and IFC loans. Approximately 10 percent of capital subscriptions are paid directly to the bank. The rest is subject to call if needed to meet obligations.

The bank has offices in more than 70 countries and approximately 25 percent of its staff resides in developing countries. In many of these countries, the staff function as policy advisors to various ministries, including the ministry of finance. The bank maintains consultative and informal ties to the world's financial markets and institutions, as well as to nongovernmental organizations in both developing and developed nations.

Loans are granted only to member nations and only for the financing of specific projects. Prior to issuing a loan, bank advisors and experts determine if the country can meet the bank's conditions, most of which are designed to ensure the loan's productive use and repayment. The borrower must be unable to secure a loan from any other source and the borrower must show that the project is technically feasible and economically sound. Repayment is ensured, via member countries guaranteeing loans made to private concerns within their territories. Subsequent to the loan being granted, periodic reports regarding the loan's use and the project's progress are required from both the borrower and the bank's own observers.

History. The bank did not begin operations until 1946, at which time its initial efforts were geared toward reconstruction of postwar Europe. In the mid-1950s, the bank began financing investments in infrastructural projects in developing nations, including roads, water facilities, and ports. Since the late 1960s, the majority of loans have been granted to developing nations in Latin America, Africa, and Asia. Starting in the 1980s, the bank began focusing on projects that would directly benefit a developing nation's poorest people. The bank attempted to accomplish this by providing loans for urban development, rural and agricultural development, and small-scale enterprises. During this time, the bank also expanded its support of projects geared toward ecological concerns and energy development.

The 1980s debt crisis played an integral role in the evolution of the bank's operations. By the early 1980s, the bank was increasingly involved in shaping economic and social policies of indebted developing countries. As a loan condition, these countries had to institute severe "structural adjustment programs," which usually required major cuts in health and education spending, liberalization of trade, deregulation of financial sectors, privatization of enterprises, and elimination of price controls. Rather than restoring economic stability, these programs often exacerbated the conditions. Learning from the debt crisis, the bank now provides financial assistance via balance-of-payment support and loans.

After the fall of communism in the late 1980s and early 1990s, the bank was a central figure in the free-market reforms of Eastern and Central Europe. The bank also provided reconstruction loans to countries suffering internal conflicts or crisis. Unfortunately, this support did not lead to the reformation of positive infrastructures, and in several instances resulted in a drastic reduction in the standard of living.

The bank is the largest multilateral creditor in the world. The result is that for many of the most indebted poor countries, the largest part of their external debt (sometimes more than 50 percent) is owed to the World Bank and its associated multilateral regional development banks. Many feel that this debt, which as per the bank's statutes cannot be canceled or rescheduled, is a major factor in the continuing economic stagnation of developing nations.

BIBLIOGRAPHY. Armand van Dormael, *Bretton Woods: Birth of a Monetary System* (Macmillan, 1978); Kevin Danaher (editor), *Fifty Years is Enough: The Case Against the World Bank and the International Monetary Fund* (South End Press, 1994); Devesh Kapur, John P. Lewis, and Richard Webb (editors), *The World Bank: Its First Half Century* (Brookings Institute, 1997); Catherine Caufield, *Masters of Illusion: The World Bank and the Poverty of Nations* (Henry Holt & Company, 1997).

S.J. RUBEL, J.D.
INDEPENDENT SCHOLAR

World Economic Forum

AN INTERNATIONAL, NON-PROFIT, and non-partisan organization, the World Economic Forum (WEF) was originally formed in January 1971, in Davos, Switzerland, as the European Management Forum (EMF). It was founded by Klaus Schwab, then professor of general management at the International Management Institute in Geneva and, since 1972, professor of business policy at the University of Geneva.

Initially, the forum brought together the executives of leading European companies to discuss the problems and the promises of the internationalization of economic activity. In 1987, the name of the EMF was changed to the World Economic Forum to reflect its focus on worldwide issues, and specifically on improving the state of the world by providing an opportunity to its members to discuss important social, economic, and political issues and problems facing the industrial and the developing world alike.

Its membership consists of approximately 1,000 large corporations that have a global focus, in countries ranging from the UNITED STATES and EUROPEAN UNION member countries, to developing countries such as Syria and Kenya. In 2003, 43 percent of the corporate members were from Europe; 26 percent from North America; 13 percent from Asia, 7 percent from Central and South America; 4.5 percent from the Middle East; 4.3 percent from Africa; and 2.2 percent from AUSTRALIA and NEW ZEALAND. Annual meetings of the WEF are traditionally held in Davos. In 2002, however, it was held in New York City to express solidarity with that city in the aftermath of the September 11, 2001, terrorist attack on the World Trade Center.

In the early 1980s, the WEF invited heads of states, cabinet ministers with high portfolios, and the directors of key international organizations such as the WORLD BANK, the INTERNATIONAL MONETARY FUND (IMF), and the WORLD TRADE ORGANIZATION (WTO) to participate in its deliberations. The WEF has been successful in initiating dialogs between ISRAEL and the Palestinian Authority, and between GREECE and TURKEY, to name a few. It has been instrumental in facilitating the transition of emerging market economies in Eastern Europe into the global economy by supporting the implementation of free-market-oriented economic, social, and political reforms.

Outreach programs of the WEF have taken various forms. For example, Global Leaders for Tomorrow aims to reach the young leaders, in politics, academia, and business. The World Arts Forum tries to foster cross-cultural appreciation and understanding.

BIBLIOGRAPHY. www.weforum.org; Klaus Schwab, Michael E. Porter, and Jeffrey D. Sachs, *The Global Competitiveness Report 2001–01: World Economic Forum* (Cambridge University Press, 2002).

M. ODEKON
SKIDMORE COLLEGE

World Trade Organization

THE WORLD TRADE Organization (WTO) is a multinational organization that defines rules for international trade, adjudicates disputes, and punishes countries that violate the rules of trade.

Established in 1995, the World Trade Organization was founded in 1995 at meetings held under the GENERAL AGREEMENT ON TARIFFS AND TRADE (GATT), an international treaty that governed trade between its signatory nations from 1948 until the WTO took over the functions of GATT.

By the 1940s, trade barriers and tariffs had become a significant block to world economic progress. GATT, based on the principle of open, non-discriminatory trade, attempted to reduce the blockage. GATT tried to discourage trade barriers, such as tariffs and import quotas, and provided a forum for resolving disputes between participating countries.

Under GATT, nations participated in regular rounds of negotiation to remedy gaps in the international trading system and attempted to reduce or eliminate trade barriers. Nations initially conducted bilateral negotiations with their main trading partners, reducing their own tariffs and trade barriers in exchange for similar reductions by their trading partners. They then offered the same terms of trade to all GATT signatories as part of GATT's encouragement of non-discriminatory trade.

By the 1970s, GATT negotiations had significantly reduced tariffs, and the only remaining barriers to trade were non-tariff barriers such as import quotas, licensing requirements, and similar measures. However, non-tariff barriers were still a major impediment to trade, and thorny disputes remained over issues such as agricultural subsidies, industrial policy, and intellectual property. These are some of the issues with which the WTO wrestles at the start of the 21st century.

The WTO incorporated all of GATT's principles. Established by the Uruguay Round (1986–94) of GATT negotiations, the WTO placed its headquarters in Geneva, SWITZERLAND and was officially launched on January 1, 1995.

GATT was focused mainly on the elimination of tariffs and traditional non-tariff barriers. The WTO extended GATT in three ways. First, as a well-defined organization rather than merely a coalition of signatories to a treaty, it was better positioned to administer the global-trading system. Second, the WTO's mission went beyond GATT: the WTO monitors national trade policies, provides technical and other assistance to developing countries, and coordinates its efforts with other international organizations such as the WORLD BANK and the INTERNATIONAL MONETARY FUND (IMF). Third, the WTO is working systematically to define global rules for international trade—not only with respect to tariffs and trade barriers, but also for intellectual property, industrial policy, environmental policy, and for specific industries.

To achieve those goals, the WTO imposes legal obligations on its members. Each member is required to submit schedules for improving the openness of its markets for international trade and must abide by WTO rules governing issues such as goods, services, industrial policy, and intellectual property. Though these moves benefit the international trading system, they are not without drawbacks to WTO member nations. In the UNITED STATES, for example, the WTO has been criticized for ruling that U.S. anti-pollution laws violate international trade rules because some foreign gasoline products fail to meet U.S. environmental standards.

Similar concerns have been raised in countries where taxes are lower and regulations less onerous than in other WTO member countries. Will countries be left free to decide on tax and regulatory policy, or will officials of the WTO usurp those decisions? It is not surprising that anti-globalizations forces target the WTO specifically as a world-corporate-government liaison and entity that threatens national and individual freedom.

The top policy-making body of the WTO is the Ministerial Conference, which consists of representatives from member countries and meets at least once every two years. Between meetings of the Ministerial Conference, the WTO General Council carries out the organization's mission. The General Council also convenes under two other names to handle specific problems:

1. The Dispute Settlement Body, which handles trade disputes between member nations. Initial rulings are made by a panel, and appeals can be made based either on facts or on points of law.

2. The Trade Policy Review Body, which reviews and assesses member nations' trade-related policies and practices.

The General Council also oversees three lower-level councils: the Council for Trade in Goods, the Council for Trade-Related Aspects of Intellectual Property Rights (TRIPS), and the Council for Trade in Services. The Trade Negotiations Committee, which is on the same level as the General Council, oversees trade negotiations and the work of specific-purpose groups such as the Committee on Agriculture.

In spite of its importance, the WTO is quite small compared to other international organizations, with its budget a fraction of those enjoyed by the World Bank, the Organization for Economic Cooperation and Development, and the International Monetary Fund. Moreover, troubling questions remain about the relation between the WTO's authority to rule on trade issues and the right of member countries to make their own decisions on domestic issues such as labor standards, anti-pollution laws, and product safety laws.

Nonetheless, the WTO's work continues to open new markets and win gradual acceptance of international trade rules by countries that previously demurred. In the 21st century, the WTO will likely be a key element in a growing and healthy system of global commerce.

BIBLIOGRAPHY. Anne Krueger, ed., *The WTO as an International Organization* (University of Chicago Press, 1998); Bernard and Martin Hoekman, Will, eds., *Developing Countries and the WTO: A Pro-Active Agenda* (Blackwell Publishers, 2001); Danaher, Kevin, ed., *Corporations Are Gonna Get Your Mama* (Common Courage Press, 1996); John Gray, *False Dawn* (The New Press, 1998).

SCOTT PALMER, PH.D.
RGMS ECONOMICS

World War I

THE EVENT THAT LED to World War I, often called The Great War, took place in Europe on June 28, 1914, when a Bosnian radical shot Archduke Franz Ferdinand, the heir to the throne of the Austro-Hungarian Empire, and his wife Duchess Sophie von Chotkova. When the government retaliated with violence, it started a chain of events that brought in other countries because of various treaties. On August 1, 1914, GERMANY declared war on RUSSIA, and other countries soon followed by declaring war on Germany. President Woodrow WILSON (1856–1924) announced that the UNITED STATES would continue its ongoing policy of isolationism. The UNITED KINGDOM became the major player on the Allied side when Germany attacked BELGIUM on August 4. In many ways, World War I illustrated that the world had become a small place interconnected by politics and finance.

Pre-war economics. Even before the United States entered the war, the lives of Americans were directly affected in many ways. On October 22, 1914, Congress passed the Emergency Revenue Act, increasing taxes on liquor and adding an excise tax to items that many Americans considered essential: toilet articles, telegraph and telephone messages, and chewing gum. Additional taxes were placed on stamps, bankers, and brokers; however, the government raised only $52 million from the new taxes rather than the $100 million that had been predicted.

Initially, the United States experienced a short decline in the output of goods; but as the war continued in Europe, American business boomed. The country produced guns, ammunition, food, and clothing for the Allies, exporting goods to the warring nations and receiving investment capital from foreign investors. England, FRANCE, and Russia often wrote off outstanding American debts in payment for goods being shipped to help them fight the war. Other means of payment included gold and gilt-edged certificates. The result of the increased export trade was prosperity and high employment for America.

Wilson had only been in office for seven months when the war began. Wilson was a scholar, and as such tended to approach politics and economics on an intellectual level. War, however, called for action. Congress had created the FEDERAL RESERVE, the country's central bank in 1913, and Wilson was almost immediately faced with the task of overseeing its implementation. Earlier in July 1914, European banks shut down, and trading increased in the United States as foreign investors hurried to liquidate. New York banks ended up with a deficit of $17 million. On July 31, the NEW YORK STOCK EXCHANGE shut down for the first time since 1873. On August 3, the secretary of the treasury announced that the government would issue $100 million in emergency funds to the New York banks and to other banks as needed. On August 4, Congress removed the limits on the amount of emergency funds that could be issued. By month's end, around $208,810,790 in new money had been circulated. The number grew to $381,530,000 by the end of November. For the first time, the Federal Reserve began to actively influence the amount of available MONEY and CREDIT, and this role would continue after the war ended.

The United States enters the war. On April 6, 1917, the United States entered the war by declaring war on Germany and followed this with a declaration of war on Austria-Hungary on December 7. As American troops were mobilized, the country needed to equip the military, and an appropriations bill was passed on June 15 to provide essentials for soldiers, such as clothing and bedding. Factories were quickly built to meet the needs of the war, and war products took precedence over other goods. Congress rarely acts quickly because of competing party and regional interests, so the lack of appropriation of funds for supplies sometimes resulted in discomfort for the military. The few individuals who tried to take advantage of the increased need for goods by charging exorbitant prices were prevented by government intervention.

The mobilization of 3,000,000 U.S. troops invigorated the war effort and helped to bring Germany to terms. Although the country was only actively involved for 17 months, the American contribution changed the course of history. Within the country, the powers of government changed almost overnight. New government agencies were created to handle different aspects of the war, and each of them had powers over resources that changed the lives of the American people. While most agencies were dismantled after the war, the role of government and the public's perceptions of its role had changed immeasurably.

Financing the war. In the United States, the national debt had remained around the $1 billion mark for the previous 30 years. By 1919, the figure would grow to $25 billion, partially because of the $32,080,266,968 that the United States spent on World War I ($9,455,014,125 of this was advanced to Allied countries). Federal spending grew from 1.5 percent of the GROSS NATIONAL PRODUCT (GNP) in 1916 to 24.2 percent of the GNP by 1918. Because of the war, the nation was close to full employment.

Economists maintain that a government can finance war in four ways: taxing the people, borrowing from the people, drafting soldiers and other resources directly from the people, and creating money that did not exist before the war. The United States government used all four methods to finance World War I. The War Reserve Act of 1917 increased both personal and corporate taxes and levied excise, excess profit, and luxury taxes. War financing consisted of 24.5 percent from taxes, 61.3 percent from funds borrowed from the public and 14.2 percent derived from creating new money. Much of the money borrowed from the public was raised through huge bond rallies, featuring such celebrities as Mary Pickford, Charlie Chaplin, and Douglas Fairbanks. Almost $7 billion of the bond sales were sold to persons with incomes of less than $2,000 a year, and even schoolchildren contributed to the war effort by buying thrift stamps at 25 cents each. The Federal Reserve possessed over $4 billion in government bonds.

Experiencing the war. A major problem for the U.S. government during World War I was to control the supply of food so that the public would be amply cared for while sending food products to American and Allied troops. Exports of agricultural products soared during the war. From December to April 1914, the United States had exported 18 million bushels of wheat. By 1915, wheat exports had risen to 98 million bushels. In August 1917, Congress passed the Lever Food and Fuel Control Act and created both a Food Administrator and a Fuel Administrator. Herbert HOOVER (1929–33) was named as Food Administrator. His task was to walk a line between serving the interests of the public and meeting the needs of the war effort. Hoover responded by inviting the public to prove their patriotism with "Meatless Mondays" and "Wheatless Wednesdays." "Victory Bread," a mix of wheat flower and lower-quality substitutes, appeared on American tables. Harry A. Garfield, the Fuel Administrator, was immediately faced with heating the country through an unusually severe cold winter. The railways, already taxed by the transportation of war-related goods, could not deliver domestic fuel quickly enough. Garfield was forced to shut down factories for a few days and on what was called "Heatless Mondays" to give the railroad time to meet demands. When factories shut down, working people lost wages, and they blamed Garfield for their problems. The lack of fuel also affected ships. During the fuel

shortage, 37 ships loaded with military supplies were stalled in a New York harbor. In addition to the Food and Fuel Agencies, Congress created a War Industries Board, and Wilson appointed Bernard Baruch to head the agency. Baruch aggressively set out to regulate the prices of key industrial products. Other prices were regulated by the Price-Fixing Committee, another wartime creation.

As business boomed in war industries and the demand for labor increased, the labor market tightened. The government had obtained contracts, financing them through both borrowed money and new money. Laborers working under government contract tended to make higher wages and enjoy better working conditions. Wilson averted most strikes by threatening dissatisfied workers with the military draft, but he nationalized the railroads rather than deal with strikes from this essential method of transportation. His move resulted in higher wages and better working conditions for railroad employees also. When the railroads returned to private ownership after the war, a number of people protested. Charged with international transportation of war goods, the shipping industry changed drastically during World War I. For instance, a section of Delaware wasteland was turned into a shipyard with 28 waterways, which often contained ships under simultaneous construction. Since large numbers of horses were shipped to Europe to be used in transporting equipment on the field, farmers switched to tractors for the first time.

Women and African-Americans and the war. Before the beginning of World War I, women demanding the right of suffrage were common on American streets, but the war seemed to make criticizing the government unpatriotic. Carrie Chapman Catt (1859–1947), the leader of the National American Woman Suffrage Association (NAWSA), encouraged the suffragettes to support both the war effort and women's suffrage. NAWSA sponsored a hospital in France, and members began knitting socks, raising and canning food, selling Liberty Bonds, and working for the Red Cross. Their hard work paid off when the 19th Amendment was ratified on August 26, 1920, granting women the right to vote. World War I did not bring larger numbers of women into the work force (around one million), but it did change the kinds of jobs that women were doing. In fact, after the war, daily newspapers published an open letter to women from the government thanking them for working beyond their natural capacities in the war effort. While most women returned to their homes after the war, the general perceptions of women's roles in society had been altered.

African-Americans had also joined the labor force during World War I. Many Southern blacks, glad to leave the discrimination of their homelands, migrated north during this period. Segregation in the American South determined what employment opportunities were open to African-Americans during the World War I boom. Since white males owned most businesses, opportunities for professional and white-collar jobs were limited. Jobs that were available tended to be low paying with few opportunities for advancement. Because of its enormous need for workers, the government offered free transportation to entice African-Americans into northern factories. White workers who resented what they saw as unfair reacted with race riots. The northern migration of African-Americans continued after the war, opening new avenues of economic opportunity.

The end of the war. Following his habit of approaching politics from an intellectual angle, Wilson spoke to Congress in January 1918 and announced his Fourteen Points, which identified the requirements for peace with Germany. Wilson's document called for a peace treaty, freedom of the seas, resumption of open trade, arms reduction, territorial adjustments, respect for national sovereignty, an international peacekeeping body and monetary compensation to the Allies. Germany ultimately agreed, and plans for a peace conference began. The major participants were David Lloyd George (1863–1945) for Great Britain, Georges Clemenceau (1841–1929) for France, Vittorio Orlando (1860–1952) for ITALY, and Wilson for the United States. Since Italy had earlier ties to Germany, the other three basically ran the show.

The Treaty of Versailles, named for the large palace in Paris in which the conference took place, was signed on June 28, 1919. However, the Republican-controlled Senate and Democratic President Wilson could not agree on terms, and the treaty was not ratified in the United States by seven votes. Wilson had been totally committed to the League of Nations established by the treaty and was devastated when it was defeated. He suffered a stroke, which virtually ended his political career, even though he technically completed his term. The League of Nations never became the reality Wilson envisioned. The Treaty of Versailles called for $33 million in Allied claims for reparation. Economist John Maynard KEYNES (1883–1946), a British representative to the conference in Versailles, argued unsuccessfully that it was an impossible requirement and contended that it would be far better to promote German production, rather than forcing Germany into a financial straightjacket (which most historians agree contributed to World War II). Contemporary sources put the total cost of World War I at around $200 billion, with $40 billion in additional property damages, and $65 billion in lost production. The cost in human life was immeasurable. Approximately 117,000 Americans died as a result of World

War I and another 204,000 were injured. At least 15 million people died in a disastrous flu epidemic during the war.

Aftermath of the war. When the Armistice was signed in November 1919, the American economy slowed down and prices soared. Despite this, the United States continued to have war-related expenses. The troops still had to be brought home, and the military had been promised veteran benefits from the government. As part of their payment for services rendered during the war, veterans had been promised postwar payments of $1 a day for domestic service and $1.25 a day for foreign service. Payment was to be made immediately if the total payment were $50 or less, and remaining benefits were to be paid in 1945. By 1932 the Great DEPRESSION was in full swing, and 32,000 businesses failed. Unemployment was near 25 percent. Since veterans and their families were often broke, they demanded payment immediately. The Bonus Army, made up of hungry and dissatisfied veterans, came to Washington, D.C., and established themselves in communities of shacks known as "Hoovervilles." The name was a slur on President Herbert Hoover for what many saw as his indifference to the country's economic crisis.

In addition to military-related expenditures, the United States was faced with dismantling the enormous bureaucracy that had grown up in response to the needs of supporting the Allies and fighting a war. The United States entered the war as a debtor nation but had finished the war as a creditor nation, possessing a good deal of the world's gold, and had become the leading industrial nation of the world.

BIBLIOGRAPHY. "Born Free," *Smithsonian* (February 2003); Elgin Grose Close, *Fifty Years of Managed Money: The Story of the Federal Reserve* (Spartan, 1966); Sara M. Evans, *Born Free: A History of Women in America* (The Free Press, 1989); Charles Gilbert, *American Financing of World War I* (Greenwood, 1970); John Steele Gordon, "The Business of America," *America Heritage* (June 2001); Natalie McPherson, *Machines and Economic Growth: The Implications for Growth Theory of The History of The Industrial Revolution* (Greenwood Press, 1984); Donald G. Nieman, *Promises to Keep: African-Americans and the Constitutional Order* (Oxford University Press, 1991); Ira Sager, "The Price of War," *Business Week* (April 4, 2003); Paul Samuelson, *Economics* (McGraw-Hill, 1973); Charles Seymour, *Woodrow Wilson and the World War* (Yale University Press, 1921); "Slouching Toward Utopia," www.j-bradford-delong.net; George Steiner, *Economic Problems of War* (John Wiley & Sons, 1942); Gary M. Walton and Hugh Rockoff, *History of the American Economy* (Dryden, 1998).

ELIZABETH PURDY, PH.D.
INDEPENDENT SCHOLAR

World War II

ECONOMIC FACTORS HAVE traditionally been considered to feature much more prominently in the causes and consequences of the First World War than the Second. The belief that modern wars invariably have their roots in capitalist rivalries attained the status of conventional wisdom among the European political left in the 1930s, and underpinned much isolationist sentiment in the UNITED STATES during the same period.

The democracies' attempt to comprehend the Nazi phenomenon was thus complicated by searches for the "powerful forces," usually identified with the more prominent figures in German heavy industry, who were thought responsible for the rise of Adolf Hitler. The course of the war itself made clear how wide of the mark such interpretations were, and the spectacular racism and brutality of the National Socialist (Nazi) regime has tended to obscure more remote causes of the conflict. Similarly, the determination of the victorious powers to ensure that the question of war debts and reparations did not overshadow the post-1945 era as it had done the interwar years—coupled with the astonishing rapidity with which nearly all the combatants made good their wartime losses—caused the economic dimensions of World War II to figure less conspicuously in popular consciousness than had formerly been the case. From the perspective of a new century, however, it is apparent that the economic consequences of World War II were far more thoroughgoing, and lasting, than those of its predecessor.

Economics and war. Although it is far too simplistic to say that the Great DEPRESSION of 1929–33 set the world inexorably on the path to war, the near-breakdown of the international economic system during these years had a profound and damaging psychological impact. Not only did the slump erode confidence in the ability of liberal-democratic policies to cope with modern problems, but the worldwide stampede toward protectionism and discriminatory trade measures that ensued, strengthened the hands of those who equated economic self-sufficiency with national security and prosperity. Autarkic measures represented an early prototype of the "siege economies" that would appear with the onset of war, and provided a justification for the acquisition, if necessary by force, of the territories and resources that would free those who controlled them from dependence upon the vagaries of the world market.

The psychological ramifications of the Depression, indeed, were in some respects perhaps more significant than its material consequences. The volume of world trade, which at the depths of the slump had fallen by 28 percent from the mark set in 1929, had recovered to its former level by 1938. Manufacturing production in Europe performed even better, surpassing its pre-slump output by 12 percent in the same year. Mass unemployment, though hardly eliminated, had been brought under control thanks in part to quasi-Keynesian measures in the United States and Scandinavia and the implementation of rearmament programs in Western Europe.

Unfortunately, these signs of recovery were not accompanied by the dismantling of the protectionist regimes created by the principal manufacturing economies in the early 1930s. The system of imperial preferences established for the British Commonwealth at the 1932 Ottawa Conference, while not the most discriminatory then existing, was bound to have a significant effect on international trade inasmuch as the Commonwealth included within its boundaries approximately a quarter of the world's population. The French Empire constituted a still more tightly protected trading area. Both Germany and Italy pursued AUTARKY and sought preferential relationships with their neighbors in southeast Europe; while America and the SOVIET UNION, secure behind high tariff walls, had become virtually self-sufficient by the end of the 1930s.

Countries waging war. The outbreak of World War II in September 1939, at once represented a continuation of this pattern, and was responsible for violently disrupting it. Compelled to rely on their own resources or those plundered from neighboring states, the Axis powers intensified their autarkic economic policies during the war. At the outset, the Allied countries likewise attempted to maintain "business as usual"; but the collapse of FRANCE in 1940, the near-bankruptcy of Britain by the spring of 1941 and the grave danger in which the United States found itself compelled them to adopt of new and radical expedients. Nonetheless, in mobilizing their economies for war, the principal belligerents found themselves driven to pursue broadly similar policies. The outcome of the war, consequently, is attributable more to the natural advantages, or otherwise, enjoyed by each of the combatants than the success or failure of their economic management.

For GERMANY and JAPAN, the ability to wage aggressive war constituted, from the mid-1930s on, the principal rationale of their economic planning. At the time of his accession to power in 1933, Hitler's first priority had been job creation. The volume of resources devoted to re-armament was initially small because there were few munitions projects that would have had a significant short-term impact on unemployment. From 1935 on, though, with full employment achieved and with the principal brake on German output becoming an increasingly acute labor shortage, re-armament took precedence over all other forms of public investment.

By the time of the Sudeten (German territorial expansion) crisis in September 1938, fully half of all public spending was being applied to military purposes. This vast re-armament project was financed largely through the manipulation of various credit instruments, supplemented by rigorous state controls—amounting almost to a complete takeover—of overseas trade. Notwithstanding the dubious nature of many of these transactions, there is little reason to believe that the German economy was heading for an inevitable crash before the war, although the comforting illusion that the rearmament effort had strained Germany to the point of collapse paradoxically helped sustain British morale, and commitment to continuing the war, after the Dunkirk defeat.

Japan, for its part, began to mobilize its economy simultaneously with its attack upon China in 1937. Japan's motives were purely predatory: To acquire by force the territories, resources and markets to which it believed it was entitled by virtue of the racial superiority and technological advancement of its people, and upon which Japan's status as a first-rate power was thought to depend. Heavily reliant on supplies of iron, steel, oil, and machine tools from America, Japan adopted a series of schemes in the late 1930s aimed at reducing import dependence and drastically increasing the output of munitions industries. No sooner had each of these plans been approved, however, than external events compelled their revision.

The outbreak of the European war in 1939 drove up the price of commodities on the world market and sharply eroded the purchasing power of Japan's already meager foreign-currency reserves. The outlook worsened still further with the U.S. suspension of scrap-metal exports in September 1940, and the German attack on the Soviet Union the following year, putting an end to shipments of goods via the Trans-Siberian Railway. Japan's occupation of southern Indochina in the summer of 1941, to which the United States, Britain, and the NETHERLANDS responded with an economic boycott, closed off all sources of external trade outside the empire and threatened Japan with imminent economic crisis. In November 1941, confronted with the alternative of foregoing its ambitions to obtain by force a hegemonic position in east Asia, or precipitating a dangerous worldwide confrontation with the United States and Britain, the Japanese government of Tojo Hideki opted for the latter course. The attacks on Pearl Harbor and the resource-rich British and Dutch East Indian colonies immediately followed.

Responding to the breakdown of the Disarmament Conference in 1934 and the growing menace of the Axis powers, the Western Allies finally moved to accelerate their own re-armament programs, albeit at an alarmingly sedate pace. British defense preparations to meet the new danger were set in motion in 1935, although, until the Sudeten crisis, the British Cabinet continued to plan on the basis that any future European conflict would be "a war of limited liability." As late as 1938, British armaments expenditure was running at a rate of £358 million, barely one-fifth of what Germany spent in the same year.

France's war preparations were still less effectual. A disproportionate share of French military spending was devoted to the maintenance—though not the completion—of the defensive Maginot Line; defense acquisition policies were uncoordinated and incoherent; and the extensive rearmament scheme inaugurated by the Popular Front government of 1936–37 was badly disrupted by a wave of strikes affecting, in particular, the crucial aircraft industry and was worsened by the persistent instability of the French franc. The outbreak of the war thus found both Allies poorly prepared, with British defense industries unable to spend all of the appropriations voted at the last moment by a panic-stricken Parliament, and the French armed services relying on equipment that was both insufficient in quantity and inadequate in quality.

The defeat of the Allies on the continent, nonetheless, was far from inevitable. The German victory in POLAND in the first weeks of the war had been accomplished only by leaving the western frontier virtually undefended against an Allied advance; while the availability of even a small mobile reserve may well have been sufficient to cut off and defeat the German advance in May 1940. But after the fall of France in June, only the intervention of an outside power could prevent a complete German victory in Europe. By the end of the year, British foreign currency reserves had been all but exhausted; and whereas the extension of Lend-Lease aid from the United States in March 1941 came as a lifeline to the hard-pressed economy, it could only have postponed, not prevented, the final outcome.

Britain persevered, less by its achievement in "standing alone"—a somewhat misleading characterization in any event, inasmuch as it benefited from the assistance of some 500 million subjects of the Empire-Commonwealth, whose consent in most cases had never been solicited—than by Hitler's monumentally misconceived action in declaring war on both the Soviet Union and the United States. Thereafter, the disparity between the rival power blocs, both in terms of population and of productive capacity, would tilt steadily in the Allies' favor.

German economic war machine. By the mid-point of the war, Germany was still capable of holding its own economically against opponents. The once-popular view that German war mobilization was less comprehensive than that of the other combatants is now being revised. Although it is true that the output of the civilian sector remained almost constant from 1939–41, up to half of the goods and services it produced were absorbed by the armed forces. Additionally, large-scale capital projects in munitions-related industries initiated in the late 1930s had not yet begun to bear fruit, providing a misleading picture of the scale of German mobilization. It was the coming stream of many of these projects that accounts in large measure for the extraordinary leap forward in German production capacity from 1942 onward.

Another significant factor was the reform of the state-planning apparatus under Fritz Todt and his successor, Albert Speer. The command economy instituted in the mid-1930s had been both bureaucratic and utterly lacking in organization, with the Ministry of Economics, the Organization for the Four-Year Plan, and the War Economy Office each issuing conflicting instructions and competing for resources. Todt's and Speer's reorganizations, devolving decision-making authority downward to individual managers, laid the foundations not only for industrial rationalization during the war, but part of the managerial structure upon which West German prosperity was built in the 1950s and 1960s.

Lastly, the thoroughness with which the Nazis stripped the occupied territories of both labor and materials—in 1943, 36 percent of French national income was being taken by Germany in the form of levies—helped sustain the war economy even as the tide of battle turned decisively toward the Allied powers.

To offset German success, however, the economies of the other Axis powers performed badly under the stress of war. Alone among the major combatants, ITALY failed to increase its output significantly above peacetime levels during the war. This was caused by a combination of raw materials shortages, with Germany competing successfully for such imports as were available; large-scale movement of labor to German munitions factories; and the innate deficiencies of the Italian manufacturing sector. The Italian armed forces do not deserve the reputation they have acquired from some critics; they fought with considerable tenacity, as is attested to by the deaths of some 290,000 servicemen during the conflict. But they were let down by poor planning, bad equipment and the lamentable performance of Italian industry: A not-so-infrequent occurrence was for basic army training to be curtailed so as to try to prevent soldiers' boots from wearing through.

Likewise, in the Far East, the material and productive imbalance between Japan and its enemies was so pronounced that, as long as the latter were determined to continue the fight, there could only be one possible outcome. Notwithstanding Japan's early successes and the ruthlessness with which it exploited the occupied territories in Korea, CHINA, Formosa, and Southeast Asia, neither the volume nor the variety of plundered supplies could substitute for the commodities previously obtained through overseas trade. A more serious problem was the increasingly acute shortage of ships to transport goods extracted from the conquered areas back to the homeland. The ill-fated Midway and Guadalcanal operations had a catastrophic impact on the Japanese merchant fleet, which by the third quarter of 1944 had dwindled to little more than half its pre-war tonnage. An increasing reliance on slave labor, female labor, and even the mobilization of children for war work failed to have a major impact on war production, sustained largely by squeezing the civilian sector almost to starvation levels.

It has been estimated that by 1944, the Japanese military accounted for a scarcely credible five-sixths of government expenditure. Efforts on this scale could not be sustained for long; nor was the Japanese economy sufficiently large for such desperate measures to have a decisive effect on the battlefield.

The Allied record, by contrast, was one of general success in meeting the challenges of mobilization. After a slow start—nearly a year after the war had begun, more than a million workers remained unemployed—the United Kingdom mounted an impressive production effort, with 55 percent of GROSS DOMESTIC PRODUCT (GDP) being devoted to war purposes by 1943. Even the Soviet Union, which saw the destruction of perhaps a quarter of its physical assets, was able to match and then exceed German output by the same year, although only at the cost of a very drastic reduction in the production of civilian goods. The Soviet Union's principal contribution to the war effort, however, was physical rather than material: For every American citizen who died in the struggle against the common enemy, more than 150 Soviet citizens lost their lives.

Effects of the war. The United States emerged from the war less affected, physically or materially, than any of the other principal combatants. Uniquely, overall levels of civilian output in the United States were maintained while a vast munitions production sector was constructed almost from scratch. The impressive growth rates that made possible such an accomplishment were achieved largely as a result of the recruitment of 17 million extra workers between 1940 and 1944; the re-allocation of Midwestern and Southern labor from agricultural to industrial processes; the increased participation of women in the labor force; and—though perhaps least importantly—increased capital investment. The immense amount of capacity latent in the manufacturing economy permitted America to maintain a military establishment of 11.4 million servicemen and women, subsidize allies to the tune of approximately $50 billion in Lend-Lease transfers, and boost real personal consumption to an all-time high by 1944.

The final defeat of the Axis powers in 1945 thus found the United States in a position of unprecedented global dominance. The course of the war had enabled it to take advantage of the financial difficulties of allies no less than enemies: American businesses benefited, for example, from the sale of British assets—often at deeply discounted prices—in the United States as well as British firms' forced withdrawal from long-established markets in Latin America. Nor was the U.S. government slow to make use of its power to secure its economic position after the return of peace. Lend-Lease was abruptly terminated after V-J Day upon 24 hours' notice; the extension of a reconstruction loan to the United Kingdom was made conditional upon the abolition of the Ottawa Agreement tariffs (although the United States did not agree to dismantle its own tariff barriers); and even U.S. reconstruction aid came with strings attached—not least the requirement of recipients to ratify the BRETTON WOODS agreements on international payments and trade.

Few in 1945 could have predicted the rapidity with which the material damage of World War II would be made good. In 1946, European industrial production stood at one-third, and agricultural production at half, of its pre-war level. Wartime damage was estimated to have destroyed 45 percent of France's total wealth; by comparison with much of Central and Eastern Europe the French had escaped lightly. Worldwide, some 50 million people had been killed in the war, and at least as many displaced from their homes.

Within 10 years, nevertheless—and in some cases much sooner—all the great powers had not merely achieved but surpassed their pre-war levels of production. There were several reasons for this. Despite the scenes of apparent devastation on every side, much of the wartime damage was not difficult to repair. A great deal of military activity had been directed against chokepoints in the enemy's economy; once these were relieved, normality was quickly restored. Wartime investment and rationalization in many cases actually left the belligerent countries with an enhanced productive capacity. Notwithstanding defeat, Germany emerged from the war with a greater stock of capital equipment than when the war began. Much of the military technology developed during the war—jet aircraft, sophisticated electronics, synthetic textiles—had valuable peacetime applications.

In retrospective assessments of the lessons to be learned from the war, the revival of the principal belligerents has most commonly been depicted as a Keynesian success story. The cancellation of inter-Allied war debts; the injection into Western Europe of $13 billion of U.S. aid under the MARSHALL PLAN; the spread of social democracy with its openness to economic interventionism; and the inauguration of a multilateral trade system have ensured that the crises of the interwar years would not be repeated. While there are fewer firm indications than was once assumed to show a cause-and-effect relationship be-

tween any of these factors and the pace of recovery, it can be said that economic integration was one of the few positive consequences of the war. The leaders of the United States saw protectionism as one of the principal causes of the conflict, and multilateralism as the cure. The post-war leaders of the former Axis powers concurred, although in the circumstances they would scarcely have been permitted to dissent.

So, too, did the leaders of the occupied countries in Europe, who attributed their swift defeat to political and economic isolationism. It is far from coincidental that the Soviet Union and Great Britain, the only countries to make serious attempts to resist the integrationist tide and preserve their prewar systems as much as possible, should have lagged behind in the pace of their respective recoveries, nor that both continued for many decades to regard the war itself rather than the peace that followed it as their "finest hour."

BIBLIOGRAPHY. M. Harrison, ed., *The Economics of World War II* (Cambridge University Press, 1998); A.S. Milward, *War, Economy and Society, 1939–1945* (University of California Press, 1977); R.J. Overy, *Why the Allies Won* (Jonathan Cape, 1995).

R.M. DOUGLAS
COLGATE UNIVERSITY

WorldCom, Inc.

TRYING TO RESURRECT itself from one of history's most massive bankruptcies and scandals caused by ACCOUNTING irregularities, WorldCom hired Michael Cappellas as chairman, president and CHIEF EXECUTIVE OFFICER (CEO) to help restore the company's solvency. The former president of Hewlett Packard and CEO of Compaq, Cappellas promised to bring back not only the customer-conscious, technically driven company that it had been, but in mid-2003, Cappellas and his team put WorldCom behind them and renamed the company MCI.

To emerge from its financial difficulties, cost-trimming measures have continued to make up for lost business time; cuts include further layoffs—more than the 17,000 workers already downsized by 2003—as well as the closing of several non-core business groups, such as its wireless resale unit.

The company has been in operation since 1983, its roots starting in Hattiesburg, Mississippi, under the name LDDS, an acronym for Long Distance Discount Services. A few rough years of red ink followed until profits began to soar in the early 1990s. The name WorldCom was inaugurated in 1995. After WorldCom purchased competitor MCI's businesses in 1998, a merger ensued and for the next two years consumers knew the company as MCI WorldCom. By the turn of the millennium the MCI part was dropped.

WorldCom continued its communications services for tens of thousands of businesses globally, and carried more international voice traffic than any other carrier. Its market share of internet communications technology was as large as its piece of the global networks market (95,000 route miles to more than 82,000 locations). As well, it owned and operated a global internet protocol backbone that provided connectivity to 2,600 cities in 100 countries, and 2,400 banking, frame, relay, and voice switches.

Part of the company's strategy to put the past behind it is to produce breakthrough products, one of which may be its WorldCom Connection, voted the 2002 Product of the Year by *Internet Telephony* trade magazine. The product consolidates a customer's entire communications needs over a single network solution, allowing for better network management, lowered costs, and use of new multimedia technology.

"We're still the same company we've always been," emphasizes the company's annual report. "The pre-eminent global communications company for the digital generation, [we] are working to regain our financial health . . . during the reorganization process."

A glimpse of the company's financials can be seen in its filing on January 29, 2003 of its November 2002 monthly operating report. During that 30-day period, it recorded $2.2 billion in revenue, an operating loss from continuing operations of $163 million and a net loss from continuing operations of $194 million.

BIBLIOGRAPHY. Lynn W. Jeter, *Disconnected: Deceit and Betrayal at WorldCom* (John Wiley & Sons, 2003); Hoover's, www.hoovers.com; WorldCom, www.worldcom.com; WorldCom press kit.

JOSEPH GERINGER
SYED B. HUSSAIN, PH.D.
UNIVERSITY OF WISCONSIN, OSHKOSH

Y-Z

Yemen

THE REPUBLIC OF YEMEN is located on the southwestern corner of the Arabian peninsula, with the Red Sea to the west, the Arabian Sea to the south, Oman in the East, and SAUDI ARABIA to the north. The capital is Sana'a.

The country's population is 18.7 million (2002), primarily ethnic Arabs. Most of the population speaks Arabic, although dialects differ from region to region. Almost the entire population is Muslim; however, a few Christians and a Jewish community have resided within Yemen since pre-Islamic times.

Yemen's relative isolation and traditionally weak economy have produced a number of long-standing social problems, including one of the lowest literacy rates in Asia and underdeveloped healthcare. Disease spreads quickly in the region due to polluted drinking water, inadequate vaccinations, and a shortage of medical personnel and facilities. Yemen plays an important role in the ongoing War on Terrorism, attracting the scrutiny of the UNITED STATES as the superpower tracks potential terrorists moving across Yemen's fluid borders. With the help of foreign aid, Yemeni leaders have made great efforts to provide social welfare to the people of Yemen. The country's GROSS DOMESTIC PRODUCT (GDP) stands at $14.8 billion, one of the poorest in the Arab world, with most of its trade coming from crude OIL exports.

Traditionally, the people of Yemen have had an economy based on subsistence agriculture and were self-sufficient. However, by the late 20th century the country began to rely heavily on cheap imported goods from Saudi Arabia and the Persian Gulf States. The PERSIAN GULF WAR of 1990–91, followed by a civil war in 1994, has led to economic hardships for Yemen, and as a result the country has suffered infrastructure damage, rampant inflation, and devaluation of the Yemeni currency.

BIBLIOGRAPHY. Paul Dresch, *A History of Modern Yemen* (Cambridge University Press, 2001); Tim Mackintosh-Smith and Martin Yeoman, *Yemen: The Unknown Arabia* (Overlook Press, 2001); Sarah Searight, *Yemen: Land and People* (Pallas Athene Publishers, 2002); *CIA World Factbook* (2002).

CHRIS HOWELL
RED ROCKS COLLEGE

yen

AS JAPAN'S OFFICIAL monetary unit since 1871, the yen (¥) has become one of the world's most important currencies. Although Chinese coins had circulated in JAPAN earlier, the first recorded Japanese coins were minted in 708 C.E. Like their Chinese counterparts, these coins were round with a square hole in the center allowing them to be strung together for easy transport. In the more recent Tokugawa period (1600–1868), the shogun's government minted gold, silver, and copper coins. The first recorded paper currency dates from around 1600, when a merchant in Ise issued paper notes to his customers.

The Tokugawa Shogunate's collapse in 1868 ushered in the Meiji regime, which was dedicated to modernizing Japan's economy. The New Currency Act, promulgated in 1871, replaced the Tokugawa gold *ryō* with the yen and created a decimal system of *sen* and *rin* to denote tenths and hundredths of a yen. The government also adopted Western style round stamped coins made of gold, silver, and copper. In 1872, a German company was contracted to print the first paper yen notes. Eager to provide additional currency for Japan's growing economy, the government also chartered private banks to print bank notes in the 1870s.

Japan's financial system had to be modified, however, after the Satsuma Rebellion contributed to rapid inflation in the late 1870s. To curb inflation and stabilize the yen, Finance Minister Matsukata Masayoshi established the BANK OF JAPAN in 1882 to centralize monetary control. The government accumulated silver to back its currency and by 1885, the Bank of Japan was prepared to issue convertible bank notes.

The 1897 Coins Law moved Japan from a silver to a gold standard. Using gold extracted from China in the Sino-Japanese War, the Japanese government made the yen redeemable for 0.75 grams of gold (one contemporary U.S. dollar contained 1.5 grams gold). In 1899, the Bank of Japan issued 10-yen gold coins and convertible banknotes.

The gold standard remained in effect until WORLD WAR I (1914–18) forced the advanced capitalist powers to halt their gold shipments. During the war, Japanese companies made windfall profits exporting to the Allied powers and to Asian markets vacated by European firms. This wartime boom rapidly increased Japanese domestic prices and forced Japan to suspend the yen's convertibility to gold. After the war, the Japanese government's attempts to restore convertibility with deflationary policies aggravated an already severe RECESSION.

The yen's convertibility to gold was finally restored in 1930, but the timing could not have been worse. The onset of the Great DEPRESSION further weakened Japanese exports resulting in mounting trade deficits. In just six months, the Japanese lost ¥250 million in gold reserves. This financial disaster contributed to Japan's nationalist rejection of the liberal international economic system in the 1930s, leading to WORLD WAR II.

After World War II, Japan participated in the BRETTON WOODS system of fixed exchange rates sponsored by the UNITED STATES to promote economic stability among its Cold War allies. In the 1950s and 1960s, the yen was pegged at ¥360 to $1. In the early 1970s, however, the financial strain of the VIETNAM WAR forced the United States to allow exchange rates to fluctuate according to currency market forces. By 1978, the yen had appreciated to ¥230 per DOLLAR. In 1985, the Bank of Japan agreed in the Plaza Accords to cooperate with other major central banks to depreciate the dollar. The Plaza agreement resulted in the yen's appreciation to ¥120 to $1 by 1988.

In the 1990s, the yen fluctuated dramatically between ¥80 and ¥160 per dollar. This exchange rate volatility generated considerable discussion of a yen-based east Asian economic group patterned on the North American Free Trade Agreement (NAFTA) and the EUROPEAN UNION, but by 2003, a yen bloc had not materialized. As of the mid 1990s, the majority of Japan's imports and exports continued to be invoiced in currencies other than the yen. Furthermore, most Asian currencies continued to have stronger ties to the dollar than to the yen, as east Asian regional trade seemed to be weakening.

BIBLIOGRAPHY. Bank of Japan, "History," *Currency Museum*, www.imes.boj.or.jp; Thomas F. Cargill, *Political Economy of Japanese Monetary Policy* (MIT Press, 1997); Edward J. Lincoln, *Arthritic Japan: The Slow Pace of Economic Reform* (Brookings Institution, 2001); Kozo Yamamura, "Then Came the Great Depression: Japan's Interwar Years," *The Great Depression Revisited* (Martinus Nijhoff, 1974).

JOHN SAGERS, PH.D.
LINFIELD COLLEGE

The Japanese currency, the yen, has been the country's monetary unit since 1871.

Zimbabwe

LOCATED IN SOUTHERN Africa, Zimbabwe is an average-sized African country, landlocked, with a total landmass of 390,680 square km, comparable to the state of Montana in the UNITED STATES. A parliamentary democracy, six areas of Zimbabwe are under provincial rule. Harare is the capital city.

With a population of 11,376,676, native Africans dominate Zimbabwe's ethnic structure with approximately 98 percent of the population from African heritage. The Shona and Ndebele ethnic groups make up 82 percent and 14 percent of the majority, respectively. Asians and whites are in the minority with about 1 percent of the population each. Zimbabwe's official language, being a former colony of the British Empire, is English, although the languages of the Shona and Ndebele are spoken as well.

Zimbabwe's per capita life-expectancy rate is extremely low, at around 35 years, mainly due to the major prevalence of AIDS in Zimbabwean society. It was recorded in 1999 that 1.5 million people, or over 10 percent of the population, had been infected with the HIV virus, and that 160,000 people each year die from the deadly disease.

Several nomadic groups are believed to be the first inhabitants of Zimbabwe, a people that would later become the Shona tribe. The Zimbabwean empire, which controlled most of southeastern Africa, experienced an era of prosperity until the 15th century, when the Shona tribes split off into self-governing states, eventually most of them banding together to form the Rozwi state. Zimbabwe experienced political turmoil for the next few centuries, with the Shona and Ndebele groups engaging in repeated power struggles. By the late 19th century, Europeans seeking mineral and other natural resources took advantage of the country's political hardships and, by 1895, Zimbabwe was under British control and a white legislature was set up. It became known as Southern Rhodesia. Conflicts over African exclusion from ownership and other widespread racial issues led to guerrilla uprisings in the mid-1900s, and in 1980 newly appointed British Prime Minister Margaret THATCHER granted Zimbabwe its independence. Robert Mugabe came to power in the democratic election of March 1980, and has retained control of the country to date in July 2003.

Mining is the main contribution to Zimbabwe's economy, with the nation specializing in coal, gold, copper, nickel, tin, clay, and numerous ores. Its main agricultural product is tobacco, which makes up approximately 30 percent of its exports, but it also specializes in wheat, coffee, sugar cane, and corn, albeit of limited quantity. Zimbabwe's exports were valued in 2002 at $2.1 billion and its imports at $1.5 billion, and its main trading partner was the neighboring nation of SOUTH AFRICA. The INTERNATIONAL MONETARY FUND (IMF) suspended financial help to the country in the wake of Zimbabwe failing to meet budgetary guidelines.

Zimbabwe's economic status has raised international concern. Inflation has risen at an alarming rate, from an annual rate of 32 percent in 1998 to 59 percent in 1999, stabilizing somewhat at 60 percent in 2000, and then reaching a new height of 100 percent in 2001. Its GROSS DOMESTIC PRODUCT (GDP) growth rate is in serious decline, at –6.5 percent by the end of 2001. Furthermore, Zimbabwe's per capita income is at $2,450, truly indicative of its poverty and unemployment level of 60 percent. Zimbabwe's economic problems stem from its lack of natural resources and limited sovereignty from the British Empire over the last century, restricting its ability to develop a successful market-based economy. Zimbabwean leader Mugabe's controversial land redistribution campaign, launched in 2000, has forced white commercial farmers to give up OWNERSHIP of their land to landless blacks without any compensation. Crippling the predominant commercial agriculture sector of the country's economy, Mugabe's tactic has come under fire and he has received international condemnation. Despite the international community's and his own peoples' staunch protest, Mugabe ran for re-election in 2002 and won by a very small margin, prompting suspicion of a rigged campaign.

BIBLIOGRAPHY. *CIA World Factbook* (2003); "Zimbabwe History," www.lonelyplanet.com; Reuters, "Landfight," www.usafricaonline.com; Sean Sheehan, *Zimbabwe* (Marshall Cavendish, 1996).

SYED B. HUSSAIN, PH.D.
UNIVERSITY OF WISCONSIN, OSHKOSH

Zurich Financial Services

DRAWING FROM ITS EXPERTISE gained over its 130 years, SWITZERLAND-based Zurich Financial Services offers a wide spectrum of solutions in financial protection, life and non-life insurance, risk management, and asset management. Customized products help to insure customers' assets, current and future, and are distributed via a number of channels, one-on-one or electronically. These channels include Zurich's immediate sales force, specific brokers and bankers, assorted partners and alliances, direct marketing programs, and the internet.

Within the list of Zurich's more popular product outlets are recognizable brand names such as Farmers Group and Kemper (in the UNITED STATES), and Allied Dunbar (in the UNITED KINGDOM).

At present, Zurich's client base totals 38 million customers who are served through 60 offices spread throughout Switzerland, continental Europe, North America, and the United Kingdom. Employees, 70,000 of them, monitor and maintain customer programs and the status of each product, whether their client is a small business, a corporation, or a multinational company.

The company dates back to 1872 with the establishment of the Zurich Insurance Company. Within a hundred years its scope widened and, with it, its turf. In 1998, the Zurich Financial Services group carried out several mergers and, by 2002, the company was ranked among the largest 100 companies in the world. Reporting revenues of $38.6 billion in 2002, Zurich faced strong competition and was re-honing its fundamental initiatives—strategic focus, operational efficiency, balance sheet and capital base. One strategic move was appointing a new CHIEF EXECUTIVE OFFICER (CEO) in 2003, PriceWaterhouseCooper's Berto Fisher, to lead these initiatives.

BIBLIOGRAPHY. "Global 500: World's Largest Companies," *Fortune* (July 2002); Hoover's, www.hoovers.com; Zurich Financial Services, www. zurich.com.

JOSEPH GERINGER
SYED B. HUSSAIN, PH.D.
UNIVERSITY OF WISCONSIN, OSHKOSH

Glossary

absolute advantage: when better natural endowments or production-related experience equip one nation with the ability to produce more of a good than another nation, even though both nations have equal quantities of resources.

accounting profit: the difference between a firm's total revenues and total costs, where total costs are measured as the firm's actual (operating) expenditures.

ad valorem tax: a tax levied on the sale of a good, where the tax on each unit sold is determined by the value or price of that unit (e.g., a sales tax).

allocative efficiency: a condition that describes the efficiency associated with how markets allocate goods and services or resources. Allocative efficiency arises when the last unit of a good is sold at a price that is equal to the economic cost of producing or providing that unit (i.e., when a good's price is equal to the good's marginal cost).

antitrust legislation: government laws aimed at preventing anticompetitive practices that firms may use to drive equally efficient rivals from an industry or to perpetuate monopoly status against otherwise equally efficient rivals.

appreciation: when the value of one country's currency increases relative to the value of another country's currency.

arbitrage: opportunistic behavior where an individual buys a good, typically a financial asset, in order to profit from selling that good elsewhere at a higher price.

asset: money or any other good with value that an individual or firm owns. Generally speaking, assets are a form of saving (non-consumption) and help to determine the wealth of an individual or firm.

autarky: when an economic system is closed to all international trade, such that domestic consumption depends solely upon domestic production.

automatic stabilizers: fiscal policy instruments enacted by government to "automatically" affect economic activity throughout the business cycle by supporting demand during recession and restrain demand during periods of inflationary pressure. Because automatic stabilizers are already in place when GDP changes, these instruments do not require any change in government policy.

average cost: the cost of the average unit of output, measured as the total economic cost divided by the number of units produced (or output).

average product: the number of units produced by the average factor of production (e.g., average laborer), measured as the total number of units produced (or output) divided by the quantity of a specific factor used to produce that output.

balance of payments: an accounting record measuring the total value of one nation's economic transactions with the other nations of the world in any given year.

barrier to entry: a long-run concept referring to the ease with which firms may enter into an industry. There are natural barriers to entry, such as significant economies of scale, and legal barriers to entry, such as patents.

barter: an economic transaction between individuals that involves the exchange of actual goods and services, rather than exchanging goods and money.

break-even: arises in microeconomic analysis when a firm's total revenues are equal to the firm's total cost, and is discussed in macroeconomics in the context of a consumer spending all disposable income on current consumption.

budget deficit: when the difference between an economic system's government expenditure and tax revenues is greater than zero (i.e., expenditures exceed tax revenues). A negative budget deficit is a budget surplus, and a budget deficit of zero is referred to as a balanced budget.

burden of a tax: the ability of a tax (e.g., per unit tax) to both increase the price paid by demanders and decrease the price received by suppliers. The change in the price paid is considered the demander's tax burden, whereas the change in the price received is considered the supplier's tax burden.

business cycle: fluctuations in the economic activity of an economic system, typically measured by changes in macroeconomic variables like real GDP and the unemployment rate.

capital account: an accounting record that measures the value of one nation's exchange of physical and financial assets with other nations in any given year.

capital flight: when the physical and financial assets of citizens from less-developed countries are invested in foreign nations.

capital stock: the cumulative value of all buildings, equipment, and machinery (i.e., capital goods) in a nation or firm at a given point in time.

capital intensive production: a production technique that utilizes more capital than another factor like labor, such as an automated production process.

cartel: price-fixing agreements whereby firms agree to decrease output and raise prices in order to increase profits to monopoly-like levels. Cartels are an overt form of collusion.

central bank: an economic institution with the responsibility of monitoring and regulating the nation's banking system, and for controlling the growth and level of the nation's money supply. In the United States, the Federal Reserve operates as the central bank.

Coase theorem: a theory stating that individuals within the private sector can resolve an externality if property rights are well defined and the bargaining costs associated with resolving the externality are low.

collective bargaining: the negotiation process by which employers and labor unions reach agreements regarding wages, fringe benefits, hiring practices, work and safety conditions, etc.

collusion: non-competitive behavior designed to maximize the profits of an entire industry or set of firms, rather than the profits of one single firm. Collusion is behavior that allows separate firms to approximate the behavior of a monopoly, thereby raising the profits of all firms within the industry.

comparative advantage: the ability of one individual, firm, or nation to produce a specific good at lower opportunity cost than another individual, firm, or nation.

complementary goods: goods related in consumption such that the two goods are purchased and consumed together (e.g., sugar and coffee). The demands for these goods are positively related, implying that increases in the demand for one good corresponds with increased demand for that good's complements.

concentration ratio: a measure calculated by summing up the squared market shares of all firms in a specific industry. The concentration ratio implies something about the degree of competition within an industry, in that greater competition is implied by lesser concentration and lesser competition is implied by greater concentration.

constant returns to scale: a condition that occurs when a firm may double the number of factors hired in the long run and consequently double the quantity of output produced.

constant-cost industry: an industry characterized by no change in long-run average cost when firms are increasing their scale of operation.

consumer goods: goods and services purchased by households (e.g., food, clothing, etc.).

consumer price index (CPI): a measure of the (weighted) average price of a particular set of consumer goods. The CPI informs consumers as to how consumer goods prices are changing over time.

consumer's surplus: the difference between the most a consumer is willing to pay and the actual price paid for a good, typically calculated for the market as a whole (i.e., for all units sold within the market, rather than for just one consumer).

consumption expenditure: the sum of all expenditures on consumer goods by households in a given period.

contestable market: a market with no barriers to entry or exit, allowing any potential firm to very easily begin or cease operations within that market.

corporation: a type of firm organization, where the firm's owners have purchased equity (stock) in the firm, with liability limited to the extent of the owner's investment in the firm.

cross-price elasticity of demand: a measure of the percentage change in the quantity of a good sold relative to the change in the price of some related good. This measure informs us of the degree of substitution.

crowding out: an economic condition that occurs when the investment expenditure of the private sector decreases as the result of increases in the expenditure of the public sector.

current account: an accounting record measuring the value of one nation's exchange of goods and services with other nations in any given year. The current account is sometimes also referred to as the trade balance.

decreasing-cost industry: an industry characterized by decreases in long-run average cost when firms are increasing their scale of operation.

deflate: the process of converting a nominal variable into a real variable (i.e., removing the effect of inflation).

deflation: a decrease in the average price of a group of goods and services.

demand curve: a graphical relationship between the price of a good and the quantity of the good consumers will buy at that price.

depreciation: the value of one country's currency decreases relative to the value of another country's currency.

deregulation: the process of removing government controls and regulations on certain industries in an attempt to improve the economic efficiency and performance of that industry.

derived demand: when the demand for one good, typically the demand for a factor of production, is dependent on the demand for another good. For example, the demand for labor is called a derived demand because the quantity of labor demanded varies with changes in the demand for the hiring firm's output.

discouraged workers: individuals who are not employed and have stopped actively looking or interviewing for a new job.

diseconomies of scale: when long-run increases in a firm's output (or scale of operation) lead to increases in long-run average cost.

disinflation: a decrease in the rate of inflation.

disposable income: the amount of income left over for consumers to use on consumption and/or saving once personal taxes are deducted.

dumping: the act of selling goods in a foreign country at a price below what is charged domestically. Dumping is a form of price discrimination.

durable goods: products designed for use in excess of one year.

economic efficiency: when goods and services are allocated in such a way as to maximize net benefit (that is, allow the most benefit to all to be achieved for the least cost).

economic cost: the sum of a firm's actual (monetary) expenditures and the opportunity cost associated with using the resources and factors making up those expenditures.

economic profit: the difference between a firm's total revenue and total economic cost. Because economic profit includes opportunity cost, economic profit provides a natural comparison between an owner's investment in a firm and the return on the next-best alternative investment.

economic system: a means of organizing demanders, suppliers, and the government in order to answer questions about what goods and services to produce, how to produce those goods and services, and then how to distribute the goods and services produced.

economies of scale: when long-run increases in a firm's output (or scale of operation) leads to decreases in long-run average cost.

elasticity: a measure of how changes in one variable respond to changes in another (related) variable, where those changes are calculated in terms of percentage change. When the response is small (i.e., less than one), the relationship is said to be inelastic, whereas when the response is larger.

entrepreneur: the individuals who bear the risk and expend the effort associated with creating profit-making (business) opportunities.

equilibrium: a state of rest or balance that exists when individuals or firms have no incentive to change their current behavior or actions.

excess capacity: a situation arising when firms produce an output level that is below minimum average cost (i.e., the minimum point on the average cost curve). Excess capacity may result from firms selling increasingly differentiated products.

exchange rate: the price of one nation's currency in terms of another nation's currency. Exchange rates may be set by the foreign exchange market (e.g., flexible exchange rates) or at specific levels by government (e.g., fixed exchange rates).

explicit costs: monetary (actual) costs of firms from producing goods and services.

exports: the quantity of goods, services, and capital assets that a country sells to other nations.

externality: when the consumption or production of a good by one individual affects the consumption or production of another individual and no compensation is made for this negative or positive effect. Externalities with negative effects, like pollution, are negative externalities and can result in overproduction or consumption, whereas externalities with positive effects, like research and development, are positive externalities and can result in underproduction or consumption.

factor market: organized markets that facilitate the exchange of factors of production (i.e., labor, land, capital) between buyers and sellers.

fiscal policy: when government chooses to affect economic activity with changes in government expenditure and/or taxation in order to accomplish specific macroeconomic goals.

fixed costs: the economic cost associated with hiring fixed inputs to produce goods and services. Fixed costs consist of both sunk costs and recoverable fixed costs, and do not change with changes in output.

foreign exchange: money or currency from different countries used to assist or facilitate international trade in goods, services, and financial assets.

free enterprise: a system that allows demanders and suppliers to freely exchange goods, services, and financial assets without government intervention.

free rider: an individual who can consume a good and avoid having to compensate the seller. Free riders may arise during the provision of public goods.

free trade: when countries engage in international trade, exchanging goods and services, but without the existence of trade barriers like quotas and tariffs.

game theory: a formal approach to analyzing strategic behavior.

gold standard: an international monetary system that allows a nation's currency to be exchanged for gold.

government expenditure: the overall expenditure by (some combination of) the various levels of government. Depending on the level of government, these expenditures include national defense, fire protection, public parks, etc.

government securities: government issued debt, including bonds and treasury bills.

gross domestic product (GDP): a measure of economic activity. GDP is calculated as the total value of all final goods and services produced in a given period within a nation's borders. When assigning value to these goods and services, one may use current prices (nominal GDP) or constant prices (real GDP).

human capital: any characteristic, such as skill level, education, etc., that improves an individual's productivity.

imperfect competition: markets that consist of firms capable of influencing the market price of a good (i.e., an industry made up of price setters).

implicit costs: the implied value of an activity in terms of what one must give up in order to engage in that activity. Within production, the implicit cost of an input would be the value of that input in some alternative use.

imports: the quantity of goods, services, and capital assets that a country buys from other nations.

income elasticity of demand: a measure of the percentage change in the quantity of a good sold relative to a percentage change in consumer income. The measure informs us as to whether consumers buy more or less of the good as their income rises (i.e., whether the good is a normal or inferior good) and whether the response is inelastic or elastic (i.e., whether the good is a necessity or luxury).

increasing returns to scale: a condition that occurs when a firm may double the number of factors hired in the long run and consequently more than double the quantity of output produced. Increasing returns to scale is consistent with economies of scale.

increasing-cost industry: an industry characterized by increases in long-run average cost when firms are increasing their scale of operation.

infant industry: a name given to new or recently formed industries made up of firms with (typically) higher unit costs than similar, more established firms producing the same good or service in other nations.

inferior good: a good characterized by a negative relationship between purchases of that good and changes in consumer income.

inflation: an increase in the average price of a group of goods and services.

inflation rate: the percentage change (or growth) in the average price of a group of goods and services. Price indexes provide an approximation of the average price of a set of goods at a moment in time, whereas percentage changes in a price index approximate the inflation rate between periods.

interest rate: the percentage of borrowed funds that must be repaid to a lender in exchange for the privilege of borrowing those funds.

investment expenditure: the sum of all private expenditures on capital goods like buildings, equipment, and machinery.

labor force: all civilian persons, typically over the age of sixteen, who are employed or actively seeking employment.

labor income: the wages or salaries received by laborers in exchange for supplying a specific amount of labor.

labor union: a group who joins together on behalf of certain laborers in order to maximize the collective benefit of those laborers regarding their wages, fringe benefits, work conditions, etc.

Laffer curve: a graphical bell-shaped relationship between (income) tax rates and tax revenues. When the tax rate is zero, and when the rate is one hundred percent, government receives no tax revenues. However, as tax rates are adjusted away from these extremes, tax revenues rise to a maximum point somewhere in between.

laissez-faire: a French phrase used to characterize economic systems with little to no government intervention in private sector markets. Laissez-faire is consistent with the concept of free enterprise.

law of demand: an observed negative relationship between the price of a good and the number of units purchased of that good. This law is used to explain why demand curves have a negative slope.

law of diminishing marginal returns: the understanding that, at some point, an individual or firm will obtain smaller increases in benefit from each additional unit consumed or produced.

law of supply: an observed positive relationship between the price of a good and the number of units purchased of that good. This law is used to explain why supply curves have a positive slope.

liability: items that one person, firm, or group potentially owe another person, firm, or group. For example, when borrowing money from a lender, that borrowed money is considered a liability for the borrower because the money must be repaid.

long run: a period of time or decision-making period where all factors of production are variable.

Lorenz curve: a graphical means of illustrating how income or wealth is distributed within an economic system. The curve is often used to measure the proportion of income earned by a cumulative percentage of the population within that economic system.

macroeconomics: the study of how the whole economy allocates goods and services across competing ends with unlimited wants. Macroeconomics focuses on the behavior of variables like GDP, inflation, unemployment, and long-run economic growth.

manager: an individual within the firm who is responsible for directing the production or sale of the firm's output.

marginal analysis: an examination of how benefits and costs change as the result of changes in certain variables. For example, when a market moves from one equilibrium to another, marginal analysis may be used to explain the direction and magnitude of that change.

marginal cost: the change in total economic cost associated with producing an additional unit of some good or service. For a firm, the marginal cost of producing additional output is calculated as the change in total cost divided by the respective change in output.

marginal product: the change in output possible from hiring an additional factor of production. For a firm, the marginal product associated with hiring additional units of a factor is calculated as the change in output divided by the respective change in the amount of factor hired.

marginal revenue: the change in revenue possible from producing and selling an additional unit of output. For a firm, the marginal revenue associated with producing and selling additional output is calculated as the change in total revenues divided by the respective change in output.

market: a collection of demanders and suppliers who exchange goods and services.

market failure: when prices fail to adjust in ways that allow the efficient distribution or production of goods and services within a market. Market failures can occur when consumers (free riders) obtain public goods without compensating the good's suppliers or when externalities are present, and can become an argument for allowing government intervention in the economy.

market power: the ability of a firm to set prices in excess of marginal cost. Market power is sometimes also referred to as monopoly power.

mercantilism: a set of policies designed to keep a nation prosperous by means of the government influencing the behavior of the private sector. For example, between the 16th and 18th centuries, major trading nations assumed that their national wealth and power were best obtained by promoting exports in exchange for precious metals (e.g., gold).

merger: when two firms join together to become a single firm. The merger is characterized as being horizontal if the two joining firms exist within the same level of production, and vertical if the two joining firms exist in different levels of production.

microeconomics: the study of how specific parts of the whole economy (e.g., individual industries) allocate goods and services across competing ends with unlimited wants. Microeconomics focuses on variables like output and price.

minimum efficient scale: the lowest level of output where minimum long-run average costs are achieved.

monetary policy: when government chooses to affect economic activity with changes in the money supply and/or interest rates in order to accomplish specific macroeconomic goals.

money: any good that fulfills the functions associated with facilitating the exchange of goods and services. Money is described as simultaneously functioning as a unit of account, a medium of exchange, and a store of value.

monopolistic competition: an industry that consists of many small firms who produce goods that are slightly different from firm to firm, but where the barriers to entry and exit are nonexistent.

monopoly: an industry that consists of one firm serving the entire market, where the barriers to entry are high enough to keep all other firms out for some period of time.

monopsony: a market with only one buyer for a particular good. Monopsony is often discussed in the context of labor markets, where only one employer for a specific type of labor exists.

moral hazard: opportunistic behavior where one person is able to take advantage of another person, because the opportunistic individual has additional information or does not bear the true cost of their actions.

multiplier effect: the overall effect of a change in expenditure on the income of an economic system. In many cases, the change in income is greater than the change in expenditure (e.g., when considering the effect of a change in investment or government expenditure on real GDP).

national debt: the sum of all of a nation's previous budget deficits. This sum represents the total amount owed by the nation's government.

natural monopoly: a monopoly with significant economies of scale (i.e., decreasing average costs) through some relevant range of market demand.

natural rate of unemployment: the level of unemployment associated with a stable or constant inflation rate. It is believed that all unemployment is voluntary at the natural rate of unemployment (i.e., workers choose to not work at the existing wage).

non-price competition: when firms compete using methods other than prices (e.g., product quality) to attract consumers.

normal good: a good characterized by a positive relationship between purchases of that good and changes in consumer income.

normative economics: economic analysis that explains or predicts outcomes on the basis of moral judgements, opinions, or beliefs.

Okun's Law: an observed negative relationship between changes in unemployment and national output which states that a one percentage point decrease in the unemployment rate is associated with a 2 to 2.5 percent increase in real GDP.

oligopoly: an industry consisting of a few large firms and fairly high barriers to entry. Oligopolistic firms are often characterized as being mutually interdependent, which implies that strategic interaction may exist within oligopolistic industries.

opportunity cost: the implicit cost of producing or consuming additional units, expressed in terms of what was given up to obtain those additional units (i.e., the value of the next-best alternative).

participation rate: the percentage of persons (civilians over the age of 16) in the population who have joined the labor force.

partnership: a type of firm organization, where two or more individuals (often) with complementary skills and knowledge, create a firm. Unlike corporations, where liability is limited to the extent of an individual's investment in the firm, partnerships are characterized as having unlimited liability.

patent: a legal means of appropriating a return on innovative activity, whereby an inventor is allowed to operate as the only seller of an innovation for a specific period of time.

per capita income: income per person, typically measured by dividing a nation's real GDP by the number of persons in the population.

perfect competition: an industry that consists of many small firms who, as individual firms, are unable to influence the market price. Perfectly competitive firms produce identical products (standardized goods) and operate in industries where the barriers to entry or exit are nonexistent.

per unit tax: a tax levied on the sale of a good, where each unit sold is taxed at the same rate (e.g., an excise tax).

Phillips Curve: an observed (graphical) relationship between unemployment rates and the rate of inflation. Economists often debate as to the nature of this relationship, in terms of whether the relationship is negative, positive, or even possibly nonexistent.

positive economics: economic analysis that explains or predicts outcomes in an objective manner. That is, analysis that is more descriptive than otherwise.

poverty: a less than acceptable level of income.

predatory pricing: the act of pricing below cost with the intent of reducing or eliminating competition within an industry.

present value: the value today of a future stream of income or payments.

price ceiling: a price control that establishes a maximum price for a good. If the price ceiling causes market prices to fall, then shortages will arise.

price control: when government imposes a specific price on an industry, often different from the price that would have otherwise arisen in the market.

price discrimination: the act of charging different prices to different consumers, but not on the basis of differences in cost.

price elasticity of demand: a measure of the percentage change in the quantity of a good sold relative to the percentage change in the price of the same good.

price floor: a price control that establishes a minimum price for a good. If the price floor causes market prices to increase, then surpluses will arise.

price leadership: an industry where one firm sets the price for the industry as a whole, where the other firms within the industry respond by selling their goods at the leader's price.

price setter: a firm that has the ability to set a specific (profit-maximizing) price for its own goods, rather than having to accept a price established by the market as a whole.

price taker: a firm that must accept the price established by the market as a whole, but who can sell as many units of output as desired at that market price.

privatization: the process of converting government-owned enterprises into private sector firms.

producer's surplus: the difference between the lowest price a producer would be willing to receive for a good and the actual price of the good, typically calculated for a market as a whole (i.e., for all units sold within the market, rather than for just one producer).

productive efficiency: a condition that describes the efficiency associated with producing goods and services at low cost. Productive efficiency occurs when goods are produced at the lowest possible opportunity cost (i.e., when firms minimize costs).

product markets: organized markets that facilitate the exchange of goods and services between buyers and sellers (also called output markets).

productivity: the average output produced per factor (e.g., labor) within a specific time period.

profit maximization: the process by which firms set output or prices in order to achieve the greatest possible profits. Firms are characterized as profit maximizing when producing where the marginal cost of a certain level of output is equal to the marginal revenue associated with selling that output.

progressive tax: a tax where persons with higher incomes pay a greater percentage of their income in taxes than do lower income groups.

property rights: the legal right to determine how a good or service is used. Private individuals, firms, and government (acting on behalf of society as a whole) may each possess the property rights for various goods and services within an economy.

proportional tax: a tax where persons with higher incomes pay the same percentage of their income in taxes as do lower income groups.

public choice: a branch of economic analysis that examines political decision-making within an economic system.

public good: any good that may be consumed by more than one individual at a specific moment in time, where one person's consumption does not exclude others from consuming the same good.

pure capitalism: an economic system where ownership and decision-making is predominantly the responsibility of private individuals, rather than the government.

pure communism: an economic system where ownership of human and nonhuman resources, as well as all decision-making is bestowed on society as a whole.

quota: a quantity restriction on the sale or importation of a good or service.

rational self interest: an assumption within economic analysis stating that individuals will behave in such a way as to maximize the net benefit of their actions.

rationing: the process of allocating goods and services among demanders, typically on the basis of one's willingness to pay a specific price to obtain the good.

recession: a fall in economic activity that can be observed through decreases in real GDP and increases in unemployment.

regressive tax: a tax where persons with lower incomes pay a greater percentage of their income in taxes than do higher income groups.

relative prices: a ratio comparing one good's price to that of other goods.

rent: payment received by a factor of production in excess of the opportunity cost associated with using that factor.

saving: the amount of disposable income not spent on current consumption, also referred to as non-consumption expenditure.

Say's Law: the belief that supply creates its own demand in that any given amount of output produced will influence demand to the degree that demanders will purchase all of any existing output.

services: any intangible good produced that has value to demanders (e.g., law services produced by lawyers).

short run: a period of time or decision-making period where at least one factor of production is fixed and cannot change.

shutdown: a short-run decision made by suppliers, typically during periods of low demand, to produce zero units of output.

social costs: the economic cost of producing or consuming a good that falls on society as a whole, and includes the actual cost of production or consumption as well as any negative effects from existing externalities that were created by that production or consumption.

socialism: an economic system where the government has ownership over most productive (nonhuman) resources, and is responsible for the predominant amount of decision-making.

sole proprietorship: a type of firm organization, where one individual becomes the owner of a firm. Like partnerships, sole proprietorships are characterized as having unlimited liability.

specialization: the act of concentrating on the production of one specific good.

spillovers: when the costs or benefits associated with providing a good fall on individuals (or society) not directly involved in producing or consuming the good.

substitute goods: goods related in consumption such that the two goods are alternatives to one another (e.g., tea and coffee). The demands for these goods are negatively related, which implies that increased demand for one good corresponds with decreased demand for that good's substitutes.

sunk costs: non-recoverable fixed costs, typically paid in advance of the decision to produce a certain level of output.

supply curve: a graphical relationship between the price of a good and the quantity of the good suppliers are willing to provide at that price.

supply of loan-able funds: a graphical relationship that illustrates how much individuals are willing to lend or save at various interest rates.

tariff: a tax levied on imported goods.

technology: the knowledge associated with producing a certain amount of output, but also a description of how factors are combined during production.

transaction costs: the economic cost of time, effort, and other resources directly related to the initiation and completion of trade and exchange. Transaction costs are also sometimes characterized as the cost of doing business.

transfer payment: a payment received by an individual from the government, where the individual is not required to compensate the government for receiving that payment. Payment may be in-kind (a transfer of non-monetary goods or resources) or monetary (a transfer of money).

transportation costs: the economic cost of transporting goods between locations in order to finalize exchange between buyer and seller.

unemployment: defined by government as all individuals without employment, but who are actively seeking employment (or waiting to begin a new job).

unemployment rate: the percentage of persons in the labor force who are not employed, but actively seeking employment (or waiting to begin a new job).

variable costs: the economic cost associated with hiring variable inputs to produce goods and services. Variable costs change with changes in output, whereas fixed costs do not change with changes in output.

wealth: the value of the physical and financial assets owned by an individual, less the accumulated liabilities (e.g., debt) incurred by that individual.

SOURCES. Peter H. Lindert and Thomas A. Pugel, *International Economics*, 10th ed. (Irwin Publishing, 1996); Paul A. Samuelson and William D. Nordhaus, *Economics*, 17th ed. (Irwin-McGraw Hill Publishing, 2001).

COMPILED AND WRITTEN BY BARRY HAWORTH
UNIVERSITY OF LOUISVILLE

Resource Guide

With more than 100 academic authors and 700 articles in the *Encyclopedia of Capitalism*, select bibliographic sources run common to a majority of topics. Certain books, authors, papers, journals, associations, websites, universities, and publishers are cited in bibliographies following the articles in this encyclopedia.

Books

A Beautiful Mind by S. Nasar (Touchstone, 1998)

A History of Capitalism, 1500–2000 by Michel Beaud (Monthly Review Press, 2001)

A History of Economic Thought by William J. Barber (Viking Press, 1967)

An Inquiry into the Nature and Causes of the Wealth of Nations by Adam Smith (Modern Library, 1974)

Business Cycles: A Theoretical, Historical, and Statistical Analysis of the Capitalist Process by Joseph A. Schumpeter (Porcupine Press, 1939)

Capital: A Critique of Political Economy by Karl Marx (Penguin USA, 1982)

Capitalism and Freedom by Milton Friedman (University of Chicago Press, 2002)

Capitalism, Socialism and Democracy by Joseph A. Schumpeter (HarperCollins, 1984)

Definitions in Political Economy by Thomas R. Malthus (Kelley & Millman, 1954)

Economic Theory in Retrospect by Mark Blaug (Cambridge University Press, 1978)

Economics: Principles and Policy by William J. Baumol and Alan S. Binder (South-Western, 2002)

Eyewitness to Wall Street: 400 Years of Dreamers, Schemers, Busts, and Booms by D. Colbert (Broadway Books, 2001)

Globalization and Its Discontents by Joseph Stiglitz (W.W. Norton, 2002)

History of the American Economy by Gary M. Walton and Hugh Rockoff (South-Western, 2001)

Human Action: A Treatise on Economics by Ludwig von Mises (Mises Institute, 1998)

Industrial Economics and Organization by Donald A. Hay and Derek J. Morris (Addison Wesley, 1999)

International Economics by Dominick Salvatore (Prentice Hall, 2002)

International Economics: Theory and Policy by Paul R. Krugman and Maurice Obstfeld (Addison Wesley, 2003)

Microeconomics by Paul A. Samuelson and William D. Nordhaus (McGraw-Hill, 2000)

Open Society: Reforming Global Capitalism by George Soros (Public Affairs, 2000)

Principles of Economics by Alfred Marshall (Prometheus Books, 1997)

Principles of Macroeconomics by Karl Case and Ray Fair (Prentice Hall, 2001)

Principles of Political Economy and Taxation by David Ricardo (Everymans Library, 1992)

Principles of Political Economy by John Stuart Mill (Augustus M. Kelley Publishers, 1999)

The Accumulation of Capital by Joan Robinson (Macmillan, 1956)

The Affluent Society by John Kenneth Galbraith (Houghton Mifflin, 1998)

The Age of the Great Depression by Dixon Wechter (Macmillan, 1948)

The Change Makers: From Carnegie to Gates by Maury Klein (Henry Holt, 2003)

The Economic Approach to Human Behavior by Gary S. Becker (University of Chicago Press, 1976)

The Fountainhead by Ayn Rand (Signet, 1996)

The General Theory of Employment, Interest, and Money by John Maynard Keynes (Prometheus Books, 1997)

The Jungle by Upton Sinclair (Bantam Classics, 2003)

The Organization of Industry by George J. Stigler (University of Chicago Press, 1983)

The Rise of Merchant Empires: Long-Distance Trade in the Early Modern World, 1350–1750 edited by James Tracy (Cambridge University Press, 1990)

The Road to Serfdom by Friedrich A. Hayek (University of Chicago Press, 1994)

The Sources of Economic Growth by Richard R. Nelson (Harvard University Press, 1995)

The Theory of Legislation by Jeremy Bentham (Prometheus Books, 1988)

The Theory of Moral Sentiments by Adam Smith (Prometheus Books, 2000)

The Theory of Political Economy by William Stanley Jevons (Transaction Publishing, 1911)

The Theory of the Leisure Class by Thorstein Veblen (Dover Publications, 1994)

War, Economy, and Society 1939–1945 by A.S. Milward (University of California Press, 1998)

Journals

American Economic Review (American Economic Association)

Applied Economics (Routledge, Taylor & Francis)

Cambridge Journal of Economics (Oxford University Press)

Cato Journal (Cato Institute)

Contemporary Economic Policy (Oxford University Press)

Econometrica (The Econometric Society)

Econometrics Journal (Royal Economic Society)

Economic History Review (Blackwell Publishing)

Economic Theory (Springer Verlag)

Emerging Markets Review (Elsevier Publishing)

Empirica (Kluwer Academic Publishers)

European Review of Economic History (Cambridge University Press)

Foreign Affairs (Council of Foreign Relations)

Global Economy Quarterly (R.T. Edwards, Inc.)

Harvard Business Review (Harvard Business School Publishing)

International Journal of Social Economics (Emerald Academic)

International Journal of the Economics of Business (Routledge, Taylor & Francis)

Journal of Applied Economics (John Wiley & Sons)

Journal of Business (University of Chicago Press)

Journal of Economic History (Cambridge University Press)

Journal of Economic Literature (American Economic Association)

Journal of Economic Perspectives (American Economic Association)

Journal of Political Economy (University of Chicago Press)

Monthly Review (Monthly Review Press)

National Institute Economic Review (Sage Publications)

New Economy (Blackwell Publishers)

Pulse of Capitalism (Commonwealth Institute)

Quarterly Journal of Economics (MIT Press)

RAND Journal Economics (Rand Publishing)

Review of International Economics (Blackwell Publishing)

World Bank Economic Review (World Bank Group)

Magazines

Advertising Age (Crain Communications, Inc.)

Adweek (VNU Business Publications)

American Demographics (Primedia Publishing)

Asia Inc. (Asia Inc.)

Black Enterprise (Earl G. Graves, Ltd.)

Bloomberg Markets (Bloomberg LP)

Business 2.0 (Business 2.0 Media, Inc.)

Businessweek (McGraw-Hill Companies, Inc.)

Euromoney (Euromoney Institutional Investor PLC)

Far Eastern Economic Review (Dow Jones & Compaay, Inc., Hong Kong)

Fast Company (Gruner + Jahr USA Publishing)

Forbes (Forbes, Inc.)

Fortune (Time Inc., AOL Time Warner)

Inc. (Gruner + Jahr USA Publishing)

Industry Week (Penton Media, Inc.)

Kiplinger's (The Kiplinger Washington Editors, Inc.)

Money (Time Inc., AOL Time Warner)

Smart Money (Dow Jones & Company)

The Economist (The Economist Group, Inc.)

Worth (Worth Media)

Newspapers

Crain's Chicago Business (Crain Communications)

Crain's New York Business (Crain Communications)

Financial Times (The Financial Times, Ltd.)

Investor's Business Daily (Investors' Business Daily, Inc.)

The International Herald Tribune (The New York Times Co.)

The New York Times (The New York Times Company)
The Wall Street Journal (Dow Jones & Company, Inc.)
The Washington Post (The Washington Post Company)

Internet websites

Almost all journals, magazines, newspapers, and associations have dedicated websites that can be easily located using standard internet search engines. One rule of caution in using internet research tools in economics and capitalism is that you should rely on "branded" media, that is, websites associated with known media and institutions. Some recommended websites include:

www.albany.edu/econ/eco_phds.html (State University of New York listing and links to university economics departments)

www.aynrand.org (Organization dedicated to the philosophy of Ayn Rand)

www.bbc.co.uk/learning/library/economics.shtml (BBC News links to economics websites)

www.capitalism.org (Independent organization promoting capitalism)

www.cia.gov/cia/publications/factbook/ (Central Intelligence Agency World Factbook)

www.commerce.gov (U.S. Department of Commerce)

www.hoovers.com (Hoover's Handbook of American Business 2003)

www.loc.gov (U.S. Library of Congress)

www.lse.ac.uk (London School of Economics)

www.nber.org (National Bureau of Economic Research)

www.stern.nyu.edu/globalmacro/ (New York University's Nouriel Roubini's website)

www.un.org/ (United Nations)

www.ustreas.gov (U.S. Treasury)

www.whitehouse.gov/omb/budget/fy2004/ (Budget of the United States)

www.worldbank.org (World Bank)

Appendix A:

International Trade by Region

THE FOLLOWING APPENDIX is provided by the World Trade Organization (© WTO) and presents comprehensive, comparable, and up-to-date statistics on trade in merchandise and commercial services for an assessment of world trade flows by country, region, and main product groups or service categories. Compiled from Section III of the WTO International Trade Statistics, the appendix retains the WTO organizational structure (i.e, charts and tables are labeled III) for easy reference within the WTO publications. For further information contact:

WORLD TRADE ORGANIZATION
Centre William Rappard, Rue de Lausanne 154,
CH-1211 Geneva 21, Switzerland • www.wto.org

1. Overview

Chart III.1

Value of world merchandise trade by region, 1994-01

(Annual percentage change in value)

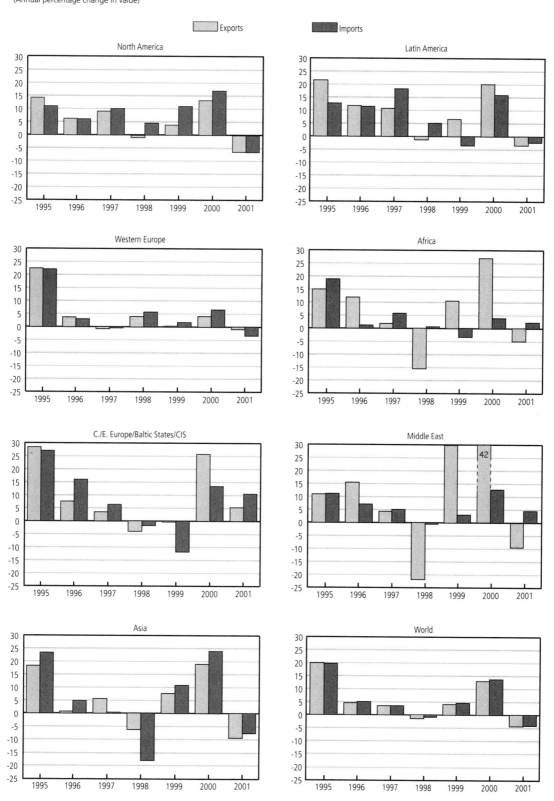

951

Chart III.2

The volume of world merchandise trade by selected region, 1994-01

(Annual percentage change)

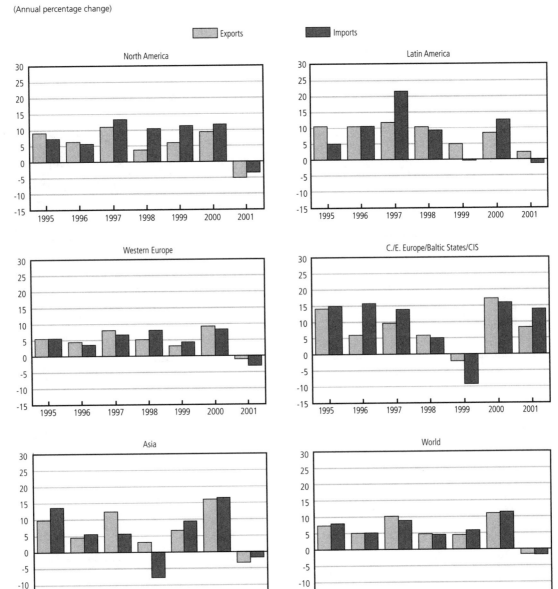

Table III.1

World merchandise exports by region, 2001

(Billion dollars and percentage)

	Value	Share		Annual percentage change			
	2001	1990	2001	1990-01	1999	2000	2001
World	5984	100.0	100.0	5	4	13	-4
North America	991	15.4	16.6	6	4	14	-6
United States	731	11.6	12.2	6	2	13	-6
Latin America	347	4.3	5.8	8	7	20	-3
Mexico	159	1.2	2.6	13	16	22	-5
Western Europe	2485	48.2	41.5	4	0	4	-1
European Union (15)	2291	44.4	38.3	4	0	3	-1
C./E. Europe/Baltic States/CIS	286	3.1	4.8	7	0	26	5
Central and Eastern Europe	129	1.4	2.2	8	1	14	12
Russian Fed.	103	-	1.7	-	1	39	-2
Africa	141	3.1	2.4	3	11	27	-5
South Africa	29	0.7	0.5	3	1	12	-2
Middle East	237	4.1	4.0	5	30	42	-9
Asia	1497	21.8	25.0	7	7	18	-9
Japan	403	8.5	6.7	3	8	14	-16
China	266	1.8	4.4	14	6	28	7
Six East Asian traders	568	7.8	9.5	7	8	19	-12
Memorandum item:							
NAFTA (3)	1149	16.6	19.2	7	5	15	-6
MERCOSUR (4)	88	1.4	1.5	6	-9	14	4
ASEAN (10)	385	4.2	6.4	9	9	19	-10

Table III.2

World merchandise imports by region, 2001

(Billion dollars and percentage)

	Value	Share		Annual percentage change			
	2001	1990	2001	1990-01	1999	2000	2001
World	6270	100.0	100.0	5	4	13	-4
North America	1408	18.3	22.5	7	11	18	-6
United States	1180	14.8	18.8	8	12	19	-6
Latin America	380	3.7	6.1	11	-3	16	-2
Mexico	176	1.2	2.8	14	14	23	-4
Western Europe	2524	48.6	40.3	4	2	6	-3
European Union (15)	2334	44.6	37.2	4	2	6	-3
C./E. Europe/Baltic States/CIS	267	3.3	4.3	6	-12	14	11
Central and Eastern Europe	159	1.4	2.5	10	-1	12	9
Russian Fed.	54	-	0.9	-	-33	13	20
Africa	136	2.8	2.2	3	-3	4	2
South Africa	28	0.5	0.5	4	-9	11	-4
Middle East	180	3.0	2.9	5	3	13	4
Asia	1375	20.3	21.9	6	10	23	-7
Japan	349	6.7	5.6	4	11	22	-8
China	244	1.5	3.9	15	18	36	8
Six East Asian traders	532	8.0	8.5	6	11	26	-13
Memorandum item:							
NAFTA (3) a	1578	19.3	25.2	8	12	18	-6
MERCOSUR (4)	84	0.8	1.3	10	-17	8	-6
ASEAN (10)	336	4.6	5.4	7	7	22	-8

a Imports of Canada and Mexico (1990-99) are valued f.o.b.

Table III.3

Intra- and inter-regional merchandise trade, 2001

(Billion dollars and percentage)

Origin	North America	Latin America	Western Europe	C./E. Europe/ Baltic States/CIS	Africa	Middle East	Asia	World
Value								
North America	391	164	188	7	13	21	207	991
Latin America	211	59	42	3	4	4	22	347
Western Europe	255	58	1677	147	63	65	195	2485
C./E. Europe/Baltic States/CIS	12	6	158	76	3	8	19	286
Africa	25	5	73	1	11	3	21	141
Middle East	39	3	39	2	9	18	112	237
Asia	376	40	252	17	24	45	722	1497
World	1308	335	2429	252	127	163	1298	5984
Share of intra- and inter-regional trade flows in each region's total merchandise exports								
North America	39.5	16.5	19.0	0.7	1.3	2.1	20.9	100.0
Latin America	60.8	17.0	12.1	0.9	1.2	1.2	6.3	100.0
Western Europe	10.3	2.3	67.5	5.9	2.5	2.6	7.8	100.0
C./E. Europe/Baltic States/CIS	4.2	2.1	55.2	26.6	1.0	2.8	6.6	100.0
Africa	17.7	3.5	51.8	0.7	7.8	2.1	14.9	100.0
Middle East	16.5	1.3	16.5	0.8	3.8	7.6	47.3	100.0
Asia	25.1	2.7	16.8	1.1	1.6	3.0	48.2	100.0
World	21.9	5.6	40.6	4.2	2.1	2.7	21.7	100.0
Share of intra- and inter-regional trade flows in world merchandise exports								
North America	6.5	2.7	3.1	0.1	0.2	0.4	3.5	16.6
Latin America	3.5	1.0	0.7	0.1	0.1	0.1	0.4	5.8
Western Europe	4.3	1.0	28.0	2.5	1.1	1.1	3.3	41.5
C./E. Europe/Baltic States/CIS	0.2	0.1	2.6	1.3	0.1	0.1	0.3	4.8
Africa	0.4	0.1	1.2	0.0	0.2	0.1	0.4	2.4
Middle East	0.7	0.1	0.7	0.0	0.2	0.3	1.9	4.0
Asia	6.3	0.7	4.2	0.3	0.4	0.8	12.1	25.0
World	21.9	5.6	40.6	4.2	2.1	2.7	21.7	100.0

Destination

Chart III.3

World trade in commercial services by selected region, 1994-01

(Annual percentage change in value)

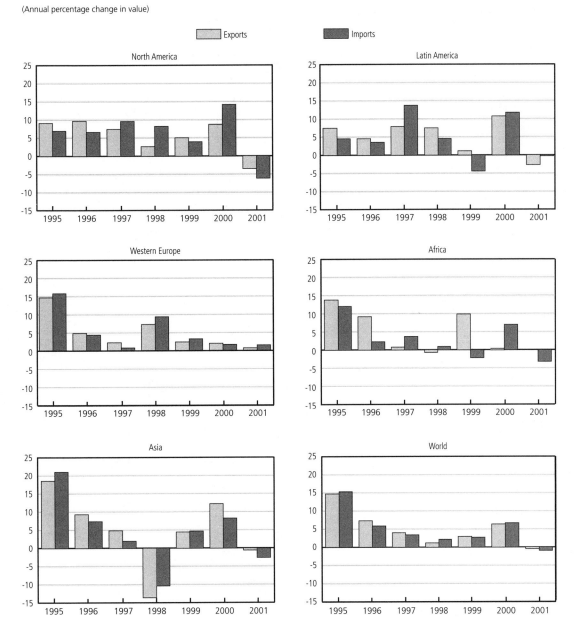

Table III.4

World exports of commercial services by region, 2001

(Billion dollars and percentage)

	Value	Share		Annual percentage change			
	2001	1990	2001	1990-01	1999	2000	2001
World	1460	100.0	100.0	6	3	6	0
North America	299	19.3	20.5	6	5	9	-3
United States	263	17.0	18.1	6	5	9	-3
Latin America	58	3.8	4.0	6	1	11	-3
Mexico	13	0.9	0.9	5	1	17	-7
Brazil	9	0.5	0.6	8	-3	29	-1
Western Europe	679	53.1	46.5	5	2	2	1
European Union (15)	612	47.2	41.9	5	4	1	1
United Kingdom	108	6.9	7.4	7	7	3	-6
France	80	8.5	5.5	2	-3	-1	-2
Germany	80	6.6	5.5	4	2	-3	-1
Italy	57	6.2	3.9	1	-13	-3	2
C./E. Europe/Baltic States/CIS	56	2.6	3.8	10	-14	11	11
Africa	31	2.4	2.1	5	10	0	0
Egypt	9	0.6	0.6	6	18	4	-9
South Africa	5	0.4	0.3	3	-4	-3	-4
Middle East	33	2.0	2.2	7	9	16	-7
Israel	11	0.6	0.8	9	19	32	-21
Asia	303	16.8	20.8	8	4	12	-1
Japan	64	5.3	4.4	4	-2	13	-7
Hong Kong, China	42	2.3	2.9	8	2	14	2
China	33	0.7	2.3	17	10	15	9
Korea, Rep. of	30	1.2	2.0	11	4	15	0
Singapore	26	1.6	1.8	7	25	13	-2
India	20	0.6	1.4	14	27	26	15

Table III.5

World imports of commercial services by region, 2001

(Billion dollars and percentage)

	Value	Share		Annual percentage change			
	2001	1990	2001	1990-01	1999	2000	2001
World	1445	100.0	100.0	5	3	7	-1
North America	229	15.4	15.9	6	4	14	-6
United States	188	12.0	13.0	6	3	16	-7
Latin America	71	4.3	4.9	7	-4	12	0
Mexico	17	1.2	1.1	5	12	19	-1
Brazil	16	0.8	1.1	8	-15	19	0
Western Europe	647	48.1	44.8	5	3	2	1
European Union (15)	605	42.9	41.9	5	3	2	2
Germany	133	9.7	9.2	5	5	-3	0
United Kingdom	92	5.5	6.3	7	9	5	-4
France	62	6.2	4.3	2	-4	-3	0
Italy	56	5.7	3.9	2	-11	-3	2
C./E. Europe/Baltic States/CIS	59	3.0	4.1	8	-8	19	13
Africa	37	3.3	2.6	3	-2	7	-3
Egypt	6	0.4	0.4	6	1	20	-10
South Africa	5	0.4	0.4	3	2	0	-8
Middle East	45	4.1	3.1	3	1	8	-7
Israel	12	0.6	0.9	9	11	16	1
Asia	355	21.9	24.6	6	5	8	-3
Japan	107	10.3	7.4	2	3	1	-7
China	39	0.5	2.7	23	17	16	9
Korea, Rep. of	33	1.2	2.3	11	11	23	0
Hong Kong, China	25	1.4	1.7	8	-5	3	-2
Taipei, Chinese	24	1.7	1.6	5	0	11	-8
India	23	0.7	1.6	13	20	15	19

Table III.6

Exports of commercial services of selected economies by selected partners, 2000

(Percentage)

	World	United States	EU (15)	Japan	Other economies
World	100	14	18	8	60
United States	100	-	33	12	55
European Union (15)	100	40	-	6	53
Japan	100	34	18	-	49
Other economies	100	8	19	8	65

Note: Excluding intra-EU trade.

Table III.7

Imports of commercial services of selected economies by selected partners, 2000

(Percentage)

	World	United States	EU (15)	Japan	Other economies
World	100	19	18	5	58
United States	100	-	37	9	54
European Union (15)	100	41	-	4	56
Japan	100	33	20	-	48
Other economies	100	15	19	5	61

Note: Excluding intra-EU trade.

Chart III.4

Trade in commercial services of selected economies by selected partners, 2000

(Billion dollars)

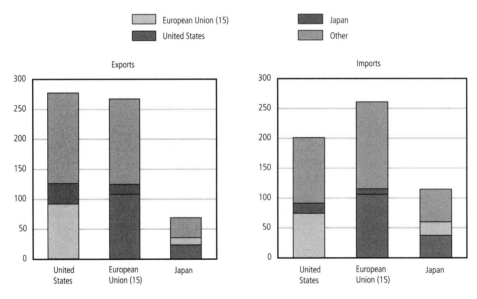

Note: Excluding intra-EU trade

2. *North America*

Table III.8

Merchandise trade of North America, 2001

(Billion dollars and percentage)

	Exports	Imports
Value	991	1408
Share in world merchandise trade	16.6	22.5
Annual percentage change		
Value		
1980-85	1	6
1985-90	11	8
1990-01	6	7
1999	4	11
2000	14	18
2001	-6	-6
Volume		
1980-85	-0.5	7.0
1985-90	8.5	5.0
1990-01	6.0	7.5
1999	6.0	11.0
2000	9.5	11.5
2001	-5.0	-3.5

Table III.9

Merchandise trade of North America by region and by major product group, 2001

(Billion dollars and percentage)

	Value		Share	
	Exports	Imports	Exports	Imports
Total	991	1408	100.0	100.0
Region				
North America	391	363	39.4	25.8
Latin America	164	218	16.5	15.5
Western Europe	188	276	19.0	19.6
C./E. Europe/Baltic States/CIS	7	16	0.7	1.1
Africa	13	28	1.3	2.0
Middle East	21	41	2.1	2.9
Asia	207	462	20.9	32.8
Product group				
Agricultural products	104	84	10.5	6.0
Mining products	74	173	7.5	12.3
Manufactures	763	1093	77.0	77.6

Chart III.5

Merchandise trade of North America, 1990-01

(Billion dollars)

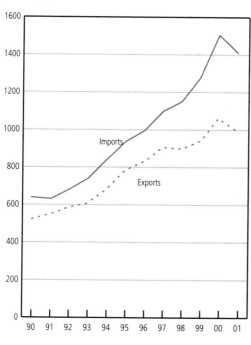

Chart III.6

Share of North America in world merchandise trade, 1990-01

(Percentage based on value data)

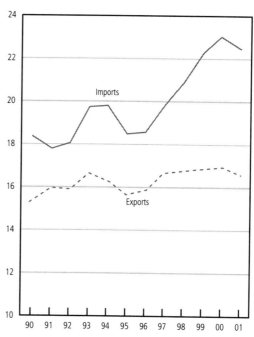

Table III.10

Merchandise exports of North America by product, 2001

(Billion dollars and percentage)

	Value	Share in exports of North America		Share in world exports		Annual percentage change			
	2001	1990	2001	1990	2001	1990-01	1999	2000	2001
Total merchandise exports	991.0	100.0	100.0	15.4	16.6	6	4	14	-6
Agricultural products	103.8	15.7	10.5	19.7	19.0	2	-3	8	-3
Food	73.5	10.2	7.4	16.9	16.8	3	-4	5	2
Raw materials	30.3	5.4	3.1	28.7	27.5	1	0	14	-12
Mining products	74.4	9.1	7.5	9.7	9.4	4	1	44	-2
Ores and other minerals	9.8	2.2	1.0	22.2	15.5	-2	-7	16	-1
Fuels	49.5	4.8	5.0	6.9	8.0	6	9	65	0
Non-ferrous metals	15.0	2.1	1.5	14.7	13.5	3	-7	17	-9
Manufactures	763.3	69.7	77.0	15.2	17.0	7	5	12	-7
Iron and steel	8.8	1.1	0.9	5.2	6.8	4	-9	14	-8
Chemicals	97.3	8.8	9.8	15.6	16.3	7	4	15	0
Other semi-manufactures	67.6	6.1	6.8	12.1	15.7	7	6	12	-6
Machinery and transport equipment	474.3	44.0	47.9	18.9	19.3	7	6	11	-9
Automotive products	118.4	11.7	11.9	19.1	21.0	6	12	4	-7
Office and telecom equipment	139.5	11.0	14.1	19.2	16.9	8	10	25	-20
Other machinery and transport equipment	216.4	21.4	21.8	18.7	20.4	6	-1	7	-2
Textiles	12.7	1.1	1.3	5.5	8.6	7	3	14	-4
Clothing	9.0	0.6	0.9	2.7	4.6	11	-4	6	-16
Other consumer goods	93.7	8.0	9.5	13.9	17.9	8	5	17	-5

Table III.11

Merchandise imports of North America by product, 2001

(Billion dollars and percentage)

	Value	Share in imports of North America		Share in world imports		Annual percentage change			
	2001	1990	2001	1990	2001	1990-01	1999	2000	2001
Total merchandise imports	1408.5	100.0	100.0	18.1	22.5	8	12	18	-6
Agricultural products	84.4	7.7	6.0	11.1	14.2	5	6	5	0
Food	64.9	5.9	4.6	11.0	13.7	5	6	5	2
Raw materials	19.5	1.9	1.4	11.2	16.4	5	7	4	-8
Mining products	172.9	15.0	12.3	18.7	20.6	6	19	62	-8
Ores and other minerals	8.1	1.2	0.6	13.2	11.2	1	-6	8	-9
Fuels	142.1	12.0	10.1	20.1	21.7	6	26	76	-7
Non-ferrous metals	22.7	1.8	1.6	16.0	19.9	6	7	25	-11
Manufactures	1093.3	73.9	77.6	19.2	23.4	8	11	14	-7
Iron and steel	19.2	2.0	1.4	11.5	13.6	4	-19	19	-22
Chemicals	102.1	5.0	7.3	10.3	16.5	11	13	16	6
Other semi-manufactures	96.9	7.0	6.9	16.1	21.1	7	12	12	-6
Machinery and transport equipment	621.9	43.0	44.2	22.3	24.6	8	13	14	-10
Automotive products	208.1	16.4	14.8	32.4	35.9	7	19	8	-4
Office and telecom equipment	197.2	11.6	14.0	24.6	23.1	9	13	22	-20
Other machinery and transport equipment	216.7	15.0	15.4	15.8	19.8	8	7	12	-5
Textiles	19.3	1.4	1.4	8.4	12.4	7	5	10	-4
Clothing	70.7	4.6	5.0	26.2	34.5	8	6	14	-1
Other consumer goods	163.1	10.9	11.6	22.5	29.3	8	11	13	-2

Table III.12

Merchandise exports of North America by destination, 2001

(Billion dollars and percentage)

	Value	Share		Annual percentage change			
	2001	1990	2001	1990-01	1999	2000	2001
World	991.0	100.0	100.0	6	4	14	-6
Intra-North America	390.7	34.2	39.4	7	10	13	-7
Asia	206.9	25.5	20.9	4	3	17	-10
Japan	62.9	10.7	6.3	1	-1	13	-12
Korea, Rep. of	23.5	3.0	2.4	4	37	21	-20
China	22.0	1.2	2.2	12	-7	26	17
Hong Kong, China	14.8	1.4	1.5	7	-3	16	-4
Western Europe	188.1	24.0	19.0	4	3	8	-4
European Union (15)	171.4	21.9	17.3	4	3	8	-4
Latin America	163.8	10.7	16.5	10	0	20	-6
Mexico	103.2	5.5	10.4	12	10	28	-9
Brazil	16.5	1.1	1.7	11	-13	15	3
Middle East	20.6	2.4	2.1	5	-10	-8	1
Africa	13.4	1.7	1.3	4	-13	9	11
C./E. Europe/Baltic States/CIS	7.3	1.0	0.7	3	-25	8	11
Inter-regional trade	600.0	65.3	60.6	5	1	14	-6

Table III.13

Merchandise imports of North America by origin, 2001

(Billion dollars and percentage)

	Value	Share		Annual percentage change			
	2001	1990	2001	1990-01	1999	2000	2001
World	1408.5	100.0	100.0	7	12	18	-6
Asia	462.3	34.4	32.8	7	11	17	-10
Japan	139.8	15.9	9.9	3	8	12	-14
China	118.2	2.7	8.4	19	17	23	2
Taipei, Chinese	37.6	4.0	2.7	4	8	14	-18
Korea, Rep. of	39.5	3.3	2.8	6	29	30	-13
Singapore	16.0	1.6	1.1	4	0	6	-22
Hong Kong, China	10.9	1.7	0.8	0	1	9	-16
Intra-North America	362.8	26.3	25.8	7	10	12	-7
Western Europe	275.8	20.3	19.6	7	12	13	-1
European Union (15)	252.3	18.4	17.9	7	12	13	0
Latin America	217.7	11.1	15.5	11	16	24	-5
Mexico	141.3	5.0	10.0	14	17	24	-3
Brazil	16.2	1.4	1.2	5	11	22	4
Middle East	40.6	3.2	2.9	4	32	54	-5
Africa	28.4	2.8	2.0	4	6	60	-9
C./E. Europe/Baltic States/CIS	16.1	0.4	1.1	17	6	38	-12
Inter-regional trade	1041.0	72.3	73.9	8	12	20	-6

Table III.14

Gross domestic product and trade in goods and services of Canada and the United States, 2001

(Billion dollars and percentage)

	Value	Annual percentage change in volume						
	2001	1990-01	1996	1997	1998	1999	2000	2001
Gross domestic product								
North America	10838	2.9	3.4	4.4	4.2	4.2	3.9	0.4
Canada	695	2.7	1.5	4.4	3.3	5.5	4.6	1.5
United States	10143	2.9	3.6	4.4	4.3	4.1	3.8	0.3
Exports of goods and services								
North America	1307	6.0	7.7	11.5	3.5	4.5	9.1	-4.3
Canada	302	7.0	5.6	8.3	8.9	9.9	7.6	-3.7
United States	1005	5.9	8.2	12.3	2.1	3.2	9.5	-4.5
Imports of goods and services								
North America	1619	7.9	7.9	13.8	10.4	9.9	12.3	-3.3
Canada	267	5.6	5.1	14.2	4.9	7.3	8.1	-5.7
United States	1352	8.1	8.6	13.7	11.8	10.5	13.4	-2.7

Table III.15

Merchandise exports and imports of Canada and the United States, 2001

(Billion dollars and percentage)

	Value	Annual percentage change							
		Value				Volume			
	2001	1990-01	1999	2000	2001	1990-01	1999	2000	2001
Exports									
North America	991	6	4	14	-6	6.0	6.0	9.5	-5.0
Canada	260	7	11	16	-6	7.5	11.0	9.0	-3.5
United States	731	6	2	13	-6	5.5	4.5	9.5	-5.5
Imports									
North America	1408	7	11	18	-6	7.5	11.0	11.5	-3.5
Canada	227	6	7	11	-7	7.5	11.0	13.0	-5.5
United States	1180	8	12	19	-6	7.5	11.5	11.5	-3.0

Table III.16

Merchandise trade of Canada by region and economy, 2001

(Billion dollars and percentage)

	Exports						Imports a				
Destination	Value	Share		Annual percentage change		Origin	Value	Share		Annual percentage change	
	2001	1990	2001	2000	2001		2001	1990	2001	2000	2001
Region						Region					
World	259.90	100.0	100.0	16	-6	World	221.35	100.0	100.0	11	-8
North America	226.63	75.1	87.2	18	-6	North America	140.88	64.6	63.6	7	-9
Asia	13.45	10.9	5.2	14	-9	Asia	31.37	14.4	14.2	18	-10
Western Europe	12.82	9.8	4.9	-4	-7	Western Europe	28.25	14.5	12.8	17	-3
Latin America	4.49	1.8	1.7	10	7	Latin America	12.16	3.4	5.5	24	-2
Middle East	1.06	0.7	0.4	15	-12	Africa	1.49	0.8	0.7	35	-20
Africa	1.00	0.8	0.4	-3	-5	Middle East	1.65	0.7	0.7	110	-4
C./E. Europe/						C./E. Europe/					
Baltic States/CIS	0.45	0.8	0.2	4	6	Baltic States/CIS	0.95	0.4	0.4	29	-22
Economy						Economy					
United States	226.59	75.0	87.2	18	-6	United States	140.87	64.6	63.6	7	-9
European Union (15)	11.80	8.5	4.5	-5	-7	European Union (15)	24.75	12.7	11.2	13	0
Japan	5.28	5.5	2.0	7	-13	Japan	9.45	7.0	4.3	10	-15
China	2.73	1.1	1.1	40	9	China	8.21	1.0	3.7	26	8
Mexico	1.75	0.4	0.7	25	28	Mexico	7.82	1.3	3.5	27	-4
Above 5	248.14	90.6	95.5	16	-6	Above 5	191.10	86.6	86.3	9	-7
Korea, Rep. of	1.28	1.1	0.5	13	-15	Korea, Rep. of	2.97	1.7	1.3	44	-14
Hong Kong, China	0.76	0.5	0.3	20	-13	Taipei, Chinese	2.85	1.6	1.3	8	-15
Australia	0.69	0.6	0.3	23	-13	Malaysia	1.22	0.3	0.6	21	-27
Taipei, Chinese	0.64	0.5	0.2	0	-17	Thailand	1.09	0.3	0.5	11	-3
Norway	0.64	0.4	0.2	3	24	Australia	1.04	0.6	0.5	28	0
Brazil	0.59	0.3	0.2	3	-18	Brazil	0.99	0.6	0.4	10	-2
Venezuela	0.52	0.2	0.2	21	23	Switzerland	0.91	0.5	0.4	11	-4
India	0.42	0.2	0.2	18	27	Venezuela	0.87	0.4	0.4	39	-8
Iran, Islamic Rep. of	0.33	0.2	0.1	21	-26	Hong Kong, China	0.79	0.8	0.4	11	-19
Indonesia	0.30	0.2	0.1	29	-37	India	0.75	0.2	0.3	21	-10
Thailand	0.29	0.3	0.1	23	16	Algeria	0.74	0.0	0.3	91	-12
Cuba	0.26	0.1	0.1	-17	15	Singapore	0.73	0.4	0.3	12	-22
Singapore	0.25	0.3	0.1	0	1	Philippines	0.63	0.1	0.3	34	-33
Chile	0.24	0.1	0.1	23	-21	Indonesia	0.62	0.1	0.3	3	3
Colombia	0.23	0.1	0.1	19	14	Iraq	0.56	0.1	0.3	319	22
Israel	0.22	0.1	0.1	5	7	Saudi Arabia	0.52	0.5	0.2	113	-16
Malaysia	0.22	0.2	0.1	-3	-19	Chile	0.41	0.1	0.2	32	10
Philippines	0.22	0.1	0.1	32	-15	Israel	0.40	...	0.2	35	0
Switzerland	0.22	0.7	0.1	5	-37	New Zealand	0.34	0.2	0.2	40	-3
Saudi Arabia	0.21	0.2	0.1	9	-3	South Africa	0.29	0.1	0.1	-19	-14
Algeria	0.19	0.2	0.1	3	-42	Colombia	0.27	0.1	0.1	19	20
Russian Fed.	0.19	0.0	0.1	11	40	Cuba	0.23	0.1	0.1	33	-15
Morocco	0.16	0.2	0.1	35	2	Russian Fed.	0.23	0.0	0.1	10	-48
New Zealand	0.14	0.1	0.1	-7	9	Argentina	0.23	0.1	0.1	17	-6
United Arab Emirates	0.13	0.0	0.1	25	-12	Jamaica	0.21	0.1	0.1	-1	58
Above 30	257.49	97.7	99.1	-	-	Above 30	211.00	95.5	95.3	-	-

a Imports are valued f.o.b.

Table III.17

Merchandise trade of the United States by region and economy, 2001

(Billion dollars and percentage)

Destination	Exports					Origin	Imports				
	Value	Share		Annual percentage change			Value	Share		Annual percentage change	
	2001	1990	2001	2000	2001		2001	1990	2001	2000	2001
Region						Region					
World	730.8	100.0	100.0	13	-6	World	1180.2	100.0	100.0	19	-6
Asia	193.5	30.2	26.5	17	-10	Asia	428.7	39.5	36.3	16	-10
Western Europe	175.1	28.7	24.0	9	-3	Western Europe	246.0	21.9	20.8	13	-1
North America	164.1	21.1	22.5	8	-7	North America	220.2	18.1	18.7	16	-5
Latin America	159.3	13.7	21.8	20	-6	Latin America	204.5	13.0	17.3	24	-5
Middle East	19.6	2.9	2.7	-9	2	Middle East	38.8	3.9	3.3	52	-5
Africa	12.4	2.0	1.7	11	13	Africa	26.8	3.3	2.3	62	-8
C./E. Europe/ Baltic States/CIS	6.9	1.1	0.9	9	12	C./E. Europe/ Baltic States/CIS	15.1	0.5	1.3	39	-11
Economy						Economy					
Canada	163.7	21.1	22.4	8	-7	European Union (15)	226.1	20.0	19.2	13	0
European Union (15)	159.4	26.3	21.8	9	-3	Canada	220.1	18.1	18.7	16	-5
Mexico	101.5	7.2	13.9	28	-9	Mexico	132.8	6.0	11.3	24	-3
Japan	57.6	12.3	7.9	14	-12	Japan	129.7	18.2	11.0	12	-14
Korea, Rep. of	22.2	3.7	3.0	22	-20	China	109.4	3.1	9.3	23	2
Above 5	504.5	70.6	69.0	13	-8	Above 5	818.1	65.4	69.3	16	-4
China	19.2	1.2	2.6	24	18	Korea, Rep. of	36.5	3.7	3.1	28	-13
Taipei, Chinese	18.2	2.9	2.5	28	-26	Taipei, Chinese	34.8	4.6	2.9	15	-18
Singapore	17.7	2.0	2.4	10	-1	Malaysia	23.1	1.1	2.0	19	-13
Brazil	15.9	1.3	2.2	16	4	Venezuela	16.1	1.9	1.4	64	-18
Hong Kong, China	14.1	1.7	1.9	16	-4	Thailand	15.6	1.1	1.3	15	-10
Australia	10.9	2.2	1.5	5	-12	Singapore	15.3	2.0	1.3	5	-22
Switzerland	9.8	1.3	1.3	19	-1	Brazil	15.3	1.7	1.3	23	4
Malaysia	9.4	0.9	1.3	21	-15	Saudi Arabia	14.4	2.1	1.2	69	-4
Philippines	7.7	0.6	1.0	22	-13	Israel	12.2	0.7	1.0	32	-8
Israel	7.5	0.8	1.0	1	-3	Philippines	11.8	0.7	1.0	13	-19
Thailand	6.0	0.8	0.8	33	-10	Indonesia	10.9	0.7	0.9	9	-3
Saudi Arabia	6.0	1.0	0.8	-21	-4	India	10.3	0.7	0.9	18	-9
Venezuela	5.7	0.8	0.8	3	2	Hong Kong, China	10.1	1.9	0.9	9	-16
Dominican Republic	4.4	0.4	0.6	9	0	Switzerland	10.0	1.1	0.8	6	-7
Argentina	3.9	0.3	0.5	-5	-16	Nigeria	9.2	1.2	0.8	139	-17
Egypt	3.8	0.6	0.5	10	13	Australia	6.8	0.9	0.6	22	0
India	3.8	0.6	0.5	-1	3	Russian Fed.	6.5	-	0.6	34	-19
Colombia	3.6	0.5	0.5	4	-2	Iraq	6.3	0.6	0.5	44	-3
Chile	3.1	0.4	0.4	12	-9	Colombia	6.1	0.7	0.5	11	-18
Turkey	3.1	0.6	0.4	17	-17	Norway	5.5	0.4	0.5	41	-8
South Africa	3.0	0.5	0.4	9	-4	South Africa	4.6	0.4	0.4	24	5
Russian Fed.	2.7	0.0	0.4	26	18	Dominican Republic	4.3	0.4	0.4	2	-4
United Arab Emirates	2.6	0.3	0.4	-16	15	Chile	4.1	0.3	0.3	12	11
Indonesia	2.5	0.5	0.3	31	-2	Angola	3.3	0.4	0.3	46	-13
Costa Rica	2.5	0.3	0.3	3	2	Argentina	3.3	0.3	0.3	19	-2
Above 30	691.6	93.0	94.6	-	-	Above 30	1114.1	94.8	94.4	-	-

Table III.18

Merchandise exports of NAFTA countries by destination, 1990-01

(Billion dollars and percentage)

Origin	Destination	United States	Canada	Mexico	NAFTA (3)	All other countries	World
Value							
United States	1990	-	83.0	28.3	111.3	282.3	393.6
	1995	-	126.0	46.3	172.3	412.4	584.7
	1999	-	163.9	87.0	250.9	441.9	692.8
	2000	-	176.4	111.7	288.1	493.0	781.1
	2001	-	163.7	101.5	265.2	465.6	730.8
Canada	1990	95.2	-	0.5	95.7	31.9	127.6
	1995	152.8	-	0.8	153.6	38.6	192.2
	1999	205.0	-	1.1	206.1	32.3	238.4
	2000	241.6	-	1.4	243.0	33.6	276.6
	2001	226.6	-	1.8	228.4	31.5	259.9
Mexico	1990	32.3	0.2	-	32.6	8.2	40.7
	1995	66.3	2.0	-	68.3	11.2	79.5
	1999	120.5	2.4	-	122.9	13.5	136.4
	2000	147.2	3.3	-	150.5	15.9	166.4
	2001	140.7	3.1	-	143.8	14.7	158.5
NAFTA (3)	1990	127.6	83.2	28.9	239.6	322.3	561.9
	1995	219.1	128.0	47.1	394.3	462.2	856.5
	1999	325.5	166.3	88.1	579.9	487.7	1067.6
	2000	388.8	179.7	113.1	681.6	542.5	1224.1
	2001	367.3	166.8	103.3	637.4	511.8	1149.2
Share							
United States	1990	-	14.8	5.0	19.8	50.2	70.0
	2001	-	14.2	8.8	23.1	40.5	63.6
Canada	1990	16.9	-	0.1	17.0	5.7	22.7
	2001	19.7	-	0.2	19.9	2.7	22.6
Mexico	1990	5.8	0.0	-	5.8	1.5	7.2
	2001	12.2	0.3	-	12.5	1.3	13.8
NAFTA (3)	1990	22.7	14.8	5.1	42.6	57.4	100.0
	2001	32.0	14.5	9.0	55.5	44.5	100.0
Annual percentage change							
United States	1990-01	-	7	14	9	5	6
	2000	-	8	28	15	12	13
	2001	-	-7	-9	-8	-6	-6
Canada	1990-01	9	-	13	9	0	7
	2000	18	-	27	18	4	16
	2001	-6	-	29	-6	-6	-6
Mexico	1990-01	16	30	-	16	6	15
	2000	22	38	-	22	18	22
	2001	-4	-6	-	-4	-8	-5
NAFTA (3)	1990-01	11	7	14	10	5	7
	2000	19	8	28	18	11	15
	2001	-6	-7	-9	-6	-6	-6

Table III.19

Trade in commercial services of Canada, 2001

(Billion dollars and percentage)

	Exports			Imports		
	Value	Share		Value	Share	
	2001	1995	2001	2001	1995	2001
Total commercial services	35.6	100.0	100.0	41.5	100.0	100.0
Transportation	6.8	20.7	19.1	9.2	24.1	22.1
Sea transport	1.6	5.7	4.4	3.4	9.0	8.2
Air transport	3.1	8.3	8.6	4.1	10.2	9.9
Other transport	2.2	6.6	6.1	1.7	4.8	4.0
Travel	10.8	31.1	30.3	11.6	31.1	28.1
Other commercial services	18.1	48.2	50.7	20.7	44.8	49.8
Communication services	1.2	5.0	3.4	1.3	3.9	3.1
Construction services	0.2	0.4	0.5	0.1	0.6	0.2
Insurance services	2.0	8.9	5.6	2.9	8.4	6.9
Financial services	1.5	2.5	4.3	1.7	2.9	4.0
Computer and information services	1.4	4.0	4.0	0.9	1.5	2.1
Royalties and licence fees	1.5	1.5	4.2	3.5	5.7	8.4
Other business services	8.9	23.0	24.9	8.9	18.8	21.4
Personal, cultural, and recreational services	1.4	2.9	3.8	1.5	3.0	3.6

Table III.20

Trade in commercial services of the United States, 2001

(Billion dollars and percentage)

	Exports			Imports		
	Value	Share		Value	Share	
	2001	1995	2001	2001	1995	2001
Total commercial services	263.4	100.0	100.0	187.7	100.0	100.0
Transportation	46.1	22.7	17.5	61.7	32.3	32.8
Sea transport	4.7	2.8	1.8	19.4	9.2	10.3
Air transport	22.6	11.2	8.6	26.8	13.5	14.3
Other transport	18.8	8.6	7.1	15.5	9.6	8.3
Travel	88.7	37.7	33.7	61.6	35.7	32.8
Other commercial services	128.6	39.7	48.8	64.5	32.0	34.3
Communication services a	4.4	1.8	1.7	5.5	6.0	2.9
Construction services a	5.5	1.3	2.1	0.2	0.3	0.1
Insurance services a	3.2	0.7	1.2	1.4	4.1	0.7
Financial services a	14.5	3.5	5.5	3.9	1.9	2.1
Computer and information services a	5.1	1.2	2.0	0.7	0.2	0.4
Royalties and licence fees	38.9	15.3	14.8	16.4	5.4	8.7
Other business services	49.6	14.6	18.8	36.3	14.0	19.3
Personal, cultural, and recreational services	7.4	1.3	2.8	0.2	0.1	0.1

a Excludes transactions between affiliates, which are recorded under "Other business services".

3. Latin America

Table III.21

Merchandise trade of Latin America, 2001

(Billion dollars and percentage)

	Exports	Imports
Value	347	380
Share in world merchandise trade	5.8	6.3
Annual percentage change		
Value		
1980-85	0	-7
1985-90	6	10
1990-01	8	11
1999	7	-3
2000	20	16
2001	-3	-2
Volume		
1980-85	5.5	-6.5
1985-90	5.0	6.0
1990-01	8.0	10.0
1999	5.0	-0.5
2000	8.5	12.5
2001	2.0	-1.0

Table III.22

Merchandise trade of Latin America by region and by major product group, 2001

(Billion dollars and percentage)

	Value	Share	
	Exports	Exports	Imports
Total	347	100.0	100.0
Region			
North America	211	60.7	48.9
Latin America	59	17.1	17.7
Western Europe	42	12.2	17.2
C./E. Europe/Baltic States/CIS	3	0.8	1.8
Africa	4	1.1	1.5
Middle East	4	1.1	0.9
Asia	22	6.4	12.0
Product group			
Agricultural products	63	18.1	9.3
Mining products	75	21.5	11.0
Manufactures	208	59.9	77.3

Note: Import shares are derived from the Secretariat's network of world merchandise trade by product and region.

Chart III.7

Merchandise trade of Latin America, 1990-01

(Billion dollars)

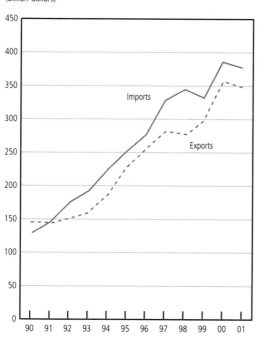

Chart III.8

Share of Latin America in world merchandise trade, 1990-01

(Percentage based on value data)

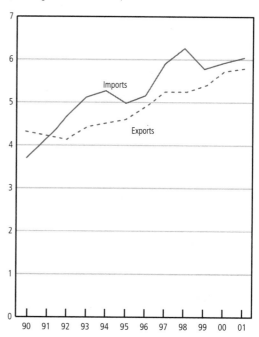

Table III.23

Merchandise exports of Latin America by product, 2001

(Billion dollars and percentage)

	Value	Share in exports of Latin America		Share in world exports		Annual percentage change			
	2001	1990	2001	1990	2001	1990-01	1999	2000	2001
Total merchandise exports	347.2	100.0	100.0	4.3	5.8	9	7	20	-3
Agricultural products	62.7	27.0	18.1	9.6	11.5	5	-8	1	2
Food	55.1	24.0	15.9	11.2	12.6	5	-9	0	3
Raw materials	7.6	3.0	2.2	4.4	6.9	6	3	14	-3
Mining products	74.7	33.3	21.5	10.0	9.4	4	22	45	-11
Ores and other minerals	10.3	5.1	3.0	14.3	16.3	3	-2	16	0
Fuels	54.0	22.7	15.6	9.2	8.8	5	36	58	-14
Non-ferrous metals	10.3	5.4	3.0	10.9	9.3	3	2	19	-9
Manufactures	207.8	38.0	59.9	2.3	4.6	14	8	19	-2
Iron and steel	7.2	4.2	2.1	5.8	5.6	2	-16	16	-12
Chemicals	16.6	4.7	4.8	2.3	2.8	9	-1	17	-2
Other semi-manufactures	18.3	4.8	5.3	2.7	4.2	10	3	13	2
Machinery and transport equipment	120.9	16.3	34.8	2.0	4.9	18	13	21	-1
Automotive products	39.3	5.0	11.3	2.3	7.0	18	4	19	3
Office and telecom equipment	39.1	3.7	11.3	1.8	4.7	22	27	25	2
Other machinery and transport equipment	42.5	7.6	12.2	1.9	4.0	14	12	20	-6
Textiles	4.0	1.5	1.2	2.2	2.8	6	0	10	-13
Clothing	20.1	2.4	5.8	3.3	10.3	19	9	15	-5
Other consumer goods	20.6	4.0	5.9	2.0	3.9	13	6	19	-1

Table III.24

Merchandise exports of Latin America by destination, 2001

(Billion dollars and percentage)

	Value	Share		Annual percentage change			
	2001	1990	2001	1990-01	1999	2000	2001
World	347.2	100.0	100.0	8	7	20	-3
North America	210.9	45.4	60.7	11	17	24	-5
Intra-Latin America	59.3	14.0	17.1	10	-12	21	-2
Western Europe	42.3	21.2	12.2	3	0	6	-3
European Union (15)	39.6	20.2	11.4	3	0	5	-2
Asia	22.3	9.5	6.4	4	3	14	5
Japan	6.6	5.1	1.9	-1	6	9	-13
China	5.0	0.8	1.4	14	-21	74	28
Other	10.7	3.7	3.1	6	8	4	10
Middle East	4.0	1.6	1.1	5	-16	8	33
Africa	3.7	1.4	1.1	5	-19	2	29
C./E. Europe/Baltic States/CIS	2.7	4.5	0.8	-8	-12	-9	17
Inter-regional trade	285.8	83.8	82.3	8	12	20	-3

Table III.25

Leading merchandise exporters and importers in Latin America, 2001

(Billion dollars and percentage)

	Value	Share				Annual percentage change			
	2001	1980	1990	1995	2001	1990-01	1999	2000	2001
Exporters									
Latin America	347.2	100.0	100.0	100.0	100.0	8	7	20	-3
Mexico	158.5	16.4	27.7	34.7	45.7	13	16	22	-5
maquiladoras	76.9	2.3	9.4	13.6	22.1	17	20	24	-3
Brazil	58.2	18.3	21.4	20.3	16.8	6	-6	15	6
Venezuela	27.4	17.5	11.9	8.0	7.9	5	17	58	-10
Argentina	26.7	7.3	8.4	9.1	7.7	7	-12	13	1
Chile	17.4	4.3	5.7	7.0	5.0	7	5	16	-4
Colombia	12.3	3.6	4.6	4.4	3.5	6	7	13	-6
Peru	7.1	3.6	2.2	2.4	2.0	7	6	15	1
Dominican Republic	5.3	1.1	1.5	1.6	1.5	9	3	12	-7
Costa Rica	5.0	0.9	1.0	1.5	1.4	12	19	-11	-15
Trinidad and Tobago	4.7	3.7	1.4	1.1	1.4	8	24	52	10
Ecuador	4.5	2.3	1.8	1.9	1.3	5	6	11	-9
El Salvador	2.9	0.9	0.4	0.7	0.8	16	2	17	-3
Guatemala	2.5	1.4	0.8	0.9	0.7	7	-7	12	-9
Uruguay	2.1	1.0	1.2	0.9	0.6	2	-19	3	-10
Netherlands Antilles	1.8	4.7	1.2	0.7	0.5	0	24	28	-1
Importers									
Latin America	379.6	100.0	100.0	100.0	100.0	11	-3	16	-2
Mexico	176.2	17.9	33.4	29.8	46.4	14	14	23	-2
maquiladoras	57.6	1.4	7.9	10.3	15.2	17	18	22	-7
Brazil	58.3	20.2	17.3	21.1	15.3	9	-15	13	-15
Argentina	20.3	8.5	3.1	7.9	5.4	16	-19	-1	-9
Venezuela	18.0	9.6	5.6	5.0	4.7	9	-11	15	-6
Chile	17.2	4.7	5.9	6.2	4.5	8	-19	20	0
Colombia	12.8	3.8	4.3	5.4	3.4	8	-27	8	-8
Dominican Republic	8.8	1.6	2.3	2.0	2.3	10	6	18	10
Peru	8.6	2.0	2.7	3.6	2.3	9	-18	9	-5
Costa Rica	6.6	1.2	1.5	1.6	1.7	11	1	1	11
Guatemala	5.6	1.3	1.3	1.3	1.5	12	-6	9	3
Ecuador	5.3	1.8	1.4	1.6	1.4	10	-46	23	1
El Salvador	5.0	0.8	1.0	1.3	1.3	13	3	21	-15
Cuba	4.9	5.3	3.5	1.1	1.3	1	3	13	-7
Trinidad and Tobago	3.6	2.6	1.0	0.7	0.9	10	-9	21	42
Jamaica	3.3	0.9	1.5	1.1	0.9	5	-4	11	2
Memorandum item:									
ANDEAN (5)									
Exports	53.7	27.8	21.2	17.2	15.5	5	11	34	-7
Imports	46.5	17.8	14.5	16.2	12.2	9	-22	12	10
MERCOSUR (4)									
Exports	87.9	26.9	31.6	30.7	25.3	6	-9	14	4
Imports	83.8	30.6	22.5	31.4	22.1	10	-17	8	-6

Table III.26

Merchandise exports of MERCOSUR countries by region, 1990-01

(Million dollars and percentage)

Origin	Destination	MERCOSUR (4)	All other regions			World
			Total	Latin America	Other regions	
Value						
Argentina	1990	1833	10520	1577	8943	12353
	1995	6780	14187	3119	11068	20967
	2000	8402	18007	4262	13745	26409
	2001	7448	19207	4852	14355	26655
Brazil	1990	1320	30094	2399	27695	31414
	1995	6154	40352	4624	35728	46506
	2000	7762	47324	6114	41210	55086
	2001	6364	51859	7141	44718	58223
Paraguay	1990	379	580	123	457	959
	1995	528	391	73	318	919
	2000	553	316	121	195	869
	2001	519	470	193	277	989
Uruguay	1990	595	1098	94	1004	1693
	1995	995	1111	130	981	2106
	2000	1024	1271	224	1047	2295
	2001	840	1220	211	1009	2060
MERCOSUR (4)	1990	4127	42292	4193	38099	46419
	1995	14457	56041	7946	48095	70498
	2000	17741	66918	10721	56197	84659
	2001	15171	72756	12397	60359	87927
Share						
Argentina	1990	3.9	22.7	3.4	19.3	26.6
	2001	8.5	21.8	5.5	16.3	30.3
Brazil	1990	2.8	64.8	5.2	59.7	67.7
	2001	7.2	59.0	8.1	50.9	66.2
Paraguay	1990	0.8	1.2	0.3	1.0	2.1
	2001	0.6	0.5	0.2	0.3	1.1
Uruguay	1990	1.3	2.4	0.2	2.2	3.6
	2001	1.0	1.4	0.2	1.1	2.3
MERCOSUR (4)	1990	8.9	91.1	9.0	82.1	100.0
	2001	17.3	82.7	14.1	68.6	100.0
Annual percentage change						
Argentina	1990-01	14	6	11	4	7
	2000	19	11	25	7	13
	2001	-11	7	14	4	1
Brazil	1990-01	15	5	10	4	6
	2000	15	15	30	13	15
	2001	-18	10	17	9	6
Paraguay	1990-01	3	-2	4	-4	0
	2000	80	-27	137	-49	17
	2001	-6	49	60	42	14
Uruguay	1990-01	3	1	8	0	2
	2000	2	3	18	1	3
	2001	-18	-4	-6	-4	-10
MERCOSUR (4)	1990-01	13	5	10	4	6
	2000	17	13	29	11	14
	2001	-14	9	16	7	4

Table III.27

Merchandise imports of MERCOSUR countries by region, 1990-01

(Million dollars and percentage)

| Destination | Origin | MERCOSUR (4) | All other regions | | | World |
			Total	Latin America	Other regions	
Value						
Argentina	1990	833	3243	516	2727	4076
	1995	4603	15519	1286	14233	20122
	2000	6881	18362	1364	16998	25243
	2001	5910	14401	1198	13203	20311
Brazil	1990	2443	20081	1551	18530	22524
	1995	7280	46503	4046	42457	53783
	2000	8182	50350	4322	46028	58532
	2001	7359	50906	3413	47493	58265
Paraguay	1990	405	947	64	883	1352
	1995	1237	1907	126	1781	3144
	2000	1132	1061	96	965	2193
	2001	1202	943	130	813	2145
Uruguay	1990	560	783	137	646	1343
	1995	1321	1546	176	1370	2867
	2000	1518	1948	275	1673	3466
	2001	1350	1711	305	1406	3061
MERCOSUR (4)	1990	4241	25054	2268	22786	29295
	1995	14441	65475	5634	59841	79916
	2000	17713	71721	6057	65664	89434
	2001	15821	67961	5046	62915	83782
Share						
Argentina	1990	2.8	11.1	1.8	9.3	13.9
	2001	7.1	17.2	1.4	15.8	24.2
Brazil	1990	8.3	68.5	5.3	63.3	76.9
	2001	8.8	60.8	4.1	56.7	69.5
Paraguay	1990	1.4	3.2	0.2	3.0	4.6
	2001	1.4	1.1	0.2	1.0	2.6
Uruguay	1990	1.9	2.7	0.5	2.2	4.6
	2001	1.6	2.0	0.4	1.7	3.7
MERCOSUR (4)	1990	14.5	85.5	7.7	77.8	100.0
	2001	18.9	81.1	6.0	75.1	100.0
Annual percentage change						
Argentina	1990-00	19	15	8	15	16
	2000	9	-4	-7	-4	-1
	2001	-14	-22	-12	-22	-20
Brazil	1990-00	11	9	7	9	9
	2000	16	13	42	11	13
	2001	-10	1	-21	3	0
Paraguay	1990-00	10	0	7	-1	4
	2000	18	12	140	6	15
	2001	6	-11	35	-16	-2
Uruguay	1990-00	8	7	8	7	8
	2000	4	3	8	2	3
	2001	-11	-12	11	-16	-12
MERCOSUR (4)	1990-00	13	9	8	10	10
	2000	12	8	26	6	8
	2001	-11	-5	-17	-4	-6

Table III.28

Merchandise exports of ANDEAN countries by region, 1990-01

(Million dollars and percentage)

Destination / Origin		ANDEAN (5)	All other regions Total	Latin America	Other regions	World
Value						
Bolivia	1990	60	866	357	509	926
	1995	222	878	213	665	1100
	2000	311	919	333	586	1230
	2001	367	918	428	490	1285
Colombia	1990	373	6393	802	5591	6766
	1995	1939	8186	1064	7122	10125
	2000	2170	10870	1682	9188	13040
	2001	2757	9500	1619	7881	12257
Ecuador	1990	189	2525	587	1938	2714
	1995	359	3948	612	3336	4307
	2000	662	4265	862	3403	4927
	2001	836	3659	662	2997	4495
Peru	1990	214	3016	283	2733	3230
	1995	405	5170	548	4622	5575
	2000	448	6580	823	5757	7028
	2001	514	6578	852	5726	7092
Venezuela	1990	489	17008	2278	14730	17497
	1995	1887	16570	4714	11856	18457
	2000	1589	30213	6515	23698	31802
	2001	1402	26007	5073	20934	27409
ANDEAN (5)	1990	1325	29808	4307	25501	31133
	1995	4812	34752	7151	27601	39564
	2000	5180	52847	10215	42632	58027
	2001	5876	46662	8634	38028	52538
Share						
Bolivia	1990	0.2	2.8	1.1	1.6	3.0
	2001	0.7	1.7	0.8	0.9	2.4
Colombia	1990	1.2	20.5	2.6	18.0	21.7
	2001	5.2	18.1	3.1	15.0	23.3
Ecuador	1990	0.6	8.1	1.9	6.2	8.7
	2001	1.6	7.0	1.3	5.7	8.6
Peru	1990	0.7	9.7	0.9	8.8	10.4
	2001	1.0	12.5	1.6	10.9	13.5
Venezuela	1990	1.6	54.6	7.3	47.3	56.2
	2001	2.7	49.5	9.7	39.8	52.2
ANDEAN (5)	1990	4.3	95.7	13.8	81.9	100.0
	2001	11.2	88.8	16.4	72.4	100.0
Annual percentage change						
Bolivia	1990-01	18	1	2	0	3
	2000	6	21	40	13	17
	2001	18	0	29	-16	4
Colombia	1990-01	20	4	7	3	6
	2000	33	9	32	6	13
	2001	27	-13	-4	-14	-6
Ecuador	1990-01	14	3	1	4	5
	2000	38	7	20	5	11
	2001	26	-14	-23	-12	-9
Peru	1990-01	8	7	11	7	7
	2000	29	14	30	12	15
	2001	15	0	4	-1	1
Venezuela	1990-01	10	4	8	3	4
	2000	30	59	15	78	58
	2001	-12	-14	-22	-12	-14
ANDEAN (5)	1990-01	15	4	7	4	5
	2000	30	34	20	38	34
	2001	13	-12	-15	-11	-9

Table III.29

Merchandise imports of ANDEAN countries by region, 1990-01

(Million dollars and percentage)

Destination	Origin	ANDEAN (5)	All other regions			World
			Total	Latin America	Other regions	
Value						
Bolivia	1990	30	657	301	356	687
	1995	111	1313	431	882	1424
	2000	157	1673	761	912	1830
	2001	179	1545	780	765	1724
Colombia	1990	474	5116	732	4384	5590
	1995	1845	12008	1604	10404	13853
	2000	1613	9926	1609	8317	11539
	2001	1401	11433	1870	9563	12834
Ecuador	1990	119	1742	302	1440	1861
	1995	705	3447	661	2786	4152
	2000	839	2882	681	2201	3721
	2001	1182	4117	883	3234	5299
Peru a	1990	515	2385	440	1945	2900
	1995	1190	6394	1439	4955	7584
	2000	1397	6018	1454	4564	7415
	2001	1150	6166	1554	4612	7316
Venezuela a	1990	213	6388	697	5691	6601
	1995	1017	9774	1638	8136	10791
	2000	1391	13193	2589	10604	14584
	2001	1898	14538	3243	11295	16436
ANDEAN (5)	1990	1351	16288	2472	13816	17639
	1995	4868	32936	5773	27163	37804
	2000	5397	33692	7094	26598	39089
	2001	5810	37799	8330	29469	43609
Share						
Bolivia	1990	0.2	3.7	1.7	2.0	3.9
	2001	0.4	3.5	1.8	1.8	4.0
Colombia	1990	2.7	29.0	4.1	24.9	31.7
	2001	3.2	26.2	4.3	21.9	29.4
Ecuador	1990	0.7	9.9	1.7	8.2	10.6
	2001	2.7	9.4	2.0	7.4	12.2
Peru	1990	2.9	13.5	2.5	11.0	16.4
	2001	2.6	14.1	3.6	10.6	16.8
Venezuela	1990	1.2	36.2	4.0	32.3	37.4
	2001	4.4	33.3	7.4	25.9	37.7
ANDEAN (5)	1990	7.7	92.3	14.0	78.3	100.0
	2001	13.3	86.7	19.1	67.6	100.0
Annual percentage change						
Bolivia	1990-01	18	8	9	7	9
	2000	2	4	11	0	4
	2001	14	-8	2	-16	-6
Colombia	1990-01	10	8	9	7	8
	2000	12	8	17	6	8
	2001	-13	15	16	15	11
Ecuador	1990-01	23	8	10	8	10
	2000	37	20	30	17	23
	2001	41	43	30	47	42
Peru	1990-01	8	9	12	8	9
	2000	35	4	24	-1	9
	2001	-18	2	7	1	-1
Venezuela	1990-01	22	8	15	6	9
	2000	48	5	34	-1	8
	2001	36	10	25	7	13
ANDEAN (5)	1990-01	14	8	12	7	9
	2000	29	7	24	3	9
	2001	8	12	17	11	12

a Imports are valued f.o.b.

Table III.30

Leading exporters and importers of commercial services in Latin America, 2001

(Billion dollars and percentage)

	Value	Share		Annual percentage change			
	2001	1990	2001	1990-01	1999	2000	2001
Exporters							
Latin America	58.2	100.0	100.0	6	1	11	-3
Mexico	12.5	24.3	21.5	5	1	17	-7
Brazil	8.7	12.5	15.0	8	-3	29	-1
Chile	3.9	6.0	6.8	7	-8	4	2
Argentina	3.9	7.6	6.7	5	-4	2	-11
Cuba a	3.0	2.1	5.1	15	…	…	…
Dominican Republic	2.9	3.7	5.0	9	14	14	-7
Colombia	2.1	5.2	3.7	3	-4	10	7
Jamaica	1.9	3.3	3.2	6	12	2	-6
Bahamas	1.9	4.9	3.2	2	18	12	-7
Costa Rica	1.8	2.0	3.1	11	13	14	6
Panama	1.8	3.1	3.1	6	-1	7	-1
Netherlands Antilles	1.6	3.8	2.7	3	-5	1	5
Peru	1.4	2.4	2.5	7	-12	0	-2
Uruguay	1.2	1.5	2.0	9	-6	7	-11
Venezuela	1.1	3.8	1.8	-1	-14	-5	-1
Importers							
Latin America	70.9	100.0	100.0	7	-4	12	0
Mexico	16.5	29.0	23.3	5	12	19	-1
Brazil	15.8	19.4	22.3	8	-15	19	0
Argentina	7.9	8.3	11.1	10	-6	3	-8
Chile	4.5	5.7	6.4	8	-3	10	4
Venezuela	4.3	6.9	6.1	6	-28	14	7
Colombia	3.5	4.9	4.9	7	-8	5	7
Peru	2.1	3.1	3.0	7	-7	3	-3
Jamaica	1.5	1.9	2.1	7	2	9	5
Ecuador	1.4	2.2	2.0	6	-8	8	16
Costa Rica	1.3	1.6	1.8	8	6	7	2
Dominican Republic	1.3	1.3	1.8	10	-6	9	-6
Panama	1.1	1.9	1.5	5	-7	0	0
El Salvador	1.1	0.9	1.5	12	11	16	14
Cuba a	0.9	0.9	1.2	10	…	…	…
Bahamas	0.8	1.5	1.2	4	-4	3	-9

a Includes Secretariat estimates.

4. *Western Europe*

Table III.31

Merchandise trade of Western Europe, 2001

(Billion dollars and percentage)

	Exports	Imports
Value	2485	2524
Share in world merchandise trade	41.5	40.3
Annual percentage change		
Value		
1980-85	-1	-3
1985-90	16	16
1990-01	4	4
1999	0	2
2000	4	6
2001	-1	-3
Volume		
1980-85	4.0	2.0
1985-90	4.5	7.0
1990-01	4.5	4.0
1999	3.0	4.5
2000	9.0	8.0
2001	-1.0	-3.0

Table III.32

Merchandise trade of Western Europe by region and by major product group, 2001

(Billion dollars and percentage)

	Value		Share	
	Exports	Imports	Exports	Imports
Total	2485	2524	100.0	100.0
Region				
North America	255	203	10.2	8.0
Latin America	58	49	2.3	1.9
Western Europe	1677	1675	67.5	66.4
C./E. Europe/Baltic States/CIS	147	153	5.9	6.0
Africa	63	76	2.5	3.0
Middle East	65	44	2.6	1.7
Asia	195	286	7.9	11.3
Product group				
Agricultural products	228	250	9.2	9.9
Mining products	179	283	7.2	11.2
Manufactures	2010	1911	80.9	75.7

Chart III.9

Merchandise trade of Western Europe, 1990-01

(Billion dollars)

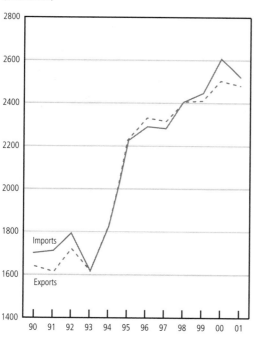

Chart III.10

Share of Western Europe in world merchandise trade, 1990-01

(Percentage based on value data)

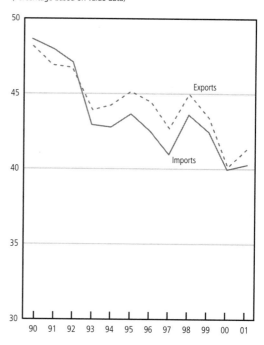

Table III.33

Merchandise exports of Western Europe by product, 2001

(Billion dollars and percentage)

	Value	Share in exports of Western Europe		Share in world exports		Annual percentage change			
	2001	1990	2001	1990	2001	1990-01	1999	2000	2001
Total merchandise exports	2485	100.0	100.0	48.2	41.5	4	2	4	-1
Agricultural products	228	11.4	9.2	45.2	41.6	2	-1	-4	-2
Food	192	9.4	7.7	48.6	43.9	2	-2	-6	0
Raw materials	36	2.1	1.4	34.3	32.4	0	6	6	-9
Mining products	179	7.2	7.2	24.2	22.7	4	12	40	-8
Ores and other minerals	16	0.9	0.6	26.9	24.5	1	1	10	-6
Fuels	120	4.3	4.8	19.4	19.5	5	21	56	-8
Non-ferrous metals	44	2.1	1.8	46.1	39.3	2	1	18	-7
Manufactures	2010	79.1	80.9	54.2	44.9	4	3	3	-1
Iron and steel	62	3.9	2.5	61.0	48.0	0	-14	9	-6
Chemicals	347	11.8	14.0	65.0	58.4	6	5	4	4
Other semi-manufactures	213	10.0	8.6	61.8	49.2	2	1	1	-3
Machinery and transport equipment	1040	37.2	41.9	50.2	42.4	5	6	4	-1
Automotive products	276	10.6	11.1	54.4	48.8	4	4	-1	0
Office and telecom equipment	248	5.8	10.0	32.0	29.9	9	10	15	-10
Other machinery and transport equipment	517	20.8	20.8	57.1	48.7	4	5	2	2
Textiles	57	3.4	2.3	53.1	38.7	0	-10	-4	-3
Clothing	56	2.9	2.3	43.6	28.9	2	-5	-5	1
Other consumer goods	234	10.0	9.4	54.5	44.5	3	3	1	-1

Table III.34

Merchandise imports of Western Europe by product, 2001

(Billion dollars and percentage)

	Value	Share in imports of Western Europe		Share in world imports		Annual percentage change			
	2001	1990	2001	1990	2001	1990-01	1999	2000	2001
Total merchandise imports	2524	100.0	100.0	48.6	40.3	4	2	6	-3
Agricultural products	250	13.1	9.9	50.3	42.1	1	-4	-3	-2
Food	201	10.0	8.0	50.3	42.5	2	-4	-6	0
Raw materials	49	3.1	1.9	50.3	40.9	-1	-3	9	-12
Mining products	283	13.0	11.2	43.3	33.6	2	8	44	-7
Ores and other minerals	28	1.7	1.1	50.4	39.4	0	-9	12	-8
Fuels	201	8.9	8.0	40.0	30.7	3	16	58	-7
Non-ferrous metals	53	2.4	2.1	54.9	46.8	3	-1	22	-7
Manufactures	1911	72.2	75.7	50.2	41.0	4	2	4	-3
Iron and steel	58	3.3	2.3	49.8	40.8	0	-16	12	-9
Chemicals	288	10.0	11.4	55.7	46.4	5	1	4	3
Other semi-manufactures	200	9.0	7.9	55.6	43.6	3	1	1	-3
Machinery and transport equipment	991	33.6	39.2	46.8	39.2	5	6	5	-5
Automotive products	246	9.5	9.7	50.1	42.4	4	3	-4	-1
Office and telecom equipment	302	8.0	12.0	45.2	35.4	8	5	16	-12
Other machinery and transport equipment	443	16.2	17.5	45.9	40.5	4	9	4	-2
Textiles	50	3.2	2.0	50.1	32.1	-1	-13	-4	-7
Clothing	85	3.6	3.4	55.2	41.5	3	-5	-3	-1
Other consumer goods	239	9.4	9.5	52.2	43.0	4	2	2	-1

Table III.35

Merchandise exports of Western Europe by destination, 2001

(Billion dollars and percentage)

	Value	Share		Annual percentage change		
	2001	1990	2001	1990-01	2000	2001
World	2485	100.0	100.0	4	4	-1
Intra-Western Europe	1677	71.4	67.5	3	2	-2
European Union (15)	1542	65.1	62.0	3	2	-1
North America	255	7.8	10.2	6	11	-1
United States	226	6.9	9.1	6	10	-3
Asia	195	7.3	7.9	5	11	-1
Japan	44	2.1	1.8	2	9	-4
China	28	0.5	1.1	12	13	16
Australia and New Zealand	17	0.8	0.7	3	-2	-3
Other	106	4.0	4.3	5	13	-3
C./E. Europe/Baltic States/CIS	147	3.8	5.9	8	9	12
Central and Eastern Europe	102	1.7	4.1	12	7	7
Russian Fed.	26	-	1.1	-	17	35
Baltic States	8	-	0.3	-	9	10
Middle East	65	2.8	2.6	3	5	5
Africa	63	3.3	2.5	1	-2	3
South Africa	12	0.5	0.5	4	5	2
Other Africa	51	3.0	2.1	0	-3	3
Latin America	58	1.8	2.3	6	5	0
Inter-regional trade	782	26.8	31.5	5	8	2

Table III.36

Merchandise imports of Western Europe by origin, 2001

(Billion dollars and percentage)

	Value	Share		Annual percentage change		
	2001	1990	2001	1990-01	2000	2001
World	2524	100.0	100.0	4	6	-3
Intra-Western Europe	1675	69.0	66.4	3	2	-2
European Union (15)	1546	63.2	61.3	3	1	-2
Asia	286	10.0	11.3	5	11	-9
Japan	72	4.3	2.8	0	5	-17
China	71	0.8	2.8	16	22	3
Australia and New Zealand	11	0.5	0.4	2	8	1
Other	132	4.3	5.2	6	10	-11
North America	203	8.2	8.0	3	9	-6
United States	184	7.3	7.3	4	8	-6
C./E. Europe/Baltic States/CIS	153	3.6	6.0	9	24	5
Central and Eastern Europe	92	1.6	3.7	12	12	10
Russian Fed.	42	-	1.7	-	50	-3
Baltic States	7	-	0.3	-	27	3
Africa	76	3.9	3.0	1	27	-2
South Africa	17	0.6	0.7	4	16	11
Other Africa	60	3.3	2.4	1	29	-5
Latin America	49	2.3	1.9	2	14	-5
Middle East	44	2.3	1.7	1	43	-17
Inter-regional trade	810	30.3	32.1	4	15	-5

Table III.37

Gross domestic product and trade in goods and services in Western Europe, 2001

(Billion dollars and percentage)

	Value	Annual percentage change in volume								
	GDP	GDP			Exports of goods and services			Imports of goods and services		
	2001	1990-01	2000	2001	1990-01	2000	2001	1990-01	2000	2001
Western Europe a	8456	2.0	3.5	1.4	6.1	11.9	1.5	5.7	11.3	-0.2
Germany	1846	1.8	3.0	0.6	5.6	13.3	1.1	5.4	10.0	0.1
France	1310	1.8	3.8	1.8	6.1	13.3	1.1	5.0	15.4	-0.2
United Kingdom	1424	2.3	3.0	2.2	5.7	10.3	1.0	6.1	10.9	2.8
Italy	1089	1.6	2.9	1.8	5.4	11.7	0.8	4.4	9.4	0.2
Spain	582	2.7	4.1	2.8	9.4	9.6	3.4	8.5	9.8	3.7
Netherlands	380	2.7	3.5	1.1	5.4	9.5	1.1	5.1	9.4	1.1
Switzerland	247	0.9	3.0	1.3	3.7	10.0	1.0	3.8	8.5	0.0
Belgium	230	2.0	4.1	1.0	4.5	9.7	-0.4	4.2	9.7	-1.3
Sweden	210	1.7	3.6	1.2	6.7	10.3	-1.4	4.6	11.5	-3.9
Turkey	148	2.2	7.4	-7.4	5.9	19.2	7.4	6.0	25.4	-24.8
Austria	189	2.6	3.0	1.0	10.5	12.2	5.5	6.4	11.1	3.6
Denmark	162	2.2	3.0	0.9	4.6	11.5	3.1	5.4	11.2	3.8
Norway	164	3.2	2.3	1.4	4.9	2.7	5.3	4.0	2.5	0.3
Finland	121	2.0	5.6	0.7	8.3	18.2	-0.7	4.6	16.2	-1.0
Greece	117	2.5	4.4	4.0	7.1	18.9	2.3	6.1	15.0	1.9
Portugal	110	2.6	3.6	1.6	5.0	8.1	3.2	6.8	6.0	0.8
Ireland	103	7.1	11.4	5.9	14.1	17.8	7.4	12.4	16.6	5.2
Memorandum item:										
European Union (15)	8430	2.0	3.4	1.6	6.3	12.2	1.4	5.8	11.6	-0.2

a Excludes the former Yugoslavia.

Table III.38

Leading merchandise exporters and importers in Western Europe, 2001

(Billion dollars and percentage)

| | Value | Share | | Annual percentage change | | | | | | | | |
| | | | | Value | | | | Volume | | | | |
	2001	1990	2001	1990-01	1999	2000	2001	1990-01	1999	2000	2001
Exporters											
Western Europe	2485.1	100.0	100.0	4	0	4	-1	4.5	3.0	9.0	-1.0
Germany	570.8	25.7	23.0	3	0	2	3	4.5	3.5	10.5	2.5
France	321.8	13.2	13.0	4	1	0	-1	4.5	5.0	6.0	-1.0
United Kingdom	273.1	11.3	11.0	4	-1	5	-4	1.5	-2.0	0.5	-5.5
Italy	241.1	10.4	9.7	3	-4	2	0	5.0	0.0	15.5	-0.5
Netherlands	229.5	8.0	9.2	5	2	7	-2	5.5	4.0	7.0	-3.5
Belgium	179.7	-	7.2	-	-	5	-5	-	-	11.0	-4.0
Spain	109.7	3.4	4.4	6	-7	10	-5	8.5	-4.5	18.5	-3.0
Ireland	82.8	1.5	3.3	12	11	9	7	12.5	19.0	16.5	3.0
Switzerland	82.1	3.9	3.3	2	2	2	1	3.5	4.0	10.5	-1.5
Sweden	75.3	3.5	3.0	2	0	3	-14	4.5	2.5	9.0	-8.0
Austria	70.3	2.5	2.8	5	3	2	4	8.0	9.0	14.5	5.5
Norway	57.9	2.1	2.3	5	13	32	-3	6.5	4.5	4.5	0.5
Denmark	51.9	2.3	2.1	3	3	2	1	4.5	6.0	9.5	3.0
Finland	42.9	1.6	1.7	4	-3	9	-7	7.0	3.0	13.5	-2.0
Turkey	31.2	0.8	1.3	8	-1	4	12	9.5	3.0	11.5	22.0
Importers											
Western Europe	2524.5	100.0	100.0	4	2	6	-3	4.0	4.5	8.0	-3.0
Germany	492.8	20.9	19.5	3	1	5	-1	4.0	3.5	6.0	-0.5
United Kingdom	331.8	13.1	13.1	4	1	6	-3	2.0	-0.5	4.5	-3.5
France	325.8	13.8	12.9	3	2	6	-2	4.0	5.5	8.5	-2.5
Italy	232.9	10.7	9.2	2	1	8	-2	4.0	5.5	12.0	-1.5
Netherlands	207.3	7.4	8.2	5	5	6	-5	5.0	8.0	4.0	-4.0
Belgium	168.7	-	6.7	-	-	8	-5	-	-	9.5	-4.5
Spain	142.7	5.2	5.7	5	-1	15	-9	7.0	0.5	16.5	-6.5
Switzerland	84.1	4.1	3.3	2	0	5	1	3.5	8.0	7.0	-0.5
Austria	74.4	2.9	2.9	4	3	2	3	5.5	5.5	10.0	2.5
Sweden	62.6	3.2	2.5	1	0	6	-14	3.5	0.0	11.0	-9.0
Ireland	50.7	1.2	2.0	8	8	9	-1	6.5	13.5	9.0	-6.0
Denmark	45.4	2.0	1.8	3	-2	0	0	4.0	1.0	8.5	1.0
Turkey	40.6	1.3	1.6	6	-11	34	-26	6.5	-1.0	32.5	-25.0
Portugal	38.0	1.5	1.5	4	4	0	-5	5.0	8.0	6.0	-5.0
Norway	32.4	1.6	1.3	2	-9	1	-6	4.0	-3.5	8.0	-5.5
Memorandum item:											
European Union (15)											
Exports	2291.4	92.2	92.2	4	0	3	-1	4.5	3.5	9.5	-1.5
Extra-exports	874.1	32.3	35.2	5	-1	7	0	4.0	0.5	13.0	0.0
Imports	2334.2	91.6	92.5	4	2	6	-3	4.0	4.5	8.0	-2.5
Extra-imports	912.8	33.9	36.2	4	4	15	-4	4.0	5.5	9.0	-2.0

Table III.39

Merchandise trade of the European Union by region and economy, 2001

(Billion dollars and percentage)

Destination	Exports					Origin	Imports				
	Value	Share		Annual percentage change			Value	Share		Annual percentage change	
	2001	1990	2001	2000	2001		2001	1990	2001	2000	2001
Region						Region					
World	2291.4	100.0	100.0	3	-1	World	2334.2	100.0	100.0	6	-3
Western Europe	1546.5	71.6	67.5	1	-2	Western Europe	1543.4	69.1	66.1	2	-2
North America	232.5	7.8	10.1	10	0	Asia	269.2	10.1	11.5	11	-8
Asia	178.6	7.2	7.8	11	-1	North America	189.3	8.2	8.1	8	-5
C./E. Europe/ Baltic States/CIS	137.8	3.7	6.0	9	12	C./E. Europe/ Baltic States/CIS	136.6	3.4	5.9	22	6
Africa	59.3	3.4	2.6	-1	3	Africa	72.2	4.0	3.1	25	-1
Middle East	58.9	2.7	2.6	5	5	Latin America	46.6	2.3	2.0	13	-4
Latin America	54.1	1.8	2.4	5	-1	Middle East	39.9	2.2	1.7	43	-17
Economies						Economies					
European Union (15)	1417.3	64.9	61.9	1	-2	European Union (15)	1421.4	63.0	60.9	1	-2
United States	210.8	6.9	9.2	10	-1	United States	172.0	7.3	7.4	7	-5
Switzerland	66.2	3.7	2.9	-2	2	China	67.3	0.8	2.9	22	4
Japan	39.2	2.0	1.7	10	-4	Japan	67.2	4.3	2.9	5	-16
Poland	31.3	0.4	1.4	1	2	Switzerland	54.4	3.0	2.3	-1	-2
Above 5	1764.7	78.0	77.0	2	-1	Above 5	1782.3	78.5	76.4	2	-2
China	26.5	0.5	1.2	14	14	Russian Fed.	34.3	0.0	1.5	49	-2
Russian Fed.	24.4	0.0	1.1	17	36	Poland	23.7	-	1.0	15	10
Czech Rep.	23.9	0.0	1.0	13	10	Czech Rep.	22.3	0.0	1.0	12	12
Norway	22.9	-	1.0	-4	-1	Hungary	21.7	0.3	0.9	7	8
Hungary	20.9	0.3	0.9	8	0	Taipei, Chinese	21.2	0.8	0.9	15	-11
Canada	19.2	0.9	0.8	8	2	Korea, Rep. of	19.2	0.6	0.8	18	-16
Hong Kong, China	18.8	-	0.8	13	1	Turkey	18.0	-	0.8	1	11
Turkey	17.7	0.7	0.8	28	-35	Brazil	16.2	0.8	0.7	14	0
Brazil	16.1	0.3	0.7	2	7	Canada	15.9	0.8	0.7	18	-6
Australia	13.7	0.6	0.6	-1	-5	South Africa	15.8	0.6	0.7	16	11
Korea, Rep. of	13.6	0.5	0.6	25	-8	Malaysia	12.4	0.3	0.5	4	-12
Mexico	13.2	0.3	0.6	17	3	Saudi Arabia	11.6	0.7	0.5	63	-21
Singapore	12.9	0.5	0.6	8	-5	Singapore	11.5	0.4	0.5	6	-17
Israel	12.2	0.5	0.5	9	-14	India	11.4	0.4	0.5	7	0
United Arab Emirates	12.1	0.3	0.5	6	12	Thailand	10.7	0.3	0.5	9	-6
Saudi Arabia	11.5	0.7	0.5	2	6	Algeria	10.5	0.6	0.4	81	-8
Taipei, Chinese	11.4	0.4	0.5	10	-14	Libyan Arab Jamahiriya	10.2	0.7	0.4	65	-16
South Africa	11.2	0.5	0.5	5	2	Indonesia	9.6	0.2	0.4	8	-5
India	10.7	0.5	0.5	13	-12	Hong Kong, China	8.9	0.7	0.4	-5	-16
Romania	9.3	0.1	0.4	20	16	Romania	8.4	0.1	0.4	15	19
Malaysia	8.2	0.2	0.4	13	8	Israel	8.3	0.3	0.4	13	-9
Slovenia	7.5	-	0.3	2	0	Australia	8.2	0.4	0.3	11	0
Tunisia	7.1	0.3	0.3	5	6	Slovak Rep.	7.3	-	0.3	2	11
Slovak Rep.	7.0	0.0	0.3	4	16	Mexico	6.4	0.0	0.3	30	0
Algeria	6.7	0.4	0.3	1	19	Iran, Islamic Rep. of	6.0	0.5	0.3	54	-23
Above 30	2123.1	-	92.7	-	-	Above 30	2132.0	-	91.3	-	-

Table III.40

Leading exporters and importers of commercial services in Western Europe, 2001

(Billion dollars and percentage)

	Value	Share		Annual percentage change			
	2001	1990	2001	1990-01	1999	2000	2001
Exporters							
Western Europe	678.7	100.0	100.0	5	2	2	1
United Kingdom	108.4	13.0	16.0	7	7	3	-6
France	79.8	15.9	11.8	2	-3	-1	-2
Germany	79.7	12.4	11.7	4	2	-3	-1
Spain	57.4	6.7	8.5	7	8	0	8
Italy	57.0	11.7	8.4	1	-13	-3	2
Netherlands	51.7	6.9	7.6	6	5	-3	0
Belgium-Luxembourg	42.6	5.9	6.3	5	10	6	-1
Austria	32.5	5.5	4.8	3	6	1	5
Denmark	26.9	3.1	4.0	7	32	21	10
Switzerland	25.2	4.4	3.7	3	1	0	-4
Sweden	21.8	3.2	3.2	4	11	2	9
Ireland	20.0	0.8	3.0	18	-7	8	20
Greece	19.4	...	2.9	...	...	...	1
Norway	16.7	3.0	2.5	3	1	8	12
Turkey	15.9	1.9	2.3	7	-30	19	-17
Importers							
Western Europe	647.2	100.0	100.0	5	3	2	1
Germany	132.6	20.2	20.5	5	5	-3	0
United Kingdom	91.6	11.4	14.1	7	9	5	-4
France	61.6	12.9	9.5	2	-4	-3	0
Italy	55.7	11.9	8.6	2	-11	-3	2
Netherlands	52.9	7.4	8.2	6	4	3	2
Belgium-Luxembourg	39.3	6.2	6.1	4	7	5	2
Ireland	34.8	1.3	5.4	19	-10	8	21
Spain	33.2	3.9	5.1	7	11	3	7
Austria	31.5	3.6	4.9	8	7	1	6
Denmark	23.5	2.6	3.6	8	17	19	6
Sweden	22.9	4.3	3.5	3	4	4	-2
Norway	15.3	3.1	2.4	2	3	-1	6
Switzerland	14.9	2.8	2.3	3	4	-1	-3
Greece	11.2	...	1.7	...	...	...	2
Finland	8.1	1.9	1.3	1	2	7	-3
Memorandum item:							
European Union (15)							
Exports	611.5	88.9	90.1	5	4	1	1
Imports	604.9	89.2	93.5	5	3	2	2

Table III.41

Trade in commercial services of France, 2001

(Billion dollars and percentage)

	Exports			Imports		
	Value	Share		Value	Share	
	2001	1995	2001	2001	1995	2001
Total commercial services	79.8	100.0	100.0	61.6	100.0	100.0
Transportation	18.1	24.6	22.6	17.4	32.9	28.2
Sea transport	4.4	4.5	5.5	5.0	7.4	8.1
Air transport	8.0	10.7	10.1	8.0	14.5	12.9
Other transport	5.6	9.5	7.1	4.4	10.9	7.1
Travel	30.5	33.2	38.1	18.1	25.4	29.3
Other commercial services	31.3	42.2	39.2	26.2	41.7	42.5
Communication services	1.6	0.6	2.0	1.5	0.6	2.5
Construction services	2.7	3.7	3.4	1.6	1.6	2.6
Insurance services	0.9	2.2	1.1	0.6	2.4	1.0
Financial services	1.1	3.1	1.3	1.4	3.6	2.3
Computer and information services	1.2	0.4	1.5	1.0	0.8	1.6
Royalties and licence fees	2.5	2.2	3.1	1.9	3.6	3.1
Other business services	20.0	28.5	25.0	16.1	27.0	26.2
Personal, cultural, and recreational services	1.4	1.4	1.8	2.0	2.1	3.2

Table III.42

Trade in commercial services of Germany, 2001

(Billion dollars and percentage)

	Exports			Imports		
	Value	Share		Value	Share	
	2001	1995	2001	2001	1995	2001
Total commercial services	79.7	100.0	100.0	132.6	100.0	100.0
Transportation	20.0	26.0	25.1	24.5	19.6	18.5
Sea transport	8.3	8.2	10.4	8.2	6.1	6.2
Air transport	8.1	12.6	10.1	6.2	6.5	4.7
Other transport	3.7	5.2	4.6	10.0	7.0	7.6
Travel	17.3	23.8	21.7	46.1	41.6	34.8
Other commercial services	42.4	50.2	53.2	62.0	38.7	46.8
Communication services	1.5	2.7	1.9	3.1	2.4	2.3
Construction services	3.1	7.0	3.9	4.6	4.7	3.5
Insurance services	0.3	1.7	0.4	0.8	1.2	0.6
Financial services	3.9	3.2	4.8	3.5	0.4	2.6
Computer and information services	4.5	1.9	5.7	5.9	1.6	4.5
Royalties and licence fees	3.0	4.2	3.8	4.8	4.7	3.6
Other business services	25.7	29.3	32.3	36.0	22.2	27.1
Personal, cultural, and recreational services	0.3	0.2	0.4	3.3	1.6	2.5

Table III.43

Trade in commercial services of Italy, 2001

(Billion dollars and percentage)

	Exports			Imports		
	Value	Share		Value	Share	
	2001	1995	2001	2001	1995	2001
Total commercial services	57.0	100.0	100.0	55.7	100.0	100.0
Transportation	8.2	17.7	14.4	11.9	24.5	21.4
Sea transport	3.9	7.5	6.8	5.3	11.9	9.5
Air transport	2.4	6.1	4.3	3.7	7.2	6.6
Other transport	1.9	4.1	3.4	3.0	5.4	5.3
Travel	25.8	47.0	45.3	14.2	27.2	25.5
Other commercial services	22.9	35.3	40.3	29.5	48.4	53.0
Communication services	1.4	0.5	2.5	2.6	1.1	4.7
Construction services	1.6	5.2	2.9	1.6	2.8	2.9
Insurance services	1.1	2.3	1.9	1.4	1.6	2.6
Financial services	0.4	4.3	0.7	0.6	8.2	1.0
Computer and information services	0.4	0.3	0.6	0.9	0.8	1.7
Royalties and licence fees	0.4	0.8	0.8	1.3	2.1	2.4
Other business services	17.0	21.5	29.9	20.0	29.7	35.9
Personal, cultural, and recreational services	0.5	0.6	1.0	1.1	2.0	2.0

Table III.44

Trade in commercial services of the United Kingdom, 2001

(Billion dollars and percentage)

	Exports			Imports		
	Value	Share		Value	Share	
	2001	1995	2001	2001	1995	2001
Total commercial services	108.4	100.0	100.0	91.6	100.0	100.0
Transportation	17.6	21.0	16.2	22.8	27.2	24.9
Sea transport	6.2	8.7	5.7	7.2	10.7	7.9
Air transport	10.1	10.9	9.4	13.5	15.1	14.7
Other transport	1.2	1.4	1.1	2.1	1.4	2.3
Travel	18.2	26.8	16.8	37.9	40.0	41.4
Other commercial services	72.6	52.2	67.0	30.9	32.8	33.7
Communication services	1.8	2.1	1.7	2.5	3.4	2.7
Construction services	0.2	0.3	0.2	0.1	0.2	0.1
Insurance services	5.5	4.8	5.1	1.1	1.3	1.2
Financial services	18.7	11.5	17.2	4.4	2.7	4.8
Computer and information services	3.5	1.6	3.2	1.1	0.7	1.2
Royalties and licence fees	8.2	7.9	7.5	5.9	8.3	6.4
Other business services	33.2	22.5	30.7	14.8	14.8	16.1
Personal, cultural, and recreational services	1.5	1.4	1.4	1.0	1.2	1.1

5. *Central and Eastern Europe, the Baltic States, and the CIS*

Table III.45

Merchandise trade of Central and Eastern Europe, the Baltic States and the CIS, 2001

(Billion dollars and percentage)

	Exports	Imports
Value	286	267
Share in world merchandise trade	4.8	4.3
Annual percentage change		
Value		
1980-85 a	0	-1
1985-90 a	3	5
1990-01	7	6
1999	0	-12
2000	26	14
2001	5	11
Volume		
1990-01	5.5	5.0
1999	-2.0	-9.0
2000	17.0	16.0
2001	8.0	14.0

a Includes the former German Democratic Republic.

Table III.46

Merchandise trade of C./E. Europe, the Baltic States and the CIS by region and by major product group, 2001

(Billion dollars and percentage)

	Value	Share	
	Exports	Exports	Imports
Total	286	100.0	100.0
Region			
North America	12	4.1	2.9
Latin America	6	2.1	1.1
Western Europe	158	55.4	58.2
C./E. Europe/Baltic States/CIS	76	26.5	30.0
Africa	3	1.1	0.4
Middle East	8	2.7	0.7
Asia	19	6.7	6.7
Product group			
Agricultural products	25	8.7	10.5
Mining products	93	32.6	13.9
Manufactures	161	56.4	74.7

Note: Import shares are derived from the Secretariat's network of world merchandise trade by product and region.

Chart III.11

Merchandise trade of Central and Eastern Europe, the Baltic States and the CIS, 1990-01

(Billion dollars)

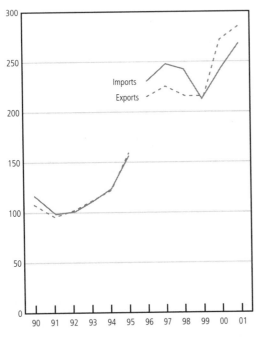

Note: New valuation in 1990 and change in area definition in 1992 and 1996.

Chart III.12

Share of Central and Eastern Europe, the Baltic States and the CIS in world merchandise trade, 1990-01

(Percentage based on value data)

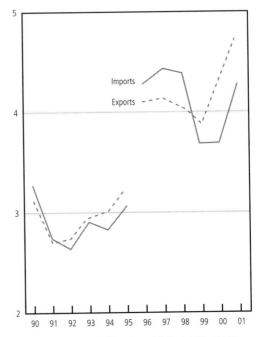

Note: New valuation in 1990 and change in area definition in 1992 and 1996.

Table III.47

Merchandise exports of C./E. Europe, the Baltic States and the CIS by major product group and main destination, 2001

(Billion dollars and percentage)

	Value	Share		Annual percentage change			
	2001	1996	2001	1998	1999	2000	2001
Central and Eastern Europe							
Total merchandise							
World	129.4	100.0	100.0	11	1	14	12
Western Europe	95.6	66.2	73.8	18	5	16	11
C./E. Europe/Baltic States/CIS	22.1	23.1	17.1	-3	-13	10	13
Manufactures							
World	107.4	100.0	100.0	16	1	15	12
Western Europe	82.0	68.7	76.4	23	5	16	12
C./E. Europe/Baltic States/CIS	16.0	20.7	14.9	-1	-14	11	15
Agricultural products							
World	10.7	100.0	100.0	-3	-8	-2	12
Western Europe	6.1	53.9	56.8	-2	3	-1	10
C./E. Europe/Baltic States/CIS	3.1	36.3	29.5	-9	-28	0	10
Mining products							
World	10.1	100.0	100.0	-11	-2	34	4
Western Europe	6.6	67.2	65.6	-9	-4	34	1
C./E. Europe/Baltic States/CIS	2.8	25.1	27.7	-11	-1	36	9
Baltic States							
Total merchandise							
World	9.9	100.0	100.0	3	-19	24	12
Western Europe	6.0	43.5	61.0	20	1	26	5
C./E. Europe/Baltic States/CIS	3.1	52.6	30.9	-13	-44	19	23
Manufactures							
World	6.4	100.0	100.0	6	-16	23	13
Western Europe	4.2	47.2	64.9	25	1	28	4
C./E. Europe/Baltic States/CIS	1.8	48.2	27.5	-14	-44	15	31
Agricultural products							
World	2.0	100.0	100.0	0	-20	6	11
Western Europe	1.2	42.2	57.3	13	1	7	-3
C./E. Europe/Baltic States/CIS	0.6	54.6	31.0	-15	-46	-2	28
Mining products							
World	1.4	100.0	100.0	-1	-26	64	11
C./E. Europe/Baltic States/CIS	0.7	72.6	45.8	-8	-41	56	1
Western Europe	0.7	25.4	49.1	7	3	76	30
Commonwealth of Independent States							
Total merchandise							
World	43.2	100.0	100.0	-12	-5	34	5
C./E. Europe/Baltic States/CIS	19.7	61.2	45.5	-19	-18	38	4
Western Europe	12.0	20.2	27.8	7	-8	42	7
Manufactures							
World	21.0	100.0	100.0	-9	-13	20	15
C./E. Europe/Baltic States/CIS	9.8	61.5	46.4	-15	-23	22	12
Western Europe	4.6	15.7	21.9	20	-14	29	13
Mining products							
World	15.6	100.0	100.0	-8	8	79	-4
C./E. Europe/Baltic States/CIS	6.3	60.3	40.6	-14	-17	84	-3
Western Europe	5.7	29.0	36.7	1	-1	77	5
Agricultural products							
World	5.8	100.0	100.0	-26	-6	5	8
C./E. Europe/Baltic States/CIS	3.4	63.8	59.2	-33	-4	17	2
Asia	0.2	5.4	4.0	-38	0	-44	-8

Table III.48

Leading merchandise exporters and importers in Central and Eastern Europe, the Baltic States and the CIS, 2001

(Billion dollars and percentage)

	Value	Share		Annual percentage change		
	2001	1996	2001	1999	2000	2001
Exporters						
C./E. Europe/Baltic States/CIS	285.6	100.0	100.0	0	26	5
Russian Fed.	103.1	41.2	36.1	1	39	-2
Poland	36.1	11.4	12.6	-3	15	14
Czech Rep. a	33.4	10.3	11.7	1	10	15
Hungary	30.5	7.3	10.7	9	12	9
Ukraine	16.3	6.7	5.7	-8	26	12
Slovak Rep. a	12.6	4.1	4.4	-4	16	6
Romania	11.4	3.8	4.0	2	22	10
Kazakhstan	8.6	2.8	3.0	3	64	-5
Belarus	7.5	2.6	2.6	-16	24	3
Bulgaria	5.1	2.3	1.8	-7	20	6
Importers						
C./E. Europe/Baltic States/CIS	267.5	100.0	100.0	-12	14	11
Russian Fed.	53.9	29.8	20.1	-33	13	20
Poland	50.3	16.1	18.8	-2	7	3
Czech Rep. a	36.5	12.0	13.6	-1	14	14
Hungary	33.7	7.9	12.6	9	15	5
Ukraine	15.8	7.6	5.9	-19	18	13
Romania	15.6	5.0	5.8	-11	24	19
Slovak Rep. a	14.8	4.8	5.5	-14	13	16
Belarus	8.0	3.0	3.0	-22	30	-7
Bulgaria	7.2	2.2	2.7	10	18	11
Kazakhstan	6.4	1.8	2.4	-15	37	26
Memorandum item:						
Central and Eastern Europe						
Exports	129.4	39.2	45.3	1	14	12
Imports	159.3	48.4	59.6	-1	12	9
Baltic States						
Exports	9.9	3.2	3.5	-19	24	12
Imports	14.1	4.4	5.3	-19	15	9
CIS						
Exports	146.3	57.6	51.2	-1	38	0
Imports	94.1	47.2	35.2	-27	16	14

a Imports are valued f.o.b.

Table III.49

Merchandise exports of selected Central and Eastern European countries by region, major trading partner and major product group, 1999-01

(Million dollars and percentage)

Destination	Origin	Bulgaria	Czech Rep.	Slovak Rep.	Hungary	Poland	Romania
				Value			
Total	1999	4005	26240	10240	25015	27405	8485
	2000	4825	28995	11870	28090	31650	10365
	2001	5105	33405	12630	30500	36090	11385
				Share in total			
Region and major trading partner							
North America	1999	4.5	2.6	1.6	5.3	2.8	4.0
	2000	4.6	3.0	1.6	5.4	3.7	4.0
	2001	6.5	3.2	1.4	5.2	2.8	3.5
Latin America	1999	0.8	0.9	0.6	0.5	1.2	1.0
	2000	1.0	0.6	0.4	0.6	1.2	0.8
	2001	1.0	0.6	0.3	0.5	1.2	1.1
Western Europe	1999	69.4	68.6	63.5	80.9	73.0	74.6
	2000	73.6	72.8	63.5	80.3	73.2	73.9
	2001	71.2	72.8	64.1	79.4	73.0	76.1
European Union (15)	1999	52.5	63.6	59.4	76.2	69.2	65.5
	2000	51.1	68.6	59.1	75.2	70.0	63.8
	2001	54.8	68.9	60.0	74.3	69.2	67.8
C./E. Europe/Baltic States/CIS	1999	17.7	21.0	31.9	9.8	18.3	9.8
	2000	13.8	19.1	32.0	10.0	17.3	11.5
	2001	10.7	19.3	32.1	11.0	18.3	9.4
Central and Eastern Europe	1999	4.2	16.5	29.0	6.8	8.4	6.6
	2000	4.0	15.9	29.3	7.2	8.0	7.7
	2001	5.0	16.2	29.1	8.0	8.4	6.6
Russian Fed.	1999	4.7	1.5	1.0	1.4	2.8	0.6
	2000	2.4	1.0	0.9	1.6	2.7	0.9
	2001	2.3	1.5	1.0	1.5	2.9	0.7
Africa	1999	2.1	1.3	0.7	0.4	1.4	3.8
	2000	1.6	0.5	0.5	0.4	1.2	3.6
	2001	1.8	0.5	0.5	0.4	1.4	2.6
Middle East	1999	2.4	2.5	0.5	0.8	0.9	4.1
	2000	3.0	1.3	0.5	0.7	1.0	3.3
	2001	3.3	1.3	0.5	1.0	0.9	3.9
Asia	1999	3.0	2.5	1.0	2.3	2.0	2.5
	2000	2.3	2.6	1.3	2.6	2.1	2.8
	2001	1.9	2.1	1.0	2.6	2.0	3.1
Major product group							
Agricultural products	1999	18.4	6.8	6.5	10.0	11.0	10.4
	2000	12.5	6.6	5.4	8.7	9.6	8.0
	2001	11.7	5.8	5.7	9.0	9.4	8.0
Mining products	1999	18.3	4.9	8.2	3.7	10.3	10.3
	2000	27.5	4.9	10.4	4.1	10.3	14.7
	2001	25.1	4.7	10.1	4.0	9.9	12.5
Manufactures	1999	59.7	88.0	84.8	86.3	78.6	78.3
	2000	58.3	88.1	83.6	87.2	80.0	76.7
	2001	61.6	89.1	83.7	86.5	80.6	79.0

Table III.50

Merchandise imports of selected Central and Eastern European countries by region, major trading partner and major product group, 1999-01

(Million dollars and percentage)

Origin \ Destination		Bulgaria	Czech Rep.	Slovak Rep a	Hungary	Poland	Romania
				Value			
Total	1999	5515	28100	11265	28010	45910	10555
	2000	6505	32110	12775	32080	48940	13055
	2001	7240	36490	14765	33680	50275	15550
				Share in total			
Region and major trading partner							
North America	1999	3.3	4.4	2.8	3.7	4.0	3.8
	2000	3.2	4.7	2.2	4.1	4.8	3.4
	2001	2.9	4.3	2.1	4.4	3.7	3.5
Latin America	1999	2.1	0.7	0.6	1.6	1.2	1.9
	2000	3.0	0.9	0.5	1.3	1.3	2.3
	2001	3.4	1.0	0.6	1.2	1.8	2.3
Western Europe	1999	54.3	67.6	54.3	67.4	68.5	65.3
	2000	49.9	65.5	51.4	61.3	64.5	61.2
	2001	55.9	65.7	52.5	60.8	65.2	62.0
European Union (15)	1999	48.6	64.2	51.7	64.4	65.0	60.4
	2000	44.0	61.9	48.9	58.5	61.2	56.6
	2001	49.4	61.8	49.8	57.8	61.4	57.3
C./E. Europe/Baltic States/CIS	1999	31.7	17.4	35.7	13.5	14.0	18.1
	2000	38.5	19.4	39.1	16.2	18.3	21.5
	2001	31.5	18.2	37.7	15.9	18.0	20.9
Central and Eastern Europe	1999	5.9	11.4	22.0	6.6	6.2	8.5
	2000	8.3	11.3	20.1	7.0	6.6	8.5
	2001	7.6	11.1	21.1	7.4	6.9	9.3
Russian Fed.	1999	20.7	4.8	12.0	5.8	5.8	6.8
	2000	24.4	6.4	17.0	8.1	9.5	8.6
	2001	19.9	5.5	14.8	7.0	8.8	7.6
Africa	1999	2.0	0.6	0.3	0.4	0.9	0.8
	2000	0.7	0.7	0.3	0.4	0.6	0.6
	2001	0.8	0.7	0.3	0.5	0.9	0.8
Middle East	1999	0.7	0.4	0.2	0.3	0.5	1.3
	2000	0.5	0.3	0.2	0.3	0.4	1.0
	2001	0.6	0.3	0.2	0.3	0.4	1.7
Asia	1999	5.8	7.3	5.3	13.1	10.7	8.3
	2000	4.2	7.4	5.4	16.5	9.8	9.7
	2001	4.9	8.0	5.8	16.8	9.7	6.3
Major product group							
Agricultural products	1999	7.5	8.0	8.3	4.8	9.0	8.8
	2000	6.6	7.0	7.5	4.4	8.1	8.4
	2001	6.8	6.6	7.4	4.5	8.2	9.0
Mining products	1999	26.5	10.1	16.4	8.6	9.8	13.3
	2000	32.4	13.2	21.2	11.1	13.7	16.0
	2001	27.2	12.5	18.9	10.8	12.8	16.0
Manufactures	1999	64.4	81.8	75.2	86.6	81.0	77.0
	2000	58.9	79.7	71.2	84.4	78.2	75.2
	2001	64.6	80.9	73.7	84.2	78.8	74.8

a Imports are valued f.o.b.

Table III.51

Relative importance of inter-regional trade in the total merchandise trade of the Baltic States, 2001

(Million dollars and percentage)

| | Exports | | | | | | Imports | | | | |
| | Value | | | Share | | | Value | | | Share | |
	World	Baltic States a	All other countries	Baltic States	All other countries		World	Baltic States	All other countries	Baltic States	All other countries
Baltic States	9895	1335	8560	13.5	86.5	Baltic States	14085	915	13170	6.5	93.5
Estonia	3310	335	2975	10.1	89.9	Estonia	4300	235	4065	5.5	94.5
Latvia	2000	275	1725	13.8	86.3	Latvia	3505	515	2990	14.7	85.3
Lithuania b	4585	725	3860	15.8	84.2	Lithuania b	6280	165	6115	2.6	97.4

a includes transit trade of fuels through Latvia and Lithuania.
b Lithuania trade recorded using the general system of trade. See Technical Notes.

Table III.52

Relative importance of inter-regional trade in the total merchandise trade of the CIS, 2001

(Million dollars and percentage)

| | Exports | | | | | | Imports | | | | |
| | Value | | | Share | | | Value | | | Share | |
	World	CIS	All other countries	CIS	All other countries		World	CIS	All other countries	CIS	All other countries
CIS	146300	30855	115445	21.1	78.9	CIS	94060	34840	59220	37.0	63.0
Armenia	340	90	250	26.5	73.5	Armenia	870	190	680	21.8	78.2
Azerbaijan	2315	225	2090	9.7	90.3	Azerbaijan	1675	445	1230	26.6	73.4
Belarus	7525	4470	3055	59.4	40.6	Belarus	8045	5585	2460	69.4	30.6
Georgia	345	145	200	42.0	58.0	Georgia	685	250	435	36.5	63.5
Kazakhstan	8645	2630	6015	30.4	69.6	Kazakhstan	6365	3250	3115	51.1	48.9
Kyrgyz Rep.	475	170	305	35.8	64.2	Kyrgyz Rep.	465	260	205	55.9	44.1
Moldova, Rep. of	570	345	225	60.5	39.5	Moldova, Rep. of	895	340	555	38.0	62.0
Russian Fed.	103100	15300	87800	14.8	85.2	Russian Fed.	53860	13190	40670	24.5	75.5
Tajikistan	650	210	440	32.3	67.7	Tajikistan	690	540	150	78.3	21.7
Turkmenistan	2620	1440	1180	55.0	45.0	Turkmenistan	2105	600	1505	28.5	71.5
Ukraine	16265	4675	11590	28.7	71.3	Ukraine	15775	9000	6775	57.1	42.9
Uzbekistan	3450	1155	2295	33.5	66.5	Uzbekistan	2630	1190	1440	45.2	54.8

Table III.53

Merchandise exports of selected economies to the CIS, 1999-01

(Million dollars)

Origin	European Union (15)			Central and Eastern Europe			Turkey		
Destination	1999	2000	2001	1999	2000	2001	1999	2000	2001
Commonwealth of Independent States	21884	25130	33125	4465	4630	5025	1533	1636	1978
Armenia	181	224	168	51	31	18	0	0	0
Azerbaijan	226	275	301	66	67	57	248	230	225
Belarus	1067	1027	1217	356	367	376	5	12	20
Georgia	175	221	240	132	127	114	114	131	144
Kazakhstan	1026	1134	1388	181	177	158	97	116	120
Kyrgyz Rep.	80	54	52	9	8	7	23	20	17
Moldova, Rep. of	267	307	335	214	255	225	21	26	28
Russian Fed.	15359	17960	24389	1825	1900	2335	589	639	924
Tajikistan	34	32	30	19	3	3	5	4	16
Turkmenistan	220	148	224	37	52	19	107	119	105
Ukraine	2719	3305	4308	1477	1559	1658	226	256	289
Uzbekistan	529	444	473	99	85	57	99	82	90

Origin	United States			Japan			China		
Destination	1999	2000	2001	1999	2000	2001	1999	2000	2001
Commonwealth of Independent States	2844	3325	3837	755	792	956	2233	3183	3477
Armenia	50	57	50	1	2	0	12	1	2
Azerbaijan	55	210	65	36	8	65	1	2	11
Belarus	26	31	35	4	3	3	5	41	9
Georgia	83	109	107	7	4	6	2	2	4
Kazakhstan	179	124	163	61	69	73	494	599	328
Kyrgyz Rep.	21	24	28	6	4	1	103	110	77
Moldova, Rep. of	11	27	36	3	1	5	0	0	2
Russian Fed.	1845	2318	2724	480	570	715	1497	2233	2710
Tajikistan	13	13	29	3	1	0	2	7	5
Turkmenistan	18	73	248	14	56	32	7	12	31
Ukraine	204	186	205	54	51	37	81	136	247
Uzbekistan	339	151	148	86	25	18	27	39	51

Table III.54

Merchandise imports of selected economies from the CIS, 1999-01

(Million dollars)

Destination Origin	European Union (15)			Central and Eastern Europe			Turkey		
	1999	2000	2001	1999	2000	2001	1999	2000	2001
Commonwealth of Independent States	29805	43418	43090	10830	16940	16625	3734	5682	4630
Armenia	101	118	67	0	0	0	0	0	0
Azerbaijan	473	904	991	11	10	113	44	96	78
Belarus	574	684	611	292	314	355	21	18	11
Georgia	127	212	269	3	4	1	93	155	127
Kazakhstan	1866	2934	2642	207	523	400	296	346	90
Kyrgyz Rep.	140	120	105	16	8	9	3	2	6
Moldova, Rep. of	145	174	205	61	54	55	11	7	3
Russian Fed.	23492	34930	34294	8871	14198	13611	2374	3880	3436
Tajikistan	59	41	54	14	44	90	4	16	14
Turkmenistan	264	204	141	21	27	74	67	98	72
Ukraine	2146	2630	3148	1233	1664	1764	774	977	758
Uzbekistan	418	467	564	101	93	153	47	86	36

Destination Origin	United States			Japan			China		
	1999	2000	2001	1999	2000	2001	1999	2000	2001
Commonwealth of Independent States	7165	9842	8326	4020	4917	4179	5282	7367	9642
Armenia	16	24	35	1	0	1	0	4	1
Azerbaijan	28	22	25	0	1	4	0	4	4
Belarus	100	113	122	6	8	14	21	73	35
Georgia	19	34	36	1	2	11	1	2	3
Kazakhstan	240	443	376	87	91	105	644	958	961
Kyrgyz Rep.	1	2	4	1	1	1	32	67	42
Moldova, Rep. of	98	115	77	0	0	0	0	8	13
Russian Fed.	6017	8038	6744	3767	4579	3850	4223	5770	7959
Tajikistan	24	9	6	0	1	0	6	10	5
Turkmenistan	9	30	51	0	1	0	2	4	1
Ukraine	586	975	790	124	154	140	340	455	610
Uzbekistan	27	37	58	34	79	53	13	12	8

6. Africa

Table III.55

Merchandise trade of Africa, 2001

(Billion dollars and percentage)

	Exports	Imports
Value	141	136
Share in world merchandise trade	2.4	2.2
Annual percentage change		
Africa		
1980-85	-8	-6
1985-90	5	6
1990-01	3	3
1999	11	-3
2000	27	4
2001	-5	2
South Africa		
1980-85	-9	-10
1985-90	8	10
1990-01	3	4
1999	1	-9
2000	12	11
2001	-2	-4
Other Africa		
1980-85	-7	-6
1985-90	4	6
1990-01	3	3
1999	14	-2
2000	32	2
2001	-6	4

Table III.56

Merchandise trade of Africa by region and by major product group, 2001

(Billion dollars and percentage)

	Value	Share	
	Exports	Exports	Imports
Total	141	100.0	100.0
Region			
North America	25	17.6	10.5
Latin America	5	3.6	2.9
Western Europe	73	51.7	49.2
C./E. Europe/Baltic States/CIS	1	0.7	2.5
Africa	11	8.0	8.9
Middle East	3	2.1	7.2
Asia	21	14.7	18.8
Product group			
Agricultural products	21	14.7	15.3
Mining products	80	57.0	11.6
Manufactures	36	25.3	70.8

Note: Import shares are derived from the Secretariat's network of world merchandise trade by product and region.

Chart III.13

Merchandise trade of Africa, 1990-01

(Billion dollars)

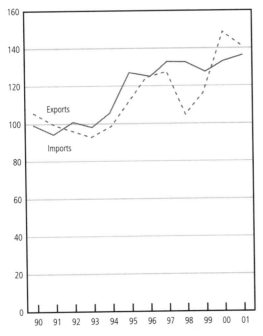

Chart III.14

Share of Africa in world merchandise trade, 1990-01

(Percentage based on value data)

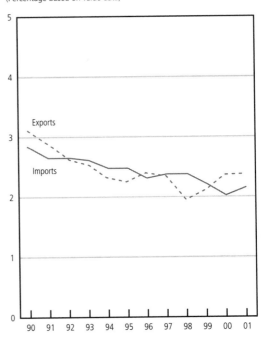

Table III.57

Merchandise exports of Africa by major product group and main destination, 2001

(Billion dollars and percentage)

	Value	Share		Annual percentage change			
	2001	1990	2001	1990-01	1999	2000	2001
Total merchandise a							
World	141.2	100.0	100.0	3	11	27	-5
Western Europe	73.0	57.6	51.7	2	5	26	-3
North America	24.8	15.2	17.6	4	7	55	-9
Asia	20.7	7.7	14.7	9	35	23	-13
Mining products							
World	80.5	100.0	100.0	3	23	50	-8
Western Europe	37.9	61.5	47.0	1	16	51	-7
North America	20.0	24.7	24.8	3	11	66	-12
Asia	12.5	5.9	15.6	13	68	42	-15
Manufactures							
World	35.7	100.0	100.0	5	2	10	2
Western Europe	21.7	62.1	60.7	5	3	12	2
Africa	4.9	11.6	13.8	7	-5	-1	-3
North America	3.8	5.9	10.7	11	-3	22	11
Agricultural products							
World	20.7	100.0	100.0	2	-4	-4	0
Western Europe	10.7	61.2	51.8	1	-10	-8	2
Asia	3.9	15.1	18.7	4	9	5	-2
Africa	2.8	11.8	13.5	3	1	1	-2

a Includes significant exports of unspecified products.

Table III.58

Merchandise exports of Africa by destination, 2001

(Billion dollars and percentage)

	Value	Share		Annual percentage change			
	2001	1990	2001	1990-01	1999	2000	2001
World	141.2	100.0	100.0	3	11	27	-5
Western Europe	73.0	57.6	51.7	2	5	26	-3
European Union (15)	67.4	52.2	47.8	2	5	23	-3
North America	24.8	15.2	17.6	4	7	55	-9
Asia	20.7	7.7	14.7	9	35	23	-13
Japan	3.5	3.0	2.5	1	-1	23	-9
Other	17.2	4.8	12.2	12	46	24	-14
Intra-Africa	11.4	5.9	8.0	6	4	9	-6
Latin America	5.1	1.5	3.6	11	32	26	12
Middle East	2.9	1.5	2.1	6	14	31	-4
C./E. Europe/Baltic States/CIS	1.1	2.2	0.7	-7	-10	-11	32
Inter-regional trade	127.7	85.7	90.4	3	11	30	-5

Table III.59

Leading merchandise exporters and importers in Africa, 2001

(Billion dollars and percentage)

	Value	Share				Annual percentage change			
	2001	1980	1990	1995	2001	1990-01	1999	2000	2001
Exporters									
Africa	141.2	100.0	100.0	100.0	100.0	3	11	27	-5
South Africa a	29.3	21.0	22.3	25.0	20.7	3	1	12	-2
Algeria	20.1	11.4	12.3	9.2	14.2	4	27	76	-9
Nigeria	19.2	21.4	12.9	11.1	13.6	3	41	51	-9
Libyan Arab Jamahiriya	11.7	18.0	12.5	8.0	8.3	-1	19	69	-13
Morocco	7.1	2.1	4.0	6.2	5.0	5	3	1	-4
Angola	6.7	1.6	3.7	3.3	4.7	5	46	53	-15
Tunisia	6.6	1.8	3.3	4.9	4.7	6	2	0	13
Egypt	4.1	2.5	3.3	3.1	2.9	2	14	32	-12
Côte d'Ivoire	3.7	2.6	2.9	3.4	2.6	2	1	-17	-4
Gabon	2.6	1.8	2.1	2.4	1.9	2	31	26	-17
Botswana	2.3	0.4	1.7	1.9	1.6	2	36	3	-15
Congo	2.1	0.8	0.9	1.1	1.5	7	6	60	-16
Equatorial Guinea	2.0	0.0	0.1	0.1	1.4	36	77	71	53
Kenya	1.9	1.0	1.0	1.7	1.4	6	-13	-1	12
Zimbabwe	1.8	1.2	1.6	1.9	1.3	0	-11	2	-8
Importers									
Africa	136.0	100.0	100.0	100.0	100.0	3	-3	4	2
South Africa a	28.4	20.1	18.5	24.2	20.9	4	-9	11	-4
Egypt	12.8	5.0	12.5	9.3	9.4	0	-1	-13	-9
Nigeria	11.2	17.1	5.7	6.5	8.2	6	-7	2	28
Morocco	11.0	4.3	7.0	7.9	8.1	4	-4	16	-5
Algeria	9.7	10.8	9.9	8.1	7.1	0	-3	0	6
Tunisia	9.6	3.6	5.6	6.2	7.0	5	1	1	11
Libyan Arab Jamahiriya	8.7	7.0	5.4	4.3	6.4	5	-21	79	12
Angola	3.4	1.4	1.6	1.2	2.5	7	50	3	4
Ghana	3.0	1.2	1.2	1.5	2.2	9	36	-15	2
Kenya	2.9	2.2	2.2	2.4	2.1	2	-11	10	-7
Côte d'Ivoire	2.6	3.0	2.1	2.3	1.9	2	9	-22	1
Botswana	2.5	0.7	2.0	1.5	1.8	2	-7	11	-1
Mauritius	2.0	0.6	1.6	1.6	1.5	2	8	-7	-4
Cameroon	1.9	1.6	1.4	0.9	1.4	3	-12	13	24
Tanzania, United Rep. of	1.7	1.3	1.0	1.3	1.2	4	7	-2	9

a Beginning with 1998, figures refer to South Africa only and no longer to the Southern African Customs Union.
Note: Recent figures for a number of traders in the region have been estimated by the Secretariat.

Table III.60

Merchandise exports of the European Union to Africa by product, 2001

(Billion dollars and percentage)

	Value	Share		Annual percentage change			
	2001	1990	2001	1990-01	1999	2000	2001
Total merchandise exports	59.3	100.0	100.0	1	-6	-1	3
Manufactures	49.1	80.9	82.8	2	-5	-4	5
Machinery and transport equipment	27.0	43.0	45.5	2	-3	-3	4
Power generating machinery	1.3	1.8	2.1	3	-7	5	-3
Other non-electrical machinery	8.3	16.1	14.0	0	-7	-13	8
Office and telecom equipment	5.0	4.9	8.4	7	-3	12	-8
Electrical machinery and apparatus	3.0	4.3	5.0	3	-2	-5	2
Automotive products	6.3	10.5	10.6	1	-1	4	22
Other transport equipment	3.2	7.4	5.4	-2	2	-11	-10
Chemicals	7.3	12.2	12.3	1	-5	-4	4
Other semi-manufactures	4.8	9.2	8.0	0	-6	-6	7
Textiles	3.4	4.7	5.7	3	-4	-6	5
Iron and steel	1.5	4.2	2.5	-3	-33	0	19
Agricultural products	7.1	14.1	12.0	0	-12	1	-2
Food	6.2	12.2	10.5	0	-13	2	-1
Mining products	2.6	3.6	4.3	3	-11	57	-17
Fuels	1.8	2.3	3.1	4	-9	81	-22

Note: The European Union accounted for 47 per cent of Africa's merchandise imports in 2001.

Table III.61

Merchandise imports of the European Union from Africa by product, 2001

(Billion dollars and percentage)

	Value	Share		Annual percentage change			
	2001	1990	2001	1990-01	1999	2000	2001
Total merchandise imports	72.2	100.0	100.0	1	2	25	-1
Mining products	35.4	58.9	49.0	0	5	66	-7
Fuels	31.1	49.3	43.1	0	8	75	-8
Ores and other minerals	2.2	4.4	3.1	-2	-9	8	1
Non-ferrous metals	2.0	5.3	2.8	-4	-10	38	2
Manufactures	23.0	17.0	31.9	7	5	5	7
Clothing	6.1	5.5	8.5	6	0	-4	5
Other semi-manufactures	6.0	4.0	8.3	8	25	26	5
Agricultural products	11.5	18.0	15.9	0	-8	-10	3
Food	8.9	13.1	12.3	1	-6	-14	6
Raw materials	2.6	4.9	3.5	-2	-13	5	-4

Note: The European Union accounted for 48 per cent of Africa's merchandise exports in 2001.

7. Middle East

Table III.62

Merchandise trade of the Middle East, 2001

(Billion dollars and percentage)

	Exports	Imports
Value	237	180
Share in world merchandise trade	4.0	2.9
Annual percentage change		
1980-85	-14	-3
1985-90	6	2
1990-01	5	5
1999	30	3
2000	42	13
2001	-9	4

Table III.63

Merchandise trade of the Middle East by region and by major product group, 2001

(Billion dollars and percentage)

	Value	Share	
	Exports	Exports	Imports
Total	237	100.0	100.0
Region			
North America	39	16.5	12.6
Latin America	3	1.3	2.4
Western Europe	39	16.3	39.8
C./E. Europe/Baltic States/CIS	2	0.7	4.7
Africa	9	3.9	1.8
Middle East	18	7.5	10.9
Asia	112	47.3	27.8
Product group			
Agricultural products	8	3.3	13.4
Mining products	175	73.8	8.1
Manufactures	52	21.8	75.2

Note: Import shares are derived from the Secretariat's network of world merchandise trade by product and region.

Chart III.15

Merchandise trade of the Middle East, 1990-01

(Billion dollars)

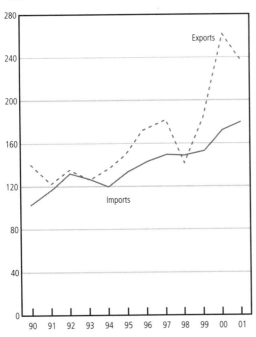

Chart III.16

Share of the Middle East in world merchandise trade, 1990-01

(Percentage based on value data)

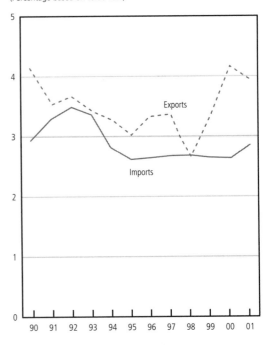

Table III.64

Merchandise exports of the Middle East by major product group and main destination, 2001

(Billion dollars and percentage)

	Value	Share		Annual percentage change			
	2001	1990	2001	1990-01	1999	2000	2001
Total merchandise							
World	236.8	100.0	100.0	5	30	42	-9
Asia	112.0	39.8	47.3	7	37	49	-11
North America	39.0	14.0	16.5	6	38	50	-5
Western Europe	38.6	26.9	16.3	0	12	31	-19
Middle East	17.7	6.3	7.5	7	8	26	8
Mining products							
World	174.8	100.0	100.0	4	38	54	-12
Asia	101.9	45.2	58.3	7	39	55	-12
Western Europe	23.8	24.9	13.6	-2	19	52	-25
North America	23.6	14.0	13.5	4	58	67	-5
Manufactures							
World	51.5	100.0	100.0	9	13	14	-1
North America	14.0	16.4	27.2	14	17	33	-6
Western Europe	12.8	32.4	24.8	6	5	4	-7
Asia	8.7	19.6	16.9	7	27	2	4
Middle East	8.1	17.9	15.7	7	0	21	12
Agriculture							
World	7.9	100.0	100.0	5	14	1	5

Table III.65

Merchandise exports of the Middle East by destination, 2001

(Billion dollars and percentage)

	Value	Share		Annual percentage change			
	2001	1990	2001	1990-01	1999	2000	2001
World	236.8	100.0	100.0	5	30	42	-9
Asia	112.0	39.8	47.3	7	37	49	-11
Japan	41.1	20.9	17.4	3	28	51	-10
Other	70.9	18.9	29.9	9	43	48	-11
Western Europe	38.6	26.9	16.3	0	12	31	-19
European Union (15)	36.4	23.9	15.4	1	13	32	-17
North America	39.0	14.0	16.5	6	38	50	-5
Intra-Middle East	17.7	6.3	7.5	7	8	26	8
Africa	9.2	3.1	3.9	7	16	40	-11
Latin America	3.0	3.7	1.3	-5	-3	36	-5
C./E. Europe/Baltic States/CIS	1.7	2.5	0.7	-6	-15	-4	11
Inter-regional trade	203.5	90.1	85.9	4	28	44	-11

Table III.66

Imports of fuels of selected regions and economies from the Middle East, 1990 and 2001

(Billion dollars and percentage)

	Value		Annual percentage change			
	1990	2001	1990-01	1999	2000	2001
North America	16.7	24.2	3	51	67	-3
United States	16.0	23.1	3	52	64	-3
Canada a	0.7	1.1	5	8	168	4
Western Europe	28.5	26.4	-1	14	55	-14
European Union (15)	25.5	24.2	0	15	55	-14
Turkey	2.5	2.0	-2	17	59	-10
Asia	50.1	88.5	5	27	67	-25
Japan	29.4	42.6	3	20	66	-10
Korea, Rep. of	4.8	22.0	15	28	84	-10
Singapore	6.3	8.9	3	20	46	-15
China	0.2	7.2	41	8	212	-17
Taipei, Chinese	2.8	6.2	8	44	71	16
Thailand	1.1	5.1	15	29	54	-7
Pakistan	1.2	2.8	8	46	73	-20
Philippines	1.4	2.7	6	25	56	-14

a Imports are valued f.o.b.

Table III.67

Leading merchandise exporters and importers in the Middle East, 2001

(Billion dollars and percentage)

	Value	Share				Annual percentage change			
	2001	1980	1990	1995	2001	1990-01	1999	2000	2001
Exporters									
Middle East	236.8	100.0	100.0	100.0	100.0	5	30	42	-9
Saudi Arabia	68.2	51.3	31.9	33.0	28.8	4	31	53	-12
United Arab Emirates	42.9	10.3	16.9	18.3	18.1	6	11	28	-2
Israel	29.0	2.6	8.7	12.6	12.3	8	12	22	-8
Iran, Islamic Rep. of	25.3	6.6	13.9	12.1	10.7	2	60	35	-11
Kuwait	16.1	9.2	5.1	8.4	6.8	8	28	59	-17
Iraq	15.9	12.4	8.9	0.3	6.7	2	132	62	-23
Oman	11.1	1.8	4.0	4.0	4.7	7	31	50	2
Qatar	10.9	2.7	2.8	2.4	4.6	10	43	61	-6
Bahrain	5.5	1.7	2.7	2.7	2.3	4	27	38	-3
Syrian Arab Republic	4.5	1.0	3.0	2.3	1.9	1	20	34	-3
Importers									
Middle East	180.0	100.0	100.0	100.0	100.0	5	3	13	4
United Arab Emirates	41.7	8.5	10.8	15.7	23.2	13	15	15	9
Israel	35.1	9.5	16.2	22.2	19.5	7	13	14	-7
Saudi Arabia	31.2	29.3	23.2	21.1	17.3	2	-7	8	3
Iran, Islamic Rep. of	17.5	11.9	19.6	10.4	9.7	-1	-11	13	22
Iraq	11.0	13.6	7.4	0.5	6.1	3	85	37	-1
Kuwait	7.7	6.4	3.8	5.8	4.3	6	-12	-6	8
Lebanon	7.3	3.6	2.4	5.5	4.1	10	-12	0	17
Oman	5.8	1.7	2.6	3.2	3.2	7	-18	8	15
Jordan	4.8	3.4	2.5	2.8	2.7	6	-3	22	7
Syrian Arab Republic	4.3	2.3	2.3	3.5	2.4	5	-2	0	13

Note: Recent figures for a number of significant traders in the region have been estimated by the Secretariat.

8. Asia

Table III.68

Merchandise trade of Asia, 2001

(Billion dollars and percentage)

	Exports	Imports
Value	1497	1375
Share in world merchandise trade	25.0	21.9
Annual percentage change		
Value		
1980-85	5	2
1985-90	13	14
1990-01	7	6
1999	7	10
2000	18	23
2001	-9	-7
Volume		
1980-85	7.5	5.5
1985-90	8.0	12.0
1990-01	7.5	7.5
1999	6.5	9.5
2000	16.0	16.5
2001	-3.5	-1.5

Table III.69

Merchandise trade of Asia by region and by major product group, 2001

(Billion dollars and percentage)

	Value	Share	
	Exports	Exports	Imports
Total	1497	100.0	100.0
Region			
North America	376	25.1	15.9
Latin America	40	2.7	1.7
Western Europe	252	16.8	15.1
C./E. Europe/Baltic States/CIS	17	1.1	1.5
Africa	24	1.6	1.6
Middle East	45	3.0	8.6
Asia	722	48.2	55.6
Product group			
Agricultural products	100	6.7	9.7
Mining products	114	7.6	18.0
Manufactures	1248	83.3	70.0

Note: Import shares are derived from the Secretariat's network of world merchandise trade by product and region.

Chart III.17
Merchandise trade of Asia, 1990-01
(Billion dollars)

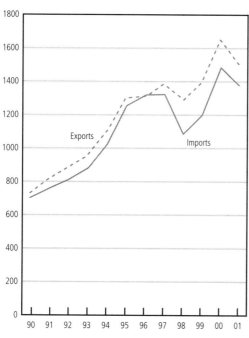

Chart III.18
Share of Asia in world merchandise trade, 1990-01
(Percentage based on value data)

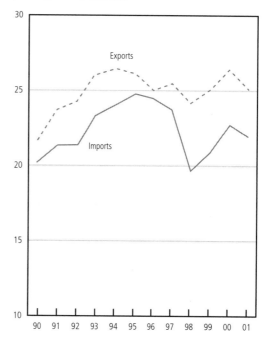

Table III.70

Merchandise exports of Asia by main product group and main destination, 2001

(Billion dollars and percentage)

	Value	Share in total merchandise		Share in product group		Annual percentage change		
	2001	1990	2001	1990	2001	1990-01	2000	2001
Total merchandise								
World	1497.4	100.0	100.0	-	-	7	18	-9
Intra-Asia	722.2	42.1	48.2	-	-	8	24	-10
Japan	147.9	10.4	9.9	-	-	6	28	-7
Other	574.2	31.7	38.3	-	-	8	24	-11
North America	375.8	28.3	25.1	-	-	5	15	-11
Western Europe	251.8	20.0	16.8	-	-	5	11	-10
All other regions	126.4	8.1	8.4	-	-	7	16	3
Manufactures								
World	1247.9	79.1	83.3	100.0	100.0	7	18	-10
Intra-Asia	551.2	28.5	36.8	36.0	44.2	9	25	-12
Japan	99.3	4.3	6.6	5.5	8.0	11	30	-7
Other	452.0	24.1	30.2	30.5	36.2	9	24	-13
North America	349.0	26.1	23.3	33.0	28.0	6	15	-12
Western Europe	224.7	17.4	15.0	22.0	18.0	5	12	-11
All other regions	106.8	6.2	7.1	7.8	8.6	8	17	2
Mining products								
World	113.8	8.9	7.6	100.0	100.0	5	38	-5
Intra-Asia	93.0	7.1	6.2	79.6	81.7	5	40	-6
Japan	28.8	3.6	1.9	40.5	25.3	1	40	-8
Other	64.2	3.5	4.3	39.0	56.4	9	40	-6
Western Europe	8.2	0.6	0.5	6.9	7.2	6	25	9
North America	6.5	0.8	0.4	8.9	5.8	1	36	-13
All other regions	4.6	0.3	0.3	2.8	4.0	9	33	11
Agricultural products								
World	99.7	9.7	6.7	100.0	100.0	3	5	-1
Intra-Asia	60.5	5.5	4.0	56.8	60.7	4	6	-2
Japan	19.0	2.3	1.3	23.2	19.1	1	5	-6
Other	41.4	3.3	2.8	33.6	41.5	5	7	-1
Western Europe	14.1	1.7	0.9	17.2	14.1	1	-1	-4
North America	13.4	1.1	0.9	11.4	13.4	5	11	-3
All other regions	11.4	1.4	0.8	14.3	11.4	1	4	8

Table III.71

Merchandise exports of Asia by product, 2001

(Billion dollars and percentage)

	Value	Share in exports of Asia		Share in world exports		Annual percentage change			
	2001	1990	2001	1990	2001	1990-01	1999	2000	2001
Total merchandise exports	1497.4	100.0	100.0	21.8	25.0	7	7	18	-9
Agricultural products	99.7	9.7	6.7	17.4	18.2	3	-2	5	-1
Food	78.5	6.8	5.2	16.0	17.9	4	-1	3	1
Raw materials	21.3	2.9	1.4	21.7	19.3	0	-4	15	-10
Mining products	113.8	8.9	7.6	13.5	14.4	5	9	38	-5
Ores and other minerals	16.6	1.5	1.1	20.5	26.2	4	2	19	6
Fuels	77.5	6.2	5.2	12.6	12.6	5	11	49	-6
Non-ferrous metals	19.7	1.3	1.3	12.8	17.8	7	7	19	-10
Manufactures	1247.9	79.1	83.3	24.4	27.9	7	9	18	-10
Iron and steel	29.2	2.8	2.0	19.5	22.6	3	-9	18	-16
Chemicals	95.2	4.6	6.4	11.4	16.0	10	12	19	-5
Other semi-manufactures	87.1	6.2	5.8	17.3	20.2	6	8	12	-6
Machinery and transport equipment	730.5	43.2	48.8	26.3	29.8	8	11	21	-13
Automotive products	107.2	9.7	7.2	22.4	19.0	4	9	9	-6
Office and telecom equipment	382.2	18.6	25.5	45.9	46.2	10	14	25	-16
Other machinery and transport equipment	241.0	15.0	16.1	18.6	22.7	7	7	20	-11
Textiles	64.7	5.0	4.3	35.3	44.0	5	3	13	-7
Clothing	88.7	6.4	5.9	43.6	45.5	6	1	14	-2
Other consumer goods	152.4	11.0	10.2	27.1	29.0	6	8	14	-7

Table III.72

Merchandise exports of Asia by destination, 2001

(Billion dollars and percentage)

	Value	Share		Annual percentage change			
	2001	1990	2001	1990-01	1999	2000	2001
World	1497.4	100.0	100.0	7	7	18	-9
Intra-Asia	722.2	42.1	48.2	8	12	24	-10
Japan	147.9	10.4	9.9	6	13	28	-7
Australia and New Zealand	37.7	2.7	2.5	6	9	5	-6
China	100.9	3.3	6.7	14	8	28	-5
Other	435.6	25.7	29.1	8	13	24	-13
North America	375.8	28.3	25.1	5	8	15	-11
Western Europe	251.8	20.0	16.8	5	1	11	-10
European Union (15)	237.6	18.6	15.9	5	4	11	-10
Middle East	45.3	2.9	3.0	7	-7	15	6
Latin America	40.3	1.8	2.7	10	-9	23	-4
Africa	23.9	1.5	1.6	7	-1	4	7
South Africa	5.9	0.2	0.4	12	-10	15	-12
Other Africa	18.0	1.2	1.2	6	2	0	16
C./E. Europe/Baltic States/CIS	16.9	1.9	1.1	2	-11	20	10
C./E. Europe	7.5	0.4	0.5	10	-1	13	5
Russian Fed.	6.6	-	0.4	-	-26	31	16
Inter-regional trade	753.9	56.4	50.4	6	3	14	-9

Table III.73

Leading merchandise exporters and importers in Asia, 2001

(Billion dollars and percentage)

| | Value | Share | | Annual percentage change | | | | | | | |
| | | | | Value | | | | Volume | | | |
	2001	1990	2001	1990-01	1999	2000	2001	1990-01	1999	2000	2001
Exporters											
Asia	1497.4	100.0	100.0	7	7	18	-9	7.0	6.5	16.0	-3.5
Japan	403.5	38.9	26.9	3	8	14	-16	1.5	2.0	9.5	-10.0
China	266.2	8.4	17.8	14	6	28	7	14.0	9.5	28.5	9.5
Hong Kong, China	191.1	-	-	8	0	16	-6	8.5	3.5	17.0	-3.0
domestic exports	20.3	3.9	1.4	-3	-9	5	-14	-3.0	-7.0	7.5	-11.0
re-exports	170.8	-	-	11	1	18	-5	12.0	5.5	18.5	-2.0
Korea, Rep. of	150.4	8.8	10.0	8	9	20	-13	14.5	12.0	21.0	3.5
Taipei, Chinese	122.5	9.1	8.2	6	10	22	-17	4.0	5.0	10.0	-14.5
Singapore	121.8	7.1	8.1	8	4	20	-12	10.0	5.5	15.5	-4.5
domestic exports	66.1	4.7	4.4	6	8	15	-16	8.0	8.0	10.0	-11.0
re-exports	55.6	2.4	3.7	11	-1	28	-6	11.5	1.5	26.5	-5.5
Malaysia	87.9	4.0	5.9	10	15	16	-10	12.0	20.0	19.5	-6.5
Thailand	65.1	3.1	4.3	10	7	18	-6	9.5	12.0	22.0	-5.5
Australia	63.4	5.4	4.2	4	0	14	-1	7.0	5.0	10.0	3.0
Indonesia	56.3	3.5	3.8	7	0	28	-9	8.5	-1.5	24.0	-5.5
India	43.6	2.4	2.9	8	7	19	3	10.5	13.0	20.0	7.0
Philippines	32.1	1.1	2.1	13	24	9	-19	16.0	28.0	13.0	-1.0
Viet Nam	15.1	0.3	1.0	18	23	25	4	...	...	...	...
New Zealand	13.7	1.3	0.9	4	3	7	3	4.5	1.5	5.5	3.0
Pakistan	9.2	0.8	0.6	5	0	6	2	4.0	12.5	12.0	...
Importers											
Asia	1374.6	100.0	100.0	6	10	23	-7	7.0	10.0	16.0	-1.5
Japan	349.1	33.2	25.4	4	11	22	-8	4.5	9.5	11.0	-1.5
China	243.6	7.5	17.7	15	18	36	8	15.0	15.0	31.5	15.0
Hong Kong, China	202.0	-	-	8	-3	18	-6	9.0	0.0	18.0	-2.5
retained imports	31.2	4.4	2.3	0	-21	22	-11	0.5	-18.5	21.0	-7.5
Korea, Rep. of	141.1	9.9	10.3	7	28	34	-12	8.5	29.0	19.0	-4.0
Singapore	116.0	8.6	8.4	6	9	21	-14	6.5	9.5	15.0	-12.5
retained imports	60.4	6.1	4.4	3	18	16	-20	...	...	...	...
Taipei, Chinese	107.3	7.7	7.8	6	6	26	-23	6.0	3.5	10.0	-12.0
Malaysia	74.1	4.1	5.4	9	11	27	-10	10.0	13.5	24.5	-8.0
Australia	63.9	5.9	4.6	4	7	3	-11	6.5	6.5	5.5	-5.5
Thailand	62.1	4.7	4.5	6	17	23	0	3.0	23.5	21.5	-10.5
India	49.6	3.3	3.6	7	9	9	-3	9.0	3.5	5.5	2.5
Philippines	31.4	1.8	2.3	8	3	4	-7	12.0	6.0	22.0	7.0
Indonesia	31.0	3.1	2.3	3	-12	40	-8	3.5	-11.5	37.0	-4.0
Viet Nam	15.6	0.4	1.1	17	1	31	2	...	...	...	...
New Zealand	13.3	1.3	1.0	3	14	-3	-4	4.5	13.5	-2.5	3.0
Pakistan	10.6	1.0	0.8	3	10	10	-6	4.0	8.0	-1.5	...
Memorandum item:											
ASEAN (10)											
Exports	385.2	19.5	25.7	9	9	19	-10	...	...	...	...
Imports	336.0	22.9	24.4	7	-25	22	-8	...	...	...	...
SAPTA (7)											
Exports	65.1	3.7	4.3	8	5	17	1	...	...	...	...
Imports	76.6	5.4	5.6	7	-2	9	10	...	...	...	...

Table III.74

Merchandise trade of Japan by region and economy, 2001

(Billion dollars and percentage)

Destination	Exports Value 2001	Share 1990	Share 2001	Annual percentage change 2000	Annual percentage change 2001	Origin	Imports Value 2001	Share 1990	Share 2001	Annual percentage change 2000	Annual percentage change 2001
Region						**Region**					
World	403.50	100.0	100.0	14	-16	World	348.61	100.0	100.0	22	-8
Asia	171.50	34.2	42.5	25	-17	Asia	165.01	35.1	47.3	27	-6
North America	129.10	34.0	32.0	11	-15	North America	71.44	26.1	20.5	8	-12
Western Europe	68.23	22.2	16.9	5	-18	Western Europe	49.18	18.2	14.1	8	-5
Latin America	11.66	2.5	2.9	15	-12	Middle East	44.25	13.3	12.7	62	-10
Middle East	10.88	3.2	2.7	-2	9	Latin America	9.10	4.0	2.6	15	-14
Africa	3.72	1.5	0.9	-7	-11	C./E. Europe/ Baltic States/CIS	5.12	1.7	1.5	25	-12
C./E. Europe/ Baltic States/CIS	2.44	1.1	0.6	25	-3	Africa	4.50	1.6	1.3	22	-9
Economy						**Economy**					
United States	122.32	31.6	30.3	11	-15	United States	63.63	22.5	18.3	7	-12
European Union (15)	64.37	20.4	16.0	5	-18	China	57.75	5.1	16.6	29	5
China	30.94	2.1	7.7	30	2	European Union (15)	44.51	16.0	12.8	9	-5
Korea, Rep. of	25.25	6.1	6.3	34	-18	Korea, Rep. of	17.16	5.0	4.9	28	-16
Taipei, Chinese	24.19	5.4	6.0	25	-33	Indonesia	14.84	5.4	4.3	30	-9
Above 5	267.06	65.5	66.2	14	-16	Above 5	197.90	54.0	56.8	16	-6
Hong Kong, China	23.23	4.5	5.8	23	-15	Australia	14.43	5.3	4.1	16	-2
Singapore	14.68	3.7	3.6	28	-29	Taipei, Chinese	14.16	3.6	4.1	40	-21
Thailand	11.86	3.2	2.9	21	-13	Malaysia	12.83	2.3	3.7	33	-11
Malaysia	10.99	1.9	2.7	25	-21	United Arab Emirates	12.82	3.9	3.7	69	-14
Philippines	8.18	0.9	2.0	17	-20	Saudi Arabia	12.30	4.5	3.5	71	-13
Australia	7.67	2.4	1.9	1	-11	Thailand	10.36	1.8	3.0	20	-2
Canada	6.55	2.3	1.6	8	-12	Canada	7.74	3.6	2.2	10	-11
Indonesia	6.40	1.8	1.6	57	-16	Philippines	6.40	0.9	1.8	36	-11
Panama	4.82	1.0	1.2	-6	-25	Qatar	6.01	0.9	1.7	70	3
Mexico	4.09	0.8	1.0	19	-22	Singapore	5.37	1.5	1.5	18	-16
Saudi Arabia	3.59	1.2	0.9	-7	16	Iran, Islamic Rep. of	5.01	1.5	1.4	71	-6
United Arab Emirates	2.56	0.5	0.6	0	1	Kuwait	4.42	0.7	1.3	66	-11
Brazil	2.47	0.4	0.6	23	-2	Russian Fed.	3.85	0.0	1.1	22	-16
Switzerland	1.96	1.0	0.5	-3	-6	Switzerland	3.28	1.7	0.9	-2	0
India	1.92	0.6	0.5	3	-23	South Africa	2.78	-	0.8	31	-7
Viet Nam	1.78	0.1	0.4	21	-10	Viet Nam	2.60	0.3	0.7	35	-1
South Africa	1.49	0.5	0.4	14	-20	Brazil	2.53	1.4	0.7	12	-15
New Zealand	1.18	0.4	0.3	-15	-7	Chile	2.43	0.7	0.7	13	-15
Korea, Dem. People's Rep. of	1.06	0.1	0.3	41	415	Oman	2.36	0.8	0.7	20	16
Israel	0.93	0.2	0.2	20	-27	India	2.21	0.9	0.6	17	-16
Iran, Islamic Rep. of	0.80	0.6	0.2	1	39	New Zealand	2.05	0.7	0.6	15	-6
Oman	0.79	0.1	0.2	11	6	Mexico	2.00	0.8	0.6	44	-16
Venezuela	0.74	0.1	0.2	26	46	Brunei Darussalam	1.69	0.5	0.5	57	2
Hungary	0.74	0.0	0.2	31	-13	Hong Kong, China	1.45	0.9	0.4	-7	-13
Turkey	0.73	0.3	0.2	33	-39	Norway	1.04	0.3	0.3	-10	-12
Above 30	388.28	94.3	96.2	-	-	Above 30	340.04	94.3	97.5	-	-

Table III.75

Merchandise exports of the United States, the European Union and Japan to China by major product, 2001

(Billion dollars and percentage)

| | Value | Share in economy's | | | | Annual percentage change | | | |
| | | total merchandise exports | | tolal exports by product group | | | | | |
	2001	1990	2001	1990	2001	1990-01	1999	2000	2001
United States									
Total merchandise exports	19.2	100.0	100.0	1.2	2.6	13	-8	24	18
Agricultural products	2.7	24.4	14.0	2.0	3.9	8	-24	88	13
Food	1.5	11.2	8.0	1.3	2.9	10	-31	98	2
Mining products	1.2	2.7	6.3	0.5	4.6	22	26	77	18
Manufactures	15.1	71.9	78.6	1.2	2.5	14	-7	14	20
Chemicals	2.2	21.9	11.5	2.7	2.7	7	6	11	-5
Other semi-manufactures	0.8	2.7	4.1	0.6	1.8	18	0	32	-1
Machinery and transport equipment	10.3	40.4	53.5	1.1	2.7	16	-13	13	27
Other non-electrical machinery	2.2	12.0	11.3	1.7	3.3	13	-5	36	20
Office and telecom equipment	3.9	5.2	20.5	0.5	3.1	28	9	44	22
Other transport equipment	2.6	16.1	13.3	2.1	4.6	12	-35	-25	44
Other consumer goods	1.6	5.1	8.4	0.7	2.1	19	10	17	31
European Union (15)									
Total merchandise exports	26.5	100.0	100.0	0.5	1.2	12	7	14	14
Agricultural products	1.0	8.4	3.8	0.4	0.5	5	36	2	-14
Food	0.4	5.7	1.5	0.3	0.2	0	13	-29	-13
Mining products	0.8	1.0	3.1	0.1	0.6	24	119	19	0
Manufactures	24.4	88.4	92.0	0.5	1.3	13	11	14	16
Chemicals	2.4	10.9	9.1	0.5	0.8	10	22	24	10
Other semi-manufactures	1.7	4.8	6.5	0.2	0.9	15	18	19	4
Machinery and transport equipment	17.6	63.6	66.6	0.8	1.8	13	10	12	16
Other non-electrical machinery	6.9	33.4	26.0	53.0	3.3	10	9	3	29
Office and telecom equipment	4.3	4.7	16.4	0.4	1.8	26	8	28	-7
Other consumer goods	1.6	4.0	6.1	0.2	0.8	16	13	22	27
Japan									
Total merchandise exports	30.9	100.0	100.0	2.1	7.7	16	16	30	2
Agricultural products	0.7	3.7	2.4	6.9	14.2	11	-4	25	16
Mining products	1.5	2.0	4.8	3.1	21.5	26	20	14	27
Non-ferrous metals	0.8	0.8	2.5	2.1	18.1	29	41	6	21
Manufactures	27.7	92.8	89.6	2.1	7.4	15	16	31	0
Iron and steel	2.1	17.3	6.7	8.5	15.3	6	1	39	-2
Chemicals	3.9	12.2	12.6	4.7	12.8	16	30	32	-2
Other semi-manufactures	1.5	6.3	4.9	2.8	8.8	13	14	28	-4
Machinery and transport equipment	15.6	43.8	50.3	1.3	5.7	17	12	32	1
Other non-electrical machinery	5.0	14.4	16.2	2.5	10.4	17	13	24	9
Office and telecom equipment	5.2	16.7	16.8	1.5	6.3	16	25	45	-1
Electrical machinery and apparatus	3.2	5.2	10.3	1.9	10.8	23	22	33	-6
Textiles	2.5	7.1	8.0	7.4	39.9	17	26	14	-4
Other consumer goods	2.2	5.9	7.0	1.5	6.2	18	26	41	3

Table III.76

Merchandise imports of the United States, the European Union and Japan from China by major product, 2001

(Billion dollars and percentage)

| | Value | Share in economy's | | | | Annual percentage change | | | |
| | | total merchandise imports | | tolal imports by product group | | | | | |
	2001	1990	2001	1990	2001	1990-01	1999	2000	2001
United States									
Total merchandise imports	109.4	100.0	100.0	3.1	9.3	21	17	23	2
Agricultural products	1.7	4.3	1.5	1.8	2.5	9	15	17	7
Food	1.3	3.6	1.2	2.0	2.5	8	17	20	11
Mining products	1.0	5.8	0.9	1.1	0.7	1	-14	67	-28
Manufactures	105.4	89.0	96.4	3.9	11.6	22	17	22	2
Chemicals	2.2	2.2	2.0	1.5	2.7	20	17	9	13
Other semi-manufactures	9.1	4.6	8.4	2.1	11.6	29	28	26	8
Machinery and transport equipment	36.5	15.6	33.4	1.2	7.2	31	24	32	0
Office and telecom equipment	22.3	8.2	20.4	2.1	12.9	33	24	32	-1
Electrical machinery and apparatus	8.8	4.1	8.0	3.4	17.1	29	22	31	1
Textiles	2.0	4.3	1.8	10.3	12.9	11	12	15	2
Clothing	9.3	22.7	8.5	13.7	14.0	10	4	15	4
Other consumer goods	45.8	39.1	41.8	11.0	32.8	22	15	16	2
Toys and games	13.7	14.7	12.6	25.0	61.8	19	7	11	-3
Footwear	10.3	9.6	9.4	15.7	64.2	21	7	9	6
Travel goods	2.4	4.6	2.1	31.4	50.8	12	4	13	-2
Furniture	5.8	1.0	5.3	3.1	28.8	43	55	39	11
European Union (15)									
Total merchandise imports	67.3	100.0	100.0	0.9	2.9	17	18	22	4
Agricultural products	2.4	12.7	3.5	1.0	1.0	3	-3	10	4
Food	1.6	7.8	2.4	0.7	0.8	4	-7	12	12
Mining products	1.4	3.0	2.1	0.4	0.5	13	-11	21	16
Manufactures	63.3	84.1	94.2	0.9	3.6	19	20	23	4
Chemicals	2.6	6.2	3.9	0.5	1.0	12	-4	9	9
Other semi-manufactures	5.4	6.4	8.0	0.6	2.9	20	21	20	6
Machinery and transport equipment	25.6	13.7	38.1	0.3	2.8	30	31	40	8
Office and telecom equipment	14.9	8.8	22.2	1.3	5.2	29	25	45	12
Electrical machinery and apparatus	6.2	2.0	9.2	0.5	6.4	37	43	36	-8
Textiles	1.8	8.5	2.7	2.3	4.0	5	-2	21	0
Clothing	8.4	21.5	12.5	7.1	10.6	11	15	4	3
Other consumer goods	19.3	27.4	28.6	2.5	8.9	18	20	17	-1
Toys and games	5.6	9.2	8.4	13.7	36.2	16	27	16	-3
Footwear	1.7	2.6	2.6	2.6	9.3	17	-4	16	2
Travel goods	2.5	4.7	3.7	19.0	46.4	15	20	10	-4
Furniture	1.2	0.8	1.8	0.7	5.1	27	36	32	4
Japan									
Total merchandise imports	57.8	100.0	100.0	5.1	16.6	17	16	29	5
Agricultural products	6.9	23.1	12.0	5.5	12.1	10	14	13	-2
Food	6.0	17.5	10.4	6.2	13.1	11	14	12	0
Mining products	2.9	28.8	5.1	4.4	3.3	-2	-5	47	-10
Manufactures	47.4	47.6	82.1	5.7	24.0	24	17	30	7
Chemicals	1.7	4.5	2.9	3.6	6.7	12	4	22	5
Other semi-manufactures	3.1	2.4	5.3	2.6	21.1	27	15	29	10
Machinery and transport equipment	15.1	3.8	26.1	1.3	15.8	42	19	41	16
Office and telecom equipment	8.1	1.4	14.1	1.5	15.5	47	19	51	26
Electrical machinery and apparatus	4.2	1.2	7.3	3.7	31.1	40	23	37	1
Textiles	2.1	6.7	3.7	19.7	44.9	10	12	18	5
Clothing	14.8	19.9	25.6	27.5	77.1	20	20	29	0
Other consumer goods	10.3	7.5	17.9	4.5	28.7	28	17	22	7
Toys and games	1.9	1.2	3.4	7.6	57.6	30	6	15	7
Footwear	2.0	1.4	3.5	12.5	66.4	28	21	13	4
Travel goods	1.3	1.0	2.3	9.6	43.2	26	22	20	4
Furniture	1.3	0.5	2.3	4.6	34.9	35	34	51	23

Table III.77

Merchandise exports of ASEAN countries by region, 1990-01

(Billion dollars and percentage)

Origin / Destination		ASEAN (10)	All other regions			World
			Total	Asia	Other regions	
Value						
ASEAN (10)	1990	28.95	115.24	...	...	144.20
	1995	81.88	239.00	...	...	320.88
	2000	103.05	324.43	...	...	427.48
	2001	90.38	294.88	...	...	385.27
Indonesia	1990	2.57	23.11	15.31	7.80	25.68
	1995	6.50	38.92	22.15	16.77	45.42
	2000	10.88	51.24	28.93	22.31	62.12
	2001	9.51	46.81	26.18	20.64	56.32
Malaysia	1990	8.62	20.83	9.65	11.18	29.45
	1995	20.41	53.51	22.83	30.68	73.91
	2000	26.06	72.08	32.93	39.15	98.14
	2001	22.13	65.79	30.47	35.33	87.92
Philippines	1990	0.59	7.58	2.59	4.98	8.17
	1995	2.36	15.14	5.04	10.10	17.50
	2000	6.24	33.54	12.42	21.12	39.78
	2001	4.99	27.14	10.97	16.17	32.13
Singapore a	1990	13.57	39.16	15.16	24.00	52.73
	1995	38.24	80.03	34.81	45.21	118.27
	2000	41.53	96.27	45.00	51.27	137.80
	2001	35.99	85.76	42.23	43.53	121.75
Thailand	1990	2.75	20.32	6.78	13.54	23.07
	1995	12.33	44.11	18.17	25.95	56.44
	2000	13.38	55.68	23.44	32.24	69.06
	2001	12.60	52.51	22.06	30.45	65.11
Share						
ASEAN (10)	1990	20.1	79.9	...	...	100.0
	2001	23.5	76.5	...	...	100.0
Indonesia	1990	1.8	16.0	10.6	5.4	17.8
	2001	2.5	12.2	15.4	11.6	14.6
Malaysia	1990	6.0	14.4	6.7	7.8	20.4
	2001	5.7	17.1	7.9	9.2	22.8
Philippines	1990	0.4	5.3	1.8	3.5	5.7
	2001	1.3	7.0	2.8	4.2	8.3
Singapore	1990	9.4	27.2	10.5	16.6	36.6
	2001	9.3	22.3	11.0	11.3	31.6
Thailand	1990	1.9	14.1	4.7	9.4	16.0
	2001	3.3	13.6	5.7	7.9	16.9
Annual percentage change						
ASEAN (10)	1990-01	11	9	...	...	9
	2000	28	16	...	...	19
	2001	-12	-9	...	...	-10
Indonesia	1990-01	13	7	5	9	7
	2000	31	27	32	21	28
	2001	-13	-9	-10	-7	-9
Malaysia	1990-01	9	11	11	11	10
	2000	29	12	19	7	16
	2001	-15	-11	-14	-10	-10
Philippines	1990-01	21	12	14	11	13
	2000	20	7	10	5	9
	2001	-20	-19	-12	-23	-19
Singapore	1990-01	9	7	10	6	8
	2000	29	17	24	11	20
	2001	-13	-11	-6	-15	-12
Thailand	1990-01	15	9	11	8	10
	2000	23	17	27	11	18
	2001	-6	-6	-6	-6	-6

a Includes significant re-exports.

Table III.78

Merchandise imports of ASEAN countries by region, 1990-01

(Billion dollars and percentage)

	Origin	ASEAN (10)	All other regions			World
Destination			Total	Asia	Other regions	
Value						
ASEAN (10)	1990	26.31	136.02	...	...	162.33
	1995	66.88	288.43	...	...	355.31
	2000	86.80	280.33	...	...	367.13
	2001	76.54	259.62	...	...	336.16
Indonesia	1990	1.88	19.96	10.12	9.83	21.84
	1995	4.22	36.41	18.13	18.29	40.63
	2000	6.49	27.03	13.76	13.27	33.52
	2001	5.46	25.50	12.82	12.68	30.96
Malaysia	1990	5.65	23.61	12.12	11.49	29.26
	1995	13.52	64.17	34.85	29.32	77.69
	2000	19.72	49.62	33.73	15.89	82.20
	2001	16.72	49.62	29.82	19.81	74.08
Philippines	1990	1.37	11.67	5.22	6.45	13.04
	1995	3.36	24.98	12.64	12.34	28.34
	2000	5.46	28.34	14.55	13.80	33.81
	2001	4.99	26.37	13.94	12.43	31.36
Singapore a	1990	12.45	48.32	20.78	27.54	60.77
	1995	31.50	93.01	44.38	48.63	124.51
	2000	39.82	94.73	41.83	52.89	134.55
	2001	34.39	81.61	33.38	48.23	116.00
Thailand	1990	4.37	28.68	15.82	12.86	33.05
	1995	9.51	61.28	32.62	28.66	70.79
	2000	10.31	51.62	26.88	24.73	61.92
	2001	10.04	52.02	25.76	26.26	62.06
Share						
ASEAN (10)	1990	16.2	83.8	...	...	100.0
	2001	22.8	77.2	...	...	100.0
Indonesia	1990	1.2	12.3	6.2	6.1	13.5
	2001	1.6	7.6	3.8	3.8	9.2
Malaysia	1990	3.5	14.5	7.5	7.1	18.0
	2001	5.0	14.8	8.9	5.9	22.0
Philippines	1990	0.8	7.2	3.2	4.0	8.0
	2001	1.5	7.8	4.1	3.7	9.3
Singapore	1990	7.7	29.8	12.8	17.0	37.4
	2001	10.2	24.3	9.9	14.3	34.5
Thailand	1990	2.7	17.7	9.7	7.9	20.4
	2001	3.0	15.5	7.7	7.8	18.5
Annual percentage change						
ASEAN (10)	1990-01	10	6	...	...	7
	2000	28	21	...	...	22
	2001	-12	-7	...	...	-8
Indonesia	1990-01	10	2	2	2	3
	2000	36	41	61	24	40
	2001	-16	-6	-7	-4	-8
Malaysia	1990-01	10	7	9	5	9
	2000	28	0	26	-31	27
	2001	-15	0	-12	25	-10
Philippines	1990-01	12	8	9	6	8
	2000	15	2	-1	6	4
	2001	-9	-7	-4	-10	-7
Singapore	1990-01	10	5	4	5	6
	2000	27	19	24	15	21
	2001	-14	-14	-20	-9	-14
Thailand	1990-01	8	6	5	7	6
	2000	29	22	25	18	23
	2001	-3	1	-4	6	0

a Includes significant imports for re-export.

Table III.79

Leading exporters and importers of commercial services in Asia, 2001

(Billion dollars and percentage)

	Value	Share		Annual percentage change			
	2001	1990	2001	1990-01	1999	2000	2001
Exporters							
Asia	302.6	100.0	100.0	8	4	12	-1
Japan	63.7	31.5	21.0	4	-2	13	-7
Hong Kong, China	42.4	13.8	14.0	8	2	14	2
China	32.9	4.4	10.9	17	10	15	9
Korea, Rep. of	29.6	7.0	9.8	11	4	15	0
Singapore	26.4	9.7	8.7	7	25	13	-2
India	20.4	3.5	6.7	14	27	26	15
Taipei, Chinese	20.3	5.3	6.7	10	3	16	2
Australia	15.7	7.5	5.2	4	7	5	-12
Malaysia	14.0	2.9	4.6	13	4	16	3
Thailand	12.9	4.8	4.3	7	11	-5	-6
Indonesia a	5.2	1.9	1.7	7	3	14	...
New Zealand	4.2	1.8	1.4	5	15	1	-2
Macao, China	3.8	1.1	1.2	9	-5	21	15
Philippines	3.1	2.2	1.0	1	...	-18	-21
Viet Nam a	2.7	...	0.9	...	-5	8	...
Importers							
Asia	355.0	100.0	100.0	6	5	8	-3
Japan	107.0	47.1	30.1	2	3	1	-7
China	39.0	2.3	11.0	23	17	16	9
Korea, Rep. of	33.1	5.6	9.3	11	11	23	0
Hong Kong, China	25.1	6.2	7.1	8	-5	3	-2
Taipei, Chinese	23.7	7.8	6.7	5	0	11	-8
India	23.4	3.3	6.6	13	20	15	19
Singapore	20.0	4.8	5.6	8	7	13	-6
Malaysia	16.5	3.0	4.7	11	13	14	0
Australia	16.4	7.5	4.6	2	6	-1	-8
Thailand	14.5	3.4	4.1	8	13	14	-6
Indonesia a	14.5	3.3	4.1	9	-3	30	...
Philippines	5.1	1.0	1.4	10	...	-19	-16
New Zealand	4.2	1.8	1.2	2	2	-1	-6
Viet Nam a	3.2	...	0.9	...	-3	7	...
Pakistan a	2.0	1.0	0.6	1	-7	11	...

a Includes Secretariat estimates.

Table III.80

Trade in commercial services of Japan, 2001

(Billion dollars and percentage)

	Exports			Imports		
	Value	Share		Value	Share	
	2001	1995	2001	2001	1995	2001
Total commercial services	63.7	100.0	100.0	107.0	100.0	100.0
Transportation	24.0	35.2	37.7	32.4	29.6	30.3
Sea transport	16.4	23.1	25.8	20.4	19.0	19.1
Air transport	7.6	12.1	11.9	11.9	10.6	11.1
Other transport	0.0	0.0	0.0	0.1	0.0	0.1
Travel	3.3	5.0	5.2	26.5	30.2	24.8
Other commercial services	36.4	59.8	57.1	48.1	40.2	45.0
Communication services	0.7	0.8	1.1	1.1	0.7	1.0
Construction services	4.8	10.3	7.5	3.8	2.6	3.6
Insurance services	-0.1	0.5	-0.2	2.6	2.1	2.5
Financial services	2.7	0.5	4.3	1.6	0.4	1.5
Computer and information services	1.4	...	2.2	2.6	...	2.5
Royalties and licence fees	10.5	9.4	16.4	11.1	7.7	10.4
Other business services	16.2	38.2	25.5	23.8	26.2	22.2
Personal, cultural, and recreational services	0.1	0.2	0.2	1.4	0.5	1.3

Table III.81

Trade in commercial services of China, 2001

(Billion dollars and percentage)

	Exports			Imports		
	Value	Share		Value	Share	
	2001	1997	2001	2001	1997	2001
Total commercial services	32.9	100.0	100.0	39.0	100.0	100.0
Transportation	4.6	12.1	14.1	11.3	35.9	29.0
Sea transport	2.0	4.0	6.1	6.9	24.5	17.7
Air transport	1.3	2.7	3.9	2.4	6.5	6.1
Other transport	1.4	5.3	4.1	2.1	4.8	5.3
Travel	17.8	49.3	54.1	13.9	29.3	35.6
Other commercial services	10.5	38.7	31.8	13.8	34.8	35.4
Communication services	0.3	1.1	0.8	0.3	1.0	0.8
Construction services	0.8	2.4	2.5	0.8	4.4	2.2
Insurance services	0.2	0.7	0.7	2.7	3.8	6.9
Financial services	0.1	0.1	0.3	0.1	1.2	0.2
Computer and information services	0.5	0.3	1.4	0.3	0.8	0.9
Royalties and licence fees	0.1	0.2	0.3	1.9	2.0	5.0
Other business services	8.4	33.7	25.7	7.5	21.5	19.2
Personal, cultural, and recreational services	0.0	0.0	0.1	0.1	0.2	0.1

Table III.82

Trade in commercial services of Taipei, Chinese, 2001

(Billion dollars and percentage)

	Exports			Imports		
	Value	Share		Value	Share	
	2001	1995	2001	2001	1995	2001
Total commercial services	20.3	100.0	100.0	23.7	100.0	100.0
Transportation	3.5	30.5	17.3	5.5	27.6	23.3
Sea transport	2.1	17.0	10.3	3.2	19.8	13.4
Air transport	1.4	13.5	7.0	2.3	7.8	9.9
Other transport	...	...	...	...	...	...
Travel	4.0	22.0	19.7	7.3	36.8	30.9
Other commercial services	12.8	47.5	63.0	10.8	35.6	45.8
Communication services	0.3	3.8	1.3	0.4	2.1	1.9
Construction services	0.1	0.7	0.5	0.4	1.2	1.7
Insurance services	0.4	2.8	2.0	0.7	2.2	3.1
Financial services	0.5	...	2.5	0.7	...	3.0
Computer and information services	0.2	...	0.8	0.3	0.2	1.1
Royalties and licence fees	0.3	1.6	1.7	1.5	4.1	6.3
Other business services	11.0	38.6	54.1	6.6	25.1	27.9
Personal, cultural, and recreational services	0.0	0.0	0.2	0.2	0.7	0.8

Table III.83

Ratio of exports of goods and commercial services to GDP of least-developed countries, 1990 and 2000

(Million dollars and percentage)

	Value	Ratio to GDP					
	GDP	Goods and commercial services		Goods		Commercial services	
	2000	1990	2000	1990	2000	1990	2000
Total LDCs	166200	17	26	14	22	2	4
Afghanistan	…	…	…	…	…	…	…
Angola	8828	38	93	38	89	1	3
Bangladesh	47106	7	14	6	14	1	1
Benin	2168	19	24	13	18	6	6
Bhutan	487	33	30	23	23	10	6
Burkina Faso	2192	11	11	10	9	1	1
Burundi	689	7	7	6	7	1	0
Cambodia	3183	…	47	…	42	…	5
Cape Verde	558	15	22	6	4	9	18
Central African Republic	963	11	18	10	17	1	1
Chad	1407	15	18	13	16	1	2
Comoros	202	10	24	7	6	2	18
Congo, Dem. Rep. of	4481	27	…	25	…	2	…
Djibouti	553	…	27	…	14	…	14
Equatorial Guinea	1341	32	97	29	96	3	1
Eritrea	608	…	14	…	4	…	10
Ethiopia	6391	8	14	4	8	4	6
Gambia	422	52	59	35	35	17	24
Guinea	3012	27	25	24	24	3	1
Guinea-Bissau	215	9	32	8	30	2	2
Haiti	4050	10	12	9	8	1	4
Kiribati	43	34	…	10	…	23	…
Lao People's Dem. Rep.	1709	10	30	9	23	1	7
Lesotho	899	15	27	10	23	6	4
Liberia	…	…	…	…	…	…	…
Madagascar	3878	15	29	10	21	4	8
Malawi	1697	24	26	22	24	2	3
Maldives	556	90	82	39	20	51	62
Mali	2298	17	27	14	24	3	4
Mauritania	935	45	40	44	37	1	3
Mozambique	3754	9	18	5	10	4	9
Myanmar	7337	11	29	8	22	3	7
Nepal	5497	11	22	6	14	5	7
Niger	1826	21	14	20	14	1	1
Rwanda	1794	5	6	4	4	1	2
Samoa	236	21	25	4	6	17	20
Sao Tome and Principe	46	12	33	7	7	5	26
Senegal	4371	23	29	16	21	6	8
Sierra Leone	636	22	8	17	6	5	2
Solomon Islands	275	42	44	33	28	9	16
Somalia	…	…	…	…	…	…	…
Sudan	11516	3	16	2	16	1	0
Tanzania, United Rep. of	9027	13	14	10	7	3	7
Togo	1219	39	47	32	43	7	4
Tuvalu	…	…	…	…	…	…	…
Uganda	6170	…	10	…	7	…	3
Vanuatu	212	46	69	9	14	37	56
Yemen	8532	30	50	29	48	2	2
Zambia	2911	41	30	38	26	3	4
Memorandum item:							
World	…	18	23	15	18	4	4

Note: Trade in goods is derived from balance of payments statistics and does not correspond to the merchandise trade statistics given elsewhere in this report. Data are estimated for most countries. See the Technical Notes.

Table III.84

Merchandise exports and imports of least-developed countries by selected country grouping, 2001

(Million dollars and percentage)

	Exports					Imports				
	Value	Annual Percentage Change				Value	Annual Percentage Change			
	2000	1990-01	1999	2000	2001	2000	1990-01	1999	2000	2001
Total LDCs	36232	7	11	28	1	41818	5	4	4	4
Oil exporters	15057	9	51	65	-10	7582	7	6	9	4
Angola	7886	5	46	53	-15	3215	7	50	3	4
Yemen	4079	15	63	67	-21	2324	3	-7	16	-3
Sudan	1807	14	31	132	-10	1510	9	-27	9	4
Equatorial Guinea	1285	36	77	71	53	533	25	20	26	31
Exporters of manufactures	11847	15	7	24	9	17125	9	6	9	3
Bangladesh	6399	13	6	17	2	8360	8	10	9	0
Myanmar	1620	19	6	44	40	2371	24	-14	3	17
Cambodia	1327	30	9	35	17	1525	23	13	26	3
Madagascar	824	10	9	41	14	997	5	7	34	17
Nepal	804	12	27	34	-8	1573	7	14	11	-6
Lao People's Dem. Rep.	330	14	-16	6	2	535	10	-5	2	3
Haiti	323	5	13	-5	-14	1036	11	29	1	-2
Lesotho	220	15	-11	28	28	728	0	-10	-7	-6
Exporters of commodities	8147	3	-5	-3	12	14780	3	3	-4	5
Senegal	920	3	6	-10	17	1521	2	5	3	-1
Guinea	750	2	-3	3	10	612	-2	2	-13	-2
Zambia	746	-4	-7	-1	17	750	-2	-11	12	28
Tanzania, United Rep. of	663	8	-8	22	18	1524	4	7	-2	9
Mali	545	7	3	-5	36	592	1	9	-28	11
Liberia	500	6	-18	0	23	290	3	4	4	0
Ethiopia	482	3	-20	7	-13	1260	0	-5	-9	-17
Uganda	461	11	4	-11	-1	1517	17	-5	13	5
Benin	392	3	2	-7	-3	613	9	11	-18	6
Mozambique	364	17	14	38	93	1158	2	44	2	-8
Togo	363	4	-1	-7	19	565	1	2	-5	10
Malawi	355	-3	-14	-20	-13	569	0	21	-18	-3
Mauritania	300	-5	7	-20	-7	320	-1	-15	5	5
Niger	283	0	-14	-1	-3	372	1	7	-8	12
Burkina Faso	213	1	-20	-16	-18	550	2	-21	-5	19
Chad	183	-1	-23	-9	-10	323	8	-11	2	96
Central African Republic	155	1	-3	6	-15	120	-2	-10	-11	8
Bhutan	116	5	7	0	0	180	8	36	-1	0
Solomon Islands	85	2	16	-42	1	125	2	-31	14	-10
Maldives	76	3	-14	19	-2	389	10	14	-3	1
Guinea-Bissau	62	10	89	22	-11	62	-3	1	-10	5
Eritrea	35	-	-29	75	-14	471	-	-6	-5	0
Vanuatu	25	-10	-24	-4	-76	57	-2	9	-41	33
Kiribati	17	21	-5	175	45	41	3	9	17	-12
Samoa	14	5	33	-30	14	106	4	19	-8	23
Djibouti	13	-6	0	8	0	165	-3	-3	8	-3
Cape Verde	11	5	20	-8	-9	238	5	9	-4	-2
Gambia	8	-11	-74	14	13	190	1	-22	-1	5
Comoros	7	-10	27	40	-14	72	5	70	-10	18
Sao Tome and Principe	3	0	-20	-25	33	22	1	-8	0	5
Tuvalu	0	-7	86	-81	68	6	2	-7	21	-8
Other LDCs a	1181	-9	-19	-12	-7	2331	-3	-7	8	1
Memorandum Item:										
World b	6430100	5	4	13	-4	6710700	6	4	14	-4

a Other LDCs comprise Congo, Dem. Rep. of, Somalia, Rwanda, Afghanistan, Burundi and Sierra Leone. Their trade data are strongly affected by conflict and civil strife.
b Includes significant re-exports or imports for re-export.
Note: Data for 2001 are largely estimated.

Table III.85

Imports of agricultural products and manufactures of European Union, Asia and North America from least-developed countries, 2001

(Million dollars and percentage)

Agricultural products

European Union (15)

	Value	Annual percentage change	
	2000	2000	2001
Total LDCs	2693	2	-8
Senegal	309	-13	-3
Tanzania, United Rep. of	255	47	-10
Madagascar	249	-1	2
Uganda	198	-21	2
Malawi	193	-14	-13
Bangladesh	186	43	-6
Ethiopia	178	12	-48
Mozambique	116	19	-13
Sudan	102	-1	-10
Mauritania	86	2	28
Liberia	80	87	13
Congo, Dem. Rep. of	58	-18	-25
Myanmar	55	5	10
Chad	52	-12	-4
Mali	45	-25	-39
Afghanistan	45	104	-64
Zambia	44	-1	14
Burkina Faso	41	-4	-8
Benin	39	13	6
Central African Republic	38	12	10
Burundi	31	-7	-49
Others (28)	292	-8	-2

Asia a,b

	Value	Annual percentage change	
	2000	2000	2001
Total LDCs	2415	4	...
Myanmar	666	20	...
Tanzania, United Rep. of	197	-3	...
Bangladesh	145	5	...
Equatorial Guinea	109	-11	...
Mozambique	97	44	...
Madagascar	92	69	...
Mauritania	91	-29	...
Lao People's Dem. Rep.	86	10	...
Sudan	74	28	...
Mali	72	-30	...
Solomon Islands	66	-39	...
Ethiopia	65	-7	...
Malawi	62	60	...
Cambodia	58	-16	...
Liberia	44	337	...
Yemen	38	61	...
Senegal	34	1	...
Togo	33	-35	...
Uganda	31	25	...
Vanuatu	20	32	...
Others (29)	336	-8	...

North America

	Value	Annual percentage change	
	2000	2000	2001
Total LDCs	531	9	-2
Bangladesh	159	27	-37
Myanmar	53	102	-4
Malawi	53	-29	40
Liberia	47	45	-6
Madagascar	44	32	99
Ethiopia	32	-5	2
Mozambique	26	188	-70
Uganda	24	7	-20
Haiti	18	0	-30
Tanzania, United Rep. of	15	-28	5
Others (39)	60	-35	20

Manufactures

European Union (15)

	Value	Annual percentage change	
	2000	2000	2001
Total LDCs	6575	13	3
Bangladesh	2666	25	5
Congo, Dem. Rep. of	746	-3	-8
Angola	646	16	-19
Cambodia	326	16	31
Myanmar	320	74	17
Liberia	300	-21	88
Madagascar	279	6	0
Guinea	171	27	-25
Central African Republic	169	8	-44
Nepal	163	1	-26
Lao People's Dem. Rep.	112	7	7
Sierra Leone	92	62	-66
Niger	84	-31	-15
Ethiopia	46	50	11
Tanzania, United Rep. of	44	98	16
Others (34)	410	-9	13

North America

	Value	Annual percentage change	
	2000	2000	2001
Total LDCs	4997	35	4
Bangladesh	2560	26	-2
Cambodia	887	39	16
Myanmar	494	104	-1
Haiti	292	-1	-10
Nepal	258	31	-15
Lesotho	151	...	53
Madagascar	122	127	63
Maldives	104	77	5
Others (41)	129	-31	2

Asia a

	Value	Annual percentage change	
	2000	2000	2001
Total LDCs	694	-21	...
Bangladesh	287	9	...
Cambodia	176	-3	...
Myanmar	111	18	...
Nepal	44	-66	...
Others (45)	75	-64	...

a China, Hong Kong, India, Japan, Malaysia, Republic of Korea, Singapore, Taipei Chinese and Thailand
b Includes Secretariat estimates for India

Table III.86

Exports of commercial services of least-developed countries by category, 2000

(Million dollars and percentage)

	Value	Share in commercial services					
	Commercial services	Transport		Travel		Other services	
	2000	1990	2000	1990	2000	1990	2000
Total LDCs	5900	29	21	35	44	36	34
Afghanistan	...	...	...	...	...	...	...
Angola	295	49	30	21	0	31	70
Bangladesh	283	13	32	6	18	81	50
Benin	126	33	13	50	60	16	27
Bhutan	30	...	...	...	...	...	...
Burkina Faso	28	37	17	34	48	29	35
Burundi	2	38	43	52	38	9	19
Cambodia	159	...	44	...	40	...	16
Cape Verde	99	50	46	20	41	30	13
Central African Republic	11	51	3	16	36	33	61
Chad	25	18	5	34	50	47	45
Comoros	36	63	13	29	80	8	6
Congo, Dem. Rep. of	...	30	...	30	...	40	...
Djibouti	75	65	57	16	9	19	33
Equatorial Guinea	10	...	1	...	81	...	18
Eritrea	61	...	...	...	...	...	...
Ethiopia	387	81	56	2	15	17	30
Gambia	101	9	9	88	78	3	13
Guinea	36	14	54	33	5	53	41
Guinea-Bissau	4	5	9	0	52	95	39
Haiti	151	20	2	79	64	1	34
Kiribati	...	40	...	13	...	47	...
Lao People's Dem. Rep.	111	75	18	24	80	1	1
Lesotho	36	14	1	51	67	35	31
Liberia	...	...	...	...	...	...	...
Madagascar	314	32	16	31	39	37	45
Malawi	44	46	18	43	78	11	4
Maldives	345	10	6	88	93	2	1
Mali	83	31	37	54	43	15	21
Mauritania	28	35	3	65	83	0	15
Mozambique	325	61	30	0	23	39	47
Myanmar	510	10	17	21	33	69	50
Nepal	410	4	15	66	38	31	47
Niger	12	5	3	59	58	35	39
Rwanda	39	56	31	33	60	11	8
Samoa	46	15	3	61	88	24	9
Sao Tome and Principe	12	14	0	59	70	28	30
Senegal	330	19	10	43	49	38	40
Sierra Leone	15	10	26	76	46	14	28
Solomon Islands	44	13	3	38	9	49	88
Somalia	...	...	...	...	...	...	...
Sudan	24	14	63	16	22	70	15
Tanzania, United Rep. of	615	20	9	36	61	44	29
Togo	46	27	24	51	13	22	63
Tuvalu	...	...	...	...	...	...	...
Uganda	182	...	13	...	82	...	5
Vanuatu	118	10	23	68	46	21	31
Yemen	174	27	12	49	42	24	46
Zambia	114	69	37	14	58	18	5
Memorandum item:							
World	1465100	29	24	34	32	38	44

Note: Data are estimated for most countries.

Appendix B:

International Trade by Sector

THE FOLLOWING APPENDIX is provided by the World Trade Organization (© WTO) and presents comprehensive, comparable, and up-to-date statistics on trade in merchandise and commercial services for an assessment of world trade flows by country, region, and main product groups or service categories. Compiled from Section IV of the WTO International Trade Statistics, the appendix retains the WTO organizational structure (i.e, charts and tables are labeled IV) for easy reference within the WTO publications. For further information contact:

WORLD TRADE ORGANIZATION
Centre William Rappard, Rue de Lausanne 154,
CH-1211 Geneva 21, Switzerland • www.wto.org

1. Overview

Chart IV.1

World merchandise exports by product, 1990 and 2001

(Share based on value)

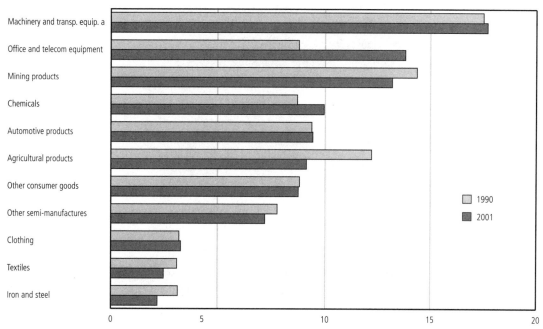

a Excluding automotive products and office and telecom equipment (throughout this report they are included with machinery and transport equipment, unless otherwise noted).

Table IV.1

World merchandise exports by product, 2001

(Billion dollars and percentage)

	Value	Share		Annual percentage change		
	2001	1990	2001	1990-01	2000	2001
All products a	5984	100.0	100.0	5	13	-4
Agricultural products	547	12.2	9.1	3	1	-1
Food	437	9.3	7.3	3	-2	1
Raw materials	110	2.9	1.8	1	10	-9
Mining products	790	14.4	13.2	4	46	-8
Ores and other minerals	63	1.6	1.1	2	14	-1
Fuels	616	10.7	10.3	5	57	-8
Non-ferrous metals	111	2.1	1.9	4	20	-9
Manufactures	4477	70.4	74.8	6	10	-4
Iron and steel	130	3.1	2.2	2	14	-8
Chemicals	595	8.7	9.9	7	9	2
Other semi-manufactures	432	7.8	7.2	5	7	-3
Machinery and transport equipment	2453	35.7	41.0	7	12	-6
Automotive products	565	9.4	9.4	5	4	-2
Office and telecom equipment	828	8.8	13.8	10	22	-14
Other machinery and transport equipment	1061	17.5	17.7	5	8	-2
Textiles	147	3.1	2.5	3	6	-5
Clothing	195	3.2	3.3	6	7	-1
Other consumer goods	525	8.8	8.8	5	8	-3

a Includes unspecified products. They accounted for 3 per cent of world merchandise exports in 2001.

Chart IV.2

World exports of commercial services by category, 1990, 1995 and 2001

(Share based on value)

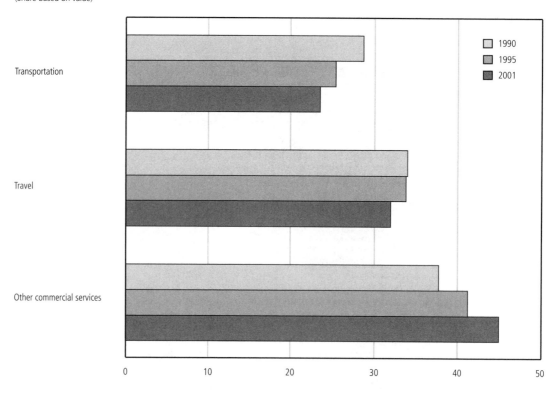

Table IV.2

World exports of commercial services by category, 2001

(Billion dollars and percentage)

	Value	Share		Annual percentage change			
	2001	1990	2001	1990-01	1999	2000	2001
All commercial services	1460	100.0	100.0	6	3	6	0
Transportation	340	28.5	23.4	4	3	8	-1
Travel	465	33.8	31.8	5	4	4	-2
Other commercial services	655	37.6	44.8	8	2	7	1

Note: Exports of transportation services are significantly under-reported. See the Technical Notes.

2. Agricultural Products

Table IV.3

World trade in agricultural products, 2001

(Billion dollars and percentage)

Value	547
Annual percentage change	
1980-85	-2
1985-90	9
1990-01	3
2000	1
2001	-1
Share in world merchandise trade	9.1
Share in world exports of primary products	40.9

Table IV.4

Major regional flows in world exports of agricultural products, 2001

(Billion dollars and percentage)

	Value	Annual percentage change		
	2001	1990-01	2000	2001
Intra-Western Europe	172.8	2	-5	-2
Intra-Asia	60.5	4	6	-2
North America to Asia	34.0	1	11	-6
Intra-North America	33.6	6	5	1
Latin America to Western Europe	17.7	3	-4	0
Latin America to North America	17.1	5	4	-7

Table IV.5

Share of agricultural products in trade in total merchandise and in primary products by region, 2001

(Percentage)

	Exports	Imports
Share of agricultural products in total merchandise		
World	9.1	9.1
North America	10.5	6.0
Latin America	18.1	9.3
Western Europe	9.2	9.9
C./E. Europe/Baltic States/CIS	8.7	10.5
Africa	14.7	15.3
Middle East	3.3	13.4
Asia	6.7	9.7
Share of agricultural products in primary products		
World	40.9	40.9
North America	58.3	32.7
Latin America	45.6	45.7
Western Europe	56.0	46.6
C./E. Europe/Baltic States/CIS	21.0	43.1
Africa	20.5	56.9
Middle East	4.3	62.2
Asia	46.7	35.0

Chart IV.3

Regional shares in world trade in agricultural products, 2001

(Percentage)

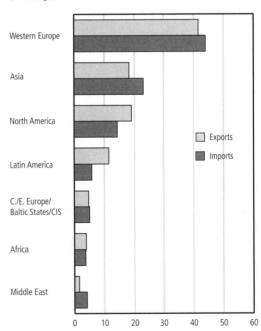

Table IV.6

Exports of agricultural products by region, 2001

(Billion dollars and percentage)

| | Value | Share in | | | | Annual percentage change | | |
| | | Region's exports | | World exports | | | | |
	2001	1990	2001	1990	2001	1990-01	2000	2001
World	547.5	-	-	100.0	100.0	3	1	-1
Western Europe								
World	227.8	100.0	100.0	45.2	41.6	2	-4	-2
Western Europe	172.8	78.2	75.8	35.3	31.6	2	-5	-2
Asia	13.6	4.8	6.0	2.2	2.5	4	1	-6
North America	12.3	4.6	5.4	2.1	2.2	3	0	0
C./E. Europe/Baltic States/CIS	11.1	3.1	4.9	1.4	2.0	6	-3	14
Africa	7.7	4.1	3.4	1.8	1.4	0	3	-1
Middle East	5.6	3.2	2.4	1.4	1.0	-1	-3	-10
Latin America	3.5	1.6	1.5	0.7	0.6	1	5	-4
North America								
World	103.8	100.0	100.0	19.7	19.0	2	8	-3
Asia	34.0	38.7	32.8	7.6	6.2	1	11	-6
North America	33.6	21.3	32.4	4.2	6.1	6	5	1
Latin America	14.9	8.4	14.3	1.7	2.7	7	8	6
Western Europe	13.8	20.4	13.3	4.0	2.5	-2	6	-7
Africa	2.9	3.2	2.8	0.6	0.5	1	4	-8
Middle East	2.8	3.3	2.7	0.6	0.5	0	13	-12
C./E. Europe/Baltic States/CIS	1.6	4.4	1.5	0.9	0.3	-7	9	14
Asia								
World	99.7	100.0	100.0	17.4	18.2	3	5	-1
Asia	60.5	56.8	60.7	9.9	11.0	4	6	-2
Western Europe	14.1	17.2	14.1	3.0	2.6	1	-1	-4
North America	13.4	11.4	13.4	2.0	2.4	5	11	-3
Middle East	4.7	5.1	4.7	0.9	0.9	2	7	3
Africa	3.1	2.7	3.1	0.5	0.6	4	-3	6
C./E. Europe/Baltic States/CIS	2.0	5.0	2.0	0.9	0.4	-5	7	21
Latin America	1.5	1.5	1.5	0.3	0.3	3	8	9
Latin America								
World	62.7	100.0	100.0	9.6	11.5	4	1	2
Western Europe	17.7	33.5	28.2	3.2	3.2	3	-4	0
North America	17.1	26.2	27.2	2.5	3.1	5	4	-7
Latin America	10.8	11.3	17.2	1.1	2.0	8	6	-2
Asia	9.6	10.1	15.4	1.0	1.8	8	7	11
Middle East	2.8	3.1	4.5	0.3	0.5	8	0	37
Africa	2.2	2.5	3.5	0.2	0.4	7	-4	35
C./E. Europe/Baltic States/CIS	2.2	13.2	3.5	1.3	0.4	-8	-23	55
Africa								
World	20.7	100.0	100.0	4.0	3.8	2	-4	0
Western Europe	10.7	61.2	51.8	2.4	2.0	1	-8	2
Asia	3.9	15.1	18.7	0.6	0.7	4	5	-2
Africa	2.8	11.8	13.5	0.5	0.5	3	1	-2
Middle East	1.3	2.3	6.2	0.1	0.2	12	11	-1
North America	1.0	5.3	4.7	0.2	0.2	1	2	-6
C./E. Europe/Baltic States/CIS	0.6	3.5	3.0	0.1	0.1	1	-20	35
Latin America	0.2	0.4	0.9	0.0	0.0	11	-5	-37
C./E. Europe/Baltic States/CIS a								
World	24.8	100.0	100.0	3.0 |	4.5	...	4	8
Western Europe	10.1	63.8	40.6	1.9	1.8	2	5	5
C./E. Europe/Baltic States/CIS	8.6	14.1 |	34.7	0.4 |	1.6	...	11	6
Asia	3.5	12.1	13.9	0.4	0.6	8	2	2
Middle East	0.7	1.6	2.7	0.0	0.1	12	-14	9
North America	0.7	2.8	2.7	0.1	0.1	6	-21	25
Africa	0.6	2.7	2.3	0.1	0.1	5	6	10
Latin America	0.1	2.7	0.5	0.1	0.0	-8	19	32
Middle East								
World	7.9	100.0	100.0	1.1	1.4	5	1	5
Middle East	4.0	25.5	50.5	0.3	0.7	12	10	13
Western Europe	1.8	46.4	22.8	0.5	0.3	-2	-7	-7
Asia	0.6	6.1	7.9	0.1	0.1	7	-5	-8
All other regions	1.0	18.5	12.2	0.2	0.2	1	-1	6

a Includes the intra trade of the Baltic States and the CIS beginning with 1996.

Table IV.7

Imports of agricultural products of selected economies by region and supplier, 2001

(Million dollars and percentage)

	Canada a						United States				
	Value	Share	Annual percentage change				Value	Share	Annual percentage change		
	2001	2001	1990-01	2000	2001		2001	2001	1990-01	2000	2001
Region						**Region**					
World	15551	100.0	5	7	2	World	68400	100.0	5	5	-1
North America	10107	65.0	6	10	2	North America	21838	31.9	7	3	1
Western Europe	1751	11.3	3	0	1	Latin America	18228	26.6	4	3	-3
Asia	1722	11.1	5	4	9	Asia	13917	20.3	5	11	-2
Latin America	1576	10.1	4	5	1	Western Europe	12230	17.9	4	3	-1
Africa	187	1.2	3	-12	-12	Africa	1110	1.6	3	7	-6
C./E. Europe/						C./E. Europe/					
Baltic States/CIS	140	0.9	13	-2	-8	Baltic States/CIS	808	1.2	8	1	11
Middle East	39	0.3	3	24	-7	Middle East	270	0.4	8	-1	19
Suppliers						**Suppliers**					
United States	10103	65.0	6	10	2	Canada	21803	31.9	7	3	1
European Union (15)	1561	10.0	3	1	-1	European Union (15)	11320	16.5	5	4	0
Australia	348	2.2	1	-1	25	Mexico	6679	9.8	31	5	2
Thailand	310	2.0	10	0	3	Thailand	2513	3.7	7	15	-10
Brazil	309	2.0	4	-12	1	Chile	2212	3.2	9	15	1
Above 5	12631	81.2	5	7	2	Above 5	44527	65.1	8	5	0
Mexico	296	1.9	6	6	6	Brazil	2105	3.1	-1	-3	-8
New Zealand	265	1.7	5	2	47	Australia	1933	2.8	3	23	10
China	236	1.5	7	22	4	Netherlands	1888	2.8	6	12	3
Chile	200	1.3	5	12	3	China	1695	2.5	8	17	7
Netherlands	171	1.1	3	11	5	New Zealand	1454	2.1	4	13	5
Colombia	132	0.8	4	12	-19	Indonesia	1399	2.0	4	0	-11
Indonesia	113	0.7	7	-7	1	Colombia	1125	1.6	1	-3	-15
Costa Rica	97	0.6	8	13	9	Ecuador	1051	1.5	1	-25	8
Argentina	93	0.6	8	11	-19	Costa Rica	1050	1.5	7	0	-2
Ecuador	79	0.5	-4	-17	3	India	1008	1.5	9	4	-11
Guatemala	79	0.5	9	42	-23	Argentina	768	1.1	3	-2	-8
India	78	0.5	10	6	-17	Guatemala	735	1.1	2	2	-11
Peru	75	0.5	19	22	34	Philippines	685	1.0	1	-2	-5
South Africa	73	0.5	8	-7	-15	Viet Nam	684	1.0	-	69	26
Uruguay	65	0.4	37	50	27	Japan	637	0.9	3	1	-9
Norway	60	0.4	17	-2	22	Taipei, Chinese	500	0.7	1	-4	-2
Viet Nam	58	0.4	15	67	5	Honduras	480	0.7	2	46	-2
Korea, Rep. of	53	0.3	6	14	8	Dominican Republic	475	0.7	2	4	3
Japan	47	0.3	-1	-2	-13	Korea, Rep. of	426	0.6	5	24	3
Russian Fed.	46	0.3	-	-24	-12	Malaysia	367	0.5	-2	1	-24
Philippines	44	0.3	3	0	-2	Turkey	361	0.5	1	-28	32
Taipei, Chinese	44	0.3	6	7	0	Russian Fed.	358	0.5	-	-13	-4
Malaysia	43	0.3	-4	3	-31	Peru	340	0.5	6	-8	7
Morocco	37	0.2	4	-19	-14	Côte d'Ivoire	255	0.4	3	-8	-14
Switzerland	37	0.2	-1	0	-3	Nicaragua	210	0.3	27	37	-14
Cuba	34	0.2	-10	-16	26	South Africa	203	0.3	8	11	-21
Hong Kong, China	33	0.2	1	3	-6	Norway	178	0.3	0	-4	-18
Côte d'Ivoire	32	0.2	5	-12	-16	Iceland	173	0.3	1	-20	-18
Iceland	30	0.2	18	-6	-33	Venezuela	162	0.2	2	4	-34
Estonia	30	0.2	-	34	-30	Panama	160	0.2	4	-21	1
Turkey	25	0.2	2	-12	9	Israel	159	0.2	5	-7	13
Jamaica	21	0.1	4	5	-9	Switzerland	146	0.2	2	40	-37
Iran, Islamic Rep. of	15	0.1	5	18	-25	El salvador	116	0.2	-1	47	-41
Singapore	14	0.1	-5	-25	17	Singapore	113	0.2	-3	-21	-19
Lithuania	10	0.1	-	-33	-29	Bangladesh	98	0.1	4	28	-36
Above 40	15396	99.0	5	7	2	Above 40	68024	99.5	6	5	-1

a Imports are valued f.o.b.

Table IV.7 *(continued)*

Imports of agricultural products of selected economies by region and supplier, 2001

(Million dollars and percentage)

European Union (15)

Region / Suppliers	Value 2001	Share 2001	Annual percentage change 1990-01	2000	2001
Region					
World	235511	100.0	1	-4	-2
Western Europe	163988	69.6	2	-5	-2
Latin America	19960	8.5	1	0	1
Asia	15275	6.5	1	0	-2
North America	13232	5.6	-2	5	-10
Africa	11471	4.9	0	-10	3
C./E. Europe/ Baltic States/CIS	9314	4.0	3	2	5
Middle East	1650	0.7	-2	4	-3
Suppliers					
European Union (15)	155728	66.1	2	-5	-2
United states	9970	4.2	-2	2	-8
Brazil	8083	3.4	3	10	10
Argentina	3778	1.6	0	-6	-1
Canada	3079	1.3	-2	15	-17
Above 5	180638	76.7	1	-4	-3
Norway	2507	1.1	0	-6	-10
China	2356	1.0	-	10	4
Australia	2102	0.9	1	4	11
Turkey	2094	0.9	3	-16	10
Russian Fed.	2030	0.9	-1	15	-1
New Zealand	1860	0.8	0	-9	10
South Africa	1825	0.8	0	-3	14
Poland	1754	0.7	-1	-1	9
Thailand	1714	0.7	0	-1	-6
Indonesia	1677	0.7	2	3	-14
Côte d'Ivoire	1641	0.7	-1	-21	3
Chile	1580	0.7	2	1	7
Switzerland	1544	0.7	0	-3	-2
Hungary	1327	0.6	0	-6	6
Malaysia	1320	0.6	-3	-4	-7
India	1279	0.5	4	5	-8
Morocco	1153	0.5	0	-6	1
Colombia	963	0.4	-3	-13	-12
Czech Rep.	945	0.4	2	-1	0
Iceland	934	0.4	-1	-9	4
Israel	810	0.3	-3	-1	-3
Ecuador	803	0.3	6	-20	6
Cameroon	796	0.3	1	-4	0
Costa Rica	778	0.3	2	-7	-4
Kenya	679	0.3	1	-10	0
Latvia	617	0.3	-	7	-6
Peru	590	0.3	6	9	0
Ukraine	528	0.2	-	19	62
Ghana	496	0.2	2	-21	3
Zimbabwe	478	0.2	3	-17	6
Mexico	455	0.2	3	3	1
Viet Nam	432	0.2	18	-7	-10
Faeroe Islands	421	0.2	1	-7	18
Philippines	412	0.2	-2	-13	2
Japan	405	0.2	-1	2	-4
Above 40	221943	94.2	1	-4	-2

Japan

Region / Suppliers	Value 2001	Share 2001	Annual percentage change 1990-01	2000	2001
Region					
World	56940	100.0	1	4	-8
Asia	22377	39.3	1	5	-8
North America	20890	36.7	0	4	-10
Western Europe	6390	11.2	3	3	-7
Latin America	3956	6.9	4	0	-9
C./E. Europe/ Baltic States/CIS	1909	3.4	5	3	-9
Africa	1326	2.3	0	0	-5
Middle East	91	0.2	1	1	-27
Suppliers					
United States	16293	28.6	-1	3	-9
China	6915	12.1	9	13	-2
European Union (15)	5517	9.7	3	4	-7
Canada	4533	8.0	1	11	-12
Australia	3804	6.7	1	5	-6
Above 5	37062	65.1	1	6	-7
Thailand	2776	4.9	3	6	-2
Russian Fed.	1662	2.9	-	3	-12
Korea, Rep. of	1592	2.8	0	-10	-18
Indonesia	1503	2.6	2	4	-6
Chile	1302	2.3	7	6	-7
New Zealand	1140	2.0	0	5	-7
Brazil	1068	1.9	2	3	-11
Taipei, Chinese	1049	1.8	-7	0	-15
Malaysia	753	1.3	-9	-5	-25
Philippines	692	1.2	-1	-1	-13
India	631	1.1	3	10	-28
Norway	620	1.1	9	-11	-4
Viet Nam	608	1.1	13	16	-1
South Africa	554	1.0	2	9	19
Mexico	433	0.8	8	5	-3
Singapore	268	0.5	2	9	-10
Morocco	260	0.5	2	5	-13
Argentina	236	0.4	-2	-22	-4
Peru	187	0.3	11	13	67
Ecuador	176	0.3	5	-9	-19
Colombia	160	0.3	1	5	-29
Korea, Dem. People's Rep. (	115	0.2	0	32	-
Sri Lanka	104	0.2	7	76	-13
Iceland	99	0.2	1	4	-31
Papua New Guinea	87	0.2	-2	-16	-36
Guatemala	69	0.1	4	0	-19
Turkey	66	0.1	-2	-5	-13
Greenland	62	0.1	-6	-6	-35
Myanmar	57	0.1	8	18	-26
Panama	54	0.1	-1	142	86
Ethiopia	45	0.1	-	-8	-24
Ghana	45	0.1	-3	-26	0
Honduras	44	0.1	-5	-19	-59
Switzerland	44	0.1	-1	3	13
Mauritania	43	0.1	-8	-31	-46
Above 40	55666	97.8	1	4	-8

Table IV.8

Leading exporters and importers of agricultural products, 2001

(Billion dollars and percentage)

	Value	Share in world exports/imports			Annual percentage change			
	2001	1980	1990	2001	1990-01	1999	2000	2001
Exporters								
European Union (15)	213.53	32.8	42.4	39.0	2	-3	-4	-2
Extra-exports	57.81	10.3	10.9	10.6	2	-5	0	-2
United States	70.02	17.0	14.3	12.8	2	-6	8	-2
Canada	33.57	5.0	5.4	6.1	4	4	7	-3
Brazil	18.43	3.4	2.4	3.4	6	-6	-3	19
China	16.63	1.4	2.4	3.0	5	-1	15	1
Australia	16.56	3.3	2.8	3.0	3	5	8	1
Argentina	12.20	1.9	1.8	2.2	5	-14	0	2
Thailand	12.06	1.2	1.9	2.2	4	2	4	-2
Mexico	9.07	0.8	0.8	1.7	9	0	12	0
Russian Fed. a	8.17	-	-	1.5	-	1	19	9
New Zealand	7.97	1.3	1.4	1.5	3	1	4	4
Malaysia	7.19	2.0	1.8	1.3	0	-3	-13	-10
Indonesia	7.02	1.6	1.0	1.3	5	-2	3	-10
Chile	6.97	0.4	0.7	1.3	9	6	8	9
India b	6.41	0.8	0.8	1.2	6	-6	10	...
Above 15	445.80	72.8	80.0	81.4	-	-	-	-
Importers								
European Union (15)	235.51	42.9	47.1	39.7	1	-4	-4	-2
Extra-imports	79.78	21.2	17.5	13.5	0	-6	-2	-1
United States	68.40	8.7	9.0	11.5	5	6	5	-1
Japan	56.94	9.6	11.4	9.6	1	6	4	-8
China	20.12	1.9	1.8	3.4	9	10	41	3
Canada c	15.55	1.8	2.0	2.6	5	2	7	2
Mexico	12.79	1.2	1.2	2.2	8	4	...	11
Korea, Rep. of	12.50	1.5	2.2	2.1	3	19	16	-3
Russian Fed. a	11.40	-	-	1.9		-25	-5	17
Hong Kong, China	11.06	-	-	-	3	-11	4	-6
retained imports	6.43	1.0	1.0	1.1	3	-10	4	-1
Taipei, Chinese	6.99	1.1	1.4	1.2	1	0	1	-11
Switzerland	5.65	1.2	1.3	1.0	0	-1	-4	-3
Indonesia	5.35	0.6	0.5	0.9	9	16	5	-7
Saudi Arabia	5.01	1.5	0.8	0.8	3	2	13	-12
Malaysia	4.83	0.5	0.5	0.8	7	8	3	5
Thailand	4.83	0.3	0.7	0.8	4	6	13	8
Above 15	472.32	73.6	81.0	79.6	-	-	-	-

a Includes Secretariat estimates.

b 2000 instead of 2001.

c Imports are valued f.o.b.

Table IV.9

Exports of agricultural products of selected economies, 1990-01

(Million dollars and percentage)

	Value					Share in economy's total merchandise exports	
	1990	1995	1999	2000	2001	1990	2001 a
World	414610	583000	547960	552240	547460	12.2	9.1
Argentina	7482	11349	11968	11933	12199	60.6	45.8
Australia	11628	14717	15292	16446	16563	29.3	26.1
Bangladesh	329	446	386	418	503	19.7	7.7
Belize	99	131	143	...	...	91.7	86.3
Bolivia	245	328	395	457	428	26.5	33.3
Brazil	9779	15673	15980	15467	18431	31.1	31.7
Bulgaria	...	1304	736	605	600	...	11.8
Cameroon	723	839	816	659	666	36.1	38.1
Canada	22339	32214	32599	34789	33574	17.5	12.9
Chile	2779	5922	5917	6399	6966	33.2	39.9
China	10060	14997	14209	16384	16626	16.2	6.2
Colombia	2514	3695	3341	3121	2884	37.2	23.5
Costa Rica	927	1848	1951	1812	1668	64.0	33.3
Côte d'Ivoire	2374	2793	2800	2308	...	77.3	59.4
Czech Rep.	-	2072	1773	1901	1942	-	5.8
Ecuador	1236	2389	2579	1948	2219	45.5	49.4
Egypt	669	552	591	...	635	19.2	15.4
El Salvador	237	574	497	577	433	40.8	15.1
Ethiopia	...	362	409	406	...	...	84.2
European Union (15)	175847	238990	227014	218592	213533	11.7	9.3
Intra-exports	130571	174404	167995	159636	155728	13.3	11.0
Extra-exports	45276	64586	59019	58956	57805	8.6	6.6
Guatemala	849	1342	1517	1622	1337	73.0	54.2
Honduras	680	813	595	767	691	81.8	52.4
Hong Kong, China	4556	7451	5531	5693	5032	5.5	2.6
domestic exports	821	881	424	454	402	2.8	2.0
re-exports	3735	6570	5107	5240	4630	7.0	2.7
Hungary	2558	3054	2502	2445	2747	25.6	9.0
Iceland	1274	1371	1411	1257	1306	80.0	65.6
India	3506	6322	5835	6405	...	19.5	15.1
Indonesia	4154	8197	7544	7764	7024	16.2	12.5
Israel	1327	1358	1264	1182	1094	11.0	3.8
Japan	3299	4656	4212	4395	5147	1.1	1.3
Kenya	559	1158	1089	1062	...	54.2	61.3
Korea, Rep. of	2985	4448	4228	4298	3948	4.6	2.6
Madagascar	224	346	294	412	456	70.2	61.6
Malaysia	7495	11571	9214	8015	7190	25.4	8.2
Mauritius	396	456	388	283	389	33.2	25.6
Mexico	3466	7189	8145	9100	9073	8.5	5.7
Morocco	1228	1643	1699	1745	1560	28.8	21.9
New Zealand	5966	8306	7330	7641	7972	63.5	58.1
Nicaragua	295	389	431	547	428	89.5	70.7
Norway	3077	4120	4560	4244	4084	9.0	7.1
Pakistan	1081	1272	1205	1234	1160	19.2	12.5
Paraguay	863	738	624	699	824	90.0	83.4
Peru	813	1701	1578	1911	1880	25.2	26.5
Philippines	1683	2457	1778	2026	1958	20.7	6.1
Poland	2268	3036	3022	3050	3392	15.8	9.4
Romania	184	783	885	828	916	3.7	8.0
Russian Fed. b	-	3534	6251	7467	8174	-	7.9
Singapore	4095	5949	3862	3723	3303	7.8	2.7
domestic exports	1182	1578	1189	1202	1155	3.4	1.7
re-exports	2912	4371	2673	2521	2148	16.3	3.9
South Africa	2881	3433	3540	3060	3109	12.2	10.6
Sri Lanka	758	941	1031	1093	1014	39.7	21.1
Sudan	367	502	456	...	...	98.1	58.5
Switzerland	2244	3032	2563	2571	2496	3.5	3.0
Taipei, Chinese	3732	5640	3011	3512	3205	5.6	2.6
Thailand	7786	13911	11762	12242	12057	33.8	18.5
Tunisia	418	570	685	548	575	11.8	8.7
Turkey	3300	4541	4442	3828	4318	25.5	13.8
United States	59404	80435	65941	71408	70017	15.1	9.6
Uruguay	1025	1244	1344	1278	1132	60.6	54.9
Zimbabwe	754	926	1141	1146	...	43.7	59.6

a Or nearest year.
b Includes Secretariat estimates.

Table IV.10

Imports of agricultural products of selected economies, 1990-01

(Million dollars and percentage)

	Value					Share in economy's total merchandise imports	
	1990	1995	1999	2000	2001	1990	2001 a
Algeria	2766	3518	2750	2815	...	28.3	30.8
Argentina	326	1509	1639	1597	1471	8.0	7.2
Australia b	2707	3794	3928	4234	3558	6.8	5.9
Bangladesh	835	1124	2215	1446	1263	23.1	15.0
Belarus	-	...	1003	1226	...	-	14.2
Brazil	2691	7218	5130	5163	4230	11.9	7.3
Cameroon	315	215	276	294	308	22.5	16.6
Canada b	9009	12204	14281	15272	15551	7.7	7.0
Chile	461	1252	1360	1421	1376	5.9	8.0
China	7855	16099	13853	19544	20125	14.7	8.3
Colombia	593	1657	1615	1736	1792	10.6	14.0
Croatia	-	1017	766	777	948	-	11.8
Cyprus	405	802	747	754	688	15.8	17.5
Czech Rep. b	-	2367	2237	2240	2397	-	6.6
Egypt	4793	4160	4350	...	3902	38.6	30.6
El Salvador	158	441	652	692	743	12.5	14.8
European Union (15)	208502	267194	249783	240170	235511	13.4	10.1
Intra-imports c	130913					13.3	
Extra-imports	77589	92789	81788	80534	79783	13.5	8.7
Ghana	...	...	433	444	634	...	20.9
Guatemala	196	440	640	673	860	11.9	15.3
Honduras	108	237	459	511	526	11.5	18.0
Hong Kong, China	8325	13798	11319	11728	11063	9.8	5.5
retained imports	4591	7228	6212	6488	6433	14.6	20.6
Hungary	1158	1362	1343	1424	1519	11.2	4.5
India	1721	3003	4862	3351	...	7.3	6.5
Indonesia	2126	6103	5476	5727	5350	9.7	17.3
Iran, Islamic Rep. of d	...	...	2933	2943	2929	...	16.7
Israel	1565	2307	2288	2288	2302	9.3	6.6
Jamaica	314	442	555	544	...	16.3	16.9
Japan	50460	74772	59750	62185	56940	21.4	16.3
Jordan	709	839	865	942	954	27.3	19.7
Korea, Rep. of	9530	14727	11084	12837	12504	13.6	8.9
Kuwait	589	1296	1354	1263	...	14.8	17.6
Lebanon	...	...	1310	1210	1362	...	18.7
Madagascar	71	99	96	140	150	11.0	15.3
Malaysia	2404	4631	4455	4610	4830	8.2	6.5
Mauritius	255	395	363	346	362	15.8	18.2
Mexico e	5374	6250	9972	11565	12795	12.3	6.7
Morocco	1096	2210	1802	1941	1925	15.8	17.6
Nepal	126	157	271	240	...	18.7	15.2
Norway	2090	3106	3128	2956	3010	7.7	9.3
Oman	506	876	1088	1158	1383	18.9	23.9
Pakistan	1568	2687	2269	1882	1682	21.2	15.8
Peru	668	1171	1145	998	1113	25.4	15.2
Philippines	1665	2994	3219	3104	3087	12.8	9.8
Poland	1253	3727	4133	3940	4141	10.8	8.2
Romania	1249	1109	933	1093	1401	16.4	9.0
Russian Fed. d	-	12702	10280	9747	11402	-	21.2
Saudi Arabia	3487	4861	5030	5663	5011	14.5	16.0
Senegal	494	425	496	394	497	40.6	32.9
Singapore	4698	6810	4985	4890	4677	7.7	4.0
retained imports	1786	2439	2312	2369	2529	4.2	4.2
Slovak Rep. b	-	974	930	953	1086	-	7.4
South Africa b	1219	2404	1667	1650	1465	7.3	5.8
Sri Lanka	549	962	879	934	873	20.4	14.7
Switzerland	5920	6770	6071	5807	5655	8.5	6.7
Syrian Arab Republic	791	942	883	850	...	32.9	22.3
Taipei, Chinese	6203	9995	7779	7888	6985	11.3	6.5
Thailand	3227	5575	3962	4473	4826	9.8	7.8
Tunisia	819	1322	929	968	1058	14.9	11.1
Turkey	2806	4493	3398	4133	3062	12.6	7.5
United Arab Emirates d	1773	2083	2729	3030	...	15.8	7.9
United States	39966	53056	66138	69115	68400	7.7	5.8
Venezuela b	986	2026	1938	1970	2105	14.9	12.8
Zimbabwe b	116	209	222	...	...	6.3	10.5

a Or nearest year.
b Imports are valued f.o.b.
c See the Technical Notes for information on intra-EU imports.
d Includes Secretariat estimates.
e Beginning with 2000 imports are valued c.i.f.

3. Mining Products

Table IV.11

World trade in mining products, 2001

(Billion dollars and percentage)

Value	790
Annual percentage change	
1980-85	-5
1985-90	3
1990-01	4
2000	46
2001	-8
Share in world merchandise trade	13.2
Share in world exports of primary products	59.1

Table IV.12

Major regional flows in world exports of mining products, 2001

(Billion dollars and percentage)

	Value	Annual percentage change		
	2001	1990-01	2000	2001
Intra-Western Europe	140.5	4	39	-6
Middle East to Asia	101.9	7	55	-12
Intra-Asia	93.0	5	40	-6
Intra-North America	50.7	8	67	0
C./E. Europe/Baltic States/CIS to Western Europe	47.1	5	57	-1
Africa to Western Europe	37.9	1	51	-7

Table IV.13

Share of mining products in trade in total merchandise and in primary products by region, 2001

(Percentage)

	Exports	Imports
Share of mining products in total merchandise		
World	13.2	13.2
North America	7.5	12.3
Latin America	21.5	11.0
Western Europe	7.2	11.4
C./E. Europe/Baltic States/CIS	32.6	13.9
Africa	57.0	11.6
Middle East	73.8	8.1
Asia	7.6	18.0
Share of mining products in primary products		
World	59.1	59.1
North America	41.7	67.3
Latin America	54.4	54.3
Western Europe	44.0	53.4
C./E. Europe/Baltic States/CIS	79.0	56.9
Africa	79.5	43.1
Middle East	95.7	37.8
Asia	53.3	65.0

Chart IV.4

Regional shares in world trade in mining products, 2001

(Percentage)

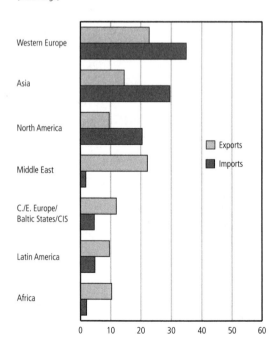

Table IV.14

Exports of mining products by region, 2001

(Billion dollars and percentage)

	Value	Share in				Annual percentage change		
		Region's exports		World exports				
	2001	1990	2001	1990	2001	1990-01	2000	2001
World	790.4	-	-	100.0	100.0	4	46	-8
Western Europe								
World	179.2	100.0	100.0	24.2	22.7	4	40	-8
Western Europe	140.5	80.0	78.4	19.4	17.8	4	39	-6
North America	19.0	8.6	10.6	2.1	2.4	6	73	-15
Asia	5.9	2.9	3.3	0.7	0.7	5	18	-16
C./E. Europe/Baltic States/CIS	4.8	1.7	2.7	0.4	0.6	8	15	9
Africa	2.7	1.7	1.5	0.4	0.3	3	55	-14
Middle East	1.6	1.2	0.9	0.3	0.2	1	32	-20
Latin America	1.4	0.5	0.8	0.1	0.2	9	15	-2
Middle East								
World	174.8	100.0	100.0	23.1	22.1	4	54	-12
Asia	101.9	45.2	58.3	10.4	12.9	7	55	-12
Western Europe	23.8	24.9	13.6	5.8	3.0	-2	52	-25
North America	23.6	14.0	13.5	3.2	3.0	4	67	-5
Africa	6.7	3.2	3.8	0.7	0.8	6	51	-14
Middle East	5.5	3.4	3.1	0.8	0.7	3	49	-1
Latin America	1.7	4.3	1.0	1.0	0.2	-9	45	-8
C./E. Europe/Baltic States/CIS	0.2	1.4	0.1	0.3	0.0	-18	-13	7
Asia								
World	113.8	100.0	100.0	13.5	14.4	5	38	-5
Asia	93.0	79.6	81.7	10.7	11.8	5	40	-6
Western Europe	8.2	6.9	7.2	0.9	1.0	6	25	9
North America	6.5	8.9	5.8	1.2	0.8	1	36	-13
Latin America	2.2	1.0	1.9	0.1	0.3	12	43	14
All other regions	2.4	1.9	2.1	0.3	0.3	6	25	8
C./E. Europe/Baltic States/CIS a								
World	93.1	100.0	100.0	8.0 l	11.8	...	56	-4
Western Europe	47.1	67.7	50.7	5.4	6.0	5	57	-1
C./E. Europe/Baltic States/CIS	29.2	17.6 l	31.4	1.4 l	3.7	...	50	-5
Asia	4.8	8.4	5.2	0.7	0.6	4	69	-12
Latin America	3.8	2.1	4.1	0.2	0.5	15	89	-19
Middle East	3.4	0.9	3.6	0.1	0.4	23	360	21
All other regions	3.5	3.2	3.8	0.3	0.4	10	17	-28
Africa								
World	80.5	100.0	100.0	11.5	10.2	3	50	-8
Western Europe	37.9	61.5	47.0	7.0	4.8	1	51	-7
North America	20.0	24.7	24.8	2.8	2.5	3	66	-12
Asia	12.5	5.9	15.6	0.7	1.6	13	42	-15
Latin America	4.3	2.3	5.4	0.3	0.5	12	46	17
Africa	3.5	3.2	4.4	0.4	0.4	6	35	-11
All other regions	0.7	1.9	0.9	0.2	0.1	-4	19	-4
Latin America								
World	74.7	100.0	100.0	10.0	9.4	4	45	-11
North America	37.7	47.2	50.5	4.7	4.8	5	56	-15
Latin America	16.3	12.7	21.8	1.3	2.1	9	40	-10
Western Europe	10.4	20.7	13.9	2.1	1.3	0	22	-5
Asia	7.6	11.6	10.1	1.2	1.0	3	30	1
All other regions	1.2	3.7	1.6	0.4	0.2	-4	35	-8
North America								
World	74.4	100.0	100.0	9.7	9.4	4	44	-2
North America	50.7	44.3	68.2	4.3	6.4	8	67	0
Western Europe	8.0	20.0	10.8	1.9	1.0	-2	-15	9
Asia	7.7	25.9	10.3	2.5	1.0	-4	16	-9
Latin America	7.1	7.7	9.6	0.8	0.9	6	49	-18
All other regions	0.8	2.0	1.1	0.2	0.1	-1	21	-18

a Includes the intra trade of the Baltic States and the CIS beginning with 1996.

3.1 Fuels

Table IV.15

World trade in fuels, 2001

(Billion dollars and percentage)

Value	616
Annual percentage change	
1980-85	-5
1985-90	0
1990-01	5
2000	57
2001	-8
Share in world merchandise trade	10.3
Share in world exports of primary products	46.0

Table IV.16

Major regional flows in world exports of fuels, 2001

(Billion dollars and percentage)

	Value	Annual percentage change		
	2001	1990-01	2000	2001
Middle East to Asia	100.4	7	56	-12
Intra-Western Europe	96.1	5	55	-6
Intra-Asia	66.0	5	50	-7
Intra-North America	39.2	11	101	3
C./E. Europe/Baltic States/CIS to Western Europe	36.0	4	76	2
Africa to Western Europe	34.5	2	57	-8

Table IV.17

Share of fuels in trade in total merchandise and in primary products by region, 2001

(Percentage)

	Exports	Imports
Share of fuels in total merchandise		
World	10.3	10.3
North America	5.0	10.1
Latin America	15.6	9.2
Western Europe	4.8	8.2
C./E. Europe/Baltic States/CIS	25.2	11.2
Africa	50.7	10.0
Middle East	72.3	6.3
Asia	5.2	14.1
Share of fuels in primary products		
World	46.0	46.0
North America	27.8	55.5
Latin America	39.3	45.6
Western Europe	29.5	38.7
C./E. Europe/Baltic States/CIS	61.1	45.7
Africa	70.7	37.0
Middle East	93.8	29.5
Asia	36.3	50.8

Chart IV.5

Regional shares in world trade in fuels, 2001

(Percentage)

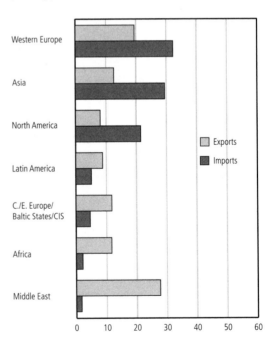

Table IV.18

Imports of fuels of selected economies by region and supplier, 2001

(Million dollars and percentage)

	Value	Share	Annual percentage change			Value	Share	Annual percentage change	
	2001	2001	2000	2001		2001	2001	2000	2001
		Canada a					United States		
Region					Region				
World	12381	100.0	75	-1	World	129014	100.0	76	-8
Western Europe	5429	43.9	75	-9	Latin America	35166	27.3	69	-17
North America	3438	27.8	76	30	North America	34713	26.9	81	9
Latin America	1235	10.0	34	-1	Middle East	23082	17.9	69	-5
Middle East	1110	9.0	168	4	Africa	18658	14.5	88	-13
Africa	976	7.9	82	-20	Western Europe	11712	9.1	91	-11
Asia	142	1.2	261	-29	Asia	4194	3.3	62	-12
C./E. Europe/					C./E. Europe/				
Baltic States/CIS	50	0.4	-27	-60	Baltic States/CIS	1490	1.2	67	-12
Suppliers					Suppliers				
United States	3438	27.8	76	30	Canada	34709	26.9	81	9
European Union (15)	3363	27.2	68	3	Venezuela	14218	11.0	73	-19
Norway	2055	16.6	82	-24	Saudi Arabia	13604	10.5	73	-4
Venezuela	798	6.4	38	-9	Mexico	10469	8.1	77	-20
Algeria	738	6.0	90	-11	Nigeria	9147	7.1	139	-17
Iraq	564	4.6	318	22	European Union (15)	7942	6.2	100	-11
Saudi Arabia	451	3.6	105	-16	Iraq	6298	4.9	44	-3
Mexico	278	2.2	49	4	Norway	3621	2.8	74	-12
Nigeria	133	1.1	56	-56	Colombia	3429	2.7	17	-20
Colombia	108	0.9	43	194	Angola	3270	2.5	46	-13
Above 10	11925	96.3	-	-	Above 10	106707	82.7	-	-
		European Union (15)					Japan		
Region					Region				
World	187702	100.0	60	-6	World	70226	100.0	55	-9
Western Europe	82107	43.7	55	-5	Middle East	42630	60.7	66	-10
Africa	31121	16.6	75	-8	Asia	24809	35.3	48	-7
C./E. Europe/					North America	1365	1.9	1	-23
Baltic States/CIS	29334	15.6	66	6	Africa	697	1.0	19	1
Middle East	24221	12.9	69	-23	C./E. Europe/				
Latin America	4363	2.3	59	-2	Baltic States/CIS	379	0.5	32	39
Asia	2668	1.4	14	34	Latin America	256	0.4	8	-45
North America	2504	1.3	15	4	Western Europe	87	0.1	-54	-18
Suppliers					Suppliers				
European Union (15)	58953	31.4	49	-5	United Arab Emirates	12618	18.0	69	-14
Russian Fed.	21976	11.7	68	4	Saudi Arabia	11977	17.1	73	-14
Norway	21612	11.5	74	-9	Indonesia	7092	10.1	47	-15
Algeria	9788	5.2	83	-11	Australia	6341	9.0	26	5
Libyan Arab Jamahiriya	9782	5.2	64	-16	Qatar	5987	8.5	70	2
Saudi Arabia	9578	5.1	78	-24	Iran, Islamic Rep. of	4948	7.0	73	-6
Nigeria	5133	2.7	126	-6	Kuwait	4418	6.3	66	-11
Iran, Islamic Rep. of	4992	2.7	65	-25	Malaysia	3356	4.8	53	2
Syrian Arab Republic	3280	1.7	41	19	Korea, Rep. of	2993	4.3	74	-12
Iraq	3101	1.7	48	-47	Oman	2345	3.3	21	16
Above 10	148195	79.0	-	-	Above 10	62077	88.4	-	-

a Imports are valued f.o.b.

Table IV.19

Imports of fuels of selected economies, 1990-01

(Million dollars and percentage)

	Value					Share in economy's total merchandise imports	
	1990	1995	1999	2000	2001	1990	2001 a
Argentina	333	844	676	910	798	8.2	3.9
Australia b	2170	2883	3814	5898	5106	5.4	8.5
Bahrain	1827	1385	1171	2108	...	49.2	45.5
Bangladesh	566	421	480	738	969	15.6	11.5
Belarus	-	...	1526	2585	...	-	29.9
Brazil	6045	6491	5846	8872	8416	26.8	14.4
Bulgaria	...	1531	1191	1741	1605	...	22.2
Canada b	7313	5948	7151	12481	12381	6.3	5.6
Chile	1099	1334	1861	3014	2730	14.2	15.8
China	1259	5127	8912	20637	17466	2.4	7.2
Costa Rica	219	273	324	486	...	11.0	7.6
Côte d'Ivoire	...	474	536	838	...	...	33.0
Croatia	-	871	859	1145	1174	-	14.6
Cyprus	270	286	315	491	471	10.5	12.0
Czech Rep. b	-	1964	1886	3089	3308	-	9.1
El Salvador	140	241	358	595	502	11.0	10.0
European Union (15)	139379	122190	125126	199942	187702	8.9	8.0
Intra-imports c	37430					3.8	
Extra-imports	101949	84700	83423	137704	128749	17.7	14.1
Ghana	...	...	532	629	716	...	23.6
Guatemala	278	410	447	620	763	16.8	13.6
Honduras	153	199	246	382	400	16.3	13.7
Hong Kong, China	1996	3705	3681	4533	4038	2.4	2.0
retained imports	1567	2126	3131	4102	3692	5.0	11.8
Hungary	1470	1805	1715	2690	2768	14.2	8.2
India	6495	8661	14343	17643	...	27.5	34.4
Indonesia	1937	3007	3726	6071	5523	8.9	17.8
Israel	1354	1673	2142	3587	3496	8.1	10.0
Jamaica	380	351	380	586	...	19.7	18.2
Japan	57453	53916	49885	77425	70226	24.4	20.1
Jordan	471	477	450	194	699	18.1	14.4
Kenya	424	413	439	642	...	19.1	20.7
Korea, Rep. of	11023	19013	22875	38077	34069	15.8	24.1
Latvia	-	385	315	392	373	-	10.7
Lebanon	...	...	555	1029	1293	...	17.7
Lithuania	-	708	713	1185	1275	-	20.3
Malaysia	1487	1736	1968	3940	3867	5.1	5.2
Mauritius	132	138	161	244	223	8.2	11.2
Mexico d	1125	1502	3089	5516	5524	2.6	2.9
Morocco	1168	1173	1324	2039	1936	16.9	17.7
Nepal	50	123	144	236	...	7.5	15.0
New Zealand	727	744	880	1446	1128	7.6	8.5
Nicaragua	121	181	142	307	308	18.9	17.3
Norway	1178	947	1033	1193	1339	4.3	4.1
Pakistan	1529	1890	2098	3598	2918	20.6	27.5
Panama	244	342	408	628	...	15.9	18.6
Paraguay	192	205	220	297	351	14.2	16.4
Peru	327	664	660	1156	970	12.4	13.3
Philippines	1943	2623	2575	4095	3586	14.9	11.4
Poland	2533	2651	3281	5308	5082	21.9	10.1
Romania	2906	2195	1067	1583	1871	38.2	12.0
Singapore	9632	10030	10080	16219	14594	15.8	12.6
retained imports	9545	9934	9966	16106	14172	22.3	23.5
Slovak Rep. b	-	1535	1457	2236	2247	-	15.2
South Africa b	...	2225	2438	3826	3736	...	14.7
Sri Lanka	333	364	306	551	447	12.4	7.5
Switzerland	3155	2317	2390	3822	3855	4.5	4.6
Taipei, Chinese	5953	7142	8170	13074	11848	10.9	11.0
Thailand	3084	4775	4830	7549	7474	9.3	12.0
Tunisia	493	572	556	902	913	8.9	9.6
Turkey	4622	4619	5375	7515	6576	20.7	16.2
Ukraine e	-	...	5305	5653	...	-	40.5
United States	68741	62984	79273	139622	129014	13.3	10.9
Zimbabwe b	288	239	245	...	...	15.6	11.5

a Or nearest year.

b Imports are valued f.o.b.

c See the Technical Notes for information on intra-EU imports.

d Beginning with 2000 imports are valued c.i.f.

e Includes Secretariat estimates.

4. Manufactures

Table IV.20

World trade in manufactures, 2001

(Billion dollars and percentage)

Value	4477
Annual percentage change	
1980-85	2
1985-90	15
1990-01	6
2000	10
2001	-4
Share in world merchandise trade	74.8

Table IV.21

Major regional flows in world exports of manufactures, 2001

(Billion dollars and percentage)

	Value	Annual percentage change		
	2001	1990-01	2000	2001
Intra-Western Europe	1312.0	3	1	-3
Intra-Asia	551.2	9	25	-12
Asia to North America	349.0	6	15	-12
Intra-North America	283.5	7	9	-9
Asia to Western Europe	224.7	5	12	-11
Western Europe to North America	221.1	7	8	0

Table IV.22

Share of manufactures in total merchandise trade by region, 2001

(Percentage)

	Exports	Imports
World	74.8	74.8
North America	77.0	79.2
Latin America	59.9	77.3
Western Europe	80.9	75.6
C./E. Europe/Baltic States/CIS	56.4	74.7
Africa	25.3	70.8
Middle East	21.8	75.2
Asia	83.3	70.0

Chart IV.6

Regional shares in world trade in manufactures, 2001

(Percentage)

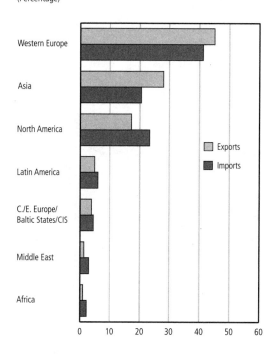

Table IV.23

Exports of manufactures by region, 2001

(Billion dollars and percentage)

	Value	Share in				Annual percentage change		
		Region's exports		World exports				
	2001	1990	2001	1990	2001	1990-01	2000	2001
World	4476.9	-	-	100.0	100.0	6	10	-4
Western Europe								
World	2009.6	100.0	100.0	54.2	44.9	4	3	-1
Western Europe	1312.0	70.6	65.3	38.3	29.3	3	1	-3
North America	221.1	8.3	11.0	4.5	4.9	7	8	0
Asia	172.8	8.2	8.6	4.4	3.9	5	11	1
C./E. Europe/Baltic States/CIS	129.8	4.1	6.5	2.2	2.9	8	10	12
Middle East	56.7	2.8	2.8	1.5	1.3	4	4	8
Latin America	52.2	2.0	2.6	1.1	1.2	7	5	0
Africa	51.7	3.4	2.6	1.8	1.2	2	-5	5
Asia								
World	1247.9	100.0	100.0	24.4	27.9	7	18	-10
Asia	551.2	36.0	44.2	8.8	12.3	9	25	-12
North America	349.0	33.0	28.0	8.1	7.8	6	15	-12
Western Europe	224.7	22.0	18.0	5.4	5.0	5	12	-11
Middle East	37.2	2.9	3.0	0.7	0.8	7	15	5
Latin America	36.3	2.0	2.9	0.5	0.8	11	23	-6
Africa	18.9	1.4	1.5	0.3	0.4	8	4	6
C./E. Europe/Baltic States/CIS	14.5	1.5	1.2	0.4	0.3	5	22	10
North America								
World	763.3	100.0	100.0	15.2	17.0	7	12	-7
North America	283.5	35.9	37.1	5.5	6.3	7	9	-9
Asia	159.2	23.1	20.9	3.5	3.6	6	19	-11
Western Europe	155.1	25.1	20.3	3.8	3.5	5	10	-4
Latin America	134.7	11.7	17.7	1.8	3.0	11	20	-7
Middle East	16.1	2.3	2.1	0.3	0.4	6	-10	3
All other regions	14.6	1.9	1.9	0.3	0.3	7	9	19
Latin America								
World	207.8	100.0	100.0	2.3	4.6	13	19	-2
North America	156.1	59.7	75.1	1.4	3.5	15	20	-2
Latin America	32.1	16.6	15.4	0.4	0.7	12	17	2
Western Europe	12.4	13.2	6.0	0.3	0.3	5	9	-5
Asia	5.0	7.4	2.4	0.2	0.1	2	8	-1
All other regions	1.8	3.1	0.9	0.1	0.0	1	14	11
C./E. Europe/Baltic States/CIS a								
World	161.0	100.0	100.0	2.1 I	3.6	...	17	11
Western Europe	98.0	43.5	60.9	0.9	2.2	15	18	11
C./E. Europe/Baltic States/CIS	37.5	32.0 I	23.3	0.7 I	0.8	...	19	14
Asia	9.1	12.3	5.6	0.3	0.2	4	5	0
North America	7.6	2.4	4.7	0.0	0.2	18	27	8
Middle East	2.9	3.4	1.8	0.1	0.1	5	24	4
Africa	1.9	2.9	1.2	0.1	0.0	3	-5	8
Latin America	1.8	3.5	1.1	0.1	0.0	1	23	-4
Middle East								
World	51.5	100.0	100.0	0.9	1.2	9	14	-1
North America	14.0	16.4	27.2	0.1	0.3	14	33	-6
Western Europe	12.8	32.4	24.8	0.3	0.3	6	4	-7
Asia	8.7	19.6	16.9	0.2	0.2	7	2	4
Middle East	8.1	17.9	15.7	0.2	0.2	7	21	12
Africa	2.2	2.6	4.3	0.0	0.0	14	17	-2
All other regions	2.3	7.5	4.5	0.1	0.1	4	11	6
Africa								
World	35.7	100.0	100.0	0.9	0.8	5	10	2
Western Europe	21.7	62.1	60.7	0.5	0.5	5	12	2
Africa	4.9	11.6	13.8	0.1	0.1	7	-1	-3
North America	3.8	5.9	10.7	0.1	0.1	11	22	11
Asia	3.0	10.5	8.4	0.1	0.1	3	4	-3
All other regions	1.9	9.4	5.3	0.1	0.0	0	21	3

a Includes the intra trade of the Baltic States and the CIS beginning with 1996.

Table IV.24

Trade in manufactures of the United States, the European Union and Japan by region, 2001

(Billion dollars and percentage)

	Exports							Imports					
Value	Share		Annual percentage change				Value	Share		Annual percentage change		
2001	1990	2001	1990-01	2000	2001		2001	1990	2001	1990-01	2000	2001
						United States						
602.4	100.0	100.0	7	13	-7	World	905.5	100.0	100.0	8	15	-6
138.6	23.4	23.0	7	7	-10	North America	139.6	16.4	15.4	8	9	-9
132.1	14.2	21.9	11	20	-7	Latin America	137.9	8.2	15.2	15	19	-1
147.9	29.9	24.6	5	9	-4	Western Europe	202.9	24.1	22.4	8	11	0
						C./E. Europe/						
4.9	0.4	0.8	13	7	14	Baltic States/CIS	9.7	0.3	1.1	22	43	-1
9.1	1.8	1.5	5	12	25	Africa	4.4	0.3	0.5	13	20	13
15.5	2.7	2.6	6	-11	3	Middle East	14.1	0.9	1.6	14	36	-6
154.1	27.6	25.6	6	18	-11	Asia	396.9	49.7	43.8	7	16	-10
						European Union (15)						
1881.9	100.0	100.0	4	3	-1	World	1760.9	100.0	100.0	4	4	-3
206.5	8.4	11.0	7	8	1	North America	164.3	8.7	9.3	5	8	-5
49.1	1.9	2.6	7	5	0	Latin America	14.9	0.8	0.8	5	23	-11
1231.0	71.1	65.4	3	1	-3	Western Europe	1201.6	74.5	68.2	3	1	-3
						C./E. Europe/						
123.2	4.0	6.5	9	10	12	Baltic States/CIS	88.2	1.8	5.0	14	13	10
49.1	3.4	2.6	2	-4	5	Africa	23.0	0.9	1.3	7	5	7
51.8	2.7	2.8	4	5	9	Middle East	13.2	0.6	0.7	7	15	-5
159.3	7.9	8.5	5	11	0	Asia	245.1	12.3	13.9	5	11	-9
						Japan						
373.7	100.0	100.0	3	14	-17	World	197.5	100.0	100.0	6	20	-7
122.0	34.5	32.6	2	11	-15	North America	45.5	30.5	23.0	4	10	-13
15.9	3.4	4.2	5	8	-16	Latin America	1.9	1.5	0.9	2	52	-11
64.6	22.5	17.3	0	4	-18	Western Europe	40.7	34.7	20.6	1	9	-4
						C./E. Europe/						
2.4	1.1	0.6	-2	25	-3	Baltic States/CIS	1.0	0.7	0.5	3	43	7
4.2	1.9	1.1	-2	-8	-12	Africa	0.7	0.4	0.3	5	40	16
10.4	3.2	2.8	1	-2	8	Middle East	1.2	1.2	0.6	0	4	-5
154.3	33.3	41.3	5	25	-19	Asia	106.6	31.0	54.0	12	29	-6

Table IV.25

Imports of manufactures of selected economies by region and supplier, 2001

(Million dollars and percentage)

	Canada a					United States			
	Value	Share	Annual percentage change			Value	Share	Annual percentage change	
	2001	2001	2000	2001		2001	2001	2000	2001
Region					**Region**				
World	182385	100.0	9	-9	World	905511	100.0	15	-6
North America	120688	66.2	6	-10	Asia	396944	43.8	16	-10
Asia	28827	15.8	19	-11	Western Europe	202871	22.4	11	0
Western Europe	20308	11.1	8	-1	North America	139618	15.4	9	-9
Latin America	8352	4.6	28	-3	Latin America	137941	15.2	19	-1
C./E. Europe/					Middle East	14051	1.6	36	-6
Baltic States/CIS	695	0.4	43	-11	C./E. Europe/				
Middle East	471	0.3	58	-19	Baltic States/CIS	9720	1.1	43	-1
Africa	224	0.1	4	-32	Africa	4359	0.5	20	13
Suppliers					**Suppliers**				
United States	120688	66.2	6	-10	European Union (15)	189623	20.9	11	0
European Union (15)	19131	10.5	8	0	Canada	139612	15.4	9	-9
Japan	9334	5.1	10	-16	Japan	124010	13.7	12	-14
China	7854	4.3	27	8	Mexico	108412	12.0	21	-2
Mexico	7200	3.9	27	-4	China	105418	11.6	22	2
Above 5	164207	90.0	8	-9	Above 5	667075	73.7	14	-5
Korea, Rep. of	2837	1.6	45	-15	Korea, Rep. of	34438	3.8	28	-13
Taipei, Chinese	2782	1.5	8	-15	Taipei, Chinese	32898	3.6	15	-19
Malaysia	1166	0.6	22	-27	Malaysia	21764	2.4	19	-12
Switzerland	842	0.5	9	0	Singapore	13783	1.5	4	-22
Thailand	771	0.4	15	-6	Thailand	12707	1.4	15	-11
Hong Kong, China	752	0.4	11	-20	Israel	11286	1.2	33	-8
Singapore	716	0.4	13	-21	Philippines	10763	1.2	14	-20
India	652	0.4	25	-11	Brazil	10574	1.2	22	10
Brazil	627	0.3	27	3	Hong Kong, China	9299	1.0	8	-16
Philippines	581	0.3	37	-35	India	8865	1.0	18	-9
Indonesia	481	0.3	3	6	Indonesia	8767	1.0	12	-1
Israel	368	0.3	35	-3	Switzerland	8354	0.9	6	-10
Australia	252	0.2	18	1	Dominican Republic	3650	0.4	2	-6
Pakistan	169	0.1	12	-3	Hungary	2911	0.3	46	9
Turkey	165	0.1	18	0	Australia	2800	0.3	14	4
Poland	162	0.1	51	4	Russian Fed.	2704	0.3	46	2
South Africa	147	0.1	-22	-22	Turkey	2660	0.3	33	-2
Bangladesh	119	0.1	20	5	Honduras	2648	0.3	10	0
Norway	117	0.1	11	-31	Bangladesh	2398	0.3	27	-2
Russian Fed.	114	0.1	20	-32	Pakistan	2352	0.3	25	4
Czech Rep.	103	0.1	27	-3	South Africa	2210	0.2	25	16
Hungary	98	0.1	71	0	Sri Lanka	2051	0.2	15	-1
Viet Nam	94	0.1	-12	9	Costa Rica	1924	0.2	-14	-25
Trinidad and Tobago	92	0.1	112	168	Guatemala	1852	0.2	18	7
Argentina	89	0.1	81	-4	El Salvador	1796	0.2	20	2
New Zealand	71	0.0	136	-58	Norway	1334	0.1	-5	8
Sri Lanka	68	0.0	58	-18	Macao, China	1254	0.1	13	-5
Romania	56	0.0	3	-17	Venezuela	1231	0.1	26	-6
Dominican Republic	52	0.0	11	-7	Colombia	1118	0.1	9	-10
Saudi Arabia	52	0.0	193	-31	Czech Rep.	1066	0.1	43	2
Macao, China	50	0.0	19	8	Argentina	1036	0.1	14	-4
Venezuela	43	0.0	166	3	Cambodia	1014	0.1	39	16
Honduras	38	0.0	-4	29	Trinidad and Tobago	980	0.1	42	23
Chile	37	0.0	53	21	New Zealand	786	0.1	34	5
Myanmar	30	0.0	157	-7	Poland	775	0.1	26	-9
Above 40	179002	98.1	-	-	Above 40	893121	98.6	-	-

Table IV.25 *(continued)*

Imports of manufactures of selected economies by region and supplier, 2001

(Million dollars and percentage)

	European Union (15)					Japan			
	Value	Share	Annual percentage change			Value	Share	Annual percentage change	
	2001	2001	2000	2001		2001	2001	2000	2001
Region					**Region**				
World	1760943	100.0	4	-3	World	197510	100.0	20	-7
Western Europe	1201572	68.2	1	-3	Asia	106641	54.0	29	-6
Asia	245128	13.9	11	-9	North America	45469	23.0	10	-13
North America	164267	9.3	8	-5	Western Europe	40666	20.6	9	-4
C./E. Europe/					Latin America	1851	0.9	52	-11
Baltic States/CIS	88182	5.0	13	10	Middle East	1174	0.6	4	-5
Africa	23028	1.3	5	7	C./E. Europe/				
Latin America	14888	0.8	23	-11	Baltic States/CIS	1025	0.5	43	7
Middle East	13205	0.7	15	-5	Africa	683	0.3	40	16
Suppliers					**Suppliers**				
European Union (15)	1121527	63.7	1	-3	China	47431	24.0	30	7
United States	153115	8.7	7	-5	United States	43633	22.1	9	-14
Japan	65837	3.7	5	-16	European Union (15)	37130	18.8	10	-4
China	63332	3.6	23	4	Taipei, Chinese	12301	6.2	45	-22
Switzerland	46637	2.6	-3	-4	Korea, Rep. of	12040	6.1	26	-17
Above 5	1450448	82.4	2	-4	Above 5	152534	77.2	19	-7
Taipei, Chinese	20889	1.2	15	-11	Malaysia	8312	4.2	33	-14
Czech Rep.	20385	1.2	12	14	Thailand	6896	3.5	24	-2
Hungary	19462	1.1	9	7	Philippines	5158	2.6	41	-8
Poland	19398	1.1	17	11	Indonesia	4707	2.4	16	-2
Korea, Rep. of	18751	1.1	18	-17	Singapore	4345	2.2	20	-16
Turkey	15157	0.9	3	12	Switzerland	3122	1.6	4	1
Singapore	11188	0.6	6	-17	Canada	1835	0.9	20	-8
Malaysia	10911	0.6	5	-12	Viet Nam	1486	0.8	36	6
Canada	9946	0.6	20	-5	Hong Kong, China	1169	0.6	-5	-14
India	9750	0.6	7	1	Mexico	1109	0.6	81	-7
Thailand	8923	0.5	11	-6	India	988	0.5	8	-8
Hong Kong, China	8650	0.5	-6	-15	Israel	767	0.4	-1	-7
Norway	8607	0.5	-2	-3	Australia	668	0.3	1	-17
Romania	7453	0.4	16	20	South Africa	577	0.3	47	21
Israel	7072	0.4	14	-9	New Zealand	447	0.2	26	-3
Indonesia	6797	0.4	10	-8	Brazil	378	0.2	17	-26
Slovak Rep.	6516	0.4	-1	15	Norway	299	0.2	-9	-1
South Africa	6424	0.4	30	3	Hungary	288	0.1	31	-14
Russian Fed.	5709	0.3	18	-1	Saudi Arabia	273	0.1	18	1
Brazil	5582	0.3	22	-12	Russian Fed.	175	0.1	9	9
Slovenia	5248	0.3	0	1	Slovak Rep.	167	0.1	523	35
Philippines	5058	0.3	4	-10	Pakistan	160	0.1	-22	-18
Tunisia	4676	0.3	0	11	Costa Rica	140	0.1	188	-11
Mexico	4357	0.2	22	6	Czech Rep.	140	0.1	75	19
Morocco	3852	0.2	-10	2	Sri Lanka	93	0.0	6	-6
Viet Nam	3462	0.2	14	8	Bangladesh	90	0.0	25	10
Bangladesh	2798	0.2	25	5	Korea, Dem. People's Rep. of	83	0.0	25	-24
Australia	2558	0.1	12	-8	Kazakhstan	82	0.0	33	19
Bulgaria	2313	0.1	13	19	Turkey	65	0.0	29	9
Pakistan	2223	0.1	1	4	Chile	65	0.0	33	15
Saudi Arabia	1959	0.1	23	-2	New Caledonia	61	0.0	45	-2
Estonia	1916	0.1	52	-7	Cambodia	61	0.0	90	36
Croatia	1733	0.1	-1	7	Poland	54	0.0	21	58
Ukraine	1616	0.1	13	9	Jordan	48	0.0	20	-38
United Arab Emirates	1418	0.1	-1	2	Romania	42	0.0	15	17
Above 40	1723204	97.9	-	-	Above 40	196886	99.7	-	-

a Imports are valued f.o.b.

Table IV.26

Leading exporters and importers of manufactures, 2001

(Billion dollars and percentage)

	Value	Share in world exports/imports			Annual percentage change			
	2001	1980	1990	2001	1990-01	1999	2000	2001
Exporters								
European Union (15)	1881.9	50.7	50.3	42.0	4	0	3	-1
Extra-exports	760.4	21.3	18.1	17.0	5	-2	7	2
United States	602.4	13.0	12.1	13.5	7	3	13	-7
Japan	373.7	11.2	11.5	8.3	3	8	14	-17
China a	235.8	0.8	1.9	5.3	16	7	28	7
Hong Kong, China	182.0	-	-	-	8	1	17	-5
domestic exports	18.8	1.2	1.1	0.4	-3	-9	6	-15
re-exports	163.2	-	-	-	12	3	18	-4
Canada	161.0	2.7	3.1	3.6	7	13	10	-8
Korea, Rep. of	135.5	1.4	2.5	3.0	8	13	20	-13
Mexico a	134.8	0.4	1.1	3.0	16	16	20	-3
Taipei, Chinese	116.4	1.6	2.6	2.6	6	8	22	-18
Singapore	102.6	0.8	1.6	2.3	10	6	19	-13
domestic exports	52.0	0.4	1.0	1.2	8	8	10	-18
re-exports	50.6	0.3	0.6	1.1	12	3	33	-7
Switzerland	75.8	2.4	2.5	1.7	2	1	0	3
Malaysia a	70.4	0.2	0.7	1.6	15	18	16	-11
Thailand	48.3	0.1	0.6	1.1	11	10	20	-7
India b	33.7	0.4	0.5	0.7	10	15	16	…
Indonesia	31.5	0.0	0.4	0.7	12	22	34	-11
Above 15	4022.6	87.2	92.5	89.8	-	-	-	-
Importers								
European Union (15)	1760.9	41.0	45.9	37.8	4	2	4	-3
Extra-imports	639.4	12.2	14.3	13.7	6	5	9	-4
United States	905.5	11.2	15.4	19.4	8	11	15	-6
Japan	197.5	2.3	4.1	4.2	6	12	20	-7
China a	189.9	1.1	1.7	4.1	15	17	28	12
Hong Kong, China	182.5	-	-	-	9	-2	20	-5
retained imports	19.3	1.1	0.9	0.4	-1	-29	30	-13
Canada c	182.4	3.7	3.8	3.9	6	8	9	-9
Mexico a	167.3	1.5	1.3	3.6	16	18	…	1
Singapore	93.2	1.2	1.8	2.0	7	8	19	-15
retained imports	42.6	0.8	1.2	0.9	3	13	7	-23
Korea, Rep. of	84.6	0.9	1.8	1.8	6	37	32	-14
Taipei, Chinese	81.8	0.9	1.5	1.8	8	10	27	-26
Switzerland	69.0	2.3	2.4	1.5	2	2	1	0
Malaysia a	59.9	0.6	0.9	1.3	9	12	25	-12
Australia c	49.3	1.3	1.3	1.1	4	8	6	-16
Thailand	46.6	0.4	1.0	1.0	6	18	20	0
Brazil	44.1	0.9	0.5	0.9	12	-16	10	3
Above 15	3951.5	70.4	84.4	84.7	-	-	-	-

a Includes significant shipments through processing zones.
b 2000 instead of 2001.
c Imports are valued f.o.b.

Table IV.27

Exports of manufactures of selected economies, 1990-01

(Billion dollars and percentage)

	Value					Share in economy's total merchandise exports	
	1990	1995	1999	2000	2001	1990	2001 a
World	2391.00	3702.00	4260.00	4685.00	4477.00	70.4	74.8
Argentina	3.57	7.10	7.39	8.49	8.64	28.9	32.4
Australia	6.90	14.27	14.94	15.16	14.52	17.4	22.9
Bangladesh	1.21	2.90	4.58	5.20	6.32	72.2	96.8
Belarus	-	...	4.43	4.88	...	-	66.5
Brazil	16.14	24.58	25.51	31.80	31.11	51.4	53.4
Bulgaria	...	3.10	2.39	2.82	3.15	...	61.6
Canada	73.31	118.22	159.03	175.64	161.05	57.4	62.0
Chile	0.83	1.86	2.47	2.79	3.18	9.9	18.3
China b	44.31	124.84	172.06	219.86	235.82	71.4	88.6
Colombia	1.70	3.49	3.44	4.26	4.84	25.1	39.5
Costa Rica b	0.39	1.69	4.84	4.17	3.45	27.0	68.8
Croatia	-	3.42	3.24	3.21	3.41	-	73.2
Czech Rep. b	-	17.73	23.09	25.55	29.77	-	89.1
Dominican Republic b, d	1.51	3.06	4.32	4.85	4.47	69.4	83.7
Egypt	1.47	1.39	1.30	...	1.36	42.4	32.9
El Salvador b	0.33	1.05	1.93	2.25	2.32	56.2	80.9
Estonia	-	1.18	1.77	2.48	2.55	-	77.1
European Union (15)	1203.33	1667.64	1846.03	1901.18	1881.91	79.8	82.2
Intra-exports	771.74	1027.52	1147.34	1154.71	1121.53	78.8	79.1
Extra-exports	431.60	640.12	698.69	746.47	760.38	81.6	87.2
Hong Kong, China	75.64	160.77	164.70	192.50	181.97	91.8	95.2
domestic exports	27.41	28.02	20.89	22.14	18.79	94.5	92.7
re-exports	48.23	132.75	143.82	170.35	163.18	90.3	95.5
Hungary b	6.28	8.70	21.58	24.49	26.39	62.8	86.5
India c	12.52	23.21	29.02	33.71	...	69.7	79.5
Indonesia	9.04	22.96	26.20	35.24	31.52	35.2	56.0
Israel c	10.43	16.96	24.06	29.55	27.46	86.3	94.6
Japan	275.13	421.62	393.14	449.69	373.68	95.7	92.6
Jordan	0.59	0.97	1.14	0.95	1.59	55.7	69.4
Korea, Rep. of	60.60	114.40	128.67	154.90	135.46	93.2	90.0
Lithuania	-	1.56	1.96	2.29	2.68	-	58.4
Macao, China	1.67	1.94	2.14	2.48	2.24	98.2	97.4
Malaysia b	15.82	55.09	67.84	78.93	70.42	53.7	80.1
Malta	1.04	1.83	1.85	2.25	1.77	91.9	92.1
Mauritius	0.80	1.08	1.17	1.20	1.13	67.3	74.2
Mexico b	26.85	61.64	115.98	138.65	134.82	66.0	85.0
Morocco b	2.21	2.43	4.90	4.76	4.67	51.8	65.6
New Zealand	2.39	4.20	3.97	3.99	4.23	25.4	30.8
Norway	11.13	13.67	14.39	13.27	13.60	32.7	23.5
Pakistan	4.39	6.77	7.06	7.80	7.86	78.2	85.0
Philippines b	5.66	13.78	32.23	34.77	29.24	69.7	91.0
Poland	8.47	16.27	21.54	25.32	29.09	59.1	80.6
Romania	3.60	6.12	6.65	7.95	8.99	72.6	79.0
Russian Fed. d	-	21.68	20.27	25.42	25.18	-	24.4
Saudi Arabia	3.66	5.70	5.09	5.96	7.48	8.2	11.0
Singapore	37.55	99.04	98.54	117.68	102.61	71.2	84.3
domestic exports	23.26	57.87	57.68	63.28	52.02	66.8	78.6
re-exports	14.28	41.16	40.87	54.40	50.59	79.8	91.0
Slovak Rep.	-	6.98	8.69	9.92	10.58	-	83.7
Slovenia	-	7.44	7.71	7.83	7.78	-	84.1
South Africa c	...	12.09	18.93	20.23	19.21	...	65.6
Sri Lanka	1.02	2.79	3.35	4.14	3.64	53.2	75.5
Switzerland	59.59	76.10	74.07	73.88	75.81	93.4	92.4
Taipei, Chinese	62.05	104.88	115.68	141.43	116.41	92.5	95.0
Thailand	14.58	41.22	43.15	51.76	48.25	63.2	74.1
Tunisia	2.42	4.35	4.61	4.50	5.42	68.6	82.0
Turkey	8.78	16.04	21.02	22.31	25.23	67.7	80.9
Ukraine d	-	...	7.39	9.38	...	-	64.3
United Arab Emirates d	2.86	6.00	6.49	7.46	...	12.1	17.1
United States	290.49	450.28	575.33	648.91	602.37	73.8	82.4

a Or nearest year.

b Includes significant exports from processing zones.

c Includes significant exports of diamonds. For the most recent year, the share of diamonds in exports of manufactures was 22 per cent for India, 32 per cent for Israel and 13 per cent for South Africa.

d Includes Secretariat estimates.

Table IV.28

Imports of manufactures of selected economies, 1990-01

(Billion dollars and percentage)

	Value					Share in economy's total merchandise imports	
	1990	1995	1999	2000	2001	1990	2001 a
Algeria	6.66	6.97	6.15	6.10	...	68.1	66.6
Argentina	3.10	17.20	22.59	22.00	17.45	76.0	85.9
Australia b	31.61	49.14	55.47	58.93	49.34	78.9	82.0
Bangladesh	1.92	3.76	4.57	4.88	5.69	53.0	67.8
Belarus	-	...	3.77	4.24	...	-	49.0
Brazil	12.62	38.18	39.24	43.00	44.10	56.0	75.7
Bulgaria	...	3.01	3.55	3.83	4.68	...	64.7
Canada b	92.90	135.70	183.52	200.75	182.38	79.7	82.4
Chile	5.29	11.80	10.41	11.86	11.80	68.4	68.5
China c	42.39	103.41	132.77	169.88	189.92	79.5	78.0
Colombia	4.28	10.78	8.41	9.19	10.40	76.5	81.0
Costa Rica c	1.50	3.54	5.58	5.45	5.66	75.3	86.2
Croatia	-	5.00	5.70	5.78	6.71	-	83.4
Cyprus	1.81	2.41	2.41	2.49	2.55	70.5	64.9
Czech Rep. b, c	-	19.68	23.00	25.59	29.50	-	80.9
Dominican Republic b, c, d	2.04	3.81	5.81	6.68	6.16	67.8	70.1
Ecuador	1.51	3.43	2.25	2.63	4.27	81.2	80.6
Egypt	6.99	7.11	9.39	...	6.97	56.3	54.6
El Salvador c	0.82	2.38	2.74	3.25	3.39	64.8	67.4
Estonia	-	1.80	2.72	3.45	3.43	-	79.7
European Union (15)	1121.53	1504.60	1756.36	1819.33	1760.94	72.0	75.4
Intra-imports e	772.63					78.7	
Extra-imports	348.89	477.07	609.02	664.62	639.42	60.5	70.0
Guatemala	1.14	2.40	3.41	3.52	3.89	69.0	69.3
Hong Kong, China	70.53	170.56	161.03	192.66	182.53	83.2	90.4
retained imports	22.30	37.81	17.21	22.31	19.35	71.2	62.0
Hungary c	7.27	11.63	24.25	27.08	28.36	70.3	84.2
India f	12.17	19.31	22.79	22.57	...	51.6	44.0
Indonesia	16.64	29.57	13.89	20.48	18.91	76.2	61.1
Iran, Islamic Rep. of d	13.64	8.84	9.16	9.96	11.76	67.1	67.2
Israel f	11.68	23.15	25.87	29.04	27.07	69.5	77.1
Japan	99.95	177.91	177.67	212.67	197.51	42.5	56.6
Jordan	1.34	2.24	2.25	2.65	3.02	51.6	62.3
Kazakhstan	-	...	2.82	3.80	4.78	-	75.2
Korea, Rep. of	44.10	89.85	74.52	98.16	84.64	63.1	60.0
Kuwait	2.61	6.29	5.95	5.95	...	65.6	83.1
Lebanon	...	...	3.82	3.48	4.23	...	58.0
Lithuania	-	2.11	3.23	3.31	4.04	-	64.3
Malaysia c	22.87	64.42	54.33	68.13	59.95	78.2	80.9
Mauritius	1.28	1.44	1.72	1.46	1.38	79.2	69.3
Mexico c, g	32.49	58.08	125.36	165.01	167.26	74.6	87.9
Morocco c	4.22	4.81	7.41	7.25	6.87	61.0	62.7
New Zealand	7.56	11.50	11.75	10.81	10.49	79.6	78.6
Norway	21.40	25.96	27.57	27.48	25.48	78.6	78.7
Oman	1.81	2.90	3.23	3.46	3.93	67.3	67.8
Pakistan	3.99	6.63	5.21	5.09	5.05	53.8	47.6
Peru	1.61	5.69	4.98	5.21	5.19	61.2	70.9
Philippines c	8.96	21.94	25.77	25.64	23.76	68.7	75.8
Poland	7.26	21.61	37.17	38.25	39.60	62.8	78.8
Romania	2.95	6.48	8.13	9.82	11.63	38.8	74.8
Russian Fed. d	-	28.45	26.14	30.40	37.71	-	70.0
Saudi Arabia	18.23	20.67	20.47	22.05	23.29	75.7	74.6
Singapore	44.42	103.32	92.41	109.78	93.18	73.1	80.3
retained imports	30.13	62.15	51.55	55.39	42.59	70.3	70.5
Slovak Rep. b	-	5.75	8.48	9.09	10.88	-	73.7
Slovenia	-	7.00	8.01	7.68	8.28	-	81.7
South Africa b	13.43	20.81	18.29	19.14	17.96	80.2	70.6
Sri Lanka	1.71	3.51	4.07	4.90	4.14	63.5	69.9
Switzerland	58.01	68.29	68.09	69.01	68.99	83.3	82.1
Taipei, Chinese	36.77	76.85	87.27	110.62	81.81	67.1	76.3
Thailand	24.83	56.70	38.89	46.57	46.58	75.1	75.1
Tunisia	3.91	5.75	6.65	6.46	7.28	70.9	76.7
Turkey	13.63	24.41	29.93	38.16	27.11	61.1	66.8
Ukraine d	-	...	5.51	6.97	...	-	49.9
United Arab Emirates d	8.87	18.31	17.02	18.78	...	79.2	49.2
United States	375.65	607.82	842.84	968.21	905.51	72.7	76.7
Venezuela b	5.05	8.24	11.02	11.81	13.36	76.5	81.3

a Or nearest year.
b Imports are valued f.o.b.
c Includes significant imports into processing zones.
d Includes Secretariat estimates.
e See the Technical Notes for information on intra-EU imports.
f Includes significant imports of diamonds. For the most recent year, the share of diamonds in total imports of manufactures was 23 per cent for India and 23 per cent for Israel.
g Beginning with 2000 imports are valued c.i.f.

4.1 Iron and Steel

Table IV.29

World trade in iron and steel, 2001

(Billion dollars and percentage)

Value	130
Annual percentage change	
1980-85	-2
1985-90	9
1990-01	2
2000	14
2001	-8
Share in world merchandise trade	2.2
Share in world exports of manufactures	2.9

Table IV.30

Major regional flows in world exports of iron and steel, 2001

(Billion dollars and percentage)

	Value	Annual percentage change		
	2001	1990-01	2000	2001
Intra-Western Europe	46.0	0	8	-8
Intra-Asia	20.1	4	18	-15
C./E. Europe/Baltic States/CIS to Western Europe	6.5	7	35	3
Intra-North America	5.4	6	13	-13
Intra-C./E. Europe/Baltic States/CIS	4.6	15	34	8
Western Europe to North America	4.5	0	26	-18

Table IV.31

Share of iron and steel in trade in total merchandise and in manufactures by region, 2001

(Percentage)

	Exports	Imports
Share of iron and steel in total merchandise		
World	2.2	2.2
North America	0.9	1.4
Latin America	2.1	1.9
Western Europe	2.5	2.3
C./E. Europe/Baltic States/CIS	6.6	3.3
Africa	1.6	3.0
Middle East	0.5	3.3
Asia	2.0	2.2
Share of iron and steel in manufactures		
World	2.9	2.9
North America	1.1	1.7
Latin America	3.5	2.5
Western Europe	3.1	3.1
C./E. Europe/Baltic States/CIS	11.7	4.5
Africa	6.3	4.2
Middle East	2.2	4.4
Asia	2.3	3.2

Chart IV.7

Regional shares in world trade in iron and steel, 2001

(Percentage)

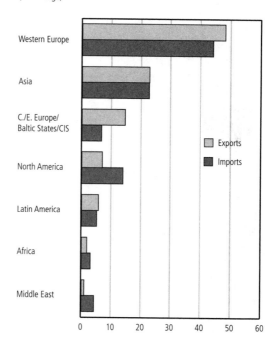

Table IV.32

Exports of iron and steel by principal region, 2001

(Billion dollars and percentage)

	Value	Share in				Annual percentage change		
		Region's exports		World exports				
	2001	1990	2001	1990	2001	1990-01	2000	2001
World	129.6	-	-	100.0	100.0	2	14	-8
Western Europe								
World	62.2	100.0	100.0	61.0	48.0	0	9	-6
Western Europe	46.0	74.9	73.9	45.7	35.5	0	8	-8
North America	4.5	6.8	7.2	4.1	3.5	0	26	-18
C./E. Europe/Baltic States/CIS	3.6	3.5	5.8	2.2	2.8	4	9	15
Asia	3.2	5.8	5.2	3.5	2.5	-1	12	7
Middle East	1.8	3.6	2.9	2.2	1.4	-2	2	12
Africa	1.7	3.7	2.7	2.2	1.3	-3	-3	18
Latin America	1.2	1.7	2.0	1.1	0.9	1	4	2
Asia								
World	29.2	100.0	100.0	19.5	22.6	3	18	-16
Asia	20.1	63.8	68.7	12.5	15.5	4	18	-15
North America	3.7	17.7	12.7	3.5	2.9	0	12	-29
Western Europe	2.0	4.9	6.8	1.0	1.5	6	33	-21
Middle East	1.5	5.7	5.2	1.1	1.2	2	1	21
Latin America	0.9	2.2	3.2	0.4	0.7	7	27	-12
All other regions	0.7	3.8	2.3	0.7	0.5	-1	-2	6
Japan								
World	13.5	100.0	100.0	11.8	10.5	1	10	-9
Asia	9.7	60.5	71.5	7.2	7.5	2	15	-13
North America	1.5	19.3	11.1	2.3	1.2	-4	-6	-9
Western Europe	0.8	5.2	5.6	0.6	0.6	1	1	21
Middle East	0.7	6.2	5.4	0.7	0.6	-1	-15	38
Latin America	0.6	3.1	4.4	0.4	0.5	4	27	-9
All other regions	0.3	5.7	2.1	0.7	0.2	-8	-9	-1
Other economies in Asia								
World	15.7	100.0	100.0	7.7	12.1	6	24	-22
Asia	10.4	69.0	66.3	5.3	8.0	6	20	-17
North America	2.2	15.2	14.1	1.2	1.7	5	24	-38
Western Europe	1.2	4.3	7.8	0.3	0.9	12	48	-35
Middle East	0.8	4.9	5.1	0.4	0.6	7	18	10
All other regions	0.7	1.7	4.7	0.1	0.6	16	16	-5
C./E. Europe/Baltic States/CIS a								
World	18.8	100.0	100.0	6.0 I	14.5	...	24	1
Western Europe	6.5	46.7	34.5	2.8	5.0	7	35	3
C./E. Europe/Baltic States/CIS	4.6	14.8 I	24.4	0.9 I	3.5	...	34	8
Asia	3.6	26.3	19.0	1.6	2.8	7	2	-8
Middle East	1.0	5.0	5.5	0.3	0.8	11	49	1
All other regions	2.3	7.0	12.1	0.4	1.7	16	30	-19

a Includes the intra trade of the Baltic States and the CIS beginning with 1996.

Table IV.33

Iron and steel imports of the European Union and the United States by region and supplier, 2001

(Million dollars and percentage)

	European Union (15)					United States			
	Value	Share	Annual percentage change			Value	Share	Annual percentage change	
	2001	2001	2000	2001		2001	2001	2000	2001
Region					Region				
World	52699	100.0	11	-8	World	14995	100.0	18	-22
Western Europe	42873	81.4	8	-8	Western Europe	4362	29.1	19	-16
C./E. Europe/					Asia	3811	25.4	16	-27
Baltic States/CIS	4726	9.0	24	0	Latin America	2939	19.6	15	-17
Asia	1944	3.7	34	-19	North America	2518	16.8	9	-14
Latin America	1116	2.1	35	-19	C./E. Europe/				
Africa	1123	2.1	30	-6	Baltic States/CIS	943	6.3	40	-45
North America	725	1.4	9	1	Africa	383	2.6	18	-34
Middle East	120	0.2	149	-31	Middle East	39	0.3	96	-20
Suppliers					Suppliers				
European Union (15)	40161	76.2	8	-8	European Union (15)	4003	26.7	19	-16
Russian Fed.	1178	2.2	56	-16	Canada	2518	16.8	9	-14
Turkey	810	1.5	16	11	Japan	1387	9.2	-15	-8
South Africa	783	1.5	30	-9	Brazil	1196	8.0	23	-16
Czech Rep.	733	1.4	8	4	Mexico	1077	7.2	5	-19
Above 5	43666	82.9	9	-8	Above 5	10181	67.9	10	-15
Switzerland	729	1.4	8	-8	Korea, Rep. of	918	6.1	7	-19
Norway	699	1.3	-7	-7	China	490	3.3	67	-29
Poland	684	1.3	30	-4	Russian Fed.	442	2.9	25	-19
United States	635	1.2	13	1	Taipei, Chinese	384	2.6	43	-45
Ukraine	496	0.9	-2	30	South Africa	338	2.3	20	-36
Japan	486	0.9	5	15	Venezuela	305	2.0	26	-12
Slovak Rep.	453	0.9	13	18	Turkey	227	1.5	62	7
Brazil	448	0.9	25	-31	Australia	193	1.3	11	-25
Korea, Rep. of	367	0.7	20	-20	India	179	1.2	107	-58
Bulgaria	341	0.6	23	15	Ukraine	162	1.1	93	-67
Romania	308	0.6	9	0	Argentina	159	1.1	18	-15
China	269	0.5	67	-29	Trinidad and Tobago	118	0.8	-11	34
Hungary	226	0.4	19	-15	Thailand	86	0.6	113	-60
Slovenia	186	0.4	10	-1	Romania	80	0.5	22	-40
Taipei, Chinese	186	0.4	37	-39	Malaysia	70	0.5	65	-1
Argentina	174	0.3	40	6	Norway	69	0.5	4	-43
Colombia	168	0.3	55	-5	Czech Rep.	65	0.4	79	51
India	162	0.3	21	-33	Indonesia	47	0.3	-3	-63
Venezuela	141	0.3	-14	53	Kazakhstan	46	0.3	43	-75
Kazakhstan	140	0.3	22	-6	Poland	42	0.3	113	-58
Australia	136	0.3	15	15	Moldova, Rep. of	40	0.3	8	-52
TFYR Macedonia	130	0.2	51	-15	Colombia	39	0.3	96	-17
Indonesia	123	0.2	69	11	Switzerland	36	0.2	-24	-32
Egypt	108	0.2	230	24	Dominican Republic	32	0.2	59	-56
New Caledonia	105	0.2	66	-25	Egypt	26	0.2	71	117
Above 30	51566	97.9	-	-	Above 30	14716	98.1	-	-

Table IV.34

Leading exporters and importers of iron and steel, 2001

(Billion dollars and percentage)

	Value	Share in world exports/imports			Annual percentage change			
	2001	1980	1990	2001	1990-01	1999	2000	2001
Exporters								
European Union (15)	57.87	52.9	57.0	44.7	0	-16	9	-7
Extra-exports	17.71	22.0	17.5	13.7	0	-20	13	-2
Japan	13.54	20.4	11.8	10.5	1	-9	10	-9
Russian Fed. a	6.00	-	-	4.6	-	-15	33	-10
United States	5.97	4.2	3.3	4.6	5	-10	16	-6
Korea, Rep. of	5.83	2.2	3.4	4.5	4	-18	13	-13
Ukraine a, b	4.88	-	-	3.5	-	-14	30	...
Taipei, Chinese	3.77	0.4	0.8	2.9	14	11	30	-18
China c	3.15	...	1.2	2.4	9	-19	65	-28
Brazil	3.14	1.1	3.4	2.4	-1	-15	17	-14
Canada	2.80	2.3	1.9	2.2	3	-8	11	-13
Turkey	2.47	0.0	1.4	1.9	5	-5	6	34
South Africa	2.18	1.6	2.0	1.7	0	-5	19	-21
Hong Kong, China	1.49	-	-	-	9	-18	4	-21
domestic exports	0.01	0.0	0.0	0.0	-12	-20	-18	-42
re-exports	1.48	-	-	-	10	-18	4	-21
Czech Rep. c	1.41	-	-	1.1	-	-21	6	15
India b	1.37	0.1	0.2	1.0	19	25	35	...
Above 15	114.37	85.3	86.6	87.9	-	-	-	-
Importers								
European Union (15)	52.70	36.4	45.2	37.2	0	-16	11	-8
Extra-imports	12.54	6.2	7.6	8.8	4	-21	23	-6
United States	14.99	10.1	9.5	10.6	3	-21	18	-22
China c	10.75	...	2.5	7.6	13	15	29	11
Korea, Rep. of	4.42	1.2	2.9	3.1	3	42	33	-17
Canada d	4.12	1.6	2.0	2.9	6	-10	24	-22
Mexico c	3.81	2.2	1.0	2.7	12	-7	...	-11
Taipei, Chinese	3.00	1.4	2.5	2.1	0	-4	11	-36
Japan	2.78	1.1	4.1	2.0	-4	-8	24	-24
Thailand	2.58	0.6	2.4	1.8	0	40	3	-7
Hong Kong, China	2.52	-	-	-	5	-15	6	-21
retained imports	1.04	0.8	0.8	0.7	1	-10	9	-21
Malaysia c	2.19	0.8	1.3	1.5	4	25	-1	3
Turkey	1.78	0.4	1.1	1.3	3	-30	53	-26
Russian Fed. a	1.71	-	-	1.2	-	-30	31	-2
Iran, Islamic Rep. of a, b	1.60	...	...	1.0	...	-9	36	...
Poland	1.60	1.5	0.3	1.1	15	-14	14	11
Above 15	109.08	59.4	75.6	76.9	-	-	-	-

a Includes Secretariat estimates.
b 2000 instead of 2001.
c Includes significant shipments through processing zones.
d Imports are valued f.o.b.

4.2 Chemicals

Table IV.35

World trade in chemicals, 2001

(Billion dollars and percentage)

Value	595
Annual percentage change	
1980-85	1
1985-90	14
1990-01	7
2000	9
2001	2
Share in world merchandise trade	9.9
Share in world exports of manufactures	13.3

Table IV.36

Major regional flows in world exports of chemicals, 2001

(Billion dollars and percentage)

	Value	Annual percentage change		
	2001	1990-01	2000	2001
Intra-Western Europe	229.5	5	3	3
Intra-Asia	60.9	10	24	-8
Western Europe to North America	40.8	11	10	7
Intra-North America	28.4	9	12	0
Western Europe to Asia	28.3	4	4	-1
North America to Western Europe	25.8	7	15	3

Table IV.37

Share of chemicals in trade in total merchandise and in manufactures by region, 2001

(Percentage)

	Exports	Imports
Share of chemicals in total merchandise		
World	9.9	9.9
North America	9.8	7.0
Latin America	4.8	11.9
Western Europe	14.0	11.7
C./E. Europe/Baltic States/CIS	6.9	11.0
Africa	3.6	10.7
Middle East	6.0	8.5
Asia	6.4	9.2
Share of chemicals in manufactures		
World	13.3	13.3
North America	12.7	8.8
Latin America	8.0	15.4
Western Europe	17.3	15.4
C./E. Europe/Baltic States/CIS	12.2	14.8
Africa	14.2	15.1
Middle East	27.4	11.3
Asia	7.6	13.1

Chart IV.8

Regional shares in world trade in chemicals, 2001

(Percentage)

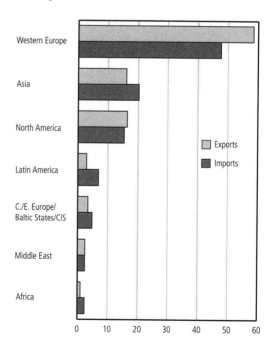

Table IV.38

Exports of chemicals by principal region, 2001

(Billion dollars and percentage)

	Value	Share in				Annual percentage change		
		Region's exports		World exports				
	2001	1990	2001	1990	2001	1990-01	2000	2001
World	595.4	-	-	100.0	100.0	7	9	2
Western Europe								
World	347.4	100.0	100.0	65.0	58.4	6	4	4
Western Europe	229.5	70.2	66.0	45.7	38.5	5	3	3
North America	40.8	6.5	11.7	4.2	6.8	11	10	7
Asia	28.3	9.2	8.2	6.0	4.8	4	4	-1
C./E. Europe/Baltic States/CIS	19.0	4.0	5.5	2.6	3.2	8	10	13
Latin America	10.1	2.6	2.9	1.7	1.7	7	3	7
Middle East	7.9	2.9	2.3	1.9	1.3	3	0	6
Africa	7.9	3.5	2.3	2.3	1.3	1	-4	4
North America								
World	97.3	100.0	100.0	15.6	16.3	7	15	0
North America	28.4	23.2	29.2	3.6	4.8	9	12	0
Western Europe	25.8	27.0	26.5	4.2	4.3	7	15	3
Asia	22.3	32.2	22.9	5.0	3.7	4	14	-6
Latin America	17.6	14.0	18.1	2.2	3.0	10	20	-1
All other regions	3.1	3.6	3.2	0.6	0.5	6	18	21
Asia								
World	95.2	100.0	100.0	11.4	16.0	10	19	-5
Asia	60.9	62.0	63.9	7.1	10.2	10	24	-8
Western Europe	13.6	16.1	14.3	1.8	2.3	9	5	0
North America	12.6	13.2	13.3	1.5	2.1	10	12	-2
Latin America	2.5	1.2	2.6	0.1	0.4	18	25	3
Middle East	2.0	1.8	2.1	0.2	0.3	12	17	1
Africa	1.9	1.3	2.0	0.1	0.3	14	14	9
C./E. Europe/Baltic States/CIS	1.1	3.0	1.2	0.3	0.2	1	41	12
Japan								
World	30.6	100.0	100.0	5.3	5.1	6	14	-13
Asia	18.1	57.0	59.1	3.0	3.0	7	20	-15
North America	6.4	16.4	20.9	0.9	1.1	9	10	-12
Western Europe	5.3	20.3	17.2	1.1	0.9	5	2	-4
Latin America	0.5	1.6	1.6	0.1	0.1	6	5	-12
All other regions	0.4	4.7	1.3	0.2	0.1	-5	3	-7
Other economies in Asia								
World	64.6	100.0	100.0	6.1	10.9	12	22	-1
Asia	42.8	66.5	66.2	4.0	7.2	12	26	-5
Western Europe	8.3	12.3	12.9	0.7	1.4	13	7	4
North America	6.2	10.3	9.7	0.6	1.0	12	15	12
Latin America	2.0	0.9	3.1	0.1	0.3	25	32	8
Middle East	1.8	1.9	2.7	0.1	0.3	16	21	2
Africa	1.8	1.7	2.7	0.1	0.3	17	14	12
C./E. Europe/Baltic States/CIS	1.0	3.8	1.6	0.2	0.2	4	44	13

Table IV.39

Leading exporters and importers of chemicals, 2001

(Billion dollars and percentage)

	Value	Share in world exports/imports			Annual percentage change			
	2001	1980	1990	2001	1990-01	1999	2000	2001
Exporters								
European Union (15)	316.36	58.4	59.0	53.1	6	2	4	3
Extra-exports	125.59	23.3	21.1	21.1	7	6	5	5
United States	82.30	14.8	13.3	13.8	7	4	15	0
Japan	30.62	4.7	5.3	5.1	6	13	14	-13
Switzerland	25.60	4.0	4.6	4.3	6	4	-5	15
Canada	14.99	2.5	2.2	2.5	8	6	15	1
China a	13.35	0.8	1.3	2.2	12	1	17	10
Korea, Rep. of	12.52	0.5	0.8	2.1	16	5	28	-9
Singapore	9.88	0.5	1.1	1.7	10	28	6	3
domestic exports	6.77	0.2	0.7	1.1	12	43	1	8
re-exports	3.11	0.3	0.4	0.5	8	4	15	-7
Hong Kong, China	9.26	-	-	-	7	-1	11	-11
domestic exports	0.70	0.1	0.3	0.1	-2	-16	11	-13
re-exports	8.56	-	-	-	8	0	12	-11
Taipei, Chinese	8.78	0.4	0.9	1.5	11	13	30	-5
Russian Fed. b	5.67	-	-	1.0	-	-1	30	1
Mexico a	5.46	0.4	0.7	0.9	9	4	19	1
Saudi Arabia	4.69	0.1	0.8	0.8	6	-10	25	11
India c	4.36	0.2	0.4	0.7	13	18	18	...
Israel	4.16	0.6	0.6	0.7	8	5	14	3
Above 15	539.45	87.8	91.6	90.6	-	-	-	-
Importers								
European Union (15)	259.18	46.4	50.6	41.8	5	0	4	3
Extra-imports	68.42	11.6	12.0	11.0	6	1	5	4
United States	81.13	6.2	7.7	13.1	12	14	18	7
China a	32.10	2.0	2.2	5.2	15	19	26	6
Japan	25.19	4.1	5.0	4.1	5	11	14	-3
Canada d	20.51	2.2	2.5	3.3	9	9	9	2
Mexico a	16.54	1.5	1.2	2.7	15	16	...	2
Switzerland	16.18	2.5	2.6	2.6	6	4	2	18
Korea, Rep. of	12.94	1.3	2.4	2.1	5	22	19	-4
Taipei, Chinese	12.17	1.3	2.3	2.0	5	7	23	-22
Hong Kong, China	11.53	-	-	-	6	-2	16	-14
retained imports	2.97	0.7	0.9	0.5	1	-7	28	-22
Brazil	10.75	2.4	1.1	1.7	11	-3	9	2
Poland	7.34	1.0	0.3	1.2	20	3	5	6
Australia d	7.33	1.2	1.2	1.2	7	9	7	-9
Singapore	6.82	0.9	1.5	1.1	3	7	16	-12
retained imports	3.71	0.6	1.1	0.6	1	10	17	-15
Thailand	6.66	0.7	1.1	1.1	6	16	20	-2
Above 15	517.80	74.4	82.6	83.6	-	-	-	-

a Includes significant shipments through processing zones.
b Includes Secretariat estimates.
c 2000 instead of 2001.
d Imports are valued f.o.b.

4.3 *Office Machines and Telecom Equipment*

Table IV.40
World trade in office machines and telecom equipment, 2001
(Billion dollars and percentage)

Value	828
Annual percentage change	
1980-85	9
1985-90	18
1990-01	10
2000	22
2001	-14
Share in world merchandise trade	13.8
Share in world exports of manufactures	18.5

Table IV.41
Major regional flows in world exports of office machines and telecom equipment, 2001
(Billion dollars and percentage)

	Value	Annual percentage change		
	2001	1990-01	2000	2001
Intra-Asia	183.7	15	33	-15
Intra-Western Europe	171.1	8	12	-11
Asia to North America	103.8	6	16	-21
Asia to Western Europe	74.8	7	19	-16
North America to Asia	51.2	9	26	-20
Latin America to North America	35.3	20	28	3

Table IV.42
Share of office machines and telecom equipment in trade in total merchandise and in manufactures by region, 2001
(Percentage)

	Exports	Imports
Share in total merchandise		
World	13.8	13.8
North America	14.1	14.2
Latin America	11.3	11.8
Western Europe	10.0	11.9
C./E. Europe/Baltic States/CIS	4.5	8.0
Africa	0.7	6.2
Middle East	2.3	7.4
Asia	25.5	20.4
Australia, Japan and New Zealand	17.5	15.0
Other Asia	29.3	22.7
Share in manufactures		
World	18.5	18.5
North America	18.3	18.0
Latin America	18.8	15.3
Western Europe	12.3	15.8
C./E. Europe/Baltic States/CIS	8.0	10.7
Africa	2.6	8.8
Middle East	10.4	9.8
Asia	30.6	29.2
Australia, Japan and New Zealand	21.5	24.1
Other Asia	34.8	31.0

Chart IV.9
Regional shares in world trade in office machines and telecom equipment, 2001
(Percentage)

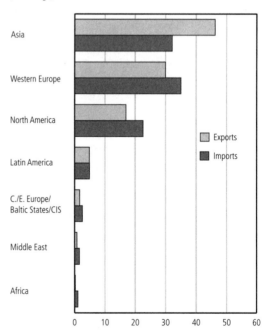

Table IV.43

Exports of office machines and telecom equipment by principal region, 2001

(Billion dollars and percentage)

| | Value | Share in | | | | Annual percentage change | | |
| | | Region's exports | | World exports | | | | |
	2001	1990	2001	1990	2001	1990-01	2000	2001
World	827.5	-	-	100.0	100.0	10	22	-14
Asia								
World	382.2	100.0	100.0	45.9	46.2	10	25	-16
Asia	183.7	29.8	48.1	13.7	22.2	15	33	-15
North America	103.8	37.9	27.2	17.4	12.5	6	16	-21
Western Europe	74.8	27.3	19.6	12.5	9.0	7	19	-16
Latin America	7.3	1.9	1.9	0.9	0.9	10	24	-12
Middle East	3.9	1.2	1.0	0.5	0.5	9	30	12
C./E. Europe/Baltic States/CIS	2.8	0.9	0.7	0.4	0.3	7	38	17
Africa	1.5	0.6	0.4	0.3	0.2	6	0	-1
Japan								
World	82.6	100.0	100.0	22.4	10.0	2	18	-24
Asia	37.1	26.7	45.0	6.0	4.5	7	28	-22
North America	25.1	38.8	30.3	8.7	3.0	0	10	-27
Western Europe	17.8	29.5	21.6	6.6	2.2	-1	16	-23
All other regions	2.6	5.0	3.1	1.1	0.3	-2	10	-19
Other economies in Asia								
World	299.6	100.0	100.0	23.5	36.2	14	27	-13
Asia	146.6	32.7	48.9	7.7	17.7	18	34	-13
North America	78.8	37.1	26.3	8.7	9.5	11	19	-19
Western Europe	57.0	25.1	19.0	5.9	6.9	11	21	-13
All other regions	13.0	4.2	4.3	1.0	1.6	15	29	3
Western Europe								
World	247.6	100.0	100.0	32.0	29.9	9	15	-10
Western Europe	171.1	76.2	69.1	24.4	20.7	8	12	-11
Asia	28.0	6.5	11.3	2.1	3.4	15	30	-9
North America	16.6	6.7	6.7	2.1	2.0	9	18	-13
C./E. Europe/Baltic States/CIS	14.8	3.3	6.0	1.1	1.8	15	28	4
Middle East	6.0	1.8	2.4	0.6	0.7	12	25	14
Africa	5.1	2.7	2.1	0.9	0.6	6	10	-8
Latin America	3.9	1.6	1.6	0.5	0.5	9	23	-10
North America								
World	139.5	100.0	100.0	19.2	16.9	8	25	-20
Asia	51.2	33.7	36.7	6.5	6.2	9	26	-20
Western Europe	29.6	32.6	21.2	6.3	3.6	4	17	-15
North America	28.1	21.4	20.2	4.1	3.4	8	31	-30
Latin America	26.9	9.5	19.3	1.8	3.3	16	27	-12
All other regions	3.7	2.8	2.7	0.5	0.4	8	9	-8

Table IV.44

Imports of office machines and telecom equipment of selected economies by region and supplier, 2001

(Million dollars and percentage)

	Canada a					United States			
	Value	Share	Annual percentage change			Value	Share	Annual percentage change	
	2001	2001	2000	2001		2001	2001	2000	2001
Region					Region				
World	23359	100.0	22	-23	World	172835	100.0	22	-20
North America	10331	44.2	16	-26	Asia	119016	68.9	18	-22
Asia	7925	33.9	21	-23	Latin America	29428	17.0	28	1
Latin America	1901	8.1	37	-5	Western Europe	12370	7.2	17	-14
Western Europe	1124	4.8	45	-47	North America	9314	5.4	51	-41
Middle East	85	0.4	62	12	Middle East	1476	0.9	87	-28
C./E. Europe/					C./E. Europe/				
Baltic States/CIS	67	0.1	136	20	Baltic States/CIS	1126	0.7	20	-27
Africa	12	0.0	31	-50	Africa	105	0.1	18	-38
Suppliers					Suppliers				
United States	10331	44.2	16	-26	Mexico	27698	16.0	32	2
Japan	2003	8.6	13	-29	Japan	25051	14.5	12	-32
Mexico	1826	7.8	41	-5	China	22272	12.9	32	-1
China	1413	6.0	45	9	Malaysia	17418	10.1	22	-14
Taipei, Chinese	1188	5.1	1	-21	Taipei, Chinese	14875	8.6	20	-22
Above 5	16760	71.7	18	-22	Above 5	92439	53.5	22	-14
European Union (15)	1079	4.6	45	-47	Korea, Rep. of	14441	8.4	33	-29
Korea, Rep. of	901	3.9	45	-24	European Union (15)	11580	6.7	17	-14
Malaysia	846	3.6	27	-32	Singapore	10563	6.1	2	-27
Singapore	538	2.3	13	-25	Canada	9314	5.4	51	-41
Philippines	381	1.6	38	-43	Philippines	6367	3.7	17	-27
Thailand	375	1.6	18	-9	Thailand	4548	2.6	9	-22
Hong Kong, China	138	0.6	25	-47	Indonesia	2071	1.2	10	-1
Indonesia	107	0.5	9	11	Israel	1469	0.8	88	-28
Israel	84	0.4	65	12	Brazil	1227	0.7	91	66
Brazil	62	0.3	-17	-11	Hong Kong, China	1170	0.7	9	-36
Hungary	43	0.2	101	10	Hungary	961	0.6	16	-31
Switzerland	24	0.1	54	-28	Costa Rica	453	0.3	-32	-57
Australia	22	0.1	47	-25	Switzerland	338	0.2	-5	-14
Estonia	16	0.1	-	61	Malta	289	0.2	60	-23
Norway	15	0.1	4	-12	Norway	155	0.1	-3	4
Above 20	21393	91.6	-	-	Above 20	157385	91.1	-	-

Table IV.44 *(continued)*

Imports of office machines and telecom equipment of selected economies by region and supplier, 2001

(Million dollars and percentage)

	European Union (15)					Japan			
	Value	Share	Annual percentage change			Value	Share	Annual percentage change	
	2001	2001	2000	2001		2001	2001	2000	2001
Region					**Region**				
World	285536	100.0	16	-12	World	52477	100.0	38	-14
Western Europe	159831	56.0	12	-11	Asia	35815	68.2	46	-11
Asia	75306	26.4	18	-14	North America	11821	22.5	20	-19
North America	30856	10.8	20	-16	Western Europe	3853	7.3	34	-19
C./E. Europe/					Latin America	658	1.3	120	-10
Baltic States/CIS	9309	3.3	38	10	C./E. Europe/				
Middle East	1698	0.6	30	-13	Baltic States/CIS	204	0.4	28	-13
Latin America	1680	0.6	39	-31	Middle East	120	0.2	-21	-9
Africa	503	0.2	-23	0	Africa	6	0.0	48	-56
Suppliers					**Suppliers**				
European Union (15)	156587	54.8	12	-11	United States	11388	21.7	19	-20
United States	28910	10.1	17	-15	China	8117	15.5	51	-14
Japan	17264	6.0	13	-24	Taipei, Chinese	6889	13.1	66	-27
China	14933	5.2	45	12	Malaysia	5313	10.1	41	-17
Taipei, Chinese	11337	4.0	25	-10	Korea, Rep. of	5140	9.8	42	-20
Above 5	229031	80.2	15	-11	Above 5	36847	70.2	54	-14
Korea, Rep. of	7242	2.5	34	-24	European Union (15)	3761	7.2	35	-19
Malaysia	7184	2.5	2	-14	Philippines	3542	6.8	54	-10
Singapore	7109	2.5	8	-25	Singapore	3051	5.8	26	-19
Hungary	5010	1.8	24	5	Thailand	2278	4.3	38	-8
Philippines	3712	1.3	5	-9	Indonesia	1006	1.9	37	19
Thailand	2705	0.9	13	-14	Mexico	500	1.0	-4	-8
Hong Kong, China	2257	0.8	-5	-24	Canada	432	0.8	81	-15
Canada	1944	0.7	71	-28	Hong Kong, China	421	0.8	97	1
Czech Rep.	1713	0.6	66	94	Hungary	182	0.3	23	-16
Switzerland	1372	0.5	7	-16	Costa Rica	132	0.3	219	-13
Israel	1332	0.5	41	-18	Israel	118	0.2	-22	-9
Mexico	1295	0.5	64	18	Switzerland	71	0.1	22	-22
Indonesia	1125	0.4	27	-5	Brazil	24	0.0	4990	-63
Poland	1037	0.4	2	14	Australia	24	0.0	-22	-56
Turkey	903	0.3	21	4	Viet Nam	23	0.0	57	-18
Above 20	274971	96.3	-	-	Above 20	52413	99.9	-	-

a Imports are valued f.o.b.

Table IV.45

Leading exporters and importers of office machines and telecom equipment, 2001

(Billion dollars and percentage)

	Value	Share in world exports/imports			Annual percentage change			
	2001	1980	1990	2001	1990-01	1999	2000	2001
Exporters								
European Union (15)	241.76	35.9	31.1	29.2	9	8	15	-10
Extra-exports	85.17	12.4	9.1	10.3	11	7	22	-9
United States	126.69	19.5	17.3	15.3	8	10	22	-17
Japan	82.60	21.1	22.4	10.0	2	7	18	-24
Singapore	61.78	3.2	6.4	7.5	11	5	22	-16
domestic exports	31.80	2.5	4.9	3.8	7	5	8	-23
re-exports	29.98	0.7	1.5	3.6	19	6	47	-7
China a	52.26	0.1	1.0	6.3	29	19	44	20
Hong Kong, China	50.16	-	-	-	13	5	30	0
domestic exports	3.02	2.0	1.6	0.4	-4	-16	11	-24
re-exports	47.14	-	-	-	17	8	32	2
Taipei, Chinese	45.83	3.2	4.7	5.5	11	16	30	-21
Malaysia a	44.87	1.4	2.7	5.4	17	28	18	-14
Korea, Rep. of	44.18	2.0	4.8	5.3	11	35	37	-25
Mexico a	34.38	0.1	1.5	4.2	20	22	29	1
Philippines a	20.75	0.8	0.6	2.5	25	29	5	-17
Thailand	16.21	0.0	1.2	2.0	15	7	23	-13
Canada	12.84	2.0	1.9	1.6	8	8	47	-38
Hungary a	6.80	0.5	0.2	0.8	27	28	31	-5
Indonesia	5.94	0.1	0.0	0.7	42	26	145	-18
Above 15	799.92	91.8	97.6	96.7	-	-	-	-
Importers								
European Union (15)	285.54	41.5	42.3	33.5	8	8	16	-12
Extra-imports	128.95	20.1	21.9	15.1	6	8	22	-13
United States	172.84	15.9	21.1	20.3	10	13	22	-20
Hong Kong, China	57.47	-	-	-	15	1	36	-3
retained imports	10.33	1.7	1.4	1.2	8	-18	52	-22
Japan	52.48	2.6	3.7	6.2	15	21	38	-14
China a	49.56	0.6	1.3	5.8	26	38	46	12
Singapore	44.20	2.6	4.5	5.2	11	14	28	-18
retained imports	14.22	1.9	2.9	1.7	4	24	7	-35
Mexico a	32.83	0.9	1.5	3.9	19	26	...	10
Taipei, Chinese	29.12	1.4	2.5	3.4	13	23	33	-25
Malaysia a	27.64	1.6	1.9	3.2	15	16	28	-15
Korea, Rep. of	26.33	1.3	2.6	3.1	12	49	38	-23
Canada b	23.36	4.1	3.5	2.7	8	10	22	-23
Thailand	13.40	0.2	1.1	1.6	13	21	44	-5
Philippines a	11.26	0.8	0.7	1.3	17	4	-5	-6
Australia b	8.23	1.5	1.4	1.0	6	19	17	-24
Brazil	7.18	0.7	0.5	0.8	15	-5	33	-9
Above 15	794.29	77.5	90.0	93.2	-	-	-	-

a Includes significant shipments through processing zones.
b Imports are valued f.o.b.

Table IV.46

Exports of office machines and telecom equipment of selected economies, 1990-01

(Million dollars and percentage)

	Value					Share in economy's total merchandise exports	
	1990	1995	1999	2000	2001	1990	2001 a
World	298540	604110	786310	959630	827530	8.8	13.8
Australia	738	1882	1617	1781	1658	1.9	2.6
Brazil	692	749	1345	2376	2397	2.2	4.1
Canada	5622	11544	14040	20631	12843	4.4	4.9
China b	3126	14506	30139	43498	52263	5.0	19.6
Costa Rica b	0	...	2576	1688	...	0.0	28.8
Czech Rep. b	-	481	690	1280	2451	-	7.3
European Union (15)	92894	163917	232558	268413	241759	6.2	10.6
Intra-exports	65803	109031	156323	175117	156587	6.7	11.0
Extra-exports	27091	54886	76235	93296	85172	5.1	9.8
Hong Kong, China	12886	34051	38418	50066	50158	15.6	26.3
domestic exports	4772	5935	3610	3997	3020	16.5	14.9
re-exports	8114	28116	34808	46069	47138	15.2	27.6
Hungary b	505	537	5432	7132	6799	5.1	22.3
Indonesia	124	2281	2976	7280	5937	0.5	10.5
Israel	1226	2369	4880	6939	5816	10.2	20.0
Japan	67007	106611	91372	108179	82604	23.3	20.5
Korea, Rep. of	14339	33217	42918	58686	44184	22.1	29.4
Lithuania	-	115	129	181	224	-	4.9
Malaysia b	8207	32721	44268	52382	44869	27.9	51.0
Malta	472	1064	1059	1556	1057	41.7	55.2
Mexico b	4535	11616	26485	34042	34376	11.1	21.7
Morocco b	114	252	534	506	449	2.7	6.3
Norway	655	955	1162	1142	1186	1.9	2.1
Philippines b	1835	7564	24040	25138	20750	22.6	64.6
Poland	342	406	1141	1271	1590	2.4	4.4
Romania	33	21	148	513	594	0.7	5.2
Singapore	19235	60322	60601	73820	61782	36.5	50.7
domestic exports	14685	40318	38615	41523	31798	42.2	48.1
re-exports	4549	20004	21986	32297	29984	25.4	53.9
Slovak Rep.	-	109	334	365	453	-	3.6
Slovenia	-	139	129	168	522	-	5.6
Switzerland	1520	2257	2730	2967	2604	2.4	3.2
Taipei, Chinese	14105	32568	44769	58074	45833	21.0	37.4
Thailand	3520	11660	15240	18681	16214	15.3	24.9
Turkey	259	255	821	1008	1040	2.0	3.3
United States	51658	97990	125664	153399	126689	13.1	17.3

a Or nearest year.
b Includes significant exports from processing zones.

Table IV.47

Imports of office machines and telecom equipment of selected economies, 1990-01

(Million dollars and percentage)

	Value					Share in economy's total merchandise imports	
	1990	1995	1999	2000	2001	1990	2001 a
Algeria	253	586	450	444	...	2.6	4.8
Argentina	305	1919	2899	3568	2234	7.5	11.0
Australia b	4262	8123	9241	10771	8229	10.6	13.7
Brazil	1514	5230	5922	7900	7181	6.7	12.3
Canada b	10475	19815	24884	30418	23359	9.0	10.6
Chile	456	1076	1553	1681	1477	5.9	8.6
China c	4058	14352	30489	44427	49565	7.6	20.3
Colombia	364	1343	1026	1048	1207	6.5	9.4
Costa Rica c	84	170	686	977	...	4.2	15.3
Croatia	-	400	349	418	600	-	7.5
Czech Rep. b, c	-	1948	2153	2790	3350	-	9.2
Ecuador	57	156	175	200	425	3.1	8.0
Egypt	226	368	712	...	606	1.8	4.7
European Union (15)	127230	198660	278905	324098	285536	8.2	12.2
Intra-imports d	61513					6.3	
Extra-imports	65717	89629	122582	148981	128949	11.4	14.1
Guatemala	61	158	384	419	400	3.7	7.1
Hong Kong, China	12326	40214	43554	59370	57466	14.5	28.4
retained imports	4212	12098	8746	13301	10328	13.4	33.1
Hungary c	670	1015	4434	6034	6380	6.5	18.9
India	662	1199	2077	...	...	2.8	4.4
Indonesia	892	1725	413	705	784	4.1	2.5
Iran, Islamic Rep. of	...	...	478	530	...	...	3.7
Israel	939	2556	3594	4894	4110	5.6	11.7
Japan	11259	37678	44060	60866	52477	4.8	15.0
Jordan	56	106	130	201	357	2.1	7.4
Kazakhstan	-	...	208	261	339	-	5.3
Korea, Rep. of	7741	16467	24729	34012	26328	11.1	18.7
Kuwait	128	341	438	...	...	3.2	5.7
Lebanon	...	...	267	254	353	...	4.8
Lithuania	-	151	244	267	351	-	5.6
Macao, China	64	113	81	104	182	4.1	7.6
Malaysia c	5744	22164	25233	32405	27641	19.6	37.3
Malta	488	964	993	1422	866	24.8	33.4
Mexico c, e	4640	9563	21362	29826	32832	10.7	17.2
Morocco c	306	240	905	1212	...	4.4	10.5
New Zealand	905	1515	1514	1618	1270	9.5	9.5
Norway	1732	2968	3251	3352	3225	6.4	10.0
Pakistan	236	308	299	372	391	3.2	3.7
Panama	65	143	283	244	...	4.2	7.2
Paraguay	320	585	211	224	183	23.7	8.5
Peru	100	687	603	656	685	3.8	9.4
Philippines c	2044	6788	12591	11982	11259	15.7	35.9
Poland	784	1816	4170	4559	4053	6.8	8.1
Romania	211	523	769	1257	1381	2.8	8.9
Russian Fed. f	-	...	2537	2954	4647	-	8.6
Saudi Arabia	811	1203	1398	1242	1327	3.4	4.3
Singapore	13392	43769	42281	54107	44201	22.0	38.1
retained imports	8842	23765	20295	21810	14217	20.6	23.5
Slovak Rep. b	-	565	693	746	929	-	6.3
Slovenia	-	449	591	556	205	-	2.0
South Africa b	...	2693	3255	3364	2967	...	11.7
Switzerland	4797	6521	7604	8206	7152	6.9	8.5
Taipei, Chinese	7438	18766	29173	38721	29118	13.6	27.1
Thailand	3421	10368	9752	14055	13398	10.4	21.6
Tunisia	149	256	289	318	373	2.7	3.9
Turkey	1234	1677	4325	5522	2383	5.5	5.9
United Arab Emirates f	717	2042	2430	3240	...	6.4	8.5
United States	63365	139927	176840	215544	172835	12.3	14.6
Venezuela b	367	682	1133	1189	1201	5.6	7.3
Zimbabwe b	59	131	123	...	...	3.2	5.8

a Or nearest year.

b Imports are valued f.o.b.

c Includes significant imports into processing zones.

d See the Technical Notes for information on intra-EU imports.

e Beginning with 2000 imports are valued c.i.f.

f Includes Secretariat estimates.

4.4 Automotive Products

Table IV.48

World trade in automotive products, 2001

(Billion dollars and percentage)

Value	565
Annual percentage change	
1980-85	5
1985-90	14
1990-01	5
2000	4
2001	-2
Share in world merchandise trade	9.4
Share in world exports of manufactures	12.6

Table IV.49

Major regional flows in world exports of automotive products, 2001

(Billion dollars and percentage)

	Value	Annual percentage change		
	2001	1990-01	2000	2001
Intra-Western Europe	199.2	4	-4	-2
Intra-North America	87.7	6	0	-10
Asia to North America	53.4	4	13	-4
Latin America to North America	31.0	18	23	2
Western Europe to North America	28.5	6	0	3
Intra-Asia	19.6	4	27	-10

Table IV.50

Share of automotive products in trade in total merchandise and in manufactures by region, 2001

(Percentage)

	Exports	Imports
Share of automotive products in total merchandise		
World	9.4	9.4
North America	11.9	15.4
Latin America	11.3	9.8
Western Europe	11.1	10.0
C./E. Europe/Baltic States/CIS	7.1	8.6
Africa	1.4	8.3
Middle East	0.8	10.2
Asia	7.2	3.0
Australia, Japan and New Zealand	17.2	4.7
Other Asia	2.4	2.2
Share of automotive products in manufactures		
World	12.6	12.6
North America	15.5	19.4
Latin America	18.9	12.7
Western Europe	13.7	13.2
C./E. Europe/Baltic States/CIS	12.6	11.5
Africa	5.4	11.7
Middle East	3.5	13.5
Asia	8.6	4.2
Australia, Japan and New Zealand	21.0	7.5
Other Asia	2.9	3.1

Chart IV.10

Regional shares in world trade in automotive products, 2001

(Percentage)

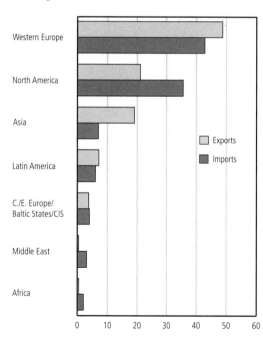

Table IV.51

Exports of automotive products by principal region, 2001

(Billion dollars and percentage)

	Value	Share in				Annual percentage change		
		Region's exports		World exports				
	2001	1990	2001	1990	2001	1990-01	2000	2001
World	564.6	-	-	100.0	100.0	5	4	-2
Western Europe								
World	275.6	100.0	100.0	54.4	48.8	4	-1	0
Western Europe	199.2	78.2	72.3	42.6	35.3	4	-4	-2
North America	28.5	8.9	10.3	4.9	5.0	6	0	3
C./E. Europe/Baltic States/CIS	16.6	1.3	6.0	0.7	2.9	20	14	16
Asia	13.1	5.7	4.7	3.1	2.3	3	14	5
Africa	6.5	3.1	2.4	1.7	1.2	2	4	22
Latin America	6.1	1.1	2.2	0.6	1.1	11	4	6
Middle East	5.3	1.5	1.9	0.8	0.9	7	28	18
North America								
World	118.4	100.0	100.0	19.1	21.0	6	4	-7
North America	87.7	77.6	74.1	14.8	15.5	6	0	-10
Latin America	15.5	7.7	13.1	1.5	2.8	11	36	-3
Western Europe	7.8	6.3	6.6	1.2	1.4	7	-7	14
Asia	4.7	5.9	3.9	1.1	0.8	2	23	-17
All other regions	2.7	2.5	2.3	0.5	0.5	5	15	27
Asia								
World	107.2	100.0	100.0	22.4	19.0	4	9	-6
North America	53.4	51.1	49.8	11.5	9.5	4	13	-4
Asia	19.6	17.8	18.2	4.0	3.5	4	27	-10
Western Europe	16.9	21.4	15.7	4.8	3.0	1	-10	-15
Middle East	8.1	4.1	7.5	0.9	1.4	10	11	15
Latin America	5.2	2.4	4.8	0.5	0.9	10	23	-6
Africa	2.5	2.5	2.3	0.6	0.4	3	-5	-13
C./E. Europe/Baltic States/CIS	1.1	0.3	1.1	0.1	0.2	16	-27	-14
Japan								
World	80.2	100.0	100.0	20.8	14.2	2	6	-9
North America	43.9	51.5	54.8	10.7	7.8	2	9	-7
Asia	13.3	16.9	16.5	3.5	2.3	2	23	-12
Western Europe	11.8	22.1	14.7	4.6	2.1	-2	-13	-20
Middle East	5.4	4.2	6.7	0.9	1.0	6	3	16
Latin America	3.6	2.5	4.5	0.5	0.6	8	14	-7
Africa	1.6	2.5	1.9	0.5	0.3	-1	-4	-17
C./E. Europe/Baltic States/CIS	0.6	0.3	0.8	0.1	0.1	12	19	-13
Latin America								
World	39.3	100.0	100.0	2.3	7.0	17	19	3
North America	31.0	70.5	78.9	1.6	5.5	18	23	2
Latin America	6.0	12.7	15.4	0.3	1.1	19	29	3
Western Europe	1.6	14.3	4.1	0.3	0.3	4	-35	-8
All other regions	0.6	2.5	1.6	0.1	0.1	12	11	89

Table IV.52

Imports of automotive products of selected economies by region and supplier, 2001

(Million dollars and percentage)

	Value	Share	Annual percentage change			Value	Share	Annual percentage change	
	2001	2001	2000	2001		2001	2001	2000	2001
		Canada a					United States		
Region					Region				
World	41946	100.0	2	-9	World	165157	100.0	9	-3
North America	33342	79.5	-1	-11	North America	52858	32.0	-1	-10
Asia	4185	10.0	12	0	Asia	52081	31.5	15	-1
Latin America	2642	6.3	41	-2	Western Europe	29642	17.9	6	2
Western Europe	1607	3.8	5	-5	Latin America	29633	17.9	27	1
All other regions	19	0.0	14	-3	All other regions	943	0.6	64	60
Suppliers					Suppliers				
United States	33342	79.5	-1	-11	Canada	52858	32.0	-1	-10
Japan	3294	7.9	7	-6	Japan	42358	25.6	11	-5
Mexico	2461	5.9	40	-5	European Union (15)	29451	17.8	6	2
European Union (15)	1591	3.8	6	-5	Mexico	28342	17.2	28	0
Korea, Rep. of	711	1.7	52	38	Korea, Rep. of	7102	4.3	61	28
Above 5	41397	98.7	-	-	Above 5	160110	96.9	-	-
		European Union (15)					Mexico		
Region					Region				
World	229209	100.0	-5	-1	World	20962	100.0	56	-6
Western Europe	188420	82.2	-5	-1	North America	15633	74.6	48	-11
Asia	16975	7.4	-11	-13	Western Europe	2784	13.3	55	23
C./E. Europe/					Asia	1295	6.2	189	-3
Baltic States/CIS	14801	6.5	16	12	Latin America	1227	5.9	130	22
North America	6114	2.7	-7	10	All other regions	13	0.1	171	68
Latin America	1642	0.7	-9	-4					
All other regions	1215	0.5	-8	16					
Suppliers					Suppliers				
European Union (15)	184390	80.4	-6	-1	United States	14542	69.4	47	-13
Japan	12349	5.4	-12	-16	European Union (15)	2758	13.2	54	23
United States	5849	2.6	-6	11	Canada	1091	5.2	58	8
Hungary	4970	2.2	0	13	Brazil	1039	5.0	129	25
Czech Rep.	4189	1.8	20	8	Japan	1021	4.9	197	-12
Above 5	211747	92.4	-	-	Above 5	20451	97.6	-	-

a Imports are valued f.o.b.

Table IV.53

Leading exporters and importers of automotive products, 2001

(Billion dollars and percentage)

	Value	Share in world exports/imports			Annual percentage change			
	2001	1980	1990	2001	1990-01	1999	2000	2001
Exporters								
European Union (15)	270.90	52.8	53.8	48.0	4	1	-1	0
Extra-exports	86.51	19.5	14.3	15.3	6	-3	9	4
Japan	80.17	19.8	20.8	14.2	2	7	6	-9
United States	63.42	11.9	10.2	11.2	6	3	7	-6
Canada	54.97	6.9	8.9	9.7	6	24	0	-9
Mexico a	30.68	0.3	1.5	5.4	19	20	18	0
Korea, Rep. of	15.43	0.1	0.7	2.7	19	15	17	2
Czech Rep. a	5.45	-	-	1.0	-	22	13	17
Hungary a	5.32	0.6	0.2	0.9	21	23	1	12
Brazil	4.82	1.1	0.6	0.9	8	-26	21	3
Poland	4.23	0.6	0.1	0.7	25	20	80	6
Thailand	2.66	0.0	0.0	0.5	34	69	37	11
Turkey	2.29	0.0	0.0	0.4	28	80	5	51
Australia	2.27	0.2	0.2	0.4	11	33	19	5
Slovak Rep.	2.27	-	-	0.4	-	-3	27	-5
Argentina	2.06	0.1	0.1	0.4	24	-43	17	-2
Above 15	546.93	94.5	97.2	96.9	-	-	-	-
Importers								
European Union (15)	229.21	37.5	46.9	39.5	4	4	-5	-1
Extra-imports	44.82	5.3	7.3	7.7	6	13	-3	0
United States	165.16	20.3	24.7	28.5	7	20	9	-3
Canada b	41.95	8.7	7.7	7.2	5	13	2	-9
Mexico a	20.96	1.8	1.6	3.6	13	22	...	-6
Japan	9.22	0.5	2.3	1.6	2	10	16	-7
Australia b	7.19	1.3	1.2	1.2	6	8	10	-16
Switzerland	6.54	1.8	1.9	1.1	1	6	-3	3
China a	4.91	0.6	...	0.8	...	23	50	29
Saudi Arabia	4.84	2.7	0.9	0.8	5	-4	48	27
Poland	4.69	0.9	0.1	0.8	25	2	-10	7
Brazil	4.27	0.3	0.2	0.7	21	-36	5	-1
Russian Fed.	3.34	-	-	0.6	-	-50	26	43
Czech Rep. a, b	3.05	-	-	0.5	-	15	9	21
United Arab Emirates c	2.80	0.4	0.3	0.5	11	-14	12	...
Norway	2.59	0.6	0.4	0.4	6	-14	-4	0
Above 15	510.71	77.1	88.5	88.1	-	-	-	-

a Includes significant shipments through processing zones.
b Imports are valued f.o.b.
c 2000 instead of 2001.

Table IV.54

Exports of automotive products of selected economies, 1990-01

(Million dollars and percentage)

	Value					Share in economy's total merchandise exports	
	1990	1995	1999	2000	2001	1990	2001 a
World	318960	456420	556460	576750	564560	9.4	9.4
Argentina	200	1374	1806	2105	2061	1.6	7.7
Australia	719	1053	1809	2151	2268	1.8	3.6
Belarus	-	...	662	740	...	-	10.1
Brazil	2034	2955	3868	4682	4819	6.5	8.3
Canada	28442	43064	60531	60656	54971	22.3	21.2
China b	...	621	1040	1581	1892	...	0.7
Colombia	6	83	75	226	433	0.1	3.5
Czech Rep. b	-	1509	4120	4665	5448	-	16.3
European Union (15)	171579	235523	274123	270116	270896	11.4	11.8
Intra-exports	125828	166324	197869	186735	184390	12.8	13.0
Extra-exports	45751	69199	76254	83381	86506	8.6	9.9
Hong Kong, China	354	1147	745	764	920	0.4	0.5
domestic exports	27	10	25	23	14	0.1	0.1
re-exports	328	1137	720	741	906	0.6	0.5
Hungary b	648	659	4715	4765	5323	6.5	17.5
India	198	568	463	...	...	1.1	1.3
Japan	66230	80680	82733	88082	80169	23.0	19.9
Korea, Rep. of	2301	9166	13035	15194	15428	3.5	10.3
Mexico b	4708	14258	26039	30655	30677	11.6	19.3
Norway	305	469	469	459	493	0.9	0.9
Oman	119	459	512	605	...	2.2	5.6
Philippines b	23	218	456	583	634	0.3	2.0
Poland	374	996	2211	3973	4228	2.6	11.7
Romania	354	153	161	195	229	7.1	2.0
Russian Fed. c	-	...	723	1050	1039	-	1.0
Singapore	348	886	633	678	649	0.7	0.5
domestic exports	82	106	92	90	91	0.2	0.1
re-exports	266	780	541	588	558	1.5	1.0
Slovak Rep.	-	344	1880	2394	2267	-	17.9
Slovenia	-	970	1120	1075	1202	-	13.0
South Africa	...	730	1546	1708	1485	...	5.1
Switzerland	591	716	856	788	896	0.9	1.1
Taipei, Chinese	829	1674	1894	2226	1780	1.2	1.5
Thailand	108	486	1758	2401	2658	0.5	4.1
Turkey	153	642	1438	1517	2291	1.2	7.3
United States	32547	52505	62923	67195	63421	8.3	8.7

a Or nearest year.
b Includes significant exports from processing zones.
c Includes Secretariat estimates.

Table IV.55

Imports of automotive products of selected economies, 1990-01

(Million dollars and percentage)

	Value					Share in economy's total merchandise imports	
	1990	1995	1999	2000	2001	1990	2001 a
Algeria	658	477	686	615	...	6.7	6.7
Argentina	183	2309	3072	2834	1968	4.5	9.7
Australia b	3794	6173	7783	8550	7192	9.5	12.0
Brazil	532	5968	4097	4314	4265	2.4	7.3
Canada b	24640	33471	45252	46276	41946	21.1	19.0
Chile	579	1780	973	1507	1337	7.5	7.8
China c	...	2609	2538	3798	4912	...	2.0
Colombia	416	1111	435	590	725	7.4	5.6
Croatia	-	422	791	831	907	-	11.3
Cyprus	281	355	361	406	432	10.9	11.0
Czech Rep. b, c	-	1461	2310	2525	3053	-	8.4
Ecuador	157	693	186	184	612	8.5	11.6
Egypt	416	634	590	...	356	3.3	2.8
European Union (15)	150825	194033	243794	231404	229209	9.7	9.8
Intra-imports d	127496					13.0	
Extra-imports	23329	27707	45925	44669	44819	4.0	4.9
Guatemala	117	453	478	481	551	7.1	9.8
Hong Kong, China	994	4394	1755	2195	2324	1.2	1.2
retained imports	666	3257	1035	1455	1418	2.1	4.5
Hungary c	715	931	2520	2481	2543	6.9	7.6
India	260	458	445	...	...	1.1	0.9
Indonesia	1523	3139	716	1870	1607	7.0	5.2
Iran, Islamic Rep. of	...	...	657	770	...	...	5.4
Israel	871	2304	1856	2298	2155	5.2	6.1
Japan	7315	11930	8597	9957	9220	3.1	2.6
Jordan	108	297	405	519	436	4.2	9.0
Kazakhstan	-	...	349	434	480	-	7.5
Korea, Rep. of	929	2218	1393	1773	1771	1.3	1.3
Kuwait	453	1003	1216	1305	...	11.4	18.2
Lebanon	...	...	602	535	610	...	8.4
Lithuania	-	226	276	339	579	-	9.2
Malaysia c	1312	2785	1351	1833	1811	4.5	2.4
Mexico c, e	5268	4400	14299	22247	20962	12.1	11.0
Morocco c	317	314	540	471	502	4.6	4.6
New Zealand	1012	1642	1685	1480	1529	10.6	11.5
Norway	1419	2433	2712	2597	2589	5.2	8.0
Oman	429	768	800	1109	...	16.0	22.0
Peru	176	866	546	510	455	6.7	6.2
Philippines c	537	1569	826	974	937	4.1	3.0
Poland	391	1693	4852	4365	4691	3.4	9.3
Qatar	202	...	290	...	429	11.9	14.3
Romania	409	312	240	429	604	5.4	3.9
Russian Fed. f	-	...	1852	2334	3337	-	6.2
Saudi Arabia	2839	2138	2579	3815	4844	11.8	15.5
Singapore	1418	2519	1554	2417	2145	2.3	1.8
retained imports	1152	1739	1013	1829	1587	2.7	2.6
Slovak Rep. b	-	447	1260	1412	1759	-	11.9
Slovenia	-	1326	1478	1214	1083	-	10.7
South Africa b	...	3061	1165	1455	1320	...	5.2
Switzerland	6048	6467	6542	6347	6541	8.7	7.8
Taipei, Chinese	2565	4495	2253	2675	1889	4.7	1.8
Thailand	2651	5184	1448	2084	2172	8.0	3.5
Tunisia	306	462	655	595	654	5.6	6.9
Turkey	1177	1730	3303	5831	1948	5.3	4.8
Ukraine f	-	...	338	462	...	-	3.3
United Arab Emirates f	991	1983	2498	2796	...	8.8	7.3
United States	79320	108016	155723	170195	165157	15.3	14.0
Venezuela b	426	1076	1106	1451	2279	6.5	13.9
Zimbabwe b	129	321	181	...	...	7.0	8.5

a Or nearest year.
b Imports are valued f.o.b.
c Includes significant imports into processing zones.
d See the Technical Notes for information on intra-EU imports.
e Beginning with 2000 imports are valued c.i.f.
f Includes Secretariat estimates.

4.5 Textiles

Table IV.56

World trade in textiles, 2001

(Billion dollars and percentage)

Value	147
Annual percentage change	
1980-85	-1
1985-90	15
1990-01	3
2000	6
2001	-5
Share in world merchandise trade	2.5
Share in world exports of manufactures	3.3

Table IV.57

Major regional flows in world exports of textiles, 2001

(Billion dollars and percentage)

	Value	Annual percentage change		
	2001	1990-01	2000	2001
Intra-Asia	37.0	5	13	-10
Intra-Western Europe	35.9	-2	-7	-7
Western Europe to C./E. Europe/Baltic States/CIS	8.1	12	3	8
Asia to Western Europe	8.0	3	10	-6
Asia to North America	7.5	6	12	-6
North America to Latin America	5.4	15	31	2

Table IV.58

Share of textiles in trade in total merchandise and in manufactures by region, 2001

(Percentage)

	Exports	Imports
Share of textiles in total merchandise		
World	2.5	2.5
North America	1.3	1.4
Latin America	1.2	3.3
Western Europe	2.3	2.1
C./E. Europe/Baltic States/CIS	1.8	4.3
Africa	1.0	5.7
Middle East	0.8	3.9
Asia	4.3	3.2
Australia, Japan and New Zealand	1.4	1.6
Other Asia	5.7	3.9
Share of textiles in manufactures		
World	3.3	3.3
North America	1.7	1.8
Latin America	1.9	4.3
Western Europe	2.8	2.7
C./E. Europe/Baltic States/CIS	3.3	5.8
Africa	4.1	8.0
Middle East	3.7	5.2
Asia	5.2	4.6
Australia, Japan and New Zealand	1.7	2.6
Other Asia	6.8	5.3

Chart IV.11

Regional shares in world trade in textiles, 2001

(Percentage)

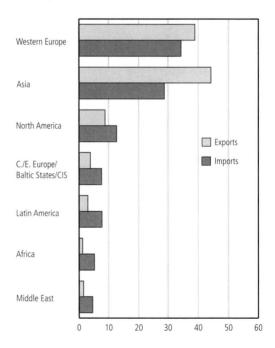

Table IV.59

Exports of textiles by principal region, 2001

(Billion dollars and percentage)

	Value	Share in				Annual percentage change		
		Region's exports		World exports				
	2001	1990	2001	1990	2001	1990-01	2000	2001
World	147.0	-	-	100.0	100.0	3	6	-5
Asia								
World	64.7	100.0	100.0	35.3	44.0	5	13	-7
Asia	37.0	57.9	57.1	20.4	25.1	5	13	-10
Western Europe	8.0	16.2	12.4	5.7	5.5	3	10	-6
North America	7.5	10.4	11.5	3.7	5.1	6	12	-6
Middle East	4.4	6.5	6.8	2.3	3.0	6	10	-1
Latin America	3.4	2.4	5.3	0.8	2.3	13	20	-8
Africa	3.2	2.9	4.9	1.0	2.2	11	16	13
C./E. Europe/Baltic States/CIS	1.2	2.5	1.8	0.9	0.8	2	24	13
Japan								
World	6.2	100.0	100.0	5.6	4.2	0	6	-12
Asia	4.7	60.3	76.7	3.4	3.2	3	10	-11
Western Europe	0.6	14.2	9.0	0.8	0.4	-4	-9	-16
North America	0.5	11.2	8.2	0.6	0.3	-2	4	-18
Middle East	0.3	9.5	4.3	0.5	0.2	-6	-7	-1
All other regions	0.1	4.7	1.7	0.3	0.1	-8	4	-4
Other economies in Asia								
World	58.5	100.0	100.0	29.7	39.8	6	13	-7
Asia	32.2	57.5	55.0	17.0	21.9	6	13	-10
Western Europe	7.5	16.6	12.8	4.9	5.1	3	12	-5
North America	7.0	10.2	11.9	3.0	4.7	7	13	-5
Middle East	4.1	5.9	7.1	1.8	2.8	8	12	-1
Latin America	3.4	2.6	5.8	0.8	2.3	14	21	-8
Africa	3.2	3.1	5.4	0.9	2.1	11	17	13
C./E. Europe/Baltic States/CIS	1.2	2.5	2.0	0.8	0.8	4	23	14
Western Europe								
World	56.9	100.0	100.0	53.1	38.7	0	-4	-3
Western Europe	35.9	78.1	63.0	41.5	24.4	-2	-7	-7
C./E. Europe/Baltic States/CIS	8.1	4.2	14.2	2.3	5.5	12	3	8
Africa	3.6	4.5	6.3	2.4	2.4	3	-7	6
Asia	3.6	5.7	6.3	3.0	2.4	1	8	0
North America	3.4	4.5	6.0	2.4	2.3	3	7	-5
Middle East	1.3	2.2	2.2	1.1	0.9	1	-5	3
Latin America	0.8	0.7	1.4	0.4	0.5	7	9	-3
North America								
World	12.7	100.0	100.0	5.5	8.6	7	14	-4
Latin America	5.4	20.2	42.4	1.1	3.7	15	31	2
North America	4.6	28.8	36.3	1.6	3.1	10	5	-5
Western Europe	1.2	25.0	9.8	1.4	0.8	-1	6	-15
Asia	1.1	19.1	9.1	1.0	0.8	0	11	-13
Middle East	0.2	4.4	1.2	0.2	0.1	-4	-27	5
All other regions	0.1	2.3	2.3	0.1	0.1	0	-5	3

Table IV.60

Textile imports of selected economies by region and supplier, 2001

(Million dollars and percentage)

Region	Canada a Value 2001	Share 2001	Annual percentage change 2000	Annual percentage change 2001	Region	United States Value 2001	Share 2001	Annual percentage change 2000	Annual percentage change 2001
World	3811	100.0	3	-8	World	15429	100.0	12	-4
North America	2426	63.7	2	-9	Asia	7675	49.7	11	-3
Asia	797	20.9	8	-8	Western Europe	3123	20.2	8	-7
Western Europe	384	10.1	1	-4	North America	1929	12.5	9	0
Latin America	143	3.8	11	3	Latin America	1909	12.4	17	-4
Middle East	24	0.6	4	-11	Middle East	453	2.9	76	8
C./E. Europe/					Africa	174	1.1	19	6
Baltic States/CIS	15	0.4	6	-12	C./E. Europe/				
Africa	14	0.4	9	17	Baltic States/CIS	166	1.1	1	-12
Suppliers					Suppliers				
United States	2426	63.7	2	-9	European Union (15)	2578	16.7	7	-7
European Union (15)	337	8.8	-1	-4	Canada	1983	12.9	15	2
China	250	6.6	25	2	China	1929	12.5	9	0
Korea, Rep. of	114	3.0	10	-13	Mexico	1516	9.8	17	-4
India	112	2.9	9	-4	India	1132	7.3	14	-6
Above 5	3239	85.0	3	-8	Above 5	9137	59.2	11	-3
Mexico	87	2.3	9	0	Pakistan	1057	6.9	24	8
Pakistan	84	2.2	9	-16	Korea, Rep. of	935	6.1	9	-5
Taipei, Chinese	79	2.1	3	-24	Taipei, Chinese	761	4.9	-2	-5
Japan	40	1.1	-4	-6	Japan	515	3.3	6	-18
Indonesia	38	1.0	-12	-18	Turkey	445	2.9	18	-2
Turkey	32	0.8	25	-2	Thailand	350	2.3	17	-4
Brazil	26	0.7	22	-3	Israel	275	1.8	12	18
Thailand	21	0.6	12	-4	Hong Kong, China	216	1.4	6	-10
Hong Kong, China	21	0.5	-21	-16	Brazil	193	1.3	31	-9
Israel	14	0.4	32	38	Indonesia	193	1.3	17	-6
Bangladesh	12	0.3	11	74	Egypt	129	0.8	22	10
Switzerland	10	0.3	8	-3	Bangladesh	121	0.8	10	16
Iran, Islamic Rep. of	9	0.2	-15	-36	Iran, Islamic Rep. of	117	0.8	-	-1
Malaysia	7	0.2	15	38	Sri Lanka	106	0.7	11	-14
Egypt	7	0.2	21	22	Philippines	100	0.6	-8	-25
Czech Rep.	7	0.2	23	2	Switzerland	82	0.5	2	-14
Dominican Republic	7	0.2	79	-11	Malaysia	66	0.4	12	-27
Colombia	7	0.2	81	80	Dominican Republic	61	0.4	5	74
Australia	6	0.2	-36	-32	Australia	49	0.3	-12	18
South Africa	6	0.1	-9	23	Nepal	39	0.3	22	-6
Viet Nam	5	0.1	-47	-1	Colombia	37	0.2	-8	-6
Chile	4	0.1	115	1	South Africa	35	0.2	12	5
Haiti	4	0.1	-55	99	El Salvador	33	0.2	0	1
Uruguay	3	0.1	-13	-14	Czech Rep.	32	0.2	1	-20
Norway	3	0.1	51	-17	Uzbekistan	26	0.2	67	29
Romania	2	0.1	-2	-26	United Arab Emirates	20	0.1	60	-6
Peru	2	0.1	-49	11	Romania	19	0.1	15	35
Philippines	2	0.1	32	-18	Bahrain	19	0.1	696	1
Sri Lanka	2	0.1	23	-35	Poland	18	0.1	37	0
New Zealand	2	0.0	-17	3	Cambodia	18	0.1	261	206
Nepal	2	0.0	54	0	New Zealand	18	0.1	13	-19
Poland	2	0.0	10	-32	Russian Fed.	17	0.1	-24	-42
Russian Fed.	1	0.0	49	-5	Saudi Arabia	16	0.1	96	-23
United Arab Emirates	1	0.0	-	-	Guatemala	14	0.1	5	4
Saudi Arabia	1	0.0	-	-	Peru	14	0.1	26	-42
Above 40	3793	99.5	-	-	Above 40	15284	99.1	-	-

Table IV.60 *(continued)*

Textile imports of selected economies by region and supplier, 2001

(Million dollars and percentage)

	European Union (15)					Japan			
	Value	Share	Annual percentage change			Value	Share	Annual percentage change	
	2001	2001	2000	2001		2001	2001	2000	2001
Region					**Region**				
World	45620	100.0	-5	-6	World	4747	100.0	9	-4
Western Europe	32020	70.2	-7	-8	Asia	3635	76.6	10	-3
Asia	7807	17.1	3	-5	Western Europe	723	15.2	1	-2
C./E. Europe/					North America	305	6.4	9	-14
Baltic States/CIS	2884	6.3	12	9	Latin America	30	0.6	0	-11
North America	1281	2.8	-3	-15	Middle East	28	0.6	3	-30
Africa	716	1.6	10	-3	C./E. Europe/				
Middle East	626	1.4	-3	-13	Baltic States/CIS	16	0.3	18	-17
Latin America	240	0.5	-5	11	Africa	10	0.2	17	0
Suppliers					**Suppliers**				
European Union (15)	28545	62.6	-8	-9	China	2131	44.9	18	5
Turkey	2005	4.4	0	6	European Union (15)	667	14.1	0	-3
China	1833	4.0	21	0	Korea, Rep. of	312	6.6	3	-22
India	1763	3.9	2	-2	Indonesia	304	6.4	3	-6
United States	1209	2.7	-2	-14	United States	296	6.2	9	-14
Above 5	35355	77.5	-6	-7	Above 5	3711	78.2	10	-2
Switzerland	1039	2.3	-9	-6	Taipei, Chinese	237	5.0	8	-15
Pakistan	995	2.2	-3	2	India	182	3.8	10	5
Czech Rep.	883	1.9	12	12	Pakistan	109	2.3	-28	-29
Korea, Rep. of	803	1.8	10	-7	Thailand	109	2.3	7	-9
Japan	587	1.3	-8	-14	Viet Nam	92	1.9	20	-2
Poland	587	1.3	12	8	Malaysia	85	1.8	14	-8
Indonesia	518	1.1	-4	-8	Philippines	30	0.6	9	10
Taipei, Chinese	464	1.0	-10	-18	Switzerland	27	0.6	10	5
Thailand	285	0.6	-10	-15	Iran, Islamic Rep. of	26	0.5	10	-29
Hungary	273	0.6	6	5	Turkey	25	0.5	30	22
Iran, Islamic Rep. of	252	0.6	-13	-19	Brazil	16	0.3	-2	-13
Egypt	242	0.5	17	-18	Hong Kong, China	16	0.3	8	30
Slovak Rep.	214	0.5	9	8	Bangladesh	10	0.2	13	-25
Slovenia	213	0.5	0	9	Canada	8	0.2	14	11
Tunisia	190	0.4	18	26	Uzbekistan	8	0.2	19	-32
Israel	187	0.4	-8	-10	Peru	7	0.2	36	22
Romania	187	0.4	18	27	Egypt	6	0.1	-9	-18
Estonia	134	0.3	27	7	Mexico	6	0.1	19	-4
Lithuania	130	0.3	1	-1	Australia	6	0.1	-9	-33
Bangladesh	126	0.3	14	6	Macao, China	4	0.1	103	18
Brazil	121	0.3	5	11	Malta	4	0.1	-	1129
Russian Fed.	121	0.3	44	3	South Africa	2	0.0	-22	44
Malaysia	110	0.2	-17	1	Singapore	2	0.0	-4	-35
Morocco	110	0.2	19	14	Sri Lanka	2	0.0	6	-22
Norway	91	0.2	-9	-1	Tanzania, United Rep. of	1	0.0	49	-17
Bulgaria	86	0.2	-6	34	Romania	1	0.0	-8	-15
Nepal	78	0.2	-12	-23	Saudi Arabia	1	0.0	20	-31
Syrian Arab Republic	77	0.2	102	-3	Russian Fed.	1	0.0	27	9
Hong Kong, China	76	0.2	4	13	Lithuania	1	0.0	250	72
Latvia	74	0.2	2	-15	Israel	1	0.0	-50	-55
Canada	72	0.2	-8	-24	Czech Rep.	1	0.0	-15	126
South Africa	66	0.1	-5	-12	New Zealand	1	0.0	2	-40
Uzbekistan	63	0.1	26	14	Nepal	1	0.0	24	-14
Viet Nam	61	0.1	4	17	Myanmar	1	0.0	5	-11
Croatia	58	0.1	4	1	Belarus	1	0.0	-71	268
Above 40	44928	98.5	-	-	Above 40	4741	99.9	-	-

a Imports are valued f.o.b.

Table IV.61

Leading exporters and importers of textiles, 2001

(Billion dollars and percentage)

	Value	Share in world exports/imports			Annual percentage change			
	2001	1980	1990	2001	1990-01	1999	2000	2001
Exporters								
European Union (15)	50.54	49.4	48.7	34.4	0	-8	-4	-4
Extra-exports	22.00	15.0	14.5	15.0	3	-6	1	1
China a	16.83	4.6	6.9	11.4	8	2	24	4
Hong Kong, China	12.21	-	-	-	4	-6	10	-9
domestic exports	1.05	1.7	2.1	0.7	-6	-12	-4	-11
re-exports	11.16	-	-	-	6	-5	11	-9
Korea, Rep. of	10.94	4.0	5.8	7.4	5	3	9	-14
United States	10.49	6.8	4.8	7.1	7	3	15	-4
Taipei, Chinese	9.92	3.2	5.9	6.7	4	-2	9	-17
Japan	6.19	9.3	5.6	4.2	0	11	6	-12
India b	5.90	2.1	2.1	3.8	10	12	16	...
Pakistan	4.53	1.6	2.6	3.1	5	-1	6	0
Turkey	3.91	0.6	1.4	2.7	9	-2	6	6
Indonesia	3.20	0.1	1.2	2.2	9	28	16	-9
Canada	2.16	0.6	0.7	1.5	11	6	9	-2
Mexico a	2.09	0.2	0.7	1.4	10	13	12	-19
Thailand	1.89	0.6	0.9	1.3	7	3	8	-4
Switzerland	1.44	2.8	2.5	1.0	-5	-9	-7	-6
Above 15	131.07	87.5	91.7	89.0	-	-	-	-
Importers								
European Union (15)	45.62	46.5	46.7	29.2	-1	-9	-5	-6
Extra-imports	17.08	14.0	13.2	10.9	2	-7	2	-2
United States	15.43	4.5	6.2	9.9	8	6	12	-4
China a	12.57	1.9	4.9	8.0	8	0	16	-2
Hong Kong, China	12.18	-	-	-	2	-7	9	-11
retained imports	1.01	3.7	3.8	0.6	-12	-17	-4	-30
Mexico a	6.02	0.2	0.9	3.9	18	43	...	-3
Japan	4.75	2.9	3.8	3.0	1	4	9	-4
Canada c	3.81	2.3	2.2	2.4	5	-1	3	-8
Korea, Rep. of	3.07	0.7	1.8	2.0	4	35	12	-9
Poland	2.62	0.5	0.2	1.7	24	-7	-3	6
Romania	2.01	...	0.1	1.3	36	9	7	17
Turkey	1.91	0.1	0.5	1.2	12	-18	11	-10
United Arab Emirates b, d	1.81	0.8	0.9	1.1	6	-14	7	...
Thailand	1.54	0.3	0.8	1.0	5	16	21	-6
Bangladesh	1.53	0.2	0.4	1.0	12	-12	3	11
Morocco a	1.46	0.2	0.3	0.9	14	-3	-3	7
Above 15	105.15	64.9	73.7	67.2	-	-	-	-

a Includes significant shipments through processing zones.
b 2000 instead of 2001.
c Imports are valued f.o.b.
d Includes Secretariat estimates.

Table IV.62

Exports of textiles of selected economies, 1990-01

(Million dollars and percentage)

	Value					Share in economy's total merchandise exports	
	1990	1995	1999	2000	2001	1990	2001 a
World	104330	151580	146230	154740	146980	3.1	2.5
Argentina	158	292	237	257	222	1.3	0.8
Australia	152	383	389	347	290	0.4	0.5
Bangladesh	343	432	413	...	...	20.5	7.6
Belarus	-	...	345	410	...	-	5.6
Brazil	769	999	822	900	855	2.4	1.5
Bulgaria	...	173	120	121	137	...	2.7
Canada	687	1377	2032	2205	2163	0.5	0.8
Chile	33	85	98	116	116	0.4	0.7
China b	7219	13918	13043	16135	16826	11.6	6.3
Colombia	133	278	237	268	264	2.0	2.2
Croatia	-	124	82	87	85	-	1.8
Czech Rep. b	-	1323	1098	1218	1327	-	4.0
Egypt	554	570	355	...	290	15.9	7.0
European Union (15)	50795	62198	55365	52923	50542	3.4	2.2
Intra-exports	35672	40218	33912	31246	28545	3.6	2.0
Extra-exports	15123	21980	21453	21677	21997	2.9	2.5
Hong Kong, China	8213	13815	12271	13442	12214	10.0	6.4
domestic exports	2171	1814	1223	1176	1051	7.5	5.2
re-exports	6042	12001	11048	12266	11164	11.3	6.5
Hungary b	249	286	366	371	408	2.5	1.3
India	2180	4358	5086	5899	...	12.1	13.9
Indonesia	1241	2713	3019	3505	3202	4.8	5.7
Iran, Islamic Rep. of c	510	610	781	766	656	2.6	2.6
Israel	270	399	477	490	534	2.2	1.8
Japan	5859	7178	6598	7023	6186	2.0	1.5
Korea, Rep. of	6076	12313	11618	12710	10941	9.3	7.3
Latvia	-	119	107	105	118	-	5.9
Lithuania	-	163	221	212	208	-	4.5
Macao, China	136	169	228	272	278	8.0	12.1
Malaysia b	343	1129	1120	1270	1056	1.2	1.2
Mexico b	713	1283	2303	2571	2091	1.8	1.3
Morocco b	203	177	133	123	142	4.8	2.0
Nepal	82	166	175	182	...	40.4	22.7
Pakistan	2663	4256	4258	4532	4525	47.4	49.0
Peru	221	172	115	128	115	6.8	1.6
Philippines b	132	280	262	297	255	1.6	0.8
Poland	284	512	727	769	796	2.0	2.2
Romania	125	178	165	196	232	2.5	2.0
Russian Fed. c	-	374	390	495	454	-	0.4
Singapore	903	1496	853	907	731	1.7	0.6
domestic exports	141	263	249	293	251	0.4	0.4
re-exports	762	1233	604	614	480	4.3	0.9
Slovak Rep.	-	375	374	319	341	-	2.7
Slovenia	-	322	286	286	365	-	3.9
South Africa	167	238	235	240	233	0.7	0.8
Sri Lanka	25	164	206	...	...	1.3	4.5
Switzerland	2557	2267	1641	1533	1443	4.0	1.8
Taipei, Chinese	6128	11882	10906	11896	9917	9.1	8.1
Thailand	928	1937	1818	1960	1888	4.0	2.9
Tunisia	112	165	129	154	201	3.2	3.0
Turkey	1440	2527	3478	3672	3907	11.1	12.5
United States	5039	7372	9510	10961	10491	1.3	1.4
Uruguay	85	90	59	65	54	5.0	2.6

a Or nearest year.
b Includes significant exports from processing zones.
c Includes Secretariat estimates.

Table IV.63

Imports of textiles of selected economies, 1990-01

(Million dollars and percentage)

	Value					Share in economy's total merchandise imports	
	1990	1995	1999	2000	2001	1990	2001 a
Argentina	53	428	632	656	526	1.3	2.6
Australia b	1442	1790	1667	1635	1292	3.6	2.1
Bangladesh	452	1481	1342	1383	1531	12.5	18.2
Brazil	252	1362	898	1112	982	1.1	1.7
Bulgaria	...	299	417	505	...	...	7.8
Canada b	2325	3204	3996	4132	3811	2.0	1.7
Chile	203	479	381	431	383	2.6	2.2
China c	5292	10914	11079	12832	12573	9.9	5.2
Colombia	75	383	413	558	553	1.3	4.3
Croatia	-	210	160	249	355	-	4.4
Czech Rep. b, c	-	928	1122	1198	1269	-	3.5
Egypt	211	280	334	...	198	1.7	1.6
El Salvador c	111	224	286	364	367	8.8	7.3
European Union (15)	50370	57227	51037	48706	45620	3.2	2.0
Intra-imports d	36133					3.7	
Extra-imports	14237	17009	17125	17460	17075	2.5	1.9
Hong Kong, China	10182	16859	12562	13717	12177	12.0	6.0
retained imports	4140	4858	1514	1451	1014	13.2	3.2
Hungary c	270	888	1146	1078	1073	2.6	3.2
Indonesia	785	1308	866	1251	1088	3.6	3.5
Israel	474	820	758	759	675	2.8	1.9
Japan	4106	5985	4547	4939	4747	1.7	1.4
Jordan	107	128	113	172	304	4.1	6.3
Korea, Rep. of	1946	3959	3001	3359	3067	2.8	2.2
Kuwait	168	262	206	...	...	4.2	2.7
Latvia	-	62	111	132	147	-	4.2
Lithuania	-	189	361	363	380	-	6.1
Macao, China	619	698	803	902	841	40.2	35.2
Malaysia c	951	1535	1015	1115	936	3.3	1.3
Mauritius	350	442	417	411	368	21.6	18.5
Mexico c, e	992	1768	4899	6219	6022	2.3	3.2
Morocco c	361	399	1400	1364	1455	5.2	13.3
Nepal	42	70	120	138	...	6.3	8.8
New Zealand	396	480	400	370	334	4.2	2.5
Norway	554	616	546	509	493	2.0	1.5
Peru	17	148	139	165	176	0.6	2.4
Philippines c	910	1245	1238	1250	1153	7.0	3.7
Poland	245	2165	2544	2478	2615	2.1	5.2
Romania	67	933	1599	1715	2013	0.9	12.9
Russian Fed. f	-	691	985	1183	1256	-	2.3
Saudi Arabia	1312	1229	996	986	969	5.5	3.1
Singapore	1778	2109	1119	1275	1020	2.9	0.9
retained imports	1016	876	515	661	540	2.4	0.9
Slovak Rep. b	-	214	513	536	643	-	4.4
Slovenia	-	335	353	346	330	-	3.2
South Africa b	561	736	562	570	510	3.4	2.0
Sri Lanka	412	1144	1331	1483	1331	15.3	22.5
Switzerland	1849	1884	1467	1354	1291	2.7	1.5
Syrian Arab Republic	168	327	330	399	...	7.0	10.5
Taipei, Chinese	1013	1790	1477	1454	1039	1.8	1.0
Thailand	898	1534	1345	1631	1535	2.7	2.5
Tunisia	790	1289	1332	1207	1435	14.3	15.1
Turkey	567	1811	1907	2124	1910	2.5	4.7
Ukraine f	-	...	342	462	...	-	3.3
United Arab Emirates f	1009	2023	1697	1811	...	9.0	4.7
United States	6730	10441	14305	16008	15429	1.3	1.3
Uruguay	37	93	88	88	74	2.8	2.4
Venezuela b	112	273	250	286	294	1.7	1.8

a Or nearest year.
b Imports are valued f.o.b.
c Includes significant imports into processing zones.
d See the Technical Notes for information on intra-EU imports.
e Beginning with 2000 imports are valued c.i.f.
f Includes Secretariat estimates.

Index

NOTE: *Page numbers in boldface refer to volume numbers and major topics. Article titles are in boldface.*

A nous la liberté, **1**:293
Abdallah, King of Jordan, **2**:448
Abdullah, Crown Prince of Saudi Arabia, **3**:736
abolitionists, **2**:494, **3**:763
Abramovitz, Moses, **3**:829
absolute advantage, **1**:82, 155, 275
abstinence theory of profit, **3**:749
Accessory Transit Company, **3**:892
accounting, 1:1–4
    accrual basis, **1**:3, **2**:405–406
    basic financial statements, **1**:2–4
    cash basis, **1**:3, **2**:406
    cash flow information, **1**:125
    Certified Public Accountants, **1**:2, 4, 340
    cost, **1**:178–179
    double entry, **1**:3
    financial, **1**:2, 179
    GAAP, *See* **Generally Accepted Accounting Principles (GAAP)**
    managerial, **1**:2
    matching concept in, **1**:3, **2**:405–406
    users of information, **1**:1
accounting equation, **1**:3
Accounting Principles Board (APB), **1**:4, 125
accrual basis accounting, **1**:3, **2**:405–406
Accumulation of Capital, The (Luxemburg), **2**:506
acquisitions and mergers, *See* mergers and acquisitions
Acton, Lord J. E. E. D., **1**:267
Adams, Abigail Smith, **1**:5
Adams, John, 1:4–6, 28, 164
    American independence and, **1**:5, 27, 199, 281
    presidency, **1**:5–6, **2**:367, 513
Adams, John Quincy, 1:6–7, 2:367, 437
    Monroe Doctrine and, **2**:574–575

Adams, Sam, **1**:281, **2**:365
Addams, Jane, **2**:490, 502
addictive goods, **1**:170
Administrative Behavior (Simon), **3**:756
Adolphus, King Gustav of Sweden, **3**:839
adverse opinion of auditors, **1**:53
adverse selection, **1**:295–296, 298
    in insurance markets, **1**:299, **2**:422–423
advertising, **1**:150–151, **2**:527
    consumer behavior and, **1**:166, 170, 327
    of drugs, **1**:218
Aeropostale, **1**:14, 15
Affluent Society, The (Galbraith), **1**:327
Afghanistan, 1:7, 210
    Soviet invasion and occupation of, **1**:123, 352
    terrorist training camps in, **1**:104
AFLAC, **1**:191
Aflak, Michel, **1**:40, 41–42
AFL-CIO, **3**:807, 868
Africa:
    European colonialism in, **1**:147, 149
    G8 summits and, **1**:326
    globalization and, **1**:347
    pan-Africanism, **2**:605, 606
    slavery, *See* **slavery**
    See also individual countries
African Americans:
    civil rights, *See* civil rights
    slavery, *See* **slavery**
    during World War I, **3**:925–926
    See also names of individuals
Afrocentrism, 1:7–10
    debate over, **1**:9
    as method of critiquing Eurocentrism, **1**:9
Age of Diminished Expectations, The (Krugman), **2**:468
Agenda 21, **3**:819

aggregate demand, **1:**198, **2:**515
  multiplier effect, **1:**246, 247
  Say's Law, *See* **Say's Law**
  stimulating, **1:**106, **2:**688
Aghion, P., **2:**419
Agilent Technologies, **2:**379
Agnew, Spiro T., **1:**305
agrarian economies, **2:**442, 481–482
  early U.S., **3:**850, 875, 876, 877
Agricultural Adjustment Act (AAA), **2:**491, 537, 592, **3:**879
Agricultural Market Act of 1929, **2:**387
agriculture, 1:10–13, **2:**411–412
  American hegemony and, **1:**12
  colonialism's effect on, **1:**11–12
  early, **1:**10–11
  globalization and, **1:**347
  Green Revolution, **1:**12–13
  international food system, **1:**11–12
  physiocracy's encouragement of, **2:**648, 691–692
  price supports, **2:**660, 661, **3:**818
  Schultz's work on problems of Third World, **1:**742
  subsidies, **3:**809
Ahmed, Eqbal, **2:**626
Air France, **1:**14
Airbus, **1:**16, 91
airlines, 1:13–16
  commerce and diplomacy, **1:**15
  deregulation of, **1:**16
  early technology, **1:**13–14
  government aid to, **1:**14–15
  jet age, **1:**16
  Simon's solution to overbooked flights, **3:**757
  subsidies, **3:**809
  World War II and its legacies, **1:**15–16
air-traffic controller's (PATCO) strike, **3:**807
AIS, **1:**346
Akerlof, George A., 1:16–17, 180, **3:**797
Aksum Kingdom, **1:**10–11
al-Arsuzi, Zaki, **1:**41
Alaska:
  oil reserves, **2:**619
  U.S. purchase of, **2:**517
Albania, **1:**58
Alcan Aluminum, **1:**110
Alchian, Armen, **1:**159, **3:**755
Alchian-Allen effect, **1:**170
ALCOA, **1:**257
alcoholic beverages, **2:**497
  liquor, *See* **liquor**
al-Din al-Baytar, Salah, **1:**41
Aldrich-Vreeland Act of 1908, **1:**285
Alémán, Miguel, **2:**546
Alexander II, Emperor of Russia, **2:**729
Alfonsín, Raúl, **1:**45
Alger, Horatio, Jr., 1:17–18

Algeria, **1:**18–19, **1:**147, 192, 309, **2:**619
Al-Husri, **1:**42
Alien and Sedition Act, **1:**6
alienation, 1:19, **3:**920
Al-Kuwatly, Shukry, **1:**41
Allais, Maurice, 1:20–21
Allais Paradox, **1:**20
Allen, Ethan, **1:**27
Allen, Paul, **1:**334, 335, **2:**549
Allen, William, **1:**16
Allen, Woody, **1:**293
Allende, Salvador, **1:**132
Allianz, 1:21
al-Rahman Shahbandar, Abd, **1:**41
Altman, Edward, **1:**225
Altman's Z-score, **1:**225
Altria (Philip Morris), 1:21–22, **3:**844
Amazon.com, **3:**896
America Online, *See* **AOL Time Warner**
American Accounting Association, **1:**2, 4
American Airlines, **1:**14
American Capitalism (Galbraith), **1:**327
American Civil War, 1:22–24, 47, **2:**413, 482, 516
  cost of, **1:**24
  economic significance of slavery, **1:**22–23
  Fillmore's stand during, **1:**292
  Grant's role in, **1:**354
  Lincoln's leadership, **1:**99, 292, 354, **2:**495–496
  Pennsylvania oil industry and, **2:**615
American Constitution, *See* Constitution of the United States
American Dilemma: The Negro Problem and Modern Democracy, An (Myrdal), **2:**580
"American Dream," **1:**18, 62, 282
American Economic Association, **3:**901
American Economic Review, **3:**771
American Electric Power (AEP), 1:24–25
American Express, **3:**915
American Federation of Labor (AFL), **2:**555, **3:**807, 867, 868
American Fur Company, **1:**51
American Institute of Certified Public Accountants (AICPA),
  1:2, 4, 54, 254, 339
American International Group (AIG), 1:25–26
American International Underwriters (AIU), **1:**25
American Management Association, **1:**33
American Marketing Association, **2:**674
American Mercury, **2:**370–371
American Motors Corporation, **1:**61
American Party ("Know-Nothings"), **1:**292
American Revolution, 1:5, 26–28, 314, **2:**364, 481, **3:**849, 874
  chronology of, **1:**27–28
  economic consequences of, **1:**28
  Faneuil Hall meetings to plan, **1:**281–282
  financing of, **1:**28
  taxes and, **1:**26–27, 28, **3:**849
American Stock Exchange (Amex), 1:28–30, 205, **3:**801, 802

American System of Henry Clay, **1:**140, 141, 164, **3:**829, 855

American Telephone and Telegraph, *See* **AT&T (American Telephone and Telegraph)**

American Tobacco Company, **2:**414, **3:**792

American Trust Company, **3:**916

Ameritech Corp., **1:**78

Amin, Samir, **2:**625, 627

Amistad, **1:**7

Amoco Corporation, **3:**792

Anatolia, **1:**115

Anciennes Mutuelles, **1:**64

ancient capitalism, 1:114–117

Andean Group, **2:**644

Ando, Albert, **1:**247

Andorra, 1:30

Andrews, Samuel, **2:**720

Andropov, Yuri, **1:**352

Angell, Norman, 1:30–31

Angelli family, **1:**291

angels (startup company investors), **1:**77

annual report, 1:31–32

Anthracite Coal Strike of 1902, **2:**728

anti-globalization, 1:32–35, 347–348, **2:**475

    Conference of Montreal and, **1:**162

    cultural imperialism and, **1:**33–34, 212, 313, 346

    G7/G8 summits and, **1:**326

    globalization debate, **1:**34–35

    kleptocracy and, **2:**461

    Stiglitz's criticisms, **3:**798

    terrorism and, **1:**346

    transnational expansion and, **1:**32–33

    World Trade Organization protests, **1:**32, 34, 35, 317, 318

    See also **globalization**

Anti-Saloon League of America (ASL), **2:**498–499

Anti-Slavery Societies, **3:**763

antitrust, 1:14, 35–38, 157, 256–257, 356

    AT&T suit, **1:**53

    Clayton Antitrust Act, **1:**36, 37, 163, 288, **3:**918

    Federal Trade Commission, *See* **Federal Trade Commission (FTC)**

    Federal Trade Commission Act, **1:**36, 286, 287

    formal cartels and, **1:**122, **123**

    international laws, **1:**38

    Microsoft suit, **1:**37–38, 161, **2:**525–526, 550

    Northern Securities Company, **2:**577, 578, 727–728

    "rule of reason" reversal, **1:**36–37

    Sherman Antitrust Act, *See* Sherman Antitrust Act

    Standard Oil investigation, **1:**278

    Theodore Roosevelt as trust buster, **2:**578, 727–728, **3:**792

    U.S. Justice Department, *See* U.S. Justice Department, Antitrust Division

    See also **conglomerate**

AOL Time Warner, 1:32, 38–39, 78, 293, 335, **2:**550

Appeal to Reason, **3:**758

Apple Computer, **1:**160, 162, **2:**445–446, 549

Aquila, 1:39

Arab League, **3:**837

Arab nationalism, 1:39–43

    Arab wa Ajam, **1:**40–41

    capitalism and, **1:**42

    future prospects, **1:**42

    Islam and, **1:**41–42

    Nasserism, **1:**41

    social, political, and intellectual antecedents to, **1:**40

Arabism, **1:**40, 41, 42

Arafat, Yasser, **2:**433

arbitrage, 1:43–44, 230, 232, 273

Area Redevelopment Act of 1961, **2:**453

Argentina, 1:44–46, **2:**424

    hyperinflation in, **2:**416

Aristotle, **1:**266, 267, **3:**793, 890

Arkwright, Richard, **3:**865–866

Armenia, 1:46

Armey, Dick, **1:**171

Arnold, Benedict, **1:**27

Arnold, Henry "Hap, " **1:**15

Arnold, Mathew, **1:**8

Arrow, Kenneth J., 1:46–47, 193, 262, **2:**379

Arthur, Chester A., 1:47–48

Arthur Anderson, **1:**254

Articles of Confederation, **1:**199, 289, **2:**513

arts, subsidies for the, **3:**809

Ashenfelter, Orley, **3:**806

Asia Life Insurance Company, **1:**25

Asian developmental state, 1:48–49

Asian financial crisis, 1:38, 49–50, 143, 346

    Hong Kong economy and, **2:**385

    Stiglitz's criticism of the IMF, **3:**798

    Vietnam and, **3:**901

    weakness in Thailand's financial system and, **3:**834

Askin, Steve, **2:**461

Aspen Skiing Co. v. Aspen Highlands Skiing Corp., **1:**37

assembly line, **1:**306, **2:**414, **3:**831

assets, **1:**2–3, 300

Assicurazioni Generali, 1:50

Association of Caribbean States (ACS), **1:**187

Association of Licensed Automobile Manufacturers (ALAM), **1:**60

Association of South East Asian Nations, **1:**276, **3:**837, 850

Assyrians, **1:**115

Astor, John Jacob, 1:51–52

asymmetric information, **1:**17, 295–297, 298, 299, **3:**797

    auctions and, **3:**901

    strikes and, **3:**806

athletics, *See* **sports**

Atlas Shrugged (Rand), **2:**699, 700

atomic bomb, **3:**852, 853

AT&T (American Telephone and Telegraph), 1:37, 52–53, 799, **3:**900

auction theory, **3:**771, 901

audit, **1**:53–54, 340
> CPAs and, **1**:4

audit opinion, **1**:53

audit risk, **1**:54

auditor's report, **1**:53

Auguste Comte and Positivism (Mill), **2**:550

Australia, 1:54–56
> privatization in, **2**:667

Austria, 1:56

Austrian Institute of Business Cycle Research, **1**:57

Austrian School, 1:56–58, 91, 231, 232, **2**:539, 540
> on capital, **1**:92, 112
> on competition, **1**:158
> profit theory, **2**:681–682

Austro-Hungarian Empire, **1**:50, 56

autarky, 1:58

Autobiography (Franklin), **1**:199, 314

Autobiography (Mill), **2**:550

automobiles, 1:59–63
> the assembly line, **1**:306, **2**:414, **3**:831
> consumerism and, **1**:62
> from craft production to mass production, **1**:59
> energy crisis' effect, **1**:62
> fuel-cell powered, **1**:305
> golden age of, **1**:61
> reorganization and internationalization of, **1**:62–63
> rise of General Motors, **1**:59–60
> unionization, **1**:60–61, 307
> *See also individual manufacturers*

Aviva, 1:63

AXA, 1:63

Azad, Abul Kalam, **3**:837

Babbage, Charles, **1**:160

Babbitt, Irving, **1**:165

"Baby Bells," **3**:900

Babylonia, **1**:115

Bacon's rebellion, **3**:762

Bagehot, Walter, **1**:234

Bahamas, 1:65

Bahrain, 1:65–66, **2**:618

Baker, Ray Stannard, **3**:758

Baktin, Mikhail, **1**:8

balance of payments crisis, **1**:49–50

balance sheet, 1:2–3, 264, 300

Balfour declaration, **2**:432, 634

Ballmer, Steve, **1**:335

Banco Central de Reserva del Peru, **2**:644

bank credit, **1**:184

Bank Leu, **1**:185

Bank of America Corporation, 1:66–67

Bank of England, 1:67–68
> monetary policy, **1**:68

Bank of France, 1:69–70

Bank of Italy (later Bank of America Corporation), **1**:66–67

Bank of Japan, 1:70–71, **2**:441, **3**:934
> monetary policy, **1**:70, 71
> speculative bubble and, **1**:70–71

Bank of Korea, **2**:466

Bank of Montréal, **1**:110

Bank of the United States, **2**:513–514, **3**:855, 891, 914

bank runs and bank panics, **1**:126

banking, **1**:296
> central banks, *See* **central banks**
> commercial, *See* **commercial banking**
> consumer, *See* **consumer banking**
> fractional-reserve, **1**:76, 126
> in Germany, **1**:342, 344
> globalization and, **2**:400
> history of regulation of, **1**:73, 79–80
> in Hong Kong, **2**:386
> in India, **2**:409
> investment, *See* **investment banking**
> in Italy, **2**:433–434, 435
> reserve ratio, **1**:75–76, 126, **2**:565–566, 567
> *See also individual banks*

Banking Act of 1933, **1**:298

bankruptcy, 1:80–81

Bankruptcy Act of 1898, **1**:81

Bankruptcy Reform Act of 1978, **1**:81

Baran, Paul A., **1**:201, **3**:791

Barbados, **3**:761, 762

Barca, Fabrizio, **2**:433

Barclays Bank, 1:81–82

Bargaining and Market Behavior: Essays in Experimental Economics (Smith), **3**:771

Barkai, Avraham, **1**:284

Barnes, Harry Elmer, **1**:84

Barro, Robert J., **1**:195, **2**:562

Barron, Clarence, **1**:215, **3**:910

Barron's Financial Weekly, **3**:910

Barron's National Business and Financial Weekly, **1**:215

barter, 1:82–83, 322, **2**:519, **3**:739, 770
> beginnings of trade, **3**:849

Baruch, Bernard, **3**:925

baseball, **3**:785, 786–787

basketball, **3**:787

Bastiat, Frédéric, 1:83–84

Basu, Kaushik, **2**:410

Bates Clark medal, **2**:468

battery, invention of the, **2**:414

Baudrillard, Jean, **1**:166

Bauman, Zygmunt, **1**:167

Baumol, William, **1**:257, **2**:569, **3**:753

Bay of Pigs, **1**:187, **2**:454

Bayh-Dole Act of 1980, **2**:641

Beard, Charles Austin, 1:84

Beard, Mary Ritter, **1**:84

Bébéar, Claude, **1**:64

Becker, Gary, 1:85, 129, **2**:384, 492

Begin, Menachem, **1:**123

Belarus, **1:**352, **3:**865

Belgium, 1:85–86, 147, **3:**924

Bell, Alexander Graham, **1:**52, **2:**414

Bell, John, **3:**881

Bell, Patrick, **2:**415

Bell Atlantic, **3:**900

Bell Canada Enterprises, **1:**110

Bell Laboratories, **1:**52

Bell Telephone Company, **1:**52–53

Ben Bella, Ahmed, **1:**18, 40

Benelux economic union, **1:**86, **2:**505

Benhabib, J., **2:**418

Benoist, Thomas, **1:**13

Bentham, Jeremy, 1:86–87, **2:**382, 715, **3:**890

    utilitarianism and, **1:**86–87, 227, 231, **2:**478, 490, **3:**883, 884

Benz, Karl, **1:**59

Bergstrasser, Charles Milford, **1:**215, **3:**910

Berkmann, Alexander, **1:**319

Berkshire Hathaway, **1:**32, **3:**799

Berle, Adolf A., 1:87

Berlin, Isaiah, **1:**267

Berlin Wall, **2:**454

    fall of, **1:**345, **2:**474, **3:**864

Bernstein, Eduard, **2:**506, **3:**771–772

Berthollet, Claude, **2:**413

Bertrand, Joseph, **2:**410

    oligopoly theory, **2:**620, 621

Bessemer, Henry, **2:**412, 414

Best Linear Unbiased Estimator (BLUE), **1:**224

Best Uses of Economic Resources, The (Kantorovich), **2:**452

Bethel, Slingsby, **1:**186

Bethlehem Steel Corporation, **3:**883

Bettman, Gary, **3:**787

Beveridge, William H., **3:**773

Bhagwati, Jagdish, **2:**556, **3:**752, 753

Bicycle Thief, **1:**293

Bill of Rights, **2:**366, 442, 513

BINAC, **1:**160

Biodiversity Convention, **3:**819

Bird, Larry, **3:**787

Birmingham Political Union, **3:**866

Bismarck, Otto von, 1:87–88

Bitner, Mary J., **3:**751

Black, Fischer, **1:**205, **3:**742

    See also Black-Merton-Scholes stock option pricing formula

black market, 1:88–89, 212, **2:**702, **3:**858

Black-Merton-Scholes stock option pricing formula, **1:**205, 297, **2:**545, **3:**741, 742

black nationalism, **1:**40

Blaine, Jams G., **1:**142

Blair, Tony, **2:**457, **3:**772, 849, 873

Blake, Luther Lee, **3:**791

Blank, Arthur, **2:**383

Bloch, Ivan S., **1:**30

Bloch, Marc, **1:**290

Blue Sky Laws, **3:**745

BNP Paribas, 1:90

board of directors, 1:31, 90, 130

    relationship to stockholders to, **3:**803

Boeing, 1:13, 91

    aircraft, **1:**13, 15–16

Boeing, William, **1:**14, 91

Böhm-Bawerk, Eugen von, 1:57, 91–92, **2:**431, 540, **3:**743

    Austrian School, **1:**57, 91

    capital theory, **1:**92, 112, 137, 139

Bolivia:

    black market in, **1:**89

    hyperinflation in, **2:**416

Bolsheviks, **2:**474, 484, 732–733, **3:**775, 864

Bombardier, **1:**110

Bonaparte, Napoleon, **1:**309, 319

bonds, 1:92–93, 194

    arbitrage and, **1:**43

    credit ratings, **1:**93

    default, **1:**93

    entities issuing, **1:**93

    key features of, **1:**92–93

    risk-free rate, **1:**93

    term structure of interest rates, **1:**194

    war bonds, **3:**925

Bonelli, Franco, **2:**433

Bonus March of 1932, **2:**387

Boody, Elizabeth, **3:**744

book building, **1:**77

bookkeeping, **1:**1

Booth, John Wilkes, **2:**497

bootlegging, **2:**499

Borgia, Cesare, **2:**508

Bosnia-Herzegovina, 1:93–94

Boston Massacre, **1:**26, **2:**365

Boston Tea Party, **1:**26, 282

Boumedienne, Houari, **1:**18

Bourdieu, Pierre, **2:**527

Bourghiba, Habib, **1:**42

Bourland, Tom, **1:**256

bourse, 1:94–95

Boutros-Ghali, Boutros, **2:**607

Boxer Rebellion, **2:**537

Boyer, Robert, **1:**204

BP (British Petroleum), 1:95, 248, **2:**618, 622

Brabazon Committee, **1:**15, 16

Brady, Dorothy, **1:**321

brands, **2:**674

    dilution, **2:**675

Braniff, **1:**16

Braudel, Fernand, **3:**784

Braverman, Harry, **1:**228

Brazil, 1:95–97, 147, 219, **2:**424, 655

    hyperinflation in, **2:**416

Brazil (cont'd)
   strikes in, **3**:807
Brecher, Michael, **2**:604
Brecht, Bertolt, **3**:840
Breckenridge, John, **1**:99
Breguet, **1**:14
Bretton Woods, 1:97–98, **2**:316
   "adjustable pegs, " **1**:97
   creation of IMF and World Bank at, **1**:97, **2**:425, 457, **3**:850
   fixed-exchange rate system implemented at, **1**:97, 213, 273–274, 349, **3**:934
   Nixon's abandonment of fixed exchange-rate system, **1**:98, 214, 274, 349, **2**:440, **3**:934
Brezhnev, Leonid, **1**:352
bribery, 1:98–99
Bricklin, Dan, **1**:160
Briggs, Asa, **1**:149
Brill, Ronald, **2**:383
Britain, *See* **United Kingdom**
British East India Company, *See* **East India Company, British**
British Petroleum (BP), *See* **BP (British Petroleum)**
Bronfman family, **2**:499–500
Brown, Alan, **3**:804–805
Brown, Edmund, **2**:703
Brown, J. J., **2**:556
Brown, John, **1**:22, 99
Brown, Walter Folger, **1**:14
Brown-Forman Corporation, **2**:500
Brue, Stanley L., **1**:245
Bryan, William Jennings, **1**:142, **2**:537, **3**:780
Buchanan, James, 1:99, **2**:649
Buchanan, James M., 1:58, **100**, **2**:462, 492
Buckley, William, **1**:165
Buddhism, **1**:133
budget deficit, **1**:194, 302
   constitutional restrictions on government spending, **1**:321
Budget Reinforcement Act of 1990, **1**:302
Buffet, Warren, **1**:32, **3**:799
Buick Motor Company, **1**:338
Bullfinch, Charles, **1**:282
Bunau-Varilla, Philippe, **2**:634
Burke, Edmund, 1:101, 164
Burke, Peter, **1**:149
Burns, Dr. Arthur, **1**:183, 320, **2**:391
Burr, Aaron, **2**:449
Bush, George H. W., 1:101–103, 129, 317, **3**:880
   foreign policy, **3**:880
Bush, George W., 1:103–104, 317, **2**:628
   Friedman's Lifetime Achievement Award, **1**:321
   tariff on steel imports, **3**:826
Business @ the Speed of Thought (Gates), **1**:335
business cycles, 1:57, **104–107**, 204, **2**:512, 704
   defined, **1**:104, 225
   depression, *See* **depression**
   effects of, **1**:105–106

   example, **1**:104
   Hayek's analysis of, **1**:57, **2**:369
   inflation's relationship to, **1**:106
   Keynes on, **1**:106
   Kuznets' analysis of, **1**:204, **2**:469
   length of, **1**:104–105
   Mill on, **2**:552
   Minsky on, **2**:557
   naming the contractionary phase, **1**:105
   new classical school of economics, view of, **3**:816
   recession, *See* **recession**
   relationship between expansionary and contractionary phases, **1**:105
   Schumpeter on, **3**:742, 743
Business Cycles: A Theoretical, Historical, and Statistical Analysis of Capitalist Process (Schumpeter), **3**:743
Buttonwood Agreement, **1**:29, **2**:595
Bygrave, William, **3**:899

Cabral, Amilcar, **3**:837
Caffentzis, George, **1**:141
Calculus of Consent, The (Buchanan and Tullock), **1**:100
Calhoun, John, **1**:6, **3**:855, 891
California, statehood for, **3**:829, 876
Callaghan, James, **3**:872
Calvin, John, **2**:684, 685
Cambodia, 1:109, **3**:903
Cambridge Controversy over capital, **1**:112, **3**:790
Canada, 1:109–111
   liquor business in, **2**:499–500, 501
   NAFTA and, **1**:111, **2**:581, 583, **3**:850
Canada-U.S. Tree Trade Agreement, **1**:111
Canadian dollar, **1**:110–111
Canadian Tire, **1**:312
Canavan, Francis, **1**:101
Cantillon, Richard, **2**:648, 682
Capellas, Michael, **3**:930
capital, 1:111–113, **2**:401, 403
   controversies, **1**:112–113
   defining, **1**:111
   films about, **1**:293
   financial, **1**:111
   marginal efficiency of, **1**:113
   Smith's theory of, **1**:111, 113–114, 118, **3**:770
   theories, **1**:92, 111–112, 138, **3**:853–854
Capital (Marx), **1**:19, **228–229**, **2**:471, 483, 533
   on capital accumulation, **1**:228–229, **2**:666
   Cleaver on, **1**:141
   on services, **3**:752
   on value of services, **3**:752
capital accumulation, 1:113–114, **3**:738, 770
   Capital on, **1**:228–229, **2**:666
   consumers and, **1**:169
   Wealth of Nations on, **1**:113–114, **3**:770
Capital and Interest (Bohm-Bawerk), **2**:540

Capital Asset Pricing Model (CAPM), **1:**44, 225, **2:**530, **3:**755

capital goods defined, **1:**111

capitalism:

ancient, **1:114–117**

political, **1:117–118**

Capitalism and Underdevelopment in Latin America (Frank), **1:**201

Capitalism, Socialism, and Democracy (Schumpeter), **1:**232, **3:**743

Capone, Al, **1:**333, **2:**499

Card David, **3:**806

Cárdenas, Lázaro, **2:**546, 616, 642

Cardoso, Fernando H., **1:**201

Caribbean Community and Common Market (CARICOM), **1:**276

Carlson, Kenneth, **1:**239

Carlyle, Thomas, **2:**551, **3:**919

Carnegie, Andrew, 1:52, **119–120**, 164, **2:**414, 478, 482

steel industry and, **1:**119–120, 319, **3:**883

Carnegie Steel Company, **1:**119

Carnegie-Mellon University, **2:**539

carrying capacity, 1:120–121

cartel, 1:35, **121–123**

OPEC as, **1:**122

tacit collusion, **1:**123

Carter, Jimmy, 1:123–124

economic policy, **1:**124, **3:**880

foreign policy, **1:**123–124, **2:**635, **3:**880

Panama and, **1:**123, **2:**635

presidential elections, **1:**104, 123, 124, 305, **2:**460–461, 703

Cartier, Jacques, **1:**109–110

Case, Steve, **1:**39, 335

Casey, Jim, **3:**874

cash basis accounting, **1:**3, **2:**406

cash flow, 1:3–4, **124–125**

statement of cash flows, **1:**3–4, 124, 300

casino gambling, **1:**328–330

Castilla, Ramon, **2:**644

Castro, Cipriano, **2:**617

Castro, Fidel, **1:**187, **2:**454, 605, **3:**837, 838

casualty insurance, **1:**299

Catt, Carrie Chapman, **3:**925

Ceausescu, Nicolae, **2:**474

Celler-Kefauver Act of 1950, **1:**37, 163

Census of Retail Trade in the United States, **2:**712

Center for Study of the Economy and the State, **3:**797

central banks, 1:126–127

monetary policy, **1:**126, **2:**565–567

opponents of, **2:**443

See also individual central banks, e.g. **Bank of England; Bank of Japan**

Central Intelligence Agency, **1:**102

Central Pacific Railroad, **2:**556

central planning, **2:**558, **3:**782

quotas used in, **2:**692

in Soviet Union, **3:**775

certificates of deposit (CDs), **1:**75

Certified Public Accountant (CPA), **1:**2, 4, 340

Césaire, Aimé, **1:**8, **2:**397

CGNU Insurance, **1:**63

chaebol, **1:**48

Chamberlain, Neville, **2:**455

Chamberlin, E. H., **1:**231, **2:**671

Champlain, Samuel de, **1:**110

Chandler, Alfred, **1:**259

Chandler Act of 1938, **1:**81

Chang, Ha-Joon, **3:**798

Chaplin, Charlie, **1:**293, **3:**925

Charles I, King of England, **1:**252–253, **3:**800–801

Charles II, King of England, **1:**253

Charles X, King of France, **1:**309

Chartism, **3:**763, 866

Chase, Salmon P., **1:**79, **2:**449

Chase Manhattan Corporation, **2:**449

Chavez, Cesar, **3:**838

Chávez, Hugo, **3:**805, 896

checkable deposits, **1:**75

Chemical Bank of New York, **2:**449

Chernenko, Konstantin, **1:**352

Chernov, Victor, **2:**733

Chevron Corporation, **2:**622, **3:**792

Chevron Texaco, 1:127, 248

Texas oil boom and, **2:**616

Chiang Kai-shek, **1:**134, 135, **3:**824

Chicago Board of Trade, 1:128–129, **2:**487, 553

Chicago Mercantile Exchange, **1:**205, **2:**553

Chicago School, 1:129–130, 320, **2:**462, **3:**797, 850

chief executive office (CEO), 1:31, 130

chief financial officer (CFO), 1:131

children:

child labor, **1:**267–268, **2:**412, **3:**762, 859, 866

health care for, **2:**374

as slaves, **3:**762

tobacco sales to, **3:**843

Children's Online Privacy Protection Act of 1998, **1:**287

Chile, 1:131–132, 317

China, 1:132–136, 211, **3:**837

Bush as U.S. liason to, **1:**102

civil war in, **1:**135, **3:**824

Cultural Revolution, **1:**135

early societies in, **1:**133

formal recognition by the U.S., **1:**124

founding of People's Republic, **1:**135

groundwork of communism in, **1:**134–135

Hong Kong policies, **2:**385

Hundred-Days Reform, **1:**134

Japanese aggression against, **1:**134, 137, **3:**928

Jiang Zemin, **2:**444–445

May Fourth Movement, **1:**134

nationalization in, **2:**588

New Culture Movement, **1:**134

Nixon's visit to, **3:**824, 903–904

Open Door policy, **1:**133, 147, **2:**537

China (cont'd)
    Opium Wars, **1:**133, 147, **2:**623–624
    recent history, **1:**135–136, **2:**444–445
    socialism and, **3:**775
    Taiwan and, **3:**824–825
    Vietnam War and, **3:**903
    World Trade Organization membership, **1:**143, 317
    See also **Taiwan**
China National Petroleum Corporation (CNPC), 1:136
China Petroleum and Chemical Corporation, *See* **Sinopec**
    Corporation
Christian Arabs, **1:**40, 41–42
Chrysler Corporation, **1:**60–63, 191, **3:**809
Churchill, Winston, **2:**455, **3:**852
Ci Xi, Empress Dowager, **1:**134
circulation of elites theory, **2:**636
Cisco Systems, **3:**896
Citicorp, **1:**73, 78, 80, 137
Citigroup, 1:73, 136–137
Citizen Kane, **1:**293
Civil Aeronautics Act of 1938, **3:**852
civil rights, **1:**8, 9, **2:**453
    Eisenhower and, **1:**242
    Lyndon Johnson and, **2:**447, 448
    legislation, **1:**242, **2:**447, 448
Civil Rights Act of 1960, **1:**242
Civil Rights Act of 1964, **2:**448
Civil Service Commission, **1:**47
civil service reform, **1:**334
Civil War in America, *See* **American Civil War**
Civil War in England, *See* **English Civil War**
Civil Works Administration, **2:**537, 593
Civilian Conservation Corps, **2:**491, 537, 592
Civilization and Capitalism (Braudel), **3:**784
Clair, René, **1:**293
Clark, John Bates, 1:137–138, 231
Clark Maurice B., **3:**792
"Clash of Civilizations, The," **2:**628
class structure, 1:138–140
classical economic theory, **1:**226–227
    on competition, **1:**158
    employment theory, **1:**245–246
    founders of, **1:**228, 230, **2:**705
    main ideas of, **1:**226–227, 230–231, **2:**705, **3:**849
    on profit, **2:**681
    transition to neoclassical economic theory from, **1:**231
Clay, Henry, 1:6, 140–141, 164, **2:**437, **3:**855
Clayton, Henry De Lamar, **1:**36
Clayton Antitrust Act, **1:**36, 37, 163, 288, **3:**918
Clean Air Act of 1990, **1:**24–25
Cleaver, Harry M., Jr., 1:141
Clemenceau, Georges, **2:**456, **3:**926
Cleveland, Grover, 1:141–142, **2:**517, 537
climate change, **1:**10, 11, 249
    Kyoto Protocol, **1:**348

Clinton, William Jefferson, 1:142–44, 356
    economic policy, **1:**143, 317, 321, **3:**783
    foreign policy, **1:**143, **3:**880
    presidential elections, **1:**103, 142, **3:**772
cliometrics, **1:**303
    revolution in economic history, **2:**609–610
Clive, Robert, **1:**222
club goods, **2:**689
coal, **1:**248–249, 319
    mining of, **2:**412, 554, **3:**758
Coal Question, The (Jevons), **2:**444
Coase, Ronald H., 1:129, 144, 154, 278, **2:**630, **3:**793
Coase Theorem, **1:**278, **2:**630, 686
Coca-Cola, **1:**32, 211
Cockerill, William, **1:**86
coincident economic indicators, **1:**225–226
Colbert, Jean-Baptiste, 1:145, **2:**542, 648, 691
Colbertism, **1:**145, **2:**648, 691, **3:**853
Cold War, **3:**879
    Asian developmental states and, **1:**49
    détente, **1:**352
    Eisenhower and, **1:**242
    Kennedy and, **2:**453, 454
    non-aligned nations, *See* **non-alignment**
Coleridge, Samuel Taylor, **2:**551
Colfax, Schuyler, **1:**354
collateral, **1:**194
Collected Papers of Kenneth J. Arrow (Arrow), **1:**47
collective bargaining, *See* **unions**
Collins, Carole, **2:**461
collusion, **1:**157
    tacit, **1:**123
Colombia, 1:145–146, **2:**728
Colonial Air Transport, **1:**15
colonialism, 1:11–12, 40, 146–149
    agriculture affected by, **1:**11–12
    capitalism and, **1:**147–148
    dependency theory and, **1:**202
    history of, **1:**146–147
    white man's burden view of, **1:**148–149
    See also **imperialism;** *individual countries*
Colt, Samuel, **3:**917
Columbian Exchange, **2:**481
Columbus, Christopher, **1:**65, **3:**761, 778, 895
Comanor, S. William, **3:**883
Comcast, **1:**53
Commerce Defended (Mill), **3:**739
commercial banking, 1:71–74, 298, 299
    bank uses of funds, **1:**72–73
    history of bank regulation, **1:**73
    rescue of banks too big to fail, **1:**73–74
    sources of funds, **1:**71–72
Commission for Labor Cooperation, **2:**581
Committee for European Economic Cooperation (CEEC),
    2:531

commodities:

arbitrage, **1:**44

"composite," **3:**790

fetishism of, **1:**19

futures and futures options trading, **1:**128–129, 297

See also **goods**

common stock, **1:**263

Commonwealth Games, **3:**786

Commonwealth of Independent States (CIS), **3:**837

communication, 1:149–153

communism, **1:**38

Cold War, *See* Cold War

containment policy, **1:**345

fascism compared to, **1:**283

Communist International, **1:**283

Communist Manifesto (Marx and Engels), **1:**139, 251, 345, **2:**473, 478, 533, 534, 535, **3:**829, 920

Communist Party of the USA, **3:**879

Community and Association (Tonnies), **1:**165

Compaine, Benjamin, **1:**152

company, 1:153–155

Compaq Computers, **2:**379

comparative advantage, 1:155–156

dynamic, **1:**156

Ricardo's analysis of, **1:**82, 155, 227, 275, 316, **2:**551, **3:**770, 849

in service sector, **3:**752, 753

comparative dynamics, **3:**796

comparative statics, **3:**796

competition, 1:156–157

illegal, **1:**156–157

perfect, **1:**156, 158, 159

competitive economics, 1:157–159

compliance audit, **1:**53

Comprehensive Smokeless Tobacco Health Education Act of 1986, **1:**287

Compromise of 1850, **1:**140–141, 292, **3:**829

computers, 1:159–62

business, **1:**160

globalization and, **1:**346

long waves of technological change, **3:**831–832

personal computing, **1:**160–162

software, **1:**160, 161

See also **information revolution; technology**

Comte, Auguste, **1:**165, **2:**551

Concorde, **1:**16

Condition of the Working Classes in England (Engels), **1:**251

conditional logit model, **2:**536

Conference of Montreal, 1:162

conglomerate, 1:162–163

Congress of International Organizations (CIO), **3:**807, 868

conjectural variations hypothesis, **2:**380

Connor, Steven, **1:**166

Conrad, Joseph, **2:**625

Conscience of a Conservative, The (Goldwater), **1:**165

conservatism, 1:164–165

Conservative Mind, The (Kirk), **1:**165

Considerations of Representative Government (Mill), **2:**550

Consolidated Foods Corporation, **1:**163

conspicuous consumption, **1:**10, **3:**894

Constitution, U.S.S., **3:**913

Constitution of the United States, **1:**5, 164, 199, **2:**513, 574, 705

Beard's economic interpretation of, **1:**84

Bill of Rights, **2:**366, 442, 513

classical liberalism and, **1:**227

13th Amendment, **2:**497

14th Amendment, **2:**446, 497

15th Amendment, **2:**497

16th Amendment, **3:**823

18th Amendment, **2:**499, **3:**918

19th Amendment, **2:**414, **3:**918

21st Amendment, **2:**499

Constitutional Convention of 1787, **1:**314, **2:**364, 513, **3:**914

consumer, 1:166–167

the American way of life, **1:**166–167

culture of the, **1:**167

Federal Trade Commission powers for protecting the, **1:**286, 287

Green, **1:**167

influences on the, **1:**166

consumer banking, 1:74–76

history of, **1:**76

investment banking distinguished from, **1:**74

method of operation, **1:**75–76

types of consumer banks, **1:**74–75

consumer behavior, 1:62, 168–171, 247, 2:469

capital accumulation and, **1:**169

factors other than price affecting, **1:**169–170

full price of, **1:**170–171

Galbraith on, **1:**169, 327

law of demand, **1:**168–169

Consumer Confidence Index, **1:**167

Consumer Leasing Act, **1:**287

Consumer Price Index (CPI), **2:**646

revisions to, **1:**353

"Consumerism and its Contradictions, " **1:**167

consumption function, **2:**561

contagion, 1:50, 171–172

Continental Airlines, **1:**81

Continental Congress, **1:**5, 26, 27, 28, **2:**513, 574, **3:**875

Continental Illinois Bank, **1:**73–74

Continental T.V. Inc. v. GTE Sylvania, Inc., **1:**37

Continuous-Time Finance (Merton), **2:**544

contracts, 1:172–174

overturned by outside authorities, **1:**172–174

promise distinguished from, **1:**173

types of valid, **1:**172

unconscionability doctrine, **1:**174

contrarian style of investing, **2:**524

contributed capital, **1:**3

"Contribution to the Theory of Economic Growth, A," **3:**775

Convertibility Plan, **1:**45–46

Cook, Thomas, **3:**846

Cooke, Jay, **1:**79

Coolidge, Calvin, 1:174–175, **2:**387, 539, **3:**816

    economic policy, **2:**478

Cooper, Peter, 1:176

Cooper, Sherry, **1:**111

Cooper Flies, The (Cooper), **1:**111

Cooper Union School for the Advancement of Science, **1:**176

Cootner, Paul, **3:**742

copyright, **3:**776

Cornwallis, Charles, **1:**27

Cornwallis, George, **3:**914

corporate leverage, **2:**486–487, 552, 561

corporations, **1:**154, **3:**877

    Berle's promotion of government supervision of, **1:**87

    compared to other forms of business organization, **2:**637, 638

    incorporation, *See* **incorporation**

corporatism, *See* **political capitalism**

corruption, 1:176–178

    bribery, **1:**98–99

    consequences of, **1:**177–178

    essential characteristics of, **1:**176

    factors affecting, **1:**177

    fighting, **1:**178

    insider trading, *See* insider trading

    levels of, **1:**176–177

    Russian economic reforms of 1990s and, **2:**731

Cortelyou, George, **1:**209

cost accounting, 1:178–179

cost of information, 1:179–181

cost theory, 1:181–182

cotton gin, **2:**413, **3:**917

Coulisse, **1:**95

Council for Trade-Related Aspect of Intellectual Property (TRIPS), **3:**923

Council of Economic Advisors, 1:183, **3:**797, 844

Counterrevolution and Revolt (Marcuse), **2:**518

Cournot, Antoine, **1:**231, **2:**410

    oligopoly theory, **1:**158, 332, **2:**620, 621

Cowles Commission for Research in Economics, **1:**46–47

Cox, James Middleton, **2:**366, 725

Crawford, William H., **2:**437

credit, 1:183–184

    poverty's effect on access to, **2:**657

credit cards, **1:**72, 166

Credit Mobilier scandal, **1:**334, 354

credit or truck system, **1:**273

Credit Suisse Group, 1:184–185

credit unions, **1:**74, 75, 298

Crisis in German Social Democracy, The (Luxemburg), **2:**506

Crocker, Charles, **2:**556

Crocker National Bank, **3:**916

Cromwell, Oliver, 1:185–186, 253, **2:**542

crony capitalism, **1:**48–49

Cross, Richard Asheton, **1:**210

Crowther, Geoffrey, **1:**235

Cruikshank, Margaret, **1:**235

Cuba, 1:186–187

    Kennedy's policies, **2:**454

    Pierce's policies, **1:**99, **2:**516–517, 649

    socialism and, **3:**775

    Spanish-American War and, **2:**517, 537, **3:**779–780

Cuban Missile Crisis, **2:**454

Cullinan, "Buckskin Joe, " **1:**127

cultural imperialism, **1:**33–34, 212, 313, 346

Culture and Imperialism (Said), **2:**626

Culture of Contentment, The (Galbraith), **1:**327

Cumberland, Richard, **3:**884

currency, 1:187–190

    appreciation, **1:**189

    Asian financial crisis, *See* **Asian financial crisis**

    coins, **1:**187–188, 273

    crises, **1:**49–50

    defined, **1:**187

    depreciation, **1:**189

    devaluation, **1:**189

    exchange between different currencies, **1:**188–189

    exchange rates, *See* **exchange rates**

    notes or paper money, **1:**28, 188

    optimum, **2:**579

    reserve, **1:**189, 213, 214, 270

    revaluation, **1:**189–190

    stabilization measures, **1:**190

    as store of value, **1:**188

    swaps, **1:**206

Currency Act of 1764, **1:**26

currency board regime, **1:**190

custom unions, **1:**276

Cyclical Fluctuations (Kuznets), **2:**469

Czech Republic, 1:190

da Gama, Vasco, **3:**783

Dai-ichi Mutual Life Insurance Company, 1:191, **2:**600

Daimler, Gottlieb, **1:**59, **2:**414

DaimlerChrysler, 1:191–192, **2:**558

D'Arcy, William Knox, **1:**95

Darden Restaurants, **1:**312

Darwin, Charles, **2:**490, 532, **3:**781

    natural selection applied to economics, **1:**159, 165

Darwish, Mehmud, **3:**837

Davies, Marion, **1:**293

Davis, Al, **1:**38

Davis, Lance, **2:**610

Dayton, George, **3:**825

de Gaulle, Charles, 1:192–193, 311, **3:**872

de Havilland, **1:**15

de la Madrid, Miguel, **2:**546–547

de la Rúa, Fernando, **1:**46

De Legibus Naturae (Cumberland), **3:**884

de Lesseps, Ferdinand Marie, **2:**634, **3:**811, 812

De Sica, Vittorio, **1:**293

dead-weight losses, **1:**122–123, **2:**693

Dearborn Independent, **1:**307

Debreu, Gerard, 1:193, 262

debt, 1:194–196

    contracts, **1:**194

    default and renegotiation of, **1:**195–196

    defined, **1:**194

    government, **1:**194–195

    instruments, **1:**194

    international, **1:**194, 195–196, 326, 347

    national (government), **1:**48, 194–195

decision-making process in economic organizations, Simon's contribution to, **3:**756

Declaration of Independence, **1:**5, 227, 266, 314, **2:**365, 442, 490

Declaration of the Rights of Man and Citizen, The (Jellinek), **2:**685

Declaration of the Rights of Man and the Citizens, **1:**318, 319

Declaratory Act of 1766, **1:**26

declining balance method of depreciation, **1:**203

deductive logic, **1:**57

Deere, John, **2:**412

defenestration of Prague, **3:**839

Defense Advanced Research Projects Agency (DARPA), **1:**161

della Vida, Samuele, **1:**50

demand, 1:196–198

    aggregate, *See* aggregate demand

    deriving, **1:**196–198

    law of, **1:**168–169

    Say's law, *See* **Say's Law**

demand deposits, **1:**75

democracy, 1:198–200, **3:**875

    capitalism and, **1:**198–199, 266–267

    free trade and, **1:**199–200

    social democracy, *See* **social democracy**

    socialism as workers', **3:**774–775

Democracy in America (Tocqueville), **1:**200

Democratic People's Republic of Korea, *See* **North Korea**

Deng Xiaoping, **2:**445

Denison, Edward, 1:200

Denmark, 1:201

Denning, Michael, **2:**378

dependency theory, 1:201–203, 290

deposit accounts, **1:**71

depreciation, 1:203

    of currency, **1:**189, 203

    methods of measuring, **1:**203

depression, 1:45, 203–205

    Great Depression of 1873-96, **1:**204–205

    Great Depression of 1930s, *See* Great Depression of 1930s

    See also **business cycles; recession**

Depression of 1893, **1:**142

deregulation, **1:**345, **2:**835

    of airlines, **1:**16

Deregulation and Monetary Control Act of 1980 (DIDMCA), **1:**73

derivatives, **1:**205–206, **2:**487

    valuation of, **2:**545

Des Forges, Bruno, **2:**597

Desert Land Act of 1877, **3:**877

DeSoto, Hernando, 1:206–207, **2:**657–658

Deutsche Bank, 1:207

Deutsche Bundesbank, **1:**344

Deutsche Telecom, 1:207, 344

developing countries, *See* Third World

Dewey, John, **2:**490

dialectic branch of philosophy, **2:**376

Dìaz, Porfirio, **2:**546

Dickens, Charles, **3:**919

Dickens, William T., **1:**17

Diem, Ngo Dinh, **3:**902

Digital Research, Inc., **1:**161

diminishing marginal substitution, **1:**168

diminishing returns, *See* **principle of diminishing returns**

direct sales, **1:**212

disabled, health care for the, **2:**374

Disarmament Conference of 1934, **3:**928

disclaimer of opinion, auditors, **1:**53

discount, 1:207–208

discount rate, 1:126, 208–209, 285, **2:**567

Discourses on the First Ten Books of Titus Livy (Machiavelli), **2:**509

discrimination, *See* civil rights

Disraeli, Benjamin, 1:209–210

distribution, 1:210–213

    aggressive strategies, **1:**211

    black markets, *See* **black market**

    blockbuster strategy, **1:**212

    direct sales, **1:**212

    of films, **1:**212, 294

    of foreign products, **1:**211

    globalization and cultural hegemony, **1:**212

    penetration, **1:**211

    spice trade, **3:**784

Distribution of Wealth, The (Clarke), **1:**137

dividend, *See* **stock dividend**

Dodge, Joseph, **2:**440

Dole, Robert, **1:**305

dollar, 1:213–215

    global trade and internationalization of, **2:**520

    as reserve currency, **1:**189, 213, 214, 349

dollar diplomacy, **2:**388

dollarization, **1:**190

Domar, Evsey, **1:**360, **2:**368

Dominican Republic, **3:**918

Donaldson, Lufkin & Jenrette, **1:**64

Dorfman, Joseph, **3:**894

Dostoyevsky, Fyodor, **2:**628

dot-com boom and bust, **1:**356, **2:**585–586

    venture capital and, **3:**896–897

Doubleday, Abner, **3:**785

double-entry accounting, **1:**3

Douglas, Donald, **1:**15

Douglas, Stephen, **1:**99, **2:**446, 495

Douglas aircraft, **1:**13, 15–16

Dow, Charles Henry, **1:**215, **3:**910

Dow Jones, 1:215–216

Dow Jones and Company, **3:**910

Dow Jones Index, **1:**215–216

Dow Jones Industrial Average (DJIA), **1:**216

Downing Street Years and The Path to Power, The (Thatcher), **2:**836

Dragon's Teeth (Sinclair), **3:**758

Drake, Edwin L., **3:**792

Drake, Sir Francis, **2:**541

Dred Scott v. Sanford, **1:**22, 99

Dresdner Bank, **1:**21

Drew, Daniel, **1:**353, **3:**892, 893

Drexel, Anthony, **1:**79

Drexel Burnham Lambert, **1:**78

Drouot, **1:**64

drugs, 1:216–218

  generic, **1:**217

  marketing of, **1:**218

  patent protection, **1:**217–218

  price regulation, **1:**217

  regulation of, **1:**217–218

  research and development, **1:**216–217

Du Bois, W. E. B., **1:**8, 9

duality theory, **2:**536

Duby, Georges, **1:**290

Duhalde, Eduardo, **1:**46

Duke Energy, 1:218

Dunoyer, Charles, **2:**697

Durant, William C., **1:**60, 338

Durkheim, Emile, **1:**165

Duryea, Charles, **1:**59

Duryea, Frank, **1:**59

Dutch auction, **3:**771

Dutch East India Company *(Verenigde Oost Indische Compagnie)* (VOC), **1:**147, 154, **2:**409, 410, 591, **3:**783–784, 800

Dutch West India Company, 1:219

Duvalier, Baby Doc, **2:**462

dynamic analysis, **3:**795–796

Dynergy, 1:219

E.ON Energie, 1:221

Ea-Nasir, **1:**115

earned capital, **1:**3

earned income tax credit, **3:**818

earnings per share (EPS), **2:**406

EASDAQ, **3:**801

East Germany, **1:**341–343, **2:**532

East India Company, British, 1:147, 154, 186, **221–223**, **2:**543, 623, **3:**759, 784, 800

Eastern Air Transport, **1:**14

eBay, **3:**896

Ebla, kingdom of, **1:**115

Echeverría, Luis, **2:**546

Eckert, J. Presper, **1:**160

ecological footprint concept, **1:**120–121

Econometric Society, **3:**842, 901

econometrics, 1:223–225, **2:**452

  business applications of, **1:**224–225

  determining the fit of the model, **1:**223–224

  estimation, **1:**223

  Frisch on, **1:**321

  multiple regression model, **1:**223

  probability theory, **2:**363

  properties of a good estimator, **1:**224

  selection problem, **2:**375

  statistical significance, **1:**224

  Tinbergen's contributions to, **3:**842

Economic and Monetary Union (EMU), **1:**268–269

Economic Census of the United States, **3:**751

Economic Community of West African States (ECOWAS), **3:**837

Economic Consequences of Peace (Keynes), **1:**234

Economic Cooperation Act (ECA), **2:**532

Economic Fluctuations in the United States, 1921-42 (Klein), **2:**460

economic geography, **2:**467

Economic Growth of the United States, 1790-1860, The (North), **2:**609

economic indicators, 1:225–226

Economic Indicators, **1:**183

Economic Interpretation of the Constitution, An (Beard), **1:**84

Economic Opportunity Act of 1964, **2:**680, **3:**879

Economic Reports, president's annual, **1:**183

Economic Stabilization Act of 1970, **2:**603

economic theory:

  classical, *See* **classical economic theory**

  Marxian, *See* **Marxian economic theory**

  neoclassical, *See* **neoclassical economic theory**

  new classical or modern economics, **2:**511–512, 562, **3:**816

Economic Value of Man, The (Engel), **1:**250

Economics: An Introductory Analysis (Samuelson and Nordhaus), **1:**129, **3:**735–736

Economics and Evolution (Hodgson), **1:**261

Economics in One Lesson (Hazlitt), **2:**370, 371

Economics of the Peace, The (Keynes), **2:**456

economies of scale, 1:232–233, 298

  small businesses and, **3:**766

Economist, The **magazine, 1:**233–236, **2:**382

Economy and Interest (Allais), **1:**20

Edgell, Stephen, **3:**894

Edgeworth, Francis, **1:**158, **2:**551, 620

Edison, Thomas Alva, 1:236–237, **2:**414

  electric lighting and, **1:**237, **2:**414, **3:**916

education, 1:237–240

  correlation between health and, **2:**371–372

  desegregation of schools, **1:**242

  as investment in human capital, **1:**237, 742

  of the labor force, **1:**237–238

  school vouchers, **1:**239

society's investment in, 1:238–239

subsidies, 3:808–809

unresolved problems in, 1:239–240

Edwards, Ruth Dudley, 1:235

efficiency, 1:20

scarcity and, 3:741

Efficient Markets Hypothesis (EMH), 2:522, 523–524

Egypt, 1:41, 42, 147, 240–241

history of trade, 3:849

nationalization of Suez Canal, 2:588, 3:811, 812

non-alignment policy, 2:604, 605–606

Ehrlich, Paul, 2:554, 3:757

Einstein, Albert, 2:490

Eire, Republic of, See Ireland

Eisenhower, Dwight D., 1:29, 241–242, 2:602

civil rights and, 1:242

domestic policy, 1:242, 3:879, 880

foreign policy, 1:242, 3:902

Lyndon Johnson and, 2:447

Eisenstein, Serguey, 1:293

El Paso Corporation, 1:242–243

elderly, health care for the, 2:374

Electoral College, 1:164

electricity, 3:831

Edison and electric lighting, 1:237, 2:414, 3:916

Franklin's experiments with, 1:314

industry, 1:249

Westinghouse's contribution to, 3:916–917

Electronic Data Systems, 1:63, 338

Elements of Pure Economics (Walras), 3:911, 912

Elements of the Philosophy of Right (Hegel), 2:377

Elizabeth I, Queen of England, 2:541, 3:849

Elkington, John, 1:167

Elliot, Charles, 2:623

Ellison, Ralph, 1:8

Emancipation Proclamation, 1:23, 24, 2:496–497

Emergency Fleet Corporation, 2:380

Emergency Price Control Act of 1942, 2:663

Emergency Revenue Act, 3:924

employee benefits, 1:243–244

Employment Act of 1946, 1:183

employment theory, 1:244–247

classical school on, 1:245–246

Keynesian view, 1:246

monetarist view, 1:247

new classical economics on, 1:247

service sector employment, 3:753

See also unemployment

Encyclopaedia of Philosophical Sciences (Hegel), 2:377

energy, 1:39, 248–249

crises, 1:62, 124, 2:618–619, 622

oil, See oil

policy, 1:249

Engel, Ernst, 1:250

Engel curves, 1:250

Engels, Friedrich, 1:250–251, 2:473

Capital and, 1:228

Communist Manifesto, See Communist Manifesto (Marx and Engels)

"wage slavery, " 3:908

Engel's Law, 1:250

Engerman, Stanley, 1:304

England, See United Kingdom

English auction, 3:771

English Civil War, 1:252–253

Enhanced Caribbean Basin Initiative, 2:385

ENI, 1:253

ENIAC, 1:160

Enlightenment, 2:490, 3:769

Enron, 1:39, 81, 253–255, 340

Ente Nazionale Idrocarburi (National Hydrocarbon Board) (ENI), 1:253

enterprise, 1:255–257

evolution of, 1:255–256

free market, 1:255

innovative enterprises, 1:256

political, 1:255, 256–257

the price system under free enterprise, 1:255

entrepreneur, 1:57, 257–261, 2:403, 3:765

capitalism and the, 1:257–258

decision-making by, 1:260–261

role of the, 1:258

Schumpeter on entrepreneurial activity, 1:258–259, 267, 3:742, 743, 766

social value of entrepreneurship, 1:259–260

See also small business

environment, 1:11

climate change, See climate change

ecological footprint concept, 1:120–121

Eisenhower and, 1:242

G8 summits and, 1:326

government's role in regulating, 2:686–687

mining and the, 2:556

sustainable development, See sustainable development

technological change and, 3:830

Theodore Roosevelt's policies, 2:728

tourism and degradation of the, 3:847

Epicureans, 3:884

Equal Credit Opportunity Act, 1:287

Equation of Capitalism (Walras), 3:912

equilibrium, 2:379

Debreu's reformulation of theory of, 1:193

disequilibrium economics, 1:263

general, 1:229, 230, 261–262, 3:770, 911

Locke on, 2:503

market failure, 1:262–263

partial, 1:229, 261, 262

Vernon Smith's experiments on, 3:771

Equitable, 1:64

equity, 1:263–264

Erie Canal, **2**:596

Erie Railroad, **1**:303, 353, **3**:893

Eritrea, **1**:268

Eros and Civilization (Marcuse), **2**:518

Escher, Alfred, **1**:184

Essay concerning Human Understanding (Locke), **2**:502

"Essay on Commerce," **2**:648

Essay on Liberation, An (Marcuse), **2**:518

Essay on Naval Discipline, An (Hodgskin), **2**:382

Essay on the Principle of Population (Malthus), **2**:515, 554

estate tax, **3**:827, 828

Estonia, 1:264

  black market in, **1**:89

ethics, 1:264–268

Ethiopia, 1:268, 284

euro, 1:268–270, 272

  benefits of, **1**:269

  countries converting to the, **1**:268, 301, **2**:429, **3**:778

  creation of, **1**:68, 268, 342

  German financial system and, **1**:342

  global trade and internationalization of, **2**:520

  impact on international business markets, **1**:270

  naming of, **1**:268

  problems with, **1**:269–270

  reasons for creation of, **1**:269

  as reserve currency, **1**:270

  rise of the, **1**:214–215

Eurocentrism, 1:148, 2:627–629

  Afrocentrism as method of critiquing, **1**:9

Euro-dollars, **1**:214

Euronext, **1**:95

European Association of Securities Dealers Automated Quotation market (EASDAQ), **3**:801

European Central Bank (ECB), 1:269, 270–271

  creation of, **1**:68, 270

  functions of, **1**:270–271

European Coal and Steel Community, **1**:86, **2**:505, **3**:871

European Economic Community, **1**:272, 311, 345, **3**:872

European Free Trade Association (EFTA), **1**:272, **3**:872

European Management Forum (EMF), **3**:922

European Monetary Union (EMU), **1**:86, **2**:655

European System of Central Banks (ESCB), **1**:270–271

European Union (EU), 1:271–272, 276, **3**:850

  creation of, **1**:20

  Germany's central role in, **1**:341, 342

  headquarters, **1**:86

  membership, **1**:18, 56, 201, 264, 272, 301, 341, 355, **2**:429, 448, **515, 627–629**, 655, **3**:778, 854

  states with formal associations with, **1**:30, 272, **2**:579

European Union Commission for Competition, **1**:163

Evans, Peter, **1**:201

Event Study, **2**:524

evolution, **3**:795–796

Exchange Rate Mechanism (ERM) of European Monetary System, **3**:873

exchange rates, 1:189, 273–274, 2:425–426

  arbitrage and, **1**:43–44

  Bretton Woods system, *See* **Bretton Woods**

  determinants of, **1**:273

  fixed, **1**:45–46, 273–274, 349

  floating, **1**:274

  interest-rate parity theory of, **1**:273

  pegged, **1**:49

  purchasing power theory of, **1**:273

  target zone, **2**:467

excise taxes, **3**:826

"Existence of a Competitive Equilibrium for a Competitive Economy," **1**:193

expected utility theory, **2**:717

export and import, 1:274–276

  economic development and, **1**:276

  globalization, *See* **globalization**

  Leontief's Paradox, **2**:485

  quotas, *See* **quotas**

  by Roman Empire, **3**:849

  specialized, **1**:275, **3**:850

  tariffs, *See* **tariff**

  U.S. economic growth and, **3**:876

  See also **free trade**

externalities, 1:277–278

  arguments against privatization and, **2**:667

  Coase Theorem, *See* Coase Theorem

  defined, **1**:277

  environment and, **3**:820

  equilibrium theory and, **1**:263

  in health care markets, **2**:372

  negative and positive, **1**:277

  non-pecuniary, **1**:277

  pecuniary, **1**:277

  role of the government and, **1**:277–278, **2**:686–687

Exxon Corp., **1**:78, **2**:622, **3**:792

ExxonMobil, 1:248, 278–279

Fabian, Tibor, **2**:530

Fabianism, **2**:381

Factor Price Equalization, **2**:376

Fair, James, **2**:556

Fair Credit Billing Act, **1**:287

Fair Credit Reporting Act, **1**:287

Fair Deal, **2**:478, 491

Fair Debt Collection Practices Act, **1**:287

Fair Labor Standards Act, **2**:594, **3**:817

Fairbanks, Douglas, **3**:925

Faisal, King of Saudi Arabia, **2**:619

Faiz, Faiz Ahmed, **3**:837

family limited partnership, **2**:637

Faneuil, Peter, 1:281–282

Faneuil Hall, **1**:281–282

Fannie Mae, 1:282, 2:389

Fanon, Frantz, **1:**8, **3:**837, 838
Faraday, Michael, **2:**414
Fargo, William, **3:**915
Farley, James, **1:**14
Farm Security Administration, **2:**594
fascism, 1:282–285
in Italy, **1:**282–83, 284, **2:**434
Fast Food Nation (Schlosser), **3:**758
"fast track" trade authority, **1:**317
Fatal Conceit, The (Hayek), **1:**264–265
Fay, C. N., **1:**175
Fazzari, Steven, **2:**557
Federacion Internationale de Football, **3:**785–786
Federal Coal Mine Health and Safety Act, **2:**555
Federal Communications Commission (FCC), **2:**593
Federal Deposit Insurance Corporation (FDIC), **1:**73, **2:**491, 537,
    592
    creation of, **1:**79, 298
Federal Deposit Insurance Corporation Improvement Act (FDICIA),
    1:73
Federal Emergency Relief Administration, **2:**592
Federal Express, **3:**882
Federal Farm Board, **2:**387
federal funds rate, **1:**71, **2:**566, 567
Federal Home Loan Bank (FHLB), **2:**389, 390
Federal Housing Administration (FHA), **2:**389, 390
    creation of, **2:**593
Federal National Mortgage Association, *See* **Fannie Mae**
Federal Open Market Committee (FOMC), **2:**567
Federal Reserve, 1:285–286, 356
    Board of Governors, **1:**286
    chairmen of, *See names of individuals, e.g.* **Greenspan, Alan;**
        Volcker, Paul A.
    discount rate, **1:**126, 208–209, 285, **2:**567
    district banks, **1:**285
    federal funds rate, **1:**71, **2:**566, 567
    housing and, **2:**391
    monetary policy and, **1:**285, 302, **2:**565–567, **3:**880, 924
    regulatory powers over member banks, **1:**73
    reserve requirements, **1:**75–76, 126, **2:**565–566, 567
    Wilson and, **3:**918, 924
Federal Reserve Act of 1913, **1:**209, 285, **3:**918, 924
Federal Savings and Loan Associations, **2:**390
Federal Savings and Loan Insurance Corporation (FSLIC), **1:**74
Federal Savings and Loan Insurance Fund, **2:**392
Federal Trade Commission (FTC), 1:36, **286–288, 3:**883
    conglomerates and, **1:**162–163
    creation of, **3:**918
    enforcement powers, **1:**286, 287–288
    structure of, **1:**286–287
Federal Trade Commission Act of 1914, **1:**36, 286, 287
federalism, 1:288–289, 3:875
    George Washington and, **3:**913–914
Federalist Papers, **1:**199, 289, **2:**364, 513
Federici, Silvia, **1:**141

Female Society for Birmingham, **3:**763
fetishism of commodities, **1:**19
feudalism, 1:10, 11, 198, **289–291, 2:**394–395, 479
    contemporary, **1:**290–291
    described, **1:**290
    as economic system, **1:**290
Fiat, 1:291, 338
Field, Sally, **1:**293
Fillmore, Millard, 1:292
film and film industry, 1:292–294
    distribution strategies, **1:**212, 294
filter rule, **2:**524
finance, 1:294–297
    academic research in field of, **1:**297
    arbitrage and, **1:**44
    asymmetric information and, **1:**295–297
    direct, **1:**295, 296
    financial institutions, *See* **financial institutions**
    financial markets, **1:**294, 295
    indicators of economic development, **1:**295
    indirect, **1:**295, 296, 297
    risk traders, **1:**297
Finance Accounting Standards Board (FASB), **1:**2, 4
financial accounting, *See* **accounting**
Financial Accounting Standards Board (FASB), **1:**339
Financial Innovations and Market Volatility (Merton), **2:**553
financial institutions, 1:294, 295, 296, **297–299**
    balancing of demands for credit with their available funds,
        1:298
    depository, **1:**298, **299**
    federal regulation of, **1:**298–299
    non-depository, **1:**298, **299**
    reflexivity in financial markets, **3:**776–777
    See also banking
financial liberalization, **1:**49
financial market theory, **3:**754–755
Financial Services Modernization Act of 1999, **1:**73, 80, 298–299
financial statements, 1:300
    accounting information and, **1:**1–4
    audit of, **1:**53–54
Financial Times, **2:**474
Findlay, R., **2:**418
Finland, 1:300–301
Firm, the Market, and the Law, The (Coase), **2:**630
First Boston (CSFB), **1:**185
First Maroon War, **3:**762
first-price sealed auction, **3:**771
fiscal policy, 1:246, **301–302, 3:**772–773, 816
    to end recessions, **2:**704
    interaction with monetary policy, **1:**301–302
    Mundell-Fleming model, **2:**579
Fisher, Berto, **3:**936
Fisher, Irving, 1:231, **302–303, 2:**431
    interest theory, **1:**92, 112–113, 303
    quantity theory of money and, **1:**303, **2:**562

Fisk, James, Jr., **1:**303, **3:**877
    railroad stock manipulation, **1:**303, 353, **2:**578, **3:**893
Fitzgerald, F. Scott, **3:**894
Five-Dollar Day, **1:**59, 63
Flagler, Henry M., **2:**720, **3:**792
FLN (Front de Liberatíon Nationale), **1:**18
Flood, Curt, **1:**37–38
Flood, James, **2:**556
Fogel, Robert, **1:**129, 303–304, **2:**609
    on railroad and capitalist development, **2:**698
football, **3:**786
Ford, Bill, Jr., **1:**305
Ford, Edsel, **1:**306, 307
Ford, Gerald R., 1:102, 305, 356, **2:**703, **3:**880
Ford, Henry, 1:59, 60, 63, 304, **306–307, 2:**414, 611, **3:**831, 917
Ford, Henry, II, **1:**307
Ford Motor Company, 1:59–63, **304–305,** 306–307, **3:**831
Fordney-McCumber tariff of 1922, **1:**316
forecast, 1:307
    errors, **1:**307
foreign-exchange market, **1:**43–44
    See also exchange rates
Fortis, 1:308
forwards, **2:**487
Foss, Murray, **1:**237–238
Foucault, Michael, **3:**774
Foundations of Economic Analysis (Samuelson), **1:**231, **3:**735
Fourteen Point, **3:**918
Fox, Vincente, **2:**547, 583, 642
fractional-reserve banking, **1:**76, 126
Fragment on Government (Bentham), **1:**227
France, **1:**309–311, **3:**837
    central bank, **1:**69–70
    colonialism, **1:**147, 309–310, **3:**902
    de Gaulle's Free French resistance movement, **1:**192
    Hundred Years' War, **2:**394–395
    import-substitution strategy, **1:**276
    Indochina and, **3:**903
    liberalism in, **2:**490
    mercantilism, **1:**145, **2:**540, 541–542
    nationalization in, **1:**311, **2:**588
    privatization in, **2:**667
    railroads in, **1:**310, **2:**696–697
    Suez Canal crisis and, **3:**812
    World War II, **3:**928, 929
France Telecom, 1:308–309
franchising, 1:312–313, **3:**765
Franco, Francisco, **3:**779, 807
Frank, Andre Gunder, **1:**201
Franklin, Benjamin, 1:5, 28, **314–315, 2:**414, 685
    Autobiography, **1:**199, 314
    postal system and, **3:**881
Frankston, Bob, **1:**160
Franz Ferdinand, Archduke, **3:**924
Freame, John, **1:**82

Freddie Mac, **1:**282, **2:**389
free trade, 1:314–318
    absolute advantage, **1:**82, 155, 275
    agreements to promote, *See individual agreements, e.g.* **NAFTA (North American Free Trade Agreement)**
    autarky and, **1:**58
    classical economists and, **1:**315–316, **3:**849
    comparative advantage, *See* **comparative advantage**
    democracy and, **1:**199–200
    in early 20th century, **1:**316, 345
    "fast track" trade authority, **1:**317
    future of, **1:**317–318
    GATT, *See* **General Agreement on Tariffs and Trade (GATT)**
    history of debate over, **1:**275
    Smith on, **1:**315, 316, **3:**770, 849
    See also **export and import**
Free Trade Area of the Americas, (FTAA), **2:**581, 583, **3:**813
Free Trade Commission, **2:**581
Freeman, Christopher, **1:**204
free-rider problem, **2:**687, 689, **3:**808
French and Indian War, **1:**26, 147, **3:**914
French East India Company, **1:**222
French Revolution, 1:309, 310, **318–319, 2:**490, **3:**914
    Burke's opposition to, **1:**101, 164
French West Indies, **2:**542
Freud, Sigmund, **2:**490
Frick, Henry Clay, 1:119–120, **319, 2:**539
Friedman, David, 2:492
Friedman, Milton, 1:320–321, 347, **2:**469, 553
    Chicago School and, **1:**320**1:**129, **2:**462, **3:**850
    competition theory, **1:**159
    as critic of Keynesian economics, **2:**458, 459, 511
    on disagreements about public policy, **1:**267
    on homo economicus, **2:**384
    as libertarian, **1:**320, **2:**492
    monetarism and, **1:**129, 247, 320, **2:**562, 563, 565, **3:**850
    Reagan economic policy and, **2:**456
    school vouchers, **1:**239
    on Stigler, **3:**796
fringe benefits, *See* **employee benefits**
Frisch, Ragnar, 1:321, **3:**842
"From Containment to Enlargement," **2:**628
Fugger family in Augsburg, **1:**154
Fugitive Slave Act, **1:**141, 292, **2:**649
Fujitsu Limited, 1:322
Full Employment and Balanced Growth Act of 1978, **1:**183
Fulton, Robert, **2:**415, **3:**892
functions of money, 1:322–323, **2:**567
Fundamental Analysis, **2:**524
fur trade, **1:**51, 110
Further Considerations concerning Raising the Value of Money (Locke), **2:**503
futures, **1:**205–206, 297, **2:**487
    trading of, **1:**128–129

G7 Summit, 1:325, 326
G8 Summit, 1:325–326
GAAP, *See* Generally Accepted Accounting Principles (GAAP)
Gadsden Purchase, 2:649
Galbraith, John Kenneth, 1:327–328, 2:604
    on business cycle, 1:105
    on consumer behavior, 1:169, 327
    on inflation, 1:328
Gallegos, Romulo, 3:895
Gamble, James, 2:669
Gamble, James Norris, 2:669
gambling and lotteries, 1:328–330
game theory, 1:231, 330–332, 2:411
    anatomy of a game, 1:330–331
    bargaining problem, 1:332
    complete information games, 1:331
    constant-sum game, 1:331
    cooperative games, 1:331
    economic applications of, 1:332
    games with coalition formation, 1:331–332
    incomplete information games, 2:368–369
    Nash's contribution to, 1:330–332, 2:368, 411, 586–587, 3:748
    non-cooperative, 2:411, 586–587
    oligopoly and, 2:620–621
    Prisoners' Dilemma game, 1:331
    Selten's contributions to, 1:339, 3:748
    zero-sum game, 1:330–331
Gandhi, M. K., 3:837, 838
gangsters, 1:332–333
    Prohibition and, 2:499
Garfield, Harry A., 3:925
Garfield, James A., 1:18, 47, 333–334
Garment, Leonard, 1:356
Garner, John Nance, 2:447
Garn-St. Germain Act, 1:73
Gates, Bill, Jr., 1:52, 160, 334–335, 2:549, 550
Gates, Henry Louis, Jr., 1:8
GATT, *See* General Agreement on Tariffs and Trade (GATT)
Gay, Paul du, 2:530
GDP, *See* gross domestic product (GDP)
Gehrig, Lou, 3:785
G8 Summit, 1:110
Geisst, Charles, 1:29
Gelderlen, J. van, 1:204
General Agreement on Tariffs and Trade (GATT), 1:276, 316–317, 335–337, 2:427, 520–521, 3:922–923
    creation of, 3:850
    members of, 2:547
    Uruguay round, 1:276, 317, 325, 335, 336, 2:693, 3:850, 923
    See also World Trade Organization (WTO)
General Competitive Analysis (Arrow and Han), 1:47
General Electric, 1:337
general equilibrium, *See* equilibrium, general
General Mills, 1:312

General Motors, 1:59–63, 293, 306–307, 338–339, 3:868
    Fiat and, 1:291, 338
General Motors Acceptance Corporation, 1:60
general partnership, 2:636
General Theory of Employment, Interest, and Money (Keynes), 1:230, 246, 2:456, 457, 509, 569, 580, 3:740
Generally Accepted Accounting Principles (GAAP), 1:2, 3, 4, 339–340, 2:405–406
    accounting scandals of early 2000s, 1:340
    audits and, 1:53, 54, 340
    development of, 1:339
    GAAP hierarchy, 1:339
Genesis of Capitalism, The (Sombart), 2:685
Geneva Accord of 1954, 3:902
George, King of England, 1:281
Georgia, 1:341
German Historical School, 1:57
Germany, 1:296, 341–344, 2:474
    Austria and, 1:56
    Bismarck's contributions to, 1:87–88
    central bank, 1:344
    European Union and, 1:341, 342
    hyperinflation in, 1:83, 2:415–416
    National Socialist, 1:235, 283–285, 341, 3:927–930
    post-war occupation of, 1:241
    privatization in, 2:667
    reparations, 1:311, 2:456, 539, 3:926
    reunification of, 1:342
    stock exchanges, 1:342–343
    Thirty Years' War and, 3:839–840
    Weimar Republic, 1:341
    World War I, 3:918, 924, 926
    See also East Germany; West Germany
Getty Oil, 1:127
Ghandi, Mohandas, 2:408
Ghosn, Carlo, 2:602
GI Bill, 2:594, 3:879
Giannini, A. P., 1:66–67
Gibbons, Thomas, 3:892
Gibbons v. Ogden, 3:892
Gibrat's Law of Proportionate Effect, 3:766
Giddens, Anthony, 3:772
Giffen goods, 1:351
Gilded Age, 1:119, 3:878, 120
Gilligan, James Patrick, 1:29
Gin Act of 1736, 2:498
Gini coefficient, 2:402
Giolitti, Giovanni, 2:434
Gladstone, William, 1:234
glasnost, 1:352, 3:864
Glass-Steagall Act, 1:73, 74, 79, 80, 137, 2:449, 577, 592
Global Leaders for Tomorrow, 3:922
global warming, *See* climate change
globalization, 1:344–348, 2:399–400, 468
    Conference of Montreal and, 1:162

globalization (cont'd)
    cultural hegemony and, 1:33–34, 212, 313, 346
    early, 1:345
    G8 summits and, 1:325, 326
    International Monetary Fund and, 2:426–427
    "McDonald-ization of society," 1:313
    modern, 1:345–346
    underground economy and, 3:860
    of venture capital, 3:898–899
    Washington consensus, 1:345, 346, 2:668, 3:798
    See also **anti-globalization**
Globalization: The Destruction of Growth and Employment (Allais), 1:20
Glorious Revolution, 2:477, 489–490
GNP, *See* **gross national product (GNP)**
Goddard, John, 3:806
Goethe, Johann Wolfgang von, 2:551
gold rush, 1:349, 2:413, 555, 3:892, 915
gold standard, 1:334, 348–349, 356, 2:537
    benefit of, 1:348–349
    Bretton Woods, *See* **Bretton Woods**
    history of, 1:97, 164, 348, 349
    J. P. Morgan and, 2:578
    Nixon's actions removing the U.S. from the, 1:98, 214, 274, 349,
        2:440, 3:934
    placed on hold during World War I, 1:349, 2:537
    yen and, 3:934
Goldberger, Arthur, 2:460
Goldwater, Barry, 1:165, 321, 2:448, 703
Golf of Tonkin Resolution, 3:903
Gomery, Douglas, 1:153, 212, 293
Gómez, Juan Vicente, 2:617
Gompers, Samuel, 3:867
Goodrich, Carter, 2:698
goods, 1:349–351
    capital, 1:350–351
    complementary, 1:351
    consumer, 1:350–351
    defined, 1:349
    economic value of, 1:349
    Giffen, 1:351
    public, *See* **public goods**
    substitutes, 1:351
    See also **services**
Gorbachev, Mikhail, 1:102, 341, 351–352, 2:835
    collapse of Soviet Union and, 1:352, 2:396, 3:864, 865
Gordon, Robert J., 1:352–353
Gospel of Wealth and Other Timely Essays, The (Carnegie), 1:119, 164
Gould, Jay, 1:353, 3:807, 877
    railroad stock manipulation, 2:578, 3:893
Gould, Thomas, 1:82
Gournay, Vincent de, 2:691
government:
    aid to airlines, 1:14–15
    Asian developmental states and, 1:48–49
    classical economic theory on functions of, 1:226
    federalism, 1:288–289
    fiscal policy, *See* **fiscal policy**
    monetary policy, *See* **monetary policy**
    monopolies run by, 2:573
    regulation, *See* **regulation**
    Spencer's belief about role of, 3:782
    See also **public;** public finance; public goods; public policy; **state**
Governmental Accounting Standards Board (GASB), 1:2, 4
Grameen Bank in Bangladesh, 3:860
Gramm, Phil, 1:356
Gramm-Leach-Bliley Financial Services Modernization Act, 1:287, 2:449
Gramm-Rudman-Hollings Act, 1:302
Gramsci, Antonio, 2:377–378, 3:789
Grant, Ulysses S., 1:23, 47, 334, 354, 2:596
Great Depression of 1873-96, 1:204–205
Great Depression of 1930s, 1:45, 105, 204, 205, 227, 244–245, 286,
    303, 2:491, 509, 3:926
    auto industry and, 1:60–61
    conditions leading to World War II, 3:927
    failure of laissez-faire economics, 2:479
    Hoover's presidency during, 2:386, 387–388, 878–879, 3:926
    housing policy, 2:390–391
    New Deal and, *See* **New Deal**
    tariffs and, 2:317
    World War II government spending and end of, 3:879
Great Illusion, The (Angell), 1:30–31
Great Railway Strike of 1877, 2:369, 370
Great Society, 2:448, 479, 491, 3:904
Greece, 1:354–355
    ancient, 1:116, 198, 267, 354–355, 3:785, 793
    Truman Doctrine and, 3:853
Green, Bill, 2:555
Green Consumer, The (Elkington et al.), 1:167
Greenhouse effect, *See* climate change
Greenspan, Alan, 1:183, 286, 356
Greg, William, 1:234
Greifeld, Robert, 2:586
Grenada, island of, 3:880
Grenville, Lord, 3:763
Griffiths, Sir Percival, 2:398
gross domestic product (GDP), 1:356–358
    Asian financial crisis and, 1:49
    definition of, 1:356–357
    factors adversely affecting the accuracy of, 1:358
    gap between actual and potential, *See* **Okun's Law**
    as imperfect measure of economic well-being, 1:357–358
    measurement of, 1:357, 359–360
    nominal vs. real, 1:357, 360
gross national income (GNI), *See* **gross national product (GNP)**
gross national product (GNP), 1:358–360, 2:401
    per capita, 2:401
Grossman, Michael, 2:371

Growenewegen, Peter, 2:533
growth, 1:360–361
  Denison's contributions to understanding, 1:200
  endogenous growth theory, 2:361
  Harrod-Domar Growth Theory, 1:360, 2:368, 3:775
  Solow on, 1:360, 3:775
Growth and Welfare in the American Past (North), 2:609
Guam, 2:517, 537, 3:780
Guang Xu, Emperor, 1:134
Guback, Thomas, 1:152, 294
Guiteau, Charles, 1:334
Guitry, Sacha, 1:293
Gulf Oil, 1:127, 2:618, 622
Gunter, Edmund, 1:160
Guomindang (GMD), 1:134, 3:824

Haavelmo, Trygve, 2:363
Habitat for Humanity, 1:124
Habre, Hissen, 2:461
Habsburg family, 3:839, 840
Hailes, Julie, 1:167
Haiti, 1:143, 3:763, 918
Hall, Stewart, 2:530
Hamilton, Alexander, 1:164, 199, 2:364
  Federalist Papers and, 1:289, 364, 2:513
  government involvement in the economy and, 1:164, 2:364, 478, 574, 3:875
  industrialization and, 2:413, 3:875
  protection of infant industries, 1:155
  as secretary of the treasury, 1:5, 2:364, 449, 3:875, 914
Han, F., 1:47
Hancock, John, 2:365–366
Hand, Billings Learned, 1:36
Hanover Bank, 2:449
Hanseatic League, 1:153
Hansen, Alvin, 2:457, 3:791
Hanushek, Eric, 1:239
Harberger Triangles, 2:619
Hardiman, Joseph, 2:584
Harding, Warren G., 1:174, 175, 2:366–367, 387, 539, 725
Harkness, Stephen, 2:720, 3:792
Harrington, James, 1:186
Harris, Jonatham M., 1:121
Harrison, Benjamin, 1:142
Harrison, William Henry, 2:367, 517, 537, 3:855, 891
Harrod, Sir Roy F., 1:360, 2:367–368, 3:884
Harrod-Domar Growth Theory, 1:360, 2:368, 3:775
Harsanyi, John, 1:330, 2:368–369, 3:748
Hart-Scott Rodino Act amendments to the Clayton Antitrust Act, 1:288, 3:883
Hawaii, U.S. annexation of, 2:517, 537
Hawkins, Sir John, 2:541
Hawley-Smoot Tariff, 1:316, 2:387
Hawtrey, R. G., 2:568
Hay, John, 2:537

Hayek, Friedrich August von, 1:58, 129, 171, 2:369, 492, 540, 558, 568, 580
  business cycles and, 1:57, 2:369
  on central planning, 3:782
  on competition, 1:158–159
  on consumer behavior, 1:169
  on decentralized decision-making of the entrepreneur, 1:260, 261
  "extended order," 1:265
  The Fatal Conceit, 1:264–265
  on knowledge, 1:158–159
  on profit, 2:681
Hayes, Rutherford B., 1:47, 334, 2:369–370, 537
Haymarket Square, strikers rally at, 3:807
Hazlitt, Henry, 2:370–371
Head Start Program, 3:879
health, 2:371–374
  Canadian health care system, 1:111
  failures in health care markets, 2:372–373
  globalization and, 1:346
  socioeconomic status and, 2:371–372, 401
  special populations, policy for, 2:374
  tobacco and, 3:843–844
health insurance, 2:372–374
  managed care, 2:373
  RAND Health Insurance Experiment (HIE), 2:373–374, 423
  universal, 2:372–373, 423
health maintenance organizations (HMOs), 1:217, 2:374
Hearst, George, 2:556
Hearst, William Randolph, 1:293, 2:556
Heart of Darkness (Conrad), 2:625
Heath, Edward, 3:835
Heavily Indebted Poor Countries (HIPC) initiative, 2:385
Heckman, James, 2:375, 535
  on educational expenditure and earnings, 1:239
Hecksher, Eli, 2:375–376
  Ohlin and, 2:613, 614
Hecksher-Ohlin Factor Endowment Theory, 2:614
Hecksher-Ohlin-Samuelson theorem, 1:275
hedonistic theory of value, 3:883–884
Hee, Park Chung, 2:465
Hegel, Georg W. F., 1:19, 2:376–377
hegemony, 2:377–378
Heidenheimer, Arnold, 1:176
Heilbroner, Robert, 3:894
Henderson, David R., 1:47
Henry, Patrick, 2:513, 574
Hepburn Act, 2:728
Hernandez Galicia, Joaquin "La Quina," 2:547
Hertz Corporation, 1:304
Hewlett, William, 2:379
Hewlett-Packard, 1:160, 2:379
Heyrick, Elizabeth, 3:763
Hichcock, F., 2:452
Hichcock Transportation Problem, 2:452

Hicks, Sir John R., **1:**46, 168, 231, **2:**379–380, 452
  IS-LM model, **2:**379, 457, 458, 509
  theory of strikes, **3:**806
Hidden Persuaders: What Makes Us Buy, Believe, and Even Vote the Way We Do, The (Packard), **2:**526
Hideki, Tojo, **3:**928
"High Price of Bullion, A Proof of the Depreciation of Bank Notes, The," **2:**715
Higher Learning in America (Veblen), **3:**895
highways, building of interstate, **2:**391, **3:**879
Hikmat, Nazim, **3:**837
Hill, T. P., **3:**751
Himmelfarb, Gertrude, **2:**532
Hirschmann, Albert, **2:**575
Hirst, F. W., **1:**234
History and Critique of Interest Theories (Böhm-Bawerk), **1:**57
History of Britain Under the House of Stuart (Hume), **2:**393
History of Economic Analysis (Schumpeter), **3:**744
History of Fascism (Payne), **1:**284
History of the Railroads of the United States and Canada, The, **3:**791
Hitachi, Ltd., 2:380–381
Hitler, Adolf, **1:**283–285, 341, **2:**376, **3:**779, 786, 905, 927
  German economy and, **3:**927–928
  Lebensraum and, **1:**285
  as military strategist, **3:**928
Ho Chi Minh, **3:**837, 902, 903
Hobbes, Thomas, **1:**164, 226, **2:**489, **3:**793
Hobsbawm, Eric, **2:**397
Hobson, John Atkinson, 2:381–382
hockey, **3:**787
Hodgskin, Thomas, 1:234, **2:**382
Hodgson, Geoffrey, **1:**261
Hodson, Harry, **1:**235
Hogg, Sarah, **1:**235
Holderlin, Friedrich, **2:**376
Holland, *See* **Netherlands, the**
Hollywood blacklist, **3:**879
Holt, Douglas, **1:**166, 167
Holy Roman Empire, **3:**839, 840
Home Depot, 2:383
Home Loan Bank Board (FHLB), **2:**390
Home Owner's Loan Corporation (HOLC), **2:**390, 537
Homestead Act of 1862, **3:**877
homo economicus, 2:383–384, 522, **3:**756
Honda Motor Company, Ltd., 1:48, 61, 62, **2:**384, 440
Honduras, 2:385
Hong Kong, 2:385–386
  export-promotion strategy, **1:**276
Hoover, Herbert, 1:14, 175, 333, **2:**386–388, 539, 726
  early political career, **2:**386–387
  as Food Administrator in World War I, **2:**386–387, **3:**925
  Great Depression and, **2:**386, 387–388, 390, **3:**878–879, 926
Hopkins, Mark, **2:**556
Hopper, Admiral Grace Murray, **1:**160

housing, **1:**62, **2:**388–392
  the Fed's influence on, **2:**391
  history, **2:**389–391
  nature of the market, **2:**389
  secondary mortgage market, **1:**282, 389
  suburbia's creation, **2:**391
Houthakker, Henrik, **1:**250
Howe, Elias, **2:**413
Howitt, P., **2:**419
HSBC Holding, 2:392
Hu Jintao, **2:**445
Hubbard, Gardiner, **1:**52
HubCo, 2:633
Hudson Bay Company, **1:**51, 110, 154
Hudson River Railroad (HRRR), **3:**892–893
Hughes, Charles Evans, **3:**918
Hughes, Howard, **1:**15
Hughes Aircraft, **1:**63
Hull, Cordell, **2:**588
Human Action (Mises), **1:**57, **2:**558
Human Capital (Becker), **1:**85
Hume, David, 1:86, **2:**392–394, 503, 567
Humphrey, Hubert H., **2:**448, 602, **3:**903
Hundred Years' War, 2:394–395
Hungary, 2:395–396, 474
  hyperinflation in, **2:**416
Huntington, Collis P., **2:**556
Huntington, Samuel, **2:**628
Husayn, Sharif, **1:**41
Hussein, King of Jordan, **2:**448
Hussein, Saddam, **1:**102, 348, **2:**448, 462, 643
Hussey, Obed, **2:**413
Hwan, Chun Doo, **2:**465
HypoVereinsbank (HVB Group), 2:396
Hyundai Group, **1:**48

IBM, **1:**37, 160, **2:**379
  antitrust case against, **1:**37, 160, 163
  personal computing and, **1:**161
Ibn Saud, King, **2:**618
Ibuka, Masaru, **2:**440, **3:**776
Ideas for a Science of Good Government... (Cooper), **1:**176
Identity Theft Assumption and Deterrence Act of 1998, **1:**287
Illinois Power, **1:**219
Immediate not Gradual Abolition, **3:**763
immigration, **3:**878
impeachment, **2:**446
imperialism, 2:397–401
  development of capitalism and, **2:**398–400
  Disraeli's policy of, **1:**210
  dynamics of growth and inequality, **2:**397–398
  future challenges, **2:**400–401
  Hobson's theory of, **2:**381
  See also **colonialism**
Imperialism: A Study (Hobson), **2:**381

import substitution industrialization, **1:**157, **3:**875

imports, *See* **export and import**

Impossibility Theorem, **1:**47

In Quest of an Economic Discipline, Part 1, Pure Economics (Allais), **1:**20

In the American Grain (Williams), **1:**314

INCO, **1:**110

income, 2:401–403

classes of, **2:**401

international view of income per capita, **2:**401–402

measuring inequality of, **2:**402–403

redistribution of, **1:**47, **2:**706

technological change and growth of per capita, **3:**829

income distribution theories, 2:403–405

income statement, 1:3, 300, **2:405–406**

income taxes, **3:**826–827, 918

16th Amendment, **3:**823

Incomes from Independent Professional Practice (Friedman and Kuznets), **1:**321

incorporation, 2:406–407

See also **corporations**

indenture system, **2:**394–395, **3:**761–762

Independent Auditor's Report, **1:**4

Independent Treasury System (Sub-Treasury), **3:**891

Index of Leading Economic Indicators, **3:**791–792

India, **2:**407–409, **3:**837

British East India Company, *See* **East India Company, British**

information technology in, **2:**409

mercantilism in, **2:**408, 543

nationalization in, **2:**588

non-alignment, **2:**604, 605

indifference curve analysis, **1:**196, 197, **3:**885

Indochina, **3:**904, 928

Indonesia, 2:409–410

non-alignment policy, **2:**605, 606

industrial organization, 2:410–411

Stigler's work on, **3:**796, 797

Industrial Organization Workshop, **3:**797

Industrial Revolution, 1:12, **2:411–415**, 490, **3:**761

in Belgium, **1:**86

early stages of, **2:**412–413, **3:**866

information revolution compared to, **2:**417–418

new industrial workers, **2:**414–415

in the New World, **2:**413–414

railroads and, **2:**696

trade and, **3:**849

in United Kingdom, **2:**412, 696, **3:**761, 774, 849, 866, 869–871

Industrial Workers of the World (IWW), **3:**867

inequality, **1:**266

globalization and, **1:**346–347

imperialism and, **2:**397–398

Kuznets' U hypothesis, **2:**469–470

measuring income inequality, **2:**402–403

poverty's dynamics and, **2:**656–657

social security and, **3:**774

inflation, **1:**96, **2:**415–416, **3:**880

business cycle and, **1:**106

Galbraith on, **1:**328

hyperinflation, **1:**83, **2:**415–416

OPEC and, **1:**62

productivity and, **2:**680

unemployment and, *See* **Phillips curve**

"Influence of Foreign Trade on the Distribution of Income, The, **2:**376, 614

information:

asymmetric, *See* **asymmetric information**

cost of, *See* **cost of information**

incomplete information games, **2:**368–369

market for, **1:**181

perfect, **1:**179–180

problems, **1:**180–181

revolution, *See* **information revolution**

Information Economics, **2:**369

information revolution, 2:399–400, 416–419

income differences among nations and, **2:**418

Industrial Revolution compared to, **2:**417–418

nature of information, **2:**418–419

new economy and, **2:**417

potential costs, **2:**419

See also **computers; technology**

ING Group, **2:**419

initial public offerings (IPOs), **1:**77, **3:**802, 898, 899

Initiative for Public Dialogue, **3:**798

input-output theory, **2:**485, 486

insider trading, 1:176, **2:420–421**, 524

installment credit, **1:**60, 72, 184

Institute Aerotechnique, **1:**14

Institute of Liberty and Democracy (ILD), **1:**206

Institutional Change and American Economic Growth (North and Davis), **2:**609–610

institutional investors, **3:**804

Institutionalism, **3:**894

Institutions, Institutional Change, and Economic Performance (North), **2:**610

insurance, 1:50, 63, 64, **2:421–423**

adverse selection in, **1:**299, **2:**422–423

moral hazard, **1:**299, **2:**373, 422–423, 575–576

See also individual companies

Intel, **1:**34, **3:**896

intellectual property rights, **1:**11–12, **3:**923

copyright, **3:**776

patents, *See* **patents**

Inter-American Development Bank (IDB), 2:423–424

interchange parts, **2:**413, 414

interchangeable parts, **3:**831, 917

Interdisciplinary Center for Experimental Science (ICES), George Mason University, **3:**771

interest rate, 1:194, **2:424–425**

arbitrage, **1:**43

Böhm-Bawerk's theory, **1:**92

interest rate (cont'd)
  equilibrium, **2:**424–425
  Fisher's theory, **1:**92, 112–113, 303
  interest-rate parity theory of exchange rates, **1:**273
  in Islamic banking, **2:**430–432
  marginal utility and, **1:**57
  monetary policy, *See* **monetary policy**
  swaps, **1:**206
  Turgot's interest theory, **3:**854
International Accounting Standards (IAS), **1:**2
International Accounting Standards Board, **1:**2
International Accounting Standards Committee (ISAC), **1:**2
International Air Transport Association, **1:**16
International Assurance Company, **1:**25
International Bank for Reconstruction and Development, **2:**457, **3:**921
International Business Machines, *See* IBM
International Center for the Settlement of Investment Disputes (ICSID), **2:**581, 582, **3:**921
International Criminal Court, **1:**348
International Development Association (IDA), **2:**599, **3:**921
International Economic Review, **2:**460
International Federation of Accountants (IFAC), **1:**2
International Finance Corporation (IFC), **2:**669, **3:**921
International Labor Organization, **3:**859, 860
International Monetary Fund (IMF), 1:336, 345, **2:**425–427, 448, 456
  anti-globalization protests, **1:**32, 35, **2:**475
  Britain's loan from, **3:**872
  creation of, **1:**97, 274, **2:**316, 457, **3:**850
  globalization and, **2:**426–427
  loan conditions, **1:**346, **2:**399
  Mexican debt crises and, **2:**546–547, 617
  Nigeria and, **2:**599
  Pakistan's disputes with, **2:**633
  Peru and, **2:**644
  purposes of, **1:**274, **2:**425
  Stiglitz's criticism of, **3:**798
  structural adjustment program, **1:**346, **2:**475
International Paper, **1:**256
International Petroleum Company, **2:**644
international trade, *See* **export and import**
International Trade Centre (ITC), 2:427
International Trade Organization (ITO), **1:**336
International Workingmen's Association, **2:**473
Internet, 1:38–39, 161–162
"Interregional and International Trade," **2:**614
Interstate Commerce Act, **1:**142, **3:**878
Interstate Commerce Commission, **2:**728, **3:**823–824, 874, 878
Interstate Highway Act of 1956, **3:**879
intra-industry trade in differentiated products, theoretic explanation of, **2:**467
Introduction to the Principles of Morals and Legislation, An (Bentham), **1:**86, **3:**884
investment:
  accounting information and, **1:**1
  cash flow information and, **1:**125
  corruption's effect on, **1:**177
  reaction of investors to bad news, **1:**50
Investment Advisors Act of 1940, **3:**745
Investment Bankers Association of America, **3:**896
investment banking, 1:76–80, 299, **3:**801–802
  consumer banking distinguished from, **1:**74
  history of, **1:**79–80
  initial public offerings (IPOs), **1:**77, **3:**802
  leveraged buyouts, **1:**78
  mergers and acquisitions, **1:**77–78
  private placements, **1:**77
  regulation of services of, **1:**77
  role of, **1:**76
  securitization, **1:**78
  venture capital funds, **1:**77
  See also **commercial banking; consumer banking;** *individual investment banks*
Investment Company Act of 1940, **3:**745
invisible hand, **1:**144, 159, 230, 277
  Nozick on, **3:**794
  as Smith's concept, **1:**227, 267, 315, **2:**393, 686, **3:**769
Invisible Man (Ellison), **1:**8
IPOs, *see* initial public offerings (IPOs)
Iran, 2:427–428, 588
  hostage crisis, **1:**124, **2:**703, **3:**880
  -Iraq War, **2:**619, 622
  oil exports, **1:**95, **2:**428, 619
  Iran-Contra Affair, **1:**102
Iraq, 2:428–429, 618
  -Iran War, **2:**619, 622
  Persian Gulf War, **1:**102, **2:**428, 468, 619, 622, **642–643,** **3:**880
  War on Terrorism and, **1:**104, 215, 348, **3:**880
Ireland, 2:429–430, 835
  Disraeli's policies and, **1:**210
Irish National Land League, **1:**210
iron industry, **1:**176, **2:**412, **3:**878
iron law of wages, *See* **Ricardo, David,** iron law of wages
Irving, Julius, **3:**787
Islam, **1:**40–43
  Hajj, **3:**736, 846
  view of gambling, **1:**330
Islamic banking, 2:430–432, **3:**736
Islamic fundamentalists, **1:**104, 124
Island, The, **1:**293
IS-LM model, **2:**379, 457, 458, 509, **509–510**
Israel, 2:432–433
  Balfour declaration, **2:**432, 634
  Camp David peace accord, **1:**123
  Six-Day War of 1967, **3:**811, 812
  Suez Canal crisis and, **3:**812
  Yom Kippur War, **1:**62, **2:**432–433, 448, 619, 622
Isuzu, **1:**62, 338
Italy, 1:50, 147, **2:**433–435**

banking in, 2:433–434, 435

export-led growth policies, 1:276

fascism in, 1:282–83, 284, 2:434

Italian Republic, 2:434–435

World War II, 3:929

Iwai, Bunsuke, 2:602

Iwai & Company, 2:602

J. P. Morgan Chase & Co., 1:79, 2:449, 578

Jackson, Andrew, 1:6, 2:367, 437–438, 482, 513, 3:891, 913

Tyler and, 3:855

Jackson, Thomas P., 1:37

Jacobs, David, 1:29

Jacobs, Jane, 1:265

James, C. L. R., 1:141, 3:837

James I, King of England, 1:252, 3:849

Japan, 1:296, 2:438–441

aggression against China, 1:134, 147, 3:928

as Asian developmental state, 1:48–49

birth of capitalism in, 2:438–439

central bank, See Bank of Japan

complacency in, 2:440–441

Gentleman's Agreement, 2:728

Hiroshima and Nagasaki, 3:852

import-substitution strategy, 1:276

Indochina occupation by, 3:902, 928

Manchuria invaded by, 2:388

Meiji restoration, 2:438, 3:933

Ministry of International Trade and Industry (MITI), 1:48, 2:440

nationalism in the 1930s, 2:439–440

Nikkei Stock Average, 2:599–600

oil imports, 2:618, 619

Pearl Harbor, See Pearl Harbor

Perry's mission to open trade relations with, 1:292

personal savings rate in, 3:738

protection of infant industries, 1:156

rapid growth of 1950s to early 1970s, 2:440

Russo-Japanese War, 2:728, 729

systemic crisis and challenges for, 2:441

U.S. occupation and postwar recovery, 2:439–440, 507–508

World War II, 1:84, 2:439, 618, 726, 3:927–929, 934

yen, 3:933–934

Jarvie, Ian, 1:294

Jay, Douglas, 1:235

Jay, John, 1:5, 289, 2:513

Jay Treaty of 1794, 3:913, 914

JDS Uniphase, 1:110

Jefferson, Thomas, 1:5, 199, 2:364, 442–443, 477–478, 481, 490, 3:914

agrarian democracy and, 3:850, 875

Embargo Act of 1807 and, 3:913

Louisiana Purchase, 2:443, 513, 574

Jellinek, Georg, 2:685

Jenkins, Simon, 2:462

Jevons, William Stanley, 1:57, 245, 2:383–384, 444, 540

marginal utility theory of value, 1:228, 231, 3:890

Jiang Zemin, 2:444–445

Joanne, Adolph, 2:697

Job Corps, 3:879

Jobs, Steve, 2:445–446

Johnson, Andrew, 1:292, 354, 2:446, 497

Johnson, Earvin "Magic, " 3:787

Johnson, George E., 3:806

Johnson, Lyndon B., 1:327, 2:446–448

economic policy, 2:448, 476, 478, 491, 3:879–880, 904

Vietnam War and, 2:447, 448, 491, 3:879, 902–903, 904

Johnson, Ross, 1:256

joint ventures, 1:33

joint-stock companies, 3:784, 800

Jones, C., 2:419

Jones, Edward D., 3:910

Jones, Homer, 1:320

Jordan, 2:448

Jordan, Hamilton, 1:144

Jordan, Michael, 3:787

Journal of Economic History, 2:609

Journal of Law and Economics, 1:144

Journal of Political Economy, 3:771, 797

Juan Carlos I, King of Spain, 3:779

Juárez, Benito, 2:546

Julius Caesar, 2:722

Jungle, The (Sinclair), 3:757–758

junk bonds, 1:78

Kahn, Alfred, 3:757

Kahn, Richard, 3:804

Kahneman, Daniel, 2:384, 451, 3:771

Kang Youwei, 1:134

Kangas, Steve, 1:129

Kansas-Nebraska Act, 1:22, 2:649

Kantorovich, Leonid, 2:451–452, 463

Karr, Herb, 2:530

Karzai, Hamid, 1:7

Kaufman, Henry, 3:905

Kautsky, Karl, 2:506, 626

keiretsu, 1:48

Keller, Kevin Lane, 2:674

Kellner, Douglas, 1:312

Kelly, William, 2:412

Kelly Act of 1925, 1:14

Kennedy, Edward, 1:124, 2:455

Kennedy, John F., 1:142, 327, 2:453–454, 455, 476, 602, 604, 3:880

assassination of, 1:305, 2:447, 448, 453, 454, 597

foreign policy, 2:453–454, 3:879, 902

Kennedy, Joseph P., 2:454–455, 593

Kennedy, Robert, 3:903

Kennedy, Scott, 1:121

Kent State University, 3:903

Kenya, 2:455–456

Key, Francis Scott, **3**:913

Keynes, John Maynard, 1:94, 171, **2**:368, 456–457, 479, 563, **3**:908
    on business cycles, **1**:106
    capital theory, **1**:113
    Economic Consequences of Peace, **1**:234
    General Theory of Employment, Interest, and Money, See Gen-
        eral Theory of Employment, Interest, and Money (Keynes)
    Hobson's influence on, **2**:381
    Mises' writings and, **2**:558
    origins of macroeconomics, **1**:227, **2**:509
    Say's Law and, **3**:739, 740, 815–816
    social security and, **3**:773
    Sraffa and, **3**:789
    Stone and, **3**:804
    on tariffs, **1**:316
Keynesian Cross Model, Samuelson's, **2**:457–458
Keynesian economics, 1:230, **2**:425, 457–460, 475–476, 687–688,
    705, 706, **3**:850, 908
    background, **2**:457
    Cambridge Keynesians, **1**:231
    on causes of depression, **1**:204
    employment theory, **1**:246
    neo-Keynesians, **2**:457–458, **3**:775
    New-Keynesians, **1**:129, **2**:459
    post-Keynesians, **2**:459, 705, 706
Keynesian Revolution, The (Klein), **2**:460
Khan, Abdul Ghaffar, **3**:837
Khatami, Mohammed, **2**:428
Khmer Rouge, **1**:109
Khomeini, Ayatollah, **1**:124
Khrushchev, Nikita, **2**:454
Kierkegaard, Soren, **2**:490
Kildall, Gary, **1**:161
Kilgore, Bernard "Barney," **1**:215, **3**:910
Kim Chong-il, **2**:465
Kim Dae-Jung, **2**:465
Kim Il Sung, **2**:463
Kim Young Sam, **2**:465
King, Martin Luther, Jr., **3**:837–838, 903
Kingsbury Commitment of 1913, **1**:52
Kipling, Rudyard, **2**:625
Kirchner, Israel M., **1**:58
Kirk, Russell, **1**:165
Kissinger, Henry, **1**:132, **3**:904
Kitchin, Joseph, **1**:204
Kleberg, Richard M., **2**:447
Klein, Lawrence, 2:363, 460–461, **3**:842
kleptocracy, 2:461–462
Knight, Anne, **3**:763
Knight, Frank H., 1:129, **2**:462–463, **3**:797
    on entrepreneurial activity, **1**:259–260
    on perfect competition, **1**:158
    theory of profit, **2**:462, 682
Knights of Labor, **3**:867
Kohlberg, Kravis, Roberts, & Company (KKR), **1**:78

Kolakowski, Leszek, **1**:139
Kolko, Gabriel, **1**:117
Koltikoff, Lauren, **3**:737
Komansky, David H., **2**:544
Kondratiev, N. D., **1**:204
Koopmans, Tjalling, 1:47, **2**:452, 463
Koopmans' Theorem, **2**:463
Korea, *See* Korean War; North Korea; South Korea
Korean War, **1**:242, **2**:447, 464, 465, 508, **3**:824, 853, 879
Kornilov, General Lavr, **2**:732
Korry, Edward, **1**:132
Kosovo, **3**:880
Kotler, Philip, **2**:672
Kraft Foods, **1**:21
Kramers, Hans, **2**:463
Kroger, 2:466–467
Kroger, Henry "Barney," **2**:466
Krueger, Anne, **2**:693
Krugman, Paul, 2:467–468
Kuttner, Robert, **1**:129
Kuwait, 1:102, **2**:468, 622, 643
Kuznets, Simon, 1:30, 204, 321, 357, **2**:469–470, 561
Kyoto Protocol, **1**:348
Kyu, Choi, **2**:465

labor:
    Industrial Revolution, *See* **Industrial Revolution**
    labor, 2:401, 403, 470–475
    alienation from, **1**:19, **3**:920
    anti-globalization and, **1**:32–33
    child, **1**:267–268, **2**:412, **3**:762
    employee benefits, **1**:243–244
    films about, **1**:293
    market, **1**:17
    NAFTA opposed by, **2**:582, 583
    poverty and, **2**:656, 657
    productivity of, *See* **productivity**
    Senior's ideas on long work hours and, **3**:749
    signaling theory, **1**:238, **3**:780–781
    Smith on, **1**:227, 350, 360, **2**:472, **3**:769–770, 830, 908
    socialist, **2**:473–474, **3**:774–775
    specialization of, **1**:10, **3**:830
    strikes, *See* **strikes**
    Taft-Hartley Act, *See* Taft-Hartley Act
    technological change and nature of, **3**:830
    trade unions, *See* **unions**
    unfair practices, **1**:13, 33
    value of, **1**:111, 228, 350, **2**:472–473, 503, **3**:890, 891, 908, 920
    women in the labor movement, **2**:414
    work as a theoretic concept, **2**:471–472
    See also **worker**
Labor Defended Against the Claim of Capital (Hodgskin), **2**:382
Laffer, Arthur, **1**:175, **2**:475
Laffer curve, 2:475–476, **3**:816
lagging economic indicators, **1**:226

laissez-faire, 2:388, 476–479, 691, 705
  Bastiat as proponent of, 1:83–84
  distortions of, 2:478
  Hamilton's rejection of, 2:364
  in Japan, 2:439
  Jeffersonian capitalism, 2:443
  Knight's views on, 2:462
  libertarian view of capitalism, 2:292
  Locke's philosophy, 2:477, 705
  physiocracy and, 2:648
  politics and, 1:164, 165, 2:478–479
  Smith as proponent of, 2:477, 686, 3:849
Laissez-Faire: Pro and Con (Knight), 2:463
Lake, Anthony, 2:628
Lancaster, Kelvin, 1:169
land, 2:401, 403, 479–482
  historical role in rise of capitalism, 2:479–482
  private property, *See* private property
Land Grant Act of 1850, 3:876
Landauer, Carl, 1:283
Landry, Peter, 2:376
Landsburg, Steven, 2:518
Lang, Fritz, 1:293
Las Vegas, Nevada, gambling in, 1:330
Latin America:
  features of feudalism in, 1:290, 291
  globalization and, 1:347
  import-substitution strategy in, 1:275
  See also individual countries
Latin America: Underdevelopment or Revolution (Frank), 1:201
Latin American Free Trade Association (LAFTA), 3:837
Latin American Integration Association (LAIA), 1:276, 2:644
Lattimer Massacre of 1897, 2:554
Latvia, 2:483
Law, John, 1:94
law of one price, 1:43, 44
Layton, Walter, 1:235
Le Duan, 3:901
Le Duc Tho, 3:904
Le Play, Frédéric, 1:250
leading economic indicators, 1:225, 226
League of Nations, 1:31, 335, 345, 2:448, 539, 3:918, 926
Lebensraum, 1:285
Lebow, Victor, 1:166
Lee, Robert E., 1:23, 354, 2:497
Leguia y Salcedo, Augusto, 2:644
leisure, value of, 3:889–890
Leland, Henry M., 1:338
Lend-Lease, 2:726, 3:928, 929, 930
Lenin, Vladimir, 2:483–485, 588, 732–733, 3:775, 864
Leo XIII, Pope, 3:893
Leonardo, Alex, 2:386
Leontief, Wassily, 1:262, 2:485–486, 3:775
Lester, Normand, 1:110
Lever Brothers, 3:863

Lever Food and Fuel Control Act, 3:925
leverage, 2:486–487
  in futures markets, 1:206
leveraged buyouts, 1:78, 3:896
Leviathan (Hobbes), 3:793
Levin, Joshua, 3:787
Levitan, R., 2:6212
Levitt, Arthur, Jr., 2:585
Levy, Philip, 1:58
Lewinsky, Monica, 1:144
Lewis, Sir Arthur, 1:742, 2:487–489, 3:810
Lewis, John L., 2:555, 3:868
liabilities, 1:3, 300
liberalism, 1:45, 2:489–491
  early American, 2:490
  in England, 2:489–491, 3:849
  French, 2:490
  Locke's philosophy, 1:266, 2:489–490, 502, 705, 3:919
  political, 2:491
  Wealth of Nations as expression of, 1:266, 3:769
Liberia, 2:491–492
libertarian, 2:492–493
Libya, 2:434, 493, 619, 835
licensees, 1:312
Liebknecht, Karl, 2:506
Liechtenstein, 2:493–494
life insurance, 1:299
light bulb, invention of electric, 2:414
limited liability partnership, 2:637, 638
limited partnership, 2:637, 638
Lin, Cindy, 3:894
Lin Zexu, 2:623, 624
Lincoln, Abraham, 2:494–497
  assassination of, 2:446, 497
  -Douglas debates, 2:495
  economic policy, 2:478
  Emancipation Proclamation, 2:496–497
  Reconstruction plans, 2:497
  secession and Civil War, 1:22, 23, 24, 99, 292, 354, 2:495–496
  on slavery, 2:494, 495–497
Lindbeck, Assar, 3:755
Lindbergh, Charles, 1:14, 15
Lindhal, E., 1:57
Lintner, John, 2:530
Lipper, Kenneth, 1:293
Lipset, Seymour Martin, 2:686
liquidity preference theory, 2:563
liquor, 2:497–501
  advertising, 2:500
  bootlegging, 2:499
  Prohibition, *See* Prohibition
  taxes on, 2:498, 500
Lithuania, 2:501
Livingston, Robert, 3:892
Lloyd, Henry Demarest, 2:501–502

Lloyd, Mary, **3**:763

Lloyd George, David, **2**:491, **3**:926

lobbying, **1**:257

local exchange trading systems (LETS), **2**:519

Lochner v. New York, **1**:174

Locke, John, 1:199, **2**:442, **502–504**

    classical economic theory and, **1**:226

    Glorious Revolution, **2**:477, 489–490

    laissez-faire philosophy, **2**:477, 705

    liberalism and, **1**:266, **2**:489–490, **2**:502, 705, **3**:919

    social contract, **3**:793

    theory of property, **1**:226, **2**:489–490, 503–504

Lockheed, **1**:13, 14, 15

Lodge, Henry Cabot, **3**:918

logic of action, **1**:57

Logic of Scientific Discovery, The (Popper), **1**:57

London Interbank Offer Rate (LIBOR), **1**:71

London Naval Conference of 1930, **2**:387–388

London School of Economics, **2**:379–380

London Working Men's Association, **3**:866

Long-Term Capital Management, **3**:742

López Portillo, José, **2**:546, 642

Lorenzo the Magnificent, **2**:508, 509

lotteries, *See* **gambling and lotteries**

Lotus, **3**:896

Louis XVI, King of France, **1**:318

Louisiana Purchase, **1**:22, **2**:443, 513

LTV, **1**:81, **3**:766

Lucas, Robert, 1:129, **2**:504–505, 562

    endogenous growth theory, **2**:361

    rational expectations hypothesis, **1**:247, **2**:458–459, 504

Lucent Technologies, **1**:53

Luddites, **3**:830

Ludlow Massacre of 1914, **2**:554

Lufthansa, **1**:13, 14–15

Lusitania, **3**:918

Luther, Martin, **2**:684, 685

Luxembourg, 2:505

Luxemburg, Rosa, 2:505–506

Maastricht Treaty, **1**:68, 271

MacArthur, Douglas, 2:507–508, **3**:853

Macartney, Lord George, **2**:623

Macaulay, Lord Thomas Babington, **2**:625

Machad, Garado, **1**:15

Machiavelli, Niccolo, 2:508–509

Machlup, Fritz, **1**:58, **2**:558

MacIntyre, Alasdair, **1**:265, 267

Mackay, R. W. G., **3**:872

Mackey, John, **2**:556

Macrae, Huigh, **1**:256

macroeconomics, 2:509–512

    coining the term, **1**:321

    dynamic disequilibrium approach to, **2**:511

    Keynes and origins of, **1**:227, **2**:509

    Klein's macroeconomic models, **2**:460–461

    microeconomics compared to, **2**:548–549

    modern or new classical, *See* new classical or modern economics

    monetarist counterrevolution of the 1970s, **2**:510–511

    in post-World War II years, **2**:509–510

Macroeconomics: A Neoclassical Introduction (Merton), **2**:553

Madero, Francisco L., **2**:546

Madison, James, 1:5, **2**:442, 443, 512–514, **3**:914

    Federalist Papers and, **1**:199, 289, **2**:513

    War of 1812 and, **3**:913

Maeda, Terunobu, **2**:559

Mafia, **1**:332

Maine (battleship), **2**:517, 537, **3**:780

Major, John, **3**:873

Major League Baseball (MLB), **1**:37–38, **3**:786–787

Makower, Joel, **1**:167

Malaysia, 2:514

Malaysian Federation, **3**:759

Malcolm X, **1**:8, **3**:836, 837

Malta, 2:515

Malthus, Thomas Robert, 1:227, **2**:515, 666, 705, 715

    general glut controversy, **3**:739

    on inadequacy of aggregate demand, **2**:515

    on population growth and food supply, **1**:120, 227, 360, **2**:515, 533, 554, 710, **3**:810

    on scarce resources, **2**:515, 554, 706, **3**:919

    on wages, **3**:908

    on workers, **3**:919

Man Versus the State (Spencer), **3**:782

management reports, **1**:2

managerial accounting, **1**:2

Manchuria, **2**:388

Mandel, Ernest, **1**:204, **2**:398

Mandela, Nelson, **2**:605, **3**:837, 838

Mandeville, Bernard, **2**:402

Manhattan Project, **3**:852

manifest destiny, 2:516–517, 654

Manjunath, Pendakur, **1**:294

Manne, Alan S., **2**:530

Mann-Elkins Act, **3**:823–824

manorial system, *See* **feudalism**

Manpower Development and Training Act of 1962, **2**:453, 680

Manufacturers Hanover Trust Company, **2**:449

Mao Zedong, **1**:134–135, **3**:837, 838–839

Marathon Oil Company, **1**:248

Marconi, Guglielmo, **2**:414

Marcos, Ferdinand, **2**:462

Marcus, Bernard, **2**:383

Marcuse, Herbert, 2:517–518

Margarine Unie, **3**:863

marginal analysis, 1:169, **2**:518–519

marginal productivity, **1**:231

    theory of income distribution, **2**:403–405

Marginal Rate of Substitution (MRS), **3**:886

marginal revenue, **2**:368

marginal utility, **1:**56–58, 196–197, **2:**540, **3:**885, 886–887, 890, 915
  principle of diminishing, **2:**444
  theory of value, **1:**228, 231, **2:**540
market, **1:**229, **2:**519–523
  barter and local exchange trading systems, *See* **barter**
  capitalism's relationship to, **2:**523
  in cyberspace, **2:**520
  free trade, *See* **free trade**
  global, **2:**519–520
  interaction with other social processes, **2:**521
  political boundaries and, **2:**520–521
  in theory and in practice, **2:**522
market efficiency, 2:523–525
"Market for 'Lemons': Qualitative Uncertainty and the Market
  Mechanism," **1:**180
market power, 2:525–526
marketing, 2:526–530
  of drugs, **1:**218
  of entertainment, media, and culture, **2:**529
  ethical issues, **2:**528
  history of, **2:**527
  institutional advertising and, **2:**528
  new economy, **2:**528–529
  opposing concepts of, **2:**526–527
  of people, **2:**529
  of services that cannot be advertised, **2:**528–529
  strategies of persuasion, **2:**527–528
marking to market, **1:**206
Markowitz, Harry M., 1:44, **2:**530, 552, **3:**754, 755
Marquez, Gabriel Garcia, **3:**837
Marschak, Jacob, **1:**46
Marschak, Thomas, **2:**530
Marshall, Alfred, 2:384, 410, 532–533, 551, **3:**749
  contributions to neoclassical economics, **1:**231, 232
  demand and supply ("scissors") model, **1:**231, 262
  Principles of Economics (Marshall), **1:**251, **2:**532, 533
  quasi-rent, **2:**681
  on regional policy promoting endogenous development, **3:**765
  on Herbert Spencer, **3:**781
Marshall, George C., **2:**531, 532
Marshall Plan, 1:97, 291, **2:**531–532, **3:**850, 853, 930
  attacks on, **2:**371
Martin, Glenn, **1:**15
Martin, William McChesney, Jr., **2:**597
Marx, Karl, 1:310, **2:**382, 473, 478, 490, 533–535, 625
  alienation and, **1:**19, **3:**920
  Capital, See Capital (Marx)
  Communist Manifesto, **1:**139, 251, 345, **2:**473, 478, 533, 534,
    535, **3:**829, 920
  on consumerism, **1:**166
  on exploitation of workers, **3:**919–920
  on feudalism, **1:**290
  principle of self-emancipation, **3:**775
  on root causes of war, **1:**30
  Senior's ideas on long work hours and, **3:**749

on social production, **2:**678
socialism and, **3:**774–775
on wages, **3:**908
Marxian economic theory, 1:228–229, **2:**403, 522, 533–535, 705,
  706, **3:**741
  autonomist tradition of, **1:**141
  on capital, **1:**111–112
  disproportionality theories, **1:**229
  fascists and, **1:**283–284
  hegemony and, **2:**378
  of income distribution, **2:**403, 404
  on labor and labor power, **1:**228, 350, **2:**471–473, 534, **3:**890,
    920
  on private property, **1:**232
  on profit, **1:**229, **2:**681
  Ricardo's influence on, **2:**715
  on social security, **3:**773
  surplus value, **1:**228, 251, 258, **2:**404, 534, **3:**810, 841
  transformation problem, **1:**228
  underconsumptionist theories, **1:**229
Mary Queen of Scots, **1:**252
Masayoshi, Matsukata, **3:**934
Mass Strike, the Political Party, and Trade Unions, The (Luxem-
  burg), **2:**506
MasterCard, **3:**916
matching concept in accounting, **1:**3, **2:**405–406
materialism, **1:**266
materiality, **1:**54
Mathematical Investigations in the Theory of Value and Prices
  (Fisher), **1:**303
*Mathematical Method of Production Planning and Organization,
  The* (Kantorovich), **2:**452
Mathematical Theories of Social Classes (Walras), **3:**912
Matsunaga, Yasuzaemon, **2:**439
Matsushita, Konosuke, **2:**535
Matsushita Electrical Works, 2:535
Mauchly, John, **1:**160
Maupassant, Guy de, **2:**697
Max Havelaar: The Coffee Auctions of the Dutch Trading Company,
  2:410
Maximilian of Hapsburg, **2:**546
Mayer, Colin, **3:**899
Mayer, Martin, **1:**29
Mazui, Ali, **1:**40
MCA, **2:**500
McCarthy, Joseph, **1:**165, 242, **3:**879
McColl, Hugh, **1:**67
McCormick, Cyrus, **2:**413
McCormick, Edward R., **1:**29
McCormick, Edward T., **1:**29
McDonald, Ramsay, **2:**491
McDonald's, **1:**312–313
McDonnell Douglas, **1:**91
McFadden, Daniel L., 2:535–536
McFadden Act of 1927, **1:**73

McGovern, George, **2:**603

McGraw-Hill, **3:**792

MCI, **3:**930–931

McKesson, John, **2:**536

McKesson Corporation, 2:536–537

McKinley, William, 1:142, 164, **2:**537–538, 727, **3:**780

McNary Waters Act of 1930, **1:**14

McRoberts, Kenneth, **1:**110

Meade, James, **2:**614, **3:**804

Meadows, Donella, **2:**554

Means, Gardiner C., **1:**87

Measurement of Consumers' Expenditure and Behaviour in the United Kingdom, The (Stone), **3:**804

Meat Inspection Act, **2:**728

Mechanics' Union of Trade Associations, **3:**867

Mecherle, George J., **3:**794

Medicaid, **3:**879

Medicare, **3:**879

Medici, Cosimo De, 2:538

Medici family, **1:**154

Meeker, Mary, **2:**586

Megginson, William L., **3:**899

Mehfouz, Nagib, **3:**837

Mellon, Andrew, 1:175, **2:**538–539

Mencken, H. L., **2:**371

Menem, Carlos S., **1:**45–46

Menger, Anton, **2:**539–540

Menger, Carl, 2:539–540, 567, 671

    disequilibrium economics and, **1:**263

    marginal utility theory of value, **1:**57, 228, 231, **2:**540, **3:**890

Mennon, Krishna, **2:**604

Mensch, Gerhard, **1:**204

Mensheviks, **2:**484, 733, **3:**864

mercantilism, **2:**489, 540–543, 705, **3:**784–785

    British, **2:**477, 480, 481, 540, **3:**849

    Colbert and, *See* **Colbert, Jean-Baptiste**

    as form of political capitalism, **1:**118

    Hecksher's work in, **2:**375–376

    India's economic system, **2:**408, 543

    Smith's views on, **1:**199, 227, 275, 315, **2:**686, 705

Mercedes-Benz, **1:**62, 63

Merchant Adventureres Company of London, **1:**153

Merck, Frederic Jacob, **2:**543

Merck & Company, 1:31–32, **2:**543

Mercosur, **1:**45, 276

mergers and acquisitions, **1:**77–78

    antitrust efforts, *See* **antitrust**

    premerger notification filings, **1:**288

    See also **conglomerate**; *individual companies, e.g.* **AOL Time Warner; ExxonMobil**

Meriwether, John, **3:**742

Merrill Lynch, 1:78, **2:**543–544

Merton, Robert C., 1:205, **2:**544–545, **3:**741, 742

    See also Black-Merton-Scholes stock option pricing formula

Merton Miller on Derivatives (Miller), **2:**553

Mesopotamia, **1:**114–115

Methods of Ethics (Mill), **3:**884

Metro, 2:545

Metro-Goldwyn-Mayer, **1:**293

Metropolis, **1:**293

Mexican-American War of 1848, **1:**5, 22, 354, **2:**482, 516, 546, 654

    Lincoln's opposition to, **2:**495

    Taylor and, **3:**828–829

Mexico, 2:424, 545–547, **3:**918

    debt crises, **1:**195, **2:**546–547, 617

    hyperinflation in, **2:**416

    NAFTA and, **2:**547, 581–583, **3:**850

    oil in, **2:**546, 616–617, 642

    Pemex, **2:**642

    Revolution in, **2:**546, 588, 616

Michaud, Yves, **3:**804

microeconomics, 2:458, 547–549

    coining the term, **1:**321

    extension of its methods to other disciplines, **2:**548

    individual behavior, **2:**547–548

    interaction and aggregate behavior, **2:**548

    macroeconomics compared to, **2:**548–549

    as normative science, **2:**548

Microsoft, 1:160, 161, 334–335, **2:**445, 549–550

    Justice Department suit against, **1:**37–38, 161, **2:**525–526, 550

    migration to urban areas, **1:**12

Milken, Michael, **1:**78

Mill, James, **3:**739

Mill, John Stuart, 1:137, **2:**550–552, 715, **3:**749

    classical economic theory and, **1:**227, **2:**478, 490, 551, 705, **3:**849

    on government-provided relief for the poor, **3:**782–783

    Industrial Revolution and, **2:**411

    on patents, **2:**640

    on redistribution of wealth, **2:**551, 706

    on Say's Law, **3:**740

    utilitarianism described by, **3:**883, 884

    wage fund doctrine and, **1:**227, **2:**551–552, **3:**908

    on workers, **3:**919

Miller, Merton H., 1:44, 129, **2:**486, 530, 552–553

Modigliani-Miller theorem, *See* Modigliani-Miller theorem

Miller, Phineas, **3:**917

Miller, Toby, **1:**212

millionaires, **1:**51–52

Mills, James, **2:**382, 550

Minc, Hilary, **2:**653, 654

minimum wage, **2:**453, 665, **3:**817–818

    laws, **1:**173, **2:**660, 661

mining, 2:412, 553–556

    in South Africa, **3:**777, 778

Minsky, Hyman P., 2:556–557

Mints, Lloyd, **1:**320

Mirabeau, Marquis, **2:**648

Mirrlees, James A., 2:557, **3:**901

Mises, Ludwig von, **1:**57, 58, 125, **2:**492, 540, 557–558
on central planning, **3:**782
Mises Institute, **1:**57
Mississippi Bubble, **3:**801
Missouri Compromise, **1:**22, 140, **2:**574, 649
Mitsubishi Motors Corporation, 2:558–559
Mitsui & Company, Ltd., 2:559
Mitterand, François, **1:**311
mixed economies, **1:**58
Mizuho Holdings, 1:191, **2:**559
Mobil Oil, **1:**78, 278, **2:**622, **3:**792
See also **ExxonMobil**
Mobutu Sese Seko, **2:**461, 462
Modern Corporation and Private Property, The (Berle and Means), **1:**87
Modern Times, **1:**293
modernization theory, 1:290, **2:**560–561
Modigliani, Franco, 1:247, **2:**469, 486, 552, **561,** **3:**742
life-cycle theory of saving, **2:**561, **3:**737
Modigliani-Miller theorem, **1:**296, **2:**486, 487, 552, 561
Molasses Act of 1733, **2:**542
"Molly Maguires," **2:**554
Molotov, Vyacheslav, **2:**531
momentum of stock prices, **2:**523–524
Monaco, 2:561–562
monetarism, **2:**511, 562–565
on causes of depression, **1:**204
employment theory, **1:**247
Friedman and, *See* **Friedman, Milton,** monetarism and
Monetary Control Act of 1980, **1:**209
Monetary Equilibrium (Myrdal), **2:**580
monetary policy, 1:20, 246, **2:**565–567
of Bank of England, **1:**68
of Bank of Japan, **1:**70, 71
to end recessions, **2:**704
Federal Reserve actions affecting the money supply, **1:**285, 302, **2:**565–567, **3:**880, 924
interaction with fiscal policy, **1:**301–302
Mises on the money supply, **2:**558
monetary base, **2:**565–566
Mundell-Fleming model, **2:**579
nominal money supply, **2:**565
money, 2:567–570
evolution of theories about, **2:**567–568
functions of, **1:**322–323, **2:**567
Keynesian revolution, **2:**569
quantity theory of, **1:**320, **2:**503, 562, 569
money market mutual funds, **1:**299
Monopolies and Restrictive Practices Commission (Britain), **1:**38
monopoly, **1:**51, **2:**410, 525, 570–573
barriers to entry, **2:**571
benefits of, **2:**572
costs associated with, **2:**571–572
defined, **2:**570

Demarest's view of, **2:**501–502
government-run, **2:**573
natural, **1:**233, **2:**573, 687, 696
See also **antitrust**
Monroe, James, 1:6, **2:**513, 574–575
Monroe Doctrine, **1:**6, 199, **2:**516, 575, 728
Montesquieu, Charles de, 2:442, 575
Moore, Michael, **1:**293
moral hazard, 1:260, 298, **2:**575–576
of bank loans, **1:**296
in health care markets, **2:**373
as information problem, **1:**180–181
in insurance markets, **1:**299, **2:**373, 422–423, 575–576
rescue of large banks, **1:**74
morality, *See* **ethics**
Moran, Bugs, **1:**333
More, Paul Elmer, **1:**165
Morgan, John Pierpont, 1:120, **2:**482, 577–578, 596, **3:**882
rescue of U.S. Treasury, **1:**78, 142, 209, **2:**577, 578
Morgan Stanley, 1:79, **2:**577
Morgan Stanley Dean Witter, **1:**78, 79, **2:**577
Morgenstern, Oskar, **1:**58, 231, 330, **2:**558, 587
Morita, Akio, **3:**776
Morita, Tomijiro, **1:**191
Morocco, 2:578–579
Morris, Robert, **1:**28
Morse, Samuel, **2:**414
mortgage-backed securities, **1:**78
mortgages, **1:**73
interest rates on, **2:**391
secondary mortgage market, **1:**282, 389
Moscovy Company of Russia, **1:**154
Mossin, Jan, **2:**530
Mother Courage and Her Children, **3:**840
Mother Jones, **2:**555
Motion Picture Association of America (MPAA), **1:**293
moving average rule, **2:**524
"Mr. Keynes and the 'Classics'", **2:**458, 509
muckrakers, **2:**502, **3:**757–758
Mugabe, Robert, **3:**935
Muhammad, Elijah, **1:**40
Muhammad, Prophet, **1:**40
Muksoud, Clovis, **1:**40
multicollinearity, **1:**223
Multilateral Investment Guaranty Agency (MIGA), **3:**921
multilateralism, **3:**880
multiple regression model, **1:**223
Mummery, A. F., **2:**381
Mundell, Robert, 2:579
Mundell-Fleming model, **2:**579
Munich Re, 2:580
Murray, Albert, **1:**8, 9
Murray, Charles, **2:**492
Musharraf, General Pervez, **2:**633
Musick, Eddie, **1:**15

Mussolini, Benito, **1:**283–85, 291, **3:**779
Muth, John, **2:**458, 570
mutual funds, **1:**299, **3:**804
mutual savings banks, **1:**74
Myers, Stewart, **3:**742
Myon, Chang, **2:**464–465
Myrdal, Gunnar, 2:568, **2:**580
Mystery of Capital: Why Capitalism Triumphs in the West and Fails Everywhere Else (DeSoto), **1:**206

Nader, Ralph, **1:**61
NAFTA (North American Free Trade Agreement), 1:132, 200, 276, **2:**581–583
    Clinton policy, **1:**143, 317
    effect on trade law, **2:**581–582
    history of, **2:**581
    quotas and, **2:**693–694
    signatories, **1:**111, 317, **2:**547, 581, **3:**850
    treaty provisions, **2:**581
Nanjing Treaty of 1842, **1:**133–134, 147
Napoleon, **1:**44–45, 69, 94
Napoleonic Wars, **1:**96, 147, **3:**913
NASDAQ, 1:29, **2:**583–586, **3:**801, 802, 803
Nash, John, 1:231, **2:**586–587
game theory, **1:**330–332, **2:**368, 411, 586–587, **3:**748
Nash Motors, **1:**61
Nasser, Gamal Abdel, **1:**41, **2:**604, 605–606, **3:**811, 812, 837, 838
Nathan, Robert, **2:**469
Nation, **2:**370
National Academy of Sciences, **3:**901
National Advisory Committee for Aircraft (NACA), **1:**13, 14
National American Woman Suffrage Association (NAWSA), **3:**925
National Association of Securities Dealers Automated Quotation (NASDAQ), *See* **NASDAQ**
National Association of the United Traders for the Protection of Labor, **3:**866
National Basketball Association (NBA), **3:**786, 787
National Bureau of Economic Research, **1:**104, 105, 353, **3:**755
National City Bank, **1:**136–137
National Commission on Social Security Reform, **1:**356
national debt, **1:**48, 129
National Economic Council, **1:**183
National Football League (NFL), **1:**38, **3:**786
National Gallery of Art, **2:**539
National Hockey League (NHL), **3:**786, 787
national income accounts, **3:**804–805
National Industrial Recovery Act (NIRA), **3:**868, 879
National Labor Relations Board (NLRB), **2:**593, 726
National Labor Union, **3:**867
National Liberation Front (NLF), **3:**902
National Observer, **3:**910
National Recovery Act of 1933, **1:**60, **2:**537, 593, 594
National Recovery Administration, **2:**592
National Review, **1:**165
National Science Foundation, **3:**833

National Steel Corporation, **3:**883
National War Labor Board, **2:**726, **3:**868
National Youth Administration, **2:**593, 594
nationalism, fascism and, **1:**283–284, 285
nationalization, 1:311, **2:**587–589, 617, 642, 644
    fascism and, **1:**284
NationsBank, **1:**67
Native Americans, **3:**876
NATO, *See* North Atlantic Treaty Organization (NATO)
Natural and Artificial Right of Property Contrasted, The (Hodgskin), **2:**382
natural gas, **1:**248
Natural Gas Clearinghouse, **1:**219
natural law, **2:**503–504
    physiocracy and, **2:**648, 691
natural monopolies, **1:**233, **2:**573, 687, 696
natural rate hypothesis, **2:**458, 459
Nature and Essence of Theoretical Economics, The (Schumpeter), **3:**743
Nature of the Firm, The (Coase), **1:**144
Nava, Mica, **1:**167
Navigation Acts, **1:**186, 199, **2:**477, 542, **3:**849
Nazism, *See* **Germany,** National Socialist
NCR, **1:**53
Neale, Thomas, **3:**881
NEC, 2:589
Nechyba, Thomas J., **1:**239
Nef, John, **3:**797
Negri, Antonio, **1:**141
Nehru, Jawaharlal, **1:**41, 42, **2:**604, 605, **3:**837, 839
Nelson, Jack L., **1:**239
Nelson, R., **2:**418
neo-Arabism, **1:**42
neoclassical economic theory, 1:229–232
    on competition, **1:**158
    criticism of, **1:**231–232
    on growth, **2:**368
    as historical legacy, **1:**230–231
    as method of economics, **1:**230
    quantity theory of money, *See* quantity theory of money
    as structure of thought, **1:**229–230
    transition from classical economic theory to, **1:**231
    on worker productivity, **1:**244
Neo-institutionalism, **1:**100
Neo-Malthusians, **2:**554
neo-mercantilism, **1:**48–49
Neruda, Pablo, **3:**837
Nestlé, 2:589–590
net income (earnings), **1:**3
net loss, **1:**3
Netherlands, the, 1:147, **2:**590–591, **3:**849
    econometric modeling in, **3:**842
    mercantilism, **2:**540, 541
    "tulip mania" in, **3:**800

Netscape, 1:38, 3:896

Neumann, George R., 3:806

Neummann, John von, 1:231, 330, 2:587

new classical or modern economics, 2:511–512, 562, 3:816

   employment theory, 1:247

   supply side analysis, 3:816

New Deal, 1:14, 36, 60, 2:388, 390, 478, 482, 491, **591–594**

   Keynesian economics and, 2:456

   opponents, 2:370, 462

   phases of, 2:592–594, 726, 3:879

   support of the banking system, 2:588, 592, 726

new economy, 1:161, 353

   dot-com boom and bust, 1:356, 2:585–586, 3:896–897

   information revolution and, 2:417

   marketing and, 2:529–530

New Freedom (Wilson platform), 3:918

New Frontier, 2:478

New Global Partnership for Development (NEPAD), 1:326

New Humanism, 1:165

New Industrial State, The (Galbraith), 1:327

"New Pacifist" movement, 1:30–31

new trade theory, 2:467

New York and Harlem (NY&H) railroad, 3:892, 893

New York Central Railroad, 1:79, 3:893

New York Curb Market, 1:29

New York Stock Exchange (NYSE), 1:28–29, 103, **2:595–597**, 3:801, 802

   history of, 2:595–597, 3:924

New Zealand, **2:597–598**

   privatization in, 2:667

Newcomen, Thomas, 2:415

Newlands Act, 2:728

Newsweek, 2:371

NeXT, 2:445

Nicaragua, 1:102, 2:388, **598–599**, 3:918

Nicholas II, Tsar, 2:484, 729, 732

Nietzsche, Friedrich, 2:490

Nigeria, **2:599**

   black market in, 1:89

Nihon Keizai Shimbun, Inc, 2:600

Nike, 1:33, 3:789

Nikkei, **2:599–600**

Nile River Valley, 1:10

Nippon Life Insurance, **2:600–601**

Nippon Telegraph & Telephone Corporation, **2:601**

Nissan Motor Car Company, **2:601–602**

Nissho Iwai, **2:602**

Nixon, Richard M., 1:211, **2:602–603**

   Bretton Woods fixed-exchange rate system abandoned by, 1:98, 214, 274, 349, 2:440, 3:934

   George H. W. Bush and, 1:102

   China policy, 3:824, 903–904

   foreign policy, 2:602, 3:824, 903–904

   on Keynesian economics, 2:458, 476

   pardon of, 1:305

   presidential elections, 1:165, 241, 321, 356, 2:447, 453, 602, 603, 703, 3:903

   wage and price freeze, 2:603, 3:880

   Watergate scandal, 1:102, 305, 2:603

Nkrumah, Kwame, 2:604, 605, 606, 3:837

Nobel, Ludwig, 2:615

Nobel family, 2:615

Nobel Peace Prize, 1:124, 352, 2:465, 728

Nobel Prize in Economic Sciences, winners of, 1:321, 3:748

Nobel Prize in Economics, winners of:

   George A. Akerlof, 1:17

   Maurice Allais, 1:20

   Norman Angell, 1:30, 31

   Kenneth J. Arrow, 1:46, 2:379

   AT&T Bell Laboratories as home of, 1:52

   Gary Becker, 1:100

   James M. Buchanan, 1:100

   Ronald Coase, 1:100, 144

   Gerard Debreu, 1:193

   Robert Fogel, 1:100, 303

   Milton Friedman, 1:100, 320

   Trygve Haavelmo, 2:363

   Daniel Hahneman, 2:451

   John Harsanyi, 1:330, 2:368

   Friedrich August von Hayek, 1:57, 129, 2:369

   Sir John R. Hicks, 1:46, 2:379

   Leonid Kantorovich, 2:452, 463

   Lawrence Klein, 2:460

   Tjalling Koopmans, 2:452, 463

   Simon Kuznets, 2:469

   Wassily Leontief, 2:485

   Sir Arthur Lewis, 2:488

   Robert E. Lucas, Jr., 2:504

   Harry Markowitz, 1:44, 2:530

   Daniel L. McFadden, 2:535

   James Meade, 2:614

   Robert C. Merton, 2:544, 3:741

   Merton H. Miller, 1:44, 100, 2:552

   James A. Mirrlees, 2:557

   Robert Mundell, 2:579

   Gunnar Myrdal, 2:580

   John Nash, 1:330, 2:586–587

   Douglass North, 2:609

   Bertil Ohlin, 2:376, 613, 614

   Paul A. Samuelson, 3:735

   Myron S. Scholes, 3:741

   Theodore Schultz, 1:100, 2:488, 3:742

   Reinhart Selten, 1:330

   Amartya Sen, 3:748

   William Sharpe, 1:44

   William F. Sharpe, 3:754

   Herbert A. Simon, 3:756

   Vernon L. Smith, 3:771

   Robert Solow, 3:775

   A. Michael Spence, 1:17

Nobel Prize in Economics, winners of (cont'd)
George Stigler, 1:100
George J. Stigler, 3:796
Joseph E. Stiglitz, 1:17, 3:797
Sir Richard Stone, 3:804
Jan Tinbergen, 3:842
James Tobin, 3:844
William Vickrey, 3:900
Leon Walras, 3:911
Nol, Lon, 1:109
non-alignment, 2:603–608
founders of, 2:604–606
key elements in defining, 2:604
milestones, 2:606–607
objectives of, 2:607
origins of the concept, 2:604
primary motivations of, 2:605
role in world politics, 2:607–608
"Non-Cooperative Games," 2:586–587
nonprofit organizations, 2:608–609, 683
Nordhaus, William, 3:735
Noriega, Manuel, 1:102
Norma Rae, 1:293
Nortel Networks, 1:110
North, Douglass, 1:303, 2:609–610, 3:793
North American Commission for Environmental Cooperation, 2:581
North American Development Bank, 2:581
North American Free Trade Agreement, See NAFTA (North American Free Trade Agreement)
North Atlantic Treaty Organization (NATO), 1:241
membership, 1:264, 355, 2:396, 483
North Korea, 2:463–464, 465
See also Korean War
North Vietnam, 3:902–904
See also Vietnam; Vietnam War
Northern Ireland, 2:835
Northern Securities Company, 2:577, 578, 727–728
Northwest Ordinance, 2:482
Norway, 2:610
Norwest, 3:916
Notes on the State of Virginia (Jefferson), 2:477
Novikov, Jacques, 1:30
NOW (negotiable order of withdrawal) accounts, 1:71, 73, 75
Nozick, Robert, 1:266, 2:492, 3:794
nuclear power plants, 1:249
nuclear weapons:
antiballistic missile treaties, 1:348
Intermediate Nuclear Forces (INF) arms limitation treaty, 1:352
SALT II, 1:123
test ban treaties, 2:454
Nusbaum, Aaron F., 3:744
Nye, Joseph, 1:346
NYNEX, 3:900

O'Brien, William, 2:556
occupation, 2:611–613
Oceana (Harrington), 1:186
Odaira, Namihei, 2:380
O'Daniel, W. Lee, 2:447
O'Donnell, Guillermo, 1:201
Office of Management and Budget (OMB), 1:302
Office of Price Administration (OPA), 1:327, 328, 2:663
O'Guinn, Thomas, 1:152
Ohlin, Bertil, 2:376, 613–614
oil, 1:248, 2:614–619
early oil booms in the U.S. and Russia, 2:615–616
in Mexico, 2:546, 616–617, 642
Middle East, 2:617–619
OPEC and the oil shocks, 1:61–62, 204, 205, 2:618–619, 622, 3:772, 880
in Saudi Arabia, 2:618, 3:736–737
in Venezuela, 2:617, 3:895–896
See also individual oil companies
Okun's Law, 2:619–620
Olcott, Charles, 2:536
Olds, Ransom E., 1:59, 60, 338
oligopoly, 1:153, 2:620–621
Cournot's theory of, 1:158, 332, 2:620, 621
game theory and, 2:620–621
in Russia, 2:731
Oliver Twist (Dickens), 3:919
Olympics, 3:785, 786, 788–789
On Liberty (Mill), 2:550
On the Proper Sphere of Government (Spencer), 3:781
On the Spirit of the Laws (Montesquieu), 2:575
Onassis, Aristotle, 1:355
O'Neal, Stanley C., 2:543
One-Dimensional Man (Marcuse), 2:518
O'Neill, Tip, 1:305
OPEC (Organization of Petroleum Exporting Countries), 1:278, 2:618–619, 621–623, 3:837, 895–896
as legal cartel, 1:122
the oil shocks and, 1:61–62, 204, 205, 2:618–619, 622, 3:772, 880
production quotas, 2:468, 692
Saudi Arabia's role in, 3:737
OPEC Fund for International Development, 2:619
open market operations, 1:126, 285, 2:566, 567
"Open Society and Its Enemies, The," 3:776
Open Society Institute, 3:776
operational audit, 1:53
Opium Wars, 1:133, 147, 2:623–624
opportunity cost, 1:57, 83–84, 182, 208
optimorum of market, 2:624
optimum currency, 2:579
option pricing theory, 2:487
options, 1:205, 297, 2:487
options contracts, 1:128, 205, 297
Ordinary Least Squares (OLS), 1:223, 224

Oregon territory, 3:855

Organization for Economic Co-Operation and Development (OECD), **1**:98, 162, **3**:768

Organization of African Unity (OAU), **3**:837

Organization of American States, **3**:813

Organization of Islamic Countries (OIC), **3**:837

Organization of Petroleum Exporting Countries (OPEC), *See* **OPEC (Organization of Petroleum Exporting Countries)**

organized crime, **1**:332–333

Orientalism, 2:625–627

Eurocentrism and, **2**:629

Orlando, Vittorio, **3**:926

Oser, Jacob, **1**:245

Osgood, Samuel, **3**:881

Ostend Manifesto, **1**:99

O'Sullivan, John, **2**:516

Other Path: The Economic Answer to Terrorism, The (DeSoto), **1**:206

Ottawa Conference of 1932, **3**:927, 930

Our Common Future, **3**:819

Outline of the Science of Political Economy, An (Senior), **3**:749

Owen, Robert, **2**:473, **3**:866, 919

Owens, Jesse, **3**:786

owners' equity, **1**:3

ownership, 2:629–631

agency problem, *See* principal-agent problem

economic efficiency and, **2**:630–631

important components of, **2**:629

private or collective, **2**:629–630

truncation by taxation and regulation, **2**:631

Pacific Northwest Pipeline Corporation, **1**:163

pacifism, **1**:30–31

Packard, David, **2**:379

Packard, Vance, **2**:526

Pakistan, 2:633

Palestine, 2:432, 633–634

Palestine Liberation Organization (PLO), **2**:433

Palestinian Arabs, **2**:432–433, 448, 634

Palonsky, Stuart, **1**:239

Pan Am, **1**:15, 16

Pan American Games, **3**:786

Pan Arabism, **2**:605, 606

Panagra, **1**:15

Panama, **1**:102, **2**:728, **3**:880

Panama Canal, 2:415, 634–635, 728

Carter and, **1**:123, **2**:635

pan-Arabism, **1**:41–42

Panch Sheel, **2**:606

Panetta, Leon, **1**:143

Panic of 1837, **2**:367, **3**:891

Panic of 1873, **2**:370, 596

Panic of 1907, **1**:209, 285

Pappas, Doug, **3**:787

Paramount Pictures Corporation, **1**:293

Pareto, Vilfredo, **1**:231, 262, **2**:383, 384, 635–636, **3**:884

Pareto optimality, 1:230, 262, 2:522, 624, 635–636, 710, 3:884

externalities and, **1**:277

Paris stock exchange, **1**:94–95

Parker, Judge Alton B., **2**:728

Parsons, Talcott, **2**:560, 686

partial equilibrium, *See* **equilibrium, partial**

Partido Revolucionario Institucional (PRI), **2**:546, 547

partnerships, 2:636–638

compared to other forms of business organization, **2**:407, 637–638

types of, **2**:636–637

patents, 2:638–642

criteria for, **2**:639–640

drug patent protection, **1**:217–218

duration of, **2**:639

early advocates of, **2**:640–641

on plants, **1**:11–13

productivity and international licensing of, **2**:679

role in research and development, **2**:641–642, **3**:832–833

patronage, **1**:47–48, **3**:881

Payne, Stanley, **1**:284

PDVSA, **2**:617

Peace Corps, **2**:453

Pearl Harbor, **1**:84, **2**:439, 618, 726, **3**:928

Pease, Elizabeth, **3**:763

Peckham, Rufus W., **1**:35–36

Peel, Sir Robert, **1**:210

Pemex, 2:642

Pendergast, Thomas J., **3**:852

Pendleton Act of 1883, **1**:47, 334

Pennsylvania Gazette, **1**:314

Pennzoil, **1**:127

Penrose effect, **3**:767

pension annuities, **1**:299

pension funds, **1**:299, **3**:755

pension plans, individually funded, **3**:738, 774

pension systems, national, **3**:738

Social Security, *See* Social Security

Penzias, A. A., **1**:52

Peoples Natural Gas, **1**:39

Pepsi Cola Enterprises, **1**:312

Pepsi, **1**:211

perestroika, **1**:352, **2**:835

Pérez, Andrés, **2**:617

Pérez Alfonso, Juan Pablo, **2**:619

Perón, Juan D., **1**:45

Perot, Ross, **2**:583

Perry, Commodore, **1**:292

Perry, George L., **1**:17

Persian Gulf War, 1:102, 2:448, 468, 619, 622, 642–643, 3:880

Persian Letters (Montesquieu), **2**:575

Peru, 1:206, 2:643–644

Pétain, Maréchal, **1**:311

Petras, James, **1**:201

Petri, Elio, **1:**293

petro-dollars, **1:**214

Petróleos de Venezuela (PDVSA), See PDVSA

Petróleos Mexicanos (PEMEX), **2:**616, **642**

petroleum, *See* **oil**

Pettinato, Giovanni, **1:**115

Peugeot Citroën, 2:644–645

Pfizer Inc., **1:**78

pharmaceuticals, *See* **drugs**

Phelps, Edmund, **2:**418

Phenomenology of Spirit, The (Hegel), **2:**377

Philadelphia Stock Exchange, **1:**205

Philby, H. A. R. "Kim," **1:**236

Philip Morris, *See* **Altria (Philip Morris)**

Philippines, 2:517, **645, 3:**823

in World War II, **2:**507

Philips, **2:**591

Phillips, A. W., **2:**416, 510, 563, 569–570, 646

Phillips curve, 2:416, 458, 459, 510, 511, 563–564, 569–570, **645–647**

expectations-augmented, **2:**646–647

Gordon's contributions, **1:**353

Phillips-Tosco, **1:**248

Phoenicia, **1:**115–116

physiocrats, 2:477, **647–648,** 705, **3:**739, 849

capital as viewed by, **1:**111

Quesnay's founding and leadership of, *See* **Quesnay, Francois**

Physiology of Industry, The (Hobson and Mummery), **2:**381

Pickett, George, **1:**23

Pickford, Mary, **3:**925

Pierce, Franklin, 1:99, **2:649**

Pigou, A. C., **1:**277, **2:**689

Pinochet, Augusto, **1:**132

Pipes, Richard, **1:**283

Pitt, William, **3:**763

Pixar Animation Studios, **2:**445

planning, 2:649–653

concept of, **2:**649–650

contextual model, **2:**652

information support for, **2:**651–652

instrumental model, **2:**652

the plan, **2:**651

process of, **2:**650–651

rationality of, **2:**650

substantive model, **2:**652

testing, evaluation, and implementation, **2:**651

Plant, Arnold, **1:**144

plant genetic material, **1:**11–13

Plato, **3:**793

Platt, Lewis, **2:**379

Platt Amendment, **1:**186

Plekhanov, Georgi, **2:**483

Poland, 2:474, **653–654, 3:**928

Polisensky, Josef, **3:**840

Polish United Workers' Party (PZPR), **2:**653, 654

Political and Financial Opinions of Peter Cooper, with an Autobiography of His Early Life (Cooper), **1:**176

political capitalism, 1:117–118

Political Discourses (Hume), **2:**393

Political Economy (Hodgskin), **2:**382

Political Economy of Development and Underdevelopment, The (Wilber), **1:**201

Political Economy of Growth, The (Baran), **1:**201

political enterprise, **1:**255, 256–257

Polk, James K., 2:516, 654, **3:828–829**

Pompadour, Madame de, **2:**691

Poor, Henry Varnum, **3:**791

Poor Richard's Almanac, **1:**314

Poor's Publishing Company, **3:**791

Popper, Sir Karl, **1:**57, **3:**776, 820

Popular Political Economy (Hodgskin), **2:**382

population growth:

aggregate demand and, **2:**515

Ehrlich-Simon "Bet, " **3:**757

Malthus's theories, *See* **Malthus, Thomas,** on population growth and food supply

Populists of the 1890s, **2:**478, 502

Porsche, Ferdinand, **3:**905

portfolio employment, **3:**860–861

Portfolio Theory and Capital Market (Sharpe), **3:**755

Portugal, 2:540, 655

Brazil and, **1:**95–96, 147, 219

spice trade, **3:**783, 785

Posher, Edwin, **1:**29

Positive Theory of Capital, The (Bohm-Bawerk), **1:**57, **2:**540

"Post-Mortem on Transition Predictions of National Product, A," **2:**460

Post Office Act of 1792, **3:**881

pound sterling:

as reserve currency, **1:**189, 213

Soros' bet against the, **3:**776

poverty, 2:655–658

absolute, **2:**655–656

demographic characteristics of, **2:**656–657

effects of, **2:**657

G8 summits and, **1:**326

gap, **3:**748

globalization and, **2:**400

policies options, **2:**657–658

relative, **2:**655

Smith on, **1:**266

social welfare programs and, *See* welfare (social programs)

threshold line, **2:**656, **3:**748

See also inequality

predation, **1:**157, 163

preferred stock, **1:**263

Presbyterianism, **1:**252

President's Commission on Privatization of 1988, **3:**882

price, 2:658–661, 3:770

clearing the market, **1:**350, **2:**548

equilibrium, *See* **equilibrium**

Marshall's theory of, **2:**533

Price, Roger, **1:**309, 311

price and distribution theory, **1:**56–58

price ceilings, 2:662, **665, 3:**817

price controls, 2:660, **661–663, 3:**880

costs and benefits of, **2:**662–663

Galbraith on, **1:**328

price ceilings, **2:**662, 665, **3:**817

price floors, **2:**662, 664–665, **3:**817

quality of goods affected by, **2:**662

price differentials, **1:**43–44

price discrimination, 2:663–664

price floors, 2:662, **664–665, 3:**817, 818

Prices and Production (Hayek), **2:**568

primary deficit or surplus, **1:**195

prime rate, **1:**72

Prince, The (Machiavelli), **2:**508–509

Princeton University, **3:**918

principal-agent problem, **1:**181, **2:**631

in insurance markets, **2:**423

principle of diminishing returns, 1:231, **2:**666–667

Ricardo and, **1:**114, **2:**666

Principles of Biology (Spencer), **3:**781

Principles of Economics (Marshall), **2:**532, 533

Principles of Economics (Menger), **1:**57, **2:**539, 540

Principles of Economy (Mill), **2:**706

Principles of Political Economy (Malthus), **2:**515

Principles of Political Economy (Mill), **1:**227, **3:**740

Principles of Political Economy and Taxation (Ricardo), **1:**155, 316, **2:**715, **3:**908

Principles of Political Economy, with Some of Their Applications to Social Philosophy (Mill), **2:**550, 551, 552

Prisoners' Dilemma game, **1:**331

private placements, **1:**77, 267

private property, **1:**265

Locke's theories, **1:**266, **2:**489–490, 503–504

privatization, 2:462, **667–669**

argument against, **2:**667

definitions of, **2:**667

in developing countries, **2:**668–669

ideological arguments for, **2:**667

in United Kingdom, **2:**667, 835, **3:**772

probability theory, **2:**363

Problem of Budgetary Reform, The (Hicks), **2:**380

"Problem of Social Cost, The," **1:**278

Procter, William, **2:**669

Procter & Gamble, 1:163, **2:**669–670

producer surplus, 2:670–671

product, 2:671–676

brands, **2:**674, 675

characteristics, **2:**672–673

classifications, **2:**672

differentiation, **2:**673–674

hierarchy, **2:**673

lines, **2:**675

in macroeconomics, **2:**671, 672

management, **2:**674–676

in microeconomics, **2:**671

proliferation, **2:**675

structure of, **2:**673

product life cycle (PLC), **2:**675

product line extension mergers, **1:**163

production:

individual, **2:**677–678

social, **2:**678–679

Production of Commodities by Means of Commodities, The (Sraffa), **1:**112, 231, **3:**789

production possibilities, 2:676–677

production possibility frontier (PPF), **2:**676–667

productivity, 1:47, **2:**468, **679–680**

Gordon's studies of, **1:**353

marginal productivity theory of income, **2:**403

profit maximization and, **2:**684

in service sector, **3:**753

worker wages and, **1:**244

Professional Golf Association (PGA), **3:**786, 787–788

Profiles in Courage (Kennedy), **2:**453

profit, 1:3, 57, **2:**405, **680–683**

abstinence theory of, **3:**749

Austrian School theory of, **2:**681–682

classical theory of, **2:**681

entrepreneurial approach to, **2:**682–683

gross, **2:**681

Marxian theory of, **1:**229, **2:**681

neoclassical theory of, **2:**681

net, **2:**681

normal, **2:**680

producer surplus, **2:**670–671

super-normal or economic, **2:**680

widely accepted views of, **2:**682–683

profit and loss statement, *See* **income statement**

profit maximization, 2:683–684

roles in capitalist societies of, **2:**684

Progressives, early 20th century, **2:**478, 502, **3:**758, 823–824

Theodore Roosevelt, **2:**596, 727, 728, **3:**823, 824, 918

Woodrow Wilson, **2:**490, 725, **3:**918

Prohibition, **1:**88, 212, 333, **2:**454, 498–499, **3:**918

Promotional Culture (Wernick), **1:**166

property, **1:**267

See also **land**

property insurance, **1:**299

property taxes, **3:**827, 828

prospectus, **1:**77

prosperity, **1:**266

Protestant Ethic and the Spirit of Capitalism, The (Weber), **1:**264, **2:**684–686

Protestant Reformation, **1:**199, 252

Protestantism, 2:684–686

Prussia, **1:**87

PSI, **1:**39

psychology and economic decision-making, **2:**451

public, 2:686–688

public choice theory, **2:**667–668, 688

public finance, **2:**686

public goods, 1:351, **2:**687, **688–689**

    exclusion and club goods, **2:**689

    government provision of, **2:**689

    incentives for private provision of, **2:**689

Public Health Cigarette Smoking Act of 1969, **1:**287

public policy, **2:**687–688

    moral issues and, **1:**267–268

    Senior's views on, **3:**749

    small business and, **3:**767–768

public sector, **2:**686, 688

Public Utility Holding Company Act (PUHCA), **1:**25, **3:**745

Public Works Administration, **2:**491, 537, 593

public works programs:

    fascists and, **1:**284

    federal, **2:**387

Puerto Rico, **2:**517, 537, **3:**780

Purchasing Power of Money, The (Fisher), **1:**303

Purchasing Power Parity (PPP), **1:**44

Pure Food and Drug Act, **2:**728, **3:**757

pure risk-less arbitrage, **1:**43

Puritanism, **1:**314

Qianlong, Manchu Emperor, **2:**623

qualified opinion, auditor's, **1:**53

quantity theory of money, **1:**303, 320, **2:**503, 562, 569

"Quantity Theory of Money: a Restatement," **2:**563

quantum mechanics, **2:**463

quasistatic changes, **3:**796

Quattrone, Frank, **2:**586

Québec, province of, **1:**110, 111

Québécor World, **1:**110

Quesnay, Francois, 2:691–692

    laissez-faire and, **2:**686

    physiocracy and, **2:**647, 648, **691–692**

Quételet, Adolphe, **1:**250

quotas, 1:275–276, **2:**520, **692–694**, **3:**851

    economic, **2:**692

    negative impact on efficiency, **2:**693

    voluntary export restraints (VERs), **3:**851

R. J. Reynolds, **3:**844

Rabin, Yitzhak, **2:**433

Radford, R. A., **2:**567

"rags-to-riches," **1:**17–18, 51–52, **3:**745, 892

railroads, 1:142, 310, **2:**370, **695–699**, **3:**830

    airlines and, **1:**14

    cartel, **1:**121

    debates over who runs the, **2:**696–697

    early, **2:**695–696

    Great Railway Strike of 1877, **2:**369, 370

    indispensability to capitalist development, **2:**697–698

    Industrial Revolution and, **2:**696

    invention of steam engine, **2:**415

    manipulation of railroad stocks, **1:**303, 353, **2:**578, **3:**893

    safety of, **2:**697

    social effects of, **2:**697

    in the 20th century, **2:**698–699

    westward expansion in the U.S. and, **3:**876–877

    See also individual railroads

Railroads and American Economic Growth (Fogel), **1:**304

Railway Labor Act (RLA), **1:**175

Rand, Ayn, 1:356, **2:**492, **699–700**

RAND Health Insurance Experiment (HIE), **2:**373–374, 423

random utility model, **2:**536

random walk, **2:**523

Ransome, Robert, **2:**412

rational choice model, **1:**85

rational expectations hypothesis, **1:**332, **2:**512, 564–565, 570

    Lucas's contribution to, **1:**247, **2:**458–459, 504

    Modigliani's contribution to, **2:**561

rationing, 2:701–702

Rauschning, Hermann, **1:**284

Rayburn, Sam, **2:**447

Re, Jerry, **1:**29

Readers' Digest, **1:**212

Reading "Capital" Politically (Cleaver), **1:**141

Reagan, Ronald, 1:356, **2:702–703**, 704

    conservative movement and, **1:**165

    economic policy, **1:**129, 175, **2:**402, 456, 474, 475, 667, 703, **3:**816

    entry into politics, **2:**703

    foreign policy, **1:**124, **2:**461, 598, 703, 835, **3:**880

    presidential campaigns, **1:**102, 104, 124, 129, 305, **2:**703

real-bills doctrine, **2:**563

reaper, mechanical, **2:**413

recession, 1:105–106, 107, 204, 245, **2:704**

    definitions of, **2:**704

    energy crisis and, **1:**62

    See also **business cycles**

reciprocal purchase agreements, **1:**163

Reconstruction, **1:**292, **2:**370, 497

Reconstruction Finance Corporation (RFC), **2:**387, **3:**767

Reder, Melvin, **3:**806

Reebok International, **3:**789

Reed, John, **3:**775

Rees, William E., **1:**120

Reflections on the Formation and Distribution of Riches (Turgot), **3:**853

Reflections on the Revolution in France (Burke), **1:**101

Reform or Revolution (Luxemburg), **2:**506

registration statement, **1:**77

regulation, 2:704–706

    under German National Socialism, **1:**284

Regulation Q, **1:**71, 73

Reid, Margaret, **1:**321

REITS (Real Estate Investment Trusts), **2**:482

Reliant Energy, 2:706–707

Remillard, Gil, **1**:162

Renaissance, **1**:200

rent control, **2**:660, 661, 662, 665

replacement-cost depreciation, **1**:203

Repsol-YPF, 2:707

Republic (Plato), **3**:793

Republic of Korea, *See* **South Korea**

Republican National Committee, **1**:102

repurchase agreement, **1**:71

research and development (R&D), 2:418–419, 707–708

    monopolies' ability to finance, **2**:573

    role of patents in, **2**:641–642, **3**:832–833

    technological change and, **3**:832–833

reserve currencies, **1**:189, 213, 214, 270

reserve ratio, **1**:75–76, 126, **2**:565–566, 567

residual interest (equity), **1**:3

resources, 2:709–710

    central question of resource economics, **2**:709–710

    classification of, **2**:709

    Ehrlich-Simon "Bet" and, **3**:757

retail, 2:710–715

    evolution, **2**:712–713

    functions, **2**:711

    management, **2**:713

    performance, **2**:714

    space, **2**:711–712

    trends, **2**:714–715

    types of, **2**:712

retail banking, *See* **consumer banking**

retained earnings, **1**:3, 263–264, 300

Reuther, Walter, **1**:59

reversal of stock prices, **2**:523

Revision of Demand Theory, A (Hicks), **2**:380

Revolutionary War, *See* **American Revolution**

Reynolds Metal Company, **1**:163

Rhee, Syngman, **2**:464

Ricardian equivalence, **1**:195

Ricardian Socialists, **2**:382

Ricardo, David, 1:195, 2:393, 522, 533, 715–716, 3:789

    on capital, **1**:111, **2**:472

    comparative advantage, **1**:82, 155, 227, 275, **2**:551, **3**:770, 849

    iron law of wages, **1**:227, 327, **2**:705–706, 715, **3**:810, 908

    labor theory of value, **1**:228, **3**:890

    principle of diminishing returns, **1**:114, **2**:666

    rent theory, **1**:114

    on scarcity of resources, **2**:710, 715

    on workers, **3**:919

Rickenbacker, Eddie, **1**:15

Right to the Whole Produce of Labour, The (Menger), **2**:539–540

Rio Declaration on Environment and Development, **3**:819

Rise of American Civilization (Beard and Beard), **1**:84

Rise of the Western World, The (North and Thomas), **2**:610

risk, 1:297, 2:716–719

    managing, **2**:718–719

    price of, **2**:716–717

    uncertainty of, **2**:717–718

risk capital, *See* **venture capital**

risk premium, **1**:194

Risk, Uncertainty and Profit (Knight), **1**:158, **2**:462

Ritt, Martin, **1**:293

Ritzer, George, **1**:166, 167, 313

RJR Nabisco, **1**:78

Road Ahead, The (Gates), **1**:335

Road to Serfdom, The (Hayek), **1**:58, **2**:369

robber barons, **2**:502, **3**:877

Robbins, Lionel, **2**:384, 558

Robertson, D. H., **2**:568

Robertson, J. C., **2**:382

Robespierre, Maximilian, **1**:319

Robinson, Joan, 1:112, 2:368, 719

    theory of imperfect competition, **1**:231, **2**:719

Robinson-Patman Act of 1936, **1**:36, **3**:767

Rockefeller, John D., 1:35, 52, 129, 256, 278, 2:719–721, 3:758, 792, 877

Rockefeller, William D., **2**:720

Rockne, Knute, **3**:785

Roebuck, Alvah Curtis, **3**:744

Roger and Me, **1**:293

"Role of Monetary Policy, The, " **2**:458

Roman Catholic Church, **3**:893

Roman d'un tribheur, Le, **1**:293

Roman Empire, 2:721–723, 3:849

Romania, 2:724

Rome, ancient, **1**:116–117, **3**:800

Romer, Paul, **2**:419

    endogenous growth theory, **2**:361

Roops, John J. R., **1**:121

Roosevelt, Eleanor, **2**:725

Roosevelt, Franklin Delano, 1:60, 200, 2:447, 724–727

    brain trust, **1**:87

    free trade and, **2**:316

    as governor of New York, **2**:725

    New Deal, *See* **New Deal**

    presidential elections, **2**:388, 455, 725–726

    price controls, **2**:663

    Truman and, **3**:852

    World War II, **1**:84, **2**:618

Roosevelt, Theodore, 1:36, 2:727–728

    Federal Reserve and, **1**:285

    foreign policy, **2**:728

    muckrakers and, **2**:502, **3**:757

    Progressives and, **2**:596, 727, 728, **3**:823, 824, 918

    in Spanish-American War, **2**:727, **3**:780

    Square Deal, **2**:727

    as trust buster, **2**:578, 727–728, **3**:792

Rosen, Harvey S., **1**:238

Rosenberg, Nathan, **3:**832

Rosenwald, Julius, **3:**744

Rostow, Walt W., **1:**204, 304

Rothbard, Murray, **1:**58, **2:**492

Rothschilds, **2:**615

Rousseau, Jean Jacques, **2:**394, 490, **3:**793

Rowe, Alan J., **2:**530

Royal Aircraft Factory, **1:**13

Royal Dutch Shell, 2:591, 618, 622, 728–729

    Texas oil boom and, **2:**616

    Venezuelan oil boom and, **2:**617

rugged individualism, **2:**387

Rural Electrification Administration, **2:**593–594

Ruskin, John, **2:**381

Russell, Bertrand, **2:**490

Russia, 1:352, **2:**729–731, **3:**864–865

    black market in, **1:**89

    as colonialist power, **1:**147

    G8 summits and, **1:**325, 326

    history prior to 1917, **2:**729

    institutional structure of new capitalism in, **2:**730

    oil production, **2:**615, 616

    oligarchic pressure groups in, **2:**731

    organized crime in, **1:**333, **2:**731

    parallel economy in, **2:**731

    problems with economic reforms of 1990s, **2:**730–731

    railroads in, **2:**698

    socialism in, **3:**775

    trade unions in, **2:**473–474, 484

    See also **Union of Soviet Socialist Republics (Soviet Union)**

Russia Company, **3:**800

Russian Revolution, 2:474, 484–485, 506, 732–733, **3:**775, 864

    China influenced by, **1:**134

Russian Revolution, The (Luxemburg), **2:**506

Russo-Japanese War, **2:**728, 729

Ruth, Babe, **3:**785

Rwanda, **1:**143

RWE, 2:733

SABMiller, **1:**21

Sachs, Jeffrey, **1:**34

Sadat, Anwar, **1:**123

Said, Edward, **1:**8, 40, **2:**626, 627, **3:**837

Said Pasha, **3:**811

Saint Domingue, **3:**763

Sakurai, Takahide, **1:**191

sales taxes, **3:**826, 827

Salinas de Gortari, Carlos, **2:**547

Salomon Smith Barney, **1:**78, 137

Sam's Club, **3:**909–910

Samuelson, Paul, 1:129, 231, **2:**376, 452, **3:**735–736

    Keynesian Cross model, **2:**457

    neoclassical synthesis and, **2:**509, 510, **3:**736

    Phillips Curve and, **2:**458

Sandanista National Liberation Front, **2:**598

Sanders, Thomas, **1:**52

Sarbanes-Oxley Act, **1:**254, **3:**745

Sargent, Thomas, **2:**562

Sargon of Akkad, **1:**115

Saro-Wiwa, Ken, **2:**728

Saudi Arabia, 1:42, **3:**736–737

    oil industry, **2:**618, **3:**736–737

Saul, Ralph, **1:**29

saving, 3:737–738

    aggregate, **3:**737–738

    government policy and, **3:**738

    Modigliani's life-cycle theory of, **2:**561, **3:**737

    personal savings rate, **3:**737–738

    primary reasons for, **3:**737

savings and loan associations, **1:**74, 298, **2:**390, 391–392

    failures of 1970s and 1980s, **1:**73, 78

savings banks, **1:**298

Say, Jean-Baptiste, **1:**227, **2:**456, 476, **3:**739, 890

Say's Law, 1:227, 245, **2:**552, 568, **3:**739–740, 815–816

    general glut controversy, **3:**739–740

SBC Communications, 1:78, **3:**740

scarcity, 1:229, 232, 327, **2:**554, **3:**740–741

    defined, **3:**740

    efficiency and, **3:**741

    Ehrlich-Simon "Bet" and, **3:**757

    Malthus on, *See* **Malthus, Thomas Robert,** on scarcity

Scarf, Herbert, **1:**262

Schanzer, Ken, **3:**787

Schechter Poultry Corporation v. United States, **1:**36

Scherer, F. M., **3:**883

Schiffrin, André, **1:**212

Schivelbusch, Wolfgang, **2:**697

Schlaet, Arnold, **1:**127

Schlosser, Eric, **1:**89, **3:**758

Schoenbaum, David, **1:**284

Scholes, Myron, 1:205, **2:**544, 553, **3:**741–742

    See also Black-Merton-Scholes stock option pricing formula

Schor, Juliet, **1:**166, 167

Schröder, Gerhard, **1:**342, **3:**772

Schultz, Henry, **1:**320–321

Schultz, Theodore, 1:129, 742, **2:**488, **3:**797

Schumpeter, Joseph, 1:57–58, 204, **2:**399, 419, 533, 613

    concept of competition, **1:**158

    on entrepreneurial activity, **1:**258–259, 267, **3:**742, 743, 766

    on static models, **1:**232, **3:**743

    theory of economic development, **1:**295, **2:**682–683, **3:**742, 743

    on Turgot's interest theory, **3:**854

    on Walras, **3:**911

Schwab, Charles, **3:**882

Schwab, Klaus, **3:**922

Schwarzkopf, General Norman, **2:**643

Science of Logic, The (Hegel), **2:**377

Scotland, **2:**499

Scott, General Winfield, **2:**649

Screen Actor's Guild, **2:**702

Sculley, John, **2:**445

Seagram Company, Ltd., **2:**499–500

Sears, Richard W., **3:**744

Sears, Roebuck & Company, 3:744

Seasonal Variations in Industry and Trade (Kuznets), **2:**469

secession powers of the states, **2:**438, 446, 495–496

Second Bank of the United States, **1:**140, **2:**367, 438, **3:**913

Second Continental Congress, **2:**365, **3:**914

Second Treatise on Civil Government (Locke), **2:**477, 489

secondary mortgage market, **1:**282, 389

Secular Movements in Production and Prices (Kuznets), **2:**469

Securities Act of 1933, **3:**745, 746–747

Securities and Exchange Commission (SEC), 1:29, 39, **3:**745–747

    accounting and, **1:**2, 4, 125, 339

    anti-fraud rules, **3:**745, 747

    creation of, **1:**80, **2:**537, 593, **3:**745

    enforcement actions, **3:**745, 746

    GAAP standards and, **1:**339

    insider trading and, **2:**420–421

    jurisdiction over interstate public offerings, **1:**77

    Joseph Kennedy as first chair of, **2:**455, 593

    registration requirements, **3:**745, 746–747

    structure of, **3:**746

Securities Exchange Act of 1934, **1:**79–80, **2:**420, **3:**745, 747

securitization of debt instruments, **1:**78

Segal, P., **1:**293

segregation, *See* civil rights

Seidl, Irmy, **1:**120

Selassie, Haile, **1:**268

Selden Patent, **1:**60

selection problem in econometrics, **2:**375

Selten, Reinhard, 1:330, **2:**368, **3:**748

Sen, Amartya, 2:461, **3:**748, 860

Senghor, Leopold, **3:**837

Senior, Nassau, 3:749

sensitivity analysis, **3:**796

separation of powers, **2:**575

September 11th terrorist attacks, **1:**16, 103–104, 240, **2:**597

    anti-globalization and, **1:**346

    stock markets and, **3:**803

Serbia and Montenegro, 3:750

serfdom, **1:**290, 291

Serious Fall in the Value of Gold, A (Jevons), **2:**444

services, 3:750–754

    as category of goods, **3:**750–751

    classification of, **3:**752

    definitions of, **3:**750–751

    economic issues, **3:**752–753

    management issues, **3:**753–754

    the service sector, **3:**751–752

    trends in service sector, **3:**753

    See also **goods**

Seven Years' War, **1:**26, 222

sewing machine, invention of, **2:**413

shareholder, *See* **stockholder**

Sharpe, William F., 1:44, **2:**530, **3:**754–755

    Capital Asset Pricing Model, **2:**552, **3:**755

Shay's Rebellion, **1:**28, **2:**366

Sheffield Female Society, **3:**763

Sherman, John, **1:**35, 334

Sherman, William Tecumseh, **1:**23

Sherman Antitrust Act, **1:**35–36, 37, 286, 287–288, **2:**687, **3:**792, 878, 882

    cartels prohibited by, **1:**121–122

    Northern Securities Company and, **2:**577, 578, 727–728

Shevardnadze, Edouard, **1:**341

Shindo, Kaneto, **1:**293

Shining Path, **1:**206

Shoyama, Etsuhiko, **2:**380–381

Shubik, M., **2:**621

Shultz, George, **2:**603

Sidgwick, Henry, **3:**883, 884

Siebert, Muriel, **2:**597

Siegel, "Bugsy," **1:**333

Siemens, 3:755–756

signaling theory, **1:**238, **3:**780–781

Sihanouk, King Norodom, **1:**109

Silicon Valley area, venture capitalism in, **3:**899

Silk Road, **3:**783

Simmel, Georg, **1:**167

Simmons, Hardwick, **2:**586

Simon, Herbert A., 2:384, 552, **3:**756

Simon, Julian, 2:554, **3:**757

Simons, Henry, **2:**557, **3:**797

Sinclair, Upton, 3:757–758

Singapore, 1:317, **3:**759–760

    as Asian developmental state, **1:**48–49

    export-promotion strategy, **1:**276, **3:**759

Singer, Isaac, **2:**413

Sinopec Corporation, 3:760

Sismondi, J. C. L. Simonde de, **3:**739

Skidelsky, Robert, **2:**457

Slater, Don, **1:**151, 167

Slater, Samuel, **2:**413

slavery, **1:**11, 12, **2:**413, 442, 481, 516, **3:**761–763, 849

    abolitionists, **2:**494, **3:**763

    John Quincy Adams and, **1:**7

    Compromise of 1850, **1:**140–141, 292, **3:**829

    decentralized federalism in the U.S. and, **3:**875

    Dred Scott v. Sanford, **1:**22, 99

    economic significance of, **1:**22–23, **3:**875, 876, 877

    Emancipation Proclamation, **1:**24, **2:**496–497

    Fillmore's views on, **1:**292

    Fogel's books on, **1:**304

    Franklin's position on, **1:**314

    Fugitive Slave Act, **1:**141, 292, **2:**649

    invention of the cotton gin and, **3:**917

    Lincoln on, **2:**494, 495–497

    Missouri Compromise, **1:**22, 140, **2:**574, 649

slavery (cont'd)

in the New World, 3:761–762

origins of, 3:761

Pierce's policies, 2:649

rebellions, 3:762–763

the scale and conditions of, 3:761, 762

Soviet slave labor camps, 3:775

Texas' annexation and, 3:855

Thirteenth Amendment, 2:497

trade in early civilizations and, 3:849

Slavery Abolition Act of 1833 (Britain), 3:763

Sloan, Alfred P., 1:338

small business, 3:763–768

economic issues, 3:765–766

management issues, 3:766–767

public policy, 3:767–768

sector, 3:764–765

trends, 3:768

See also **entrepreneur**

Small Business Act, 3:764

Small Business Administration, 3:764, 3:767, 768

Small Business Innovation Research (SBIR) program, 3:768

Small Business Investment Company (SBIC), 3:767, 768

Small Time Crooks, 1:293

Smaller War Plants Corporation, 3:767

Smart Money, 1:215

Smibert, John, 1:281

Smith, Adam, 2:364, 383, 522, 705, **3:769–770**

absolute advantage, 1:82, 155, 275

Burke and, 1:101

capital theory, 1:111, 113–114, 118, 3:770

on competition, 1:158

industrial organization and, 2:410

on innovative methods of production, 3:832

invisible hand, 1:227, 267, 315, 2:393, 686, 3:769

on labor, 1:227, 350, 360, 2:472, 3:769–770, 830, 890, 908

laissez-faire, 2:477, 686, 3:849

on mercantilism, 1:199, 227, 275, 315, 2:686, 705

monetary theory, 2:567–568

on moral significance of prosperity, 1:266

on physiocracy, 2:691

on services, 3:752

on the state's duties, 3:793

on taxes, 2:475, 705

Wealth of Nations, See **Wealth of Nations, An Inquiry Into the Nature and Causes of the** (Smith)

on workers, 3:919

Smith, Alfred, 2:725

Smith, John F. Jr., 1:338

Smith, Roger, 1:293

Smith, Vernon L., 2:369, 451, 558, **3:771**

smoking, *See* **tobacco**

Smoot-Hawley tariff of 1930, 1:316, 2:387

Socal, 2:618

soccer, 3:785–786, 788

social assistance programs, *See* **social security**; welfare (social programs)

Social Class and Individual Values (Arrow), 1:47

Social Darwinism, 1:164–165, 2:478, 3:782, 813

social democracy, 3:771–773

Bismarck's attack on, 1:87–88

spread of, 3:772, 930

the Third Way, 3:772–773

Social Economics (Wieser), 1:57, 2:540

Social History of the Media, From Gutenberg to the Internet, A (Briggs and Burke), 1:149

social production, 2:678–679

social security, 2:453, 3:738, 773–774, 879

dual meanings of, 3:773

program in the United States, 2:594, 3:773

Social Security Act, 2:491, 726

Social Security Administration, 3:773

Social Statics (Spencer), 3:782

socialism, 3:774–775

alienation and, 1:19

Arab nationalism and, 1:40, 41, 42

Austrian School and, 1:57

Bismarck's attack on, 1:87–88

in India, 2:408

Luxemburg's views, 2:505–506

Marx and, 3:774, 920

nationalization under, 2:588

revisionist, 2:506

Schumpeter on, 3:742, 743

Sinclair's advocacy of, 3:757

social democracy as alternative to, 3:771

in the United States, failure in the, 3:920

Socialism (Mises), 1:57, 2:558

Society for the Abolition of Slavery, 3:763

Society of Friends, 3:763

sole proprietorships, 2:407, 637

Solow, Robert, 1:360, 2:368, 458, **3:738, 775**

on technology, 3:829, 831

Somalia, 1:143

Sombart, Werner, 2:685

Some Consideration of the Consequences of the Lowering of Interest and Raising the Value of Money (Locke), 2:503

Some Unsettled Questions in Political Economy (Mill), 2:550

Sompo Japan, 1:191

Sons of Liberty, 1:26

Sony, 1:48, 2:440, **3:776**

Sony Pictures Entertainment, 1:293

Soros, George, 1:129, **3:776–777**

Souter, Justice David, 1:102

South Africa, 1:147, **3:777–778**

dismantling apartheid in, 1:102, 3:777

South African/European Union Trade, Development and Cooperation Agreement, 3:778

South Asian Association for Regional Cooperation (SAARC), 3:837

South Korea, 2:464–466

as Asian developmental state, 1:48–49

export-promotion strategy, **1:**276

political strike of 1997, **3:**805

protection of infant industries, **1:**156

See also Korean War

South Seas Bubble, **3:**801

South Vietnam, **3:**902–904

See also **Vietnam; Vietnam War**

Southern Africa Customs Union (SACU), **3:**778

Southern African American Development Coordination Council (SAADCC), **3:**837

Southern African Development Community (SADC), **3:**778

Southern Rhodesia, **3:**935

See also **Zimbabwe**

Soviet Union, *See* **Union of Soviet Socialist Republics (Soviet Union)**

Sowell, Thomas, **2:**492

Spain, 3:778–779

Civil War, **3:**779

mercantilism, **2:**540, 541

Mexican independence, **2:**545–546

privatization in, **2:**667, **3:**779

railroads in, **2:**698

strikes in, **3:**807

Spanish-American War, 1:147, 186, **2:**517, 537, **3:**779–780

Theodore Roosevelt and, **2:**727, **3:**780

special-interest groups, **3:**782

specialization of labor, **1:**10

Specie Circular of 1836, **2:**438, **3:**891

Speer, Albert, **3:**929

Spence, A. Michael, 1:17, **3:**780–781, 797

signaling theory, **1:**238, **3:**780–781

Spencer, Herbert, 1:234, **2:**381, **3:**781–783, 813

Spengler, Joseph J., **3:**739

spheres of influence, **1:**134, **2:**397

spice trade, 3:783–785

Spiegel, M., **2:**418

spinning mill, invention of, **2:**413

spoils system, **1:**142

sports, 3:785–789

business of, **3:**786

marketing, **3:**789

Sports Authority, **3:**789

Sprint, **1:**19

Square Deal, **2:**727

Sraffa, Pierro, 1:112, 231, **3:**789–790

stagflation, **1:**62, 205, **2:**459, 476, 510, 564, **3:**880

stagnation, 3:790–791

Stalin, Josef, **1:**283, 341, **2:**485, 653, 729, **3:**775, 852, 853

Stamp Act, **1:**26, **2:**365

Standard and Poor's, 3:791–792

S&P 500, **3:**791–792

Standard Oil Company, 1:278, **2:**414, 501, 502, **3:**792

establishment of, **2:**615, 720

railroads and, **2:**698

Standard Oil Company of Ohio, **2:**720, **3:**792

Standard Oil Co. v. United States, **1:**35–36, 127

Standard Oil of New Jersey, **2:**617, **3:**792

Standard Statistics Bureau, **3:**791

Stanley, Harold, **1:**228, **2:**577

Starbucks, **3:**896

Starr, Cornelius Vander, **1:**25

"Star-Spangled Banner, " **3:**913

state, 3:793–794

See also **government**

State Farm Insurance Companies, 3:794

statement of cash flows, **1:**3–4, 124, 300

statement of income, *See* **income statement**

Statement of Principles for Sustainable Management of Forests, **3:**819

Statements of Financial Accounting Standards, **1:**4

static and dynamic analysis, 3:795–796

statistical significance, **1:**224

steam engine, **2:**415, **3:**830

steamships, **2:**415

steel industry, **1:**176, 319, **3:**877, 878

Bessemer process, **1:**319, **2:**412, 414

Carnegie and, **1:**119–120, 319, **3:**883

tariffs under George W. Bush administration, **3:**883

Steffens, Lincoln, **3:**758

Stein, Herbert, **1:**237–238

Stephenson, George, **1:**86

Stevens, John F., **2:**634

Stevenson, Adlai, **1:**241, 327, **3:**839

Stewart, Dugald, **2:**393

Stewart, Margaret, **1:**235

Stigler, George, 1:129, **2:**462, 492, 553, 621, **3:**796–797

Stiglitz, Joseph, 1:17, 183, **2:**487, **3:**797–798

Stimson, Henry L., **2:**388

stock:

concept of, **3:**800

See also **stock dividend; stock market; stockholder**

stock dividend, 3:798–799, 802

stock market, 3:799–803

contemporary markets, **3:**802–803

growth of world markets, **3:**801–802

history of the markets, **3:**799, 800–801

non-economic events affecting, **3:**802–803

risk and reward theories, **2:**530

rumors, **3:**801

See also individual exchanges

stock market crash of 1929, **1:**36, 205, **2:**386, 387, 390, 593, 597, **3:**745, 878

stock market crash of 1987, **1:**129, **2:**553

stockholder, 3:803–804

advocacy for interests of, **3:**804

relationship to board of directors, **3:**803

stockholders' equity, **1:**3, 263–264

stock-keeping unit (SKU), **2:**675–676, 714

Stone, Oliver, **1:**293

Stone, Richard, **2:**363

Stone, Sir Richard, 1:357, **3:**804–805

Storrow, James J., **1:**338

straight line method of depreciation, **1:**203
Strike, **1:**293
strikes, **2:**474–475, 728, **3:**805–808, 868
    air-traffic controller's (PATCO), **3:**807
    contract, **3:**805, 806
    Coolidge administration and, **1:**174, 175
    economic theories of, **3:**805–806
    first nationwide, by federal employees, **3:**882
    history, **3:**807
    at Homestead steel works, **1:**119–120, 319
    political, **3:**805
    Pullman strike of 1894, **1:**142, **3:**807
    recognition, **3:**805, 806–807
    significance of, **3:**806–807
    in socialist Russia, **3:**775
    trends internationally, **3:**807–808
    during Truman administration, **3:**852
    wildcat, **3:**805
Stromberg, Joseph, **1:**118
Structure and Change in Economic History (North), **2:**610
Structure of the American Economy, 1919-1929 (Leontief),
    2:485–486
Studebaker, **1:**61
Studies in the Law of Corporation Finance (Berle), **1:**87
Study in the Theory of Economic Evolution, A (Haavelmo), **2:**363
Subaru, **1:**62
Subgame Perfect Equilibrium (Selden), **3:**748
Subjection of Women, The (Mill), **2:**550–551
subsidies, **3:**808–809
subsistence theory, **3:**810
suburbanization, **1:**62
Suez Canal, **1:**242, **2:**415, **3:**811, 812
Suez Company, **1:**210, **2:**588, **3:**811–812
Sugar Act of 1764, **1:**26
Sukarno, Ahmad, **2:**604, 606, **3:**837
Sumer, **1:**114–115
Sumitomo Corporation, **3:**812
Sumitomo Life, **2:**600
Summers, Lawrence, **3:**737
Summit of the Americas, **3:**812–813
Sumner, William Graham, **1:**165, **3:**813, 850
Sun Microsystems, **3:**896
Sun Oil Company, **2:**616
Sun Yat-sen, **1:**134
sunk costs, **1:**182
supply, **3:**814–816
    economic policy and, **3:**815–816
    macroeconomic analysis, **3:**814–815
    microeconomic analysis, **3:**814
    Say's Law, *See* **Say's Law**
supply-side economics, **1:**175, **2:**475, 476, 511, 703, **3:**772–773, 816
Supreme Court, U.S., **1:**7, 22, 333, **3:**776, 852
    antitrust cases, **1:**35–37, 163, **3:**792, 882
    appointments to, **1:**102
    Gibbons v. Ogden, **3:**892

    Native American tribe gaming rights, **1:**329
    Franklin D. Roosevelt and, **2:**593, 594, 726
surplus, **3:**817–818
    labor markets and, **3:**817–818
    market forces and, **3:**817
surplus value, Marxian theory of, **1:**228, 251, 258, **2:**404, 534,
    3:810, 841
sustainable development, **3:**819–820
    G8 summits and, **1:**326
    globalization and, **2:**400–401
Sutherland, Thomas, **2:**392
Suzuki, Iwajiro, **2:**602
Suzuki & Company, **2:**602
Swan, Trevor, **3:**775
swaps, **1:**205, 206
sweatshops, **3:**877
Sweden, **3:**820–821
    liquor sales and production in, **2:**499
    nationalization in, **2:**588
Swedish School, **1:**57
Sweezy, P., **3:**791
Swiss Bank Corporation, **3:**857
Switzerland, **3:**752, 821–822
Sylos-Labini, P., **3:**791
Syria, **3:**822
System of Logic, A (Mill), **2:**550

Tableau économique de la France (Quesnay), **2:**471, 648, 691
Taft, Robert, **1:**241
Taft, William Howard, **1:**36, **2:**728, **3:**823–824, 918
Taft-Hartley Act, **1:**61, **2:**447, 603
    Truman and, **3:**852–853
Tagliabue, Paul, **3:**786
Tagore, Rabindernath, **3:**837
Taiwan, **1:**124, 135, **3:**824–825
    as Asian developmental state, **1:**48–49
    export-promotion strategy, **1:**276
    history of, **3:**824
    protection of infant industries, **1:**156
    See also **China**
Taliban, **1:**7
tamkarum or temple/palace model of capitalism, **1:**114–115
Tammany Hall, **1:**142, **2:**501, 725
Taosim, **1:**133
Tarbell, Ida, **3:**758
Target Corporation, **3:**825
target zones, **2:**467
tariff, **1:**275, 316, 345–346, **2:**437–438, 453, 520, 660, **3:**825–826
    ad valorem, **3:**825, 851
    to attract tariff-jumping investment, **3:**826
    Dingley, **2:**537
    in early U.S. history, **3:**850, 875
    GATT, *See* **General Agreement on Tariffs and Trade (GATT)**
    under Harrison, **2:**367
    Hawley-Smoot Tariff, **1:**316, **2:**387

McKinley Tariff of 1890, **2:**537
under mercantilism, *See* **mercantilism**
Payne-Aldrich Act, **3:**823
production-sharing law, **3:**826
revenue, **3:**825
Smith's view of, **1:**315
states' right to nullify, **2:**437–438
steel industry, under George W. Bush administration, **3:**883
temporary, compensating, **3:**826
Underwood Tariff Act, **3:**918
Tariff Act of 1828, **1:**6
Tariki, Abdullah, **2:**619
Tax Reduction Act of 1964, **2:**448
Taxation and Wealth (Hicks), **2:**380
taxes, 3:826–828
accounting information and, **1:**1
American Revolution and, **1:**26–27, 28, **3:**849
choice between raising, and debt financing, **1:**195
under Coolidge administration, **1:**175
defined, **3:**826
fair taxation, **3:**827–828
fees compared to, **3:**826
fiscal policy, *See* **fiscal policy**
income, *See* income taxes
Laffer Curve, **2:**475–476, **3:**816
on liquor, **2:**498, 500
Mirrlees' work on optimal taxation, **2:**557
Pigou, **2:**689
poverty reduction policies, **2:**658
proportionate, **3:**828
regressive, **3:**828
16th Amendment authorizing the income tax, **3:**823
Smith on, **2:**475, 705
taxation without representation, **1:**27, 28, **3:**849
on tobacco, **3:**843–844
types of, **3:**826–827
underground economy, *See* **underground economy**
Taylor, A. J. P., **2:**699
Taylor, Frederick Winslow, **2:**414, 611
Taylor, Zachary, 1:141, 292, **2:**495, 516, **3:**828–829
technical analysis of stock prices, **2:**523
technological optimists, **2:**554–555, **3:**757, 775
technology, 3:829–834
Asian developmental state and, **1:**48–49
Ehrlich-Simon "Bet" and, **3:**757
intellectual property rights, *See* intellectual property rights
long waves and technological change, **3:**830–832
opposition to technological change, **3:**829–830
rate and direction of technical change, **3:**832–834
research and development, *See* **research and development (R&D)**
underground economy and, **3:**861
unprecedented pace in capitalist economies, **3:**829
See also **computers; information revolution**
telecommunications, **3:**831, 832
Telecommunications Act of 1996, **3:**740, 900

telegraph, invention of the, **2:**414
Telemarketing and Consumer Fraud and Abuse Prevention Act of 1994, **1:**287
telephones, **1:**52–53, **2:**414
Temporary Assistance for Needy Families, **3:**783
Tennessee Valley Authority, **2:**537, 592–593, **3:**879
terrorism, **1:**16
Luxor attacks near the Pyramids, **1:**240
September 11th terrorist attacks, *See* September 11th terrorist attacks
War on Terrorism, **1:**104, 214, 348, **3:**880, 933
Tesla, Nikola, **3:**916
Texaco, **1:**81, 127, **2:**618
See also **Chevron Texaco**
Texas:
annexation of, **3:**855
oil boom, **2:**615–616
Texas Oil & Gas Corporation, **3:**882
textile industry, **1:**85, **2:**412, **3:**875
in Japan, **2:**439
putting-out system, **2:**611
Thailand, 3:834–835
Thatcher, Margaret, 3:835–836
economic policy, **2:**402, 457, 474, 564, 667, **3:**772, 835, 849, 872–873
foreign policy, **2:**835
Zimbabwe independence and, **3:**935
Theory and Measurement of Demand (Schultz), **1:**320–321
Theory of Economic Development (Schumpeter), **1:**57–58, **3:**743
Theory of Economic Growth, The (Lewis), **2:**488
Theory of Games and Economic Behavior (Neumann and Morgenstern), **1:**330, **2:**587
Theory of Interest (Fisher), **1:**303
Theory of Money and Credit, The (Mises), **1:**57, **2:**557–558
Theory of Monopolistic Competition (Chamberlin), **2:**671
Theory of Moral Sentiments (Smith), **1:**266
Theory of Political Economy, The (Jevons), **2:**444
Theory of the Business Enterprise, The (Veblen), **3:**895
Theory of the Consumption Function (Friedman), **1:**321
Theory of the Leisure Class, The (Veblen), **3:**894
Theory of Value, The (Debreu), **1:**193
Thieme, Carl, **2:**580
Thinking as a Science (Hazlitt), **2:**370
Third Way, The (Giddens), **3:**772
third world:
dependency theory, **1:**201–203
globalization and, **1:**346–348
import substitution industrialization, **1:**157
Lewis' theories on underdeveloped economies, **2:**487–489
modernization theory, **2:**560–561
non-alignment, *See* **non-alignment**
in postwar period, **1:**345
privatization in, **2:**668–669
Schultz's work on problems of, **1:**742
strikes in, **3:**807

third world (cont'd)

World Bank's role in, *See* **World Bank**

See also individual countries

Third World Internationalism, 2:836–839

Third Worldism, 3:836–837

Thirty Years' War, 3:839–840

Thomas, Justice Clarence, 1:102

Thomas, Paul, 2:610

Thompson, E. P., 2:475

Thompson, James E., 2:386

Thornton, Henry, 2:568

Thoughts and Details on Economic Scarcity (Burke), 1:101

Tiananmen Square protests, 1:136, 2:445

Tilden, Samuel J., 2:370

Timber Culture Act of 1873, 3:877

Timber Stone Act of 1878, 3:877

time, 3:840–842

time deposits, 1:75

Time Inc., 1:38

Time on the Cross: The Economics of American Negro Slavery (Fogel and Engerman), 1:304

Time Warner, 1:78

See also **AOL Time Warner**

Time-Life, 1:212

Timmons, Jeffrey, 3:899

Tinbergen, Jan, 1:321, 3:842

Tisdell, Clem, 1:120

Tito, Marshal Josep, 2:604, 605, 606

tobacco, 3:843–844

Tobin, James, 2:569, 3:844

Tobin Tax, 2:658, 3:844

Tocqueville, Alexis de, 1:200, 289, 2:575

Todt, Fritz, 3:929

Tokyo Electric Power Company, 3:844–845

Tokyo stock exchange, 1:71, 2:441

Tokyo Telecommunications Engineering Corporation (Tokyo Tsushin Kogyo), 3:776

Tolstoy, A., 2:452

Tommy Boy, 1:293

Tonnies, Ferdinand, 1:165

Torrens, Robert, 2:666

Torrijos, General Omar, 2:635

Torrio, Johnny, 1:333

Toshiba Corporation, 3:845

TotalFinaElf, 3:845–846

totalitarianism, 1:283

tourism, 3:846–848

tournament theory, 2:403

Toussaint L'Ouverture, 3:763

Townsend Acts of 1767, 1:26

Toynbee, Arnold, 1:235, 2:411

Toyoda, Kiichiro, 3:848

Toyota, 1:61, 62

Toyota Motor Corporation, 3:848

trade, 3:849–850

Asian developmental state's view of, 1:48–49

autarky and, 1:58

comparative advantage, *See* **comparative advantage**

export and import, *See* **export and import**

free trade, *See* **free trade**

Hecksher-Ohlin Factor Endowment Theory, 2:614

history of, 3:849

imperialism and, *See* **imperialism**

mercantilism, *See* **mercantilism**

Mill's contributions to trade theory, 2:551

Montesquieu on, 2:575

quotas, *See* **quotas**

tariffs, *See* **tariff**

theory, 3:849–850

treaties, *See individual treaties*

before World War II, 3:927

trade barrier, 3:851

quotas, *See* **quotas**

tariff, *See* **tariff**

trade credit, 1:184

trade unions, *See* **unions**

Traite d'économie politique (Say), 3:739

Transcontinental and Western Airlines, 1:14

transistor radios, 2:440, 3:776

transnational corporations, 1:32–35

Transparency, International, 1:98, 177

Trans-World Airlines (TWA), 1:14, 15, 16

Travelers Group Inc., 1:73, 78, 80, 137

Travels in the North of Germany (Hodgskin), 2:382

Treatise of Human Nature (Hume), 2:393

Treatise of Political Economy (Say), 1:227

"Treatise of Probability," 2:456

Treaty of Brest-Litovsk, 2:733

Treaty of Detroit, 1:61

Treaty of European Union of 1992, 1:269

Treaty of Ghent, 3:913

Treaty of Guadalupe-Hidalgo, 3:829

Treaty of Paris of 1783, 1:5, 3:874

Treaty of Paris of 1898, 3:780

Treaty of Tianjin, 2:623

Treaty of Versailles, 1:234, 3:918, 926

Treaty on Economic and Monetary Unification, *See* Maastricht Treaty

Trembling Hand Perfect Equilibrium (Selden), 3:748

triangular trade, 3:762

trickle-down economics, *see* supply-side economics

Trippe, Juan, 1:15, 16

TRIPS (Trade Related Aspects of Intellectual Property), 2:642

Troeltsch, Ernst, 2:685

Tronti, Mario, 1:141

Tropicana Juice Beverages, 2:500

Trotsky, Leon, 3:775

Truman, Harry S, 1:241, 2:663, 704, 3:851–853, 879

Fair Deal, 2:478, **491**

free trade and, **2**:316
    Korea and, **2**:447, 508
Truman Doctrine, **3**:853
Trust Indenture Act of 1939, **3**:745
trusts, *See* **antitrust; monopoly**
Truth in Lending Act, **1**:287
Truth in Securities Act of 1933, **1**:79
Tucker, Albert, **1**:331
Tullock, Gordon, **1**:100
Turgot, Baron Anne Robert Jacques, 2:666, **3**:853–854
Turkey, 3:854
    Truman Doctrine and, **3**:853
Turkish Petroleum Company, **2**:618
Turner, Frederick Jackson, **2**:517
Turner, Ted, **1**:38
Turner Broadcasting System, **1**:38
Tuskegee Institute, **2**:414
Tversky, Amos, **2**:384, 451
Tweed, "Boss," **2**:501
Twentieth Century Fox Film Corp., **1**:293
Two Treatises on Government (Locke), **2**:502, **2**:503
Tyco International, **1**:125
Tyler, John, 2:516, **3**:855
Tyre, city-state of, **1**:116

UBS, **3**:857
Ukraine, 1:352, **3**:857–858, 865
    black market in, **1**:89
unconscionability doctrine, **1**:174
under-consumptionist theories, **2**:381
underdeveloped economies, Lewis' theories on, **2**:487–489
underground economy, 3:858–861
    future prospects for, **3**:860–861
    in less-developed countries, **3**:858
    making the informal sector formal, **3**:860
    omitted from measurement of GDP, **1**:358
    reasons for participating in, **3**:859–860
    social aspects of, **3**:859
    varieties of activities, **3**:858–859
Understanding Popular Culture (Fiske), **1**:151
Underwood Tariff Act, **3**:918
unemployment, 3:861–863
    costs of, **3**:862
    cyclical, **3**:862
    employment theory, *See* **employment theory**
    frictional, **3**:862
    during Hoover administration, **2**:388
    inflation and, *See* **Phillips curve**
    job rationing and, **3**:863
    job search and, **3**:863
    measurement of, **3**:861–862
    natural rate of, **2**:564, 570, 647
    sticky wages theory, **3**:863
    structural, **3**:862
UNESCO Universal Declaration of Cultural Diversity, **1**:212, 213

Unilever, **3**:863
Unión Cívica Radical (UCR), **1**:45
Union des Assurances de Paris (UAP), **1**:64
Union of Soviet Socialist Republics (Soviet Union), 1:46, 211,
    2:729–730, **3**:864–865
    Afghanistan invasion and occupation, **1**:123, 352
    Cold War, *See* Cold War
    collapse of, **1**:345, 352, **2**:396, 474, 729–730, **3**:864–865
    Cuba and, **1**:187
    detente, **1**:123
    economic growth in 1930s, **2**:509
    Georgia and, **1**:341
    oil production in, **2**:615
    prices in, **2**:659–660
    Reagan foreign policy, **2**:703, 835
    socialism in, **3**:775
    Vietnam and, **3**:903
    in World War II, **1**:285, **3**:928, 929
    See also **Russia;** *individual leaders*
Union Trust, **3**:916
unions, 3:865–869
    anti-globalization and, **1**:33
    Asian developmental states and, **1**:48
    auto industry, **1**:59, 61, 62–63, 307
    birth of, **3**:866–867
    British trade unions, **3**:807, 835
    early labor organization, **3**:865
    ebb and flow of power of, **3**:867–868
    emergence of trade unions, **2**:473, **3**:878
    Mill on, **2**:551–552
    post-World War II, **3**:868–869
    right to form, **1**:175
    rise of modern manufacturing, **3**:865–866
    Russian trade unions, **2**:473–474, 484
    in Soviet Union, **3**:775
    strikes, *See* **strikes**
    Wilson and, **3**:867, 918, 925
    See also individual unions
United Airlines, **1**:13, 14
United Auto Workers (UAW), **1**:59, 61, 62–63, 307
United Bank of Switzerland, **3**:857
United Kingdom, 3:869–873
    American Revolution, *See* **American Revolution**
    Burke's opposition to colonial policy in North America, **1**:101
    central bank, *See* **Bank of England**
    civil war, **1**:252–253
    classical economic theorists, *See* **classical economic theory**
    colonialism, **1**:147, **3**:759, 761
    Corn Laws, **1**:233–234, **2**:542, 666, 706, **3**:749, 849
    English Civil War, **1**:252–253
    European Community and, **3**:871–872
    Glorious Revolution, **2**:477, 489–490
    Hundred Years' War, **2**:394–395
    Industrial Revolution in, **2**:412, 696, **3**:761, 774, 849, 866,
        869–871

United Kingdom (cont'd)
Kuwait as protectorate of, **2**:468
liberalism in, **2**:489–491, **3**:849
mercantilism, **2**:477, 480, 481, 540, **3**:849
nationalization in, **2**:588, 699
Navigation Acts, **1**:186, 199, **2**:477, 542, **3**:849
Nigeria and, **2**:599
Palestine and, **2**:432, 634
Poor Laws, **3**:919
privatization in, **2**:667, **3**:772, 835
railroad industry and Industrial Revolution in, **2**:696
slavery and, **3**:761, 762–763
strikes in, **3**:807
Suez Canal crisis and, **3**:812
Thatcherism in, *See* **Thatcher, Margaret,** economic policy
Third Way, **3**:873
trade history, **3**:849
trade unions in, **3**:807, 835
Transjordan mandate, **2**:448
War of 1812, *See* **War of 1812**
in World War I, **3**:871, 924
in World War II, **3**:871, 928, 929
United Mine Worker Association (UMWA), **2**:554, **3**:867
United Nations, **1**:348
creation of, **1**:345
General Assembly, **1**:346, **3**:774, 824
Security Council, **2**:432, **3**:880
Truman and, **3**:852
Universal Declaration of Human Rights, **3**:774
United Nations Conference for Environment and Development (UNCED), **3**:819, 820
United Nations Framework, Convention on Climate Change, **3**:819
United Nations Security Council, **2**:643
United Parcel Service (UPS), **3**:874, 882
United States, **3**:874–880
Constitution, *See* Constitution of the United States
economic history of, **3**:874–880
See also individual leaders, economists, and economic concepts related to the United States
United States Housing Corporation, **2**:389
United States Postal Service, **1**:13, 14, 15, **3**:880–882, 915
history of, **3**:880–882
UPS and FedEx and, **3**:874, 882
United States v. Aluminum Company of America, **1**:36–37
United States v. American Tobacco Co., **1**:35–36
United States v. E. C. Knight Co., **1**:35
United States v. General Dynamics Corp., **1**:37
U.S. Bureau of Alcohol, Tobacco, and Firearms, **2**:501
U.S. Bureau of Labor Statistics, **1**:238, **2**:679
U.S. Bureau of Mines, **2**:555
U.S. Census Bureau, **2**:656
U.S. Defense Department, **1**:161
U.S. Department of Agriculture (USDA), **1**:12
U.S. Department of Housing and Urban Development, **2**:448

U.S. Department of Transportation, **2**:448
U.S. International Trade Commission (USITC), **3**:883
U.S. Justice Department, **1**:288
Antitrust Division, **1**:35, 36, 37–38, 78, 161, 163, 288, **2**:525–526, 550, 585, **3**:883
Arthur Anderson and, **1**:254
U.S. Steel Corporation, **1**:79, **2**:578, **3**:766, 868, 882–883
antitrust case against, **3**:882
Carnegie and, **1**:120, 319
U.S. Treasury, J. P. Morgan's prevention of collapse of, **1**:79, 142, 209, **2**:577, 578
U.S. Veterans Administration (VA), **1**:62, **2**:389
UNIVAC, **1**:160
Universal Declaration of Human Rights, **3**:774
universal product code (UPC), **2**:676
Universal Studios, **1**:293, **2**:500, **3**:776
Unsafe at Any Speed (Nader), **1**:61
UPS, *See* **United Parcel Service (UPS)**
Ur, **1**:115
urbanization and the underground economy, **3**:860
USA Networks, **2**:500
"Use of Knowledge in Society, The," **2**:369
USSR, *See* **Union of Soviet Socialist Republics (Soviet Union)**
usury laws, **2**:660
USX, **3**:766, 882–883
See also **U.S. Steel**
UtiliCorp United, **1**:39
utilitarianism, **2**:478, 490, **3**:883–884
act vs. rule, **3**:884
Bentham and, **1**:86–87, 227, 231, **2**:478, 490, **3**:883, 884
Utilitarianism (Mill), **3**:884
utility, **1**:20, **3**:885
cardinal, **3**:885
defined, **3**:885
marginal, *See* marginal utility
ordinal, **3**:885
theory, **1**:196–197, **3**:890, 891
utility maximization, **2**:522, **3**:886–887

Vallance, Aylmer, **1**:235
Valletta, Vittorio, **1**:291
value added tax (VAT), **3**:826–827
Value and Capital (Hicks), **2**:380
value of leisure, **3**:889–890
value theory, **1**:57, **3**:890–891
implications of, **3**:890–891
labor, *See* **labor,** value of
marginal utility theory of value, *See* **marginal utility,** theory of value
subjective basis of value, **1**:57
surplus value, *See* surplus value, Marxian theory of
utility approach, *See* **utility**
Van Buren, Martin, **1**:102, **3**:891–892
Vanderbilt, Cornelius, **1**:52, 353, **3**:877, 892–893
Vanderbilt, William H., **1**:79, **3**:893
Vargas, Getúlio, **1**:96

Vatican Bank, 3:893
Vavilov, Nikolai, 1:10
VEBA, 1:221
Veblen, Thorstein, 1:169, 231–232, 327, 3:893–895
  conspicuous consumption and, 1:10, 3:894–895
  on entrepreneurial interests and community welfare, 1:259
Venetian spice trade, 3:783
Venezuela, 3:895–896
  general strikes of 2000 in, 3:805
  oil boom in, 2:617, 3:895–896
venture capital, 1:39, 77, 3:896–900
  acquisition financing, 3:896
  business, 3:896–897
  cyclical nature of the industry, 3:900
  expansion financing, 3:896
  future of the field, 3:899–900
  globalization of the industry, 3:898–899
  leverage-buyout financing, 3:896
  seed financing, 3:896
  start-up financing, 3:896, 897
  U.S. venture capital industry, 3:897
  venture capital funds, 3:898
  vitality of, 3:897–898
Verizon Communications, 3:900
Vermeer Technologies, 2:550
Versailles Peace Conference, 2:456
Versailles Treaty, 1:234, 3:918, 926
vertical integration, 1:154, 2:720
Veterans Administration (VA), 1:62, 2:389
VIAG, 1:221
Vickers, 1:15
Vickrey, William, 2:557, 3:900–901
Victor Emmanuel, King, 1:283
Vienna School, 1:56–58
Vietminh, 3:902
Vietnam, 3:901
  nationalization in, 2:588
Vietnam War, 1:84, 305, 3:902–904
  French war with the Vietminh, 3:902
  Johnson and, 2:447, 448, 491, 3:879, 902–903, 904
  Kennedy and, 2:454, 3:902
  Nixon administration and, 3:903–904, 924
  Tet offensive, 3:903
  Thai economy and, 3:834
  value of the dollar and, 1:214
  Vietnamization of, 3:903
Villa, Francisco, 2:546
Villa, General Pancho, 3:918
Ville, Simon P., 2:698
Viner, Jacob, 1:129, 320, 3:797
VisiCalc, 1:160, 161
Vivendi Universal, 3:904
VOC, See Dutch East India Company (Verenigde Oost Indische Compagnie) (VOC)
Vodafone Airtouch, 3:900

Volcker, Paul A., 3:904–905
Volkswagen, 1:61, 3:905–906
Volta, Ilatian Alessandro, 2:414
Voluntary Export Restraint (VER), 2:693
voluntary export restraints (VERs), 3:851
von Haberler, Gottfried, 1:58
von Schelling, Friedrich W. von, 2:376
Von Stackelberg, H., 2:620
Voting Rights Act of 1965, 2:448

W. R. Grace Company, 1:15
Wade, John, 2:382
wage, 3:907–908
  Mill on wage fund doctrine, 1:227, 2:551–52, 3:908
  minimum wage, See minimum wage
  Ricardo and iron law of wages, 1:227, 327, 2:705–706, 715, 3:810, 908
wages:
  under Stalin, 3:775
Wagner Act, 1:60, 2:594, 3:868, 879
Walker, William, 3:892
Wall Street (film), 1:293
Wall Street Journal, 1:215, 216, 3:910–911
Wallace, Henry A., 1:12
Wallerstein, Immanuel, 1:290–291
Wal-Mart, 3:909–910
Walras, Leon, 1:94, 2:540, 3:911–912
  on capital, 1:112
  general equilibrium, 1:261, 3:911
  marginal utility theory of value, 1:57, 228, 231, 3:890
Walt Disney Company, 1:212, 293, 3:776
Wang, An, 3:912
Wang Laboratories, 3:912
War Industries Board, 3:925
War of 1812, 1:51, 2:367, 437, 513, 3:912–913
  Battle of New Orleans, 3:913
War on Terrorism, 1:104, 214, 348, 3:880, 933
War Production Board, 2:726
War Reserve Act of 1917, 3:925
Ward, Barbara, 1:235
Warner Bros., 1:38, 293
Warner Lambert, 1:78
Warren, Fred, 3:758
Warren, Dr. Joseph, 1:281
Warren Commission, 1:305
Warsaw Pact, 2:396
Washington, Booker T., 2:414
Washington, George, 1:5, 12, 27, 28, 3:913–914
  at Constitutional Convention, 2:513, 3:914
  presidency, 3:913–914
  Whiskey Rebellion and, 2:498, 3:914
Washington Consensus, 1:345, 346, 2:668, 3:798
Wasko, Janet, 1:294
Watergate scandal, 1:102, 305, 2:603
Watt, James, 2:415, 3:830

Wattenberg, Ben, **3:**905

Way to Will Power (Hazlitt), **2:**370

Wealth Against Commonwealth (Lloyd), **2:**502

Wealth of Nations, An Inquiry Into the Nature and Causes of the
    (Smith), **1:**230–231, **2:**471, 479, 490, 543, 648, 715, **3:**739,
    769–770

    absolute advantage theory, **1:**82, 155

    on capital accumulation, **1:**113–114, **3:**770

    classic liberalism and, **1:**266, **3:**769

    classical economics and, **2:**705

    on exchange creating wealth, **3:**769–770

    on free trade, **1:**315, 316, **3:**770, 849

    general equilibrium, **1:**261, **3:**770

    on labor, **1:**111, **3:**769–770, 890, 908

    laissez-faire and, **2:**477

    on mercantilism, **1:**199, 227, **2:**686, 705

    on patents for inventors, **2:**640

Weatley, John, **2:**393

Webb, Beatrice, **2:**490

Webb, Sidney, **2:**490

Weber, Max, **1:**165, 264, **2:**627, 684–686

    on Benjamin Franklin, **1:**314–315

Weiner, Richard, **1:**312

welfare (economics), **3:**748, 884, **914–915**

welfare (social programs), **3:**772, 782–783

    cycle of dependency on, **2:**658, 688

    as form of social security, **3:**773

    poverty and, **2:**658, **3:**782, 809

    workfare, **2:**658, 688, **3:**774

welfare theory, **2:**379

Welles, Orson, **1:**293

Wells, Henry, **3:**915

Wells Fargo, 3:915–916

Wendy's International, **1:**312

Wernick, Andrew, **1:**166

West, Edward, **2:**666

West Germany, **1:**341–343, **2:**531–532

    export-led growth policies, **1:**276

West-Indische Compagnie (WIC), *See* **Dutch West India Company**

Westinghouse, George, 3:916–917

Westinghouse Electric Company, **3:**916

Westminster Review, **3:**884

Weston, J. Fred, **3:**755

"What Is Seen and What Is Not Seen," **1:**83–84

Wheeler-Lea Act of 1938, **1:**287

Wheeler-Truman Act, **3:**852

Whiskey Rebellion, **2:**498, **3:**914

White, Edward D., **1:**35–36

Whitney, Eli, 1:22, **2:**413, **3:917**

Who Owns the Media? (Gomery), **1:**212

Wicksell, Knut, **1:**57, **2:**431

    on capital, **1:**112, 113

    on marginal productivity, **1:**231

    monetary theory, **2:**568

Wicksell Effect, **1:**112

Wieser, Friedrich von, **1:**57, **2:**540, **3:**743

Wilber, Charles K., **1:**201

Wilberforce, William, **3:**763

Wilensky, Uri, **1:**232

Will Dollars Save the World (Hazlitt), **2:**371

Williams, Raymond, **1:**151

Williams, Walter, **2:**492

Williams, William Carlos, **1:**314

Williams v. Walker-Thomas Furniture Co., **1:**174

Wilmot Proviso, **2:**495

Wilson, James, **1:**233–234, **2:**382

Wilson, R. W., **1:**52

Wilson, William, **2:**555

Wilson, Woodrow, 1:13, **2:**386–387, **3:**824, **917–918**

    economic policies, **2:**491, **3:**918

    Federal Reserve and, **1:**285

    foreign policy, **3:**918, 924

    free trade and, **1:**199–200

    liberal internationalism and, **1:**345

    presidency during World War I, **3:**918, 924–926

    presidential elections, **1:**36, **2:**728, **3:**918

    as Progressive, **2:**490, 725, **3:**918

    unions and, **3:**867, 918, 925

Wise, D. A., **1:**238

Without Consent or Contract (Fogel), **1:**304

Witter, Jean, **3:**899

Wittfogel, Karl, **2:**625

Witzel, Morgen, **2:**527

women:

    equal rights, **2:**550–551

    as factory workers, **2:**414

    members of New York Stock Exchange, **2:**597

    poverty among, **2:**656

    in sports, **3:**786

    voting rights, **2:**414, **3:**918

Woo, Roh Tae, **2:**465

Word Processing System, Wang's introduction of, **3:**912

worker, 3:919–920

    socialism as workers' democracy, **3:**774–775

    See also **labor**

Working Class Goes to Heaven, The, **1:**293

Works Progress Administration, **2:**491, 592, 726

World Arts Forum, **3:**922

World Bank, 1:7, 336, 345, **2:**399, 401, 461, **3:920–922**

    anti-globalization protests, **2:**475

    board of directors, **3:**921

    creation of, **1:**97, **2:**316, 426, 457, **3:**850, 920

    decision-making process, **3:**921

    history of, **3:**921–922

    institutions that comprise, **3:**921

    Morgan Stanley's promotion of, **2:**577

    ownership of, **3:**921

    poverty and, **2:**656, 658

    Private Sector Development Strategy (PSDS), **2:**668–669

    purpose of, **3:**921

qualification for loans from, 1:346, 3:921

Stiglitz and, 3:797, 798

structural adjustment program, 1:346, 2:475

World Commission for Environment and Development, 3:819

World Conservation Strategy, 3:819

World Cup, 3:785–786, 788

World Economic Forum, 3:922

World Social Forum, 1:348

World Trade Center attacks, *See* September 11th terrorist attacks

World Trade Organization (WTO), 1:345, 2:399, 3:851, 922–923

anti-globalization and, 1:32, 34, 35, 317, 318

creation of, 1:276, 317, 335, 2:521, 3:850, 922–923

membership, 1:143, 264, 317, 2:448, 501, 3:778

mission of, 3:923

policy making, 3:923

steel tariff of George W. Bush administration challenged by, 3:883

World War I:

aftermath of, 3:926

financing of, 3:924–925

Hoover's role in, 2:386–387, 3:925

opposition to, 1:30–31

Treaty of Versailles, 1:234, 3:918, 926

unions during, 3:867, 925

Wilson's presidency during, 3:918, 924–926

World War II, 2:469, 3:927–930, 934

aftermath of, 3:930

airlines and, 1:15–16

black market activity during, 1:89

Eisenhower and the D-Day invasion, 1:241

end of Great Depression and, 3:879

Germany's attack on Soviet Union, 1:285, 3:928

globalization and, 1:345

lend-lease, 2:726, 3:928, 929, 930

oil and, 2:618

Pearl Harbor, 1:84, 2:439, 618, 726, 3:928

Truman administration and end of, 3:852

unions and, 1:61

Worldcom, Inc., 1:81, 340, 3:930–931

world-systems theory of Wallerstein, 1:290–291

Wozniak, Steve, 2:445

Wyse, Lucien, N. B., 2:634

Xerox, 1:340

Xerox-Parc, 1:160, 2:445, 549

X-inefficiency, 2:572

Yahoo!, 3:896

Yalta Conference, 2:653, 3:852

Yellen, Janet, 1:17, 183

Yeltsin, Boris, 1:102, 352, 3:864–865

Yemen, 3:933

yen, 3:933–934

global trade and internationalization of, 2:520

Yew, Lee Kuan, 3:759

Yom Kippur War, 1:62, 2:432–433, 448, 619, 622

Young, John, 2:379

Yrigoyen, Hipólito, 1:45

Yuan Shikai, 1:134

Yugoslavia, 1:83, 93, 3:749, 837

Yum! Brands, 1:312

Zaharias, Babe Didrikson, 3:786

Zaire, 2:461

Zappata, Emiliano, 2:546

Zarb, Frank G., 2:585

Zedillo, Ernesto, 2:547

Zeithaml, Valarie, 3:751

Zhou Enlai, 3:837

Zimbabwe, 3:934–935

Zola, Émile, 2:697

Zurich Financial Services, 3:935–936